THE ROUTLEDGE HANDBOOK OF THE PSYCHOLOGY OF LANGUAGE LEARNING AND TEACHING

This state-of-the-art volume is the first to capture a hybrid discipline that studies the role and linguistic implications of the human mind in language learning and teaching. This *Handbook* considers individual as well as collective factors in language learners and teachers from an array of new empirical constructs and theoretical perspectives, including implications for practice and "myths, debates, and disagreements" in the field, and points to future directions for research. This collection of stellar contributions is an essential resource for researchers, advanced students, and teachers working in applied linguistics, second language acquisition, psychology, and education.

Tammy Gregersen is Professor of TESOL at the American University of Sharjah in the United Arab Emirates.

Sarah Mercer is Professor of Foreign Language Teaching and Head of ELT at the University of Graz, Austria.

ROUTLEDGE HANDBOOKS IN APPLIED LINGUISTICS

Routledge Handbooks in Applied Linguistics provide comprehensive overviews of the key topics in applied linguistics. All entries for the handbooks are specially commissioned and written by leading scholars in the field. Clear, accessible, and carefully edited *Routledge Handbooks in Applied Linguistics* are the ideal resource for both advanced undergraduates and postgraduate students.

The Routledge Handbook of Forensic Linguistics
Second Edition
Edited by Malcolm Coulthard, Alison May and Rui Sousa-Silva

The Routledge Handbook of Corpus Approaches to Discourse Analysis
Edited by Eric Friginal and Jack A. Hardy

The Routledge Handbook of World Englishes
Second Edition
Edited by Andy Kirkpatrick

The Routledge Handbook of Language, Gender and Sexuality
Edited by Jo Angouri and Judith Baxter

The Routledge Handbook of Plurilingual Language Education
Edited by Enrica Piccardo, Aline Germain-Rutherford and Geoff Lawrence

The Routledge Handbook of the Psychology of Language Learning and Teaching
Edited by Tammy Gregersen and Sarah Mercer

The Routledge Handbook of Language Testing
Second Edition
Edited by Glenn Fulcher and Luke Harding

For a full list of titles in this series, please visit www.routledge.com/series/RHAL

THE ROUTLEDGE HANDBOOK OF THE PSYCHOLOGY OF LANGUAGE LEARNING AND TEACHING

Edited by Tammy Gregersen and Sarah Mercer

NEW YORK AND LONDON

First published 2022
by Routledge
605 Third Avenue, New York, NY 10158

and by Routledge
2 Park Square, Milton Park, Abingdon, Oxon OX14 4RN

Routledge is an imprint of the Taylor & Francis Group, an informa business

© 2022 Taylor & Francis

The right of Tammy Gregersen and Sarah Mercer to be identified as the authors of the editorial material, and of the authors for their individual chapters, has been asserted in accordance with sections 77 and 78 of the Copyright, Designs and Patents Act 1988.

All rights reserved. No part of this book may be reprinted or reproduced or utilised in any form or by any electronic, mechanical, or other means, now known or hereafter invented, including photocopying and recording, or in any information storage or retrieval system, without permission in writing from the publishers.

Trademark notice: Product or corporate names may be trademarks or registered trademarks, and are used only for identification and explanation without intent to infringe.

Library of Congress Cataloging-in-Publication Data
A catalog record for this title has been requested

ISBN: 9780367337230 (hbk)
ISBN: 9781032074795 (pbk)
ISBN: 9780429321498 (ebk)

DOI: 10.4324/9780429321498

Typeset in Bembo
by Newgen Publishing UK

CONTENTS

Notes on Contributors   *viii*

Introduction   1

PART 1
Perspectives on Psychology   **5**

1   The Cognitive Approach   7
Yuichi Suzuki

2   Sociocultural Theory   22
Remi A. van Compernolle

3   The Humanistic Approach   36
Jane Arnold and José Manuel Foncubierta

4   The Complex Dynamic Approach   48
Elizabeth Hepford

5   Positive Psychology   61
Peter D. MacIntyre and Samantha Ayers-Glassey

6   Psycholinguistics   74
Simone E. Pfenninger and Julia Festman

PART 2
Constructs: Teacher and Learner Psychologies — 87

7 Identity — 89
   Ron Darvin and Bonny Norton

8 Self-efficacy — 100
   Kay Irie

9 Personality — 112
   Jean-Marc Dewaele

10 Motivation — 124
   Christine Muir

11 Engagement — 137
   Hayo Reinders and Sachiko Nakamura

12 Attitudes and Beliefs — 149
   Amy S. Thompson

13 Attributions and Mindsets — 161
   Xijia Zhang, Nigel Mantou Lou, Kimberly A. Noels, and Lia M. Daniels

14 Emotion — 178
   Rebecca L. Oxford

15 Well-being — 191
   Kyle Read Talbot

16 Resilience — 205
   Phil Hiver and Ana Clara Sánchez Solarte

17 Self-regulation — 218
   Isobel Kai-Hui Wang

18 Vision and Goal Self-Concordance — 231
   Alastair Henry

19 Autonomy and Agency — 245
   Paula Kalaja and Maria Ruohotie-Lyhty

20 Willingness to Communicate in an L2 — 260
   Tomoko Yashima

PART 3
Groups and Communities   273

21 Teacher-Learner Relationships   275
    Christina Gkonou

22 Group Dynamics   285
    Tim Murphey, Yoshifumi Fukada, Tetsuya Fukuda, and Joseph Falout

23 Culture and Intercultural Communication   300
    Tony Johnstone Young, Sara Ganassin, and Alina Schartner

24 Social Interaction   313
    Jim King and Sam Morris

25 Prosocial Behavior and Social Justice   325
    M. Matilde Olivero

PART 4
Myths, Debates, and Disagreements   337

26 Trait and State Perspectives of Individual Difference Research   339
    Kata Csizér and Ágnes Albert

27 The Social/Cognitive Split   350
    Anne Feryok

28 The Mind-Body split   362
    Steven G. McCafferty

29 What Counts as Evidence?   378
    Yasser Teimouri, Ekaterina Sudina, and Luke Plonsky

30 Language Aptitudes   391
    Zhisheng (Edward) Wen

31 Psychology of Learning versus Acquisition   406
    Miroslaw Pawlak

Index   *419*

NOTES ON CONTRIBUTORS

Ágnes Albert is Assistant Professor at the Department of English Applied Linguistics at Eötvös University, Budapest and holds a PhD in Language Pedagogy. Her research interests include task-based language learning and individual differences in foreign language learning, in particular learner creativity and positive emotions associated with language learning.

Jane Arnold was Professor of Language Teaching Methodology at the University of Seville (Spain) from 1989 until 2016 when she retired and now is Honorary Assistant. She is a member of the research group REALL (Research in Affective Language Learning). She has numerous publications in important journals, as well as books published with Cambridge University Press and Helbling Languages. She has given plenaries and workshops in many countries. Her main research area is the affective domain of language learning and teaching.

Samantha Ayers-Glassey, is a BSc graduate from Cape Breton University (Canada) currently pursuing a Master's degree in Psychology at the University of Waterloo (Canada). Her general research interests include cognitive neuroscience, attention, and emotion regulation.

Kata Csizér is Associate Professor at Eötvös Loránd University, Budapest. Her main field of research interest is the social psychological aspects of L2 learning and teaching, as well as foreign language motivation. She has published over 100 academic papers and has co-authored several books, including the recent *Second Language Motivation in a European Context: The Case of Hungary* with Springer Nature.

Lia M. Daniels is Professor of Educational Psychology in the Faculty of Education at the University of Alberta. She investigates motivation, emotions, and outcomes like achievement, perceived success, and well-being in students and teachers across all levels of schooling with the aim of creating adaptive learning environments.

Ron Darvin is Assistant Professor of Applied Linguistics at The Chinese University of Hong Kong. His research interests include identity, investment, digital literacies, and social class, and his work has been published in *Annual Review of Applied Linguistics, TESOL Quarterly,* and *Journal of Language, Identity, and Education.*

Jean-Marc Dewaele is Professor of Applied Linguistics and Multilingualism at Birkbeck, University of London. He has published widely on individual differences in Second Language Acquisition and

Multilingualism. He is former president of the *International Association of Multilingualism* and the *European Second Language Association* and he is General Editor of *Journal of Multilingual and Multicultural Development*.

Joseph Falout, Associate Professor at Nihon University (Japan), has published 60-plus papers and chapters on language learning or teaching, including topics such as demotivation, remotivation, past and future selves, ideal classmates, group dynamics, present communities of imagining, and critical participatory looping. He has been awarded five times for his publications and presentations by the Japan Association for Language Teaching.

Anne Feryok is Senior Lecturer at the University of Otago. Much of her research is within socio-cultural theory and complex dynamic systems theory and is about second language teacher cognition and development. Her work has appeared in a number of journals and edited collections.

Julia Festman is Professor of Multilingualism at University College of Teacher Education Tyrol in Innsbruck. Her main research focus is on multilingualism on the individual, cognitive, and educational level. She combines psycholinguistic, neurolinguistic, and neuroscientific methods for investigating the learning and processing of multiple languages. She has a particular interest in the effects of multilingualism on cognition and in the bilingual advantage debate.

José Manuel Foncubierta is Professor of Linguistics at the Department of Hispanic Philology in Universidad of Huelva. He is a member of the research group REALL (Research in Affective Language Learning). He has various publications in academic journals and books on learning Spanish, and he has conducted plenaries and workshops in many countries. His main research areas are the affective domain of language learning and teaching and musical aptitude in L2 reading process.

Tetsuya Fukuda is Instructor at International Christian University in Tokyo, Japan. Tetsuya received his PhD from Temple University Japan. His research interests include L2 motivation, school belonging, group dynamics, school engagement, and learning strategies. He has authored and co-authored about 30 papers mainly on these topics, including seven book chapters.

Yoshifumi Fukada (EdD) is Professor at Meisei University (Japan). His main research interests are L2 learners' and users' dynamic identities, as in their agency in their English-learning and social interactions. His recent publications include 'Whole language approach' (*The TESOL Encyclopedia of English Language Teaching*, Wiley-Blackwell, 2018) and *L2 learning during study abroad: The creation of affinity spaces* (Springer, 2019).

Sara Ganassin is Lecturer in Applied Linguistics and Communication at Newcastle University in the UK where she teaches and researches intercultural communication and education. Her research interests include the interplay of language, culture, and identity in contexts of migration, displacement, and mobility, as well as the internationalization of higher education.

Christina Gkonou is Associate Professor of TESOL and MA TESOL Program Leader in the Department of Language and Linguistics at the University of Essex, UK. Her research interests are in language learner and teacher emotions, and the relational dimensions of learning and teaching. She has published extensively on these areas.

Tammy Gregersen is Professor of TESOL at the American University of Sharjah in the United Arab Emirates. She has published extensively on individual differences, teacher education, nonverbal communication in language classrooms, positive psychology, and language teacher well-being. She was awarded two Fulbright Scholar opportunities in Costa Rica and Chile.

Alastair Henry is Professor of Language Education at University West, Sweden. His work on motivation for language learning has focused largely on multilingualism, perseverance, engagement in L2 classrooms, and technology use. Other recent work has involved teacher identities and willingness to communicate in contexts of migration.

Elizabeth Hepford is Assistant Professor of the Practice in TESOL at Wesleyan University. Her research focuses on the interaction of complexity, accuracy, and fluency under the theoretical framework of Complex Dynamic Systems Theory. She also conducts research in non-native English speakers' ability to understand the Miranda Warning.

Phil Hiver is Assistant Professor in the School of Teacher Education at Florida State University. His published research focuses on leveraging individual differences and learner variation to reduce achievement disparities in L2 instructional settings. He also writes on the contribution of complexity/dynamic systems theory (CDST) to language education research.

Kay Irie is Professor at the Faculty of International Social Sciences, Gakushuin University, Tokyo. She is teaching in the language program to support the EMI curriculum. She also teaches at the Graduate College of Education at Temple University Japan. Her research interests include language learning psychology and learner autonomy.

Paula Kalaja is Professor Emerita at University of Jyväskylä, Finland. She specializes in second language learning and teaching. She has co-authored and -edited (among others) *Beliefs about SLA* (2003), *Beliefs, Agency and Identity in Foreign Language Learning and Teaching* (2016), and *Visualising Multilingual Lives* (2019), as well as (text)books for the local market.

Jim King is based at the University of Leicester where he directs the institution's campus-based postgraduate taught courses in applied linguistics and TESOL. His most recent books include *The Emotional Rollercoaster of Language Teaching* (with Christina Gkonou and Jean-Marc Dewaele, Multilingual Matters, 2020) and *East Asian Perspectives on Silence in English Language Education* (with Seiko Harumi, Multilingual Matters, 2020).

Peter D. MacIntyre is Professor of Psychology at Cape Breton University (Canada). His research focuses on the psychology of language and communication, including research on anxiety, motivation, and willingness to communicate. His research interests focus on the psychology of communication, including positive psychology, motivation, nonverbal communication, and individual differences.

Nigel Mantou Lou received his PhD in Psychology from the University of Alberta. His research focuses on the psychology of language learning, immigration, and intercultural communication. He is an associate editor in *Frontiers in Psychology* and a co-editor of a special issue on "Growth mindsets and language learning" in *Innovation in Language Learning and Teaching*.

Sarah Mercer is Professor of Foreign Language Teaching and Head of ELT at the University of Graz. She is the author, co-author, and co-editor of several books in the field of language learning psychology. In 2018, she was awarded the Robert C Gardner Award for excellence in second language research.

Notes on Contributors

Steven G. McCafferty is Professor of Applied Linguistics at the University of Nevada, Las Vegas. His research has centered on applications of sociocultural theory to second language development, and of particular interest to him is the study of L2 thought and language, which includes the study of multimodal ensembles.

Sam Morris is Lecturer in the Center for Foreign Language Education and Research at Rikkyo University (Japan). He is interested broadly in the affective dimension of teacher psychology. His principal focus is on the situated emotion regulation actions that teachers employ during their work.

Christine Muir is Assistant Professor in Second Language Acquisition at the University of Nottingham. She has published on varied topics relating to the psychology of language learning and teaching, particularly in the area of individual and group-level motivation. Recent publications include *Directed motivational currents and language education: Exploring implications for pedagogy* (2020, Multilingual Matters).

Tim Murphey holds a PhD from the Université de Neuchâtel, Switzerland and is TESOL's *Professional Development in Language Education* series-editor, co-author of *Group Dynamics in the Language Classroom*, co-editor of *Meaningful Action*, and author of *Music and Song, The Tale that Wags, Language Hungry,* and *Voicing Learning* (CandlinMynard, 2021). He has been plenary speaker 21 times since 2010 and is Visiting Professor at RILAE-KUIS.

Sachiko Nakamura is Lecturer at International Education Center, Tokai University, Japan. She holds a PhD in Applied Linguistics from King Mongkut's University, Thailand. Her research interests include emotions, task engagement, and strategy instruction.

Kimberly A. Noels is Professor of Psychology at the University of Alberta, Canada. Her research focuses on the social psychology of language learning (including foreign, second, heritage, and classical languages) across diverse socio-cultural and interpersonal contexts, and the implications of language learning for social identities, intercultural communication, and acculturation.

Bonny Norton (FRSC) is University Killam Professor in the Department of Language and Literacy Education, University of British Columbia. Her primary research interests are identity, language learning, and international development. She is a Fellow of the Royal Society of Canada and American Educational Research Association. Her website is faculty.educ.ubc.ca/norton/.

M. Matilde Olivero holds a PhD in Second Language Acquisition from the University of South Florida, USA. She is a teacher educator and researcher in the English Teacher Education Program at Universidad Nacional de Río Cuarto, Argentina. Her main research interests include individual differences and peacebuilding approaches in second language education.

Rebecca L. Oxford holds two degrees in languages and two (including a PhD) in educational psychology and has been a language teacher, language teacher educator, program director in language teacher education and in psychology and counseling, and author/editor of works on language teaching and learning, psychology, and peace.

Miroslaw Pawlak is Professor of English at Adam Mickiewicz University, Kalisz, Poland, and State University of Applied Sciences, Konin, Poland. His research interests include classroom interaction, form-focused instruction, corrective feedback, learner autonomy, language learning strategies, motivation, willingness to communicate, boredom, pronunciation teaching, and study abroad.

Notes on Contributors

Simone E. Pfenninger is Associate Professor of Second Language Acquisition and Psycholinguistics at the University of Salzburg. Her principal research areas are multilingualism, psycholinguistics, and variationist SLA, especially in regard to quantitative approaches and statistical methods. She is co-editor of the Second Language Acquisition book series for Multilingual Matters, Vice President of the International Association of Multilingualism, and Vice President of the European Second Language Association.

Luke Plonsky is Associate Professor of Applied Linguistics at Northern Arizona University. His work, focusing primarily on SLA and research methods, has appeared in over 90 articles, book chapters, and books. He is Associate Editor of *SSLA* and Managing Editor of *Foreign Language Annals*, and Co-Director of the IRIS Database.

Hayo Reinders (www.innovationinteaching.org) is TESOL Professor and Director of Research at Anaheim University, USA, and Professor of Applied Linguistics at KMUTT in Thailand. He is founder of the global Institute for Teacher Leadership and editor of Innovation in Language Learning & Teaching. His interests are in out-of-class learning, technology, and language teacher leadership.

Maria Ruohotie-Lyhty is Senior Lecturer in Applied Linguistics at the Department of Language and Communication Studies, University of Jyväskylä, Finland, and is responsible for foreign language teacher education in her department. Her research focuses on language teacher and learner identities, agency and emotions, language teacher education, and narrative research.

Ana Clara Sánchez Solarte is Associate Professor at Universidad de Nariño in Pasto, Colombia. She is a foreign language teacher educator. Her research interests include second and foreign language methodology, L2 teachers' well-being, L2 teachers' emotions, and teacher preparation. She is currently a PhD candidate at Florida State University.

Alina Schartner is Lecturer in Applied Linguistics at Newcastle University in the UK where she teaches and researches intercultural communication. Her research interests include the internationalization of higher education and intercultural transitions of internationally mobile groups (e.g., international students, refugees), as well as the social psychology of communication.

Ekaterina Sudina is a PhD candidate in Applied Linguistics at Northern Arizona University. Her research interests include second language acquisition, the psychology of second and foreign language (L2) learning and teaching (particularly individual differences), quantitative research methods, and L2 reading and writing.

Yuichi Suzuki is Associate Professor at Kanagawa University. He received the Valdman's Award from *Studies in Second Language Acquisition* (2017) and the IRIS Replication Award (2018). He co-edited the special issue of the *Modern Language Journal* "Optimizing Second Language Practice in the Classroom" (2019) with Tatsuya Nakata and Robert DeKeyser.

Yasser Teimouri is Assistant Professor of Applied Linguistics at Boğaziçi University, Department of Foreign Language Education. His main areas of interest include psychology of language learning and teaching, research methodology, and task-based language learning and teaching.

Amy S. Thompson is Professor of Applied Linguistics and Department Chair of World Languages, Literatures, & Linguistics at West Virginia University. Her research interests involve Individual Differences in SLA and the relationship to bi-/multilingualism, as well as advocacy against native-speakerism in language teaching. See the following website for examples of recent publications: worldlanguages.wvu.edu/faculty-staff/administration/amy-thompson

Notes on Contributors

Remi A. van Compernolle is Associate Professor of Second Language Acquisition and French and Francophone Studies at Carnegie Mellon University. His research interests center around second language development in educational contexts, language and cognition, concept formation, and classroom discourse and interaction.

Isobel Kai-hui Wang is a senior research fellow and teacher educator at the University of Graz, Austria. Her research interests lie in the areas of language learner strategies and intercultural communication. She is the author of *Learning Vocabulary Strategically in a Study Abroad Context*, published by Palgrave Macmillan.

Kyle Read Talbot is a language teacher and researcher in Applied Linguistics. He taught ESL at the University of Iowa in the United States before enrolling as a PhD student at the University of Graz in Austria. He holds an MA in TESOL/Applied Linguistics from the University of Northern Iowa, in Cedar Falls, IA. His current research and thinking interests include the psychology of language learning and teaching, well-being, bilingual and multilingual education and CDST and applied complexity science.

Tomoko Yashima is Professor of Applied Linguistics and Intercultural Communication at Kansai University in Japan. Her research interest includes L2 motivation, affect, and willingness to communicate. Her studies have been published in international journals including *Modern Language Journal, Language Learning, Psychological Reports, and International Journal of Intercultural Relations*.

Tony Johnstone Young is Professor of Applied Linguistics and Communication at Newcastle University in the UK. His work explores aspects of intergroup and intercultural communication in health, language education, and higher educational contexts, and is informed (he hopes) by a strong social inclusion and social justice agenda.

Xijia Zhang is a PhD student in Psychology at the University of Alberta, Canada. Her research interests include language learning and language teaching motivation, as well as the interaction between students' and teachers' motivation.

Wen Zhisheng (Edward) is currently Associate Professor in the School of Languages and Translation at Macao Polytechnic Institute in Macau, China. His teaching and research interests lie in second language acquisition, task-based language teaching and learning, psycholinguistics, and cognitive science, with a particular focus on the roles of working memory and language aptitude in SLA.

INTRODUCTION

The Psychology of Language Learning (PLL) represents an interdisciplinary blend of linguistics, psychology, and education that examines areas of psychology as enacted and experienced in the context of language learning and teaching. As a field experiencing rapid growth in both theory and practice, interest from teachers, learners, and researchers alike has surged. As an interdiscipline, PLL is expanding our understandings of the psychological experience of key stakeholders in language education by drawing on a myriad of theoretical perspectives, constructs, and methodological approaches (see also Mercer & Ryan, 2016). Its plurality of perspectives is indeed one of its characteristic strengths.

This handbook represents the state of the art in this field. It is explicitly and actively interdisciplinary in character. Indeed, there is generally a growing trend towards interdisciplinary perspectives on complex life problems such as the teaching and learning of languages, and this book reflects that contemporary ethos. Interdisciplinarity can counter the blinkered blindness that can overcome a discipline when it fails to engage with related work in other fields. It can lead to fresh insights and perspectives that challenge traditional disciplinary norms and cultures. However, interdisciplinary work has inherent challenges as well as benefits. Mercer and Ryan (2016) discussed at length the early challenges faced by the field. One of the most notable is the need to have expertise in more than one discipline. We have kept that challenge in the forefront of our minds as we put the collection together and have structured the chapters in a way which ensures a deliberate engagement with the literature and perspectives of both the core parent disciplines of applied linguistics and psychology. However, we also recognize that this field of inquiry is unique with its own specific identity, which we hope to have accommodated in integrating perspectives and allowing flexibility within the structure of the chapters. The identity of PLL is not one in crisis (Al-Hoorie, Hiver, Kim, & De Costa, 2020), but rather one which is open to diversity and plurality to reflect each scholar's own professional trajectories, experiences, and interests in more than one discipline. In line with the move towards a blurring of domain boundaries in notions of pluralism, Marshall and Moore (2018, p. 22) explain that, "a person's languages and cultures are not viewed as separate and compartmentalized but instead are seen as interrelating in complex ways that change with time and circumstances, and which depend on individuals' biographies, lived experiences, social trajectories, and life paths" (Marshall & Moore, 2018, p. 22).

While it is important to support work in this specific area as distinct, we are cautious not to build barriers between areas. Indeed, one of the strengths of interdisciplinary work is it is often innovative, original, and unique in character as it creates new vistas in those in-between spaces beyond traditional disciplinary boundaries. So, while on the one hand, we want to actively support work in this area by giving it credence, space, voice, and community, we see its boundaries as permeable and conceive it as a welcoming global village open to interconnections with other areas of scholarship and disciplines. As Larsen-Freeman (2019) cautions, the establishing of the PLL field is not intended to create an isolated community and thereby further fragment the field. Rather, given its inherently interdisciplinary character, we hope this will ensure scholars in this area remain even more welcoming of connections across areas to permit further growth and innovation.

In light of this, it is perhaps important at this point to address the distinctions between PLL and the notion of individual differences (ID) within SLA as the two have a shared heritage but are developing in slightly different directions. The field of SLA assimilates the area conventionally framed as IDs. ID work covers core constructs such as motivation and beliefs, which are also included in this collection and are very much part of the field. However, PLL has also more readily embraced other less familiar constructs that have typically been underrepresented in applied linguistics such as those emerging from positive psychology (e.g., emotions, resilience, well-being, etc.). However, perhaps more notably, PLL is typically concerned with generating understandings from a more holistic perspective, focusing on the psychological experiences involved in language learning and teaching beyond the typical emphasis in SLA on the effectiveness of these processes. In addition, PLL not only examines the learner, but also focuses on the teacher and their psychology as a key determinant of language learning and teaching processes. As one of the main stakeholders in language education, it is perhaps surprising that there is comparatively little research examining teachers and the full range and complexity of their psychologies (Mercer & Kostoulas, 2018). Indeed, even within this collection, most chapters predominantly focus on learners, although many authors also make conscious reference to the respective situation for teachers. PLL as a field has enabled the emergence of a body of work on teacher psychology building on existent work on cognition and identity but extending this to a broader range of constructs, perspectives, and populations, although it remains comparatively in its infancy.

PLL has also fostered a more conscious and explicit focus on the social and collective dimensions of psychology looking beyond the individual as is indicated in the final set of chapters in this collection as well as the social perspectives within many chapters. Rather than isolating psychological variables removed from social and interactional contexts, PLL also incorporates a considerable body of work which seeks to situate psychological variables as lived by "persons-in-context" (Ushioda, 2009). As such, the field has also drawn on a wide range of theoretical lenses including complexity theory and sociocultural theory, among others that emphasize a relational perspective—blending the interaction between the individual and contexts or affordances. Consequently, the field has also evinced extensive methodological variety covering especially qualitative and mixed method approaches. Indeed, the chapters reflect this spread of methodological designs and understandings of psychology stretching from strictly cognitive to strongly socially constructed.

Thus, although the field has much overlap with IDs in SLA, there are also some characteristics, investigative spaces, and epistemological approaches which differ. Nevertheless, for some constructs, the distinction may not be sustained and especially with the growth of interest in Instructed SLA (ISLA), there is an especially fertile potential for interesting collaborations and fresh perspectives on the complex field of language learning and teaching (cf. Hiver, Al-Hoorie, & Mercer, 2021). The community of PLL is necessary for supporting scholarship in this area, especially for early-career academics who may need to connect with a recognizable community and body of work, particularly if their host institution does not actively promote interdisciplinary research in this area. As the field of PLL expands rapidly in light of new theoretical developments and an increasing openness to cross-disciplinary work, this handbook can help to establish the state-of-the-art and point towards future directions and areas for collaborations across areas of scholarship. It is an exciting, diverse, and vibrant field of inquiry with rich potential for future growth and expansion.

Outline of the Sections and Chapter Format

This handbook covers an extensive collection of 31 chapters divided into four sections. The first explores empirical and theoretical perspectives in the field and considers how these have shaped approaches to the study of language learning and teaching. It covers more familiar perspectives such as cognitive, psycholinguistic, and humanistic perspectives, as well as approaches grounded in positive psychology and dynamic complex systems theory. This section provides the broad frameworks on which subsequent sections are built. It is important to highlight that there is not one single approach to PLL, but many different lenses can inform both teaching and researching in this area. The psychology of learning and teaching a language is far too complex to be covered by one single theory alone (cf. Block, 1996). Instead, PLL represents a field of inquiry, and this first section illustrates some of the theoretical lenses which can be used to inform empirical work in this area.

In Section 2, the handbook addresses specific psychological constructs involved in language learning and teaching. In using the word "construct" to label the elements in this section, we are drawing on the Britannia dictionary definition of "a tool used to facilitate understanding of human behavior" (Binning, 2016). Section 2 covers a range of constructs from the more familiar, such as motivation, beliefs, and identity, to the less familiar, such as personality, emotions, and well-being, among others. Here the broad range of different constructs addressed reveals the scope of the field in terms of the diverse factors known to influence language learning and teaching. It is hoped that by bringing them together, we can also facilitate an overview ensuring that work on individual constructs does not itself become isolated, but that scholars remain aware of the connection to other related constructs and the breadth of complexity inherent in human psychology.

Section 3 considers the psychology of language learners and teachers in groups and communities. This section highlights that psychology is not only an individual experience, but that it emerges in groups and is inherently socially situated contrary to many misconceptions that only conceive of psychology as being cognitively contextualized. While one can focus on the cognitive aspects of psychology, the field of psychology itself is diverse and multifaceted, including many social, collective, and interactionist perspectives. In particular, this section examines relationships that emerge between the teacher and learner(s), among learners themselves, among groups, and within a society, and how such relational connections mutually influence the individual and the group.

The concluding section offers new insights into some of the controversial topics currently being debated that fall within the scope of the volume. Many of the disputes are generated by individuals taking a "this or that" perspective: Are individual differences traits or states? Is a given phenomenon social or cognitive? Does embodiment facilitate the functionality of the mind? Do quantitative or qualitative measures provide more accurate evidence? Is a language learner endowed with aptitude to learn effectively or are they doomed to struggle? Is language proficiency most effectively heightened through learning or acquisition? The contributors to this section of the handbook took on the challenge of clarifying such "this or that" argumentation and countered the dichotomous perspectives perpetuated in competing perspectives.

Organization Within the Chapters

Readers will find a similar organizational pattern among the chapters in each of the four sections of the handbook (e.g., Perspectives; Constructs; Groups and Communities; and Myths, Debates, and Disagreements). Beginning with an introduction of the perspective, construct, group, or debate, each topic is then contextualized, defined, and outlined in the wider discipline of psychology and then subsequently in SLA, or sometimes, depending on the chapter, in the reverse order. Once this backdrop is established, authors highlight how each of their topics integrates perspectives from both psychology and SLA. That is to say, they describe the psychological insights from their topic that have been integrated into language learning and teaching and vice versa. At times, authors contemplate synergies that would be beneficial to transfer across fields but as of yet have not occurred. Given the diversity of topics addressed in the handbook, it is natural that these sections are not of equal length across chapters and that tends to reflect whether the predominance of perspective from authors is given to one body of literature or the other. All authors bring their own perspectives and professional interdisciplinary identities to bear, but all engage consciously and explicitly with both "parent" disciplines, albeit to differing degrees. Next, from the review of the literature, implications for practice in language education and research are drawn—this is the portion in each chapter that seeks to connect the handbook to classroom contexts and offer insights of relevance to practicing language teachers. Each contribution concludes with future directions, often by drawing upon lessons learned from the past. Readers with a desire to engage more deeply with a topic will benefit from reflection questions posed by the authors as well as recommended readings.

The handbook offers an innovative and wide-reaching perspective on an increasingly influential field within applied linguistics and is an essential resource for all those working in this area as well as in neighboring or related disciplines. Its innovation lies in the presence of a variety of dynamic interacting synergies. Authors explored the interface of teaching and learning; they established theoretical foundations from which they made practical pedagogical and research applications; they linked multiple disciplines like SLA, psychology, education, and applied linguistics; they explored the interconnectedness of constructs as well as individuals and contexts. In sum, this handbook hopes to engender further research in this fascinating and exciting investigative space. The psychology of language learning and teaching is the foundation of what happens in practice and it is hoped that this collection of chapters can further inspire research in the field and the conscious efforts to keep connected to practice. Psychology is at the heart of what it means to be human and PLL is at the heart of language learning and teaching. We look forward to many years of further exciting interdisciplinary scholarship.

References

Al-Hoorie, A. H., Hiver, P., Kim, T.-Y., & De Costa, P. I. (2020). The identity crisis in language motivation research. *Journal of Language and Social Psychology (Advanced access)*.

Binning, J. F. (2016, February 22). *Construct. Encyclopedia Britannica*. Retrieved November 13, 2020, from www.britannica.com/science/construct.

Block, D. (1996). Not so fast: Some thoughts on theory culling, relativism, accepted findings and the heart and soul of SLA. *Applied Linguistics, 17*(1), 63–83.

Hiver, P., Al-Hoorie, A., & Mercer, S. (2021). *Student engagement in the language classroom*. Multilingual Matters.

Larsen-Freeman, D. (2019). Thoughts on the launching of a new journal: A complex dynamic systems perspective. *Journal for the Psychology of Language Learning, 1*(1), 67–82.

Marshall, S., & Moore, D. (2018). Plurilingualism amid the panoply of lingualisms: Addressing critiques and misconceptions in education. *International Journal of Multilingualism, 15*(1), 19–34.

Mercer, S., & Ryan, S. (2016). Stretching the boundaries: Language learning psychology. *Palgrave Communications, 2*, 1–5.

Ushioda, E. (2009). A person-in-context relational view of emergent motivation, self and identity. In Z. Dörnyei & E. Ushioda (Eds.), *Motivation, language identity and the L2 self* (pp. 215–228). Multilingual Matters.

PART 1

Perspectives on Psychology

1
THE COGNITIVE APPROACH

Yuichi Suzuki

In this chapter, second language (L2) learning processes are elucidated from cognitive perspectives gained from psychology and second language acquisition (SLA) research. While L2 acquisition involves complex cognitive mechanisms, these are naturally embedded in social contexts, and the importance of social, affective, and conative factors and their interaction is widely recognized. Yet, the internal or cognitive mechanisms and processes presumably share some key commonalities across all L2 learners with different affective and motivational levels in various social contexts. Thus, it is worth investigating and seeking to understand the cognitive underpinnings of L2 learning.

Historically, theories of L2 learning have drawn upon cognitive approaches. For instance, in their edited book, *Theories in second language acquisition: An introduction*, Vanpatten and Williams (2015) presented ten "mainstream" L2 theories, eight of which were cognitive (e.g., usage-based approaches, skill acquisition theory, input-processing model, declarative/procedural model, processability theory). These eight theories are not exhaustive even within cognitive approaches. Over a decade ago, Long (2007) pointed out that there are "as many as 60 theories, models, hypotheses, and theoretical frameworks" (p. 4). As such, an extensive list cannot be addressed within a single chapter; here, focus will be placed on skill acquisition theory, as this cognitive theory is deeply rooted in psychology literature and is highly relevant for language learning.

In what follows, the foundational concepts of memory and knowledge in cognitive psychology are briefly outlined. Next, skill acquisition theory is delineated from SLA perspectives and several key issues are highlighted. Last, an integrated perspective of SLA and cognitive psychology—the main theme of this chapter—is presented.

Cognitive Perspectives in Psychology

Many essential constructs in SLA stem from cognitive psychology, which is the scientific study of human mental processes, such as perception, attention, consciousness, memory, automatization, and language. Two related constructs—memory and knowledge—are posited to play critical roles in learning. Psychologists have a particular interest in *memory*, i.e., the underlying mechanisms that support diverse forms of learning. While memory was once considered a unitary system, it is now generally believed to be multi-componential (Baddeley, Eysenck, & Anderson, 2014). Declarative and nondeclarative memory (e.g., Squire & Zola, 1996), as well as working memory (Baddeley, 2012), are the most influential conceptualizations of human long-term memory not only for psychologists but also for L2 researchers. Declarative memory is used for the learning of factual information and events, whereas the nondeclarative type of memory is involved in procedural, priming, conditioning, and non-associative learning. A well-known concept, working memory, is responsible for temporarily storing and manipulating information for carrying out complex cognitive tasks. From a cognitive perspective, these memory systems form the foundation for acquiring *knowledge* that is dedicated to specific processes by experiencing and encoding events from the environment (e.g., Anderson, 1996). For instance, L2 learners need to process and analyze L2 input such that they develop mental representations—L2 knowledge—that can be used for communication.

A number of empirical studies in the field of cognitive psychology and education have also provided valuable insights into the effectiveness of various teaching techniques in promoting learning in general (e.g., feedback, distributed learning, and individualized instruction). In the effort to promote the "science of learning," Hattie and Yates (2013) synthesized the meta-analyses of cognitive psychology findings regarding effective teaching and learning strategies that can be utilized in research-informed classroom teaching (see also Horvath, Lodge, & Hattie, 2016).

Although psychology research has generated a number of insights that could be applied in education, in most cases, researchers tended to examine simple tasks (Wulf & Shea, 2002) that are only remotely related to L2 learning. Consequently, the findings pertaining to the effectiveness of certain techniques in psychology may not always be applicable to L2 learning. While some cognitive psychologists are interested in L2 learning, the scope of L2 learning examined in such studies is often limited. In the past, for instance, L2 learning was equated simply with vocabulary acquisition (e.g., Donovan & Radosevich, 1999). Historically, psychologists rarely delved into the complexity of L2 learning; however, this situation changed dramatically in the past decade. Recently, L2 researchers have started incorporating and testing findings reported by psychologists (Suzuki, Nakata, & DeKeyser, 2019b), and this emerging field will be discussed in depth in the "Integrating Perspectives" section.

Cognitive Perspectives in SLA

Skill Acquisition Theory

A particularly useful cognitive theory for elucidating L2 learning processes from a cognitive perspective is skill acquisition theory (DeKeyser, 2015). It stems from Anderson's adaptive control of thought-rational (ACT-R) theory in psychology (Anderson, Bothell, Byrne, Douglass, Lebiere, & Qin, 2004). In an overview of the field of psychology and SLA, Dörnyei (2009, 2019) identified this theory as one of the most useful frameworks that offers a concrete approach to studying L2 learning from a psychology perspective.

According to skill acquisition theory, knowledge has declarative and procedural forms. In L2 learning, declarative knowledge consists of exemplars and rules that L2 learners are usually aware of, while procedural knowledge is used by applying declarative knowledge to behaviors/skills, such as L2 comprehension and production. For instance, when learners possess declarative knowledge of third person *s*, they can explain when the morpheme *-s* is used at the end of the verb. Using this declarative rule as a crutch, they practice producing or comprehending sentences by paying attention to the target morpheme *-s* that is embedded in its surrounding linguistic information. Engaging in this type of deliberate practice leads to proceduralization. Further fine-tuning of linguistic knowledge requires substantial practice, and this gradual process is described as automatization. Automatization leads to faster, more consistent and efficient utilization of acquired skills. In sum, the theory presupposes three stages of L2 learning: declarative–procedural–automatization.

The key long-term memory systems—declarative and procedural memory—are also highlighted in Michael Ullman's declarative/procedural model (Ullman, 2015, 2016). According to this neurobiological L2 learning model, learners gradually shift from the declarative to the procedural stage as their L2 proficiency increases. Unlike skill acquisition theory, the declarative/procedural model does not seem to distinguish between the procedural and automatization phases. What is important for L2 researchers and teachers, however, is that both theories can provide a theoretical neuro-cognitive foundation for the way L2 learners develop their knowledge and skills.

This dual-memory system view of L2 knowledge can easily be linked to explicit and implicit knowledge, which are key constructs in both SLA and psychology. Declarative and procedural knowledge corresponds to explicit and implicit knowledge in most cases; however, some discrepancies in operational definitions utilized by L2 researchers do exist, which has led to long-lasting controversies fueled by confusion. The distinction between explicit and implicit knowledge is based on the criterion of awareness. Explicit knowledge is conscious, whereas implicit knowledge is used without awareness (DeKeyser, 2003; Williams & Paciorek, 2015). In contrast, declarative knowledge and procedural knowledge are often distinguished, irrespective of awareness, by the neurobiological long-term memory systems involved: declarative memory (hippocampus and medial temporal lobe) and procedural memory (frontal-basal ganglia circuits), respectively (Paradis, 2009; Ullman, 2015, 2016).

From a pedagogical perspective, the declarative–procedural–automatization distinction, rather than the explicit–implicit distinction, fulfills the purposes and is perhaps more useful in analyzing cognitive underpinnings of L2 learning processes in most classroom contexts. This is because highly advanced L2 learners can develop conscious, explicit knowledge and are able to access it quickly (Suzuki & DeKeyser, 2015; Suzuki, 2017). In other words, these advanced L2 learners can use speeded-up or automatized explicit knowledge that is presumably useful for communication, and the acquisition of unconscious, implicit knowledge, unless it is highly automatized, may be of less concern, at least for practitioners. Automatization of implicit knowledge necessitates extensive L2 exposure and may take a number of years to develop typically beyond classroom contexts, and only some portion of L2 grammatical knowledge may ultimately become implicit in the sense of non-awareness, even in naturalistic settings (Paradis, 2009; Suzuki & DeKeyser, 2017c).

Rather than the idea of "implicit" learning without awareness, proceduralization may be a construct that is more applicable to analyzing L2 learning process and perhaps can be achieved realistically in classroom settings. According to skill acquisition theory, initial proceduralization can be achieved after just a few attempts in some cases (DeKeyser, 2015). Automatization emerges from this procedural knowledge and skill and requires a long learning process, which is a useful conceptualization for tracking the L2 learning progress from a longitudinal perspective. The discussions presented in this chapter primarily focus on the transition from the declarative to the procedural learning phase, and finally to automatization, irrespective of awareness, as this learning mode is likely to be most relevant in the majority of L2 learning classroom settings.

Key Issues and Research from the Skill Acquisition Perspective

The chief objective of research guided by skill acquisition theory is elucidating how declarative–explicit knowledge, which is initially acquired deductively or inductively, supports proceduralization and automatization. In the seminal study conducted by DeKeyser (1997), participants were exposed to artificial grammar rules during the course of 22 sessions delivered across 11 weeks. After participants acquired declarative (metalinguistic) knowledge about target rules, they engaged in systematic comprehension or production practice involving 1,440 sentences. Analysis of their performance showed that accuracy and speed gradually improved with the number of practice opportunities, as indicated by the Power of Law learning curve

While many empirical studies rooted in skill acquisition theory are conducted in controlled laboratory settings, Sato and McDonough (2019) carried out their investigation in an English-as-a-Foreign-Language (EFL) classroom. They examined the role of declarative knowledge in proceduralization of wh-questions through contextualized speaking practice. The participants (EFL learners) engaged in a variety of teacher–student information–gap tasks (e.g., spot-the-difference tasks, interview tasks, story completion), with the aim of acquiring procedural knowledge of wh-questions, over five weekly sessions.

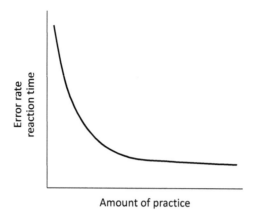

Figure 1.1 Power of Law Curve

Note: Error rate and reaction time decreases dramatically in the initial study sessions and the decline becomes asymptotical over time.

The authors found that accuracy, speech rate, and mean pause length significantly improved over the five sessions, confirming that the "practice effects" previously observed in the lab can be extended to contextualized practice in the classroom. Although declarative knowledge was not a significant predictor of performance change from the first to the final (fifth) session, declarative knowledge allowed the learners to engage in using the target structure accurately in the initial stages of proceduralization. This research is an exemplary descriptive study in that it satisfied, to a large extent, both ecological validity and methodological rigor, as it was carried out in the classroom over an extended period of time using a pedagogically useful interactive task that systematically targeted wh-question formation.

An important prediction that skill acquisition theory makes is the skill specificity (Anderson, 1993; DeKeyser, 2015). In other words, it is postulated that the procedural knowledge gained through dedicated practice of one skill is fine-tuned to that specific skill (e.g., comprehension) and is unlikely to be used for different skills (e.g., production). According to this theory, skill transfer is possible only through declarative knowledge, which is a more general system that can be applied for different skills. The skill specificity effect has been confirmed across different types of L2 skills and linguistic domains in subsequent studies (see Li & DeKeyser, 2017; Suzuki & Sunada, 2019 for recent progress in this area).

A new line of research from the perspective of skill acquisition theory has recently emerged, whereby the researchers started exploring the optimal conditions that are conducive for proceduralization and automatization of L2 knowledge. Optimal practice scheduling is a particularly burgeoning research area and is inspired by cognitive psychology research. L2 researchers have started to reveal the optimal timing to repeat L2 practice activities for proceduralization and automatization (see the "Integrating Perspectives" section for details).

Another key issue is the role of explicit instruction on proceduralization or automatization, which is a central topic in instructed SLA (e.g., Norris & Ortega, 2000). More recently, McManus and Marsden (2017, 2019) adopted the skill acquisition perspective to examine the role of explicit information for practicing the target L2 French grammar of *Imparfait*. In addition to explicit information about L2 target structure, they also presented explicit information about how participants' L1 (English) expresses the L2 target structure (e.g., how English expresses ongoingness and habitualness). Their findings indicated that the provision of L1 explicit information had additive benefits for accurate and faster processing (proceduralization) of target grammar.

Furthermore, researchers have started to investigate individual differences that play an important role in engaging in efficient proceduralization and automatization (Ettlinger, Bradlow, & Wong, 2014; Morgan-Short, Faretta-Stutenberg, Brill-Schuetz, Carpenter, & Wong, 2014; Pili-Moss, Brill-Schuetz,

Faretta-Stutenberg, & Morgan-Short, 2019; Suzuki, 2018). Morgan-Short et al. (2014) focused on individual differences in declarative and procedural memory (part of the long-term memory system) in their laboratory research on artificial grammar learning. Their findings revealed that individual differences in declarative memory, measured by Part V of the Modern Language Aptitude Test (paired associate) (see Chapter 30) and the continuous visual memory task (Buffington & Morgan-Short, 2019, p. 30) predicted the disparities in the earlier stage of grammatical knowledge acquisition. In contrast, procedural memory, measured by the Tower of London and weather prediction tasks (Buffington & Morgan-Short, 2019), predicted the later stages of grammar knowledge. Pili-Moss et al. (2019) subsequently reanalyzed the performance data gathered during the training sessions conducted by Morgan-Short et al. (2014). They found that automatization of grammatical knowledge was predicted by procedural memory only among learners with superior declarative memory. Furthermore, Suzuki's (2018) laboratory experiment also revealed the significant role of procedural memory (measured by the Tower of London task) in automatization of novel L2 morphological structures through repeated systematic practice with the support of declarative knowledge. These findings suggest that automatization can be facilitated by higher levels of declarative and procedural memory. While these studies are well-controlled laboratory studies using an unfamiliar artificial/miniature language, Faretta-Stutenberg and Morgan-Short (2018) focused on American university students who were studying Spanish in an at-home classroom or a study-abroad context. Individual differences in procedural memory ability, as well as working memory capacity, significantly predicted the grammatical development over one semester in the study-abroad context, but not in the at-home context. Cognitive abilities are recruited differentially depending on the quality of L2 learning experiences catered by different settings, indicating the need to explore the complex interactions between cognitive mechanisms and social contexts.

Integrating Perspectives

Optimizing L2 Practice from Cognitive Psychology Perspectives

The goal of this section is to provide an overview of emerging intersections between SLA and cognitive psychology. Based on the skill acquisition perspective, several researchers have attempted to connect SLA and cognitive psychology to inform L2 education (DeKeyser, 2007; Lyster & Sato, 2013; Suzuki et al., 2019b). The central idea of this intersection is *practice*. The term *practice* is widely used in both L2 and psychology studies on skill acquisition. Here, practice is defined, from the L2 skill acquisition perspective, as "specific activities in the second language, engaged in systematically, deliberately, with the goal of developing knowledge of and skills in the second language" (DeKeyser, 2007, p. 1). This broader conceptualization departs from the narrower, more traditional Audiolingual idea of practice (e.g., decontextualized drill and exercises) and embraces both form-focused and meaning-focused activities where learners engage in systematic and deliberate use of L2 knowledge. Meaning-focused practice, for instance, involves extensive reading and listening, interactive information–gap activities, discussion tasks, etc. More importantly, form-focused activities that are widely used in foreign language context, such as oral reading and shadowing (Kadota, 2019), but are often treated as marginal in some approaches (e.g., task-based language teaching) can be included as practice activities.

Findings yielded by empirical L2 research informed by cognitive psychology shed light on the ways practice can be optimized. In what follows, three key sub-areas of L2 practice that are closely tied to psychology of learning are highlighted to provide implications for L2 teaching and learning.

Retrieval Practice and Overlearning: Maximizing Deliberate Vocabulary Learning

Cognitive psychology research (e.g., Karpicke & Roediger, 2008) has shown that *testing* facilitates learning and retention. In this context, testing is not limited to paper-and-pencil assessments,

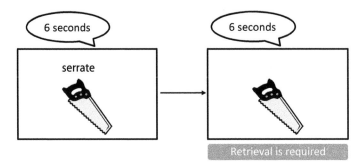

Figure 1.2 An Illustration of Retrieval Practice in Barcroft (2007)

but rather relates to *retrieval*, referring to the general process of accessing previously stored information. Cognitive psychologists found the benefits of retrieval practice for learning a variety of materials, such as word lists, paired associates, passages, and trivia facts (Chan, Meissner, & Davis, 2018).

Barcroft (2007) examined the effects of retrieval opportunities for deliberate vocabulary learning by English native speakers of L2 Spanish. As shown in Figure 1.2, in the retrieval condition, participants saw both target word and picture for six seconds (e.g., *serrate* and a picture of "saw") and then saw the picture only (e.g., the picture of saw) for another six seconds, which provided an opportunity for retrieving the word form (e.g., *serrate*). In the non-retrieval condition, participants saw both the word and the corresponding picture for 12 seconds. The advantage of retrieval practice was demonstrated in the immediate posttest and it was found to persist for up to seven days.

Van Den Broek, Takashima, Segers, and Verhoeven (2018) extended the research on the retrieval practice effect to the contextualized L2 vocabulary learning. Participants in their study were exposed to novel words (e.g., *funguo*) through reading either an uninformative text (e.g., "I need the *funguo*.") which necessitated retrieval of the word meaning from memory, or an informative text ("I want to unlock the door: I need the *funguo*.") where word meaning was inferable and retrieval was not required. The results achieved by these two conditions on the seven-day delayed posttest showed that retrieval practice using the uninformative texts led to more correct recalls.

Furthermore, Nakata (2017) examined an interesting question regarding frequency of retrieval practice. In his study, both *effectiveness* (posttest score) and *efficiency* (posttest score divided by study time) of deliberate vocabulary learning were examined. The Japanese university students studied unfamiliar English words using a retrieval technique in a single session, while the frequency of retrieval practice was varied from one, three, five, to seven. The author found that the higher retrieval practice frequency, the greater the number of words recalled correctly on both immediate and delayed posttests. However, in terms of efficiency, the single retrieval practice opportunity was found to be the most optimal. These findings suggest that when learners want to make most of their time, they do not have to repeat retrieval practice within the single study session but should rather distribute it across multiple study sessions (Rohrer, Taylor, Pashler, Wixted, & Cepeda, 2005).

These results corroborate the findings in psychology on *overlearning* (Rohrer et al., 2005). Overlearning refers to the continued practice beyond one successful performance of a certain task. It is the means of ensuring long-term retention most commonly recommended in textbooks about education and training. Although a meta-analysis (Driskell, Willis, & Copper, 1992) suggests the medium-effect benefit of overlearning in the short term (one week or less), overlearning may not necessarily be effective, particularly for long-term retention (Rohrer et al., 2005). As Nakata (2017) pointed out, most word learning seems to occur during the first retrieval practice. Thus, it is unlikely that practicing retrieval multiple times within the same study session would be justified by its cost (i.e., spending more study time within the same session).

Research on overlearning has important implications for L2 teachers and learners, as it informs their decision on how much L2 learners should practice their skill to maximize the effectiveness and efficiency of skill and knowledge retention. Yet, extant research on this topic in both psychology and L2 research is limited in scope, focusing primarily on vocabulary learning (cf. Lambert, Kormos, & Minn, 2017).

Distributed Practice: Best Timing of Repeated Practice

As previously pointed out, overlearning may not be effective for long-term retention. Instead, in cognitive psychology research, distributing practice opportunities over multiple study sessions has been proven to be more valuable for long-term retention (e.g., Cepeda, Pashler, Vul, Wixted, & Rohrer, 2006). Therefore, identifying optimal study schedules that can enhance L2 learning is an important issue. It is no wonder that this topic has recently attracted extensive attention by L2 researchers. Distributed practice effects have been examined in both laboratory and classroom settings in studies focusing on different linguistic domains: vocabulary (Kanayama & Kasahara, 2017; Nakata, 2015; Nakata & Suzuki, 2019a; Rogers & Cheung, 2020; Schuetze, 2015; Serrano & Huang, 2018), pronunciation (Li & DeKeyser, 2019), and grammar (Bird, 2010; Kasprowicz, Marsden, & Sephton, 2019; Rogers, 2015; Suzuki, 2017; Suzuki & DeKeyser, 2017a).

In a most comprehensive study in the field of psychology, Cepeda, Vul, Rohrer, Wixted, and Pashler (2008) demonstrated that the optimal spacing is determined by the ratio of inter-session interval (ISI) and retention interval (RI) (see Figure 1.3).

Participants in this study remembered trivial facts (e.g., What European nation consumes the spiciest Mexican food? "Norwegians") under different relearning schedules. The findings reported by Cepeda et al. (2008) indicate that the longer the RI, the longer the optimal ISI. The optimal ratios for memory recall and recognition were similar except for the seven-day RI (see Figure 1.3).

L2 researchers have explored the extent to which findings reported by Cepeda et al. (2008) are applicable to L2 learning. In L2 grammar learning, which is the most debated and examined linguistic domain, some empirical experiments (Bird, 2010; Rogers, 2015) indicate that the optimal ISI-RI ratio is consistent with that obtained by Cepeda et al. (2008). However, experiments conducted by other authors (Kasprowicz et al., 2019; Suzuki, 2017; Suzuki & DeKeyser, 2017a) suggest that the optimal ISI-RI relationship is different for L2 grammar learning.

The discrepancy in the findings may be attributed to several moderating factors, including complexity of target skills (Donovan & Radosevich, 1999); experimental context, such as laboratory versus classroom (Rogers & Cheung, 2020); frequency of study sessions and posttests (Suzuki, 2017); skill/knowledge type, such as declarative and procedural (Li & DeKeyser, 2019; Suzuki & DeKeyser, 2017a); and individual differences in learners' aptitudes (see Chapter 30), such as working memory

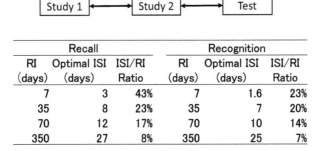

	Recall			Recognition	
RI (days)	Optimal ISI (days)	ISI/RI Ratio	RI (days)	Optimal ISI (days)	ISI/RI Ratio
7	3	43%	7	1.6	23%
35	8	23%	35	7	20%
70	12	17%	70	10	14%
350	27	8%	350	25	7%

Figure 1.3 Optimal Intersession (ISI) to Retention Interval (RI) Ratio Found in Cepeda et al. (2008)

and language analytic ability (Kasprowicz et al., 2019; Suzuki, 2019; Suzuki & DeKeyser, 2017b). Further investigations in both laboratory and classroom contexts are thus needed to obtain a more nuanced picture of distributed practice effects from theoretical and pedagogical points of view.

Interleaved Practice: Optimizing Exemplar Presentation Order

Another issue related to the practice schedule is whether to use blocked or interleaved schedules. Interleaved practice refers to a teaching technique where multiple exemplars from different categories are presented in a mix (e.g., ABCDCADBACBD), whereas blocked practice involves a sequence of exemplars blocked by category (e.g., AAABBBCCCDDD). Cognitive psychology research shows that interleaving results in better retention than blocking (Kang, 2016; Taylor & Rohrer, 2010).

Based on their recent meta-analysis of studies on interleaving effects, however, Brunmair and Richter (2019) suggested that the effectiveness of blocking and interleaving depends on features of the learning materials. For instance, blocking does indeed seem more effective than interleaving for learning unfamiliar pronunciations that widely differ across categories (Carpenter & Mueller, 2013). In their study on pronunciation learning, Carpenter and Mueller (2013) asked participants to read French words for which lexico-phonological rules were very different (e.g., *bateau, vernis, brumeux*). Blocked presentation of exemplars from the same category (e.g., *bateau, carreau, corbeau, fardeau*) seemed to have facilitated noticing the common features (e.g., *eau*) among the exemplars presented in a row.

On the other hand, findings yielded by recent research indicate that interleaved practice is beneficial for L2 grammar learning (Nakata & Suzuki, 2019b; Pan, Tajrana, Lovelett, Osuna, & Rickard, 2019; Suzuki & Sunada, 2019; Suzuki, Yokosawa, & Aline, 2020). Figure 1.4 illustrates sample sequences of 24 practice items on relative clauses under blocked and interleaved schedules (Suzuki & Sunada, 2019). In the blocked schedule, exemplars of subjective relative clauses (SR) *who* are presented, followed by a block of SR *which* exemplars, object relative clause (OR) *whom*, and OR *which*. In contrast, in the interleaved practice schedule, these exemplars of four syntactic categories are randomized.

The categories of these target linguistic features (e.g., SR *which* and OR *which*) are similar to each other, and interleaved practice can facilitate the discrimination of those similar features by highlighting subtle differences (Kang & Pashler, 2012). The advantage of interleaving was found in the acquisition of English tense–aspect–mood distinction (Nakata & Suzuki, 2019b) and Spanish past-tense morphology (Pan et al., 2019), as well as in English relative clause/adverb construction (Suzuki & Sunada, 2019; Suzuki et al., 2020).

Furthermore, Suzuki and colleagues (Nakata & Suzuki, 2019b; Suzuki & Sunada, 2019) recently explored the effectiveness of hybrid (increasing) practice, whereby blocked and interleaved practices were combined, as shown in Figure 1.4. Theoretically, when hybrid practice schedule is adopted, the difficulty of practice can be increased gradually from blocking to interleaving in order to optimally challenge learners for better retention of knowledge and skills—desirable difficulty (Schmidt & Bjork, 1992; Suzuki, Nakata, & DeKeyser, 2019a; see also Figure 1.5). The empirical findings related to the effectiveness of this method are presently limited as well as mixed. While Nakata and Suzuki (2019b) failed to establish the advantage of hybrid practice, Suzuki and Sunada (2019) found it superior to blocked or interleaved practice alone. As in the case of distributed practice, there are several key moderating factors that need to be taken into account for optimizing the sequence of exemplars (Fuhrmeister & Myers, 2020; Suzuki et al., 2020).

Implications for Practice and Research

The L2 teaching and learning techniques introduced in this section have obvious pedagogical implications for enhancing learning from SLA and cognitive psychology perspectives. Implications of many of the findings are somewhat straightforward (e.g., incorporating more retrieval practice). Interestingly, however, many teachers and students are unaware of the benefits of retrieval, distributed,

Blocked schedule

SR-who	SR-who	SR-who	SR-who	SR-who	SR-who	SR-which	SR-which	SR-which	SR-which	SR-which	SR-which
OR-whom	OR-whom	OR-whom	OR-whom	OR-whom	OR-whom	OR-which	OR-which	OR-which	OR-which	OR-which	OR-which

Interleaved schedule

SR-who	SR-which	OR-whom	OR-which	OR-whom	SR-which	SR-who	OR-which	SR-which	SR-who	OR-which	OR-whom
SR-which	OR-whom	OR-which	SR-who	SR-which	OR-which	SR-who	OR-whom	SR-who	OR-whom	SR-which	OR-which

Hybrid (increasing) schedule

SR-who	SR-who	SR-who	SR-which	SR-which	SR-which	OR-whom	OR-whom	OR-whom	OR-which	OR-which	OR-which
SR-which	OR-whom	OR-which	SR-who	SR-which	OR-which	SR-who	OR-whom	SR-who	OR-whom	SR-which	OR-which

Sample sentences
- SR-who: That is the boy who is kissing the dog.
- SR-which: That is the kangaroo which is massaging the boy.
- OR-whom: That is the man whom the woman is pushing.
- OR-which: That is the bird which the cat is watching.

Figure 1.4 Blocked and interleaved practice of relative clauses. From Suzuki and Sunada (2019)

and interleaved practice (Karpicke, 2009; Karpicke, Butler, & Roediger III, 2009; Nakata & Suzuki, 2019b). This means that L2 learners and teachers need to become aware of and take advantage of these effective techniques for learning. One way to achieve this is to provide strategy-based instruction for promoting the use of effective techniques. Another approach may be to create materials and computerized programs that automatically optimize the practice formats and learning schedules using portable devices such as smartphones (e.g., Lin & Lin, 2019).

In order to advance a research agenda for a more systematic investigation of L2 practice, Suzuki et al. (2019b) proposed an overarching framework for L2 practice shown in Figure 1.5. This framework stipulates that three factors—(a) practice condition, (b) linguistic difficulty, and (c) learner-related difficulty—determine the overall difficulty levels of L2 practice. It is, therefore, useful for researchers aiming to establish the optimal values of multiple variables for achieving the levels of difficulty that would yield the best learning outcomes (Schmidt & Bjork, 1992).

For instance, Nakata and Suzuki (2019a) examined whether the effectiveness of massed and spaced vocabulary learning (practice condition) was moderated by semantic relatedness of vocabulary (linguistic feature). Studying semantically related words (e.g., baboon, badger, otter, raccoon) induces interference effect (i.e., generating an incorrect lexical item in the same semantic category such as confusing "baboon" with "otter"), which presumably increases learning difficulty and creates a optimally challenging learning condition. Nakata and Suzuki (2019a) found that spaced learning reduced the semantic interference of studying semantically related words, which resulted in less knowledge retention compared to semantically unrelated words. This suggests that the effectiveness of practice

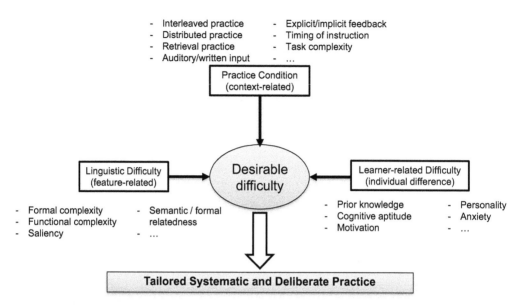

Figure 1.5 An Overarching Theoretical Framework for Systematic and Deliberate L2 Practice from Suzuki, Nakata, and DeKeyser (2019a)

condition should be evaluated by taking into account relevant aspects of linguistic difficulty (e.g., semantic relatedness).

Furthermore, the effectiveness of distributed practice is also influenced by a set of cognitive aptitudes (see Chapter 30) such as working memory and language analytic ability (Kasprowicz et al., 2019; Suzuki, 2019; Suzuki & DeKeyser, 2017b). Compared to cognitive factors like aptitude, however, relatively little attention has been given to the affective and motivational factors for research on L2 practice. Given that practice should be done repeatedly and extensively for developing knowledge and skills, motivation is an important moderating factor of the amount and potentially effectiveness of practice (de Bruin, Kok, Leppink, & Camp, 2014; see Chapter 10). It is thus important to investigate how learners' intrinsic motivation, such as interest, enjoyment, and satisfaction (e.g., McEown & Oga-Bladwin, 2019), can be engaged and sustained during practice over an extended period of time.

This overarching framework of L2 can capture the complexity of cognitive, affective, and conative factors involved in L2 practice in a variety of social settings. As there is no single best method of practice for all learners, the framework will provide a foundation for understanding how the key factors can be modulated to create optimal practice conditions for learning a particular linguistic feature for a group of learners with particular characteristics in a given setting (see Suzuki, Nakata, & DeKeyser, 2020 for more detail). In sum, the implications of these findings stemming from cognitive psychology and L2 research are not only informative for teachers, learners, and material developers, but also for researchers who can find stimulating synergies between cognitive psychology and L2 research.

Future Directions

In this chapter, an overview of cognitive underpinnings and research findings of L2 learning was provided from the perspective of one cognitive L2 theory—skill acquisition theory. In cognitive approaches, memory and knowledge are treated as the key systems underlying learning. Research guided by skill acquisition theory has thus largely focused on declarative–procedural–automatized

L2 knowledge. Due to the need to impose methodological control over the experimental treatment in empirical research, attention is typically given to a single target linguistic point while participants are subjected to decontextualized practice using single sentences. This limitation is critical when attempting to elucidate the pedagogical implications of the findings yielded for teaching because such highly controlled study protocols have little resemblance to actual L2 use for communication.

In order to overcome this limitation, an emerging line of investigations aims to broaden the scope of research by integrating the idea of distributed/interleaved practice to a task-based language teaching (TBLT) perspective (e.g., Ellis, Skehan, Li, Shintani, & Lambert, 2020). For instance, Bui, Ahmadian, and Hunter (2019) examined the distributed practice effects of task repetition practice in which EFL learners engaged in oral picture description task twice. Their findings indicated that different amounts of spacing (0-day, 1-day, 3-day, 7-day, and 14-day ISIs) influence complexity−accuracy−fluency (CAF) performance in speaking tasks. Similar efforts were made by Suzuki (under review), who examined fluency development in speaking skills and compared blocked practice and interleaved practice. In this study, EFL learners engaged in six-frame cartoon narrative task nine times over three study sessions under either blocked (Day 1: Cartoon AAA, Day 2: Cartoon BBB, Day 3: Cartoon CCC) or interleaved condition (Day 1: ABC, Day 2: ABC, Day 3: ABC). Their posttest performance indicated that the blocked practice led to significant gains in some aspects of utterance fluency (e.g., faster articulation rate). In addition to the investigation into the acquisition of a specific linguistic structure, the effects of repeated practice need to be examined from a more global perspective including CAF analysis as in Bui et al. (2019) and Suzuki (2021) and, ideally, in conjunction with other affective and motivational factors that are discussed in this handbook.

This line of research is promising for both theoretical and pedagogical reasons. Theoretically, these attempts are considered transdisciplinary, as cognitive psychology findings are tested in the context of TBLT (e.g., Ellis et al., 2020). Pedagogically, the findings will be particularly useful in formulating task sequencing guidelines for teachers for maximizing students' L2 skill development. In order to make these findings substantial and reliable for L2 education stakeholders (e.g., teachers, learners, and policy makers), researchers continue to seek the generalizability of empirical findings in both classroom-based and laboratory-based longitudinal studies.

In this chapter, the strengths of a cognitive approach in psychology and L2 research were highlighted—strong theoretical and psychological foundations in memory and knowledge that serve as the basis for effective teaching and learning. From an L2 acquisition perspective, skill acquisition theory was presented to postulate that learning process occurs in three stages, i.e., it follows the declarative−procedural−automatization sequence. Furthermore, an emerging interdisciplinary research area linking SLA and cognitive psychology was highlighted and situated in the broader conceptualization of L2 practice. The focused review of three main research streams—retrieval practice, distributed practice, and interleaved practice—were presented, and these pedagogical techniques on L2 learning are highly relevant for L2 classrooms and are useful for maximizing the effectiveness of L2 practice. Finally, an overarching theoretical framework of L2 practice for creating desirable difficulty and optimizing L2 learning was presented, which can inform not only research but also L2 curriculum and material development, as well as digital learning.

Reflection Questions

- What aspect of L2 learning can skill acquisition theory explain most directly?
- How do other perspectives and constructs described in this handbook resonate with the cognitive view of L2 learning (e.g., declarative−explicit and procedural−implicit knowledge, desirable difficulty)?
- How can L2 teachers incorporate cognitive psychology/L2 research findings on retrieval, distributed, and interleaved practice into their classroom practices?

Recommended Reading

DeKeyser, R. M. (2015). Skill acquisition theory. In B.VanPatten & J.Williams (Eds.), *Theories in second language acquisition: An introduction* (2nd ed., pp. 94–112). Routledge.
This book chapter provides an authoritative account of skill acquisition theory in L2 learning. It also explains how skill acquisition theory contributes to the explicit–implicit debate.

Suzuki,Y., Nakata,T., & DeKeyser, R. M. (2019b). Optimizing second language practice in the classroom: Perspectives from cognitive psychology. *The Modern Language Journal*, 103, 551–561.
This special issue of *The Modern Language Journal* showcases empirical studies that approach L2 practice from a perspective of cognitive psychology. This introductory paper gives an overview of the state-of-the-art empirical research on various practice-related topics, such as retrieval practice, distributed practice, interleaved practice, integrated practice, and individual differences.

Horvath, J. C., Lodge, J. M., & Hattie, J. (2016). *From the laboratory to the classroom: Translating science of learning for teachers*. Routledge.
This edited book provides a comprehensive overview of research in the field of science of learning. As the title indicates, its aim is to build a bridge between laboratory research findings and real classroom practice in various cognitive and other aspects of learning.

References

Anderson, J. R. (1993). *Rules of the mind*. Lawrence Erlbaum Associates.
Anderson, J. R. (1996). ACT: A simple theory of complex cognition. *American Psychologist*, 51, 355–365.
Anderson, J. R., Bothell, D., Byrne, M. D., Douglass, S., Lebiere, C., & Qin,Y. (2004). An integrated theory of the mind. *Psychological Review*, 111, 1036–1060.
Baddeley, A. D. (2012). Working memory: Theories, models, and controversies. *Annual Review of Psychology*, 63, 1–29.
Baddeley, A. D., Eysenck, M., & Anderson, M. (2014). *Memory*. Psychology Press.
Barcroft, J. (2007). Effects of opportunities for word retrieval during second language vocabulary learning. *Language Learning*, 57, 35–56.
Bird, S. (2010). Effects of distributed practice on the acquisition of second language English syntax. *Applied Psycholinguistics*, 31, 635–650.
Brunmair, M., & Richter, T. (2019). Similarity matters: A meta-analysis of interleaved learning and its moderators. *Psychological Bulletin*, 145, 1029–1052.
Buffington, J., & Morgan-Short, K. (2019). Declarative and procedural memory as individual differences in second language aptitude. In Z. Wen, P. Skehan, A. Biedroń, S. Li, & R. L. Sparks (Eds.), *Language aptitude: Advancing theory, testing, research and practice* (pp. 215–237). Routledge.
Bui, G., Ahmadian, M. J., & Hunter, A. M. (2019). Spacing effects on repeated L2 task performance. *System*, 81, 1–13.
Carpenter, S. K., & Mueller, F. E. (2013). The effects of interleaving versus blocking on foreign language pronunciation learning. *Memory & Cognition*, 41, 671–682.
Cepeda, N. J., Pashler, H., Vul, E., Wixted, J. T., & Rohrer, D. (2006). Distributed practice in verbal recall tasks: A review and quantitative synthesis. *Psychological Bulletin*, 132, 354–380.
Cepeda, N. J., Vul, E., Rohrer, D., Wixted, J. T., & Pashler, H. (2008). Spacing effects in learning a temporal ridgeline of optimal retention. *Psychological Science*, 19, 1095–1102.
Chan, J. C. K., Meissner, C. A., & Davis, S. D. (2018). Retrieval potentiates new learning: A theoretical and meta-analytic review. *Psychological Bulletin*, 144, 1111–1146.
De Bruin, A. B. H., Kok, E. M., Leppink, J., & Camp, G. (2014). Practice, intelligence, and enjoyment in novice chess players: A prospective study at the earliest stage of a chess career. *Intelligence*, 45, 18–25.
DeKeyser, R. M. (1997). Beyond explicit rule learning. *Studies in Second Language Acquisition*, 19, 195–221.
DeKeyser, R. M. (2003). Implicit and explicit learning. In C. J. Doughty & H. M. Long (Eds.), *The handbook of second language acquisition* (pp. 312–348). Blackwell Publishers.
DeKeyser, R. M. (2007). *Practice in a second language: Perspectives from applied linguistics and cognitive psychology*. Cambridge University Press.

DeKeyser, R. M. (2015). Skill acquisition theory. In B. VanPatten & J. Williams (Eds.), *Theories in second language acquisition: An introduction* (2nd ed., pp. 94–112). Routledge.
Donovan, J. J., & Radosevich, D. J. (1999). A meta-analytic review of the distribution of practice effect: Now you see it, now you don't. *Journal of Applied Psychology, 84*, 795–805.
Dörnyei, Z. (2009). *The psychology of second language acquisition*. Oxford University Press.
Dörnyei, Z. (2019). Psychology and language learning: The past, the present and the future. *Journal for the Psychology of Language Learning, 1*, 27–41.
Driskell, J. E., Willis, R. P., & Copper, C. (1992). Effect of overlearning on retention. *Journal of Applied Psychology, 77*, 615–622.
Ellis, R., Skehan, P., Li, S., Shintani, N., & Lambert, C. (2020). *Task-based language teaching: Theory and practice*. Cambridge University Press.
Ettlinger, M., Bradlow, A. R., & Wong, P. C. M. (2014). Variability in the learning of complex morphophonology. *Applied Psycholinguistics, 35*, 807–831.
Faretta-Stutenberg, M., & Morgan-Short, K. (2018). The interplay of individual differences and context of learning in behavioral and neurocognitive second language development. *Second Language Research, 34*, 67–101.
Fuhrmeister, P., & Myers, E. B. (2020). Desirable and undesirable difficulties: Influences of variability, training schedule, and aptitude on nonnative phonetic learning. *Attention, Perception, & Psychophysics, Advanced Access*.
Hattie, J., & Yates, G. C. (2013). *Visible learning and the science of how we learn*. Routledge.
Horvath, J. C., Lodge, J. M., & Hattie, J. (2016). *From the laboratory to the classroom: Translating science of learning for teachers*. Routledge.
Kadota, S. (2019). *Shadowing as a practice in second language acquisition*. Routledge.
Kanayama, K., & Kasahara, K. (2017). What spaced learning is effective for long-term L2 vocabulary retention? *ARELE: Annual Review of English Language Education in Japan, 28*, 113–128.
Kang, S. H. (2016). The benefits of interleaved practice for learning. In J. C. Horvath, J. M. Lodge, & J. Hattie (Eds.), *From the laboratory to the classroom: Translating science of learning for teachers* (pp. 79–93). Routledge.
Kang, S. H., & Pashler, H. (2012). Learning painting styles: Spacing is advantageous when it promotes discriminative contrast. *Applied Cognitive Psychology, 26*, 97–103.
Karpicke, J. D. (2009). Metacognitive control and strategy selection: Deciding to practice retrieval during learning. *Journal of Experimental Psychology: General, 138*, 469–486.
Karpicke, J. D., Butler, A. C., & Roediger III, H. L. (2009). Metacognitive strategies in student learning: Do students practise retrieval when they study on their own? *Memory, 17*, 471–479.
Karpicke, J. D., & Roediger, H. L. (2008). The critical importance of retrieval for learning. *Science, 319*, 966–968.
Kasprowicz, R., Marsden, E., & Sephton, N. (2019). Investigating distribution of practice effects for the learning of foreign language verb morphology in the young learner classroom. *The Modern Language Journal, 103*, 580–606.
Lambert, C., Kormos, J., & Minn, D. (2017). Task repetition and second language speech processing. *Studies in Second Language Acquisition, 39*, 167–196.
Li, M., & DeKeyser, R. M. (2017). Perception practice, production practice, and musical ability in L2 mandarin tone-word learning. *Studies in Second Language Acquisition, 39*, 593–620.
Li, M., & DeKeyser, R. M. (2019). Distribution of practice effects in the acquisition and retention of L2 mandarin tonal word production. *The Modern Language Journal, 103*, 607–628.
Lin, J.-J., & Lin, H. (2019). Mobile-assisted ESL/EFL vocabulary learning: A systematic review and meta-analysis. *Computer Assisted Language Learning, 32*, 878–919.
Long, M. H. (2007). *Problems in SLA*. Lawrence Erlbaum Associates.
Lyster, R., & Sato, M. (2013). Skill acquisition theory and the role of practice in L2 development. In M. García Mayo, Gutierrez-Mangado, J., & Martínez Adrián, M. (Eds.), *Contemporary approaches to second language acquisition* (pp. 71–92). John Benjamins Publishing Company.
McEown, M. S., & Oga-Baldwin, W. L. Q. (2019). Self-determination for all language learners: New applications for formal language education. *System, 86*, 102–124.
McManus, K., & Marsden, E. (2017). L1 explicit instruction can improve L2 online and offline performance. *Studies in Second Language Acquisition, 39*, 459–492.
McManus, K., & Marsden, E. (2019). Signatures of automaticity during practice: Explicit instruction about L1 processing routines can improve L2 grammatical processing. *Applied Psycholinguistics, 40*, 205–234.
Morgan-Short, K., Faretta-Stutenberg, M., Brill-Schuetz, K. A., Carpenter, H., & Wong, P. C. M. (2014). Declarative and procedural memory as individual differences in second language acquisition. *Bilingualism: Language and Cognition, 17*, 56–72.
Nakata, T. (2015). Effects of expanding and equal spacing on second language vocabulary learning: Does gradually increasing spacing increase vocabulary learning? *Studies in Second Language Acquisition, 37*, 677–711.

Nakata, T. (2017). Does repeated practice make perfect? The effects of within-session repeated retrieval on second language vocabulary learning. *Studies in Second Language Acquisition, 39*, 653–679.

Nakata, T., & Suzuki, Y. (2019a). Effects of massing and spacing on the learning of semantically related and unrelated words. *Studies in Second Language Acquisition, 41*, 287–311.

Nakata, T., & Suzuki, Y. (2019b). Mixing grammar exercises facilitates long-term retention: Effects of blocking, interleaving, and increasing practice. *The Modern Language Journal, 103*, 629–647.

Norris, J. M., & Ortega, L. (2000). Effectiveness of L2 instruction: A research synthesis and quantitative meta-analysis. *Language Learning, 50*, 417–528.

Pan, S. C., Tajrana, J., Lovelett, J., Osuna, J., & Rickard, T. (2019). Does interleaved practice enhance foreign language learning? The effects of training schedule on Spanish verb conjugation skills. *Journal of Educational Psychology*, Advance online publication.

Paradis, M. (2009). *Declarative and procedural determinants of second languages.* John Benjamins Publishing Company.

Pili-Moss, D., Brill-Schuetz, K. A., Faretta-Stutenberg, M., & Morgan-Short, K. (2019). Contributions of declarative and procedural memory to accuracy and automatization during second language practice. *Bilingualism: Language and Cognition*, 1–13.

Rogers, J. (2015). Learning second language syntax under massed and distributed conditions. *TESOL Quarterly, 49*, 857–866.

Rogers, J., & Cheung, A. (2020). Input spacing and the learning of L2 vocabulary in a classroom context. *Language Teaching Research, 24*(5), 616–641.

Rohrer, D., Taylor, K., Pashler, H., Wixted, J. T., & Cepeda, N. J. (2005). The effect of overlearning on long-term retention. *Applied Cognitive Psychology, 19*, 361–374.

Sato, M., & McDonough, K. (2019). Practice is important but how about its quality? Contextualized practice in the classroom. *Studies in Second Language Acquisition, 41*, 999–1026.

Schmidt, R. A., & Bjork, R. A. (1992). New conceptualizations of practice: Common principles in three paradigms suggest new concepts for training. *Psychological Science, 3*, 207–217.

Schuetze, U. (2015). Spacing techniques in second language vocabulary acquisition: Short-term gains vs. Long-term memory. *Language Teaching Research, 19*, 28–42.

Serrano, R., & Huang, H. Y. (2018). Learning vocabulary through assisted repeated reading: How much time should there be between repetitions of the same text? *TESOL Quarterly, 52*, 971–994.

Skehan, P. (2003). Task-based instruction. *Language Teaching, 36*, 1–14.

Squire, L. R., & Zola, S. M. (1996). Structure and function of declarative and nondeclarative memory systems. *Proceedings of the National Academy of Sciences, 93*, 13515–13522.

Suzuki, Y. (2017). The optimal distribution of practice for the acquisition of L2 morphology: A conceptual replication and extension. *Language Learning, 67*, 512–545.

Suzuki, Y. (2018). The role of procedural learning ability in automatization of L2 morphology under different learning schedules: An exploratory study. *Studies in Second Language Acquisition, 40*, 923–937.

Suzuki, Y. (2019). Individualization of practice distribution in second language grammar learning: A role of metalinguistic rule rehearsal ability and working memory capacity. *Journal of Second Language Studies, 2*, 170–197.

Suzuki, Y. (2021). Optimizing fluency training for speaking skills transfer: Comparing the effects of blocked and interleaved task repetition. *Language Learning*, 71, 285–325.

Suzuki, Y., & DeKeyser, R. M. (2017a). Effects of distributed practice on the proceduralization of morphology. *Language Teaching Research, 21*, 166–188.

Suzuki, Y., & DeKeyser, R. M. (2017b). Exploratory research on L2 practice distribution: An aptitude x treatment interaction. *Applied Psycholinguistics, 38*, 27–56.

Suzuki, Y., & DeKeyser, R. M. (2017c). The interface of explicit and implicit knowledge in a second language: Insights from individual differences in cognitive aptitudes. *Language Learning, 67*, 747–790.

Suzuki, Y., Nakata, T., & DeKeyser, R. M. (2019a). The desirable difficulty framework as a theoretical foundation for optimizing and researching second language practice. *Modern Language Journal, 103*, 713–720.

Suzuki, Y., Nakata, T., & DeKeyser, R. M. (2019b). Optimizing second language practice in the classroom: Perspectives from cognitive psychology. *Modern Language Journal, 103*, 551–561.

Suzuki, Y., Nakata, T., & DeKeyser, R. M. (2020). Empirical feasibility of the desirable difficulty framework: Toward more systematic research on L2 practice for broader pedagogical implications. *The Modern Language Journal, 104*(1), 313–319.

Suzuki, Y., & Sunada, M. (2019). Dynamic interplay between practice type and practice schedule in a second language: The potential and limits of skill transfer and practice schedule. *Studies in Second Language Acquisition, 42*, 169–197.

Suzuki, Y., Yokosawa, S., & Aline, D. (2020). The role of working memory in blocked and interleaved grammar practice: Proceduralization of L2 syntax. *Language Teaching Research,* Early View.

Taylor, K., & Rohrer, D. (2010). The effects of interleaved practice. *Applied Cognitive Psychology, 24*, 837–848.

Ullman, M. T. (2015). The declarative/procedural model: A neurobiologically-motivated theory of first and second language. In B. VanPatten & J. Williams (Eds.), *Theories in second language acquisition: An introduction* (2nd ed., pp. 135–158). Routledge.

Ullman, M. T. (2016). The declarative/procedural model: A neurobiological model of language learning, knowledge, and use. In G. Hickok & S. L. Small (Eds.), *Neurobiology of language* (pp. 953–968). Academic Press.

Van Den Broek, G., Takashima, A., Segers, E., & Verhoeven, L. (2018). Contextual richness and word learning: Context enhances comprehension but retrieval enhances retention. *Language Learning, 68*, 546–585.

VanPatten, B., & Williams, J. (2015). *Theories in second language acquisition: An introduction* (2nd ed.). Routledge.

Williams, J. N., & Paciorek, A. (2015). Indirect tests of implicit linguistic knowledge. In A. Mackey & E. Marsden (Eds.), *Advancing methodology and practice* (pp. 37–54). Routledge.

Wulf, G., & Shea, C. H. (2002). Principles derived from the study of simple skills do not generalize to complex skill learning. *Psychonomic Bulletin & Review, 9*, 185–211.

2
SOCIOCULTURAL THEORY

Remi A. van Compernolle

This chapter examines the integration and expansion of Vygotskian sociocultural theory in the domain of additional language (LX) development. Throughout this chapter, I will use the term *cultural-historical psychology* (CHP). Although *sociocultural theory*, or SCT, is widely used in the LX field, it has created some confusion as it is not just a theory of the social and the cultural (see Lantolf & Thorne, 2006). The CHP terminology is a way of focusing on the theory's interest in studying and explaining human psychology and its development. The central tenet of the theory, as originally formulated by L. S. Vygotsky (e.g., Vygotsky, 1978, 1986), is that the study of human development must be based on a dialectical understanding of the relationship between biologically endowed psychological functions (e.g., declarative and procedural memory) and the use of cultural tools (e.g., language). Researchers working within the theory explore the ways in which the latter transform the former into higher forms of specifically human psychological functioning (e.g., voluntary memory, logical reasoning) as well as the processes by which symbolic artifacts are internalized by children and adult learners as they are assisted by more competent people in their environment. CHP has a long history in LX research, where it has been used as a lens through which to understand the psycholinguistic processes and consequences of LX acquisition, language socialization, and formal instruction and assessment.

Vygotskian Theory in Psychology

Vygotsky's theory was originally developed during the so-called crisis in psychology of the early twentieth century. The crisis was characterized by a debate between behaviorist theories (e.g., Pavlov, Wundt, Watson), focused as they were on explaining material stimulus-response reactions, and Gestalt psychology, which was primarily interested in describing human consciousness (Cole & Scribner, 1978). Vygotsky (1997) criticized both schools of psychology as reductive. While behaviorists reduced human psychology to the social environment (e.g., habit formation through reinforcement) and ignored consciousness, Gestalt psychologists reduced psychological functioning to lower-level biological processes without reference to larger social and cultural processes (Zinchenko, 2002). Vygotsky sought to create a new psychology that was capable of both *describing* the relationship between consciousness and concrete behavior in the material world and *explaining* its development. In so doing, the aim was to overcome the dualistic thinking of his contemporaries in psychology, but "his solution was not predicated on a recipe approach that called for a pinch of nature and a pinch of nurture"

(Lantolf, 2006, p. 69). Instead, Vygotsky (1978, 1986) focused on the ways in which lower, biologically endowed processes were transformed into higher, specifically human processes through the internalization of cultural tools (e.g., language). It is important to note that Vygotsky regarded internalization as bidirectional—while artifacts are taken in from the outside to mediate internal functioning, they are also outward-facing inasmuch as they mediate human behavior in the concrete material world (Frawley, 1997; Zinchenko, 2002).

Mediation and Internalization

Vygotsky's (1978) proposal of the concept of mediation was central to overcoming the nature-versus-nurture problem in psychology. Although focused on explaining behavior in the material world, Vygotsky rejected the idea that humans acted out of direct stimulus-response (S-R) processes. Instead, he argued, humans internalize culturally constructed artifacts that interrupt the S-R process to create an indirect, or mediated, relationship between the person and their environment. The result, according to Vygotsky, is that humans are able "to control their behavior *from the outside*" (p. 40, italics in original), which in turn "creates new forms of a culturally based psychological process" (ibid.).

One of the primary examples Vygotsky (1986) gave was the use of speech/language. Children first acquire speech as a social tool for communication (e.g., parent-child interaction), but it is subsequently directed inwardly as externalized private speech and eventually as nonverbalized inner speech to regulate mental functioning and behavior (John-Steiner, 2007). In this way, what was once a purely social tool (i.e., used between people) is internalized to mediate psychological processes on the internal plane (i.e., used within the person). For instance, while humans are born with the same biologically endowed neural circuitry for perception, evidence in cognitive science suggests that there are cross-cultural variations in the perception of time, space, and motion due to differences in the linguistic resources that are made available across cultures (Boroditsky, 2018). In other words, the internalization of language, which has its origins in social-communicative speech, transforms a basic biological process into a culturally based process for perceiving the world around us.

Vygotsky (1978) described this movement from social to individual (or external to internal) in terms of a general genetic law of development:

> Every function in the child's cultural development appears twice: first, on the social level, and later, on the individual level; first, *between* people (*interpsychological*) and then *inside* the child (*intrapsychological*). This applies equally to voluntary attention, to logical memory, and to the formation of concepts. All the higher functions originate as actual relations between human individuals.
>
> *p. 57; italics in original*

It is important to note that internalization was not meant to be synonymous with the passive acquisition of ready-made tools. Rather, Vygotsky's focus on the "actual relations between human individuals" (p. 57) foregrounds active participation (Sfard, 1998) in sociocultural activities in which children are supported in using appropriate mediating artifacts under the guidance of more competent persons. In other words, children are made able to perform with support from others before they are competent individuals (cf. Cazden's 1981 notion of performance before competence). And it is this engagement in sociocultural activities that begins the "process of coming to understand the meaning and functional significance of the [mediating artifacts] that one has been using all along" (Wertsch, 2007, p. 186). To return to the earlier example of perception, the development of a culturally based perceptual process results not from the passive acquisition of linguistic items (e.g., cardinal vs. relative direction vocabulary) but from participating in concrete activities in which adults use perceptual language and guide children's perception so that children begin to see things the ways adults do. As children interpret and begin to use relevant language with adults, it becomes part of their internal psychological system (i.e., internalization).

Zone of Proximal Development

One of Vygotsky's most widely recognized contributions to psychology and, by extension, to education is the Zone of Proximal Development (ZPD). Often described as the difference between what a person can do alone and what becomes possible when appropriate assistance is made available (Vygotsky, 1978), the ZPD was in part Vygotsky's attempt to address the problem of age in relation to development (Vygotsky, 1998) and in a more general sense a shorthand device for describing the messy transitional zones between the more stable forms of cognitive functioning that psychologists tend to focus on (Vygotsky, 1978, 1986, 1997). In other words, the ZPD represents a stage in the development of some higher function (cf. internalization of a new mediating artifact) where it is no longer what it was in a past stable stage, but neither has it matured into a qualitatively new function (Valsiner & van der Veer, 2014).

The ZPD is an expression of Vygotsky's dialectical approach to addressing the relationship between the biological and the cultural bases for development. While Vygotsky (1998) proposed an age-referenced periodization scheme with reference to biological maturation, he was careful to underscore the foundational role of the social environment, and especially cooperation with others, as the primary source and driver of the development of higher functions (cf. mediation and internalization). In so doing, Vygotsky invoked the ZPD concept as both a diagnostic tool for evaluating development and an educational construct for determining appropriate forms of instruction in school. It is important to note that the normative references for age-levels are not wholly equivalent to biological maturation. Each age period depends on previous neoformations that are culturally based. For example, the development of communicative speech in early childhood (typically around 1-2 years old) is a prerequisite for the appearance of intellectual speech used for self-regulation in the preschool years (typically around 3-5 years old).

At the same time, age-related developmental benchmarks vary across time and place. The advent of widespread public education in privileged societies during the early twentieth century dramatically changed literacy and numeracy rates and, by extension, what it means to be a functioning person in the adult world (e.g., having at a bare minimum basic reading and math abilities). In other words, human cultures have not only created tools such as language, scripts, numbers, and so on but also large institutions specifically designed to handle the "artificial" (i.e., intentional, culturally based) development of the individual (Vygotsky, 1997. While Vygotsky's own work focused primarily on child development from birth to about age 17, his colleagues and later interpreters extended the ZPD concept to the domain of adult development (e.g., Luria, 1976; Saxe, 1982; Scribner & Cole, 1981; Tulviste, 1991). This research and the many studies across disciplines that have followed since the 1990s have shown that psychological functioning can continue to develop as adults internalize new, and often more sophisticated, mediating artifacts through educational opportunities. In this sense, the ZPD concept is not about age periods in adults since they are already biological mature; instead, it helps to describe the transition from one culturally based way of thinking to another, more sophisticated one. This is often characterized by the shift from thinking through everyday or spontaneous concepts to thinking through academic or scientific concepts (Vygotsky, 1986, 1997), which may become more complex and sophisticated through higher education (e.g., the shift from high school to university, to graduate school, and so on).

Unity of Affect, Intellect, and Environment

Following from the ZPD concept and the importance assigned to the social environment of development, Vygotsky (1994) sought to understand the unitary nature of intellect and affect. His argument was simple: thinking and feeling, while distinct dimensions of consciousness, are never separate from one another. Instead, higher forms of psychological functioning result from the synthesis of intellectual and affective processes (Chaiklin, 2002; Davydov, 1995; Zinchenko, 2009). Vygotsky's (1971, 1994, 1998) use of the term *perezhivanie*, or "the process of experiencing and the state of 'living-through'" (Valsiner & van der Veer, 2014, p. 160; see also González Rey & Martínez, 2016; Smagorinsky, 2011), underscored the unity of intellect, affect, and environment in his work. The internalization of mediating artifacts occurs as people participate in and experience *affectively and intellectually* the sociocultural activities that shape their lives. Such a view on development compels psychologists to take a *unitary* approach to analysis rather than the more typical approach wherein a phenomenon of interest in separated into its constituent elements for analysis (Vygotsky, 1986).

Of special importance in the concept of *perezhivanie* is Vygotsky's understanding that the environment does not simply impact upon the individual's development in a unidirectional manner. Rather, development results in a reconfiguration of the relationship between the individual and their environment (Vygotsky, 1994, 1998): The transitions from infancy to early childhood, to preschool age, to school age, to puberty, and finally to adulthood all carry with them transformations in the psychological tools required to perform age-period-appropriate functions as well as the formation of new social relations between caregivers and parents, teachers, friends, romantic partners, and so on as the child grows into an individual functioning in their social world. What Vygotsky was getting at with the unit of *perezhivanie* was that development was not just about the growth of distinct psychological functions, but the continuous negotiation of the social-relational roles we play as we participate in life with others, roles that involve a functional system of socioculturally mediated intellectual and emotional processes. Extended to contexts of education, the concept of *perezhinvanie* provides a holistic unit of analysis for understanding the mediating role of the environment on learning as well as the consequences of learning for the individual's relationship with the environment (i.e., development of new functions and social relations) (González Rey & Martínez, 2016; Smagorinsky, 2011; Valsiner & van der Veer, 2014).

Educational Praxis

Vygotsky's (1978) ZPD concept holds important implications for education, especially regarding the assessment of learner capabilities. As noted above, Vygotsky (1998) made reference to age periods in child development when discussing the ZPD and its usefulness for diagnosing the psychological or developmental age of children as opposed to their biological age. In the context of schooling, the ZPD provides a shorthand device for essentially describing the relationship between an individual student and grade-level expectations. For example, while two 7-year-old children (i.e., second graders in the US school system) may both be able to master second-grade-level texts in independent reading tasks, one may be able to handle reading materials normally reserved for fifth graders when given a little support, while the other may only comprehend texts at the third grade level with support. In this example, an assessment that included the ZPD (i.e., what becomes possible with support) would conclude that the children are both able to read texts that are more difficult than their biological age would suggest. In addition, the assessment would reveal that they are also very different from one another in terms of their developmental ages, even though their solo performances were very similar.

The idea of using the ZPD concept as an assessment tool has been taken up under the term *dynamic assessment* (DA) (Haywood & Lidz, 2007; Lidz, 2000) or sometimes *dynamic testing* (Sternberg & Grigorenko, 2002). The essence of DA is that teaching is integrated into the assessment process so that a dual evaluation of the learner is possible: 1) what the learner can do alone (i.e., current developmental level), and 2) what becomes possible with intervention (i.e., the ZPD). In some models, DA is carried out in a test-teach-retest format, akin to a pretest-intervention-posttest design, while in others DA might involve teaching throughout a single assessment task. In addition, teaching may be standardized across learners (e.g., using prescribed prompts when the test-taker encounters difficulty) or it may be dialogically negotiated with the learner through interaction. A full review of the various models of DA and their advantages and disadvantages is beyond the scope of this chapter (see Poehner, 2008). It suffices to say that approaches using the test-teach-retest procedures and/or standardized forms of support lend themselves better to psychometric evaluative criteria and can be scaled up for use with large numbers of students, whereas more open-ended forms of DA that allow for continuous and/or dialogically negotiated support through interaction may be rather labor intensive but can be more sensitive to individual learners' ZPDs.

Vygotsky (1997) also paid special attention to the role of formal instruction in driving what he referred to as the *artificial,* or *intentionally organized,* development of the individual. Vygotsky noted that in the everyday world outside of school, children develop through direct empirical experience, and from these experiences they begin to abstract concepts that may be transferable from one context to the next. By contrast, formal education is organized around sets of academic or scientific concepts that represent the collective knowledge of a field of study. Such concepts require no direct experience to acquire because they are abstract. For instance, a child may learn that plants need sunlight and water to thrive through the experience of gardening with parents at home, but in school they are taught the concept of photosynthesis, which requires no experience with gardening. To be sure, Vygotsky conceived of the development of everyday and scientific concepts complementary processes:

> In working its slow way upward, an everyday concept clears a path for the scientific concept and its downward development. It creates a series of structures necessary for the evolution of a concept's more primitive, elementary aspects, which give it body and vitality. Scientific concepts, in turn, supply structures for the upward development of the child's spontaneous concepts toward consciousness and deliberate use.
>
> *Vygotsky, 1986, p. 194*

Thus, experience with—or at least some knowledge of—gardening in the everyday world provides concrete exemplars that help to make sense of the scientific concept of photosynthesis, which in turn reorganizes the person's understanding of their prior experiences in the everyday world. As such, the goal of formal education is to provide a context for the internalization of scientific knowledge and to connect that knowledge with its practical use in the world.

This line of inquiry was extended by one of Vygotsky's collaborators, Piotr Gal'perin (1989, 1992), who developed the pedagogical approach known as systemic theoretical instruction (STI). Gal'perin established a theory of the formation of mental actions that includes three processes. The first is an orientation process, which involves planning one's actions. The second is the execution of the action, in which the orientation is carried out. The third process in turn involves control over one's action in that the execution is monitored, evaluated, and possibly revised in relation to the orientation and potentially changing circumstances. Gal'perin's research showed that the quality of the orientation was critical: Scientifically grounded orientations to action led to better executions and control over action than did orientations based on everyday concepts. Education, then, should focus on developing students' scientific understandings of school subjects.

Gal'perin's STI model does exactly this by leading learners toward the internalization of scientific concepts through three basic processes: the materialization of the concepts in the form of a Schema for the Complete Orienting Basis for Action, or SCOBA, verbalization, and performance (see Haenen, 1996, 2001). The SCOBA is a visual/multimodal representation of the essence of the concept that provides a motive for accomplishing some action (i.e., why is it important?) and that reminds the learner of how to orient to the action's execution (i.e., how can it be done?). SCOBAs can be used during learning activities (e.g., problem-solving tasks) as quick references/guides to support task completion, and they are to be withdrawn as the learner internalizes the concept. Verbalization supports internalization in two ways. First, learners use self-explanation to develop an awareness of the concept, what they understand, and importantly what they do not understand. Second, learners perform concurrent and/or retrospective think-alouds during learning tasks in which they explain performance in relation to the concept/SCOBA. Performance (i.e., learning tasks) supports internalization because it gives learners a concrete context in which to put their developing conceptual knowledge to use and in turn to use their conceptual knowledge to reflect on their performance.

Vygotskian Theory in LX Development

Vygotsky's theory has been taken up in LX research and practice since the early 1980s. In what follows, I provide brief overviews of four principal, albeit broad and relatively diverse, areas that have emerged during that time.

Intrapsychological Functions of Speech and Gesture

Some of the earliest LX work in the theory focused on the ways in which first and additional languages might mediate cognition within the person (i.e., intrapsychological functioning), that is, as inner and private speech (for in-depth review, see Guerrero, 2018). The research of Frawley and Lantolf (1985; Lantolf & Frawley, 1984), for example, suggested that while language learners at lower levels of proficiency are unable to use the LX to regulate their psychological functioning, some learners at higher proficiency levels and with considerable experience in the LX culture are able to use the language to self-regulate. Examples include the use of tense and aspect to gain perspective on tasks (e.g., for orientation purposes) and the use of discourse particles (e.g., *oh, let me VERB*) to maintain control over thinking processes. Additional research in this area has examined the multifunctionality of private speech in social-collaborative learning tasks (e.g., DiCamilla & Antón, 2004; Steinbach-Kohler & Thorne, 2011). This research suggests that while speech may indeed be produced for self-regulatory purposes, because it is publicly produced/verbalized, it is available for an interlocutor to act upon (e.g., by offering assistance). It should be noted that while Frawley and Lantolf's studies focused on private speech in the LX, much later work examined private/self-directed L1 use, especially among lower-proficiency learners. The use of L1 during an LX task or communication has often been interpreted as evidence that the development of social-communicative speech functions outpaces the internalization of the LX as private/intrapsychological tool for thinking (i.e., as inner speech). Indeed, Ushakova (1994) has gone so far as to claim that the L1 creates a lasting foundation for thinking that is not changed by the acquisition of additional languages. However, additional research has challenged this assertion by investigating conceptual restructuring in bilingualism (Guerrero, 2018; Pavlenko, 2005).

A related strand of research has extended McNeill's (1992, 2005) work on co-speech gestures to LX contexts. McNeill's theory contends that while speech is analytic and therefore parses thinking into linear units (i.e., morphemes, words, phrases, clauses, etc.), gestures maintain the holistic or synthetic nature of thought. Together, they form an integrative system for mental functioning (See Chapter 28). Following from questions about inner and private speech, LX research has sought to examine whether, and to what extent, co-speech gestures can provide insight into LX internalization and self-regulatory behavior. For example, a number of studies (see Stam, 2018 for an overview) have investigated motion events in speakers whose L1 and LX provide different resources for doing so (i.e., verb-framed vs. satellite-framed languages). Findings suggest that while LX speakers may be able to produce grammatically correct and even nativelike utterances in speech, their gestures often follow an L1 pattern or a kind of L1-LX hybrid. In other words, it seems that at least some aspects of inner speech, as externalized through co-speech gestures, remain influenced, if not fully mediated, by the L1, despite highly proficient social-communicative speech in the LX.

Assistance and the ZPD

Vygotsky's theory is frequently associated with the concepts of assistance (or assisted performance) and scaffolding. In LX research, for example, there is a long history of research into the role of teacher feedback, seen as regulation (or mediation) (Aljaafreh & Lantolf, 1994), and peer scaffolding (Donato, 1994) in supporting development (See Chapters 21 and 22). The ZPD is often invoked as a theoretical grounding for this work, drawing on Vygotsky's (1978) well known formulation of the concept as the difference between what one is able to do alone and what is possible with assistance from another person, typically a caregiver or a teacher who is capable of guiding the child or learner through a difficult task. In other words, assistance from another person can support a learner in accomplishing tasks that are beyond their independent abilities, which in turn may facilitate development by working within the learner's ZPD.

A good deal of research has examined the verbal and nonverbal interactional practices that can observed in classroom and tutoring settings (e.g., Ohta, 2001; van Compernolle, 2015) as well as in study abroad contexts (Kinginger, Lee, Wu, & Tan, 2016). In such work, the focus has been on the ways in which teachers and peers may provide support to learners in using and understanding target linguistic forms (e.g., vocabulary, syntax, pragmalinguistics) and, somewhat less frequently, in internalizing semantic, pragmatic, or cultural concepts (see below for a focus on CBLI). While there are often overlaps with more cognitivist SLA theories (see Chapter 1) in terms of corrective feedback (e.g., recasts, metalinguistic hints, overt correct), albeit reinterpreted as mediation or other-regulation, this research has drawn attention to the multimodal and dialogically negotiated, interpsychological nature of assistance, or what van Compernolle (2015) has referred to as co-regulation. This perspective highlights the fact that assistance is achieved *between* people as opposed to an act done by one person to another. In addition, because Vygotsky's interest in assistance was in its relevance to development (i.e., the formation of new psychological functions) (see Chaiklin, 2003), Vygotskian-inspired LX research has begun to focus more on the internalization of psychological mediators (e.g., concepts, gestures, self-regulation strategies) than on the role of assistance on task performance. Indeed, this is the distinction drawn between assisted performance/scaffolding and mediation in recent interaction-focused work in the field (van Compernolle, 2015).

A particularly salient example of the emphasis on the relevance of assistance for development, which is also explicitly grounded in the ZPD concept, is dynamic assessment (DA). By integrating teaching into a testing situation, DA has the potential to provoke (traces of) the development one is interested in observing. In other words, any assistance provided by the test administrator—also known as the mediator—has the explicit goal of setting developmental processes in motion through teaching (Poehner, 2008). For example, offering prompts, hints, and providing metalinguistic feedback have—among other strategies—been used in DA literature as means of supporting learners in assessment tasks when they encounter difficulties. Following Vygotsky's (1978) logic, DA enables one to arrive at a dual evaluation of the learner: what is possible in solo performance and what capacities are still developing, as revealed through assistance. DA has been implemented in a wide range of adult (i.e., university language learners) classrooms and formal assessment contexts as well as within educational programs grounded in Vygotskian principles (see Poehner, 2018 for review). In addition, DA has been used in more clinical settings for diagnostic purposes (Antón, 2018) and with children in second language contexts (Peña & Greene, 2018).

Concept-Based Language Instruction

Negueruela's (2003) doctoral work marked an important shift in Vygotskian LX research by moving beyond using the theory as a lens through which to interpret LX development and toward its use as framework for intervening in pedagogical processes. He extended Gal'perin's (1989, 1992) model of STI to the teaching of Spanish grammar (i.e., tense, aspect, and mood). In so doing, he argued that grammar instruction should be centered around the teaching of conceptual categories of meaning rather than form. In other words, the semantics (meaning) and functions (pragmatics) of communication are given a leading role in pedagogy, and forms serve to illustrate how and why speakers choose between the available forms during communicative activity. This work, often referred to as concept-based language instruction (CBLI), has since been expanded in a relatively large number of studies, including genre in ESL writing (Ferreira, 2005), narrative literacy in French (Buescher, 2015), pragmatics in French (van Compernolle, 2014, van Compernolle & Henery, 2014) and Spanish (van Compernolle, Gomez-Laich, & Weber, 2016), and legal writing and thinking for international Master of Laws students (Hartig, 2017; Kurtz, 2017). Collectively, the body of CBLI research has shown very positive outcomes with regard to metalinguistic, metapragmatic, and metacommunicative (van Compernolle, 2018) awareness as well as positive outcomes for communicative performance. It is important to note that CBLI studies often report that concept formation outpaces performance accuracy. This is to say that students' ability to use the relevant linguistic forms they are learning lags behind their capacity to interpret and think through new conceptual categories of meaning. However, the argument is that once learners have a strong conceptual foundation for learning new forms, their communicative performances typically improve in a relatively short period of time.

A particularly important strand of CBLI research that has recently emerged focuses on the pedagogical interactions around conceptual materials in problem-solving and communication tasks. Drawing on Vygotsky's emphasis on the role of inner and private speech, as well as Swain's (2006) extension of the concept of languaging, CBLI research has often focused on the ways in which self-directed speech (i.e., verbalization; see above) can assist in the internalization process. Building on this idea, van Compernolle (2014) argued that while monologic verbalization can help learners to realize what they do and do not understand about the concepts they are appropriating, dialogic verbalization is also necessary so that an expert can push the learner and provide more explicit instruction as needed. Thus, van Compernolle's (2014) research on concept-based pragmatics instruction linked Gal'perin's (1989, 1992) STI model of materials and task design to the kinds of on-the-ground interactive pedagogical practices found in the literature on dynamic assessment. This was done in both concept-based and problem-solving tasks as well as in dynamic strategic interaction scenario tasks (van Compernolle, 2018) that focus on communication. In parallel, Poehner and Infante (2015) have recently proposed the concept of mediated development as a framework for planning and carrying out concept-based pedagogical tasks, with an emphasis on the intermental nature of task interaction (i.e., co-constructed thinking and performance).

Affect and Perezhivanie

A relatively less common extension of Vygotsky's theory to LX development, but one that is gaining traction, is the relevance of affect/emotion to LX learners and the notion of *perezhivanie* (Mahn & John-Steiner, 2002; Mok, 2015; Swain, 2013; van Compernolle, 2019; Veresov & Mok, 2018). This work has attempted to reunite affective and cognitive processes as two sides of human consciousness, a unity that was central to Vygotsky's work but, as Swain (2013) pointed out, was somehow forgotten for a number of years as researchers focused primarily of the cognitive aspects of LX development in isolation from the affective processes that permeate them. Researching affect and *perezhivanie* has led investigators to adopt a wider range of methods for examining LX development than has often been used in Vygotskian research, including ethnography, diary and interview studies, and discourse analysis of emotive language use (see Veresov & Mok, 2018), to complement the more cognitive data that have traditionally been the focus of LX research (e.g., results of metalinguistic and performance tasks).

Integrating Perspectives

As noted above, Vygotsky's theory has been well integrated into LX development research for a number of years. Indeed, over a decade ago, it was already considered one of the "new mainstream" theories in the field (Swain & Deters, 2007). The work has garnered considerable attention as a theoretical framework for interpreting LX development processes as well as for designing LX assessments and educational programs. However, the contribution of LX work to the general theory is less clear because most of us who work within the theory have used it to address LX questions rather than to use the LX development context to ask more general questions about human psychology and development. In this section, I will turn my attention to the question of what LX research has contributed, or has the potential to contribute, to Vygotskian psychology.

The clearest example of a contribution to psychology more generally is research on inner speech (Guerrero, 2018). Because Vygotsky (1986) ascribed such importance to the internalization of communicative speech as a tool for mediating one's own thinking, the role and consequences of LX development on internal mental functioning is a natural point of integration between LX and the general theory. Indeed, Pavlenko's (2005) work on conceptual restructuring has provided important evidence that LX development has interesting consequences for cognition. For example, in color-naming tasks, Pavlenko (2005) found that while monolingual speakers of Russian identify the distinction between dark-blues and light-blues (an obligatory distinction in the language—there is no Russian word that covers all shades/hues of blue) with a very high degree of agreement, Russian speakers who have become highly proficient in and have lots of experience living in English (e.g., immigrants to the United States) are less able to identify the boundary between dark and light blues. The argument is that since English has no obligatory distinction (they are all shades of blue), bilingual speakers inhabit a kind of hybrid space that is distinct from monolingual speakers of Russian and monolingual speakers of English. In other words, a consequence of LX development is a change in inner speech, which leads to a change in the speakers' perception of color. In addition, as noted earlier, a similar finding has been found in studies of speech-gesture synchrony, at least in terms of motion events, where bilinguals may adopt LX speech patterns that are native-like but exhibit an L1 or L1-LX hybrid pattern in their gestures, suggesting that their inner speech is either L1 mediated or at least influenced by both languages simultaneously (Stam, 2018).

There have also been fruitful integrations of LX research into general psychology with regard to children in contexts of immigration. Mahn and John-Steiner (2002) focused on the affective dimensions of being an English Language Learner (ELL) in a public school, and how teachers and learners provided support for the development of self-confidence. In addition, a large body of work has used DA as a means of providing more accurate diagnoses of ELLs' needs, especially by distinguishing difficulties arising from typical LX development from those that are linked to more general language impairments (e.g., dyslexia) (Peña & Greene, 2018). Such a fine-grained assessment has important consequences for the kinds of school-based support provided to children (e.g., developing an individualized education program for a student).

There are, of course, a number of insights from LX research that have not yet transferred to general psychology but would be beneficial to the field more generally. A primary example is the insight from studies of interaction that assistance (or mediation) is an intricately negotiated phenomenon that is coordinated in real time between interlocutors. Because LX researchers are often trained as applied linguists, they have brought approaches to discourse analysis and conversation analysis to bear on classroom, tutoring, and dynamic assessment interactions that provide in-depth empirical and theoretically grounded analyses of intermental functioning (e.g., van Compernolle, 2015). Unfortunately, much of the work in the general theory focuses on psychometric data (e.g., test scores) or, when interaction is considered, very superficial descriptions of the content of verbal exchanges.

Implications for Practice and Research

The review of literature above presents several implications for practice and research. In line with recent calls to overcome the research/practice divide in favor of a praxis-driven agenda (Lantolf & Poehner, 2014), I will outline some of the major contributions of Vygotskian theory to the field.

A first issue is the role of inner speech in LX development and, by extension, the consequences of LX development on inner speech. As noted, there appears to be a possible bidirectional relationship: L1 inner speech may continue to exert an influence on cognition during LX development while at the same time internalizing an LX may lead to changes in inner speech (e.g., an L1-LX hybrid). This finding implies that pedagogies should be sensitive to similarities and differences in semantic encoding and not simply focus on forms. In addition, research into instructed LX development ought to consider underlying cognitive processes and not simply communicative performance data. Such data might include metalinguistic knowledge, perceptual tasks, and/or analyses of speech-gesture activity as a means of looking into LX learners' inner speech.

Second, pedagogies centered around meaning—especially CBLI—seem to help learners to orient to conceptual categories of meaning that are relevant to the LX language and culture, which may or may not work in the same way in their L1. The implication is that by making concepts visible to learners and the object of explicit pedagogy, learners may be able to use and eventually internalize a new conceptualization system. As noted, concepts typically precede forms in CBLI, so teachers and researchers should be sensitive to the fact the learners may at first control only a limited number of forms. However, with practice—especially in communication tasks that involve support in controlling forms (van Compernolle, 2014, 2018)—the development of communicative abilities proceeds relatively quickly.

Third, assessment practices—whether in clinical, educational, or purely research contexts—would do well to include the kind of ZPD-inspired dual evaluation of learners embodied by DA. In this way, teachers and researchers alike are able to distinguish already formed abilities from those capacities that are in the process of developing. For teaching purposes, such information can provide instructors with valuable information relevant to developing course materials, individualized learning plans, remedial as well as enhancement programs, and so on. For research purposes, this kind of information can provide a window into the developmental processes under study as well as the possible variation between learners. For instance, using a DA can distinguish learners who fail to respond at all to a particular intervention from those who responded well but happened not to make enough progress to control a target language feature independently.

Finally, a fourth overarching implication of Vygotskian LX research is that educators and researchers alike need to attend to the affective and experiential processes that underpin LX development and may lead to individual variation in outcomes. At a bare minimum this means understanding affect and experience (i.e., perezhivanie) as a context for the more linguistic or cognitive phenomena one is interested in. Ideally, following through with Vygotsky's commitment to educating the whole person as a unity of affect and intellect requires us to rethink LX educational practices and research so that they foreground emotion and experience as an integral part of the development process, and not just as a set of independent factors that may impact the linguistic and cognitive phenomena we are interested in.

Future Directions

There are many directions for future research to take. Here, I will simply sketch out a few of the main questions that arise from the review above.

First, more research is needed on the role of inner speech in LX development and the consequences of LX development on inner speech. The latter is especially interesting for the study of human consciousness beyond the LX field. Such research may involve laboratory experiments (e.g., perceptual tasks), elicited discourse tasks with a focus on speech as well as gesture patterns, or naturalistic discourse analysis. Indeed, all three kinds of studies would go far toward understanding the L1-LX inner speech relationship.

Second, while work in dynamic assessment and concept-based language instruction has yielded positive outcomes, these studies tend to be more descriptive than comparative. In other words, while DA and CBLI seem to be effective, we have little information on the relative effectiveness of them in comparison to more traditional/nondynamic approaches to assessment or language instruction. For instance, does the added information about still-developing capacities in DA actually help to better predict future LX outcomes or learning potential compared with non-DA tests? Does the internalization of conceptual categories of meaning in CBLI lead to better communicative outcomes compared to other approaches to implicit or explicit language teaching?

Third, additional work on affect and perezhivanie is needed. Ideally, this work would combine multiple sources of data (e.g., interviews, diaries, observation, discourse tasks) and address historical, environmental, and intramental processes involved in LX development. Importantly, this research would need to strive to maintain the unity of affect and intellect, with the understanding that affective and intellectual processes, though not the same thing, operate in parallel to mediate human consciousness.

Reflection Questions

- What are some implications for your research and/or teaching of the finding that inner speech may remain dominated by a learner's L1 or may continue to exert an influence as part of a L1-LX hybrid system?
- How might an understanding of assistance as intermental functioning inform language instruction and/or assessment practice in the language(s) you research and/or teach?
- Think of a context in which you conduct LX research. How could you expand your methods to include affect and/or perezhivanie as a dimension of your work?

Recommended Reading

Lantolf, J. P., & Poehner, M. E. (2014). *Sociocultural theory and the pedagogical imperative in L2 education: Vygotskian praxis and the research/practice divide.* Routledge.
This book highlights Vygotsky's commitment to praxis—the unity of theory and practice—in psychology. Drawing primarily on examples from concept-based language instruction and dynamic assessment, the authors argue that LX research should be conducted in educational contexts in order to improve language education and at the same time answer fundamental questions about the nature of LX development through educational intervention.

Lantolf, J. P., & Poehner, M. E. (Eds.), with M. Swain. (2018). *The Routledge handbook of sociocultural theory and second language development.* Routledge.
This is the first handbook focused on Vygotskian theory and its extension to LX development. It includes contributions from leading scholars in the field and covers an expansive range of topics, including current debates within the general theory, private and inner speech, concept-based language instruction, dynamic assessment, teacher education, and social justice.

Van Compernolle, R. A. (2015). *Interaction and second language development: A Vygotskian perspective.* John Benjamins.
This book outlines an approach to understanding pedagogical interaction in classroom and tutoring contexts, with specific focus on Vygotskian educational programs such as dynamic assessment and concept-based language instruction. The main contribution of the book is to illustrate how multimodal conversation analysis can be used as a means of elucidating the moment-to-moment coordination of intermental functioning in LX development.

References

Aljaafreh, A., & Lantolf, J. P. (1994). Negative feedback as regulation and second language learning in the zone of proximal development. *Modern Language Journal, 78,* 465–483.
Antón, M. (2018). Dynamic diagnosis of second language abilities. In J. P. Lantolf & M. E. Poehner (Eds.) with M. Swain, *Routledge handbook of sociocultural theory and second language development* (pp. 210–323). Routledge.
Boroditsky, L. (2018). 7,000 universes: How the languages we speak shape the way we think. Doubleday.

Buescher, K. (2015). *Developing narrative literacy in a second language through concept-based instruction and a division-of-labor pedagogy* [Unpublished doctoral dissertation]. The Pennsylvania State University.

Cazden, C. (1981). Performance before competence: Assistance to child discourse in the zone of proximal development. *Quarterly Newsletter of the Laboratory of Comparative Human Cognition, 3*(1), 5–8.

Chaiklin, S. (2002). A developmental teaching approach to schooling. In G. Wells & G. Claxton (Eds.), *Learning for life in the 21st century: Sociocultural perspectives on the future of education* (pp. 167–180). Blackwell.

Chaiklin, S. (2003). The zone of proximal development in Vygotsky's analysis of learning and instruction. In A. Kozulin, B. Gindis, V. Ageyev, & S. Miller (Eds.), *Vygotsky's educational theory in cultural context* (pp. 39–64). Cambridge University Press.

Cole, M., & Scribner, S. (1978). Introduction. In M. Cole, V. John-Steiner, S. Scribner, & E. Souberman (Eds.), *L. S. Vygotsky. Mind in society: The development of higher psychological processes* (pp. 1–14). Harvard University Press.

Davydov, V. V. (1995). The influence of L. S. Vygotsky on education theory, research, and practice (trans. S. T. Kerr). *Educational Researcher, 24*(3), 12–21.

Dewaele, J.-M. (2018). Why the dichotomy "L1 versus LX user" is better than "native versus non-native speaker." *Applied Linguistics, 39*, 236–240.

DiCamilla, F. J., & Antón, M. (2004). Private speech: a study of language for thought in collaborative interaction of language learners. *International Journal of Applied Linguistics, 14*, 36–69.

Donato, R. (1994). Collective scaffolding in a second language. In J. P. Lantolf & G. Appel (Eds.), *Vygotskian approaches to second language research* (pp. 33–56). Ablex Press.

Ferreira, M. M. (2005). *A concept-based approach to writing instruction: From the abstract to the concrete performance* [Unpublished doctoral dissertation]. The Pennsylvania State University.

Frawley, W., & Lantolf, J. P. (1985). Second language discourse: A Vygotskian perspective. *Applied Linguistics, 6*, 19–44.

Frawley, W. (1997). *Vygotsky and cognitive science. Language and the unification of the social and computational mind.* Harvard University Press.

Gal'perin, P. Y. (1989). Mental actions as a basis for the formation of thoughts and images. *Soviet Psychology, 27*(3), 45–65.

Gal'perin, P. Y. (1992). Stage-by-stage formation as a method of psychological investigation. *Journal of Russian and Eastern European Psychology, 30*(4), 60–80.

González Rey, F. L., & Martínez, A. M. (2016). Perezhivanie: Advancing on its implications for the cultural-historical approach. *International Research in Early Childhood Education, 7*, 142–160.

Guerrero, M. C. M. de. (2018). Private and inner speech in L2 learning: The impact of Vygotskian sociocultural theory. In J. P. Lantolf & M. E. Poehner (Eds.) with M. Swain, *Routledge handbook of sociocultural theory and second language development* (pp. 152–164). Routledge.

Haenen, J. (1996). *Piotr Gal'perin: Psychologist in Vygotsky's footsteps*. Nova Science Publishers.

Haenen, J. (2001). Outlining the teaching–learning process: Piotr Gal'perin's contribution. *Learning and Instruction, 11*, 157–170.

Hartig, A. J. (2017). *Connecting language and disciplinary knowledge in English for specific purposes: Case studies in law*. Multilingual Matters.

Haywood, H. C., & Lidz, C. S. (2007). *Dynamic assessment in practice. Clinical and educational applications*. Cambridge University Press.

John-Steiner, V. P. (2007). Vygotsky on thinking and speaking. In H. Daniels, M. Cole, & J. V. Wertsch (Eds.), *The Cambridge Companion to Vygotsky* (pp. 136–152). Cambridge University Press.

Kinginger, C., Lee, S. H., Wu, Q., & Tan, D. (2016). Contextualized language practices as sites for learning: Mealtime talk in short-term Chinese homestays. *Applied Linguistics, 37*, 716–740.

Kurtz, L. (2017). *Vygotsky goes to law school: A concept-based pedagogical intervention to promote legal reading and reasoning development in international L.L.M. students.* [Unpublished doctoral dissertation]. The Pennsylvania State University.

Lantolf, J. P. (2006). Sociocultural theory and L2. *Studies in Second Language Acquisition, 28*, 67–109.

Lantolf, J. P., & Thorne, S. L. (2006). *Sociocultural theory and the genesis of second language development*. Oxford University Press.

Lantolf, J. P., & Frawley, W. (1984). Second language performance and Vygotskyan psycholinguistics: Implications for L2 instruction. In A. Manning, P. Martin, & K. McCalla (Eds.), *The Tenth LACUS Forum 1983* (pp. 425–440). Hornbeam Press.

Lantolf, J. P., & Poehner, M. E. (2014). *Sociocultural theory and the pedagogical imperative in L2 education. Vygotskian praxis and the research/practice divide*. Routledge.

Luria, A. R. (1976). *Cognitive Development. Its Cultural and Social Foundations*. Harvard University Press.

Mahn, H., & John-Steiner, V. (2002). The gift of confidence: A Vygotskian view of emotion. In G. Wells & G. Claxton (Eds.), *Learning for life in the 21st century: Sociocultural perspectives on the future of education* (pp. 46–58). Blackwell.

McNeill, D. (1992). *Hand and mind. What gestures reveal about thought*. University of Chicago Press.
McNeill, D. (2005). *Gesture & thought*. University of Chicago Press.
Mok, N. (2015). Toward an understanding of perezhivanie for sociocultural SLA research. *Language and Sociocultural Theory, 2*, 139–159.
Negueruela, E. (2003). *A sociocultural approach to the teaching-learning of second languages: Systemic-theoretical instruction and L2 development* [Unpublished doctoral dissertation]. The Pennsylvania State University.
Ohta, A. S. (2001). *Second language acquisition processes in the classroom: Learning Japanese*. Erlbaum.
Pavlenko, A. (2005) Bilingualism and thought. In A. De Groot & J. Kroll (Eds.), *Handbook of bilingualism: psycholinguistic approaches* (pp. 433–453). Oxford University Press.
Peña, E. D., & Greene, K. J. (2018). Dynamic assessment of children learning a second language. In J. P. Lantolf & M. E. Poehner (Eds.) with M. Swain, *Routledge handbook of sociocultural theory and second language development* (pp. 324–339). Routledge.
Poehner, M. E., & Infante, P. (2015). Mediated development: Inter-psychological activity for L2 education. *Language and Sociocultural Theory, 2*, 161–183.
Poehner, M. E. (2008). *Dynamic assessment: A Vygotskian approach to understanding and promoting L2 development*. Springer Verlag.
Saxe, G. B. (1982). Developing forms of arithmetical thought among the Oksapmin of Papua New Guinea. *Developmental Psychology, 18*, 583–594.
Scribner, S., & Cole, M. (1981). *The psychology of literacy*. Harvard University Press.
Sfard, A. (1998). On two metaphors for learning and the dangers of choosing just one. *Educational Researcher, 27*(2), 4–13.
Smagorinsky, P. (2011). Vygotsky's stage theory: The psychology of art and the actor under the direction of perezhivanie. *Mind, Culture, and Activity, 18*, 319–341.
Stam, G. (2018). Gesture as a window onto conceptualization in second language acquisition: A Vygotskian perspective. In J. P. Lantolf & M. E. Poehner (Eds.) with M. Swain, *Routledge handbook of sociocultural theory and second language development* (pp. 165–178). Routledge.
Steinbach-Koehler, F., & Thorne, S. L. (2011). The social life of self-directed talk: A sequential phenomenon? In J. Hall, J. Hellermann, & S. Pekarek Doehler (Eds.), *L2 interactional competence and development* (pp. 66–92). Multilingual Matters.
Sternberg, R. J., & Grigorenko, E. L. (2002). *Dynamic testing. The nature and measurement of learning potential*. Cambridge University Press.
Swain, M. (2006). Languaging, agency and collaboration in advanced language proficiency. In H. Byrnes (Ed.), *Advanced language learning: The contribution of Halliday and Vygotsky* (pp. 95–108). Continuum.
Swain, M. (2013). The inseparability of cognition and emotion in second language learning. *Language Teaching, 46*, 195–207.
Swain, M., & Deters, P. (2007). "New" mainstream SLA theory: Expanded and enriched. *Modern Language Journal, 91*(S1), 820–836.
Tulviste, P. (1991). *The cultural-historical development of verbal thinking*. Nova Science Publishers.
Ushakova, T. (1994). Inner speech and second language acquisition: An experimental-theoretical approach. In J. P. Lantolf & G. Appel (Eds.), *Vygotskian approaches to second language research* (pp. 135–156). Ablex.
Valsiner, J., & van der Veer, R. (2014). Encountering the border: Vygotsky's zona blizhaishego razvitia and its implications for theories of development. In A. Yasnitsky, R. van der Veer, & M. Ferrari (Eds.), *The Cambridge handbook of cultural-historical psychology* (pp. 148–173). Cambridge University Press.
van Compernolle, R. A. (2014). *Sociocultural theory and L2 instructional pragmatics*. Multilingual Matters.
van Compernolle, R. A. (2015). *Interaction and second language development: A Vygotskian perspective*. John Benjamins.
van Compernolle, R. A. (2018). Focus on meaning and form: A Vygotskian perspective on task and pragmatic development in dynamic strategic interaction scenarios. In M. Ahmadian & M. P. G. Mayo (Eds.), *Recent trends in task-based language learning and teaching* (pp. 79–97). Mouton De Gruyter.
van Compernolle, R. A. (2019). The qualitative science of Vygotskian sociocultural psychology and L2 development. In J. W. Schwieter & A. Benati (Eds.), *The Cambridge handbook of language learning* (pp. 62–83). Cambridge University Press.
van Compernolle, R. A., & Henery, A. (2014). Instructed concept appropriation and L2 pragmatic development in the classroom. *Language Learning, 64*, 549–578.
van Compernolle, R. A., Gomez-Laich, M. P., & Weber, A. (2016). Teaching L2 Spanish sociopragmatics through concepts: A classroom-based study. *Modern Language Journal, 100*(1), 341–361.
Veresov, N., & Mok, N. (2018). Understanding development through *perezhivanie* of learning. In J. P. Lantolf & M. E. Poehner (Eds.) with M. Swain, *Routledge handbook of sociocultural theory and second language development* (pp. 89–101). Routledge.
Vygotsky, L. S. (1971). *The psychology of art*. MIT Press.

Vygotsky, L. S. (1978). *Mind in society: The development of higher mental processes*. Harvard University Press.
Vygotsky, L. S. (1986). *Thought and language*. MIT Press.
Vygotsky, L. S. (1994). *The problem of the environment*. In R. van der Veer & J. Valsiner (Eds.), *The Vygotsky reader* (pp. 338–354). Blackwell.
Vygotsky, L. S. (1997). *Educational psychology*. Nova Science.
Vygotsky, L. S. (1998). The problem of age. In R. W. Rieber (Ed.), *The collected works of L. S. Vygotsky. Volume 5: Child Psychology*. Plenum.
Wertsch, J. (2007). Mediation. In H. Daniels, M. Cole, & J. Wertsch (Eds.), *The Cambridge companion to Vygotsky* (pp. 178–192). Cambridge University Press.
Zinchenko, V. P. (2002). From classical to organic psychology. *Journal of Russian and East European Psychology, 39,* 32–77.
Zinchenko, V. P. (2009). Consciousness as the subject matter and task of psychology. *Journal of Russian and East European Psychology, 47,* 44–75.

3

THE HUMANISTIC APPROACH

Jane Arnold and José Manuel Foncubierta

The humanistic approach to education has significantly influenced the field and while much has been written about its advantages, there have also been some criticisms. Humanistic psychology, which has made contributions in educational contexts, according to Underhill (1989), "is a general term given to a loose, overlapping confederation of explorations in the field of human potential that share some common beliefs and values, but which do not work from a single articulated theory" (p. 250). In language teaching, the humanistic perspective is an attempt to place the learner at the center of the process of target language acquisition. According to Sanchez Calvo (2007), an "undeniable root of learner-centred teaching seems to be the humanistic approach" (p. 191). Unlike the approaches centered only on the contents of the language, a humanistic orientation promotes freedom and learner initiative, considering the learner as an active figure in the process of learning. In this chapter, we will review the importance of humanistic aspects of psychology in education in general and specifically in language teaching and we will see how this has been incorporated in language classrooms.

Humanism in Educational Psychology

Moving away from psychoanalysis and behaviorism (both considered to limit a person's control over motivational factors), Carl Rogers was one of the founders of humanistic psychology, a perspective which emphasizes the importance of self-actualization and reaching one's potential. He contributed influential ideas for education, such as the need for unconditional positive regard in which learners feel accepted and thus have more confidence. Amini and Amini (2012) comment that, for Rogers, "a precondition for learning to take place is that the subject of learning be relevant to the learner and stimulate active participation of the learner" (p. 102). In his book *Freedom to Learn,* Rogers (1969) points out that if what is done in the classroom does not relate in some way to the learners and what they want to achieve, this learning "… involves the mind only. It is learning which takes place from the neck up. It does not involve feelings or personal meanings; it has no relevance for the whole person" (pp. 3–4). He proposed five elements of significant learning: personal involvement, self-initiation, pervasiveness (affecting behavior and attitudes), evaluation by the learner (who knows if it leads toward what they want to know), and meaningfulness (p. 5). Gadotti (1994) says, "Education should have a vision of the pupil as a complete person, who has feelings and emotions" (p. 12).

Rogers saw the teacher not just as someone who presents the subject matter but as a facilitator. Underhill (1989) describes the three qualities of a teacher/facilitator that Rogers considered support whole-person learning—genuineness, unconditional acceptance, and empathy:

> Teachers exercising the quality of genuineness are able to be authentically themselves in the act of teaching, rather than playing the role of teacher… A teacher with the quality of unconditional acceptance is able to respect and accept her learners for what they are, in an unconditional way… This teacher who is empathic… is able to identify with others and to feel what it's like for them at any point in a lesson.
>
> *p. 258*

Abraham Maslow was also important in the development of humanistic psychology. In his theory of a hierarchy of needs, Maslow (1943) focused on the development of human potential and how people reach important achievements. The hierarchy is typically represented as a pyramid with different levels of needs—physiological, safety, love, belonging, esteem, and self-actualization—with the most basic needs at the bottom of the pyramid. For the highest level, self-actualization, Maslow (1943) notes that, "It refers to the person's desire for self-fulfillment, namely, to the tendency for him to become actualized in what he is potentially" (p. 382). Later, Maslow also included cognitive needs, aesthetic needs, and transcendence. His theory has been useful in psychology and in educational contexts, especially in understandings of motivation, even though it was not based on empirical research. A valuable contribution of his work is his holistic view of education, which takes into account all aspects of the learner—physical, social, and emotional, as well as intellectual.

In a posthumous book synthesizing many of his ideas, Maslow (1971) stated that a humanistic educational approach would produce people who are:

> …stronger, healthier, and would take their own lives into their hands to a greater extent. With increased personal responsibility for one's personal life, and with a rational set of values to guide one's choosing, people would begin to actively change the society in which they lived.
>
> *p. 95*

Implications for the classroom abound in many of his theories. For students to reach their potential, not only are their cognitive needs important to consider but they also need to feel physically and emotionally comfortable in the classroom to make the necessary effort to reach their potential as learners.

Similar humanistic ideas are also found in the relatively new field of Positive Psychology (PP) (see Chapter 5). Two of its founders, Seligman and Csíkszentmihályi (2000) consider that, "Psychology is not just the study of pathology, weakness and damage, it is also the study of strength and virtue" (p. 7), and they mention "four different personal traits that contribute to positive psychology: subjective well-being, optimism, happiness, and self-determination" (p. 9). If in the process of studying a language, students experience these positive factors, then this is likely to benefit their learning as well as their lives more broadly. In their research with university students, Macaskill and Denovan (2013) found that in a group where they incorporated a psycho-educational intervention that supported the psychological strengths related to confidence (which they measured in relation to self-efficacy and self-esteem), there were significant increases both in confidence measures and autonomous learning in comparison to the control group which did not receive the intervention. As can be seen, there is considerable overlap and resonance between the themes addressed in positive psychology and those which lie at the heart of humanism.

Humanistic Perspectives in Language Learning

In the 1960s and 1970s, humanism was a term being used in diverse contexts. Its exact meaning was not always clear. The term was taken up by experts in many areas of foreign/second language teaching. In his book, *Humanism in Language Learning*, Stevick (1990, pp. 23–4) proposes five components of humanism:

Feelings. This includes both personal emotions and aesthetic appreciation.
Social relations. This side of humanism encourages friendship and cooperation, and opposes whatever tends to reduce them.
Responsibility. This aspect accepts the need for public scrutiny, criticism, and correction.
Intellect. This includes knowledge, reason, and understanding and fights against whatever interferes with the free exercise of the mind.
Self-actualization. This is the quest for full realization of one's own deepest true qualities.

In a humanistic approach to language teaching, affective factors are very important. They include both intrapersonal aspects, such as learners' motivation and confidence, and also the group relationships established in the learning context. Stern (1983) wrote that, "the affective component contributes at least as much and often more to language learning than the cognitive skills" (p. 386). According to related neurobiological research, the two areas cannot be separated. For example, neuroscientist Antonio Damasio (1994) explained that the affective component of learning needs to be considered when discussing the neurological conditions which lead to the effective functioning of the brain. Schumann (1994) states that, "the brain stem, limbic and frontolimbic areas, which comprise the stimulus appraisal system, emotionally modulate cognition such that, in the brain, emotion and cognition are distinguishable but inseparable. Therefore, from a neural perspective, affect is an integral part of cognition" (p. 232).

The rise of Positive Psychology, whose roots are firmly planted in humanism, balances what is good in life with life's adversities, and it works to promote positive experiences and to focus on positive principles in institutions. It has also influenced how second language practitioners approach SLA. As Dewaele, Chen, Padilla, and Lake (2019) point out, "For many years, a cognitive perspective had dominated research in applied linguistics. Around the turn of the millennium researchers became increasingly interested in the role of emotions in foreign language learning and teaching." This has led to diverse applications of PP in the second language acquisition context such as those MacIntyre and Mercer (2014) discuss; they consider that, "PP has been designed to address three topic areas: the workings of positive internal experiences such as emotions, positive individual characteristics such as traits associated with living well, and institutions that enable people to flourish" and so "PP aims to contribute another perspective to psychology by studying what we can do to increase strengths and attributes such as resiliency, happiness, optimism and the like in the general population" (pp. 154–155). While important in any educational context, such attributes are even more significant in language learning where affective factors can strongly influence the results of the learning process. For example, students speaking in front of others in a language that they do not always control well is an inherent feature of second language acquisition contexts and it may produce anxiety in learners, inhibiting production and comprehension of language. Thus, it is especially important to establish a classroom atmosphere for language learning that contributes to learners' sense of confidence and security. MacIntyre and Mercer (2014) comment:

> Many language educators are aware of the importance of improving individual learners' experiences of language learning by helping them to develop and maintain their motivation, perseverance, and resiliency, as well as positive emotions necessary for the long-term undertaking of learning a foreign language. In addition, teachers also widely recognise the

vital role played by positive classroom dynamics amongst learners and teachers, especially in settings in which communication and personally meaningful interactions are foregrounded.

p. 156

An aspect of positive psychology that has also been important for Humanistic Language Teaching (HLT) is Self-Determination Theory which centers on three psychological needs: A need for a sense of competence, a sense of belonging, and a sense of autonomy (Deci & Ryan, 2001). All of these are relevant in language teaching, but a sense of autonomy has played an especially central role in understandings of the language learning process and related pedagogy. Arnold and Fonseca (2017) suggest that, "what matters most for the development of autonomy is often invisible, not innovative technology or teaching materials, important as they may be, but rather what happens inside and between the participants in the learning community we create in the classroom" (p. 49). According to the Common European Framework of Reference (CEFR), language learning autonomy "can be promoted if 'learning to learn' is regarded as an integral part of language learning, so that learners become increasingly aware of the way they learn, the options open to them and the options that best suit them" and then they can be "brought increasingly to make choices in respect of objectives, materials and working methods in the light of their own needs, motivations, characteristics and resources" (Council of Europe, 2001, pp. 141–142).

Diverse humanistic factors play an important role in the language acquisition process: learners' feelings about themselves such as confidence, anxiety, boredom, and interest; how they see the relationship of the language and their academic and personal goals; and if learning is personally meaningful. Learners' feelings are always present, though they may or may not be taken into consideration by the teacher. However, when they are, the learning process will be more effective. As Oxford (2013, pp. 99–100) states, "emotions are powerful motivators for cognition." Also, when considering the learning process, ideally, there needs to be a commensurate focus on teachers' emotions and a humanistic perspective would imply a consideration of the teacher as a whole person as well as their relationship to learners (see Chapter 21). According to Moskowitz and Dewaele (2021, p. 118), this "can lead to a deeper, more nuanced understanding of the student/teacher relationship and by extension, the FL learning process itself." One of the conclusions of the research of Cuéllar and Oxford (2018, p. 67), which was designed to draw teachers' emotions out of the shadows, is that their emotions are important and that "they can manage their emotions to serve the learning process." Teachers need to be aware of how their own emotions are going to affect what goes on in the classroom and, as Dewaele, Gkonou, and Mercer (2018, pp.126–7) explain, teachers "should be able to regulate their own emotions to ensure they are in the right frame of mind to create positive rapport with learners, generate enjoyment and manage any anxieties," and they continue by pointing out the need to "work towards a deeper understanding of language teacher psychology including in particular how they manage the emotional complexity of the FL classroom for themselves and their learners." Although there is increasing recognition of the importance of the teacher as a holistic, emotional being, the emphasis in humanism has tended to largely focus on the learner.

Integrating Perspectives

In a humanistically focused class, the teacher is sensitive to learners' affective experiences. Teachers typically seek to accentuate the positive affective elements such as interest and enjoyment, while at the same time, managing any negative emotions such as fear of speaking in front of others. According to the Affective Filter Hypothesis (Krashen, 1985), just as negative affect can close down the mind and prevent learning, positive affect can provide invaluable support for language learning. This is also reflected in the broaden-and-build theory, which explains how positive emotions broaden thought action repertoires, and in so doing build personal resources (Fredrickson, 2004) (see Chapter 14). As such, positive emotions are not just desirable outcomes; they are desirable input states as they have the potential to create a positive upward spiral.

One important emotional factor for teachers to develop is empathy with students. Teachers do not need to always agree with their students, but they do need to try to understand how they are feeling, to listen to them—not just the language they produce but also the person who is speaking. In this way, interaction with students can be more meaningful. In their research, McAllister and Jordan Irvine (2002) found that, "an empathetic disposition led to more positive interactions with their students, supportive classroom climates, and student-centered pedagogy" (p. 442), all factors reminiscent of the core features of a humanistic approach.

One of the authors who dealt most directly with humanistic language teaching in its early stages was Gertrude Moskowitz. Her work is related in diverse ways to concepts from psychology such as self-actualization where learners are encouraged to know themselves better and reach their potential. This connection with psychology has strongly influenced the development of diverse pedagogical approaches in language teaching. Although some activities she proposed may not be applicable in all educational situations, the principles she presents in the introduction to her book, *Caring and Sharing in the Foreign Language Class: A Sourcebook on Humanistic Techniques,* relate to many of today's insights into the role of psychology in language teaching:

- A principal purpose of education is to provide learning and an environment that facilitates the achievement of the full potential of students.
- Personal growth as well as cognitive growth is a responsibility of the school. Therefore, education should deal with both dimensions of humans—the cognitive or intellectual and the affective or emotional.
- For learning to be significant, feelings must be recognized and put to use.
- Significant learning is discovered for oneself.
- Human beings want to actualize their potential.
- Having healthy relationships with other classmates is conducive to learning.
- Learning about oneself is a motivating factor in learning.
- Increasing one's self-esteem enhances learning. (Moskowitz, 1978, p. 18)

An important influence of psychology on education reflected here is the concern for educating the whole person, taking into account both intellectual and affective aspects. Stevick (1990) discusses Moskowitz's work on humanism in education, which he notes involves "concern for personal development, for self-acceptance and acceptance by others" (pp. 24–25), something Moskowitz saw as closely related to humanistic psychology, which considers how learners feel about themselves and deals with both the intellectual and the emotional dimensions—in other words, the whole person.

Humanism was also present in the work of Wilga Rivers, an authority on language teaching and learning who made many contributions to the field. She stressed how John Dewey, psychologist and educational reformer, felt that education was not simply receiving knowledge of the subject taught but also about how to live one's life and reach one's potential. Rivers (1983) commented, "In the individualization movement of the 1970s, humanistic education continued its struggle for recognition of the primacy of the individual personality against deterministic behaviorist emphases," and she pointed out how, while "content is not neglected in a class that uses humanistic techniques, in an affective or humanistic approach, students are encouraged to talk about themselves, to be open with others, and to express their feelings" (pp. 23–24). She emphasized the emotional aspects of foreign language learning and stressed the need to make material meaningful for learners, ideas supported by key figures in psychology and education.

An advantage of taking into account the affective, humanistic dimension of learners is that it can make it much easier to address a concern that exists in many language teaching contexts today: learner diversity. Studies of inclusivity stress the importance of meeting the needs of diverse students and working sensitively with individuals from a range of backgrounds and with different needs. Research shows that this can involve things such as those indicated by Williams, Berger, and McClendon (2005):

1. Focusing on students' intellectual and social development; offering the best possible course of study for the context in which the education is offered.
2. Purposely developing and using educational resources to enhance students' learning; establishing an environment that challenges each student to achieve at high levels academically while encouraging each member of the class to contribute to students' overall learning and knowledge development.
3. Paying attention to the cultural differences diverse learners bring to the educational experience and how those cultural differences enhance the teaching and learning environment.
4. Creating a welcoming classroom environment that engages all of its diversity in the pursuit of individual and collaborative learning.

Humanistic teachers, aware of their students as individuals, can in subtle ways communicate to them acceptance of and respect for their individuality. This can lead to a positive atmosphere in the classroom, which contributes to one of the chief goals of HLT, the creation of a well-functioning group that supports the learning process. In this scenario, diversity is seen less as a problem but rather more as an interesting challenge and potential resource. Diversity is a primary factor considered by Howard Gardner (1993) in his Multiple Intelligence Theory, which proposes that intelligence is not limited to that which can be measured only by verbal and numerical means and that success in life is often determined to a great degree by other intelligences, such as musical, spatial, kinesthetic, interpersonal, and intrapersonal, which are not always taken into consideration in educational programs. There are many ways we can work in language classes to use all learning capacities and all types of intelligence in order to support language learning.

Reflection is central to humanism, and the opportunity for reflection is stressed in humanistic psychology (Schneider, Fraser Pierson, & Bugental, 2015) and education. When learners are encouraged and given time to reflect on their learning process, this can lead to deeper learning and more security. For example, completing one exercise after another in a textbook does not facilitate connections to what learners already know and it does not offer them the chance to practice self-regulation in order to see how they need to proceed in order to have greater control over the language and their learning. Reflecting individually or together with others in the class, including the teacher, needs to be part of this process. Reflection on the learning and teaching transpiring in class is also important for teachers' professional development as their systematic reflection can lead to greater professional competence. Farrell (2015, p. xi) states that with reflection, teachers "can not only improve the quality of their teaching, but also provide better opportunities for the students to learn." As Quesada Pacheco (2005) affirmed, "Reflective teaching is undoubtedly a valid means towards effective teaching practices" (p. 12).

The origins of HLT come in part from the work in the 1960s and 1970s of psychologists such as Rogers and Maslow, who showed concern for the development of the whole learner with affective and physical as well as cognitive needs. This concern is reflected in the alternative methods developed then; however, those working in HLT did not limit themselves solely to methods but rather extended their views to a broad, systemic view of experience closely related to psychology where learning, teaching, and living are interrelated. SLA and psychology have both stressed the importance of integrating affect and cognition in the learning process.

Humanism in language teaching does not require adopting one of the specific humanistic methods. Moskowitz (1978) offers "some specific ways foreign language teachers can weave humanistic strategies into their already existing curricular materials" and she states that this does not mean "total abandonment of what teachers are expected to teach, but supplementing these materials where appropriate" (p 1).

Humanistic approaches provide language teachers with options for teaching the language that can make significant differences for learners in their language learning experience.

> We can opt for teaching the language in a way that may teach the structure of [the language], but certainly nothing more (for example, an activity in which students practice question forms with superficial, non-meaningful items); alternatively, we can teach it in a way that, while practicing the same forms, permits students to share part of themselves with others, and in the process perhaps learn more about themselves and each other.
>
> *Arnold, 1998, p. 235*

In addition to general concepts, humanistic approaches include specific methods for language teaching—Community Language Learning, the Silent Way, Suggestopedia, and Total Physical Response—which incorporate aspects closely related to humanistic psychology. However, Underhill (1989) notes that often these methods have merely been considered for their colorful techniques "without serious attention to the *values*, *attitudes* and *awarenesses* that inform those practices," and he also points out that it is not essential to use one of the specific humanistic methods "in order to facilitate learning in a way that is consistent both with the values of humanistic psychology, and with our own individual awareness, knowledge and skills" (p. 250).

Even without teaching specifically following one of the humanistic methods, there are aspects related to these methods that can be of use in many language teaching contexts:

- *Learner-centered teaching.* Richards and Rodgers (2014) encourage teachers to take into account that learners learn in different ways.
- *Teachers work towards establishing learners' well-being.* In HLT, effective activities for learning are seen as those that, along with presenting the linguistic information to be learned, have personal significance for learners, take into account mind, emotions and the body, include the possibility of choice and lead to a positive atmosphere in the classroom where learners feel comfortable. MacIntyre and Mercer (2014, p.154) referring to Seligman's (2011) model of well-being describe it using the acronym PERMA "to reflect the multiple dimensions of the good life, including a focus on positive emotion (P), engagement with activities that use one's character strengths (E), developing positive interpersonal relationships (R), finding meaning by serving a cause beyond oneself (M), and recognizing areas of accomplishment and achievement (A)." Language teachers can reflect on these diverse aspects in promoting the well-being of their learners during teaching and as an outcome of it (see Chapter 15).
- *Use of music.* There are many advantages to using music in the classroom. Fonseca and Toscano (2012) point out that it can reduce stress, relax the body, keep the mind alert, stimulate creativity, improve concentration and be the basis for many types of language learning activities. Music is an important part of the HLT method Suggestopedia.
- *Use of images.* Stevick (1986) pointed out that a modification of images in the participants' minds is necessary for verbal communication to exist. Many advantages for working with images are seen in activities suggested by Arnold, Puchta, and Rinvolucri (2007): facilitating memory, critical thinking, connecting with the imagination, and making activities motivating and personally meaningful.
- *Movement.* One of the HLT methods, Total Physical Response, has movement as a central element and as Arnold and Foncubierta (2019) explain, it is beneficial for learning because it gets oxygen to the brain, strengthens concentration, leads to more participative learning, and helps to change the rhythm of the class.
- *Creation of a supportive atmosphere in the classroom.* Dörnyei and Murphey (2003) mention some possible feelings students might experience in a new language class: General anxiety and anxiety

about using the L2, doubts about understanding the teaching and knowing what to do, insecurity about their competence with the language, and general lack of confidence. However, they also present factors that will facilitate the creation of an effective learning community: The positive model of a teacher who gives space to diverse opinions, closeness, knowledge of others in the group, cooperation, and the satisfaction of completing tasks together.

Communicative language teaching (CLT**),** an approach rather than an actual method, uses communication as both the goal and the means to reach the goal. Hence, group dynamics (see Chapter 22) are especially important in that learners are expected to participate in activities where they need to interact with others in order to learn to speak the language. The field of education is rich with research on group dynamics, which Heron (1999) referred to as "the combined configuration of mental, emotional and physical energy in the group at any given time; and the way this configuration undergoes change" (p. 51). Effective classroom learning is facilitated by "great teachers who can create a positive classroom atmosphere [and] transmit insights in language and culture in such a way that learners will perceive it less as a 'transfer of knowledge' and more like a 'self-discovery of knowledge'" (Dewaele, 2011, p. 37). The focus on group dynamics is central to both HLT and successful CLT.

Within HLT, there are also a number of specific methods that have several special characteristics, which we will now consider. *Community Language Learning* (CLL) is a method developed by the psychologist Charles Curran, arising from his work with Counseling Learning but focusing specifically on language learning. As Richards and Rodgers (2014) point out, "counseling is one person giving advice, assistance and support to another who has a problem or is in some way in need. CLL draws on the counseling metaphor to redefine the roles of the teacher (the *counselor*) and learners (the *clients*) in the language classroom" which is where "the content of the language class stems from topics learners want to talk about and the teacher translates their requests into an appropriate syllabus" (p. 303). The teacher is not doing therapy, but rather recognizing that learning can be somewhat stressful and providing needed support for the students, while little by little encouraging their independence.

Feeling secure during interaction is central to the precepts of CLL. Larsen-Freeman (1986) points out the usefulness of the teacher's position in the CLL class since if the teacher sometimes moves around the class, "the threat is reduced and the students' learning is facilitated" (p. 96). Furthermore, as the teacher responds to students' language production in a non-threatening way, this encourages their confidence. Richards and Rodgers (2014) point out how in CLL the interactions between learners "deepen in intimacy as the class becomes a community of learners" (p. 306).

Suggestopedia is a method created in the 1970s by Georgi Lozanov, a psychiatrist and educator from Bulgaria. Stevick (1996) describes Lozanov's view of learning: "People are able to learn at rates many times greater than what we commonly assume to be the limits of human performance" (p. 306). Such issues are considered in what Lozanov termed "Suggestology." Positive suggestion comes from the teacher helping to remove barriers to learning; this may be direct (comments on how they will be successful in their learning process) or indirect (use of music and a pleasant environment in class).

According to O'Connell (1982), for Lozanov, "joy and relaxation are the prerequisites of all effective, fast learning. In language learning this means that students must feel comfortable, unthreatened, secure, and at the same time interested, amused and involved in meaningful activities using the new language." It is only in this state that learners will "respond to the teacher's desuggestion/suggestion, encouraging them to perform beyond their normal expectations" (pp. 111–112).

Music is a basic element used to put learners in a relaxed state. Fonseca Mora and Herrero Machancoses (2016) affirm: "Melodies and rhythm can create an attractive and enjoyable environment fostering learners' willingness to participate in the language classroom" (p. 362). According to Larsen-Freeman (1986), "On the conscious plane, the learner attends to the language; on the subconscious plane, the music suggests that learning is easy and pleasant. When there is a unity between conscious and subconscious, learning is enhanced" (p. 79).

The Silent Way, developed by Caleb Gattegno in the 1970s, concentrates more on how students learn than on how to teach. Learning is seen as creative problem solving. The method involves working with somewhat unusual things: a Fidel chart (a color-coded chart with symbols for the sounds of the language), vocabulary charts, and Cuisenaire rods (small wooden rods of different colors and different lengths) used in activities. Underhill (2014) suggests that teachers "may associate it with colored rods and word charts, but the Silent Way is neither of those things and is better seen as the language learning application of Gattegno's much larger vision for education, the Subordination of Teaching to Learning" (p. 213). However, the props used in Silent Way classes, due to their concrete, visual nature, can help learners' retention. The teacher generally speaks little. Rather than receiving explanations, students are involved in problem-solving. The teacher will speak if needed, but students generally work independently and thus become more autonomous.

McNeill (1982) points out: "The silences which occur in the lessons provide students with a chance to process thoroughly in their minds the few things that have been given by the teacher" (p. 119). All aspects of the language are dealt with but a special emphasis is placed on pronunciation. Richards and Rodgers (2014) summarize the learning hypotheses of Gattegno's theories: Learning is facilitated "if the learner discovers or creates rather than remembers and repeats what is to be learned… by accompanying (mediating) physical objects… by problem-solving involving the material to be learned" (p. 291). Learners are encouraged to trust themselves.

Total Physical Response (TPR) is a method developed by James Asher which, as its name suggests, involves movement in the classroom and stresses the importance of listening comprehension. When children are learning their first language, their parents give them many commands (e.g., *come here, get the ball…*), and before they begin to speak, they respond with movement. Asher reduced learner stress by teaching the language through physical activity wherein students were not required to produce language in the beginning, but rather just show comprehension of what they hear (stand up, put the book on the table…). Asher said that "most of the grammatical structure of the target language and hundreds of vocabulary items can be learned from the skillful use of the imperative by the instructor" (Asher, 1977, p. 4). After a while, students begin to produce the language, giving commands to other students and reading and writing the language. TPR has generally been used in the early stages of language learning, and it has been considered compatible with other methods. Thornbury (2013, p. 73) explains how TPR "exploits the physical nature of the classroom ecology," and he points out how "the embodied nature of language strongly supports a role for incorporating the kinesthetic and gestural aspects of communication in language learning."

Implications for Practice and Research

One of the main implications for language teaching from the humanistic approach is the need to develop a positive group atmosphere, something highly recommended in educational psychology. For this, it is important at the beginning of a new class to provide opportunities for students—and teachers—to get to know something about each other. Another implication is the importance of creating teaching activities that deal with the different ways that students learn, and insights from differentiation approaches can be useful here. Differentiation has been defined as "a philosophy of teaching purporting that students learn best when their teachers effectively address variance in students' readiness levels, interests, and learning preferences" (Tomlinson, 2005, p. 363). Teachers can deal with this by varying their teaching to include different ways to connect with and engage learners. For example, broadening our vision of the learning/teaching process can take us, as Foncubierta and Gant (2016) say, to "a more multisensory way of learning in the classroom," and where

> the use of images, the emphasis on the emotional gaze of the learner, along with the sensations that are awakened by musical instruments and the experience that we gain

through activities based on physical movement or through the feeling of moving through imaginary situations, can contribute to the development of a more multisensory way of learning in the classroom.

p. 150

Future Directions

Humanism is associated with many of the developments in language education from the 1960s, 1970s, and 1980s, but its relevance is just as pertinent today. Many of its principles and themes are also reflected in the emergence of the field of positive psychology within SLA. Yet, there remains work to be done to understand humanistic principles in light of contemporary educational challenges and to consider how these principles apply not only to learners and the classroom group, but also to teachers. From a relational perspective on the language classroom, it is critical to understand the teacher as well as each learner as a whole person and the relationships between all the stakeholders as holistic, feeling individuals.

Currently, in studies on second language acquisition, there is an important focus on the learner and on interaction among learners and between teacher and learners (Murphey, 2015). In learning to speak a language, it is not enough just to do exercises in a textbook; learners need to interact with the teacher and with each other. Language teaching and learning is deeply relational and interactional. Taking a holistic and humanistic perspective, teachers can consider both the cognitive and the affective dimensions of the process. There is great potential for further research on how concepts from humanistic approaches can continue to provide inspiration and positively influence the processes of language teaching and learning. As has been shown, there is a range of diverse methodological approaches to such work, such as from the neurosciences. Humanism and its related principles will continue to be relevant for language teaching practice and research.

Reflection Questions

- What can we do in class to reduce anxiety and to make learners feel more confident and more motivated?
- In education, why is it important to see psychology as dealing not only with problems but also with positive matters?
- What could we use from the research in the neurosciences to promote learning in language classes?

Recommended Reading

Arnold, J., & Murphey, T, (Eds). (2013). *Meaningful action: Earl Stevick's influence on language teaching.* Cambridge University Press.
Here there are a collection of chapters which deal with diverse ways to make learning more meaningful for teachers and learners in the language classroom.

Richards, J., & Rodgers, T. (2014). *Approaches and methods in language teaching.* Cambridge University Press.
This book provides a solid introduction to early developments in language teaching, to what they consider current approaches/methods, and to alternative twentieth-century humanistic approaches and methods, giving information about their design, syllabus, activities, and procedures, among other things.

Stevick, E. (1990). *Humanism in language learning: A critical perspective.* Oxford University Press. Stevick clarifies here terminology and concepts related to humanism and discusses how it has been used in philosophy and education and by different authors dealing with language teaching. Examples of the HLT methods developed by Curran and Gattegno are presented and humanistic elements outside the methods are also discussed.

References

Amini, D., & Amini, M. (2012). Teacher and learner in Humanistic Language Teaching. *Language in India, 12*(7), 100–112.

Arnold, J. (1998). Towards more humanistic English teaching. *ELT Journal, 52*(2), 235–242.

Arnold, J., Puchta, H., & Rinvolucri, M. (2007). *Imagine that! Mental imagery in the EFL classroom.* Helbling Languages.

Arnold, J., & Foncubierta, J. M. (2019). *La atención a los factores afectivos en la enseñanza de ELE.* Edinumen.

Arnold, J., & Fonseca-Mora, M. C. (2017). Autonomy and affect in language learning: A dynamic relationship. In M. Jimenez Raya, J. Martos Ramos, & M. Tassinari (Eds.), *Learner and teacher autonomy in higher education: Perspectives from modern language teaching,* (pp. 37–54). Peter Lang.

Asher, J. (1997). *Learning another language through actions: The complete teacher's guidebook.* Sky Oaks Productions.

Council of Europe. (2001). *Common European Framework of Reference for Languages: Learning, teaching, assessment.* Cambridge University Press. rm.coe.int/1680459f97

Cuéllar, L., & Oxford, R. (2018). Language teachers' emotions. Emerging from the shadows. In J. Martínez Agudo (Ed.), *Emotions in second language teaching. Theory, research and teacher education,* (pp. 53–72). Springer International Publishing.

Damasio, Antiono. (1994). *Descartes' error: Emotion, reason, and the human brain.* Avon Books.

Dewaele, J.-M. (2011). Reflections on the emotional and psychological aspects of foreign language learning and use. *Anglistik, 22*(1), 23–42.

Dewaele, J.-M., Chen, X., Padilla, A., & Lake, J. (2019). The flowering of positive psychology in foreign language teaching and acquisition research. *Frontiers in Psychology, 10,* 2128.

Dewaele, J.-M., Gkonou, C., & Mercer, S. (2018). Do ESL/EFL teachers emotional intelligences, teaching experience, proficiency and gender affect their classroom practice? In J. Martínez Agudo (Ed.), *Emotions in second language teaching. Theory, research and teacher education,* (pp. 125–144). Springer International Publishing.

Dörnyei, Z., & Murphey, T. (2003). *Group dynamics in the language classroom.* Cambridge University Press.

Farrell, T. (2015). *Reflection in second language education.* Routledge.

Foncubierta, J. M., & Gant, M. (2016). Awakening senses for language learning. In M. C. Fonseca Mora, & M. Gant (Eds.), *Melodies, rhythm and cognition in foreign language learning,* (pp. 142–152). Cambridge Scholars Publishing.

Fonseca-Mora, M. C., & Herrero Machancoses, F. (2016). Music and language learning: emotions and engaging memory pathways. In P. Macintyre, T. Gregersen, & S. Mercer (Eds.), *Positive psychology in SLA,* (pp. 259–373). Multilingual Matters.

Fonseca, M., & Toscano, C. (2012). La música como herramienta facilitadora del aprendizaje del inglés como lengua extranjera. *Teoría de la Educación, 24*(2), 197–213.

Fredrickson, B. (2004). The broaden-and-build theory of positive emotions. *Philosophical Transactions of the Royal Society B, 359,* 1367–1377.

Gadotti, M. (1994). *Reading Paulo Friere. His life and work.* State University of New York.

Gardner, H. (1993). *Multiple intelligences: The theory in practice.* Basic Books.

Heron, J. (1999). *The facilitator's handbook.* Kogan Page.

Krashen, S. (1985). *The input hypothesis: Issues and implications.* Longman.

Larsen-Freeman, D. (1986). *Techniques and principles in language learning.* Oxford University Press.

Lozanov, G. (1978). *Suggestology and outlines of Suggestopedy.* Gordon and Breach.

Macaskill, A., & Denovan, A. (2013) Developing autonomous learning in first year university students using perspectives from positive psychology. *Studies in Higher Education, 38*(1), 124–142.

MacIntyre, P., & Mercer, S. (2014). Introducing positive psychology to SLA. *SSLLT, 4*(2), 153–172.

McAllister, G., & Jordan Irvine, J. (2002). The role of empathy in teaching culturally diverse students: A qualitative study of teachers' beliefs. *Journal of Teacher Education, 53*(5).

Maslow, A. H. (1943). A theory of human motivation. *Psychological Review. 50*(4), 370–96.

Maslow, A. H. (1971). *The farther reaches of human nature.* Viking Press.

McNeill, A. (1982). The silent way: Evaluating an experience. *Humanistic approaches: An empirical view,* (pp. 118–123). The British Council.

Moskowitz, G. (1978). *Caring and sharing in the foreign language class. A sourcebook on humanistic techniques.* Newbury House.

Moskowitz, S., & Dewaele, J.-M. (2019). Is teacher happiness contagious? A study of the link between perceptions of language teacher happiness and student attitudes. *Innovation in Language Learning and Teaching.* 1–14.

Murphey, T. (2015). Adapting ways for meaningful action: ZPDs and ZPAs. In Arnold, J., & Murphey, T. (Eds.), *Meaningful action: Earl Stevick's influence on language teaching,* (pp. 172–189). Cambridge University Press.

O'Connell, P. (1982). Suggestopedy and the adult language learner. *Humanistic approaches. An empirical view,* (pp. 110–117). The British Council.

Oxford, R. (2013). Understanding language learner narratives. In J. Arnold, & T. Murphey (Eds.), *Meaningful action: Earl Stevick's influence on language teaching,* (pp. 95–110). Cambridge University Press.

Quesada Pacheco, A. (2005). Reflective teaching and its impact on foreign language teaching. *Revista Electrónica Actualidades Investigativas en Educación, 5,* 2–19.

Richards, J., & Rodgers, T. (2014). *Approaches and methods in language teaching* (3rd ed.). Cambridge University Press.

Rivers, W. (1983). *Communicating naturally in a second language: Theory and practice in language teaching.* Cambridge University Press.

Rogers, C. (1969). *Freedom to learn: A view of what education might become.* Charles Merrill.

Sánchez Calvo, A. (2007). A learner-centred approach to the teaching of English as an L2. *ES: Revista de Filología Inglesa, 28,* 89–196.

Schumann, J. H. (1994). Where is cognition? Emotion and cognition in second language acquisition. *SSLA, 16,* 231–242.

Schneider, K, Fraser Pierson, J., & Bugental, J. (2015). *The handbook of humanistic psychology. Theory, research and practice* (2nd ed.). Sage.

Seligman, M., & Csíkszentmihályi, M. (2000). Positive psychology: An introduction, *American Psychologist, 55*(1), 5–14.

Stern, H. H. (1983). *Fundamental concepts of language teaching.* Oxford University Press.

Stevick, E. (1986). *Images and options in the language classroom.* Cambridge University Press.

Stevick, E. (1990). *Humanism in language learning. A critical perspective.* Oxford University Press.

Stevick, E. (1996). *Memory, meaning & method. A view of language teaching* (2nd ed.). Heinle and Heinle.

Thornbury, S. (2013). The learning body. In J. Arnold & T. Murphey (Eds.), *Meaningful action: Earl Stevick's influence on language teaching,* (pp. 62–78). Cambridge University Press.

Tomlinson, C. A. (2005, November 17–19). *Differentiated instruction as a way to achieve equity and excellence in today's schools, building inclusive schools: A search for solutions* [Conference Report]. Canadian Teachers' Federation Conference, Ottawa, Ontario.

Underhill, A. (1989). Process in humanistic education. *ELT Journal, 43*(4), 250–260.

Underhill, A. (2014). Review of *How We Learn and How We Should be Taught: An Introduction to the Work of Caleb Gattegno. ELT Journal, 68*(2), 213–216.

Williams, D. A., Berger, J. B., & McClendon, S. A. (2005). *Toward a model of inclusive excellence and change post secondary institutions.* Association of American Colleges & Universities.

4
THE COMPLEX DYNAMIC APPROACH

Elizabeth Hepford

Picture a game of chess. The players know the rules. The predicted outcome is that one or the other will win or there will be a stalemate. Thus, the interesting part of the game is the process between the first move and checkmate. Each time a player moves a piece, a new set of possibilities appears to which the other player must react. With the exception of players who play chess from the same memorized playbook, each move could result in an unpredictable reaction that guides the game in different directions, but all within the confines of the rules. Therein lies the ideas that guide Complex Dynamic Systems Theory (CDST). Similar to a chess game, psychological and linguistic development progresses unpredictably within the parameters of a system. Instead of reacting to the opponent's movements on a chessboard, the system reacts to changes in the person's cognitive abilities and exposure to external influences. With each modification to the system, the conditions change, and the person adjusts, which can result in a variety of developmental paths.

This chapter aims to explain how recent research has conceptualized psychological and second language development (SLD) as complex, adaptive, and dynamic systems that self-organize in non-linear and unpredictable paths. Additionally, I will describe how scholars in these fields conduct research within this developmental paradigm, also known as complexity theory, dynamic systems theory, or complex adaptive theory to address questions that were previously overlooked. The chapter begins with an overview of the theory's concepts and terms, then examines how researchers in both fields have begun incorporating CDST, how research in both fields can be integrated, and, finally, the implications and future directions for research.

CDST differs from other scientific paradigms in that researchers focus on the development or processes of a phenomenon in an individual or small group of individuals. As such, longitudinal or time-series research designs with dense data collection are favored over large statistical analyses using intervention experiments. Moreover, researchers in CDST approach the data without a hypothesis to prove or disprove. Instead, SLD scholars approach the data retrospectively to look for emerging phenomenon (Baba & Nitta, 2014; Polat & Kim, 2014), and psychology scholars aim to create multiple models that focus on the various paths that development might follow (Bryan & Rudd, 2016; Cramer, Waldorp, van der Maas, & Borsboom, 2010). Though participants or models are often chosen because the researcher suspects a certain type of development is happening, there is not a preconception of how that development will occur. As Larsen-Freeman and Cameron (2008) explain, "We may have expectations of how a process will unfold, or even of its outcomes, based on prior experience, but essentially, adopting a complexity theory perspective brings about a separation of explanation and prediction" (p. 202).

To illustrate the point, Larsen-Freeman (2006) examined the non-linear development and individual differences of five intermediate Chinese participants studying English. She found that they developed in opposite directions (some improving and others worsening) on the same variables (accuracy, fluency, vocabulary complexity, and grammatical complexity) during the same ten-month period despite their similar backgrounds. She also showed that when the learners' scores were averaged together, the group displayed gradual improvement. Thus, the individual differences, which add insight to the learning process, were lost in the larger analysis. To emphasize that language is continually changing in unpredictable manners, Larsen-Freeman and other researchers using a CDST framework often chose the term *second language development* (SLD), as I will in this chapter, rather than second language acquisition.

Non-CDST research has shown that individual differences and experiences often result in differences in development. As demonstrated in other chapters in this book, various factors including motivation (Chapter 13), personality (Chapter 12), and willingness to communicate (Chapter 23) affect psychological and language development in various ways. However, CDST places greater emphasis on how those types of variables affect development by emphasizing the participants' *beginning states* or *initial conditions,* and how those initial states interact with cognitive development and external influences. As Smith and Thelen (2003) explain, "Even very small differences in beginning states and in developmental histories can amplify and lead to large individual differences" (p. 347). Moreover, as development occurs, systems distinctively *self-organize* and react to various inputs and influences resulting in vastly different developmental paths (Chan, Verspoor, & Vahtrick, 2015; Thelen, 1995).

Dynamic systems develop and change based on attractor states and the parameters that limit the system. *Attractor states* represent one of the many developmental paths available. *Parameters* are the constraints that determine the possibilities for changes within the system (Hiver & Al-Hoorie, 2016). They may be cognitive, such as working memory (Larsen-Freeman & Cameron, 2008) or biomechanical factors (Thelen, 1995), or they may be external influences, such as language instruction (Fogal, 2019) and counseling (Ribeiro, Bento, Salgado, Stiles, & Gonçalves, 2011). As an example, when learning past tense verbs, second language learners often experience over-generalization, or applying a standard rule to an irregular verb. In this case, the parameters have expanded, shown by the learners being cognitively ready to attempt a new verb tense. Thus, learners begin to experiment and they are likely to apply the newly learned past tense rule to irregular as well as regular verbs (goed instead of went). Based on feedback, they may even fluctuate between three attractor states: the rule incorrectly applied to an irregular verb, the correct irregular conjugation, and the present tense that they were using previously. After a period of experimentation in which the system *self-organizes,* their language will most likely stabilize into one of those attractors (not necessarily the correct one). Depending on their interaction with positive or negative feedback, the system may remain stable for a lengthy or short amount of time (Larsen-Freeman & Cameron, 2008; Waninge, Dörnyei, & de Bot, 2014).

Self-organization in a system can occur in two ways: slowly and gradually within a stable system or suddenly as the result of a system becoming unstable (de Bot, Lowie, & Verspoor, 2007). Both occur as the result of *iterative processes,* meaning that the system is exposed to the same stimulant continually with each exposure resulting in a new initial state (Larsen-Freeman, 2019). Some systems will gradually move to a new attractor state while remaining stable. Others will experience a stage of instability, fluctuating dramatically between attractor states. This may occur due to changes in the parameters that create instability, referred to as *perturbations* (i.e., cognitive development, exposure, feedback, etc.). Dramatic fluctuations occur as the system experiments with the new attractor state(s) but continues to return to the original attractor state. The fluctuation increases temporarily, and then stabilizes by either returning to its original attractor state or moving to the new attractor state. The latter is referred to as a *phase shift, phase transition,* or *bifurcation.*

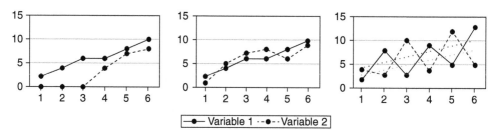

Figure 4.1 Illustration of Conditional, Cooperative, and Competitive Growers

A final noteworthy difference between traditional statistical analyses and CDST analyses is the emphasis on variable interaction. Rather than looking at causative independent variables, CDST places greater emphasis on the interaction of multiple variables over time. That interaction is often described in terms of *growers*, meaning that the variables are *coupled* and maintain a meaningful and correlated relationship over time (Smith & Thelen, 2003; Verspoor, Lowie, & van Dijk, 2008). In contrast to standard statistical correlations, grower correlations are calculated multiple times and analyzed for strengthening, weakening, or alternating relationships. Growers are classified in three ways: *conditional*, meaning one variable is dependent on the other's development before it can begin; *cooperative*, meaning a positive correlation is maintained as the variables develop; and *competitive*, meaning they are competing for the learner's attention as they develop, which results in an alternating pattern of one variable increasing while the other decreases (Verspoor et al., 2008; Verspoor & van Dijk, 2011). Figure 4.1 illustrates the three types of grower relationships.

In sum, CDST adheres to certain principles, which differ from other research paradigms. As Larsen-Freeman (1997) explains, developing systems are "dynamic, complex, nonlinear, chaotic, unpredictable, sensitive to initial conditions, open, self-organizing, feedback sensitive, and adaptive" (p. 142). Therefore, researchers using a CDST framework strive to illustrate those principles. The next two sections will describe how psychology and SLD incorporate those principles.

CDST Perspective in Psychology

A breakthrough for the dynamic systems approach in psychology originated in the work of scholars such as Thelen, Smith, Spencer, Schöner, Urich, and their colleagues in the 1990s (van Geert & Steenbeek, 2010). These scholars applied the ideas from dynamic systems research in physics and math to the qualitative aspects of human development in order to advance and explain infant motor skills and spatial perception (Smith, Thelen, Titzer, & McLin, 1999; Thelen & Smith, 1994). Previous research in this area relied heavily on the idea that cognitive development dictated the stages of motor skill development (McGraw, 1944) and that infants were endowed "with genetically programmed and pre-existing mental structures trapped in an immature body" (Smith & Thelen, 2003, p. 343). In contrast, dynamic approaches argue that, "organization arises only from the confluence of the components within a particular environmental context" (Thelen, 1995, p. 83).

As an example, Goldfield, Kay, and Warren (1993) conducted a study with eight infants to explain the process of infants learning to use a baby bouncer. Based on analyses from three videotaped sessions, they found that infants learning to move their legs depend not only on cognitive and muscular development, but also on stimulants in the environment encouraging them to explore kicking and stepping. Thus, a baby put in a baby bouncer will go through a period of exploration encouraged by feedback and resulting in fluctuating amounts of variance in the force applied to create movement. As infants find the right amount of force and movement to achieve their optimal bounce, they settle into their ideal attractor state, thus completing a phase shift. Their ability to apply force and find the appropriate timing for their movements represents the parameters of the system. Their continued practice epitomizes the iterative process of self-organization. Every infant begins with a different initial state (strength in their legs, interest in bouncing) and follows a unique path with an experimentation stage that leads to their optimal bouncing level.

Smith et al. (1999) also examined child development with CDST by re-examining the *A not B error*. Piaget (1954) found that when infants were shown a toy being hidden at location A, they would remember where it was and reach for the toy. After repeating the task a few times, if the researcher then hid the toy in location B (still in full view), infants less than 10 months old would look for the toy in location A rather than location B (the A not B error). In contrast, if the infants were older than 12 months, they would consistently look for it in location B. Piaget (1954) theorized that infants under 10 months do not understand object permanence yet. However, Smith et al. (1999) showed that the phenomenon was not that simple in a series of six experiments conducted with 30 infants within two weeks of their 8-month birthday, 40 infants between 8–10 months old, and 107 infants within two weeks of 10-month birthday. They showed that the infants' reaching choices were affected by the number of iterations of the object in location A, changes in the babies' posture or direction of infants' gaze, the novelty of the object being hidden, and the interaction of those variables. They argued that the response to the task was a soft-assembly of multiple factors. Each child adjusted to their environment and used the resources available differently. Therefore, declaring cognitive development as the sole cause of their reaching behavior did not capture the entirety of the developmental phenomenon.

Both the baby bouncer and the A not B error examples show the need to consider multicausality in human development. Accordingly, that idea has expanded into other aspects of psychological research. To show the breadth of that expansion, the last example comes from a different area of psychology, the comorbidity of mental disorders.

Comorbidity refers to patients suffering from multiple mental disorders simultaneously. To describe the phenomenon, traditional research often refers to the latent variable theory. From this perspective, observable symptoms (i.e., fatigue, weight issues, concentration problems, etc.) are caused by variables that are not directly observable (i.e., depression and anxiety). If the patient suffers from comorbidity, it is argued that a bi-directional relationship between two latent variables is causing the symptoms. Thus, the latent variable model does not allow for interaction between the symptoms. If symptoms like sleep disturbances and fatigue have a positive correlation, it is argued that they are both being caused by the latent variables. In contrast, Cramer, Waldorp, van der Maas, & Borsboom (2010) argue that disorders are "networks that consist of symptoms and causal relations between them" (p. 138). Using a dynamic perspective, connections between the symptoms and the disorders build a network of interactions that produce the symptoms and the disorders. Cramer and her colleagues argue that one might be fatigued because of sleep disturbances. Moreover, fatigue may lead to other symptoms, such as thoughts of inferiority, which create sleep disturbances. Thus, the process creates a negative spiral. The latent variable model dismisses that relationship and focuses on treating the latent variable. For example, anti-depressants are used to treat depression, which is believed to cause fatigue, sleep disturbances, and thoughts of inferiority. Notably, clinicians often acknowledge relationships between symptoms, whereas psychometric interpretations do not. In fact, Cramer and her colleagues point out that many clinicians focus on breaking cycles and the relationship between symptoms.

To illustrate their point, Cramer et al. (2010) created network models showing the relationships between major depressive disorder (MDD) and generalized anxiety disorder using data from the National Comorbidity Survey Replication (NCS-R). The computer model, created with gRbase package for R (Dethlefsen & Højsgaard, 2005), coded the variables and symptoms as nodes and relationships between them as edges (lines between them). Larger nodes indicated higher frequency and thicker edges indicated more co-occurrence of the symptoms. The findings demonstrated that symptoms are not necessarily equal in strength and that some symptoms may be more central to a disorder and as such should be considered more heavily in a diagnosis. They also found that symptoms are interconnected and suggested that diagnoses should be based on a weighted cluster of symptoms rather than a certain number of symptoms equaling a disorder as suggested by the Diagnostic and Statistical Manual of Mental Disorders, DSM-5 (American Psychiatric Association, 2013). Lastly, Cramer and her colleagues suggested that their model allows researchers to consider oscillations between the disorder and no disorder states as the patient improves or worsens (fluctuation between attractor states), the connection between symptom development (connected growers), and the effect of therapeutic interventions or other external factors (parameters). They proposed that continued research in this area may lead to deeper understanding of how the disorders work resulting in better diagnoses. Thus, just as in child development or language learning, the variables in the system are interconnected, affecting each other, fluctuating between attractor states as development occurs, and limited by the parameters of the system.

A wide variety of psychology research beyond the scope of this chapter has begun incorporating a CDST framework, including topics such as personality emergence (Nowak, Vallacher, & Zochowski, 2005) and suicide prevention (Bryan & Rudd, 2016). Most focus on developing nonlinear, interactive, and dynamic systems models to explain a variety of phenomenon. In contrast, SLD research rarely discusses modeling and typically focuses on retroactive analyses, as the next section explains.

CDST Perspective in Second Language Development

CDST was introduced to first and second language development in the 1990s in order to investigate outliers, individual development, and other developmental phenomenon that experimental statistical research could not adequately describe (Larsen-Freeman, 1997; van Geert, 1991). As de Bot et al. (2007) explain:

> Traditional statistics is meant to reveal how a group performs as a whole and may be useful to see the grand sweep of things, but if we really want to know what happens in the actual process of language acquisition we should also look at the messy little details, the first attempts, the degree of variation at a developmental stage, and the possible attrition.
>
> *p. 19*

CDST offers a framework and research methods to investigate fluctuation and interaction between SLD variables over time. The simultaneous surge in complexity, accuracy, and fluency (CAF) research (Skehan & Foster, 1999) paired well with the CDST techniques, which likely led to CDST research focusing on various combinations of CAF variables. For example, Chan et al. (2015) analyzed the differences between L1 Chinese identical twins development of syntactic complexity over eight months through a CDST lens. Though CAF continues to be a focus, CDST research in other SLD areas is increasing, such as authorial voice (Fogal, 2019), anxiety and self-efficacy (Pinel & Csizér, 2015), inner dialogue (Gregersen & MacIntyre, 2015) motivation (Waninge et al., 2014), and language advising (Castro, 2018). In addition to numerical analyses, SLD scholars have created visualization techniques to explore time-series and longitudinal data. Thus, this section begins with brief descriptions of some of those techniques:

a. *Trajectory graphs* are the most common method for beginning an analysis. The raw data from the variable being investigated is placed on the y-axis and the time of data collection is placed on the x-axis, which provides an overview of the learner's development including fluctuation over time.
b. *Polynomial trendlines* mathematically smooth the data into straight or slightly curved lines to explore emerging trends.
c. *Moving averages* are also smoothing techniques that show emerging trends but allow for more fluctuation than trendlines by using small overlapping groups (1-5 data points) over time.
d. *Min/Max graphs* establish a max-line (a moving average of maximum scores) and a min-line (a moving average of minimum scores) to explore fluctuation. The further apart the lines are, the greater the fluctuation.

e. *Progmax-regmin graphs* find developmental jumps in the data with a progressive max-line (small group averages of maximum scores starting at the first score and progressively adding data points) and a regressive min-line (small group averages of minimum scores starting with the last score and progressively adding data points toward the beginning). A phase shift is indicated when both lines "jump" to a new level.
f. *Moving Correlations* use small groups of overlapping correlation scores to show the correlation between two variables over time.

These techniques can all be created/calculated in most spreadsheet software like Excel. For more information on how to calculate these analyses, see Verspoor, de Bot, and Lowie (2011). Figure 4.2 and Figure 4.3 illustrate each of these techniques.

Polat and Kim (2014) used these techniques to investigate the non-linear development of six complexity and accuracy variables over time in Alex, an untutored L1 Turkish learner of English. They collected oral interview samples every two weeks for a year. Using trajectory graphs, moving averages, and min/max graphs (see a, c, and d below), they found that each of the variables developed

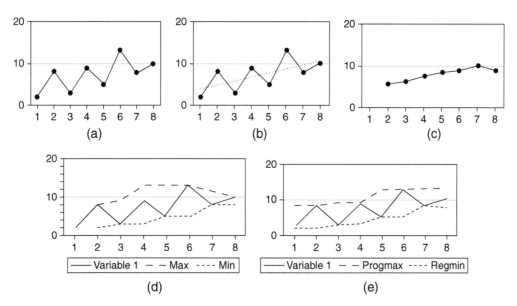

Figure 4.2 Illustration of Common CDST Graphs: a) trajectory graph, b) trajectory graph with a polynomial trendline, c) moving average graph, d) min/max graph, and e) program/regmin graph

Note The graphs were calculated from the same fictional data.

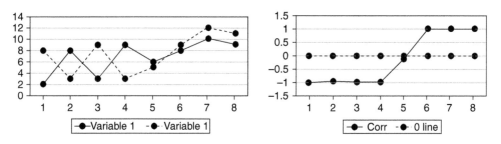

Figure 4.3 Illustration of Raw Data (f) and the Resulting Moving Correlation (g)

Note: Graphs display two fictional variables switching from a negative to a positive correlation.

differently and entered periods of fluctuation at different times. For example, lexical diversity (a measure of unique words) and grammatical accuracy showed a slight improvement, even though both were in a continual state of fluctuation. In contrast, errors related the present simple tense remained in a state of fluctuation, indicating that Alex was experimenting with the present simple for the entire year.

The analyses of grammatical complexity variables were more complicated due to changes in the amount of fluctuation and interaction between the variables. Using min/max graphs (see d above), Polat and Kim (2014) showed that clauses per AS-Unit (a measure of subordinating clauses) entered and exited two periods of fluctuation. However, rather than creating a phase shift by stabilizing in a new attractor state, Alex's language returned to the original state, meaning that his subordinate clause usage did not improve or worsen. Words per AS-Unit and words per clause (measures of vocabulary acquisition) also entered periods of fluctuation and additionally appeared to have a conditional grower relationship. More simply put, words per clause entered a period of fluctuation immediately after words per AS-Unit stabilized at a higher level, indicating that the second variable was dependent on the first one to appear. While words per AS-unit completed a phase shift by moving to a new attractor state (increased words per AS-unit), the study ended while words per clause was still in a period of fluctuation making it impossible to determine if a phase shift occurred. Polat and Kim (2014) used this data to show how an advanced untutored learners' language is dynamic rather than *fossilized*, or stationary, as non-progressing learners are often described. Even though Alex did not show drastic improvement over time, he was still going through periods of experimentation. Polat and Kim (2014) pointed out that movement to a new attractor state might have been stifled due to the limited feedback that untutored learners receive.

Spoelman and Verspoor (2010) also studied non-linear development by investigating the relationships between complexity and accuracy variables. They analyzed 54 writing samples of an L1 Dutch learner of Finnish collected over three years. Since Finnish noun cases are notoriously difficult to learn, they started by investigating grammatical case usage (total usage minus incorrect usage). Using a min/max graph (see d above), they found that accuracy rates fluctuated considerably at the beginning and gradually stabilized.

Next, they looked at the interactions between complexity variables over time. First, they used standard statistical correlations and found a negative correlation between one-word and two-word noun phrases (NP), one and two morpheme words, and noun and sentence complexity. In other words, when long words, phrases, and sentences increased in frequency, short words, phrases, and sentences decreased, and vice versa. Thus, the coupled variables were competing for attentional resources as the learner's grammatical understanding and vocabulary developed, also referred to as a competitive grower relationship. They also found positive correlations between word and sentence complexity and word and noun phrase complexity, meaning as their vocabulary increased their sentences became longer and more complex. Since these variables grew in the same direction, they exemplified a cooperative grower relationship. In contrast, the correlation between word complexity and noun case accuracy was very weak (R = -0.022), which implies that the connection between learning Finnish cases and increased vocabulary was insignificant. To investigate further, they calculated a moving correlation (see Figure 4.3 above), which showed that the variables switched between negative and positive correlations three times during the three years. After controlling for the task and learning conditions, they concluded that the switch must have been related to changes in proficiency. Lastly, they found developmental jumps in the average length of NPs using progmax-regmin graphs (see e above). The analysis showed that NPs gradually increased in length until sample 44, then jumped to a higher level, indicating a sudden improvement.

In contrast to the quantitative approaches covered so far, some CDST researchers have begun including more qualitative research. For example, MacIntyre and Legatto (2011) explored fluctuation in the willingness to communicate (WTC) and anxiety levels of six L1 English university students learning French (see Chapter 20). They began with questionnaires regarding extraversion,

WTC-traits, and language anxiety to establish general long-term trends. Next, participants were asked to respond to questions at varying levels of difficulty in French. The sessions were videotaped and observed by research assistants who noted signs of anxiety such as avoiding eye contact, fidgeting, and changes in facial expression. After the sessions were complete, participants were asked to evaluate their WTC throughout videotaped interviews by continuously clicking on a mouse to indicate rising and falling levels of WTC. When they finished, they were asked to explain sudden changes in their levels while watching the video a third time. The results showed that the task, the learner's vocabulary knowledge, and their confidence level affected their self-ratings of WTC and their anxiety-indicating behavior.

With regards to CDST, MacIntyre and Legatto (2011) found theoretical connections to premises of the theory. First, rather than labeling a learner as generally extroverted or introverted as previous research typically does, the results showed considerable fluctuation throughout the session. For example, a speaker with high WTC self-evaluations and low anxiety levels lowered her score and showed signs of anxiety when responding to a question that required vocabulary she didn't know and a topic with which she was unfamiliar. Other participants had similar increases and decreases that contradicted their initial survey results. Second, they analyzed participants' development on several timescales. They began with surveys that evaluated a lifetime of WTC and anxiety traits. Then, they looked at fluctuation within the time window of completing the task (one hour). Lastly, they looked at each task individually on ten-of-seconds and per second bases. By doing so, they were able to observe a participant fluctuating from a stable attractor state (their general trends) to a temporary state of instability when confronted with a more difficult or easier task. If this version of this task was repeated regularly, it's likely that the perturbation and resulting fluctuation in the system would begin to have an effect, such as increasing or decreasing the learners' confidence levels. Such data is easily applied to the effects of repeated tasks in a classroom environment. These studies demonstrate how SLD research investigates individual development by analyzing quantitative or qualitative data retrospectively. The next section will show how psychology has used data from case studies and how SLD has used modeling techniques.

Integrating Perspectives

Research in first language development using a CDST framework exemplifies the commonalities and differences between psychology and SLD research. Researchers in first language development consider cognitive development based on maturity factors and language acquisition. Moreover, the foundations of the methods used in second language development research are predominately based on methods from first language development including the concepts of connected growers and developmental parameters (van Geert, 1991). However, first language development and the majority of psychological studies using CDST focus on creating statistically based models and mathematical equations to explore various developmental paths, whereas SLD focuses on individual language development to study the anomalies in the data. The difference between the epistemologies may lie in the differences between their expectations. While fluency is expected to develop in a first language, balanced bilingual fluency is unusual and even the definition of second language fluency is debated. Thus, while first language scholars were defining the stages of acquisition (Chomsky, 1972), SLD scholars were studying cases of rare native-like fluency (Ioup, Boustagui, El Tigi, & Moselle, 1994). As such, it is easier to create a model when multiple examples of achievement are available and clearly defined endpoints exist. Despite their epistemological differences, there are overlaps in techniques that demonstrate what the fields could gain from considering each other's approaches.

As an example of SLD modeling, Murakami (2016) developed statistical modeling techniques to simultaneously analyze general trends, variation, and nonlinearity in SLD. Using a corpus with longitudinal data from the EF-Cambridge Open Language Database, he analyzed the development of ten groups of English learners with different L1s (N = 158). Specifically, he looked at accuracy in articles, the past tense –ed, and the plural –s. He separated the learners into two subgroups for each feature: those with the feature in their L1 and those without it. The generalized findings showed that plural –s was more accurate than article usage, students who had articles in their L1 used them more accurately than those who did not, overall accuracy improved over time, and correct article usage was correlated with proficiency, all of which could have been determined using standard statistical analyses. However, he was also able to see that despite the improving accuracy trend, some of the learners' accuracy decreased, the plural –s was slower to develop than article usage, and the amount of variance of the groups without articles in their L1 varied more than the group with articles in their L1. In other words, there was a great deal of individual variance in their developmental paths. Since researchers in SLD using the CDST framework are trying to understand variance and individual developmental paths, analyses of large databases may direct them to which linguistic features develop in particularly non-linear paths (articles) and which types of learners have more variance (those without the feature in their L1). Hence, knowing about the features of their learners' first language(s) may help second language instructors understand their students' seemingly erratic development. That being said, Larsen-Freeman (2012) warns SLD researchers to approach statistical models with caution:

> developing a computer model requires explicit statements of theory and the most accurate empirical knowledge about the real systems and processes being modeled… Inevitably, the model differs from the actual system, being idealized or simplified in some respects, approximated in others. Its potential and its limitations remain to be investigated.
>
> *p. 84*

From the psychology perspective, some developmental studies have used a small case study format to explore a phenomenon in detail. As an example, Corbetta and Bojczyk (2002) investigated why infants who have mastered adaptive reaching (using each hand independently) suddenly begin to reach with two hands again at approximately one year of age. Psychologists believed that this phenomenon was the result of neuromotor reorganization (Gesell, 1939). However, in line with dynamic system's theories on variable interaction, Corbetta and Bojczyk (2002) believed that interaction between neuromotor development and upright locomotion created the phenomenon. To test their hypothesis, they studied hand reaching in ten infants who could not yet walk once a week until they started walking and returned to adaptive reaching. To measure adaptive reaching, infants opened a lid and retrieved a toy from inside of a box. The first issue of variance appeared immediately as they all began to walk at different times. Moreover, some infants completed the entire process more quickly than others, with a range from seven to 13 weeks. Despite the variance, Corbetta and Bojczyk (2002) were able to show that the two events (walking and two-handed reaching) co-occurred in a predictable and interactive pattern. They concluded, "The process of integration might involve the dynamic reorganization of multiple systems, that is, neural, motor, sensory, and cognitive" (p. 94). Thus, the interaction between standing and walking resulted in a temporary regression in the development of independent hand movement. Once the system self-organized and stabilized, the hand reaching behavior returned to the previous attractor state. Karasik, Tamis-Lemonda, and Adolph (2011) expanded this study to a larger group of 50 infants learning to walk. In addition to reaching behavior, they also found interaction between walking and carrying or sharing objects. Similar to seminal case studies such as Schmidt (1983), which led to the Focus on Form movement in SLD, psychology could benefit from single subject or small group studies, which may lead to larger more generalizable studies.

As tools for longitudinal analyses are created and refined, the fields of psychology and SLD will discover more to share. Scholars such as Larsen-Freeman (2012) and van Geert and Steenbeek (2010) tentatively suggest that carefully constructed computer models could lead to methods for analyzing interaction between multiple variables. Van Geert and Steenbeek (2010) also suggest that clinical psychology would benefit from approaches that study the "fuzzy and dynamic boundaries between disorder and normality" (p. 175), which are more easily studied in smaller case studies, as suggested by SLD. The integration of these fields' ideas and methods could result in deeper understanding of human development in general.

Implications for Practice and Research

Research using a CDST framework offers an alternative lens with details about the processes in which psychological and SLD phenomena develop. Moving forward, scholars should consider how this research could be practically applied to teaching second languages and treating patients with developmental issues. A deeper understanding of the processes of development may help us streamline the process for those who are struggling with psychological and SLD developmental issues. In the realm of psychology, that could mean studying how treatment intervention affects individual outcomes; in the classroom, that could mean exploring how teaching methods affect individual development. This section offers examples of some already existing research in both.

In the area of clinical psychology, Ribeiro et al. (2011) applied CDST to research the effect of changes in patients' narratives over time while overcoming depression. Specifically, they looked at innovative moments (IMs), which are statements that break depressive narratives, and protonarratives, which are the themes that emerge from those IMs. To more deeply explore and validate the existing model of narrative change in psychotherapy, Ribeiro and his colleagues conducted a case study of a 20-year woman overcoming depression over a period of 12 weeks. Recordings of her sessions were coded for IMs using the Innovated Moments Coding System (Gonçalves, Ribeiro, Mendes, Matos, & Santos, 2011). The first analysis determined her current narrative, which was pessimism, and the IMs that broke from that narrative. Next, they placed the IMs from each session on *state spaced grids*, which place five types of IMs (action, reflection, protest, reconceptualization, and performing change) on the x-axis and three protonarratives themes (optimism, achievement, and balance) on the y-axis of the grid. They compared the graphs from each session and found dynamic development fitting with CDST. The participant started in a stable attractor state of reflection IMs and the protonarrative of optimism, which she only occasionally veered from until session 8. From session 8 until session 12, she began using the IMs of reconceptualization, action, protest, and performing change increasingly and in that order. She also moved freely between protonarratives. Yet, the data shows frequent returns to reflection IMs and the optimism protonarrative. By session 12, she seemed to have stabilized in the IM of reconceptualization and the protonarrative of balance. Thus, between sessions 8 and 12, she appears to be in a state of self-organization. In the end, she has moved to a new attractor state (reconceptualization and balance). Based on this data, Ribeiro and his colleagues suggested that therapists encourage clients to explore diverse protonarratives in order to construct viable alternatives, or in CDST terms, to encourage more perturbations that might destabilize the system and lead to healthier attractor states.

CDST research in SLD classrooms mainly focuses on the effects of pedagogy on SLD development. For example, Fogal (2019) explored the development of authorial voice in seven L1 Japanese learners of English during a three-week writing intervention consisting of 16 hours of instruction. Authorial voice was taught by daily analysis of texts for features of authorial voice, collaborative peer feedback on essays, and opportunities to revise their work. The data was divided into seven data collection points (including a delayed posttest four weeks later), each containing at least one essay. Development was assessed in two methods by three outside raters and the author. First, they gave each participant a score from 0-5 with 5 meaning students were able to identify and use authorial voice in and out of the context it was taught and 0 meaning they could not use it outside of the context it was taught. Next, the frequency of authorial voice markers (hedges, certainty expressions, attitude markers, authorial self-mentions, and direct reader references) was coded and counted. Using trajectory and min-max graphs, Fogal (2019) found that their development was non-linear, unique, and fluctuated over time. Despite their different paths, the group generally showed improvement. Based on comments regarding the tasks in the interview data, Fogal argued that the repeated classroom tasks created perturbations in the system, which eventually increased authorial voice.

While very different in scope, both studies show that iteration affects change. Whether the iterations are therapy sessions where patients repeatedly discuss the same issues, classroom tasks where language learners complete similar tasks, or sessions with physical therapists where patients practice similar motor skill tasks, iterations lead to perturbations that cause fluctuations in the system and may (or may not) lead to phase shifts. In addition, practitioners need to consider the effects of feedback during those iterations, which can help solidify or correct behaviors (Larsen-Freeman, 2012; Smith & Thelen, 2003). The effects of such feedback are addressed in the next section.

Future Directions

Researchers in both psychology and SLD have suggested that external influences affect cognitive development; yet, the research about perturbations created by outside influences on internal development is limited. Van Geert (1991) suggested the concept of an *ecosystem* for the cognitive development of first language learning. He envisioned multiple elements such as vocabulary, grammar, and problem-solving skills interacting and developing together as a cognitive ecosystem. In an effort to acknowledge external influences, scholars of SLD such as de Bot et al. (2007), and Dörnyei (2009) expanded that concept to include both the cognitive ecosystem and the social ecosystem. Using this metaphor, the *cognitive ecosystem* refers to elements within the learner such as motivation and cognitive development, whereas the *social ecosystem* refers to external influences such as language classes and therapy sessions. Other scholars such as Ushioda (2015) have created similar labels (i.e., learner and context) and research on external influences such as career ambitions (Baba & Nitta, 2014), study abroad (Irie & Ryan, 2014) and Computer Assisted Language Learning (Marek & Wu, 2014) has begun to increase.

Even though the term ecosystem mainly appears in language development research, psychology also refers to social effects on developing systems (Cramer et al., 2010; Thelen, 1995). To acknowledge the impact of social influences, both psychology and SLD would benefit from investigating the effects of topics such as family and peer pressure, changes in circumstances, and positive and negative feedback on the systems being investigated. Rather than studying each variable separately and looking for causation, the system should be investigated holistically, looking for interaction of the variables. Thus, CDST would benefit from additional approaches and methods that allow interactive analyses of qualitative and quantitative data. Such methods may lead to a deeper understanding of how social influences affect cognitive development, thereby increasing our understanding of how dynamic systems develop within language learners and the mind in general.

Reflection Questions

- How does complex dynamic systems theory (CDST) vary from traditional experimental research?
- What are the differences and similarities in CDST research in psychology and second language development?
- Could CDST contribute to your research methods, teaching practices, or general understanding of development? How?

Recommended Reading

Larsen-Freeman, D. (1997). Chaos/Complexity Science and Second Language Acquisition. *Applied Linguistics, 18*, 141–165.
This seminal article introduces the basic principles of CDST from an SLD perspective. Larsen-Freeman uses specific examples and insightful metaphors to explain the theory and features of CDST,

and compares it to other frameworks. She also explains the benefits of CDST to second language pedagogy. This is a theoretical overview and as such discusses theory rather experimental results.

Thelen, E. (1995). Motor development. A new synthesis. *The American Psychologist*.
This article explains the differences in Piaget's (1954) theories on child motor skill development and complex dynamic systems approach by examining experimental research.

Verspoor, M., de Bot, K., & Lowie, W. (2011). *A Dynamic Approach to Second Language Development: Methods and Techniques* (Vol. 29). John Benjamins.
This book is a necessity for anyone new to CDST research in SLD. The authors provide a theoretical overview and guide readers with step-by-step instructions on how to create graphs, calculate Monte Carlo simulations, and create models for development.

References

American Psychiatric Association, DSM. Task Force. (2013). *Diagnostic and statistical manual of mental disorders: DSM-5* (5th ed.. ed.): American Psychiatric Association.

Baba, K., & Nitta, R. (2014). Phase transitions in development of writing fluency from a complex dynamic systems perspective. *Language Learning, 64*(1), 1–35.

Bryan, C. J., & Rudd, M. D. (2016). The importance of temporal dynamics in the transition from suicidal thought to behavior. *Clinical Psychology: Science and Practice, 23*(1), 21–25.

Castro, E. (2018). Complex adaptive systems, language advising, and motivation: A longitudinal case study with a Brazilian student of English. *System, 74*, 138–148.

Chan, H., Verspoor, M., & Vahtrick, L. (2015). Dynamic development in speaking versus writing in identical twins. *Language Learning, 65*(2), 298–325.

Chomsky, C. (1972). Stages in language development and reading exposure. *Harvard Educational Review, 42*(1), 1–33.

Corbetta, D., & Bojczyk, K. E. (2002). Infants return to two-handed reaching when they are learning to walk. *Journal of Motor Behavior, 34*(1), 83–95.

Cramer, A. O. J., Waldorp, L. J., van der Maas, H. L. J., & Borsboom, D. (2010). Comorbidity: A network perspective. *Behav Brain Sci, 33*(2–3), 137–150.

de Bot, K., Lowie, W., & Verspoor, M. (2007). A dynamic systems theory approach to second language acquisition. *Bilingualism, 10*(1), 7–21.

Dethlefsen, C., & Højsgaard, S. (2005). A common platform for graphical models in R: The gRbase package. *Journal of Statistical Software, 14*(17), 1–12.

Dörnyei, Z. (2009). Individual differences: Interplay of learner characteristics and learning environment. *Language Learning, 59*(s1), 230–248.

Dörnyei. Z., MacIntyre, P., & Henry, A. (Eds.) (2015). *Motivational dynamics in language learning*. Multilingual Matters.

Fogal, G. G. (2019). Tracking microgenetic changes in authorial voice development from a complexity theory perspective. *Applied Linguistics, 40*(3), 432–455.

Gesell, A. (1939). Reciprocal interweaving in neuromotor development. A principle of spiral organization shown in the patterning of infant behavior. *Journal of Comparative Neurology, 70*(2), 161–180.

Goldfield, E. C., Kay, B. A., & Warren, W. H. (1993). Infant bouncing: The assembly and tuning of action systems. *Child Development, 64*(4), 1128–1142.

Gonçalves, M. M., Ribeiro, A. P., Mendes, I., Matos, M., & Santos, A. (2011). Tracking novelties in psychotherapy process research: The innovative moments coding system. *Psychotherapy Research, 21*(5), 497–509.

Gregersen, T., & MacIntyre, P. (2015). "I can see a little bit of you on myself": A dynamic systems approach to the inner dialogue between teacher and learner selves. In Z. Dörnyei, P. MacIntyre, & A. Henry (Eds.), *Motivational dynamics in language learning* (pp. 260–284). Multilingual Matters.

Hiver, P., & Al-Hoorie, A. H. (2016). A dynamic ensemble for second language research: Putting complexity theory into practice. *Modern Language Journal, 100*(4), 741–756.

Ioup, G., Boustagui, E., El Tigi, M., & Moselle, M. (1994). Reexamining the critical period hypothesis: A case study of successful adult SLA in a naturalistic environment. *Studies in Second Language Acquisition, 16*(1), 73–98.

Irie, K., & Ryan, S. (2014) Study abroad and the dynamics of change in learner L2 self-concept. In P. D. MacIntyre, Z. Dörnyei, & A. Henry (Eds.), *Motivation dynamics in language learning* (pp. 343–366). Multilingual Matters.

Karasik, L. B., Tamis-Lemonda, C. S., & Adolph, K. E. (2011). Transition from crawling to walking and infants' actions with objects and people. *Child Development, 82*(4), 1199.

Larsen-Freeman, D. (1997). Chaos/complexity science and second language acquisition. *18*(2), 141–165.

Larsen-Freeman, D. (2006). The emergence of complexity, fluency, and accuracy in the oral and written production of five Chinese learners of English. *Applied Linguistics, 27*(4), 590–619.

Larsen-Freeman, D. (2012). Complexity theory. In S. M. Gass & A. Mackey (Eds.), *The Routledge Handbook of Second Language Acquisition* (pp. 73–87). Routledge.

Larsen-Freeman, D. (2019). On language learner agency: A complex dynamic systems theory perspective. *Modern Language Journal, 103*(S1), 61–79.

Larsen-Freeman, D., & Cameron, L. (2008). Research methodology on language development from a complex systems perspective. *The Modern Language Journal, 92*(2), 200–213.

MacIntyre, P., & Legatto, J. (2011). A dynamic system approach to willingness to communicate: Developing an idiodynamic method to capture rapidly changing affect. *Applied Linguistics, 32*(2), 149–171.

Marek, M., & Wu, W. (2014). Environmental factors affecting computer assisted language learning success: A Complex Dynamic Systems conceptual model. *Computer Assisted Language Learning, 27*(6), 560–578.

McGraw, M. B. (1944). The neuromuscular maturation of the human infant. *The Journal of Nervous and Mental disease, 99*(3), 334.

Murakami, A. (2016). Modeling systematicity and individuality in nonlinear second language development: The case of English grammatical morphemes. *Language Learning, 66*(4), 834–871.

Nowak, A., Vallacher, R. R., & Zochowski, M. (2005). The emergence of personality: Dynamic foundations of individual variation. *Developmental Review, 25*(3), 351–385.

Piaget, J. (1954). *The construction of reality in the child*. Basic Books.

Pinel, K., & Csizér, K. (2015). Changes in motivation, anxiety and self-efficacy during the course of an academic writing seminar. In Z. Dörnyei, P. MacIntyre, & A. Henry, (Eds.), *Motivational dynamics in language learning*. (pp. 164–194). Multilingual Matters.

Polat, B., & Kim, Y. (2014). Dynamics of complexity and accuracy: A longitudinal case study of advanced untutored development. *Applied Linguistics, 35*(2), 184–207.

Ribeiro, A. P., Bento, T., Salgado, J., Stiles, W. B., & Gonçalves, M. M. (2011). A dynamic look at narrative change in psychotherapy: A case study tracking innovative moments and protonarratives using state space grids. *Psychotherapy Research, 21*(1), 54–69.

Schmidt, R. (1983). Interaction, acculturation and the acquisition of communicate competence: A case study of an adult. *Sociolinguistics and Language Acquisition*: 137–174.

Skehan, P., & Foster, P. (1999). The influence of task structure and processing conditions on narrative retellings. *Language Learning, 49*(1), 93–120.

Smith, L. B., & Thelen, E. (2003). Development as a dynamic system. *Trends in Cognitive Sciences, 7*(8), 343–348.

Smith, L. B., Thelen, E., Titzer, R., & McLin, D. (1999). Knowing in the context of acting: The task dynamics of the A-Not-B error. *Psychological Review, 106*(2), 235–260.

Spoelman, M., & Verspoor, M. (2010). Dynamic patterns in development of accuracy and complexity: A longitudinal case study in the acquisition of Finnish. *Applied Linguistics, 31*(4), 532–553.

Thelen, E. (1995). Motor development. A new synthesis. *The American Psychologist, 50*(2), 79.

Thelen, E., & Smith, L. B. (1994). *A dynamics systems approach to the development of cognition and action*. Bradford Books/MIT Press.

Ushioda, E. (2015). Context and Complex Dynamic Systems Theory. In Z. Dörnyei, P. MacIntyre, & A. Henry (Eds.), *Motivational dynamics in language learning* (pp. 47–54). Multilingual Matters.

van Geert, P. (1991). A dynamic systems model of cognitive and language growth. *Psychological Review, 98*(1), 3–53.

van Geert, P., & Steenbeek, H. (2010). Networks as complex dynamic systems: Applications to clinical and developmental psychology and psychopathology. *Behavioral and Brain Sciences, 33*(2–3), 174–175.

Verspoor, M., de Bot, K., & Lowie, W. (2011). *A dynamic approach to second language development: Methods and techniques* (Vol. 29). John Benjamins.

Verspoor, M., Lowie, W., & van Dijk, M. (2008). Variability in second language development from a dynamic systems perspective. *Modern Language Journal, 92*(2), 214–231.

Verspoor, M., & van Dijk, M. (2011). Visualizing interaction between variables. In M. Verspoor, M. van Dijk, & W. Lowie (Eds.), *A dynamic approach to second language development: Methods and techniques* (Vol. 29). John Benjamins.

Waninge, F., Dörnyei, Z., & de Bot, K. (2014). Motivational dynamics in language learning: Change, stability, and context. *Modern Language Journal, 98*(3), 704–723.

5
POSITIVE PSYCHOLOGY

Peter D. MacIntyre and Samantha Ayers-Glassey

> The notion that deliberate and effective interventions can be made to increase wellbeing for both individuals and communities is a central tenet in [positive psychology] and is a defining feature of education itself, with language at the very center of the process.
>
> MacIntyre, 2016, p. 6

Psychology has been influential in understanding language learning, from cognitive neuroscience to educational psychology's approaches to designing pedagogy. In return, language development and use in communication have been major topics throughout much of the history of psychology and prominent topics in many of its subfields. Positive psychology (PP) is a relatively new subfield that was developed to complement the predominantly clinical "business-as-usual" approach to psychology. As Peterson (2006a) put it,

> [PP] calls for as much focus on strengths as on weaknesses, as much interest in building the best things in life as in repairing the worst, and as much attention to fulfilling the lives of healthy people as to healing the wounds of the distressed.
>
> p. 5

By focusing on the positive sides of language learning, PP can help to avoid the trap of thinking of second language (L2) learners in terms of what they struggle to do. Rather than deficient versions of native language (L1) speakers (Byrnes, 2018), L2 learners are in the process of creating new strengths and opportunities that can be understood in positive terms.

Positive Perspective in Psychology
What is Positive Psychology?

PP is the study of "what it is to be healthy and sane, and what humans choose to pursue when they are not suffering or oppressed" (Seligman, 2019, p. 3). In other words, it is the study of what is good in life. PP was developed to complement the dominant emphasis on defining and diagnosing problems, as reflected both in psychology in general and the disease model of clinical psychology in particular, which has primarily focused on negative and psychopathological experiences such as mental illness and distress (MacIntyre & Mercer, 2014; MacIntyre, 2016; Seligman, 2019). Instead, PP was founded to focus on positive experiences (e.g. happiness, fulfillment), positive individual traits (e.g. strength of character, values), and positive institutions (e.g. families, schools, communities; MacIntyre & Mercer, 2014; Peterson, 2006a; Seligman, 2019).

A common misconception is that PP is simply the study of happiness (Peterson, 2006a). However, PP sets itself the task of empirically studying well-being, that is, using rigorous methods to gather empirical evidence about what promotes individuals' positive evaluations of how their lives are going across domains, including overall satisfaction, emotions, relationships, and positive and negative experiences (Diener & Chan, 2011). Together, evaluating the multiple different aspects of what makes up one's life experiences combines into a person's level of subjective well-being, which can then also have multiple impacts on their life experiences. For example, research shows that high levels of subjective well-being are associated with improved physical health and longevity in healthy adults (Diener & Chan, 2011). One of the reasons to focus on positive psychological processes is that they influence a variety of health behaviors, including the immune and cardiovascular systems (Diener, Pressman, Hunter, & Delgadillo-Chase, 2017).

Foundations of Positive Psychology

Peterson (2006a, referencing Boring, 1950) aptly described PP as having a short history and a long past: Although the specific field of PP is still relatively young, its foundational concepts have been present in many ancient philosophies, religions, and belief systems (Dewaele, Chen, Padilla, & Lake, 2019; MacIntyre & Mercer, 2014; MacIntyre, 2016). Therefore, it is important to acknowledge and understand the foundational roots of the field as well as its more recent developmental history.

According to Diener (2009), "in one sense, positive psychology is thousands of years old, dating back to the thoughts of ancient philosophers and religious leaders who discussed character, virtues, happiness and the good society" (p. 7). Indeed, ancient Greek philosophers Socrates and Plato sought to understand what makes life good through reason and intuition (Compton & Hoffman, 2019). Centuries later, the Renaissance period (1400–1600) revolutionized the ideas of creativity and intellectual importance in its focus on art and individualism (Compton & Hoffman, 2019; Seligman, 2019).

The beginning of the twentieth century solidified the development of the field of psychology as we know it today, led by philosopher William James (Compton & Hoffman, 2019; Froh, 2004). One of James's major contributions to the field was an interest in the breadth of human potential, "the study of optimal human functioning and its relationship to experience, a common thread woven throughout positive psychology literature" (Froh, 2004, p. 19). James's perspective influenced the formation of humanistic psychology (see Chapter 3), a holistic approach to examining individuals' lives and what makes them good, popularized in the 1950s (Compton & Hoffman, 2019; Froh, 2004; MacIntyre & Mercer, 2014). Abraham Maslow, a leading figure of humanistic psychology, sought to understand what differentiated the most respected, fully functioning, and admired persons, whom he called self-actualizers, from others. Maslow was also the first to use the term "positive psychology" in his 1954 book, *Motivation and Personality* (Compton & Hoffman, 2019). Even then, he believed that the field of psychology was not balanced in its perspectives, focusing far more on the negative, pathological aspects of human experiences and not enough on the positive, self-actualizing aspects. Maslow said, "…the science of psychology has been far more successful on the negative than on the positive side… it is as if psychology had voluntarily restricted itself to only half its rightful jurisdiction, and that the darker, meaner half" (Maslow, 1954, p. 354).

There are key differences between humanistic psychology and PP. "Although Maslow himself embraced empiricism and sought to ground his thinking in research data, humanistic psychology generally did not engage with a strongly empirical approach, which ultimately led to extensive criticism of work emerging from this branch of psychology" (MacIntyre & Mercer, 2014, p. 7). PP was developed specifically to follow the same scientific, empirical approach that has been so successfully applied in psychology's studies of anxiety, depression, schizophrenia, post-traumatic stress, and other disorders (Compton & Hoffman, 2019; MacIntyre, 2016; MacIntyre & Mercer, 2014; Seligman, 2019). Additionally, humanistic psychology often takes a predominantly optimistic approach to human nature, whereas PP "regards both the good and the bad about life as genuine" (Peterson, 2006a, p. 9). The notion of an inherent and necessary dialectical relationship between positive and negative experiences may be replacing a simpler binary view, and studies of language are helping to advance the need to understand how different cultures value different experiences (Lomas & Ivtzan, 2016). That is, experience almost always has some combination of positive and negative attributes. There is a greater appreciation emerging in PP of the need to understand how positive and negative experiences fit together.

"Inventing" Positive Psychology

In a recent publication discussing his personal accounts of the development of PP, Seligman (2019) described spending the first week of 1998 with his mentor, Ray Fowler, and colleague, Mihaly Csíkszentmiályi, "inventing" the subfield. Modern PP is most often cited as beginning during Seligman's 1998 American Psychological Association (APA) presidency, when he proposed focusing on psychological "prevention" for that year. Seligman and Csíkszentmiályi (2000) outlined their vision for the newly emerging subfield, focusing on both theory and practice, in an article for APA's flagship journal, *American Psychologist*.

Theoretical developments in the area have introduced a long list of concepts (MacIntyre & Mercer, 2014), including a systematic examination of character strengths and happiness. The Values in Action (VIA) Classification of Strengths was developed as a positive parallel to the classification of disorders compiled in the DSM-V (Diagnostic and Statistical Manual; APA, 2013), which has been the primary resource used for the diagnosis of mental health disorders since the 1950s (Peterson, 2006b). The VIA Classification consists of six overarching virtues that are broken down into 24 character strengths (see Table 5.1) with in-depth descriptions, measures, and lifetime and cultural applications for each. The VIA Classification is measured by an online survey tool that can be used in both self-assessment and formal research applications (Peterson, 2006b). According to their website, the VIA inventory has been taken by more than eight million people (www.viacharacter.org).

Understanding character strengths is one major theoretical thrust of PP; understanding happiness and well-being is another. Although happiness is a notoriously difficult concept to define and measure (Lazarus, 2003), Seligman (2011) proposed a multidimensional theory of well-being based on five key elements reflecting "…what free, nonsuffering people choose to pursue for its own sake" (Seligman, 2019, p. 9). These five elements formed PERMA:

P- Positive emotion
E- Engagement
R- Relationships
M- Meaning
A- Accomplishment

Existing measures of well-being correlated very strongly with the PERMA-profiler measure (Seligman, 2018). The multidimensional approach to well-being provided by PERMA allows for a more fine-grained, in-depth evaluation of the specific elements that make up one's sense of well-being (Kern, Waters, Adler, & White, 2015; Seligman, 2018). PERMA has been applied in studies and interventions since its development and is finding its place in second-language acquisition (SLA) literature (see *EMPATHICS* below).

In addition to theoretical developments, a major goal of PP has been to develop interventions that everyday individuals can use to improve their positive experiences (e.g. gratitude) and reduce

Table 5.1 Values in Action (VIA) Classification of Character Strengths (adapted from Peterson, 2006b).

Virtues (6)	Character Strengths (24)
Wisdom & Knowledge	Creativity
	Curiosity and interest in the world
	Judgment and critical thinking
	Love of learning
	Perspective
Courage	Bravery
	Persistence
	Authenticity/Honesty
	Vitality
Love	Intimacy
	Kindness
	Social intelligence
Justice	Citizenship
	Fairness
	Leadership
Temperance	Forgiveness/Mercy
	Humility/Modesty
	Prudence
	Self-regulation
Transcendence	Appreciation of beauty and excellence
	Gratitude
	Hope
	Humor
	Spirituality

their negative experiences (e.g. depression). The first collection of Positive Psychology Interventions (PPIs) was published on the Authentic Happiness website (www.authentichappiness.org) created by Peterson and Schulman (Seligman, 2019). The website contained measures and activities such as the "Three Blessings"/"Three Good Things" intervention, which involves writing down three positive experiences every day for a week. PPIs have been found to substantially improve subjective ratings of depressive symptoms for as long as six months (Seligman, 2019; Sin & Lyubomirsky, 2009).

The above provides a bird's-eye view of PP and its underlying rationale. Applications of PP to education in general—and language pedagogy in particular—are providing a wealth of new research and applications. Norrish, Williams, O'Connor, and Robinson (2013) wrote, "(s)chools are one of the most important developmental contexts in young peoples' lives and can be a key source of the skills and competencies that support their capacity for successful adaptation" (p. 147).

Positive Perspective in SLA

Positive Education

PP and education go hand-in-hand (MacIntyre, 2016). It has been proposed that promoting well-being in schools can function as "an antidote to depression, as a vehicle for increasing life satisfaction, and as an aid to better learning and more creative thinking" (Seligman, Ernst, Gillham, Reivich, & Linkins, 2009). The need for an application of PP to the educational context is clear.

The three primary focuses of PP—positive experiences, positive individual traits, and positive institutions—fit well into the educational context. Positive experiences, such as students' daily interactions with their peers and teachers, can have a lasting impact on the students' outlooks and perspectives related to learning and the educational environment, as well as their broader beliefs:

> To the extent that teachers convey pessimism, distrust, and a tragic outlook on life, their students' worldview will be thus fabricated. To the extent that teachers transmit optimism, trust, and a hopeful sense of the future, this will positively influence their students' perception of the world.
>
> *Seligman, 2019, p. 15*

Studies have shown a clear connection between positive mood and factors related to learning, such as academic achievement (Kern et al., 2015; Pekrun, Goetz, Titz, & Perry, 2002), creativity (To, Fisher, Ashkanasy, & Rowe, 2011), attention (Fredrickson, 2004), fewer risky behaviors, better physical health (Kern et al., 2015), and more. Therefore, fostering a positive learning environment can benefit students' day-to-day experiences outside the classroom. Positive traits such as character strengths can have direct implications on students' learning and academic and personal development. The ethos of the learning institution can also play an important role in fostering positive student experiences and long-term functioning (Norrish et al., 2013).

Positive Psychology and SLA

The formal combination of PP and SLA research was established by MacIntyre and Gregersen (2012) and solidified by MacIntyre and Mercer (2014). The articles fell on the "fertile ground" of an SLA field already pursuing lines of inquiry related to topics such as motivation, positive attitudes, and emotions, though such considerations were somewhat on the sidelines of the field dominated by cognitive models of instructed learning (Dewaele et al., 2019). In 2016, two PP-themed books appeared in the SLA literature: *Positive Psychology in SLA* (MacIntyre, Gregersen, & Mercer, 2016) and *Positive Psychology Perspectives on Foreign Language Learning and Teaching* (Gabryś-Barker & Gałajda, 2016). Through these and other publications, the importance of incorporating a PP perspective into SLA became recognized. Language learning is a long-term process with a good deal of inevitable failure and frustration along the way; it requires perseverance, optimism, and resilience among a number of other qualities highlighted within PP (MacIntyre et al., 2019a). The synergy of SLA and PP is emerging in both research and practice.

Research methods used in PP often are familiar to those in SLA. PP emphasizes the need for high-quality measurement of concepts, methodological rigor, and data-driven tests of theories/hypotheses. Methods based on survey research, classroom observation, and experimental methods are used to varying degrees across the field of SLA. One area where SLA research may be ahead of PP is in its applications of qualitative research methods, as a recent call for qualitative research was made in the *Journal of Positive Psychology* (Hefferon, Ashfield, Waters, & Synard, 2017). Developing more eclectic methods and nuanced theories is facilitating the second wave of PP research, a dialectical approach that involves theorizing about integrating positive and negative experiences (Wong, 2011). Dewaele and MacIntyre (2019) emphasized that PP can strengthen SLA "…by encouraging researchers to acknowledge that there are interactions between positive and negative phenomena and that equating the positive to 'good/motivated/successful' and negative to 'bad/unmotivated/unsuccessful' is simplistic" (p. 269).

With respect to language teaching, there are clear avenues where PPIs can be adapted to educational practice. An emphasis on participant-active approaches (i.e. Participatory Action Research [PAR]) is valued in both fields (MacIntyre & Mercer, 2014). According to MacDonald (2012), using PAR allows "qualitative features of an individual's feelings, views, and patterns [to be] revealed without control or manipulation from the researcher" (p. 34) and involves "an action researcher and community or organization members who are seeking to improve their situation" (p. 36). Qualitative methods are especially helpful for this type of inquiry as they can provide richer, more in-depth insight than quantitative methods (MacDonald, 2012; MacIntyre & Mercer, 2016; MacIntyre et al., 2019a). The use of multiple methodological approaches to evaluate SLA research and practice allows for analysis at both the group and individual levels, which can together provide information on individuals' traits and their strategic use, and the functioning and contribution of the institution.

Integrating Perspectives

In this section, we offer a brief overview of areas in which PP has been specifically integrated into SLA research and practice, including the humanistic approach, the importance of emotions for language learners and teachers, motivational models and flow, and a reinvented version of PERMA specific to the SLA context called "EMPATHICS".

A Humanistic Approach to Language Teaching

Humanistic psychology influenced the development of PP and had a role to play in SLA (MacIntyre & Mercer, 2014). Beginning in the 1970s, language learning and its participants began to be viewed holistically, including their cognitions and emotions (see Chapter 14) (Khatib, Sareem, & Hamidi, 2013; Lei, 2007). This contributed to how SLA research progressed, setting the groundwork for more PP-like perspectives. Khatib et al. (2013) summarized these changes, stating that, "the roles of teachers and learners were redefined, learners' needs were given priority and language pedagogy went through crucial modifications" (p. 45). They described three types of teachers: lecturers, who simply present educational material at a surface level; teachers, who have more in-depth knowledge of the material and understand some different ways in which the material could be presented in an educational setting; and facilitators, who understand the material in-depth and actively present and discuss the subject matter to facilitate optimal learning (Khatib et al., 2013; Lei, 2007). According to the authors, only the latter type of teacher reflects a humanistic approach to language teaching.

Approaching a language learner holistically means viewing them first as an individual, separate from the learning environment (Lei, 2007). This means "not merely developing the cognitive and linguistic abilities of the learners but also paying attention to the learners' emotions and feelings" (Khatib et al., 2013, p. 45). Therefore, the role of the teacher as a facilitator is necessary to "create a supportive psychological atmosphere for the learners so they can study independently, non-defensively and therefore, effectively" (Lei, 2007, p. 61).

Like humanistic psychology, the humanistic approach to SLA was blemished by criticisms regarding its methodologies and lack of scientific support. It did, however, leave a long-lasting impact on language-teaching and -learning research, and its core principles and approaches continue to influence how the field operates (MacIntyre & Mercer, 2014).

Positive and Negative Emotions

The topic of emotions and their potential impacts on learning activity is "taking off" in SLA, partly due to the overarching influence of PP (Dewaele et al., 2019). Prior research might have focused on single emotions such as anxiety (MacIntyre, 2017); however, it is becoming almost untenable to investigate the effects of single emotions alone, because they rarely are encountered as singular experiences. Modern studies of emotions tend to focus on a broad range of potentially applicable emotions, both negative and positive (e.g. MacIntyre & Gregersen, 2012; MacIntyre & Vincze, 2017). Consistent with the dynamics of the self, there have been a series of studies on emotional experiences which demonstrate clearly the integration of positive and negative emotion with diverse elements of goals, experiences, social interaction, present context, and additional influences negotiated and combined in real time (Dewaele, MacIntyre, Boudreau, & Dewaele, 2016; Gregersen, MacIntyre, Hein-Finegan, Talbot, & Claman, 2014; MacIntyre & Serroul, 2015). In an overview of the concept *perezhivanie*, Lantolf and Swain (2019) offer a Vygotskian account (see Chapter 2) of the necessary integration of cognition and emotion that applies to learners and teachers alike.

The focus on emotions in addition to cognitive factors within SLA has been developing along multiple pathways, even before PP was directly implicated (Prior, 2019). According to Dewaele et al. (2019), "emotions are at the heart of language learning and teaching, which were underestimated in the past because of the dominance of cognitive perspectives and the false beliefs that studying emotions is somehow unscientific" (p. 1). Although language learners have been a primary focus for SLA research on the topic, the study of teachers' emotions and their influence on learning outcomes has begun to take hold more recently (MacIntyre, Ross, Talbot, Mercer, Gregersen, & Banga, 2019b). In a recent introduction to a series of articles on emotion, Bigelow (2019) wrote,

> I am certain that work in the area of emotion holds tremendous relevancy to classroom teaching and learning, and not only from the student perspective but also that of teachers. It is high time we recognized emotion as a critical, embodied, and cognitive part all of the dimensions that touch on language teaching and learning.
>
> *p. 516*

Anxiety experienced by learners has been the predominant emotion studied in SLA, often referred to as foreign-language classroom anxiety (FLCA). However, positive emotions such as foreign-language enjoyment (FLE) have been increasingly examined alongside FLCA. Although it might seem straightforward to present positive and negative emotions such as enjoyment and anxiety as opposite ends of a continuum, moving up and down in opposite directions like a see-saw, FLCA and FLE have been shown to instead be related but independent. They are best viewed as complementary to each other:

> Consistent with the adaptive nature of emotion in general, and the narrowing effects of negative emotion and anxiety in particular, it is likely that enjoyment and anxiety will cooperate from time to time, enjoyment encouraging playful exploration and anxiety generating focus on the need to take specific action.
>
> *Dewaele & MacIntyre, 2014, p. 262*

Several studies have found students' FLE to be significantly higher than FLCA in typical L2 classrooms (Dewaele & Alfawzan, 2018; Dewaele & MacIntyre, 2014; Dewaele et al., 2016). These results have been linked to variables such as learners' age, gender, education level, L2 level, personality traits, number of languages known and being studied, perceived L2 proficiency, comprehension abilities, and other factors (Brantmeier, 2005; Dewaele & MacIntyre, 2014, 2019; Dewaele et al., 2016). Most notably, recent studies have found students' FLE to be most predicted by variables related to the learning context, such as teachers' emotional and professional skills and supportive peer interactions (Dewaele & MacIntyre, 2014, Dewaele et al., 2019).

A Focus on the Teacher

As students' well-being and success within the L2 classroom has been clearly tied to teacher performance, it is surprising that teachers have not been studied to the same extent (Hwang, Bartlett, Greben, & Hand, 2017; MacIntyre et al., 2019b; Van Petegem, Creemers, Rossel, & Aelterman, 2005). The focus on PP in SLA has brought with it a concern for teacher well-being (Gkonou, Dewaele, & King, 2020; Mercer & Kostoulas, 2018). Teachers practice a stressful profession due to the high possibility for interpersonal conflict, time pressures, heavy workloads, role conflict and ambiguity, and additional duties such as administration (MacIntyre et al., 2019b; Owen, 2016). As individuals, teachers' subjective well-being involves not only their experiences within their profession, but also in their personal lives and sense of self (Hwang et al., 2017).

Although teachers often report perceptions of the teaching environment more positively than learners, stress and other issues can still persist (Van Petegem et al., 2005). However, protective factors have been found that can mitigate these negative experiences and promote more well-being such as emotion-related personality traits (MacIntyre et al., 2019b), gender differences, and level of teaching experience (Van Petegem et al., 2005), as well as support from other teachers (Owen, 2016) and mindfulness practices (Hwang et al., 2017). Hiver (2016) provides a particularly engaging account of how teachers working in a difficult context promote trajectories of hope in their daily practice. PP is shining a spotlight on the mutually dependent relationships between teachers and students and is facilitating a long-overdue focus on the well-being of language teachers.

Motivation and Flow

Motivation has long been a foundational concept in studying the psychology of language learners (see Chapter 10) and there are obvious ties to PP. A particularly intense form of motivation, one central to PP since its inception, is flow. Flow is defined as "the state in which people are so involved in an activity that nothing else seems to matter" (Csíkszentmihályi, 1991, p. 4). Flow experiences have been linked to the positive emotions that are often associated with subjective well-being (Jackson & Marsh, 1996). In SLA research, flow has been examined to a much lesser extent than other motivational concepts (see Dewaele & MacIntyre, in press; MacIntyre, 2016). Research suggests flow in the L2 is correlated with positive outcomes such as reading engagement (Kitchhoff, 2013), computer-based language learning (Egbert, 2006), perceived accomplishment (Oxford, 2016), and motivation (Czimmermann & Piniel, 2016). As Dewaele and MacIntyre (in press) stated,

> (f)low experiences create a unique mode in which a learner's thoughts, feelings, and behaviour reflect effortless and harmonious coordination. Flow experiences are motivating and they are memorable. Best of all, the conditions for flow have been well studied in other contexts and language tasks can be designed to increase the probability of flow among learners and teachers.
>
> *p. 23*

The conditions necessary for flow can be fleeting, and perhaps the sense of the experience as ephemeral is one reason flow, like emotion, has not been as widely studied in SLA as other motivational concepts.

For a long time, thinking about motivation was dominated by Gardner's socio-educational model of L2 learning (Gardner, 1985, 2010), which proposed that motivation is based in large part on positive attitudes (see Chapter 12). More recently, Dörnyei's (2005, 2009) motivation self-system took emphasized concepts of the ideal future self, obligations carried in an ought-to self, and the influence of L2 experience. For Dörnyei (2020), the most active ingredient in motivation is a positive vision of an ideal future self, including the potentially powerful mental imagery and emotions that accompany it. "Language learning is a sustained and often tedious process with lots of temporary ups and downs, and I felt that the secret of successful learners was their possession of a superordinate vision that kept them on track" (Dörnyei, 2009, p. 25). This vision can be linked to directed motivational currents (DMCs), which themselves can be tied directly to PP concepts and principles, including positive emotions, passions, and self-control motives such as persistence, grit, hardiness, conscientiousness, and academic buoyancy (see Dörnyei, 2020). DMCs reflect a sustained period of intensive activity in pursuit of a long-term goal. Although neither Gardner nor Dörnyei explicitly tied their motivation-related concepts to PP, both theorists drew substantially on psychological theories that are now central to the study of PP, including positive attitudes, emotions, and a positive view of the self.

EMPATHICS

The development of PP in SLA has introduced a new, overarching framework that draws together many of the themes emerging from the humanistic tradition, much of the research on individual differences in language learning, and the notion of development captured by changes in dynamic systems. Although PP's PERMA framework (Seligman, 2011) can be applied in SLA, Oxford (2016) proposed a more encompassing, extended version that she suggested might be more applicable to language learning and teaching. This new framework was named "EMPATHICS" and included nine dimensions (Oxford, 2016, p. 10):

E- Emotion and empathy
M- Meaning and motivation
P- Perseverance, including resilience, hope, and optimism
A- Agency and autonomy
T- Time
H- Hardiness and habits of mind
I- Intelligences
C- Character strengths
S- Self factors (self-efficacy, self-concept, self-esteem, self-verification)

According to Oxford, the dimensions of the EMPATHICS framework are meant to "help learners achieve high well-being and progress rapidly, develop proficiency, and relish the language learning experience. At the same time, [the] components help explain why learners with low well-being crash on the rocks of frustration, anxiety or indifference" (2016, p. 10). The dimensions of EMPATHICS were not developed as a complete hierarchical model, but rather as a direction for future theories and research on the topics in SLA (MacIntyre, 2016). Several of the topics proposed in the framework have not yet been tested within SLA research, but based on previous findings in other subfields of psychology, Oxford proposed hypotheses for each dimension to "open up new vistas for theory and research, for language teaching practice and, of course, for language learning itself" (2016, p. 11; see Table 5.2).

Implications for Practice and Research

Research to date has shown that pedagogical practices link to the well-being of teachers and learners. "It is imperative that teacher training courses pay attention to these crucial emotional dimensions in order to allow teachers to create a positive climate in their classrooms" (Dewaele & Alfawzan,

Table 5.2 Oxford's (2016) Hypotheses for the Nine Dimensions of EMPATHICS.

Dimensions	Hypotheses
	Language learners with high well-being…
E	Recognize their *emotions*, manage them effectively, and show *empathy* for others
M	Seek and create *meaning*, which helps them be *motivated*
P	*Persevere* in their learning
A	Embody *agency* and *autonomy*
T	Appraise themselves *temporally* in a positive way and have a *time perspective* that fits their needs for learning
H	Develop *hardy attitudes* and *hardy action patterns* and have useful *habits of mind*
I	Recognize their own *intelligences* and take advantage of those intelligences for learning and living
C	Have a range of *character strengths* that help them in their learning and in their lives
S	Possess *self-efficacy*, positive *self-concepts*, and high *self-esteem*, and use *self-verification* positively

2018, p. 40). Mercer et al. (2018) outline the broad implications of engaging with PP in SLA for both teachers and learners. They argue it is necessary to combine non-linguistic and linguistic aims in sustainable ways, taking care not to impair the development of either skill set nor to overburden educators. There is a balance to be found between a concern for the content of language teaching and for the learner, but one lesson from PP is that ignoring how they fit together is a mistake. Language teachers function in a wide variety of contexts, sharing the core theme that teaching and learning are done by human beings whose well-being is not an optional or superfluous consideration but central to the whole process (MacIntyre et al., 2019a).

The language-learning context provides an opportunity to engage with the principles of PP. However, the stage must be set in a systematic way if the field is to fully embrace the challenge. Mercer et al. (2018) argue that

> …training is needed at in-service and pre-service levels to support teachers in understanding what wellbeing is and how it can be fostered for both themselves and their learners. We need to work towards a framework of Positive Language Education that can be empirically validated and further developed, and which can be practically implemented in diverse cultural and linguistic settings without prescriptivism and in sustainable ways… The question is whether this is especially "positive" language education, or simply what good language education ought to be anyway.
>
> *p. 24*

PP highlights the importance of balancing the perception of teacher and learner needs because it requires a focus on strengths and weaknesses, and especially how they interact over time (Oxford, 2016).

Future Directions

1. *A holistic approach integrating positive and negative.* PP shares with SLA a concern for theory, research, and practice. PP is moving toward a holistic integration of positive and negative sides of experiences. One advantage for the SLA field is the dialectical position described by second-wave PP, which may be even more consistent with the mixed-methods approach taken to research in SLA than is within the disciplinary boundaries of psychology.
2. *Research showing the facilitating role for positive experiences: How do strengths such as grit, creativity, and courage play out in specific language tasks, learning contexts, and cultural milieus?* For SLA to fully embrace PP, there will be an ongoing need to demonstrate its value of concepts such as flow, hope, courage, well-being, optimism, creativity, happiness, passion, flourishing, grit, resilience, buoyancy, positive emotions, creativity, character strengths, wisdom, health, and laughter in facilitating language-learning outcomes. Further, tests of the success of specific interventions at the level of the individual teacher/learner, classroom, institution, and beyond are necessary, but it is crucial that all of the relevant outcomes and effects, not simply the so-called linguistic outcomes, be identified and empirically studied.
3. *New pedagogical practices that integrate theory of well-being into language with an evaluation of their efficacy.* In conjunction with #2 above, there is a particular need for classroom-based research to show the variety of applications of PP as well as its results. Emerging research is showing that those outcomes are highly individual and vary from person to person (e.g. Gregersen et al., 2014).

Reflection Questions

1. How does a teacher's approach to their classroom reflect their beliefs about learner psychology? How might a teacher identify their own beliefs about their own psychology as well as what their learners might need to succeed?

2. Is it unfair, or is it absolutely necessary, to ask teachers to concern themselves with learner psychology?
3. How can teachers use the principles of empirical research (e.g., good measurement, clear definitions, systematic data collection, falsifiable hypotheses) as "amateur scientists" in their classrooms to collect data to evaluate interventions? What other ways are there to engage with the principles of PP in classroom research?

Recommended Reading

Dewaele, J.-M., Chen, X., Padilla, A. M., & Lake, J. (2019). The flowering of positive psychology in foreign/second language teaching and acquisition research. *Frontiers in Psychology, 10*, 1–13.
This article provides a thorough historical overview of the development of positive psychology in SLA with a focus on theory, empirical work, and criticisms.

MacIntyre, P. D. & Mercer, S. (2014). Introducing positive psychology to SLA. *Studies in Second Language Learning and Teaching, 4*(2), 153–172.
Although not the first to draw upon positive psychology, this paper is the first to advocate for the large-scale application of positive psychology and its concepts to the study of language learning.

MacIntyre, P. D., Gregersen, T., & Mercer, S. (2019). Setting an agenda for positive psychology in SLA: Theory, practice, and research. *Modern Language Journal, 103*(1), 262–274.
This article, in one of the leading journals in applied linguistics, outlines the work that has been done to develop positive psychology in SLA and helps to establish a foundation for future work in the area. An article by Mercer et al. (2018) provides a companion piece focusing more directly on language education.

References

American Psychiatric Association [APA]. (2013). *Diagnostic and Statistical Manual of Mental Disorders (DSM-5)*. American Psychiatric Publications.
Bigelow, M. (2019). (Re) considering the role of emotion in language teaching and learning. *Modern Language Journal, 103*(2), 515–516.
Brantmeier, C. (2005). Nonlinguistic variables in advanced second language reading: Learners' self-assessment and enjoyment. *Foreign Language Annals, 38*(4), 494–504.
Byrnes, H. (2018). Advanced-level grammatical development in instructed SLA. In P. Malovrh & A. Benati (Eds.), *The Handbook of Advanced Proficiency in Second Language Acquisition* (pp. 133–156). Wiley-Blackwell.
Compton, W. C., & Hoffman, E. (2019). *Positive Psychology: The Science of Happiness and Flourishing (3rd Edition)*. SAGE Publications.
Csíkszentmihályi, M. (1991). *Flow: The Psychology of Optimal Experience*. HarperPerennial.
Czimmermann, E., & Piniel, K. (2016). Advanced language learners' experiences of flow in the Hungarian EFL classroom. In P. D. MacIntyre, T. Gregersen, and S. Mercer (Eds.), *Positive Psychology in SLA* (pp. 193–214). Multilingual Matters.
Dewaele, J.-M., & Alfawzan, M. (2018). Does the effect of enjoyment outweigh that of anxiety in foreign language performance? *Studies in Second Language Learning and Teaching, 8*(1), 21–45.
Dewaele, J.-M., Chen, X., Padilla, A. M., & Lake, J. (2019). The flowering of positive psychology in foreign/second language teaching and acquisition research. *Frontiers in Psychology, 10*, 2128.
Dewaele, J.-M., & MacIntyre, P. D. (2014). The two faces of Janus? Anxiety and enjoyment in the foreign language classroom. *Studies in Second Language Learning and Teaching, 4*(2), 237–274.
Dewaele, J.-M., & MacIntyre, P. D. (2019). The predictive power of multicultural personality traits, learner and teacher variables on foreign language enjoyment and anxiety. In M. Sato & S. Loewen (Eds.): *Evidence-Based Second Language Pedagogy: A Collection of Instructed Second Language Acquisition Studies* (pp. 263–286). Routledge.
Dewaele, J.-M., & MacIntyre, P. D. (in press). Flow in the Spanish foreign language classroom. Unpublished manuscript. Published after translation as El flujo en el aula de español como lengua extranjera. In M. del Carmen Méndez & J. Andoni Duñabeitia (Eds.), *Factores Cognitivos y Afectivos en la Enseñanza de español como lengua extranjera (Advances in Spanish Language Teaching)*. Routledge.

Dewaele, J.-M., MacIntyre, P. D., Boudreau, C., & Dewaele, L. (2016). Do girls have all the fun? Anxiety and enjoyment in the foreign language classroom. *Theory and Practice of Second Language Acquisition, 2*(1), 41–63.

Diener, E., & Chan, M.Y. (2011). Happy people live longer: Subjective well-being contributes to health and longevity. *Applied Psychology: Health and Well-Being, 3*(1), 1–43.

Diener, E. (2009). Positive psychology: Past, present, and future. In S. J. Lopez & C. R. Snyder (Eds.): *The Oxford Handbook of Positive Psychology* (pp. 7–11).

Diener, E., Pressman, S. D., Hunter, J., & Delgadillo-Chase, D. (2017). If, why, and when subjective well-being influences health, and future needed research. *Applied Psychology: Health and Well-Being, 9*(2), 133–167.

Dörnyei, Z. (2005). *The Psychology of the Language Learner: Individual Differences in Second Language Acquisition*. Lawrence Erlbaum.

Dörnyei, Z. (2009). The L2 motivational self system. In Z. Dörnyei & E. Ushioda (Eds.), *Motivation, Language Identity and the L2 Self* (pp. 9–42). Multilingual Matters.

Dörnyei, Z. (2020). *Innovations and Challenges in Language Learning Motivation*. Routledge.

Egbert, J. L. (2006). Flow as a model for CALL research. In J. L. Egbert & G. M. Petrie, *CALL Research Perspectives* (pp. 129–140). Routledge.

Fredrickson, B. L. (2004). The broaden-and-build theory of positive emotions. *Philosophical Transactions of the Royal Society of London. Series B: Biological Sciences, 359*(1449), 1367–1377.

Froh, J. J. (2004). The history of positive psychology: Truth be told. *NYS Psychologist, 16*(3), 18–20.

Gabryś-Barker, D., & Gałajda, D. (2016). *Positive Psychology Perspectives on Foreign Language Learning and Teaching*. Springer.

Gardner, R. C. (1985). *Social Psychology and Second Language Learning: The Role of Attitudes and Motivation*. London: Edward Arnold Publishers.

Gardner, R. C. (2010). *Motivation and Second Language Acquisition: The Socio-Educational Model*. Peter Lang.

Gkonou, C., Dewaele, J.-M., & King, J. (Eds.). (2020). *The Emotional Rollercoaster of Language Teaching*. Multilingual Matters.

Gregersen, T., MacIntyre, P. D., Hein-Finegan, K., Talbot, K., & Claman, S. (2014). Examining emotional intelligence within the context of positive psychology interventions. *Studies in Second Language Learning and Teaching, 4*, 327–353.

Hefferon, K., Ashfield, A., Waters, L., & Synard, J. (2017). Understanding optimal human functioning: The "call for qual" in exploring human flourishing and well-being. *Journal of Positive Psychology, 12*(3), 211–219.

Hiver, P. (2016). The triumph over experience: Hope and hardiness in novice L2 teachers. In P. D. MacIntyre, T. Gregersen, and S. Mercer (Eds.), *Positive Psychology in Second Language Acquisition*, (pp. 168–192). Multilingual Matters.

Hwang, Y. S., Bartlett, B., Greben, M., & Hand, K. (2017). A systematic review of mindfulness interventions for in-service teachers: A tool to enhance teacher wellbeing and performance. *Teaching and Teacher Education, 64*, 26–42.

Jackson, S. A., & Marsh, H. W. (1996). Development and validation of a scale to measure optimal experience: The Flow State Scale. *Journal of Sport and Exercise Psychology, 18*(1), 17–35.

Kern, M. L., Waters, L. E., Adler, A., & White, M. A. (2015). A multidimensional approach to measuring well-being in students: Application of the PERMA framework. *Journal of Positive Psychology, 10*(3), 262–271.

Khatib, M., Sareem, S. N., & Hamidi, H. (2013). Humanistic education: Concerns, implications and applications. *Journal of Language Teaching and Research, 4*(1), 45–51.

Kitchhoff, C. (2013). L2 extensive reading and flow: Clarifying the relationship. *Reading in a Foreign Language, 25*(2), 192–212.

Lantolf, J. P., & Swain, M. (2019). Perezhivanie: The cognitive-emotional dialectic within the social situation of development. In A. H. Al-Hoorie and P. MacIntyre (Eds.), *Contemporary Language Motivation Theory: 60 Years Since Gardner and Lambert (1959)*. Multilingual Matters.

Lazarus, R. S. (2003). Does the positive psychology movement have legs? *Psychological Inquiry, 14*(2), 93–109.

Lei, Q. (2007). EFL teachers' factors and students' affect. *US-China Education Review, 4*(3), 60–67.

Lomas, T., & Ivtzan, I. (2016). Second wave positive psychology: Exploring the positive-negative dialectics of wellbeing. *Journal of Happiness Studies, 17*(4), 1753–1768.

MacDonald, C. (2012). Understanding participatory action research: A qualitative research methodology option. *Canadian Journal of Action Research, 13*(2), 34–50.

MacIntyre, P., & Gregersen, T. (2012). Affect: The role of language anxiety and other emotions in language learning. In S. Mercer, S. Ryan, and M. Williams (Eds.), *Psychology for Language Learning* (pp. 103–118). Palgrave Macmillan.

MacIntyre, P. D., & Mercer, S. (2014). Introducing positive psychology to SLA. *Studies in Second Language Learning and Teaching, 4*(2), 153–172.

MacIntyre, P. D., & Serroul, A. (2015). Motivation on a per-second timescale: Examining approach-avoidance motivation during L2 task performance. In Z. Dörnyei, P. D. MacIntyre, and A. Henry (Eds.), *Motivational Dynamics in Language Learning* (pp. 109–138). Multilingual Matters.

MacIntyre, P. D., & Vincze, L. (2017). Positive and negative emotions underlie motivation for L2 learning. *Studies in Second Language Learning and Teaching, 7*(1), 61–88.

MacIntyre, P. D. (2016). So far so good: An overview of positive psychology and its contributions to SLA. In D. Gabryś-Barker & D. Gałajda (Eds.): *Positive Psychology Perspectives on Foreign Language Learning and Teaching* (pp. 3–20). Springer International Publishing.

MacIntyre, P. D. (2017). An overview of language anxiety research and trends in its development. In C. Gkonou, M. Daubney, & J. M. Dewaele (Eds.), *New Insights into Language Anxiety: Theory, Research and Educational Implications* (pp. 11–30). Multilingual Matters.

MacIntyre, P. D., Gregersen, T., & Mercer, S. (2016). *Positive Psychology in SLA*. Multilingual Matters.

MacIntyre, P. D., Gregersen, T., & Mercer, S. (2019a). Setting an agenda for positive psychology in SLA: Theory, practice, and research. *Modern Language Journal, 103*(1), 262–274.

MacIntyre, P. D., Ross, J., Talbot, K., Mercer, S., Gregersen, T., & Banga, C. A. (2019b). Stressors, personality and wellbeing among language teachers. *System, 82*, 26–38.

Maslow, A. (1954). *Motivation and Personality*. Harper & Row Publishers.

Mercer, S., & Kostoulas, A. (Eds.). (2018). *Language Teacher Psychology*. Multilingual Matters.

Mercer, S., MacIntyre, P. D., Gregersen, T., & Talbot, K. (2018). Positive Language Education: Combining Positive Education and Language Education. *Theory and Practice of Second Language Acquisition, 4*, 11–31.

Norrish, J. M., Williams, P., O'Connor, M., & Robinson, J. (2013). An applied framework for positive education. *International Journal of Wellbeing, 3*(2), 147–161.

Owen, S. (2016). Professional learning communities: Building skills, reinvigorating the passion, and nurturing teacher wellbeing and "flourishing" within significantly innovative schooling contexts. *Educational Review, 68*(4), 403–419.

Oxford, R. L. (2016). Toward a psychology of well-being for language learners: The "EMPATHICS" vision. In P. D. MacIntyre, T. Gregersen, & S. Mercer (Eds.), *Positive Psychology in SLA* (pp. 10–87). Multilingual Matters.

Pekrun, R., Goetz, T., Titz, W., & Perry, R. P. (2002). Academic emotions in students' self-regulated learning and achievement: A program of qualitative and quantitative research. *Educational Psychologist, 37*(2), 91–105.

Peterson, C. (2006a). *A Primer in Positive Psychology*. Oxford University Press, Inc.

Peterson, C. (2006b). The Values in Action (VIA) classification of strengths. In M. Csíkszentmihályi & I. S. Csíkszentmihályi: *A Life Worth Living: Contributions to Positive Psychology* (pp. 28–29). Oxford University Press.

Prior, M. T. (2019). Elephants in the room: An "affective turn" or just feeling our way? *Modern Language Journal, 103*(2), 516–527.

Seligman, M. (2011). *Flourish*. Simon & Schuster.

Seligman, M. (2018). PERMA and the building blocks of well-being. *The Journal of Positive Psychology, 13*(4), 333–335.

Seligman, M. E. (2019). Positive psychology: A personal history. *Annual Review of Clinical Psychology, 15*, 1–23.

Seligman, M. E., Ernst, R. M., Gillham, J., Reivich, K., & Linkins, M. (2009). Positive education: Positive psychology and classroom interventions. *Oxford Review of Education, 35*(3), 293–311.

Seligman, M. E. P., & Csíkszentmihályi, M. (2000). Positive psychology (Special issue). *American Psychologist, 55*(1), 5–14.

Sin, N. L., & Lyubomirsky, S. (2009). Enhancing well-being and alleviating depressive symptoms with positive psychology interventions: A practice-friendly meta-analysis. *Journal of Clinical Psychology, 65*(5), 467–487.

To, M. L., Fisher, C. D., Ashkanasy, N. M., & Rowe, P. A. (2011). Within-person relationships between mood and creativity. *Journal of Applied Psychology, 97*(3), 599–612.

Van Petegem, K., Creemers, B. P. M., Rossel, Y., & Aelterman, A. (2005). Relationships between teacher characteristics, interpersonal teacher behaviour and teacher wellbeing. *Journal of Classroom Interaction, 40*(2), 34–43.

Wong, P. T. P. (2011). Positive psychology 2.0: Towards a balanced interactive model of the good life. *Canadian Psychology, 52*(2), 69–81.

6
PSYCHOLINGUISTICS

Simone E. Pfenninger and Julia Festman

Psycholinguistics is a scientific discipline that focuses on the study of how humans learn and use language. Acquisition, learning, and use of language are based on fundamental cognitive processes which underlie language-based skills (production/speaking, writing, perception/comprehension, reading). Psycholinguistics also entails the understanding of how language knowledge is stored, accessed, and retrieved in our mind, in particular how it is interrelated with domain-general knowledge, pragmatics, and action. These already complicated processes peak in complexity when an individual learns more than one language—the highly efficient brain learns how to handle more than one language and optimizes processes by involving other cognitive functions such as cognitive control and language control.

While interest in issues relating to language processing has been a feature of second language acquisition (SLA) research for some time (see, e.g., VanPatten, 1996), it is only recently that SLA researchers have begun using theories from psychology—such as dynamic systems theories that were derived originally from physical theories—to examine the way learners *develop* second languages (L2) in an iterated, non-linear way. Conversely, the epistemological and methodological diversity in individual differences (ID) research in psychology has too often been described in terms of opposition and conflict (e.g. nature vs. nurture), neglecting or at least downplaying the meaningfulness of inter- and intra-individual variation. This chapter illustrates how SLA research benefits from theories and methods that sit at the intersection of psychology and linguistics.

Psycholinguistics in Psychology

A psychological approach to psycholinguistics involves the study of language behavior and language learning being based on *cognitive individual processes* happening within the individual. In order to grasp these processes and to make them more evident, psycholinguists draw on systematizing basic principles and processes by putting forward systematic *models* such as models of language production (e.g., Levelt, 1989; Levelt, Roelofs, & Meyer, 1999). Bridging the linguistic and psychological ends of the continuum of psycholinguistics, these models strive to facilitate our understanding of the language input and intake of a learner or speaker in relation to their *speech environment*, characterizing the learner's/speaker's verbal output and trying to understand the underlying processes necessary for perception of input, and for thoughts to end up being produced in terms of output. While *influential prerequisites* (e.g., cognitive faculty, working memory, etc.) as well as factors characterizing the speech or learning environment (socio-economic status, etc.) play a role in psycholinguistic research on language learning, they are not an essential part of classical psycholinguistic models, albeit commonly included in empirical studies (see our discussion of *confounding variables* below).

To give an example, psycholinguistic models of language production (e.g., Levelt, 1989) suggest a number of discrete stages that occur during the preparation of speech production before a word or sound is uttered. Roughly speaking, an idea, message, or speaker intention has to pass through the stages of conceptualization (segmentation, structure of abstract information), formulation (lexical selection, grammatical encoding, and phonological encoding), and finally production (articulation) until a verbal utterance is expressed.

It needs to be mentioned that the current view on language production is essentially a monolingual one, in which language production is described for only one language at a time. A recent prominent example of such a monolingual approach is the theoretical model put forward by Pickering and Garrod (2013), which integrates language production and comprehension framed within embodied cognition. Attempts to include bilingualism have been put forward, but they are still from the lens of a monolingual bias. One example is de Bot's Bilingual Production Model (1992, 2003), which builds on Levelt's model by postulating one lexicon, in which both languages are represented together, language-specific pathways of formulation, partially overlapping conceptualizers for the different languages, and a common system for articulation.

Psychological constructs that have found their way into psycholinguistic research seem to be predominantly related to the question as to how the mind/brain handles more than one language. Arguably the most seminal model of bilingual processing is David Green's Inhibitory Control (IC) Model (1986, 1998). For Green, activation and inhibition are domain-general processes found across different neurobiological and -chemical domains in which they work as counterparties in the brain. For example, on the motor execution level, activation and inhibition are involved in choice (Praamstra & Seiss, 2005), while on the enzyme level, they act as opponents (e.g. Saboury, 2009). On the behavioral level, the idea of competition between two response alternatives has been famously investigated in the Stroop task (Stroop, 1935): By presenting a printed word to a literate adult, Stroop knew that their automatic processing would come into play as they automatically read and determined the semantic meaning of the word while simultaneously ignoring the color of the ink. In the Stroop test, the adult is, however, asked to name the print color of the word (activation) and to "ignore" the reading and meaning of the word (inhibition). This is particularly difficult in the case of incongruent color-word stimuli (e.g., the word RED printed in blue).

This observation has important repercussions for bilinguals, who constantly find themselves in communicative situations in which only one of their available languages is needed (e.g., when language use demands are created by the speech environment such as at school, at work, etc.). In such conditions, it is necessary to activate representations from the target language while simultaneously inhibiting possible lexical competitors from both the target language and from the non-target language, since both languages of a bilingual have been found to be constantly activated in parallel (Honisho & Thierry, 2011; Kroll, Bobb, Misra, & Guo, 2008). Without inhibition, cross-linguistic interference (i.e., the production of parts of the language that are currently not needed) may occur at multiple levels. In language conditions in which both languages can be used (code-switching), a relatively low level of inhibition is needed.

In order to orchestrate these complex processes, a "surveillance system" has to be in place. *Cognitive control*, a complex mental process used to manage behaviors and thoughts, is a composition of multiple subprocesses such as inhibition, shifting, updating, attention, and conflict monitoring (e.g., Green & Abutalebi, 2013; Miyake, Friedman, Emerson, Witzki, Howerter, & Wager, 2000). Abutalebi and Green (2007) postulate that language control and non-linguistic (cognitive) control both activate similar neural networks (see also Wu, Yang, Chen, Zhang, Kang, Ding, & Guo, 2019). Such a common or shared neural mechanism for language control and general cognitive control has been the focus of a line of recent studies on switching in highly proficient, balanced Russian-German bilingual university students (Festman, 2012; Festman & Münte, 2012; Festman, Rodriguez-Fornells, & Münte, 2010). Interestingly, some of the tested bilinguals were better at language control (measured via a picture-naming task with an "alternating runs paradigm" i.e., a regular switching pattern of naming two consecutive pictures in Russian, followed by two pictures in German, etc.), whereas others showed instances of cross-linguistic interference. Evidence supporting the common mechanism for language control and cognitive control was strengthened by the finding that those better at language control (termed "non-switchers") performed faster and more accurately on a number of neuropsychological tests (e.g., Flanker, Tower of Hanoi, Ruff Figural Fluency Test RFFT, go/Nogo, Wisconsin Card Sorting Test WCST, etc.) than those who showed more unintended switches in the picture naming task ("switchers"). An ERP-study with the same two groups corroborated these findings, showing that the non-switchers had less response conflict than the switchers (Festman & Münte, 2012).

Bilinguals' training in inhibiting incongruent or irrelevant information as described above has been used to endorse the so-called "bilingual advantage (BA)" in executive functions. The bilingual advantage is based on the rationale that language control activates a neural network that is responsible for general cognitive control. Bilingualism understood as "language control training" is hypothesized to give rise to the enhancement of general cognitive control abilities. The debate over a possible bilingual advantage in executive function has been prolific yet also contentious, as some studies found evidence of such an advantage in bilinguals and some did not (see, e.g., the meta-analysis by Lehtonen, Soveri, Laine, Järvenpää, de Bruin, & Antfolk, 2018). The gathering of evidence has been complicated by the revelation of a publication bias, arguably even a confirmation bias (Paap, Mason, Zimiga, Silva, & Frost, 2020). One crucial outcome of the debate so far has certainly been the necessity for a clear-cut description of the samples in question, a reduction of methodological flaws (e.g., group-wise comparisons of mono- vs. bilinguals, see our discussion below), a clear understanding of the tasks and specific measures thereof used for investigation, and the inclusion of crucial background variables of the—naturally—highly heterogeneous group of bilinguals (for an example of how to take the heterogeneity of participants into account, see Czapka, Wotschak, Klassert, & Festman, 2019).

Psycholinguistics in SLA

In the realm of SLA (as opposed to psychology), psycholinguistic research on language learning has highlighted the importance of the *learning setting*, from micro-contextual variables (neighborhood effects, classroom effects, family circumstance, peer pressure, etc.) to treatment variables (e.g., type of instruction) and macro-contextual variables. The latter include more *informal* settings such as in mother–child interaction at home or language acquisition in the target culture versus more *formal* conditions of language learning at school. As for so-called *naturalistic language acquisition*, it is considered to be characterized by *implicit* learning, while formal L2 learning has often been described as involving *explicit* learning (and teaching). Although the precise meaning of "implicit" and "explicit" in this context and the nature of their differentiation cannot be said to be universally agreed upon (cf. Mitchell, Myles, & Marsden, 2019, implicit learning is generally thought of as an automatic, non-conscious, and powerful mechanism that results in knowledge that can be accessed quickly and without effort (Dörnyei, 2009; Ellis, 1994). In contrast, explicit learning is characterized as involving "conscious awareness on the part of the learner as they attempt to understand material, seek to analyze input, or try to solve production or comprehension problems, e.g. via deliberate hypothesis-testing" (Tellier & Roehr-Brackin, 2017, p. 24). Thus, the study of informal acquisition centers on statistical learning—the process of tracking and learning co-occurrences between elements in the environment—while investigations of formal learning aim to shed light on effects of training, teacher input and feedback, scaffolding strategies, etc. Finally, in SLA, the main focus of linguists is more on characterizing input on linguistic levels (e.g., complexity of sentence structure, variability of grammatical forms, variation of lexical items, etc.). Psychologists, on the other hand, are likely to be more interested in the particular structures or *levels of language* (e.g., morphology, syntax, etc.).

We believe that a focus on individual differences (IDs) provides a unique perspective on longstanding debates in psycholinguistics and SLA, in particular the degree of interaction between hypothesized components of the linguistic system and the relationship between language and other cognitive systems (Kidd, Donnelly, & Christiansen, 2018). Traditionally, psycholinguistic theory has downplayed the possibility of meaningful differences in language across individuals. However, it is becoming increasingly evident that there is significant variation among speakers at any age as well as across the lifespan, as there is evidence of clear IDs in basic processes underlying much of cognition, such as attention, phonological short-term memory, verbal working memory (WM) and visuospatial WM, and executive function (attention, inhibition, switching, and updating, etc.), as well as language itself (Kidd et al., 2018). In first language (L1) acquisition, IDs—such as auditory brainstem responses (Chonchaiya, Tardif, Mai, Xu, Li, Kaciroti, Shao, & Lozoff, 2013) and resting-state brain activity (Brito, Fifer, Myers, Elliott, & Noble, 2016)—are frequent and wide-spread, observed early and across all domains, and notably stable across development, affecting, for instance, variable vocabulary and grammatical development, online language processing, and ultimate attainment (e.g., Bornstein & Putnick, 2012). In SLA research, emergentist approaches predict a more widespread pattern of IDs than formal linguistic approaches, due to the greater emphasis placed on the input and learning mechanisms in jointly contributing to language acquisition and use. Various scholars (e.g., Goldberg, 2006) predict meaningful interactions between levels of language that are themselves subject to IDs. For instance, there seem to be differences between statistical learning ability that may affect L2 learning (e.g., Brooks & Kempe, 2013; Granena, 2013). According to Kidd et al. (2018), IDs in statistical learning have been linked to language proficiency across the lifespan, a relationship that has been attested across multiple domains of language, including vocabulary, grammatical, and literacy development in children and L2-learning adults.

Relating IDs to environmental variables in SLA, Mitchell, Myles, and Marsden (2019) remind us that, "the L2 learner is also a social being" (p. 45). ID variables often interact with external variables (e.g., socioeconomic status or instructional foreign language settings), thus creating a joint impact on the outcome variable. What is more, variation in *input quality and quantity* in itself also has an effect on language acquisition and processing, leading to variation in language proficiency across the lifespan. This view is reflected in the so-called "social turn" in L2 research (Block, 2003; Douglas Fir Group, 2016; Ortega, 2009), which redressed the balance after decades when psycholinguistic and individualist perspectives on L2 learners dominated. There has been a long-standing preoccupation in SLA with the decontextualized individual as the source of variation—see, e.g., Ellis's (2008a) telltale characterization of the learner as "an associative network, a mechanistic processor of information, relatively unembodied, unconscious, monologic, unsituated, asocial, uncultured, and untutored" (p. 12). Although recently complexity theories take a different view of the learner (see our discussion below), its focus on individual variation nevertheless can easily fall prey to "putting the blame" on the individual learner. This is reminiscent of what cognitivists do when they cite aptitude (see Chapter 30) as, ultimately, a learner defect, rather than as something that sits at the intersection of learner and language use environment, including quite particularly the educational setting for instances of instructed L2.

A focus on the role of *experience* in interaction with IDs in language acquisition and processing provides a crucial source of evidence that bears strongly upon core issues in theories of the acquisition and processing of language. In psycholinguistics, the role of contextual influences on WM performance has come into focus recently (e.g., Brose, Schmiedek, Lövdén, Molenaar, & Lindenberger, 2010). For instance, studies have shown that the exposure to daily stress is coupled with WM performance within individuals, potentially indicating an allocation of attention to events and not to task performance (Sliwinski, Smyth, Hofer, & Stawski, 2006). In SLA, the current view offered on the age factor is that "success" in additional languages is a function of the quantity and quality of language experience rather than simply a matter of maturation—irrespective of the age of the learner. In fact, the current consensus among cognitive scientists is that the brain remains plastic *throughout* life, and that the brain is modified by experience at *any* age (Green, 2018; Pfenninger & Singleton, 2019; Schlegel, Rudelson, & Tse, 2012). Such a view is particularly appealing if we want to make a distinction between chronological age and social or "contextual" age; the former is understood to be a "predictable, even ineluctable progression along an incremental scale," while the latter is "a far less predictable ebbing and flowing, reflecting the arrival and passing of particular somatic, experiential and emotional circumstances" (Coupland, Coupland, & Giles, 1991, p. 140). In this connection, Eckert (1998) recommends a shift in focus "away from chronological age and towards life experiences that give age meaning" (p. 165). With respect to starting age (as opposed to biological age), several scholars (e.g., Muñoz & Singleton, 2011; Pfenninger & Singleton, 2019) highlight the multicausality of emerging age effects, since much of the effect of starting age is nothing else but the consequence of its co-varying relationship with non-biological factors. Thus, understanding how IDs in linguistic experience influence language can help test and refine theory.

Integrating Perspectives

Developmental theorists have proposed for a long time that the prevailing focus on stable IDs has obstructed the discovery of short-term covariations between cognitive performance and contextual influences within individuals that may help to uncover mechanisms underlying long-term change (Brose et al., 2010). As early as 1962, K. Warner Schaie, an American social gerontologist and psychologist, noted in the context of adult age changes that "[e]xperience has shown that it is a formidable task to identify the ever-changing forces which act upon the individual at any given moment as well as to identify his capacity to deal with any particular stimulus" (p. 132). He thus set the stage for a psychological perspective on cognitive development that is inherently dynamic, person-oriented, and open to experiential and historical influences (Brose et al., 2010).

Time and timing in development are also considered core constructs in SLA:

> All of the most relevant questions about SLA, including the age issue, L1 influence, individual differences, implicit versus explicit learning, the role of input, intentional versus incidental learning, and of course the order of acquisition of morphosyntax, are implicitly or explicitly about change over time.
>
> Lowie & Verspoor, 2015, p. 78

However, applied linguistics has not been exactly to the fore in employing sophisticated procedures to analyze truly longitudinal data (Ortega & Iberri-Shea, 2005). On the one hand, longitudinal data are often analyzed by recourse to the same inferential statistics that are employed in cross-sectional research, i.e., general linear models, which are unable to capture the non-linear nature of L2 learning trajectories. On the other hand, most existing longitudinal studies are product-oriented rather than process-oriented and therefore risk "decontextualizing, segregating, and atemporalizing" language development according to Larsen-Freeman and Cameron (2008, p. 252), which is regrettable for several reasons. For one, our contemporary understanding of SLA views it as a complex, dynamic, ecologically situated, multivariate phenomenon—hence the impact of theories like chaos/complexity theory (Larsen-Freeman & Cameron 2008) and dynamic systems theory (de Bot, Lowie, & Verspoor, 2007; Herdina & Jessner, 2002)—henceforth referred to as Complex Dynamic Systems Theory (see Chapter 4). Arguably "the most widely used and powerful explanatory framework in science" (van Gelder, 1998, p. 622), CDST sits at the intersection of psychology and L1/L2 acquisition, as it has been introduced into the fields of L1 development (van Geert & van Dijk, 2002), L2 development (de Bot et al., 2007; Larsen-Freeman, 1997) and cognitive science and psychology (Thelen & Smith,

1994; van Gelder & Port, 1995). CDST is a (meta)theory of change as well as a relational theory (e.g. Hiver & Al-Hoorie, 2019), with the following principal characteristics (among others):

1. Language is interrelated with and embedded in our cultural, sociological, and psychological lives.
2. Learning is a (non-linear) process rather than a product (there is no stasis, only change).
3. Free, non-systematic variation is a prerequisite of development and therefore a source of information (e.g. increased variability coincides with a developmental jump in L2).
4. A complex dynamic system is made up of many and diverse interacting components. Changes in one subsystem may affect other subsystems within the same system, and relationships between subsystems may be competitive or supportive and may show interactions between different dimensions of language proficiency.

As for point (1), it is assumed that L2 development is sensitive to many individual factors—such as the learner's attention, motivation, and the like—as well as to external factors such as the type and amount of meaningful input and interaction the learner has in the language (Verspoor & Smiskova, 2012). The view that L2 development is sensitive to many individual factors is also reflected in dynamic usage-based (DUB) theory, a term suggested by Langacker (2000). The major tenet of DUB is that, all other things being equal, frequency of input and use are major factors in language acquisition, i.e., L2 learners learn and acquire first and best what they hear and use most (Ellis, 2002). In this view, "the brain, cognition, consciousness, self, experience, communication and human interaction, society, culture, and history are all inextricably intertwined in rich, complex, and dynamic ways in language" (Ellis, 2008b, p. 232). All experience with language has an immediate impact on cognitive representations, that is, on grammar, i.e., language users' experiences with language influence mental representations on an ongoing basis, just as in other areas of cognition. Thus, language is acquired—and changes!—as it is used, in small increments repeated over and over in usage-events.

In sum, according to the social view, "everything counts" (Thelen, 2005, p. 261) when it comes to how effects are caused: "Every act in every moment is the emergent product of context and history, and no component has causal priority" (Thelen, 2005, p. 271). This view has come under criticism, considering that "[…] it is impossible to capture all relevant variables in one longitudinal study" (Lowie & Verspoor, 2015, p. 82). Thus, the question arises as to what variables should/should not be controlled for, considering that there is always also the danger of overrating the importance of controlling for possible confounders. The default practice in psycholinguistics has been to control for everything that can be measured: SES, age, gender, neighborhood, aptitude, IQ, etc.—a practice that Pearl and McKenzie (2018, p. 139) call "both wasteful and ridden with errors." The authors argue that knowing the set of assumptions that stand behind a given conclusion (measuring and adjusting for confounders, etc.) is not less valuable than attempting to circumvent those assumptions with a randomized controlled trial, which has complications of its own (see, e.g., Pfenninger & Singleton, 2017).

Point (2) above challenges the traditional assumption in SLA that the nature of the relationships among factors involved in L2 development is linear. On the one hand, this means that studying performance at one point in time may provide an inaccurate or at least an incomplete picture of language development; on the other hand, recent trends tend to see IDs as dynamic entities that change over time and may affect development differentially at different times (see e.g. Dörnyei, MacIntyre, & Henry, 2015). Of course, not all factors are equally variable, and the variability may depend on the time scale. Language learning aptitude and WM, for instance (see Chapter 30), may be considered to be relatively stable at shorter time scales but do tend to change across the life span (Waters & Caplan, 2003). Motivated behavior, on the other hand, differs across both shorter and longer timescales, from seconds (MacIntyre & Serroul, 2015) to the lifespan (Kormos & Csizér, 2008). MacIntyre and Legatto (2011), for instance, found substantial diversity in the patterns of change in willingness to communicate (see Chapter 20) both within the person over time (i.e., on a second-to-second basis) and across the different interview questions.

Related to this, point (3) highlights the *meaningfulness* of intra-learner variation. The prevailing approach to SLA up to the beginning of this century has been to focus on product-based explanations of SLA (Lowie & Verspoor, 2015), which are reflected, among other things, in the assumption that the variation in interlanguage is either rather systematic or completely random and relegated to "(white) noise." In particular, it was non-systematic, free intra-individual variation that had often been too readily dismissed as noise or measurement error or attributed it to "outliers" (see Bülow & Pfenninger, in press). According to Ellis (1985), intra-individual variation—or "interlanguage variability," as he calls it—can be categorized into systematic (situational, contextual, or psycholinguistic) variation vs. non-systematic (performance or free) variation. Non-systematic, free variation—sometimes referred to as "random variability" despite its rather non-random characteristics (see Singleton, 2021)—relates to the existence of two or more forms in the learner's mind, which he uses to realize the same range of meanings. It is this type of intra-individual variation that has recently been suggested to be the key to understanding the vertical dimension of interlanguage, i.e., language developments (e.g., van Dijk, Verspoor, & Lowie, 2011). The main premise is that a large amount of variability signals that the learner is apparently trying things out and that the subsystem under consideration is unstable (Lowie & Verspoor, 2015; van Dijk et al., 2011). Therefore, the claim is that stability and variability are indispensable aspects of human development (van Geert & Verspoor, 2015).

According to point (4), it is highly unlikely that events are completely independent, and we cannot know what the relationships will be at one level of analysis from the relationships that exist at another. As a dynamic system is never isolated from other systems, other systems that might interact with the focal system need to be identified, "with a particular need to be alert to the ways in which the focal system might adapt as a response to the interaction" (MacIntyre & Serroul, 2015, p. 424).

That said, despite close resonances between CDST and scholars' thematic areas of expertise, microdevelopment studies, which require dense data collection intervals to focus on studying change as it occurs in the data that cover the entire period during which development is studied, are still relatively rare in SLA (Lowie, 2017). In part, this might have to do with the fact the methods for "doing" CDST and researching such issues using insights from CDST have remained relatively elusive (but see Hiver & Al-Hoorie, 2019). This process-oriented, person-centered view is new to psychology, too: Most research methodology in the behavioral sciences, in particular the more-familiar experimental approaches of the cognitive sciences, have employed inter-individual analyses, which provide information about the state of affairs of the population (Kidd et al., 2018; Molenaar & Campbell, 2009). More often than not, however, inter-individual analyses that are now standardly applied in analyses of psychological processes such as personality and emotional processes have to be replaced by analyses of intra-individual variation in order to obtain valid results (Molenaar & Campbell, 2009). As Mitchell, Myles, and Marsden (2019) rightly point out, increased collaboration with researchers from linguistic perspectives is needed in order to challenge cognitive researchers to explain L2 learning phenomena that cannot be explained purely by learner-internal variables, L1 influence, or input characteristics. In turn, continued collaboration with psychologists will help explore the way and the extent to which innate cognitive mechanisms drive both L1 and L2 acquisition.

Implications for Practice and Research

Point (3) above touches on the traditional assumption in SLA that findings can be generalized from the group to the individual and vice versa: What can the group say about the individual? What can single case studies say about the group? Several researchers have addressed this question from various theoretical angles. Dewaele (2009) warned of the "dangerous assumption" in quantitative designs that "every individual in the group goes through a similar experience and displays similar behavior"

(p. 639). In Birdsong and Vanhove's (2016) work on the critical period hypothesis (CPH), they suggest that when looking at sufficiently large groups of learners from a sufficiently large distance, there may be a clear cut-off point, for example at age 12, after which it may be problematic to start learning a L2. However, at the individual level, that cut-off point like any other cut-off point is not predetermined or fixed. Within the CDST framework, in particular, scholars have discussed the issue of aggregation:

> A group trend, however significant it may be, cannot accommodate the dynamic multicausality of the emerging language system of an individual, and interpreting a developmental phenomenon on mean trends and variance of group scores at one point in time underestimates the complexity of the developmental process.
>
> *Lowie & Verspoor, 2015, p. 78*

Such findings have significant relevance for classroom research. Besides contributing to theory building—a good theory should be able to describe and explain individual developmental patterns (Larsen-Freeman, 2017)—they can inform L2 curriculum and assessment decisions about what should be learned and tested and how this knowledge should be evaluated. One important message for practitioners, for instance, is that errors are not to be viewed necessarily as a product of imperfect learning, and that we should come to accept the uncertainty surrounding change and development. A complexity theory perspective insists on acknowledging the richly differentiated and often seemingly contradictory ecology of real classrooms and proceed to building ways of understanding them in the hope of being able to enhance teaching and learning success for both teachers and learners in just such classrooms. Furthermore, there is much to be learned from a single case study in terms of learners' language development and how it is contingent on interactional environments (see, e.g., Eskildsen, 2012).

Regarding the implications for research, we think that although generalizing across learners is not necessarily the aim of CDST-related studies (Lowie & Verspoor, 2019), a relatively large number of participants might be useful (and perhaps even necessary) for yielding both more reliable and generalizable results, by comparing developmental patterns as well as the results of individual dynamic analyses across learners (see also Bulté & Housen, 2020). At the same time, looking for developmental patterns across learners does not necessarily involve averaging scores across learners (see Pfenninger, in press). In order to be able to generalize, we also need more replications of multiple individual case studies, "as each case study can be seen as a replication study to falsify or corroborate the causal relations discerned in other studies" (Lowie, 2017, p. 137).

Future Directions

A number of methodological and theoretical issues and questions are pending. For one, the monolingual bias in psycholinguistic models of language acquisition places a premium on designing a model that is truly able to capture bilingualism or multilingualism in all its complexity (from environment to speaker in interaction and the brain)—see, e.g., van Heuven and Wen's (2019) call for "a universal computational model of bilingual word recognition and word translation" (p. 695).

Furthermore, our discussion of psycholinguistic perspectives of SLA has shown that IDs result from a complex interplay of endogenous cognitive systems and the environment. Understanding the contribution of these variables allows a better understanding of the mechanisms underlying human language. What is more, since the literature on environmental effects on adult language processing and attainment highlights the typically Western Educated Industrialized Rich Democratic (WEIRD) nature of samples in adult psycholinguistic research, the likely range of IDs is larger than what might be estimated from our current evidential base (Kidd et al., 2018).

From a methodological perspective, one lesson to be learned concerns the grouping of participants into aggregate, social, non-individual entities according to various IDs, such as proficiency level (e.g., low-, advanced-, and high-proficiency L2 learners), age (e.g., 5–8-year-olds, 9–12-year-olds, 12–15-year-olds), nativelikeness (native vs. non-native) and multilingualism (monolinguals vs. bilinguals vs. multilinguals). Grouping participants comes with several issues. As with many other participant features, proficiency level or nativelikeness is not inherently categorical. That is, individuals are not simply "native" or "non-native" speakers, or low- or high-proficiency learners, but they are proficient in English to varying degrees (Birdsong, 2018). Accordingly, in order to faithfully capture the construct, proficiency level is properly operationalized and analyzed as a *continuous* (rather than categorical) subject factor. As with any other continuous variable, participant assignment to proficiency categories (low-, advanced-, and high-proficiency learners) may mask intra-group variability and result in loss of statistical power (see, e.g., Altman, 1998). Furthermore, studying the aggregate of a group to which the individual belongs raises the important question of whether the observed effect is realized in each one of the individuals to whom the treatment condition or personal attribute producing that effect applies (Furnham, 2016; Lowie, 2017), which leads us to our next point.

As far as the individual level is concerned, despite recent findings that intra-individual variation is an important source of information in addition to the mean performance in both aging and child L2 development, the empirical evidence is still far from sufficient to demonstrate the usefulness of adding a measure of variability to that of the mean level, as well as its specificity. For instance, the question of whether large intra-individual variation is dysfunctional or adaptive (pointing to resilience) is still being presently discussed in the aging domain in psycholinguistics (see, e.g., Fagot, Mella, Borella, Ghisletta, Lecerf, & de Ribaupierre, 2018).

Moreover, the meaning of large intra-individual variation is not very clear from a theoretical point of view. Bülow and Pfenninger (in press) were the first to make a systematic distinction between "intra-learner variation" and "intra-speaker variation." The former can be considered to occur when two or more *target-like* and *non-target-like* forms are in (free) variation, which has a long tradition in SLA (see, e.g., Cancino, Rosansky, & Schumann, 1978), while the latter refers to a subject making use of a variety of *target-like* forms to express an identical range of functions and meanings. This raises several important questions. First, how can we distinguish between "target language" and "non-target language"? Even if one claimed that the target was a standard form of language, it would be inadequate, i.e., a language is not a single homogeneous construct to be acquired (Larsen-Freeman, 2015). Second, how can we conceptualize and measure the threshold between non-systematic and systematic intra-individual variation in L2 learners? Third, few psycholinguistic studies have analyzed intra-individual variation across the entire lifespan, from childhood to advanced old age, using the same tasks in the different age groups or comparing tasks of varying complexity, to determine whether intra-individual variation would be larger in more complex tasks and assessing for possible interactions of age and complexity. In the future, attempts need to be made to offer a general theory for lifespan development of intra-individual variation in L2 learners, e.g., by paralleling Labov's (1964, pp. 91–93) developmental model for the acquisition of standard spoken English that comprises six stages. Similarly, in SLA, Ortega and Byrnes (2008) lament that,

> after some 40 years of disciplinary history, we know little about the longitudinal pace and pattern of development in second language and literacy, much less when development is understood to span the lifetime of multilingual and multicultural people who set out to function in several languages, including an L2.
>
> *p. 3*

We thus argue that a focus on intra-individual variation in language ability has the potential to shed new light on longstanding theoretical debates in psycholinguistics and bring us closer to a detailed mechanistic understanding of human language.

Reflection Questions

- How can we define, delimit, and empirically capture what is meant by "context" in psycholinguistics and SLA (Ushioda 2015)?
- How can we conceptualize and measure the threshold between non-systematic and systematic intra-individual variation in L2 learners?
- Which components would a psycholinguistic model of individual bi- and multilingualism need to include to truly reflect its complexity from acquisition to use and attrition (i.e., its dynamic nature) on the level of language, environment, cognition, and brain?

Recommended Reading

Birdsong, D. (2018). Plasticity, variability and age in second language acquisition and bilingualism. *Frontiers in Psychology*, 9.

Birdsong's (2018) state-of-the-art review of critical period effects vs. bilingualism effects does a remarkable job discussing the "nature-of-bilingualism" account, which posits that no bilingual speakers, regardless of the age at which they acquired their second language, will, across all measurable domains, be identical to monolingual speakers. Birdsong also provides clear and convincing arguments for the behavior of individual differences as a function of age: With increasing age of onset, the learners' L2 results become more dispersed, goals for L2 learning become more diverse, and there is an increase in inter-individual effects of progressive cognitive decline, progressive L1 entrenchment, and education on L2 attainment.

Grosjean, F. (1998). Studying bilinguals: Methodological and conceptual issues. *Bilingualism: Language and Cognition*, 1(2), 131–149.

Grosjean's compilation of critical remarks on study designs and variables in the context of empirical research on bilingualism is a must. He calls for a more careful treatment and consideration of methodological and conceptual issues due to the high diversity among bilingual participants and the complexity of bilingualism. One focus is on detailed descriptions of participants' profiles (including social-interactional aspects such as language mode), the other on specificities of tasks and stimuli used. Both foci are directly related to issues of representation and processing of two or more languages.

Lowie, W., & Verspoor, M. (2019). Individual differences and the ergodicity problem. *Language Learning*, 69(S1), 184–206.

Lowie and Verspoor examine the ergodicity assumption, that is, the often-made, highly debated, and rarely tested assumption of an equivalence of within- and between-person structures of psychological variables. The authors explain in great detail why ergodicity—a major condition for the generalization of average group scores from studies on inter-individual variation to the analysis of intra-individual variability (and vice versa)—cannot be assumed if your data is neither homogeneous in time nor homogeneous across different subjects.

References

Abutalebi, J., & Green, D. (2007). Bilingual language production: The neurocognition of language representation and control. *Journal of Neurolinguistics*, 20(3), 242–275.

Altman, D. G. (1998). Categorizing continuous variables. In P. Armitage & T. Colton (Eds.), *Encyclopedia of biostatistics* (pp. 563–567). Wiley.

Birdsong, D. (2018). Plasticity, variability and age in second language acquisition and bilingualism. *Frontiers in Psychology*, 9.

Birdsong, D., & Vanhove, J. (2016). Age of second-language acquisition: critical periods and social concerns. In Nicoladis & S. Montanari (Eds.), *Bilingualism across the lifespan: Factors moderating language proficiency* (pp. 162–181). American Psychological Association.

Block, D. (2003). *The social turn in second language acquisition*. Georgetown University Press.

Bornstein, M., & Putnick, D. L. (2012). Stability of language in childhood: a multiage, multidomain, multimeasure, and multisource study. *Dev. Psychol., 48*, 477–491.

Brito, N. H., Fifer, W. P., Myers, M. M., Elliott, A. J., & Noble, K. G. (2016). Associations among family socioeconomic status, EEG power at birth, and cognitive skills during infancy. *Dev. Cogn. Neurosci., 19*, 144–151.

Brooks, P. J., & Kempe, V. (2013). Individual differences in adult foreign language learning: The mediating effect of meta-linguistic awareness. *Memory & Cognition, 41*, 281–296.

Brose, A., Schmiedek, F., Lövdén, M., Molenaar, P. C. M., & Lindenberger, U. (2010). Adult age differences in covariation of motivation and working memory performance: Contrasting between-person and within-person findings. *Research in Human Development, 7*(1), 61–78.

Bülow, L., & Pfenninger, S. E. (in press.) Intra-speaker variation across time and space—Sociolinguistics meets psycholinguistics. *Linguistics Vanguard*.

Bulté, B., & Housen, A. (2020). A DUB-inspired case study of multidimensional L2 complexity development: Competing or connected growers? In W. Lowie, M. Michel, A. Rousse-Malpat, M. Keijzer, & R. Steinkrauss (Eds.), *Usage-based dynamics in second language development: In celebration of Marjolijn Verspoor*. Multilingual Matters.

Cancino, H., Rosansky, E., & Schumann, J. H. (1978). The acquisition of English negatives and interrogatives by native Spanish speakers. In E. M. Hatch (Ed.), *Second language acquisition. A book of readings* (pp. 207–230). Newbury House.

Chonchaiya, W., Tardif, T., Mai, X., Xu, L., Li, M., Kaciroti, N., Kileny, P. R., Shao, J., & Lozoff, B. (2013). Developmental trends in auditory processing can provide early predictions of language acquisition in young infants. *Developmental Science, 16*, 159–172.

Coupland, N., Coupland, J., & Giles, H. (1991). *Language, society and the elderly: Discourse, identity and ageing*. Blackwell.

Czapka, S., Wotschack, C., Klassert, A., & Festman, J. (2019). A path to the bilingual advantage: Pairwise matching of individuals. *Bilingualism: Language and Cognition, 23*(2), 344–354.

de Bot, K. (1992). A bilingual production model: Levelt's "speaking" model adapted. *Applied Linguistics, 13*, 1–24.

de Bot, K. (2003). A bilingual production model: Levelt's "speaking" model adapted. In *The bilingualism reader* (pp. 399–420). Routledge.

de Bot, K., Lowie, W., & Verspoor, M. (2007). A dynamic systems theory approach to second language acquisition. *Bilingualism, 10*(1), 7–21.

Dewaele, J.-M. (2009). Individual differences in Second Language Acquisition. In W. C. Ritchie & T. K. Bhatia (Eds.), *The new handbook of second language acquisition* (pp. 623–646). Emerald.

Dörnyei, Z. (2009). *The psychology of second language acquisition*. Oxford University Press.

Dörnyei, Z., MacIntyre, P. D., & Henry, A. (Eds.). (2015). *Motivational dynamics in language learning*. Multilingual Matters.

Douglas Fir Group. (2016). A transdisciplinary framework for SLA in a multilingual world. *Modern Language Journal, 100*(Supplement 2016), 19–47.

Eckert, P. (1998). Age as a sociolinguistic variable. In F. Coulmas (Ed.), *The handbook of sociolinguistics* (pp. 151–167). Blackwell Publishers.

Ellis, N. C. (Ed.). (1994). *Implicit and explicit learning of languages*. Academic Press.

Ellis, N. C. (2002). Frequency effects in language acquisition: A review with implications for theories of implicit and explicit language acquisition. *Studies in Second Language Acquisition, 24*, 143–188.

Ellis, N. C. (2008a). The psycholinguistics of the interaction hypothesis. In A. Mackey & C. Polio (Eds.), *Multiple perspectives on interaction in SLA: Second language research in honor of Susan M. Gass* (pp. 11–40). Routledge.

Ellis, N. C. (2008b). The dynamics of second language emergence: Cycles of language use, language change, and language acquisition. *Modern Language Journal, 41*(3), 232–249.

Ellis, R. (1985). Sources of variability in interlanguage. *Applied Linguistics, 6*(2), 118–131.

Eskildsen, S. W. (2012). Negation constructions at work. *Language Learning, 62*(2), 335–372.

Fagot, D., Mella, N., Borella, E., Ghisletta, P., Lecerf, T., & de Ribaupierre, A. (2018). Intra-individual variability from a lifespan perspective: A comparison of latency and accuracy measures. *Journal of Intelligence, 6*(1).

Festman, J. (2012). Language control abilities of late bilinguals. *Bilingualism: Language and Cognition, 15*(3), 580–593.

Festman, J., & Münte, T. F. (2012). Cognitive control in Russian-German bilinguals. *Frontiers in Psychology, 3*, 1–7.

Festman, J., Rodriguez-Fornells, A., & Münte, T. (2010). Individual differences in control of language interference in late bilinguals are mainly related to general executive abilities. *Behavioral and Brain Functions, 6*(5).

Furnham, A. (2016). Rerum cognoscere causas: Dependent and independent variables in psychology. In R. Harré & F. M. Moghaddam (Eds.), *Questioning causality. Scientific explorations of cause and consequence across social contexts* (pp. 67–80). Praeger.

Goldberg, A. (2006). *Constructions at work: The nature of generalization in language*. Oxford University Press.

Granena, G. (2013). Individual differences in sequence learning ability and second language acquisition in early childhood and adulthood. *Language Learning, 63*(4), 665–703.

Green, D. W. (1986). Control, activation, and resource: A framework and a model for the control of speech in bilinguals. *Brain and Language, 27*(2), 210–223.

Green, D. W. (1998). Mental control of the bilingual lexico-semantic system. *Bilingualism: Language and Cognition, 1*(2), 67–81.

Green, D. (2018). The interactional challenge: L2 learning and use in the third age. In D. Gabrys-Barker (Ed.), *Third age learners of foreign languages* (pp. 31–47). Multilingual Matters.

Green, D. W., & Abutalebi, J. (2013). Language control in bilinguals: The adaptive control hypothesis. *Journal of Cognitive Psychology, 25*(5), 515–530.

Herdina, P., & Jessner, U. (2002). *A dynamic model of multilingualism: Perspectives of change in psycholinguistics*. Multilingual Matters.

Hiver, P., & Al-Hoorie, A. (2019). *Research methods for complexity theory*. Multilingual Matters.

Hoshino, N., & Thierry, G. (2011). Language selection in bilingual word production: electrophysiological evidence for cross-language competition. *Brain Research, 1371*, 100–109.

Kidd, E., Donnelly, S., & Christiansen, M. H. (2018). Individual differences in language acquisition and processing. *Trends in Cognitive Sciences, 22*, 154–169.

Kormos, J., & Csizér, K. (2008). Age-related differences in the motivation of learning English as a foreign language: Attitudes, selves and motivated learning behavior. *Language Learning, 58*(2), 327–355.

Kroll, J. F., Bobb, S. C., Misra, M., & Guo, T. (2008). Language selection in bilingual speech: Evidence for inhibitory processes. *Acta psychologica, 128*(3), 416–430.

Labov, W. (1964). Stages in the acquisition of Standard English. In R. Shuy, A. Davis, & R. Hogan (Eds.), *Social dialects and language learning* (pp. 77–104). National Council of Teachers of English.

Langacker, R. W. (2000). A dynamic usage-based model. In M. Barlow and S. Kemmer (Eds.), *Usage-based models of language* (pp. 1–63). CSLI Publications.

Larsen-Freeman, D. (1997). Chaos/complexity science and second language acquisition. *Applied Linguistics, 18*(2), 141–165.

Larsen-Freeman, D. (2015) Complexity theory. In B. VanPatten & J. Williams (Eds.), *Theories in second language acquisition*. 2nd edition. Routledge.

Larsen-Freeman, D. (2016) Compleixity theory: The lessons continue. In L. Ortega & Z.-H. Han (Eds.), *Complexity theory and language development: In celebration of Diane Larsen-Freeman* (pp. 11–50). John Benjamins.

Larsen-Freeman, D., & Cameron, L. (2008). *Complex systems and applied linguistics*. Oxford University Press.

Lehtonen, M., Soveri, A., Laine, A., Järvenpää, J., de Bruin, A., & Antfolk, J. (2018). Is bilingualism associated with enhanced executive functioning in adults? A meta-analytic review. *Psychological Bulletin, 144*(4), 394–425.

Levelt, W. J. M. (1989). *Speaking: From Intention to Articulation*. MIT Press.

Levelt, W. J., Roelofs, A., & Meyer, A. S. (1999). A theory of lexical access in speech production. *Behavioral and Brain Sciences, 22*(1), 1–38.

Lowie, W. (2017). Lost in state space? Methodological considerations in Complex Dynamic Theory approaches to second language development research. In L. Ortega & Z.-H. Han (Eds.), *Complexity theory and language development* (pp. 123–142). John Benjamins.

Lowie, W., & Verspoor, M. (2015). Variability and variation in second language acquisition orders: A dynamic reevaluation. *Language Learning, 65*, 63–88.

Lowie, W., & Verspoor, M. (2019). Individual differences and the ergodicity problem. *Language Learning, 69*(S1), 184–206.

MacIntyre, P. D., & Legatto, J. J. (2011). A dynamic system approach to willingness to communicate: Developing an idiodynamic method to capture rapidly changing affect. *Applied Linguistics, 32*(2), 149–171.

MacIntyre, P. D., & Serroul, S. (2015). Motivation on a per-second timescale: Examining approach-avoidance motivation during L2 task performance. In Z. Dörnyei, P. D. MacIntyre, & A. Henry (Eds.), *Motivational dynamics in language learning* (pp. 109–138). Multilingual Matters.

McDonough, K., & Trofimovich, P. (2016). The role of statistical learning and working memory in L2 speakers' pattern learning. *The Modern Language Journal*, 100(2), 428–445.

Mitchell, R., Myles, F., & Marsden, E. (2019). *Second language learning theories*. Fourth Edition. Routledge.

Miyake, A., Friedman, N. P., Emerson, M. J., Witzki, A. H., Howerter, A., & Wager, T. D. (2000). The unity and diversity of executive functions and their contributions to complex "frontal lobe" tasks: A latent variable analysis. *Cognitive Psychology, 41*(1), 49–100.

Molenaar, P. C. M., & Campbell, C. G. (2009). The new person-specific paradigm in psychology. *Current Directions in Psychological Science, 18*(2), 112–117.

Muñoz, C., & Singleton, D. (2011). A critical review of age-related research on L2 ultimate attainment. *Language Teaching 44*(1), 1–35.

Ortega, L. (2009). *Understanding second language acquisition*. Routledge.

Ortega, L., & Byrnes, H. (Eds.). (2008). *The longitudinal study of advanced L2 capacities*. Routledge.

Ortega, L., & Iberri-Shea, G. (2005). Longitudinal research in SLA: Recent trends and future directions. *Annual Review of Applied Linguistics, 25*, 26–45.

Paap, K., Mason, L., Zimiga, B., Silva, Y., & Frost, M. (2020). The alchemy of confirmation bias transmutes expectations into bilingual advantages: A tale of two new meta-analyses. *Quarterly Journal of Experimental Psychology, 73*(8), 1278–1289.

Pearl, P., & Mackenzie, D. (2018). *The book of why: The new science of cause and effect*. Basic Books.

Pfenninger, S. E., & Singleton, D. (2017). *Beyond age effects in instructional L2 learning: Revisiting the age factor*. Multilingual Matters.

Pfenninger, S. E., & Singleton, D. (2019). A critical review of research relating to the learning of additional languages in the third age. *Language Teaching, 52*(4), 419–449.

Pickering, M. J., & Garrod, S. (2013). An integrated theory of language production and comprehension. *Behavioral and Brain Sciences, 36*(4), 329–347.

Praamstra, P., & Seiss, E. (2005). The neurophysiology of response competition: Motor cortex activation and inhibition following subliminal response priming. *Journal of Cognitive Neuroscience, 17*(3), 483–493.

Saboury, A. A. (2009). Enzyme inhibition and activation: A general theory. *Journal of the Iranian Chemical Society, 6*(2), 219–229.

Schaie, K. W. (1962). A field-theory approach to age changes in cognitive behavior. *Vita Humana, 5*, 129–141.

Schlegel, A. A., Rudelson, J. J., & Tse, P. U. (2012). White matter structure changes as adults learn a second language. *Journal of Cognitive Neuroscience, 24*(8), 1664–1670.

Singleton, D. (2021). The random and the non-random in intra-individual L2 variation. *Linguistics Vanguard*, 7(s2).

Sliwinski, M. J., Smyth, J. M., Hofer, S. M., & Stawski, R. S. (2006). Intraindividual coupling of daily stress and cognition. *Psychology and Aging, 21*, 545–557.

Stroop, J. R. (1935). Studies of interference in serial verbal reactions. *Journal of Experimental Psychology, 18*(6), 643.

Tellier, A., & Roehr-Brackin, K. (2017). Raising children's metalinguistic awareness to enhance classroom second language learning. In M. P. García Mayo (Ed.), *Learning foreign languages in primary school: Research insights* (pp. 22–48). Multilingual Matters.

Thelen, E. (2005). Dynamic systems theory and the complexity change. *Psychoanalytic Dialogues, 15*(2), 255–283.

Thelen, E., & L. B. Smith. (1994). *A dynamic systems approach to the development of cognition and action*. MIT Press/Bradford Books series in cognitive psychology. MIT Press.

Ushioda, E. (2015). Context and complex dynamic systems theory. In Z. Dörnyei, P. D. MacIntyre, & A. Henry (Eds.), *Motivational dynamics in language learning* (pp. 47–54). Multilingual Matters.

van Dijk, M., Verspoor, M., & Lowie, W. (2011). Variability analyses in language development. In M. Verspoor, W. Lowie, & K. de Bot (Eds.), *A dynamic approach to second language development: Methods and techniques* (pp. 55–84). John Benjamins.

van Geert, P., & van Dijk, M. (2002). Focus on variability: New tools to study intraindividual variability in developmental data. *Infant Behavior and Development, 25*, 340–374.

Van Geert, P., & Verspoor, M. (2015). Dynamic systems and language development. In B. MacWhinney, & W. O'Grady (Eds.), *The handbook of language emergence* (pp. 537–556). Wiley-Blackwell.

van Gelder, T. (1998). The dynamical hypothesis in cognitive science. *Behavioral and Brain Sciences, 21*, 615–628.

van Gelder, T. J., & Port, R. (1995) It's about time: An overview of the dynamical approach to cognition. In R. Port & T. van Gelder (Eds.), *Mind as motion: Explorations in the dynamics of cognition* (pp. 1–43). MIT Press.

Van Heuven, W. J., & Wen, Y. (2019). The need for a universal computational model of bilingual word recognition and word translation. *Bilingualism: Language and Cognition, 22*(4), 695–696.

VanPatten, B. (1996). *Input processing and grammar instruction: Theory and research*. Ablex.

Verspoor, M. H., & Smiskova, H. (2012). L2 writing Development: Multiple perspectives. In R. Manchón (Ed.), *L2 writing development: Multiple perspectives* (pp. 17–46). De Gruyter Mouton.

Waters, G. S., & Caplan, D. (2003). The reliability and stability of verbal working memory measures. *Behavior Research Methods, Instruments, & Computers, 35*, 550–564.

Wu, J., Yang, J., Chen, M., Li, S., Zhang, Z., Kang, C., Ding, G., & Guo, T. (2019). Brain network reconfiguration for language and domain-general cognitive control in bilinguals. *NeuroImage, 199*, 454–465.

PART 2

Constructs
Teacher and Learner Psychologies

7
IDENTITY

Ron Darvin and Bonny Norton

In the field of psychology and language learning and teaching, scholars interested in identity have drawn on a wide range of epistemologies and research traditions. Early work by scholars such as McNamara (1997) drew on the inter-group studies of psychologists (Giles, 1977; Tajfel, 1982; Tajfel & Turner, 1986), while more current perspectives focus on notions of the self (Kostoulas & Mercer, 2016; Mercer & Williams, 2014). Constructs such as self-efficacy (see Chapter 8), self-regulation (see Chapter 17), personality (see Chapter 9), attributions, and mindsets (see Chapter 13), to name a few, recognize the significance of individual differences and the diverse experiences, thoughts, motives, and behaviors of both language learners and teachers.

While constructs of the self focus particularly on cognitive and affective dimensions of language learning and teaching, the contemporary construct of identity highlights the self *in relation to* particular social contexts, and often unequal relations of power (Block, 2007; Darvin & Norton, 2015; Norton, 2013). By highlighting the significance of social contexts (see Chapter 23), contemporary identity research focuses on the relationship between the individual and the social world, particularly with reference to sociocultural, poststructural, and critical theory (Douglas Fir Group, 2016). Such research recognizes that when language learners speak, they are not only exchanging information with others, but are reconfiguring their relationship to the social world (Norton & De Costa, 2018). While learners and teachers can speak from multiple positions, as they perform different identities, they can also be positioned in undesirable ways, which may limit opportunities to speak and be heard. Identity categories such as race, gender, class, ethnicity, and sexual orientation can shape interaction in different language learning and teaching contexts, and relations of power influence access to communities and social networks. To assert their rightful place both within and beyond the classroom, language learners and teachers often need to claim more powerful identities from which to speak, read, write, and teach the target language.

Identity and Psychology

The poststructuralist work of Weedon (1987) has been highly influential in the work of social psychologists such as Davies and Harré (1990, p. 62), who explicitly use the term "position" as "the central organising concept for analysing how it is that people do being a person." They and other poststructuralist theorists have reminded us that identities are contingent, shifting, and context-dependent, and that while identities or positions are often given by social structures or ascribed by others, subject positions can also be negotiated by agents who wish to position themselves. As Davies and Harré note, "discursive practices constitute the speakers and hearers in certain ways and yet at the same time are a resource through which speakers and hearers can negotiate new positions" (1990, p. 62). In seeking to develop what they call "a social psychology of selfhood," Davies and Harré promote a transdisciplinary relationship between psycholinguistics and sociolinguistics:

> The recognition of the force of "discursive practices," the ways in which people are "positioned" through those practices and the way in which the individual's "subjectivity" is generated through the learning and use of certain discursive practices are commensurate with the "new psycho-socio-linguistics."
>
> *Davies & Harré, 1990, p. 43*

Recognizing the significance of individual differences, the field of social psychology has developed constructs that focus on understanding the thoughts and motives of the self, as learners negotiate both formal and informal, instruction-based and acquisition-based settings. In her monograph *Towards an understanding of language learner self-concept*, Mercer (2011) asserts:

> Each individual learner holds their own unique complex set of self-beliefs, which influence not only the way learners choose to act and the kinds of decisions they make within the present setting, but also how they interpret their past experiences and what kinds of goals and challenges they set themselves for the future. These beliefs provide learners with a sense of continuity and help them to make sense of their position in the world and their relationship to it.
>
> *pp. 1–2*

Identity and SLA

Changing conceptions of the individual, language, and learning have shifted perspectives on the psychology of the language learner. In early work on language and social psychology, Gardner (1985, p. 143) notes that Lambert's (1974) social psychological model of second language acquisition (SLA) "is a theory of bilingual development and self-identity modification." In the socio-educational model of SLA, Gardner and colleagues make the case that there is both an educational and a cultural component to learning a language. If a language were simply a "code," learning a language would be akin to learning any other school subject. However, if language is implicated in identity development, there would be individual differences if linguistic features of another community become part of the self. In a later publication, Gardner (2010) noted as follows,

> As stated many times before, an underlying assumption of the socio-educational model is that an individual's language is an important component of the individual. It serves to organize the individual's thoughts, perceptions of the world, etc. and consequently can be said to define one's self-identity.
>
> *p. 207*

When Norton's 1995 article, "Social identity, investment, and language learning" (Norton Peirce, 1995) was published, language learning research was just beginning to emerge from its predominantly cognitive orientation to examine how social factors facilitated or inhibited language learning (Firth & Wagner, 1997). These changes were raising new questions of identity, and Norton saw the need to develop social theories complementary to cognitive theories, which would capture a theory of language as "discourse" and language learning as a social, cognitive, and affective process. Her study of five immigrant women in Canada captured how large-scale migrations were transforming post-industrialist societies into more multicultural spaces (Norton, 2000). As migrants occupied a variety of spaces in their country of settlement, being able to acquire the country's official language was key to social integration and meaningful employment. Native speakers of the host community, however, often served as gatekeepers to participation in different contexts by controlling access to language resources and determining rules of use. For immigrants to claim their rightful place in a new country and to imagine better futures, immigrants had to negotiate relations of power at work, school, and other community settings, and assert more powerful identities (see Chapter 25).

Drawing on the poststructuralist work of Weedon (1987) and the social theory of Bourdieu (1977), Norton noted that language constructs both social organization and a sense of self. The individual is conceived of as a "subject," in that the individual can be subject *to* a set of relationships in one social site, or subject *of* a set of relationships in another social site. In the former, the individual would be in a relatively powerless subject position; in the latter, the individual would have greater power relative to other individuals. The central point is that the individual's "subjectivity," or what could be considered their "identity," is always constituted in relational terms; the individual never stands apart from the social world but is always an integral and constitutive part of it. To capture the plurality and fluidity that characterized this poststructuralist perspective, Norton (2000, p. 5) defined identity as "how a person understands his or her relationship to the world, how that relationship is structured across time and space, and how the person understands possibilities for the future." As Mercer (2011) notes, learners' hope and expectations of the future are important in their complex set of self-beliefs. Norton's conception of identity, with its central focus on "how a person understands possibilities for the future" includes an interest in learners' *imagined communities* and *imagined identities*, which has found resonance with psycholinguistic scholars such as Dörnyei (2005):

> It is important to introduce the intriguing concept of the "imagined community" proposed by Bonny Norton (2001). Based on Wenger's (1998) notion of "imagination" as a mode of belonging to a community, Norton conceptualizes the concept of "communities of imagination" as being constructed by a combination of personal experiences and factual knowledge (derived from the past) with imagined elements related to the future... Norton explicitly states that a learner's imagined community invites an "imagined identity."
>
> *p. 98*

While some previous language learner research defined learners in binary terms (such as motivated or unmotivated, introverted or extroverted, inhibited or uninhibited), more contemporary identity theorists see these affective descriptors as constructed in frequently inequitable relations of power between language learners and target language speakers, as variable over time and space, and sometimes co-existing in contradictory ways within a single individual. Following Norton's research, leading SLA researchers such as Toohey (2000), Pavlenko and Blackledge (2004), Block (2007), and Kramsch (2009) provided compelling evidence that language learners are not unidimensional, but have identities that are multiple, changing, and often sites of struggle.

In order to capture the historical and material relationship of learners to the target language, Norton (1995, 2000, 2013) also developed the construct of *investment*, which indexes the commitment to learn a language while navigating conditions of power in the process of aspiring for a wider range of symbolic and material resources. As a theoretical tool, investment helps examine the conditions under which social interaction takes place and the extent to which social relations of power enable or constrain opportunities for language learners to speak. Norton (2013) argued that while learners can be highly motivated to learn a language, they may not necessarily be *invested* in the language practices of a given classroom or community, particularly if they are positioned as inadequate because of characteristics such as race, social class, gender, or sexual orientation. Recognizing that language learning is a social practice, the construct of investment signals how conditions of power impinge on the desire of learners to learn and practice a target language. In this sense, commitment to learning is understood not just as a product of motivation, but a social practice that continually shifts as learners navigate different contexts and situations. In addition to asking, "Are students motivated to learn a language?", researchers and teachers are encouraged to pose the question, "To what extent are students *invested* in the language and literacy practices of a given classroom and community?" Because learners negotiate multiple identities, investment is complex, contradictory, and often in a state of flux.

Responding to these theoretical developments, Dörnyei and Ushioda (2009), in their volume, *Motivation, language identity and the L2 self,* indicated how L2 motivation was "in the process of being radically reconceptualized and re-theorised in the context of contemporary notions of self and identity" (p. 1) and assembled the first comprehensive collection of papers that marked this paradigmatic shift. In her chapter proposing a person-in-context relational view of motivation, Ushioda (2009) argues for a focus on persons located in particular cultural and historical contexts rather than an abstract theoretical notion of learners or individual differences. Aligning with poststructuralist views of identity, she recognized how context is not a pre-existing stable independent variable, but that there is a "mutually constitutive relationship between persons and the contexts in which they act—a relationship that is dynamic, complex and non-linear" (p. 218).

Two decades after Norton's (1995) original conceptualization of investment, Darvin and Norton (2015) developed a more comprehensive model of investment that responds to the new world order transformed by advancements in technology and new forms of mobility (see Figure 7.1). Through digital affordances, learners traverse online and offline translocal spaces with greater ease and speed. The dynamic nature of these spaces, the diversity of those who occupy them, and the transformation of language have enabled new possibilities for the performance of identities and language learning. The distribution of power in communicative contexts no longer rests on the simple dichotomy of native speaker and language learner. Through the affordances of social media and the internet, learners are able to participate in a wider variety of multilingual communities and assert themselves to varying degrees as legitimate speakers (Darvin, 2017; Norton, 2015). As they move across these spaces governed by different value systems, not only do they have to perform multiple identities and draw on more complex linguistic and semiotic repertoires, they are also positioned in new, often invisible ways. As new spaces of socialization and ideas of belonging continue to emerge, two distinct

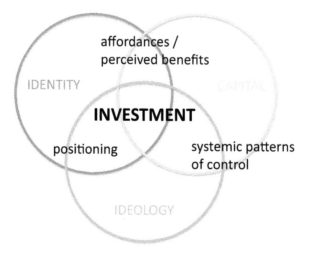

Figure 7.1 Darvin and Norton's (2015) model of identity and investment. Reproduced with permission from Annual Review of Applied Linguistics. Cambridge University Press.

questions confront educators interested in identity and investment in the twenty-first century. First, how do language learners negotiate their identities and capital as they traverse online and offline spaces with greater fluidity? Second, how does power operate within this new social landscape and impact their investment in language learning? To address these questions, Darvin and Norton's (2015) model locates investment at the intersection of identity, capital, and ideology. As a critical framework of language learning, the model challenges educational agents to examine how discrete language events are indexical of communicative practices, and how learners both position themselves and are positioned not only within the contexts of a classroom or workplace but within local, national, and global networks.

In this model, *capital* refers to power in forms that extend from the material/economic to the cultural and social (Bourdieu, 1986), and how these forms of capital are distributed represents the structure of the social world. The form the different types of capital take "once they are perceived and recognized as legitimate" (Bourdieu, 1987, p. 4) in different fields is symbolic capital. By asserting that capital has different forms and values as it travels across space and time, this model acknowledges that power is something that can be redistributed and reconfigured. This conception of power extends to Darvin and Norton's (2015) definition of *ideologies* as "dominant ways of thinking that organize and stabilize societies while simultaneously determining modes of inclusion and exclusion" (p. 72). This pluralized formulation highlights how ideologies are constructed by different structures of power and reproduced by both institutional conditions and recursive hegemonic practices. By shaping dominant material practices, ideologies determine who is at the center and the periphery of a society, or is outside the parameters of what is considered acceptable. In a more mobile world, learners and teachers are able to move fluidly across spaces where ideologies collude and compete, shaping their identities and determining the value of their capital. While ideologies make certain social practices appear universal or common sense, they themselves are porous and can be challenged by new ways of thinking.

In formulating this model of identity and investment, Darvin and Norton (2015) also added a new dimension to understanding identity. Drawing on Bourdieu's (1990) notion of habitus, they discussed how learners negotiate both disposition and desire, existing and imagined identities. Ideologies and social locations shape a learner's habitus, an internalized system "of durable, transposable dispositions" (p. 53) that allows him or her to make sense of the world. Although what learners desire can also be shaped by habitus, it is through desire that the learner is propelled to act. Whether it is because the learner wants to be part of a country or a peer group, to seek romance, or to achieve financial security, learners invest because there is something that they want for themselves—it is part of the structure of desire, as comprehensively theorized by Motha and Lin (2014). Like Dörnyei's (2005) conception of the "ought-to self," which represents someone's sense of duty, habitus compels individuals to do or aspire for what conforms with established norms or expectations. While habitus can predispose learners to think a certain way, it is through desire that they are able to imagine new possibilities for themselves, to transgress these norms and expectations, and exercise agency. Because of this duality, learners need to always interrogate their own language learning goals and understand to what extent they are shaped by hegemonic or agentive impetuses.

Integrating Perspectives from Psychology and SLA

Like the work of social psychologists Davies and Harré (1990), identity theorists in SLA highlight the diverse positions from which language learners are able to participate in social life and demonstrate how learners can, and sometimes cannot, appropriate more desirable identities with respect to the target language community. While some identity positions may limit and constrain opportunities for language learners to listen, speak, read, or write, other identity positions may offer enhanced sets of possibilities for social interaction and human agency, i.e., the possibility to take action in social settings. Identity theorists are, therefore, concerned about the ways in which power is distributed in both formal and informal sites of language learning, and how it affects learners' opportunities to negotiate relationships with target language speakers.

By asserting how an individual's sense of self is structured across time and space and negotiated through relations of power, identity as a construct has generated language learning and teaching research that highlights the significance of historical, cultural, and material contexts. While there is already an extensive body of research on identity and language learning (Norton & Toohey, 2011), research on identity and language teaching has been gaining momentum (e.g., Barkhuizen, 2017; Cheung, Said, & Park, 2015; Clarke, 2009; Dagenais, 2012; De Costa & Norton, 2017; Kanno & Stuart, 2011; Menard-Warwick, 2013; Sayer, 2012; Varghese, Motha, Trent, Park, & Reeves, 2016). Kumaravadivelu (2012) has called for a rethinking of teacher identities in this globalized world, arguing against dependency on western knowledge of production and center-based methods, a view supported by scholars such as Pennycook and Makoni (2020). Such challenges are being taken up by scholars such as McKinney (2017) in South Africa, who is interested in the relationship between language, power, and subjectivity in post-colonial schools, as well as Carazzai (2013) and Sanches Silva (2013) from Brazil, who are exploring ways in which globalization is impacting language teacher identity in tertiary language education programs. The vibrant scholarship on language teacher identity has contributed much to contemporary debates on identity research, and the ways in which teacher identities have evolved in the wake of globalization and neoliberal impulses.

Aligned with this focus, Darvin and Norton's (2015) model of identity and investment has been used as a heuristic to frame different studies of teacher identity. For example, drawing on a longitudinal study that investigates the imagined identities of a preservice English teacher in New Zealand, Barkhuizen (2016) examines how language teacher identities are constructed in and through narrative. Recognizing that "investment indexes issues of identity and imagined futures" (Darvin & Norton, 2015, p. 39), Barkhuizen analyzes the lived stories of one teacher, Sela, as they unfold across personal, institutional, and ideological contexts. Through these different scales, the researcher demonstrates how one teacher is able to invest in practices and identities that enable both agency and resistance. In another study of EFL instructors in South Korea, Gearing and Roger (2017) used the model to analyze to what extent teachers were invested in learning and using the Korean language. While their status as native English speakers provided them with symbolic capital, the participants shared how they were also positioned as outsiders by locals who did not fully accommodate non-standard pronunciation of Korean. The failed attempts of the foreign teachers to negotiate membership into these local communities, and the perceived lack of value of the L2 in terms of their long-term life trajectories, made them less invested in learning the target language.

Implications for Research and Practice

Contemporary work on identity and investment offers many possibilities for reflexive and transformative research and practice. For example, Uju Anya's award-winning monograph *Racialized identities in second language learning: Speaking blackness in Brazil* (Anya, 2017) draws extensively on Norton's theories of identity and investment. As she notes with respect to African American learners of Portuguese in a study abroad program in Brazil:

> I show that their investments (Norton, 1995, 2000, 2001, 2010, 2013) in transformative socialization, their desires to develop new language practices, the varied resources and capital they seek to gain from fluency, the social conditions and systemic patterns of control that influence the feasibility of fluency, and, most importantly, the participants' multiple, shifting identities all contribute to their participation in different communities and lead to how successful they become or are perceived to be in learning Portuguese.
>
> *Anya, 2017, pp. 54–55*

Theories of identity and investment challenge researchers and teachers to reflect on the extent to which teaching can privilege some learners while marginalizing others, and raises many critical questions for both research and practice, including those identified by Darvin (2015, p. 597):

1. To what extent do teachers recognize and respond to the material, unequal lived realities of learners and their multiple identities?
2. What dominant ideologies and systemic patterns of control circumscribe the realities and experiences of language learners and teachers? How does the worldview of teachers position learners?
3. To what extent and in what ways do teachers recognize the linguistic and cultural capital that language learners bring to class?

In addressing issues of power and inequality, these questions encourage educators to recognize the multiple identities of students in the class and develop pedagogical practices that enhance students' investment in the language practices of the classroom. Teachers are encouraged to design learning activities that recognize the rich diversity of learners and affirm the histories, languages, and identities that they bring to class. Teachers are encouraged to reflect on the conditions under which learners will speak, and which identity positions offer greater opportunities for access to powerful networks. Learners who may be marginalized by virtue of gender, race, ethnicity, social class, or sexual orientation can reframe their relationship with others in order to appropriate more powerful identities (see Chapter 23). By serving as a guide to construct inclusive and identity-affirming activities, these critical questions can also enable teachers to construct classroom activities in which the individual talents of learners are made more visible. Not only would there be greater opportunity for social interaction and language use, but such activities could affirm the identities of these learners as knowledgeable and competent individuals.

One such activity is the construction of *identity texts,* which are creative works or performances that promote enhanced investment on the part of learners (Cummins & Early, 2010). In recent years, digital stories have become a popular identity text project that encourages learners to claim authorial agency. By borrowing and repurposing texts, images, and music, learners are able to become co-authors and agents of language and literacy acquisition. In a study of the creative process of ninth-grade students, Rowsell (2012) demonstrated how their production of their own digital stories about "an odyssey of self" helped them reposition their identity. By making different multimodal choices to represent their lived histories, learners are granted individual creative expression. Because digital stories have very few structuring conditions and constraints, learners can improvise their ideas, values, and histories without critical challenge, and thus, they are able to reimagine their own self-identifications.

For Darvin and Norton (2014), digital storytelling is a powerful way to affirm the transnational identities of migrant learners, whose lives are emblematic of the fluidity of the new world order. Through a workshop where high school students produced their own stories of migration, learners were able to use their own voices and mother tongues and draw from the modalities of images and music to share their lived experiences. Kendrick, Chemjor, and Early (2012) conducted a project where rural Kenyan students were provided with digital cameras, laptops with connectivity, and voice recorders to be journalists. As students conducted interviews with government officials, their digital tools became signifiers of membership in a journalistic context. Through role-playing, students were able to ask about controversial issues like dissent and police corruption, and negotiate the performance of new, more empowered identities. By continually addressing the inequalities of learners through teacher training and reflexive practice, language teachers are able to develop a critical disposition necessary for a pedagogy that affirms and empowers the complex, multiple identities of learners (Stranger-Johannessen & Norton, 2019). Through this critical pedagogy, language learners are encouraged to invest in the language and literacy practices of their classrooms and claim their right to speak and to be heard.

Future Directions

In an increasingly mobile and digital world where learners move fluidly across spatial and linguistic boundaries, new and exciting possibilities for identity studies abound. Following the trans-turn of language learning and teaching research where translanguaging, transculturality, and transnationalism have been foregrounded, there has been increasing interest in research populations like study abroad learners, heritage language learners, and lingua franca speakers (Norton & De Costa, 2018). Examinations of the intersectionality of race, ethnicity, gender, and social class remain particularly relevant as communities become more dispersed and diverse (Block & Corona, 2014). To understand how new forms of inequality impact the social and educational trajectories of learners, the construct of scales has become increasingly generative (De Costa & Canagarajah, 2016; Maloney & De Costa, 2017). Longitudinal identity research is enhanced by a scalar approach that treats scales as a shifting category of practice and helps interpret how identities emerge from the translingual practices of people and institutions. By responding to the call of The Douglas Fir Group (2016) for more transdisciplinary SLA research, identity research can also benefit from examining further how the constructs of investment and motivation complement and enrich each other (Darvin, 2019; Norton, 2020). The bifocality of such an approach holds great possibilities in grasping the interconnectedness and interdependence of the cognitive, psychological, emotional, and social processes that constitute language learning and teaching.

As technology continues to provide new spaces of language acquisition, how learners draw on their linguistic and semiotic repertoires to construct multiple digitally mediated identities will continue to be an important area of research (Darvin, 2018; Lam & Smirnov, 2017; Thorne, Sauro, & Smith, 2015). Learners often navigate these spaces in disembodied ways, and how social categories of race, ethnicity, gender, class, and sexual orientation are performed and recognized online will be of increasing interest to identity researchers examining issues of positionality. Through the digital, not only do speech and writing converge, collapsing the boundaries of language and literacy, but online and offline spaces impinge on each other in mutually constitutive ways. The connection between bodies and devices has become more seamless, shaping not only behavior, but also modes of thinking (Pennycook, 2017). Consequently, online communicative practices are produced through the convergence of material conditions, dispositions, desires, and cultures. New and often invisible relations of power between human and non-human actors, sociotechnical structures, and algorithmic processes shape the ways learners negotiate their identities online. The dynamics of this interaction as it impacts opportunities for language learning and use presents a range of research tasks for those interested in investment.

Reflection Questions

- In what ways can identity research examine individual differences in ways that integrate cognitive and social dimensions of language learning?
- What combination of research methods can support studies that integrate motivation and investment in their theoretical framework?
- How can Darvin and Norton's (2015) model of identity and investment be used to examine language learner and teacher perspectives in diverse learning contexts?

Recommended Reading

Darvin, R., & Norton, B. (2015). Identity and a model of investment in applied linguistics. *Annual Review of Applied Linguistics, 35*, 35–56.
In response to advances in digital technology and shifts in patterns of mobility, Darvin and Norton have developed an expanded model of investment, which occurs at the intersection of identity, ideology, and capital. The article won the 2016 TESOL Distinguished Research Award.

Mercer, S., & Williams, M. (Eds.). (2014). *Multiple perspectives on the self in SLA*. Multilingual Matters.
This collection of chapters provides a comprehensive perspective on constructions of the self in second language acquisition and foreign language learning. It makes a convincing case that diverse theories of the self can enrich our understanding of identity and language learning.

Norton, B. (2020). Motivation, identity, and investment: A journey with Robert Gardner. In A. Al-Hoorie & P. MacIntyre (Eds.), *Contemporary language motivation theory: 60 years Since Gardner and Lambert (1959)* (pp. 153–168). Multilingual Matters.
This chapter traces how the psychological construct of motivation and the sociological construct of investment complement each other in examining how individuals commit to language learning.

References

Anya, U. (2017). *Racialized identities in second language learning: Speaking blackness in Brazil*. Routledge.

Barkhuizen, G. (2016). A short story approach to analyzing teacher (imagined) identities over time. *TESOL Quarterly, 50*(3), 655–683.

Barkhuizen, G. (ed.) (2017). *Reflections on language teacher identity research*. Routledge.

Block, D. (2007). The rise of identity in SLA research, post Firth and Wagner (1997). *The Modern Language Journal, 91*(5), 863–876.

Block, D., & V. Corona (2014). Exploring class-based intersectionality. *Language, Culture and Curriculum, 27*(1), 27–42.

Bourdieu, P. (1977). The economics of linguistic exchanges. *Social Science Information, 16*(6), 645–668.

Bourdieu, P. (1986). The forms of capital. In J. F. Richardson (Ed.), *Handbook of theory and research for the sociology of education* (pp. 241–258). Greenwood Press.

Bourdieu, P. (1987). What makes a social class? On the theoretical and practical existence of groups. *Berkeley Journal of Sociology, 32*, 1–17.

Bourdieu, P. (1990). *The logic of practice*. Stanford University Press.

Carazzai, M. R. (2013). *The process of identity (re)construction of six Brazilian language learners: A poststructuralist ethnographic study*. Ph.D. dissertation, Universidade Federal de Santa Catarina.

Cheung, Y. L., Said, S., & Park, K. (2015). *Advanced and current trends in language teacher identity research*. Routledge.

Clarke, M. (2009). The ethico-politics of teacher identity. *Educational Philosophy and Theory, 41*, 185–200.

Cummins, J., & Early, M. (2010). *Identity texts: The collaborative creation of power in multilingual schools*. Trentham.

Dagenais, D. (2012). Identities and language teaching in classrooms. In C. A. Chapelle (Ed.), *The encyclopedia of applied linguistics*. Wiley and Sons.

Darvin, R. (2015). Representing the margins: Multimodal performance as a tool for critical reflection and pedagogy. *TESOL Quarterly, 49*(3), 590–600.

Darvin, R. (2017). Social class and the inequality of English speakers in a globalized world. *Journal of English as a Lingua Franca, 6*(2), 287–311.

Darvin, R. (2018). Social class, and the acquisition of unequal digital literacies. *Language and Literacy, 20*(3), 26–45.

Darvin, R., & Norton, B. (2014). Transnational identity and migrant language learners: The promise of digital storytelling. *Education Matters: The Journal of Teaching and Learning, 2*(1), 55–66.

Darvin, R., & Norton, B. (2015). Identity and a model of investment in applied linguistics. *Annual Review of Applied Linguistics, 35*, 36–56.

Davies, B., & Harré, R. (1990). Positioning: The discursive production of selves. *Journal for the Theory of Social Behaviour, 20*(1), 43–63.

De Costa, P. I., & Canagarajah, A. S. (Guest Eds.). (2016). Scalar approaches to language teaching and learning (special issue). *Linguistics and Education, 34*.

De Costa, P. I., & Norton, B. (Eds.). (2017). Transdisciplinarity and language teacher identity. *The Modern Language Journal, 101*, 3–14.

Douglas Fir Group. (2016). A transdisciplinary framework for SLA in a multilingual world. *The Modern Language Journal, 100*, 19–47.

Dörnyei, Z. (2005). *The psychology of the language learner. Individual differences in second language acquisition*. Lawrence Erlbaum.

Dörnyei, Z., & Ushioda, E. (Eds.). (2009). Motivation, language identity and the L2 self. *Multilingual Matters, 36*.

Firth, A., & Wagner, J. (1997). On discourse, communication and (some) fundamental concepts in SLA research. *The Modern Language Journal, 81*(3), 285–300.

Gardner, R. C. (1985). *Social psychology and second language learning: The role of attitudes and motivation.* Edward Arnold.

Gardner, R. C. (2010). *Motivation and second language acquisition: The socio-educational model.* Peter Lang Publishing.

Gearing, N., & Roger, P. (2017). "I'm never going to be part of it": Identity, investment and learning Korean. *Journal of Multilingual and Multicultural Development, 39*(2), 155–168.

Giles, H. (1977). (Ed.). *Language, ethnicity and intergroup relations.* Academic Press.

Kanno, Y., & Stuart, C. (2011). The development of L2 teacher identity: Longitudinal case studies. *The Modern Language Journal, 95*, 236–252.

Kendrick, M., Chemjor, W., & Early, M. (2012). ICTs as placed resources in a rural Kenyan secondary school journalism club. *Language and Education, 26*(4), 297–313.

Kostoulas, A., & Mercer, S. (2016). Fifteen years of research on self & identity in System. *System, 60*, 128–134.

Kramsch, C. (2009). *The multilingual subject.* Oxford University Press.

Kumaravadivelu, B. (2012). *Language teacher education for a global society.* Routledge.

Lam, E., & Smirnov, N. (2017). Identity in mediated contexts of transnationalism and mobility. In S. Thorne & S. May (Eds.), *Language, Education and Technology, Encyclopedia of Language and Education* (Vol. 9, pp. 105–118). Springer.

Lambert, W. E. (1974). Culture and language as factors in learning and education. In F. E. Aboud & R. D. Meade (Eds.), *Cultural factors in learning and education* (pp. 91–122). Fifth Western Washington Symposium on Learning.

Maloney, J., & De Costa, P. I. (2017). Imagining the Japanese heritage learner: A scalar perspective. *Language, Discourse, & Society, 9*(1), 35–52.

McNamara, T. (1997). Theorizing social identity: What do we mean by social identity? Competing frameworks, competing discourse. *TESOL Quarterly, 31*(3), 561–567.

Menard-Warwick, J. (2013). *English language teachers on the discursive faultlines: Identities, ideologies, pedagogies.* Multilingual Matters.

Mercer, S. (2011). *Towards an understanding of language learner self-concept* (Vol. 12). Springer Science & Business Media.

Mercer, S., & Williams, M. (Eds.). (2014). *Multiple perspectives on the self in SLA.* Multilingual Matters.

McKinney, C. (2017). *Language and power in post-colonial schooling: Ideologies in practice.* Routledge.

Motha, S., & Lin, A. (2014). "Non-coercive rearrangements": Theorizing desire in TESOL. *TESOL Quarterly, 48*(2), 331–359.

Norton, B. (2000). *Identity and language learning: Gender, ethnicity and educational change.* Longman/Pearson Education.

Norton, B. (2001). Non-participation, imagined communities, and the language classroom. In M. Breen (Ed.), *Learner contributions to language learning: New directions in research* (pp. 159–171). Pearson Education.

Norton, B. (2013). *Identity and language learning: Extending the conversation* (2nd ed.). Multilingual Matters.

Norton, B. (2015). Identity, investment, and faces of English internationally. *Chinese Journal of Applied Linguistics, 38*(4), 375–391.

Norton, B. & De Costa, P. (2018). Research tasks on identity in language learning and teaching. *Language Teaching, 51*(1), 90–112.

Norton, B., & Toohey, K. (2011). Identity, language learning, and social change. *Language Teaching, 44*(4), 412–446.

Norton Peirce, B. (1995). Social identity, investment, and language learning. *TESOL Quarterly, 29*(1), 9–31.

Pavlenko, A., & Blackledge, A. (Eds.) (2004). *Negotiation of identities in multilingual contexts.* Multilingual Matters.

Pennycook, A. (2017). *Posthumanist applied linguistics.* Routledge.

Pennycook, A., & Makoni, S. (2020). *Innovations and challenges in applied linguistics from the Global South.* Routledge.

Rowsell, J. (2012). Artifactual English. In M. Grenfell, D. Bloome, C. Hardy, K. Pahl, J. Rowsell, & B. V. Street (Eds.), *Language, ethnography and education: Bridging new literacy studies and Bourdieu,* (pp. 110–131). Routledge.

Sanches Silva, J. F. (2013). *The construction of English teacher identity in Brazil: A study in Mato Grosso do Sul* [Doctoral dissertation, Universidade Federal de Santa Catarina]. Repositório Institucional. repositorio.ufsc.br/handle/123456789/105151

Sayer, P. (2012). *Ambiguities and tensions in English language teaching: Portraits of EFL teachers as legitimate speakers.* Routledge.

Stranger-Johannessen, E., & Norton, B. (2019). Promoting early literacy and student investment in the African Storybook. *Journal of Language, Identity, and Education, 18*(6), 400–411.

Tajfel, H. (1982). Social psychology of intergroup relations. *Annual Review of Psychology, 33*, 1–39.

Tajfel, H., & Turner, J. C. (1986). The social identity theory of inter-group behavior. In S. Worchel & W. G. Austin (Eds.), *Psychology of Intergroup Relations,* (pp. 7–24). Nelson-Hall.

Thorne, S. L., Sauro, S., & Smith, B. (2015). Technologies, identities, and expressive activity. *Annual Review of Applied Linguistics, 35*, 215–233.

Toohey, K. (2000). *Learning English at school: Identity, social relations and classroom practice*. Multilingual Matters.
Ushioda, E. (2009). A person-in-context relational view of emergent motivation, self and identity. In Z. Dörnyei & E. Ushioda (Eds.), *Motivation, language identity and the L2 self,* (pp. 215–228). Multilingual Matters.
Weedon, C. (1987). *Feminist practice and poststructuralist theory*. Basil Blackwell.
Varghese, M., Motha, M., Trent, J., Park, G., & Reeves, J. (Guest Eds.). (2016). Language teacher identity in multilingual settings (special issue). *TESOL Quarterly 50*(3), 541–783.

8
SELF-EFFICACY

Kay Irie

Self-efficacy is essentially a self-evaluation of how able you feel to carry out a specific task in a specific situation successfully. There may be various reasons why you might not actually take action to undertake the task. However, unless you feel that you can complete the task successfully, the likelihood that you will take that action is low. Self-efficacy also determines how much you can endure the challenge that the task or the situation brings. This sense of "can-do" is crucial in the long journey of language learning. It is considered one of the cornerstones of self-regulation (see Chapter 17) and sustained motivation (see Chapter 10). How learners maintain their enthusiasm and continue to make effort and control their learning is affected by their sense of what they feel they are able to do. Following the large body of empirical and applied evidence for the effects of self-efficacy on learning and academic performances in general education, it is understandable that interest in self-efficacy research is also increasing in SLA (e.g., Bai, Chao, & Wang, 2019; Mills, Pajares, & Herron, 2007; Mills, 2014; Zhang & Ardasheva, 2019).

To define and explain self-efficacy, I begin this chapter by looking at Bandura's (1986, 2001) Social Cognitive Theory (SCT) in which self-efficacy beliefs are the vital component. This will be followed by an outline of key findings of research in the field of psychology. Next, I discuss how self-efficacy has been applied and investigated in the field of SLA and specific areas in language learning in which research has been conducted including writing, listening, language learning strategies, self-regulated learning (SRL), and more global self-efficacy for L2 learning. Following this, I review the findings of both psychology and SLA in order to suggest implications for language education. Although I do touch on teacher self-efficacy (TSE), or how teachers evaluate their teaching skills, due to the limitation of space my main focus in this chapter will be on self-efficacy in learners.

Self-Efficacy in Psychology

Self-Efficacy within Social Cognitive Theory

Self-efficacy is a core construct in Social Cognitive Theory (SCT) in which Bandura seeks to explain the active and proactive role people play in shaping the course of their lives. The SCT triadic causal model is based on the idea that "human functioning is a product of the interplay of interpersonal influences, the behavior individuals engage in, and the environmental forces that impinge upon them" (Bandura, 2012, p. 11). That is, people are self-regulating agents who take action in response to the complex interactions among personal, behavioral, and environmental determinants. In this model, self-efficacy is a major constituent of the personal determinants that allow people to be agentic and make their own decisions, and not simply be forced by the environment.

The personal determinants are composed of the four human capabilities that facilitate personal agency: intentionality, forethought, self-reactiveness, and self-reflectiveness (Bandura, 2001, 2012). Self-efficacy beliefs belong to the fourth capability, self-reflectiveness, which enables people to evaluate their capacity to control their functioning and develop self-efficacy beliefs. Believing that they can achieve the outcome that they desire, people are motivated to take action. Thus, self-efficacy is considered to be the foundation of human agency (Bandura, 2001).

These capabilities and the function of self-efficacy may be illustrated by an example of a language student's study-abroad experience. In most cases, students do not choose to study abroad by accident. There is some kind of intention. To realize this with the ability of forethought, they think about where and when to go, as well as weighing up the costs and benefits against the goals they set up. The ability of self-reactiveness enables the students to integrate their thought into action. Once they have arrived at their stay abroad destination, they also observe and assess their action, affect, and motivation. When they notice that they are spending too much time with people from the home country, they may correct their course of action by spending more time with people from other countries. Finally, with the ability to self-reflect, they re-assess their capability to interact with people in the L2 and they self-regulate their efforts and learning to complete the study abroad program with a positive outcome. This self-assessment is necessary for developing self-efficacy, which can affect the subsequent courses of action. In other words, self-efficacy is based on learning from experiences associated with actions taken.

One of the critical concepts in SCT is learning through modeling. This comes from trial and error, the behavioral psychological perspectives of learning. SCT identifies four primary types of experiences as self-efficacy information: mastery experience (one's own experiences of successes and failures), vicarious experience, social persuasion, and physiological and affective states in the situation. In other words, self-efficacy for particular tasks can be strengthened or weakened by people's interpretation of their experiences of similar tasks, the performance of others of similar ability, feedback on their performance, and the emotions and stress as well as physical conditions felt at the time. Different interpretations may arise from the same experiences or physiological state. Amongst all information sources, Bandura (1986, 2006) regarded the interpretation of one's own experiences as the most powerful. When applied to language education, the learners' interpretation of their own experience of language use or learning activity is more likely to affect how they evaluate their capacity to carry out similar or related tasks. It is not only a matter of success or failure of the outcome but also the perceived effort and the process undertaken. Furthermore, their interpretation of the experience may change over time, regardless of the type of experience they actually had (Ryan & Irie, 2014).

In defining terms, some self-constructs can be confused with self-efficacy. Self-esteem is the overall value and feelings people have for themselves. It is considered an emotional evaluation (Carnevale, 2016). Self-esteem is a broad sense that does not involve any objective or accurate measurement of worth or capacity and is "a holistic judgement of self-worth that does not function at the domain-specific level (e.g., the domain of learning English as a foreign language)" (Mercer, 2011, p.18). Self-efficacy is a cognitive self-evaluation of the capacity with regards to a particular task. They are beliefs that are an integral part of the domain-specific self-concept beliefs. In contrast, self-esteem is viewed as a holistic judgment of self-worth that does not function at the domain-specific level (e.g., the domain of learning English as a foreign language). Thus, the assessment of self-esteem is typically done by asking the respondents to rate their general satisfaction with themselves without specifying any domains (e.g., Rosenberg, 1965).

Another related concept is self-concept, which Schunk and Pajares (2004) refer to as a perception of self, based on personal interpretations of experiences and environment that are affected by feedback from family, friends, and other people around them. It is a more general construct than self-efficacy. Self-concept can be domain-specific, such as athletic self-concept, academic self-concept, and linguistic/L2 self-concept. Although both self-concept and self-efficacy are evaluative constructs, Bong and Skaalvik (2003) point out that the measurement of self-efficacy asks respondents to rate their confidence in successfully carrying out a specific task and is typically more cognitive in content. In contrast, the scales for self-concept are intended to elicit how respondents feel, such as how much they enjoy the activities, or how difficult they would find the materials within specific domains, such as mathematics or writing in an L2.

Although the emphasis of self-efficacy is on its domain-specificity as defined in SCT, this emphasis may hinder its practical applications as formal education is structured on the expectation of skill transfer and the incremental difficulty (Schunk & Pajares, 2004). Therefore, to apply self-efficacy practically in education, it needs to be transferable beyond specific tasks. One way to do this may be to treat self-efficacy as part of the larger domain of self-concept (Mercer, 2011). By comparing academic self-concept and academic self-efficacy, Bong and Skaalvik (2003) state that the two constructs are difficult to distinguish at the domain level of specificity, and there may be considerable overlap between them. Therefore, it is possible to consider self-efficacy as "the most important building block in one's self-concept" (pp. 10–11). In language learning domains, self-efficacy can be assessed in terms of specific writing tasks or communicative tasks. Gaining confidence to complete the tasks successfully may enhance people's more general self-concept, their vision of who they are as L2 learners and users.

Empirical Evidence about Self-Efficacy in Educational Settings

Self-efficacy has been applied and investigated in both the academic and career development spheres (Blair & Lowe, 2018). Originally, Bandura (1977) proposed this construct for therapeutic behavioral change (e.g., snake phobias) and not for academic performance in educational psychology. As such, much of the earlier research was carried out in controlled settings with adults who could reasonably estimate their capacity for performing specific tasks, which led to a high correlation between self-efficacy and actual performance. On the other hand, research on self-efficacy in school settings is often carried out with children who may be less able to judge their capacity accurately. Furthermore, studies in school settings are more naturalistic and involve difficult to control diverse socio-cultural factors such as peer pressure, classroom dynamics, and individual difference factors such as socioeconomic status and academic ability (Schunk & Pajares, 2004). However, because of the relevance of the concept to education, much research has been conducted particularly on the relationship with academic achievement and performances.

Self-efficacy for students in school or academic performances has been labeled academic self-efficacy (ASE), which consists of self-efficacy for learning (self-regulation) and academic performance, that is, students' self-evaluation of their own ability to successfully meet specific educational goals (Honicke & Broadbent, 2016). According to their systematic review of ASE research in educational contexts between 2003 and 2015, Honicke and Broadbent (2016) concluded that academic self-efficacy moderately correlated with academic performance, with mediating and moderating factors that included effort regulation, deep processing strategies, and goal orientations. Amongst the published research, the Motivated Strategies for Learning Questionnaire (MSLQ) (see Pintrich, Smith, Garcia, & McKeachie, 1993 for the original) has been the most commonly used instrument to measure ASE. The most widely used criterion measurement was an official subject grade or grade-point average. The correlations between the two measures reported in the studies indicate that students with high ASE are likely to achieve high performance, take on more difficult tasks, persevere with the work, and try out different learning strategies when unsuccessful. In line with the importance of specificity highlighted in the previous section, the authors of the review pointed out that the more specific the scales are, the more reliable. This is also evident in subject-domain-level research such as mathematics. For example, Pietsch, Walker and Chapman (2003) looked into the relationship among self-concept, self-efficacy, and mathematics performance among 416 high school students in Australia. Their study shows that mathematics self-efficacy was more highly related to performance in mathematics when compared with a more general mathematics self-concept.

The essential role of self-efficacy in educational contexts is widely acknowledged, and teachers are encouraged to be mindful about not only about students' actual performance but also their self-evaluation of their competence. These are related to students' motivation and the course of actions for learning and school. Pajares (2002) stated that an unnecessary lack of confidence would negatively affect students and potentially lead to various maladaptive behaviors, such as being reluctant to engage in tasks and easily giving up. He emphasized the importance of noticing students' inaccurate estimates of their competence and changing them.

Before moving on to the next section, it should be noted that the research on teacher self-efficacy (TSE), a teacher's judgment of his or her own capacity to bring about aimed outcomes in student engagement and learning, is also growing in general education (e.g., Skaalvik & Skaalvik, 2007; Tschannen-Moran & Woolfolk Hoy, 2001). Reviewing 165 quantitative studies conducted on TSE between 1976 and 2014, Zee and Koomen (2016) report the significance of TSE in terms of managing classrooms, engaging students, and using effective instructional strategies. Their meta-analysis also reveals the importance of TSE to teachers' well-being regardless of teaching contexts. In essence, self-efficacious teachers are likely to be more resilient to negative factors such as stress and emotional exhaustion and to gain a higher sense of accomplishment, commitment, and job satisfaction. Therefore, it seems beneficial for teachers to think not only about the self-efficacy of learners but also their own.

Self-Efficacy in SLA

Self-efficacy is gradually gaining increased attention in SLA. This coincides with the exponential growth of publications on L2 motivation and self-related concepts (Boo, Dörnyei, & Ryan, 2015). Mills (2014) provides an introduction of the concept with its theoretical background and a summary of the research in SLA. The review covers some initial work done in the field of reading, listening, proficiency, language learning strategy use, anxiety, and self-regulation. It includes her pioneering work with her colleagues bridging the fields of educational psychology and SLA (Mills et al., 2007). They examined the influence of French grade self-efficacy as well as self-efficacy for SRL and other factors, such as French learning anxiety and French learning self-concept. The results of their study suggest that learners' self-efficacy for self-regulation was a better predictor of achievement than other constructs, such as self-efficacy in grade performance, L2 anxiety in listening and reading, and their French learning self-concept. This is in line with the increasing importance of self-efficacy in SRL in general education (see Wang, this volume; Pintrich, 2000; Zimmerman, 2013) as well as in the use of language strategies in language education.

In fact, most studies on self-efficacy in SLA look into the relationship with the use of learning strategies rather than a direct relationship with the actual performance or overall proficiency development. The concept of self-efficacy is particularly useful as language learning is often broken down into skills. For example, within the area of reading, Li and Wang (2010) investigated the relationship between self-efficacy and comprehension strategies with EFL university students in China. They found that those who have strong efficacious beliefs regarding reading are likely to employ more cognitive and social/affective strategies. Similarly, Rahimi and Abedi (2014) report a positive correlation between listening self-efficacy and metacognitive awareness of listening strategies, particularly planning-evaluation and problem-solving strategies, but a negative correlation with mental translation strategies.

Some research has also been conducted to explore the effectiveness of strategy instruction in increasing self-efficacy. For listening, Graham and Macaro (2008) examined the effectiveness of strategy training with lower-intermediate learners of French in the UK. Their study demonstrated its effectiveness not only in increasing the level of listening comprehension ability but also in listening self-efficacy. They cautiously point out the potential of feedback in linking strategy use and successful listening to self-efficacy. Furthermore, a study conducted by Liao and Wang (2018) focused on the instruction of reading comprehension strategies for EFL reading with university students in Taiwan. Those who received the strategy instruction increased their reading self-efficacy and improved reading proficiency significantly more than those who did not receive the instruction. These studies provide support for the effectiveness of strategy instructions and their positive relationship with the learners' beliefs in their capacity to carry out tasks in specific domains.

In addition to the relationship with strategies, another new line of inquiry is the self-efficacy formation for language learning and use. Focusing specifically on public speaking, Zhang and Ardasheva (2019) looked into the sources contributing to English public speaking self-efficacy for Chinese university students in science and liberal arts. The researchers explored the contributions of the four sources of self-efficacy information (mastery experience, vicarious experience, social persuasion, and physiological and affective states). They found that all sources except for physical and affective states contribute to the development of self-efficacy. Bai et al. (2019) also examined the relationships between self-efficacy for learning English in class and achievement amongst EFL secondary students in Hong Kong. In their study, self-efficacy was found to be the most reliable and robust factor in predicting English learning achievement, with positive feedback from parents providing a facilitative condition for developing self-efficacy in the Hong Kong context. This parental support suggests that social persuasion can come from family as well as the environment that learners are in.

Similar to the general education field, teacher self-efficacy (TSE) has also been drawing attention in language education (e.g., Choi & Lee, 2016; Malmir & Mohammadi, 2018; Phan & Locke, 2015; Thompson, 2020; Wyatt, 2010). In his systematic review of TSE of language teachers, Wyatt (2010) points out the unique factors that may negatively affect language teachers such as target language proficiency among non-native teachers, lack of understanding of L1 students among monolingual native speaker teachers, and common issues of poor student motivation in foreign language teaching contexts. Thompson (2020) states that the studies so far on language teacher efficacy have generally shown that each of the four sources of efficacy contributes to TSE, particularly in-service mastery experiences.

In summary, the research on self-efficacy in SLA is increasing, and the range of inquiry is widening. With the establishment of a strong link between self-efficacy and various SRL and language learning strategies as well as academic performance, new lines of inquiry have been emerging to explore the effectiveness of strategy training as well as the facilitation of self-efficacy. Considering the applicability to teaching, these are welcome developments that have the potential to bring research and practice closer, as will be discussed more later.

Integrating Perspectives

As I have shown in the preceding sections, empirical research provides evidence for the usefulness of self-efficacy in education. Looking at the connection between psychology and SLA, the bridge has been built by researchers from different disciplines. In the work of self-efficacy in SLA (Mills et al., 2007), Nicole Mills and Carol Herron, who both have a background in language education, worked with Frank Pajares, an educational psychologist and a specialist on self-efficacy. This interdisciplinary collaboration on the initial application of the construct to SLA helped provide an accurate theoretical understanding for the operationalization of self-efficacy in research. Another example of interdisciplinary collaboration can be seen in the development of the Questionnaire of English Self-Efficacy (QESE) by Wang and his team of language educators and educational psychologists (Wang, Kim, Bai, & Hu, 2014; Wang, Schwab, Fenn, & Chang, 2013). While Wang at el. (2013) collaborated to investigate cultural differences in the self-efficacy and SRL strategies between English learners in Chinese and German universities, Wang et al. (2014) carried out a study in China to examine the validity of the QESE. This scale has been employed in research on English language learners' self-efficacy in Korea by Wang and other psychologists (Kim, Wang, Ahn, & Bong, 2015). Likewise, SLA researchers are also referring to such studies in their exploration of self-efficacy in language education (e.g., Bai et al., 2019; Teng, Sun, & Xu, 2018; Zhang & Ardasheva, 2019). This kind of interdisciplinary collaboration is highly desirable and necessary for the development of language learning psychology (Mercer & Ryan, 2016).

Nevertheless, there are potential problems in researching self-efficacy. As Mills (2014) warned, mismeasurement of the construct still seems to be common regardless of the field of inquiry. Currently, two issues in this regard are prominent. One is the lack of specificity in measurement. The other is the use of a bipolar Likert type scale for a construct that is essentially unipolar.

For example, in Chang's study (2010) on the relationship between group process (group cohesiveness and group norms) and level of L2 motivation among Taiwanese university students, self-efficacy was used as one of the two aspects of motivation. They employed a scale, which was originally designed to measure general self-efficacy for people working in various contexts. The items included statements such as *I am proud of my English ability and skill*, which does not reflect the definition of self-efficacy. There was no significant correlation found between group process and self-efficacy. However, without a reliable measurement, no conclusion can be drawn regarding the relationship. This kind of misconstruction of measurement is likely to be connected with the lack of specificity of the skills or tasks, and it points out the potential pitfalls in self-efficacy research.

Since self-efficacy is task- and situation-specific, the scale should always be designed or adopted carefully for each study. The good news is that the statements in scales more in line with the theoretical definition of self-efficacy, such as QESE, as well as others used in various skill-specific studies, are written in the can-do form. The use of can-do statements is convenient for SLA, as they are familiar to stakeholders in the field having been used in education for a long time (e.g., Clark, 1987) and in the Common European Framework of Reference for languages (CEFR) in the early 2000s.

The second issue of mismeasurement concerns the scaling. Bandura (2011) stipulates that efficacy scales should be unipolar from zero to a maximum strength of belief (p. 16). He dismisses the use of a bipolar 5-point Likert-scale ranging from strongly disagree with negative scores below the zero or neutral point as one cannot have an assessment of capacity lower than 0. Furthermore, it does not make sense to convert the neutral point (neither agree or disagree) to a midpoint on a unipolar scale. Bipolar 5-point Likert-scales have been widely used in SLA (e.g., Sardegna, Lee, & Kusey, 2018). An example of a unipolar scale can be found in the study by Mills and Péron (2009), who used a 10-point interval scale from 0 (not confident at all) to 100 (completely confident). Another example is QESE (Wang et al., 2013; Wang et al., 2014), which uses a unipolar 7-point scale from 1 (I cannot do it at all) to 7 (I can do it very well). The issue of scaling is not just a technical detail; it affects the further development of self-efficacy research regardless of the field as, without reliable measurement, it is impossible to observe any change and accumulate the evidence for its relationship with other factors.

Finally, in both fields, most research on self-efficacy is dominated by correlation-based quantitative methods. Given the history of the psychological construct development, this is understandable, and the quantitative approach has been useful in refining the construct. However, there is a growing interest in the use of qualitative approach and mixed methods, and there also seems to be an increasing interest in expanding upon research methods, particularly in teacher training and in language education (e.g., Glackin & Hohenstein, 2018, Klassen & Durksen, 2014, see Wyatt 2010 for SLA). These studies focus on the details of the self-efficacy of individuals in certain contexts rather than the generalization of the construct's characteristics.

Implications for Practice and Research

In the previous sections, I sought to provide implications for teachers and researchers. In this section, I will discuss the importance of valid measurements and the expansion of research methods, the usefulness of four sources of self-efficacy information, and how to enhance self-efficacy for learners and teachers.

As suggested earlier, there are two issues with research methods. First, it is paramount to have appropriate measurements, and this will be a key concern for future work in the field. The significance of construct validity is obvious, but it also pedagogically helps both learners and teachers in the classroom. For students, the statements in the scale can also serve as articulated goals they can aim for. For teachers, they provide a framework for designing the course and tasks. Periodical measurements of self-efficacy can be used as self-assessment to raise students' awareness and provide feedback to the teachers on their instruction and tasks. One difficulty in using this approach is the lack of qualitative research on self-efficacy when it comes to understanding it in a local context as the definition of the construct demands. Another issue is the limited range of research methods typically used. As Ushioda (2019) states, the qualitative approach is suitable for refining the construct as its open-ended style of inquiry can help researchers to delve into learners' own perceptions of how they see themselves. More research on self-efficacy using qualitative methods should enhance understanding of how it functions for certain people in the specific contexts and how it appears to be related to the control of their behavior.

Another good focus for practice and research is on the four sources of self-efficacy: mastery experiences, vicarious experiences, social persuasion, and physiological/affective states. Out of these four information sources, according to Bandura (1986, 2006), mastery experiences can function as the most potent indicators of efficacy. Teachers can provide conditions to increase learners' confidence in using the language to complete tasks, shifting gradually from teacher-led or modeled activities to student-led activities with less scaffolding or from textbooks and modified materials to authentic materials. In order to increase the chances of mastery experience, it would be beneficial to equip students with strategies for learning as well as for self-regulation. Since it is not the experiences themselves that form efficacy but rather the interpretation of the experiences, causal attribution—or how people explain their success and failures—can be considered to play a role in developing self-efficacy (Zhang, Mantou Lou, Noels, & Daniels, this volume; Stajkovic & Sommer, 2000). Attribution theory (Weiner, 1986) suggests that where people attribute their success and failure to a cause, that cause can be something internal/external, stable/unstable, and controllable/uncontrollable. Dörnyei and Ryan (2015) mention Ushioda's (1996, 1998, 2001) findings on positive motivational thinking involving two patterns of attributions. One is attributing successes to internal (personal) factors such as ability and effort. Another is attributing failures to unstable yet controllable factors such as lack of effort and lack of L2 use opportunities (Dörnyei & Ryan, 2015, p. 83). Attribution retraining is a set of procedures to influence the individuals' beliefs about the causes of their performance of tasks. Chapman and Tunmer (2003) suggest the effectiveness of the attribution retraining employing teachers' feedback to assure the learners' effort and adequate ability along with the actual skill training.

Opportunities for vicarious experiences can be provided within a class by having students share their performances, especially when students observe the success of peers of similar proficiency. The idea is also known as near-peer role modeling in language education (Murphey & Arao, 2001). The key is for the learners to see that the people they are observing are similar to them so that their success can suggest the possibility of success for the observers, too. With videos available online today, teachers and students can share examples that can function in place of near-peer role models. Another possibility is tandem-learning amongst language learners on a common target language (Brammerts, 2003) or language exchange partnerships in which people teach each other their first language (Ahn, 2016).

Social persuasion is the third source of self-efficacy information. This is an area where teachers can contribute to students' healthy self-efficacy development through feedback. In studies by Mills and Péron (2009) as well as Chan and Lam (2010), feedback that indicated progress to the students enhanced their L2 self-efficacy in writing and vocabulary learning, respectively. Mills and Péron (2009) demonstrated that the process-writing approach for intermediate-level French students in university provides opportunities for consistent and personalized feedback to the students. Similarly, Chan and Lam (2010) reported that summative feedback that focuses on the outcome rather than formative feedback focusing on the process decreased self-efficacy for vocabulary learning among Grade 8 Chinese students. Their study also showed that self-referenced feedback focusing on the progress of the learner rather than norm-referenced feedback focusing on comparison with others in the class linked to a significant increase in self-efficacy.

Finally, the fourth source of self-efficacy information is physiological and affective states. Bandura (1995) emphasizes that it is the perception and interpretation of the physical and emotional states that is important rather than the states themselves. That is to say that students with high self-efficacy and with low self-efficacy may interpret the same elevation of heartbeat positively or negatively. Considering that language is learned through communication with others, teachers should be mindful of creating a space where students are encouraged to develop their emotional intelligence, the ability to observe their own and others' feelings and emotions, and to differentiate between them (Salovey & Mayer, 1990). Research also shows that teachers' self-efficacy partly determines classroom atmospheres and their actual instructional abilities. (Mills, 2011; Faez, Karas, & Uchihara, in press; see Zee & Koomen, 2016, for a review of teacher self-efficacy research).

Furthermore, some classroom approaches that can enhance self-efficacy have been suggested. One is working with project-based learning, as described in Mills (2009), while another is using motivation partnerships, as suggested by Cave, Evans, Dewey, and Hartshorn (2018). Both studies suggest that it is useful to provide opportunities for students to experience all four sources of information in the classroom interaction with their peers and teachers. However, it should be remembered that it is not the information itself that enhances self-efficacy, but rather it is the learners' cognitive processing and interpretation of the information that can affect their self-efficacy and subsequent learning behavior.

Future Directions

Looking forward, there remains much research to be done, and there are new areas to be explored for self-efficacy in language education. The range of research methods is clearly skewed to the quantitative side. It is highly desirable to expand the range of approaches. If we are to understand the role that self-efficacy plays in language acquisition, new studies need to be carefully designed using various methods to capture the complex relationship in which self-efficacy functions as a mediator rather than as a predictor or outcome. Interactions among self-efficacy and other constructs, such as task value and attributions, should be clarified. In particular, for obvious importance, it is vital to investigate its role in SRL or efficacy for SRL further (see Chapter 17) and other pertinent factors such as resilience and the use of coping strategies.

Collective efficacy and collective agency (Bandura, 1995, 2000) are both concepts that have not been extensively or empirically investigated in psychology and even less so in SLA. Collective agency is the sense of capacity to achieve something that cannot be done individually (Bandura, 1986, 2006). In both SLA and general education, this construct seems to be dealt with in connection with the teachers' community for professional development. Collective efficacy can be relevant when a language class or program is considered a community that can work together for common goals. This is an area with considerable potential to bridge research and practice. Teacher-researchers can bring benefits to all parties involved by researching in their own classrooms or possibly school-wide, including sociocultural environmental factors that are unique to the classroom, institution, local area, and society.

It is also appropriate to expand self-efficacy research as a construct from the perspective of positive psychology (Bandura, 2006) (see Chapter 5). Self-efficacy itself predates the emergence of positive psychology, yet it has started to attract attention as a construct that fits well within that perspective (Dewaele, Chen, Padilla, & Lake, 2019). It is incorporated in one of the hypotheses for Oxford's (2016) EMPATHICS vision of well-being for language learners and in the model of positive L2 self by Lake (2016). More empirical studies are needed to investigate the role of self-efficacy in the well-being of language learners and teachers (Helms-Lorenz & Maulana, 2016; Zee & Koomen, 2016).

Finally, so far, the vast majority of self-efficacy studies in SLA have been with language learners in formal education contexts. Since language learning is not limited to those who are in school, the scope must be widened to those who are learning outside of school, including older learners, online learners, and learners of a language for career development. If self-efficacy is vital to sustaining the long journey of language learning, this is all the more reason to investigate how it is experienced by those who choose to start and continue to learn a language of their own will.

Reflection Questions

- Consider your self-efficacy in learning any specific language. Can you identify the role played by information you gained from the four sources (mastery experience, vicarious experience, social persuasion, and physiological and affective states)?
- How would you go about helping students to adjust their perceptions in the case of gross overestimation and underestimation of their own capacity?
- Choose a task or skill in which you would like to investigate students' self-efficacy. What methodology would you choose and why?

Recommended Reading

Bandura, A. (1986). *Social foundations of thought and action: A social cognitive theory*. Prentice Hall.
The book provides a detailed theoretical account of social cognitive theory, including a wide range of areas of application. It is of historical importance, representing the paradigm shift in the view of human behavior from a simple combination of person and context in causal relationships to more complex reciprocal interactions in which self-efficacy plays a pivotal role.

Bandura, A. (2006). Guide for constructing self-efficacy scales. In F. Pajares & T. Urdan (Eds.), *Self-efficacy beliefs of adolescents* (Vol. 5, pp. 307–337). Information Age Publishing.
This book chapter offers excellent guidelines for those who are interested in developing a scale of self-efficacy for any tasks or skills relevant to their practice and research.

Mills, N., Pajares, F., & Herron, C. (2007). Self-efficacy of college intermediate French students: Relation to achievement and motivation. *Language Learning, 57*, 417–442.
This is a pioneering and exemplary interdisciplinary work on self-efficacy, bridging educational psychology and SLA.

References

Ahn, T. (2016). Learner agency and the use of affordances in language-exchange interactions. *Language and Intercultural Communication, 16*(2), 164–181.
Bai, B., Chao, G. C. N., & Wang, C. (2019). The relationship between social support, self-efficacy, and English language learning achievement in Hong Kong. *TESOL Quarterly, 53*, 208–221.
Bandura, A. (1977). Self-efficacy: Toward a unifying theory of behavioral change. *Psychological Review, 84*, 191–215.
Bandura, A. (1986). *Social foundations of thought and action: A social cognitive theory*. Prentice Hall.
Bandura, A. (1995). Exercise of personal and collective efficacy in changing societies. In A. Bandura (Ed.), *Self-efficacy in changing societies* (p. 1–45). Cambridge University Press.

Bandura, A. (2000). Exercise of human agency through collective efficacy. *Current Directions in Psychological Science, 9*(3), 75–78.
Bandura, A. (2001). Social cognitive theory: An agentic perspective. *Annual Review of Psychology, 52*, 1–26.
Bandura, A. (2006). Toward a psychology of human agency. *Perspectives on Psychological Science, 1*(2), 164–180.
Bandura, A. (2011). A social cognitive perspective on positive psychology. *International Journal of Social Psychology, 26*(1), 7–20.
Bandura, A. (2012). On the functional properties of perceived self-efficacy revisited. *Journal of Management, 38*, 9–44.
Blair, S. D., & Lowe, P. A. (2018). Self-efficacy. In B. B. Frey (Ed.), *The SAGE encyclopedia of educational research, measurement, and evaluation*. SAGE Publications.
Bong, M., & Skaalvik, E. M. (2003). Academic self-concept and self-efficacy: How different are they really? *Educational Psychology Review, 15*, 1–40.
Boo, Z., Dörnyei, Z., & Ryan, S. (2015). L2 motivation research 2005–2014: Understanding a publication surge and a changing landscape. *System, 55*, 145–157.
Brammerts, H. (2003). Autonomous language learning in tandem: The development of a concept. In T. Lewis, & L. Walker (eds.), *Autonomous language learning in tandem*. Academy Electronic Publications.
Carnevale, J. (2016). Self-esteem. In H. Miller (Ed.), *The SAGE encyclopedia of theory in psychology* (pp. 833–835). SAGE Publications.
Cave, P. N., Evans, N. W., Dewey, D. P, & Hartshorn, K. J. (2018). Motivational partnerships: Increasing ESL student self-efficacy. *ELT Journal, 72*(1), 83–96.
Chan, J. C. Y., & Lam, S. (2010). Effects of different evaluative feedback on students' self-efficacy in learning. *Instructional Science, 38*(1), 37–58.
Chang, L. Y.-H. (2010). Group processes and EFL learners' motivation: A study of group dynamics in EFL classrooms. *TESOL Quarterly, 44*, 129–154.
Chapman, J. W., & Tunmer, W. E. (2003). Reading difficulties, reading-related self-perceptions, and strategies for overcoming negative self-beliefs. *Reading & Writing Quarterly, 19*(1), 5–24.
Choi, E., & Lee, J. (2016). Investigating the relationship of target language proficiency and self-efficacy among nonnative EFL teachers. *System, 58*, 49–63.
Clark, J. L. (1987). *Curriculum renewal in school foreign language learning*. Oxford University Press.
Dewaele, J-M., Chen, X., Padilla, A. M., & Lake, J. (2019). The flowering of positive psychology in foreign language teaching and acquisition research. *Frontiers in Psychology, 10*, 2128.
Dörnyei, Z., & Ryan, S. (2015). *The psychology of the language learner revisited*. Routledge.
Faez, F., Karas, M., & Uchihara, T. (in press). Connecting language proficiency to teaching ability: A meta-analysis. *Language Teaching Research*.
Glackin M., & Hohenstein, J. (2018) Teachers' self-efficacy: Progressing qualitative analysis. *International Journal of Research & Method in Education, 41*(3), 271–290.
Graham, S. J., & Macaro, E. (2008). Strategy instruction in listening for lower-intermediate learners of French. *Language Learning, 58*(4), 747–783.
Helms-Lorenz, M., & Maulana, R. (2016). Influencing the psychological well-being of beginning teachers across three years of teaching: Self-efficacy, stress causes, job tension and job discontent. *Educational Psychology, 36*(3), 569–594.
Honicke, T., & Broadbent, J. (2016). The influence of academic self-efficacy on academic performance: A systematic review. *Educational Research Review, 17*, 63–84.
Kim, D.-H., Wang, C., Ahn, H. S., & Bong, M. (2015). English language learners' self-efficacy profiles and relationship with self-regulated learning strategies. *Learning and Individual Differences, 38*, 136–142.
Klassen, R. M., & Durksen, T. L. (2014). Weekly self-efficacy and work stress during the teaching practicum: A mixed methods study. *Learning and Instruction, 33*, 158–169.
Lake, J. (2016). Accentuate the positive: Conceptual and empirical development of the positive L2 self and its relationship to L2 proficiency. In P. D. MacIntyre, T. Gregersen, & S. Mercer (Eds.), *Positive psychology in SLA* (pp. 237–257). Multilingual Matters.
Li, Y., & Wang, C. (2010). An empirical study of reading self-efficacy and the use of reading strategies in the Chinese EFL Context. *Asian EFL Journal, 12*(2), 144–162.
Liao, H.-C., & Wang, Y.-H. (2018). Using comprehension strategies for students' self-efficacy, anxiety, and proficiency in reading English as a foreign language. *Social Behavior and Personality, 46*(3), 447–458.
Malmir, A., & Mohammadi, P. (2018). Teachers' reflective teaching and self-efficacy as predicators of their professional success: A case of Iranian EFL teachers. *Research in English Language Pedagogy (RELP), 6*(1), 117–138.
Mercer, S. (2011). *Towards an understanding of language learner self-concept*. Springer.
Mercer, S., & Ryan, S. (2016). Stretching the boundaries: Language learning psychology. *Palgrave Communications, 2*, 1–5.

Mills, N. (2009). A guide du routard simulation: Increasing self-efficacy in the standards through project-based learning. *Foreign Language Annals, 42*, 607–639.

Mills, N., & Péron, M. (2009). Global simulation and writing self-beliefs of college intermediate French students. *International journal of Applied Linguistics, 156*, 239–273.

Mills, N. (2011). Situated learning through social networking communities: The development of joint enterprise, mutual engagement, and a shared repertoire. *Calico Journal, 28*(2), 345.

Mills, N. (2014). Self-efficacy in second language acquisition. In S. Mercer & M. Williams (Eds.), *Multiple perspectives on the self in SLA* (pp. 6–22). Multilingual Matters.

Mills, N., Pajares, F., & Herron, C. (2007). Self-efficacy of college intermediate French students: Relation to achievement and motivation. *Language Learning, 57*, 417–442.

Murphey, T., & Arao, H. (2001). Changing reported beliefs through near peer role modelling. TESL-EJ, *5*(3), 1–15.

Oxford, R. L. (2016). Toward a psychology of well-being for language learners: The "EMPATHICS" vision. In T. Gregersen, P. MacIntyre, & S. Mercer (Eds.), *Positive psychology and language learning*. Multilingual Matters.

Pajares, F. (2002). *Self-efficacy beliefs in academic contexts: An outline*. Emory University. www.uky.edu/~eushe2/Pajares/efftalk.html

Pajares, F. (2003). Self-efficacy beliefs, motivation, and achievement in writing: A review of the literature. *Reading & Writing Quarterly: Overcoming Learning Difficulties, 19*(2), 139–158.

Phan, N. T. T., & Locke, T. (2015). Sources of self-efficacy of Vietnamese EFL teachers: A qualitative study. *Teaching and Teacher Education, 52*, 73–82.

Pietsch, J., Walker, R., & Chapman, E. (2003). The relationship among self-concept, self-efficacy, and performance in mathematics during secondary school. *Journal of Educational Psychology, 95*(3), 589–603.

Pintrich, P. R. (2000). The role of goal orientation in self-regulated learning. In M. Boekaerts, P. R. Pintrich, & M. Zeidner (Eds.), *Handbook of self-regulation* (pp. 451–502). Academic Press.

Pintrich, P. R., Smith, D. A. F., Garcia, T., & McKeachie, W. J. (1993). Reliability and predictive validity of the motivated strategies for learning questionnaire (MSLQ). *Educational and Psychological Measurement, 53*, 801–813.

Rahimi, M., & Abedi, S. (2014). The relationship between listening self-efficacy and metacognitive awareness of listening strategies. *Procedia: Social and Behavioral Sciences, 98*, 1454–1460.

Rosenberg, M. (1965). *Society and the adolescent self-image*. Princeton University Press.

Ryan, S., & Irie, K. (2014). Imagined and possible selves: Stories we tell ourselves about ourselves. In S. Mercer & M. Williams (Eds.), *Multiple perspectives on the self in SLA* (pp. 109–126). Multilingual Matters.

Salovey, P., & Mayer, J. D. (1990). Emotional intelligence. *Imagination, Cognition and Personality, 9*, 185–211.

Sardegna, V. G., Lee, J., & Kusey, C. (2018). Self-efficacy, attitudes, and choice of strategies for English pronunciation learning. *Language Learning, 68*, 83–114.

Schunk, D. H., & Pajares, F. (2004). Self-efficacy in education revisited: Empirical and applied evidence. In D. McInerny & S. van Etten (Eds.), *Big theories revisited* (pp. 115–138). Information Age Publishing.

Skaalvik, E. M., & Skaalvik, S. (2007). Dimensions of teacher self-efficacy and relations with strain factors, perceived collective teacher efficacy, and teacher burnout. *Journal of Educational Psychology, 99*(3), 611–625.

Stajkovic, A., & Sommer, S. (2000). Self-efficacy and causal attributions: Direct and reciprocal links. *Journal of Applied Social Psychology, 30*, 707–737.

Teng, L. S., Sun, P. P., & Xu, L. (2018). Conceptualizing writing self-efficacy in English as a foreign language contexts: Scale validation through structural equation modeling. *TESOL Quarterly, 52*, 911–942.

Tschannen-Moran, M., & Woolfolk Hoy, A. (2001). Teacher efficacy: Capturing an elusive construct. *Teaching and Teacher Education, 17*, 783–805.

Thompson, G. (2020). *Exploring language teacher efficacy in Japan*. Multilingual Matters.

Ushioda, E. (1996). Developing a dynamic concept of L2 motivation. In T. Hickey, & J. Williams (Eds.), *Language, education and society in a changing world* (pp. 239–245). IRAAL/Multilingual Matters.

Ushioda, E. (1998). Effective motivational thinking: A cognitive theoretical approach to the study of language learning motivation. In E. Alcón Soler, & V. Codina Espurz (Eds.), *Current issues in English language methodology* (pp. 77–89). Publicacions de la Universitat Jaume.

Ushioda, E. (2001). Language learning at university: Exploring the role of motivational thinking. In Z. Dörnyei, & R. Schmidt (Eds.), *Motivation and second language acquisition* (pp. 93–125). Second Language Teaching and Curriculum Center.

Ushioda, E. (2019). Researching L2 motivation: Past, present and future. In M. Lamb, K. Csizér, A. Henry, & S. Ryan (Eds.), *The Palgrave handbook of motivation for language learning* (pp. 661–682). Palgrave Macmillan.

Wang, C., Kim, D.-H., Bai, R., & Hu, J. (2014). Psychometric properties of a self-efficacy scale for English language learners in China. *System, 44*(1), 24–33.

Wang, C., Schwab, G., Fenn, P., & Chang, M. (2013). Self-efficacy and self-regulated learning strategies for English language learners: Comparison between Chinese and German college students. *Journal of Educational and Developmental, 3*, 173–191.

Weiner, B. (1986). *An attributional theory of motivation and emotion*. Springer-Verlag.

Wyatt, M. (2010). An English teacher's developing self-efficacy beliefs in using groupwork. *System, 38*(4), 603–613.

Zee, M., & Koomen, H. M. Y. (2016). Teacher self-efficacy and its effects on classroom processes, student academic adjustment, and teacher well-being: A synthesis of 40 years of research. *Review of Educational Research, 86*(4), 981–1015.

Zhang, X., & Ardasheva, Y. (2019). Sources of college EFL learners' self-efficacy in the English public speaking domain. *English for Specific Purposes, 53*, 47–59.

Zimmerman, B. J. (2013). From cognitive modeling to self-regulation: A social cognitive career path. *Educational Psychologist, 48*(3), 135–147.

9
PERSONALITY

Jean-Marc Dewaele

Second language teachers and researchers have long been fascinated by the idea that personality might be responsible for "success" in SLA: "The idea that particular behaviors, dictated by underlying personality dimensions, are more conducive to the learning of foreign languages seems intuitively appealing" (Dewaele, 2009, p. 625). Yet, as Dörnyei and Ryan (2015) explain, "the curious situation is that while all parties to the language learning process agree that personality factors play a significant role in successful L2 learning, there has been a major disconnect between this perception and research findings" (p. 29). Is it the perception that is misguided, the authors wonder, or do SLA researchers, for some reason, fail to explain the link? Thirty years ago, Furnham already pointed out that the difficulty facing both SLA researchers and psychologists is finding an appropriate level of analysis for both the psychological and the linguistic variables (Furnham, 1990). The difficulty has not disappeared since, because of a continuing absence of:

> parsimonious, consistent, fruitful theories described specifically for, or derived from, the personality markers of speech… the theories that do exist are frequently at an inappropriate level—too molecular in that they deal specifically with the relationship between a restricted number of selected variables or too molar in the sense that by being overinclusive they are either unverifiable or unfruitful in the extent to which they generate testable hypotheses.
>
> *Furnham, 1990, p. 92*

In the present chapter, I propose to briefly consider the field of personality psychology before focusing on five higher-order personality traits and a number of lower-order personality traits that have been shown to be relevant in SLA research. After that, I will look at research that has measured the effect of psychological variables on SLA and L2 performance. This will be followed by implications for practice and research, and then I will reverse the assumption of causality, asking to what extent the learning of new languages may shape the personality of the learner. I will conclude with a number of suggestions for further research and will point to some of the fundamental obstacles that need to be taken into account in this area of research.

Personality in Psychology

Cloninger (2009) traces the origins of the scientific field of personality back to Allport (1937). He points out that since then psychologists have adopted definitions that reflect the unique concerns of their perspective (psychodynamic, trait, learning, humanistic, cognitive, and biological). Allport himself defined personality as "the dynamic organization within the individual of those psychophysical systems that determine their unique adjustments to the environment" (p. 48). Cloninger (2009) explains that a frequent assumption in these definitions is that innate biological components are at the basis of personality, which can be shared with others or which are distinct because of heredity and other influences, and these tendencies are shaped over time by a multitude of other factors, including family and culture, which leads to "habitual behaviours, cognitions, emotional patterns, and so constitute personality" (p. 5). This suggests a dynamic rather than a static view of personality.

Psychologists, who adopt a trait perspective, suggest that traits "summarize a person's typical behavior" (Pervin & Cervone, 2010, p. 229) but can also include thought and emotion. Traits are assumed to be relatively stable over time and are contrasted with states, which are more transitory. Trait psychologists agree on a hierarchical organization of traits with five broad, orthogonal dimensions at the apex (the so-called Big Five: Extraversion versus Introversion; Neuroticism versus Emotional Stability; Conscientiousness versus Negligence; Agreeableness versus Disagreeableness and Openness-to-Experience/Intellect versus Unsophisticated) and a larger number of "lower-order" personality traits, which are often correlated with Big Five traits but also explain unique variance (Pervin & Cervone, 2010). These traits are universal; in other words, the same dimensions emerge from questionnaires around the world, independent of language and culture, after the use of factor analysis (a statistical technique) to numerous datasets with personality items (Pervin & Cervone, 2010).

Personality inventories extensively rely on self-report questionnaires in the form of Likert scales. Researchers calculate individual scores on the various dimensions. Traits are thus continuous dimensions of variability and scores are normally distributed. This means that most people are in fact in the middle of a dimension rather than at it poles. For example, there are more ambiverts than either extraverts or introverts.

Eysenck (1967) argued that personality could be best described by three dimensions: Extraversion, Neuroticism, and Psychoticism. He linked Extraversion and Neuroticism to physiological causes. Extraverts have low levels of cortical arousal and introverts have high levels, leading extraverts to seek out more stimulation (louder music and brighter lights at parties, for example) to be more gregarious and thrill-seeking. Introverts, on the other hand, avoid strong external stimulation which would push them over their optimal level. The optimal level of arousal is thus different for each person (Eysenck, 1994). The second personality trait to have a neurological cause according to Eysenck is Neuroticism, which depends on levels of arousal in the limbic system. Just as for Introversion, activation thresholds vary between individuals. People who score high on Neuroticism are thus more likely to exceed this threshold when exposed to minor stressors, whereas people at the opposite end of the dimension (Emotional Stability) will typically remain below the threshold, even when dealing with large stressors. This view is not shared by proponents of the Big Five approach, who think that people's position on the various dimensions is linked to genetics and environmental factors without any specifics (Costa & McCrae, 1992).

The first personality trait in Big Five Models is Extraversion. Extraverts have been described as being sociable, active, talkative, person-oriented, optimistic, fun-loving, assertive, and affectionate. They are gregarious and eager to engage in social interactions, driven by optimism and a love of taking physical and social risks. Introverts, on the other hand, are typically reserved, sober, aloof, thoughtful, task-oriented, retiring, and quiet (Costa & McCrae, 1985).

The second of the Big Five dimensions is Neuroticism versus Emotional Stability. Individuals who score high on this dimension are prone to psychological distress. They are worried, nervous, emotional, insecure, impulsive, feel inadequate, and are more likely to display angry hostility. Individuals on the opposite end of this dimension (emotional stability) are calm, relaxed, unemotional, hardy, secure, and self-satisfied (Costa & McCrae, 1985).

The third dimension is Conscientiousness. This refers to the degree of organization, persistence, and motivation in goal-directed behavior. Individuals who score high on conscientiousness tend to be organized, meticulous, reliable, hard-working, self-disciplined, punctual, scrupulous, neat, ambitious, and persistent. They display principled behavior guided or conforming to their own conscience. People who score low on conscientiousness tend to be aimless, unreliable, lazy, careless, lax, negligent, weak-willed, and hedonistic (Costa & McCrae, 1985). It has been associated with the dorsolateral prefrontal cortex.

The fourth dimension is Agreeableness. People who score high on this dimension are compliant, trusting, empathic, sympathetic, friendly, and have a cooperative nature (Graziano & Tobin, 2002).

The fifth dimension is Openness-to-experience, which is composed of two related but separable traits, Openness-to-experience and Intellect (DeYoung, Peterson, & Higgins, 2005). This reflects proactive seeking and appreciation of experience for its own sake as well as a willingness to explore the unfamiliar. It seems to be a good predictor of foreign language learning achievement. Individuals who score high on openness-to-experience have wide interests, and are imaginative and insightful. Those who score low on this dimension are conventional, down-to-earth, have narrow interests, and are inartistic and unanalytical (Costa & McCrae, 1985). Openness-to-experience is correlated with activity in the dorsolateral prefrontal cortex (DeYoung et al., 2005).

Social psychologists Van der Zee and Van Oudenhoven (2000) developed a Big Five personality inventory (the *Multicultural Personality Questionnaire - MPQ*) that was focused on multilingual and multicultural participants and was geared toward predictions of multicultural success compared with general personality questionnaires. It consists of 91 items with Likert scales. The first dimension is Cultural Empathy: the ability to empathize with cultural diversity and understanding feelings, beliefs and attitudes different from the ones one grew up with. The second dimension is Flexibility: the ability to learn from new experiences, adjusting behavior according to contingency, and enjoying novelty and change. The third dimension is Social Initiative, which shares characteristics with Extraversion, namely, the tendency to approach social situations actively, taking the initiative and engaging in social situations. The fourth dimension is Emotional Stability (i.e., the positive pole on the Neuroticism dimension): the tendency to remain calm in stressful situations, controlling emotional reactions. The final dimension is Openmindedness (close to Openness-to-experience): an open, unprejudiced attitude towards linguistic and cultural diversity. Even the MPQ dimensions that closely correspond with Big Five scales are more specifically focused on aspects that are relevant to multicultural experience. Cultural Empathy, for example, is quite similar to Agreeableness but also includes empathizing with and understanding the feelings of members of different cultural groups. Van der Zee, Van Oudenhoven, Ponterotto, and Fietzer (2013) examined the construct validity of the MPQ short form (40 items) and found positive and significant relationships with scales for well-being and emotional intelligence. They concluded that the short form was sufficiently reliable and showed sufficient content overlap with the original scales.

An intensely researched lower-order personality trait is Emotional Intelligence (see Chapter 14), sometimes defined as an ability (Salovey & Mayer, 1990), more frequently defined as a trait (Petrides & Furnham, 2000). It is defined as a constellation of emotional perceptions located at the lower levels of personality hierarchies. It concerns people's self-perceptions of their emotional abilities. Petrides (2017) pointed out that Trait Emotional Intelligence is the only definition that recognizes the inherent subjectivity of emotional experience. Petrides maintains that Emotional Intelligence is not a mental ability or competence (that can be trained) but a trait. It consists of fifteen facets organized under four main factors: well-being, emotionality, self-control, and sociability (Petrides, 2017). The factor well-being is characterized by the ability to feel cheerful and satisfied with life (happiness), to be self-confident (self-esteem), and to look on the bright side of life (optimism). The emotionality factor is related to the ability of taking someone else's perspective (empathy), of being clear about people's feelings (emotional perception), of communicating feelings to others (emotional expression), and of maintaining fulfilling personal relationships (relationships). The self-control factor refers to the ability to control emotions (emotional regulation), to not give in to urges (impulsiveness), and to withstand pressure and regulate stress (stress management). The final factor is sociability, and it refers to the ability to influence other people's feelings (emotional management), to stand up for one's rights (assertiveness), and to establish networks thanks to social skills (social awareness).

Tolerance/intolerance of ambiguity is a personality trait that was defined as the "tendency to perceive ambiguous situations as desirable" (Budner, 1962, p. 29). Ambiguous situations entail three characteristics: novelty, complexity, and insolubility (Budner, 1962). An ambiguous situation is thus one with which an individual is unfamiliar and requires attention to multiple cues for how to behave, some or all of which may be contradictory or conflicting in some way. Tolerance of ambiguity reflects a person's comfort with dealing with novel, unfamiliar situations in which multiple, and sometimes conflicting, cues are present. Individuals who are intolerant of ambiguity are less likely to engage with ambiguous information or stimuli (Furnham, 1994).

Anxiety has been considered as a trait (see Chapter 26), namely, a general propensity to be anxious and also as a temporary state varying in intensity. To measure these concepts, Spielberger, Gorssuch, Lushene, Vagg, and Jacobs (1983) developed the *State-Trait Anxiety Inventory*, consisting of 40 items with Likert scales that measure the strength of a person's feelings of anxiety. Trait anxiety has been defined as feelings of stress, worry, and discomfort that individuals experience across typical situations that everyone experiences on a daily basis. State anxiety has been defined as temporary fear, nervousness, discomfort, and the result of the arousal of the autonomic nervous system induced by specific situations that individuals perceive as dangerous.

Personality in SLA

Dörnyei and Ryan (2015) highlight how confused SLA researchers can feel when faced with "a plethora of personality factors that sometimes differ only in label while referring to nearly the same thing, or—which can be more confusing—have the same label while measuring different things" (p. 17). I have compared those who went in search for the Holy Grail of the psychological profile of the good language learner (myself included) to "Arthur's knights, stumbling through the night, guided by a stubborn belief that something must be there, glimpsing tantalizing flashes of light from a distance, only to discover that their discoveries looked rather pale in the daylight" (Dewaele, 2009, p. 625). The fact that findings have been relatively modest is probably linked to expectations that were (or are) unrealistic, the difficulty of carrying out solid interdisciplinary research between personality psychology and SLA, and the fact that SLA is a volitional activity that implies that learners with specific personality profiles many behave atypically, adding noise to the data. In other words, there is no psychological determinism in SLA. Having the "right" learner profile is no guarantee for successful L2 learning or achievement (Dewaele, 2012).

I have reported how random events can trigger a sudden desire or motivation to learn a new language, independent of the personality of the learner (Dewaele, 2013a, p. 9). The fictional character Raimund Gregorius, in Pascal Mercier's wonderful philosophical-linguistic book *Night Train to Lisbon* (2008), is a bilingual Swiss-German teacher of Latin, ancient Greek, and Hebrew with little interest in modern languages, who, one morning on his way to school in Bern, comes across a mysterious woman who is about to jump off a bridge. He convinces her to come down and to accompany him to class. Chatting in French, he discovers that she is a native speaker of Portuguese. The word "Português" acts as trigger: "The *o* she pronounced surprisingly as a *u*; the rising, strangely constrained lightness of the *e* and the soft *sh* at the end came together in a melody that sounded much longer than it really was, and he could have listened to all day long" (Mercier, 2008, p. 7). His passion for Portuguese starts right there and transforms his personality. The grumpy teacher who preferred the silence of dead languages discovers language desire, investment, a high motivation, combined with a social and geographical displacement (the journey to Lisbon). He learns to control his communicative anxiety in Portuguese and becomes both braver and wiser. The enthusiasm at his new-found linguistic skills connects him with the world and alters his sense of self.

Given the complex interaction of personality variables of language learners with dynamic socio-educational contexts, it becomes very difficult to isolate the effect of personality among the cognitive, social, and situational variables that contribute to SLA and L2 production (Dörnyei & Ryan, 2015). Indeed, the effect of some personality traits can remain hidden in some situations or tasks, but may reveal itself in other circumstances. My own research, for example, has shown that while extraverts and introverts are roughly undistinguishable in terms of fluency in a relaxed conversation in the L2, the introverts' fluency drops significantly in a more stressful oral exam situation (Dewaele & Furnham, 1999).

Integration of Psychological Concepts in SLA Research

Ehrman (2008) is one the main studies in SLA to have delved into the psychological profile of "good" language learners. Her 62 learners had obtained the highest level (i.e., "full professional proficiency, with few if any limitations on the person's ability to function in the language and culture" (p. 64) on an oral interview test. They were selected from a group of 3000 learners and thus represent "the true elite of good language learners" (p. 61). She used the *Myers-Briggs Type Indicator* (MBTI) to establish personality types. There are four scales—extraversion–introversion, sensing–intuition, thinking–feeling, judging–perceiving—combining into sixteen possible four-letter types. Since these variables are nominal, she used crosstabs analyses to determine which personality type was most frequent. She found that INTJ types (introverted–intuitive–thinking–judging) were the most frequent in her sample (p. 64), leading her to conclude that "the best language learners tend to have introverted personalities, a finding which runs contrary to much of the literature, and, even, to pedagogical intuition. The best learners are intuitive and they are logical and precise thinkers who are able to exercise judgment" (Ehrman, 2008, p. 70).

Extraversion has been the first choice of SLA teachers and researchers for its potential effect on SLA. They felt intuitively that the more talkative, gregarious extravert learners would have an edge over their more introverted peers. Unfortunately, research on the role of extraversion in SLA got off on the wrong foot, with an influential and partially flawed study by Naiman, Fröhlich, Stern, and Todesco (1978) on personality and language learning. The authors expected that the more extraverted of their Canadian secondary school students learning French as an L2 would score higher on a Listening Test of French Achievement and an Imitation Test. When no significant relationship emerged, the authors questioned the independent variable, namely the construct validity of the *Eysenck Personality Inventory* which was used to measure extraversion (Naiman et al., 1978, p. 67) rather than questioning the adequacy of their dependent variables. Their widely publicized result turned applied linguists away from personality and Extraversion in particular. Dewaele and Furnham (1999) lamented that Extraversion had unjustly become an "unloved" variable in SLA research. They suggested that test results and written language were less likely to correlate with Extraversion than linguistic variables that reflected oral language. Indeed, extraverts have been found to be typically more fluent in oral L2 production, with higher speech rates, fewer disfluencies, lower values of lexical richness, more implicit/deictical speech styles, and shorter utterances than the introverts (Dewaele & Furnham, 2000; Wakamoto, 2009). Extraversion was not significantly linked to morpholexical accuracy rates, meaning that extraverts were not necessarily "better" language learners. The effect of extraversion was stronger in a formal conversation during an oral exam rather than in informal classroom conversations. Dewaele and Furnham (2000) argued that these differences are linked to the increased cognitive load that L2 production entails. In contrast, L1 production is more automatic and requires less Short Term Memory capacity. Because introvert L2 users have less STM capacity, it causes a slowdown in processing and in fluency. Extravert L2 users are more stress resistant and have more Short Term Memory capacity, which means they experience less disruption in L2 processing in stressful formal situations, and are able to remain flexible and fluent. To reach the optimal level of arousal, introverts prefer quiet familiar learning environments while extraverts prefer something more stimulating. This was demonstrated in MacIntyre, Clément, and Noels's (2007) study of the interaction between learning situation and extraversion on vocabulary test scores of Canadian French L2 learners. The introverts performed best after having studied in a very familiar situation, while the extraverts performed best in a situation that involved a moderate degree of novelty (2007, p. 296). MacIntyre and Charos (1996) found that introversion was linked to L2 anxiety among their 92 Anglo-Canadian students of French. A similar pattern was observed in Dewaele and MacIntyre (2019), who investigated the link between personality traits and FLCA (as well as FL enjoyment) among 750 FL learners from around the world. Social Initiative was found to be a strong negative predictor of FLCA (explaining 16 percent of variance) and a positive predictor of FL Enjoyment (9 percent of variance).

Neuroticism and anxiety have been linked to foreign language (classroom) anxiety (FLCA), defined by Horwitz (2017) as a

> specific anxiety[y] [that has] characteristics of both trait and state anxieties. When individuals experience Language Anxiety, they have the trait of feeling state anxiety when participating in language learning and/or use. It is also likely that individuals who experience Language Anxiety would feel anxious simply thinking about language learning and/or use.
>
> *p. 33*

No direct relationship was found between Neuroticism and Flemish students' foreign language grades (Dewaele, 2009). MacIntyre and Charos (1996) found that Neuroticism was negatively linked to integrativeness, which the authors interpret as an unwillingness to engage with members of the L2 community, possibly because their own anxiety is interpreted as evidence that something about the target language community makes them nervous. Dewaele (2013b) investigated the link between Eysenck's three global personality traits (Psychoticism, Extraversion, and Neuroticism) and levels of FLCA in the second (L2), third (L3), and fourth (L4) language of a group of 86 students from London, and a second group of 62 students from Mallorca who were all were studying at least two foreign languages. Correlation analyses revealed a significant positive link between Neuroticism and FLCA in the L2 and L3 of both groups. In other words, Neuroticism and FLCA shared between 9 percent and 25 percent of variance, which can be described as small to moderate effect sizes. Dewaele and Al Saraj (2015) investigated the link between Neuroticism and FLCA among 348 Arabic learners of English in the Arab world. They found that FLCA was significantly and negatively correlated with Emotional Stability (the positive end of the Neuroticism dimension), sharing 21.1 percent of variance. Muehlfeld, Urbig, Van Witteloostuijn, and Garagalianou (2016) established a significant link between FLA in English L2 and Emotionality (which includes trait anxiety) among 320 adult Dutch L1 speakers (10 percent of shared variance). Tests of discriminant validity showed that trait anxiety was psychometrically distinct from FLA. Dewaele and MacIntyre's (2019) investigation showed that Neuroticism was the strongest predictor of FLCA (explaining 28 percent of variance). Thematic analysis of participants' descriptions of classroom episodes in which they had experienced intense FLCA showed that the most frequent cause of FLCA was the self in the social context of the classroom.

British FL learners of French who scored high on Conscientiousness have been found to be more likely to complete the course successfully than peers who scored low in this dimension (Wilson, 2008). Ehrman's (2008) description of her exceptional FL learners combining high scores on intuition and thinking corresponds to high Conscientiousness. These learners are merciless with themselves, working hard to gain mastery of the FL. They develop long-term metacognitive strategies (goal-setting, self-assessment, self-monitoring) to progress quickly and strive to be accurate in vocabulary use, idiomatic expressions, and grammar rules (2008).

Openness-to-experience/intellect has been found to be linked to perceived competence in French L2 (MacIntyre & Charos, 1996). Ehrman (2008) pointed out that openness to experience is linked to intuition. FL learners with high scores on this dimension "concentrate on meaning, possibilities, and usually accept constant change" (p. 66). They love to discover hidden patterns, are excellent readers, and can pick up L1-like ways of self-expression (2008). Openmindedness was also found to be a predictor of FL Enjoyment in Dewaele and MacIntyre (2019), explaining 10 percent of variance.

Agreeableness was one of the factors included in MacIntyre and Charos (1996) and was found to predict Willingness to Communicate in the L2. In other words, being pleasant increases the chances of wanting to have pleasant interactions with users of the L2.

Trait Emotional Intelligence has been linked to a number of positive outcomes in SLA. Ożańska-Ponikwia (2013) found that among her sample of 107 Poles who had settled in the UK and Ireland, those who scored high on TEI were more likely to engage in conversations in English L2. One possible explanation is that they suffered less from FLCA and were more confident about their ability to use the L2. Such results emerged from the analysis of an international sample of 465 multilinguals from around the world (Dewaele, Petrides, & Furnham, 2008). High TEI multilinguals reported lower levels of anxiety when speaking their various languages, including their L1, which the authors attributed to their better ability to gauge the emotional state of their interlocutor. Similarly, Shao, Yu, and Ji (2013) also found that 510 Chinese EFL learners who scored high on TEI generally experienced a lower level of FLCA, and scored higher on English achievement and self-rated English proficiency. Li (2019) found that those of her 1307 Chinese EFL students who scored higher on TEI reported experience more FL Enjoyment and less FLCA. She also discovered that TEI and L2 learning achievement is partially mediated by FLCA and FL enjoyment. Li and Xu (2019) confirmed this relationship in a database of 1718 Chinese EFL high school students. Similarly, Resnik and Dewaele (2020) found positive relationships between TEI and Enjoyment in both German L1 and EFL classes of 768 secondary- and tertiary-level students. Resnik and Dewaele (2021) found a similar pattern in both in-person and online EFL classes of 510 European tertiary-level students. Choosing a qualitative approach, Gregersen, MacIntyre, Finegan, Talbot, and Claman (2014) observed spontaneous displays of EI on one FL learner and one pre-service FL teacher, to see how they mobilized aspects of their EI, such as awareness and regulation of their own emotions.

Second Language Tolerance of Ambiguity (SLTA) is an advantage in SLA because learners who are comfortable with uncertainty are more likely to try out their guesses and accept that "change is an integral part of the language learning process" (Rubin, 2008, p. 11). Ely (1989) and Ehrman and Oxford (1990) defined SLTA as a cognitive style. Using the *Myers-Briggs Type Inventory* (MBTI), Ehrman and Oxford (1990) suggested that sensers, judgers and thinkers have less SLTA than intuitive, perceiving, and feeling types, respectively (p. 319). Oxford and Ehrman (1992) argue that learners who have higher SLTA have a better risk-taking ability, guessing meaning based on background knowledge, which is useful and helpful in SLA. The authors point out that risk-avoiding behavior to avoid self-criticism or anticipated criticism from others may restrict language practice. Doughty, Campbell, Mislevy, Bunting, Bowles, & Koeth (2010) argued that learners who score high on SLTA may have a superior ability to retain incongruous fragments of input in memory, which may become important later on in the learning process. Learners with moderate to high levels of SLTA are more likely to persist in SLA (Ely, 1989). Ely (1995) summed up the advantages that the learner with moderate to high levels of SLTA has, being

> neither inhibited by low tolerance of ambiguity nor oblivious to linguistic subtleties. The student who is aware of, but not threatened by, linguistic differentiation, and who treats it as an occasion for introspection, experimentation and, ultimately, learning, is the one for whom tolerance of ambiguity will be a help, not a hindrance.
>
> *p. 93*

Dewaele and Shan Ip (2013) used an online survey to collect data from 73 secondary school EFL students in Hong Kong. They found that students with higher SLTA were less anxious in their EFL classes and they also felt more proficient.

To conclude, SLA researchers have gained a better understanding of psychological dimensions that might affect learner progress and performance and they have also adjusted their expectations about their explanatory power. It has become clear that just as there is no established psychological profile of millionaires, there is no neat psychological profile of the successful second language learner.

Implications for Practice and Research

The implications of research on personality and SLA are relatively limited for practice in language education. There are two main reasons for this: Firstly, any language class will consist of learners with unique profiles. Some will be talkative extraverts; others will be silent, shy, and anxious introverts. It would be absurd to create groups on the basis of personality dimensions for three main reasons: (a) Most students would have a score in the middle of dimensions so how would they have to be grouped?; (b) It would be impossible to decide on the dimensions to select for constituting different groups; and (c) It would be a highly ideological and logistical nightmare to organize. The only thing that teachers can draw from the literature on personality in SLA is the realization that different learners have different personality profiles that the teacher may be required to accommodate individually in interactions with students, depending on their profile. Crucially, all learners have the potential to make good progress. Teachers thus need to create a safe place, with a positive emotional atmosphere, where all students feel they belong, and where all get the opportunity to try out their new language skills with sufficient encouragement from teacher and peers (Dewaele & MacIntyre, 2019).

Secondly, because personality traits are quite stable, there is nothing the teacher can do to change this (See however, Moyer, 2021). In other words, a highly talkative student might be told to allow a less talkative peer to participate in the discussion, but there is no magic formula to transform the personality of learners. I remember how during my time as a French L2 teacher, I sometimes had anxious students who stuttered. Having established group solidarity, I would appeal to students in the middle of a heated debate to be quiet for a moment, to allow the anxious student to express an opinion and hence participate, however briefly, in the group interaction. This worked well because it was understood that fairness, inclusiveness, and collaboration was at the heart of the language learning journey.

Some lessons for research can be drawn from the literature review so far. The dominant view in psychology and much of SLA research on individual differences is that personality predicts students' learning and acquisition of new languages. In other words, personality is seen as the cause of learner behavior. I have argued that causality could in fact be bi-directional (Dewaele & Van Oudenhoven, 2009). In other words, the number of languages a person has acquired—or is in the process of acquiring—and the level of mastery attained in these different languages may very well shape their personality. Research suggests that this is indeed the case (for an overview see Dewaele & Botes, 2020). Of the four studies that used the *Multilingual Personality Questionnaire*, all reported a positive link between the degree of multilingualism and Openmindedness, two reported a positive relationship between multilingualism and Social Initiative, one reported a positive link between multilingualism and Flexibility, and one found a positive link between multilingualism and Cultural Empathy. The link between multilingualism and Emotional Stability is less straightforward, with one study finding a positive link, the other a negative link. Dewaele and Botes (2020) pointed out that the consistent positive relationship between multilingualism and Openmindedness is no coincidence as it a trait that shares characteristics with the lower-order trait Tolerance of Ambiguity—on which people knowing more languages also score higher (Dewaele & Li, 2013; Van Compernolle, 2016; Wei & Hu, 2018)—and with Social Flexibility (Ikizer & Ramírez-Esparza, 2017). In other words,

> multilinguals know from very early on that their own linguistic, cultural values, and practices may not be shared by the people with whom they interact. The awareness and the interest

in these differences could lead to self-reflection and ultimately to acceptance that different people may have different values.

Dewaele & Botes, 2020, p. 820

Interestingly, no significant relationships have been uncovered between multilingualism and Trait Emotional Intelligence (Dewaele, 2021), but knowing more languages was linked to lower levels of anxiety in all the languages (Dewaele, Petrides, & Furnham, 2008). Finally, Tracy-Ventura, Dewaele, Köylü, and McManus (2016) found that the personality profile of 58 British undergraduate students changed after spending a year abroad. The researchers collected data through the *Multilingual Personality Questionnaire* pre-departure and post-return. Reflective interviews were also conducted on return to investigate whether students noted any personality changes. Participants were found to score significantly higher on Emotional Stability. More than three-quarters of participants confirmed that they felt more confident after their residence abroad, not just in the L2 but in their lives in general.

Future Directions

One of the intriguing questions is why there has not been more research published on personality and SLA. A possible answer is that a lot of studies did not lead to publication because the relationships between psychological and linguistic variables were too weak. The authors may have decided against submitting the paper to a (good) journal, or they may have tried and failed because editors and reviewers are typically less interested in null result papers. Another reason is that higher-order personality traits that may have significant relationships with a linguistic variable typically explain (very) small amounts of variance. The reason for this is probably the fact that the relationship is mediated by a number of intermediate variables and diluted by confounding variables. As Dörnyei and Ryan (2015) point out, "the relationship between personality factors and learning achievement is often not direct and linear but indirect as it is mediated by various modifying variables" (p. 27).

A particular psychological dimension may only have an effect when the learner is performing an activity in a specific modality, in a specific situation, and at a specific moment. In other words, no effect might be detected in written speech, when the learner feels comfortable surrounded by friendly peers and a supportive teacher, performing a satisfying task at a moment of feeling fully engaged and motivated. Any variation in the intensity and/or alignment of independent variables could reduce the effect of a psychological variable. Also, because the emerging linguistic system and the emotions of the learner are in a permanent state of flux, it is very hard to measure exactly what has an in/direct effect on what, at any specific point of time as it is difficult to measure the learner's unpredictable volition. That is also why personality variables have relatively limited predictive value in SLA. So many potentially important variables fall outside the inevitably narrow window of research designs. Metaphorically, the SLA researcher could be compared to an astronomer gazing at the night sky from behind a porthole window. It is therefore important to abandon simplistic research designs (Dörnyei & Ryan, 2015, p. 27) and exaggerated expectations. Qualitative approaches can do more justice to the richness and the complexity of the phenomena, but they do not allow generalization. Ideally, they need to be combined with a quantitative component, offering SLA researchers binocular vision of the glittering stars and meteor showers outside their porthole window (Dewaele, 2019b).

Reflection Questions

- Does the fact that learners have their own unique personality profile mean that they cannot enjoy the same classroom activities to the same extent?
- Could you develop a mixed-methods research design to focus on the effects of a single personality dimension on a linguistic variable in an L2?

- To what extent is the field of personality and SLA research constrained by the instruments used to measure personality and linguistic performance or progress?

Recommended Reading

Dörnyei, Z. (2009). *The Psychology of Second Language Acquisition*. Oxford University Press.
This is the original book that brought an excellent overview of the main psychological areas and theories in SLA research. Dörnyei includes psycholinguistic and neuropsychological topics including neuroimaging, the role of explicit/implicit learning and memory, the distinction between procedural and declarative knowledge, individual differences including personality traits, the critical period hypothesis, and educational psychology.

Dörnyei, Z., & Ryan, S. (2015). *The Psychology of the Language Learner Revisited*. Routledge.
This is the revised edition of the original book and is by far the best source in the field. The authors explain that the concept of individual differences had evolved fundamentally since the first edition, moving away from a "classic," static definition to a more dynamic conception inspired by the Complex Dynamic Systems Approach: "the study of individual differences is in a theoretical turmoil, with powerful arguments suggesting that individual differences do not exist as such and also that they do" (p. xiii). They also devote more attention to the role of emotions in SLA.

Norton, B., & Toohey, K. (2001). Changing perspectives on good language learners. *TESOL Quarterly, 35*(2), 307–322.
In this Forum piece, the authors criticize the traditional "modernist" conception of the profile of the good language learner in the late twentieth century and defend a sociocultural and poststructural approach that privileges case studies. It stands in marked contrast with the views of the social psychological paradigm in SLA research.

References

Allport, G. W. (1937). *Personality: A psychological interpretation*. H. Holt.
Budner, S. (1962). Intolerance of ambiguity as a personality variable. *Journal of Personality, 30*(1), 29–50.
Cloninger, S. (2009). Conceptual issues in personality theory. In P. J. Corr & G. Matthews (Eds.), *The Cambridge handbook of personality psychology* (pp. 3–26). Cambridge University Press.
Costa, P. T., & McCrae, R. R. (1985). *The NEO personality inventory manual*. Psychological Assessment Resources.
Costa, P. T., & McCrae, R. R. (1992). Four ways five factors are basic. *Personality and Individual Differences, 13*(6), 653–665.
Dewaele, J.-M. (2009). Individual differences in Second Language Acquisition. In W. C. Ritchie & T. K. Bhatia (Eds.), *The new handbook of Second Language Acquisition* (pp. 623–646). Emerald.
Dewaele, J.-M. (2012). Personality traits as independent and dependent variables. In S. Mercer, S. Ryan, & M. Williams (Eds.), *Psychology for language learning: Insights from research, theory and practice* (pp. 42–58). Palgrave Macmillan.
Dewaele, J.-M. (2013a). *Emotions in multiple languages* (2nd ed.). Palgrave-MacMillan.
Dewaele, J.-M. (2013b). The link between Foreign Language Classroom Anxiety and Psychoticism, Extraversion, and Neuroticism among adult bi- and multilinguals. *The Modern Language Journal, 97*(3), 670–684.
Dewaele, J.-M. (2019). The vital need for ontological, epistemological and methodological diversity in applied linguistics. In C. Wright, L. Harvey, & J. Simpson (Eds.), *Voices and practices in applied linguistics: Diversifying a discipline* (pp. 71–88). White Rose University Press.
Dewaele, J.-M. (2021). Multilingualism and Trait Emotional Intelligence: An exploratory investigation. *International Journal of Multilingualism, 18*(3), 331–351.
Dewaele, J.-M., & Al Saraj, T. (2015). Foreign Language Classroom Anxiety of Arab learners of English: The effect of personality, linguistic and sociobiographical variables. *Studies in Second Language Learning and Teaching, 5*, 205–230.
Dewaele, J.-M., & Botes, E. (2020). Does multilingualism shape personality? An exploratory investigation. *International Journal of Bilingualism, 24*(4), 811–823.

Dewaele, J.-M. & Furnham, A. (1999). Extraversion: The unloved variable in applied linguistic research. *Language Learning, 49*(3), 509–544.

Dewaele, J.-M. & Furnham, A. (2000). Personality and speech production: A pilot study of second language learners. *Personality and Individual Differences, 28*, 355–365.

Dewaele, J.-M., & Li, W. (2013). Is multilingualism linked to a higher tolerance of ambiguity? *Bilingualism: Language and Cognition, 16*(1), 231–240.

Dewaele, J.-M., & MacIntyre, P. D. (2019). The predictive power of multicultural personality traits, learner and teacher variables on foreign language enjoyment and anxiety. In M. Sato & S. Loewen (Eds.), *Evidence-based second language pedagogy: A collection of Instructed Second Language Acquisition studies* (pp. 263–286). Routledge.

Dewaele, J.-M., Petrides, K.V., & Furnham, A. (2008). The effects of trait emotional intelligence and sociobiographical variables on communicative anxiety and foreign language anxiety among adult multilinguals: A review and empirical investigation. *Language Learning, 58*(4), 911–960.

Dewaele, J.-M., & Shan Ip, T. (2013). The link between Foreign Language Classroom Anxiety, Second Language Tolerance of Ambiguity and self-rated English proficiency among Chinese learners. *Studies in Second Language Learning and Teaching, 3*(1), 47–66.

Dewaele, J.-M., & Van Oudenhoven, J. P. (2009). The effect of multilingualism/multiculturalism on personality: No gain without pain for third culture kids? *International Journal of Multilingualism, 6*(4), 443–459.

DeYoung, C. G., Peterson, J. B., & Higgins, D. M. (2005). Sources of openness/intellect: cognitive and neuropsychological correlates of the fifth factor of personality. *Journal of Personality, 73*(4), 825–58.

Dörnyei, Z., & Ryan, S. (2015). *The psychology of the language learner revisited*. Routledge.

Doughty, C. J., Campbell, S. G., Mislevy, M. A., Bunting, M. F., Bowles, A. R., & Koeth, J. T. (2010). Predicting near-native ability: The factor structure and reliability of Hi-LAB. In M. T. Prior, Y. Watanabe, & S.-K. Lee (Eds.), *Selected proceedings of the 2008 Second Language Research Forum: Exploring SLA perspectives, positions, and practices* (pp. 10–31). Cascadilla.

Ehrman, M. (2008). Personality and the good language learner. In C. Griffiths (Ed.), *Lessons from the good language learner* (pp. 61–72). Cambridge University Press.

Ehrman, M., & Oxford, R. (1990). Adult language learning styles and strategies in an intensive training setting. *The Modern Language Journal, 74*(3), 311–327.

Ely, C. M. (1989). Tolerance of ambiguity and use of second language strategies. *Foreign Language Annals, 22*, 437–446.

Ely, C. M. (1995). Tolerance of ambiguity and the teaching of ESL. In J. M. Reid (Ed.), *Learning styles in the ESL/EFL classroom* (pp. 216–217). Heinle & Heinle.

Eysenck, H. J. (1967). *The biological basis of personality*. Thomas.

Eysenck, H. J. (1994). Creativity and personality: Word association, origence, and psychoticism. *Creativity Research Journal, 7*(2), 209–216.

Furnham, A. (1990). Language and personality. In H. Giles & W. P. Robinson (Eds.), *Handbook of language and social psychology* (pp. 73–95). John Wiley & Sons.

Furnham, A. (1994). A content, correlational and factoranalytic study of 4 Tolerance of Ambiguity questionnaires. *Personality and Individual Differences, 16*, 403–410.

Graziano, W. G., & Tobin, R. M. (2002). Agreeableness: Dimension of personality or social desirability artifact? *Journal of Personality, 70*(5), 695–727.

Gregersen, T., MacIntyre, P. D., Finegan, K. H., Talbot, K., & Claman, S. (2014). Examining emotional intelligence within the context of positive psychology interventions. *Studies in Second Language Learning and Teaching, 4*(2), 327–353.

Horwitz, E. K. (2017). On the misreading of Horwitz, Horwitz, and Cope (1986) and the need to balance anxiety research and the experiences of anxious language learners. In C. Gkonou, M. Daubney & J.-M. Dewaele (Eds.), *New insights into language anxiety: Theory, research and educational implications* (pp. 31–47). Multilingual Matters.

Ikizer, E. G., & Ramírez-Esparza, N. (2017). Bilinguals' social flexibility. *Bilingualism: Language and Cognition, 21*(5), 957–969.

Li, C. (2020). A Positive Psychology perspective on Chinese EFL Students' Trait Emotional Intelligence, Foreign Language Enjoyment and EFL learning achievement. *Journal of Multilingual and Multicultural Development, 41*(3), 246–263.

Li, C., & Xu, J. (2019). Trait Emotional Intelligence and classroom emotions: A Positive Psychology investigation and intervention among Chinese EFL Learners. *Frontiers in Psychology. Language Sciences*.

MacIntyre, P. D., & Charos, C. (1996). Personality, attitudes, and affect as predictors of second language communication. *Journal of Language and Social Psychology, 15*, 3–26.

MacIntyre, P. D., Clément, R., & Noels, K. A. (2007). Affective variables, attitude and personality in context. In D. Ayoun (Ed.), *Handbook of French applied linguistics* (pp. 270–298). John Benjamins.

Mercier, P. (2008). *Night train to Lisbon*. Grove Press.

Moyer, A. (2021). *The gifted language learner. A case of nature of nurture?* Cambridge University Press.
Muehlfeld, K., Urbig, D., Van Witteloostuijn, A., & Garagalianou, V. (2016). Foreign language anxiety in professional contexts. A short scale and evidence of personality and gender differences. *Schmalenbach Business Review*, *17*(2), 195–223.
Naiman, N., Fröhlich, M., & Stern, H. H. (1978). *The Good Language Learner: A Report.* Toronto: Ontario Institute for Studies in Education.
Oxford, R., & Ehrman, M. (1992). Second language research on individual differences. *Annual Review of Applied Linguistics*, *13*, 188–205.
Ożańska-Ponikwia, K. (2013). *Emotions from a bilingual point of view. Personality and emotional intelligence in relation to perception and expression of emotions in the L1 and L2.* Cambridge Scholars.
Pervin, L. A., & Cervone, D. (2010). *Personality: Theory and research* (11th ed.). John Wiley & Sons.
Petrides, K. V. (2017). Intelligence, emotional. *Reference module in neuroscience and biobehavioral psychology*.
Petrides, K. V. (2000). On the dimensional structure of emotional intelligence. *Personality and Individual Differences*, *29*, 313–320.
Resnik, P., & Dewaele, J.-M. (2020). Trait emotional intelligence, anxiety and enjoyment in first and foreign language classes. *System*, *94*.
Resnik, P., & Dewaele, J.-M. (2021). Learner emotions, autonomy and trait emotional intelligence in "in-person" versus emergency remote English Foreign Teaching in Europe. *Applied Linguistics Review*.
Rubin, J. (2008). Reflections. In C. Griffiths (Ed.), *Lessons from good language learners* (pp. 10–15). Cambridge University Press.
Salovey, P., Mayer, J. (1990). Emotional intelligence. *Imagination, Cognition and Personality*, *9*(3), 185–211.
Shao, K., Yu, W., & Ji, Z. (2013). An exploration of Chinese EFL students' emotional intelligence and foreign language anxiety. *Modern Language Journal*, *97*(4), 917–929.
Spielberger, C. D., Gorssuch, R. L., Lushene, P. R., Vagg, P. R., & Jacobs, G. A. (1983). *Manual for the state-trait anxiety inventory.* Consulting Psychologists Press.
Tracy-Ventura, N., Dewaele, J.-M., Köylü, Z., & McManus, K. (2016). Personality changes after a year abroad? A mixed-methods study. *Study Abroad Research in Second Language Acquisition and International Education*, *1*(1), 107–126.
Van Compernolle, R. A. (2016). Are multilingualism, tolerance of ambiguity, and attitudes toward linguistic variation related? *International Journal of Multilingualism*, *13*(1), 61–73.
Van der Zee, K. I., & Van Oudenhoven, J. P. (2000). The Multicultural Personality Questionnaire: A multicultural instrument for multicultural effectiveness. *European Journal of Personality*, *14*, 291–309.
Van der Zee, K., Van Oudenhoven, J. P., Ponterotto, J. G., & Fietzer, A. W. (2013). Multicultural personality questionnaire: Development of a short form. *Journal of Personality Assessment*, *95*(1), 118–124.
Wakamoto, N. (2009). *Extroversion/introversion in foreign language learning: Interactions with learner strategy use.* Peter Lang.
Wei, R., & Hu, Y. (2018). Exploring the relationship between multilingualism and tolerance of ambiguity: A survey study from an EFL context. *Bilingualism: Language and Cognition*, *22*(5), 1209–1219.
Wilson, R. (2008). *"Another language is another soul": Individual differences in the presentation of self in a foreign language* [Unpublished PhD dissertation]. University of London.

10
MOTIVATION

Christine Muir

Understanding motivation is central to understanding the way in which we interact with both each other and with the world around us. Motivation—or lack of motivation—influences the goals that we choose to work towards and the choices that we make. It impacts the level of effort that we invest in goal striving, and the length of time and the intensity of our persistence in following up these choices. In mainstream psychology, considerable work into the study of motivation can be found across diverse subdisciplines, including cognitive psychology (see Chapter 1), social psychology, and educational psychology. A dedicated line of research investigating motivation specifically in the context of language learning (LLing) has followed a unique developmental trajectory and, as a result, has evolved into a distinct subdiscipline; there are no comparable fields of research investigating motivation in the context of other educational subject domains (Lamb, Csizér, Henry, & Ryan, 2019).

There are areas of both convergence and divergence in the research histories of mainstream motivational psychology and LLing. Sometimes the changing emphases and areas of interest have occurred nearly in parallel, particularly in more recent decades. At other times, developments in thinking have occurred out of step with each other. A good example of this is the "cognitive revolution" witnessed in mainstream motivational psychology around the start of the second half of the twentieth century, but not identifiable in the context of LLing until the 1990s. However, it has not always been the case that LLing motivation research has aligned itself with the dominant concerns in mainstream psychology. As Dörnyei and Ushioda (2011) have noted, social-contextual perspectives central to the genesis of the field of LLing motivation research only emerged much later as a core site for investigation elsewhere.

Research into motivation in the context of LLing has a relatively short history, emerging as a novel site for investigation in the 1960s. However, what is remarkable about this short history has been its continued voracity (Boo, Dörnyei, & Ryan, 2015). Since Gardner and Lambert's 1959 article "Motivational variables in second language acquisition," widely considered as the genesis of motivation research in the context of LLing, Lamb et al. note the remarkable fact that, "at no stage in its history has the field shown signs of stagnation" (2019, p. 12). The field is instead characterized "by seemingly unceasing theoretical and methodological innovation, and by inventive proposals for pedagogical interventions" (Lamb et al., 2019, p. 12). As an inherently *applied* discipline, theoretical innovation and pedagogical relevance vie for attention.

I begin this chapter with an overview of the ways motivation has been defined in both mainstream psychology and in the context of LLing, before going on to overview theories and approaches that have integrated the two fields. Also foregrounded here are several motivation constructs developed in the context of LLing that do not have direct parallels in mainstream motivational psychology. The chapter continues by highlighting specific implications for practice and research, concluding by highlighting key directions for future work and by offering a curated set of reflection questions and recommendations for further reading.

Motivation in Psychology

Providing a clear definition of "motivation" is not a straightforward task. As Weiner encapsulates: "The most encompassing definition of the subject matter of the field of motivation is *why human and sub-human organisms think and behave as they do*" (Weiner, 1992, p. 1). Weiner goes on to reflect:

> Motivational psychologists therefore observe and measure what the individual is doing, or *choice* behavior; how long it takes before the individual initiates that activity when given the opportunity, or the *latency* of behavior; and how hard the individual is working at that activity, or the *intensity* of behavior; what length of time the individual will remain at that activity, or the *persistence* of behavior; and what the individual is feeing before, during, or after the behavioral episode, or *emotional* reactions.
>
> *1992, p. 2*

Reduced to its most fundamental principle, motivational psychologists are interested in understanding the *whys* of human behavior (Weiner, 1992).

The single term "motivation" belies the fact that research encompasses a multitude of interrelated lines of inquiry, with each distinct line of research seeking to gain understanding into this complex phenomenon from discrete approaches and perspectives. In their introduction to *The Cambridge Handbook of Motivation and Learning*, Hidi and Renninger (2019) describe some of the avenues that motivation researchers have followed:

> Historically, research on motivation explores conscious as well as unconscious (implicit) responses to social and cultural circumstances, the will to engage (connect, participate), the influence of feelings about the self (self-concept, self-efficacy) and the work needed to address those feelings (self-regulation, self-motivation). It includes whether and when information search, rewards, incentives, or choice are operative, as well as the contributions of interest and internal motivation, curiosity and boredom, and goals and values.
>
> *2019, p. 1*

Throughout its formative years, research in the field was governed by behaviorist ideas and principles, and this view retained its dominance throughout much of the twentieth century. This perspective foregrounded the importance of *environment* in shaping action, largely excluding consideration of any internal processes that may account for it. This "*black box* thinking," to use Ryan's turn of phrase (Ryan, 2019b, p. 4), describes a system that "is analyzed exclusively in terms of its inputs and outputs" (Ryan, 2019b, p. 4). Many of the ideas and research strands continuing to dominate to this day have their roots in the trajectories that emerged during the following "cognitive revolution," which questioned the predominance of behaviorist perspectives, and was concerned instead with "cognitive mediators between environmental inputs and behavioural outputs" (Ryan, 2019b, p. 4).

The field has since moved on to incorporate various phenomenological and experiential phenomena such as flow, interest, and curiosity (see Ryan, 2019a). Focus has also widened from looking purely to psychological constructs in search of understanding, to embracing the investigation of various physiological and biological mechanisms mediating the relationship between behavior and environment (for example, the growing interest in motivational neuroscience; Reeve & Lee, 2019). Ryan concludes: "In the early twenty-first century, empirical research is, it appears, resoundingly focused on what is inside the black box. We have travelled beyond mere functionalism to a science that has explanatory power, depth, and consilience" (Ryan, 2019b, p. 6).

Motivation in SLA

The definition of motivation arguably most commonly cited in the context of LLing is that put forward by Dörnyei and Ushioda (2011, p. 4):

"Perhaps the only thing about motivation most researchers would agree on is that it, by definition, concerns the *direction* and *magnitude* of human behavior, that is:

- The *choice* of a particular action
- The *persistence* with it
- The *effort* expended on it

In other words, motivation is responsible for

- *Why* people decide to do something
- *How long* they are willing to sustain the activity
- *How hard* they are going to pursue it."

LLing motivation research faces the same definitional challenges, with debate continuing as to whether motivation should be considered a *trait*, a *state*, or a *process* (cf. Dörnyei, 2020) (see Chapter 26). Initially conceptualized as an individual difference variable (see Ryan, 2019), Dörnyei and Ryan (2015) have more recently looked towards McAdams's work in personality psychology and the "new big five" (see McAdams & Pals, 2006). They foreground in particular the middle three levels of McAdams's five level model: *Dispositional traits* (more stable personality features), *characteristic adaptations* (more dynamic, situated responses), and *integrative life narratives* (encapsulating life stories individuals create in order to broker understanding of the world and build identity). Such an understanding fits well within the *complexity approaches* (see Chapter 4) to research that are currently prevailing throughout the field of LLing, and indeed the field of applied linguistics as a whole (cf. Larsen-Freeman & Cameron, 2008). The notion of *motivational conglomerates*—a compilation of factors that act together as a single "whole" (Dörnyei & Ushioda, 2011)—similarly reflects this revised conceptualization: Rather than seeking to identify and trace the influences of distinct motives, this approach to understanding recognizes the *fundamental interrelationships* between motivation, emotion, and cognition (Storbeck & Clore, 2007). One example of such a motivational conglomerate is that of *interest*: "besides its obvious *motivational* connotations, the notion of interest also involves a salient *cognitive* aspect—the curiosity in and engagement with a specific domain—as well as a prominent *affective* dimension concerning the joy associated with this engagement" (Dörnyei & Ushioda, 2011, p. 93; italics added).

As in mainstream motivational psychology, broad stages are likewise identifiable in the developmental trajectory of motivation research in the context of LLing (see Dörnyei & Ushioda, 2011, for a detailed categorization and history). The pioneering work of Robert Gardner and colleagues set the compass for the first several decades of work in the field. Rationale for this unique trajectory was rooted in the argument that motivation to learn a language is *fundamentally unique* compared to the learning of other school subjects; learning a language "involves making features of another cultural community part of one's own repertoire" (Gardner, 2010, p. 3). Gardner describes the initial genesis of his *socio-educational model* (1985) as, "simple and straightforward; to identify the characteristics of people that could account for differences in their interest and success in learning a second language" (Gardner, 2019, p. 21). Adopting an affective rather than a cognitive or behavioral perspective, Gardner's research was also ground-breaking in its argumentation that *language aptitude* (see Chapter 30) is associated with LLing achievements.

The socio-educational model incorporates four complex variables: *motivation, integrativeness, attitudes towards the learning situation*, and *language anxiety. Motivation* is assessed via three separate measures: motivational intensity (the amount of effort invested in language learning), the desire to learn the language, and attitude towards learning the language (Gardner, 2010). The notion of integrativeness—related to an individual's identification with, interest in, and desire to engage with a target language community—has been an enduring legacy of this work, as has the influence of the Attitude and Motivation Test Battery (AMTB) in setting the bar for the rigor required of quantitative research in the field (for further reading see Al-Hoorie & MacIntyre, 2020). Indeed, the strength of this legacy has been such that its fundamental assumption—that at its heart, language learning is fundamentally different to the study of other educational subjects—has only recently begun to be deliberately and thoroughly empirically investigated (see Al-Hoorie & Hiver, 2020).

The cognitive revolution of the 1990s saw the inclusion of a broad array of cognitive theories from mainstream psychology integrated into the theoretical approaches used in LLing motivation research. The impetuses for this included a desire for increased emphasis on *foreign language* learning contexts (as opposed to the *second language* context of bilingual Canada, which was the birthplace of LLing motivation research), and the foregrounding of questions and issues related to language *pedagogy*. Around the turn of the century, researchers began to recognize the importance of motivation as a process playing out *over time* (see Williams & Burden, 1997). This development occurred in step with a similarly marked rise in a more *situated, contextually-rooted* understanding of motivation, alongside the increase in the use and status of *qualitative* research methodologies (see Ushioda, 1994, 2009). The current "socio-dynamic period" (Dörnyei & Ushioda, 2011) has seen the broad acceptance of many underpinning principles of a complex, dynamic systems approach to research and understanding (Hiver & Papi, 2019), and as a consequence this has ushered in a state of methodological diversification, required to investigate the issues emerging through the glass of this newly focused lens on LLing motivation (Dörnyei, MacIntyre, & Henry, 2015).

Integrating Perspectives

Since the emergence of the novel field of LLing motivation research, there has been significant integration of ideas between research conducted in this context and that carried out within mainstream motivation research. This is most marked in the direction of LLing motivation research "returning to the mainstream" (Lamb et al., 2019, p. 13), and becoming increasingly aligned with research in mainstream motivational psychology. In this section, I overview key areas of integration between the two fields, before highlighting two theories that have emerged in the field of LLing that do not have direct counterparts elsewhere.

The "Cognitive Revolutions"

Whereas behavioral perspectives posit that an individual's actions should be understood as a function of their environment (i.e., as related to the stimuli and reinforcement individuals are exposed to), cognitive perspectives centrally position individuals' personal agency and the notion of *choice*. As Dörnyei and Ushioda explain, "Cognitive theories of motivation focus on the instrumental role of mental structures, beliefs and information-processing mechanisms in shaping individual behaviour and action" (2011, pp. 12–13). At the point of the "cognitive revolution" in LLing, cognitive perspectives were already dominant in mainstream motivational psychology, and a number of theories that emerged in mainstream psychology over these years continue to be highly influential to the present day. These include frameworks rooted in the fundamental dichotomy of *approach* versus *avoidance motivation* (founded in the recognition that we tend to approach pleasure, and seek to avoid pain; Atkinson, 1957). Other *expectancy-value models*, in which an individual's motivation is a function of their expectancy of success and their subjective appraisal of a task's intrinsic, attainment, and utility value, along with relative costs (cf. Eccles, 2005), continue to be similarly prominent. Critically, expectancies and task values have been demonstrated to be "critical predictors of educational outcomes" across all levels of compulsory education and across many academic domains (Rosenzweig, Wigfield, & Eccles, 2019, p. 625). An individual's expectancy of success is also related to their *self-efficacy beliefs* (Bandura, 1997) (see Chapter 8), and an individual's present engagement is furthermore affected by successes and failures in *past* engagement (see Chapter 11), and to what they *attribute* these outcomes (cf. Weiner, 1992). (For a fuller overview of these theoretical approaches and related research findings in education, see Schunk, Meece, & Pintrich, 2014).

In the context of LLing, several 1990s models drew on these and other cognitive theories of motivation that had emerged in mainstream psychology. Williams and Burden's (1997) tripartite model emphasized three discrete aspects of motivated action—*reasons for doing something*, *deciding to act*, and *sustaining the effort or persisting*—and posited that each of these stages would be variably affected by different psychological processes. For example, they argued that an individual's decisions both to act and sustain motivation would in part be affected by their *self-efficacy beliefs* and past *attributions*. Crookes and Schmidt (1991, p. 502) adopted "a definition of motivation in terms of choice, engagement, and persistence, as determined by interest, relevance, expectancy, and outcomes" (drawing, for example, on *expectancy-value* models). Dörnyei's (1994, p. 280) tripartite model offered a basis for future work by delineating three discrete levels for investigation: a *language level*, a *learner level*, and a *learning situation level*, which included *course*, *teacher* and *group-specific* motivational components (see Chapters 21 and 22). In addition to many of the cognitive theories highlighted throughout this section, Dörnyei also foregrounded the important role of specific affective factors (such as language learner *anxiety*). A final theory of note is *self-determination theory* (SDT; Deci & Ryan, 1985), spearheaded in the context of LLing by Kimberly Noels (cf. Noels, Lou, Lascano, Chaffee, Dincer, Zhang, & Zhang, 2019), and rooted in one of the most well-known dichotomies across all fields of motivation research: *intrinsic* and *extrinsic motivation*. SDT has been extensively researched across both mainstream and LLing motivational contexts. There has been an explosion of interest in the context of LLing over the past half-decade in particular (Noels et al., 2019), further fueled via its application in conceptualizing our understanding of language learner *engagement* (cf. Mercer, 2019).

It is pertinent to note, however, that even with this comprehensive turn towards cognitive psychology both throughout the 1990s and in the years since, the integration of mainstream cognitive theories into LLing motivation research has occurred in a relatively patchwork manner.

Individual vs. Social Motivation and the Importance of Context

Gardner's social-psychological framework was also seminal in that it "distinguished second language motivation research from the individual-cognitive perspectives then dominating mainstream motivational psychology" (Ushioda, 2013, p. 1). Although the cognitive revolution went on to align the focus of research in LLing motivation with the predominantly individual-cognitive perspectives in psychology, in the following years, the importance of the *social* and *contextual* aspects of our understanding of motivation regained their position the fore. Rooted in social psychology and Vygotsky's (1978) *sociocultural theory* (cf. Lantolf & Thorne, 2006) (see Chapter 2), research perspectives in the context of LLing characterized motivation "as a fundamentally sociohistorically situated process, emergent through the interactions among participants, context and sociocultural activity" (Dörnyei & Ushioda, 2011, p. 34). Positioning individuals in a *dynamic, two-way* relationship with their surrounding context, such a perspective "takes the view that people are not just products but also *active producers* of their own social and cultural environments" (Dörnyei & Ushioda, 2011, p. 34; emphasis added). Ushioda's (2009) *person-in-context relational view* of motivation—which situates learners as culturally and historically situated beings, viewing them holistically as people not merely as "language learners"—similarly foregrounds the importance of a wholly rooted, situated interpretation of motivational understanding. Instead of viewing context as an independent variable, researching a person-*in*-context, allows us "to capture the mutually constitutive relationship between persons and the contexts in which they act—a relationship that is dynamic, complex and non-linear" (Ushioda, 2009, p. 218).

Possible Selves & the L2 Motivational Self System

Although it lacks direct parallels, the L2 motivational self system (L2MSS; Dörnyei, 2009), and its partner body of research investigating language learner and teacher vision (Dörnyei & Kubanyiova, 2014), have deep roots in social psychology. Drawing on Markus and Nurius's (1986) theory of *possible selves* and on Higgins's (1987) *self-discrepancy theory*, the L2MSS comprises three discrete elements: the *ideal L2 self*, the *ought-to L2 self*, and the *L2 learning experience* (see Csizér, 2019). Providing a conceptual link between motivation and cognition, "Possible selves are the cognitive components of hopes, fears, goals, and threats, and they give the specific self-relevant form, meaning, organization, and direction to these dynamics" (Markus & Nurius, 1986, p. 954). When the content of these imagined future selves is at odds with our current self-state, this causes us to experience specific types of discomfort, pushing us to act in order to reduce this discrepancy (in the context of LLing, see also Papi, Bondarenko, Mansouri, Feng, & Jiang, 2018 and Teimouri, 2017).

Since its introduction to the field, a significant body of amassed research has drawn on the L2MSS as a theoretical framework (Boo et al., 2015). The ideal L2 self has tended to emerge (and to be positioned) as the central element of this model, although it may be that recent developments will be capable of facilitating a more appropriately balanced research emphasis by, for example, incorporating issues such as *regulatory focus* into our understanding of the ought-to L2 self (Papi et al., 2018; Teimouri, 2017; in mainstream psychology see Higgins, 1998). A more dedicated focus on the L2 learning experience (both at a conceptual level of understanding and in absolute terms with regards to research output) could similarly prove to be highly valuable (Csizér & Kálmán, 2019). Csizér (2019, p. 87) has recently concluded that the "simplicity and adaptability" of the L2MSS framework have been key factors in underpinning its remarkable rise and enduring prominence within the field, and that the complex relationships both within the model itself, and between discrete aspects of the model and specific individual and contextual factors, means that its relevance with regards to future work in the field continues to remain high.

Directed Motivational Currents & Long-Term Motivation

The notion of *directed motivational currents* (DMCs) has recently been proposed to encapsulate a unique motivational phenomenon, occurring when "a significant personal goal is accompanied by an appropriate pathway of action, resulting in a match that actually works to *amplify* the energy released by the goal" (Dörnyei, Henry, & Muir, 2016, p. 20). Although lacking a direct parallel, the theoretical roots of DMCs are firmly planted in well-established research findings across multiple fields of psychology (see Dörnyei et al., 2016). DMCs are not the norm in the context of goal striving, yet their motivational basis is argued to be "made up of the same building blocks as the motivational basis which energises long-term behaviors in general" (Dörnyei et al., 2016, p. 33). There is initial evidence indicating their broad relevance across diverse contexts and in support of potential practical application in the context of language pedagogy (Muir, 2020).

DMCs represent an "*optimal form* of engagement with an extended project" (Dörnyei et al., 2016, p. 20). In educational psychology, student engagement has recently been described as the "holy grail of learning" (Sinatra, Heddy, & Lombardi, 2015, p. 1), and DMCs have been positioned as potentially forming "a first step" in the development of a "holistic framework" capable of bringing together diverse strands of research in order to facilitate the development of understanding relating to different aspects of engagement (Mercer, 2019, p. 6). DMC theory also builds "on understandings about the facilitative function of positive emotions" (Henry, 2019, p. 151) (see Chapter 14). The rise of positive psychology (see Seligman & Csíkszentmihályi, 2000) (see Chapter 5) is likewise mirrored in a parallel increase in research focus in the context of LLing (MacIntyre, Gregersen, & Mercer, 2016), and DMCs represent just one example of a motivational construct with the experience of positive emotions at its very heart (and a further example of a *motivational conglomerate*, highlighting again the interwoven relationships between cognition, emotion, and motivation).

DMCs highlight another ongoing challenge, common to motivation research in both mainstream psychology and in the context of LLing: the difficulty of incorporating the notion of *time*. Although a considerable amount of work has investigated motivational antecedents, there is a relative dearth of research investigating the subsequent processes required to support the *continuation* of motivation (Dörnyei et al., 2016). DMCs represent a very specific type of long-term goal striving, yet research into other types and aspects of long-term motivation, for example *persistence* (e.g. Dörnyei, 2020) or *regulatory focus* (e.g. Henry & Davydenko, 2020), is likely to contribute to an area already poised to gain further traction and increased research momentum in the coming years.

Implications for Practice and Research

Rooted in any field of inquiry—whether mainstream educational psychology or the context of LLing—motivation research is a fundamentally *applied* discipline. Yet, although empirical work often concludes by suggesting tangible practical implications, a longstanding concern is that this rarely makes it into the hands of practicing language teachers (Marsden & Kasprowicz, 2017). In this section, I highlight three areas of study with particular practical relevance.

Motivational Strategies

In educational psychology, much of the discourse surrounding these applied issues has been incorporated within a growing narrative centered around student *engagement* (see Christenson, Reschly, & Wylie, 2012), and research on student engagement is likewise gaining ground in the context of LLing (Hiver, Al-Hoorie, & Mercer, 2020; Mercer & Dörnyei, 2020). Much of the work completed to date investigating issues related to motiva*ting* language learners has built on Dörnyei's work on motivational strategies (cf. Dörnyei, 2001a), and there is a parallel body of strategy research working beyond Dörnyei's taxonomy (see Lamb, 2017). A key, concise, yet crucial, finding of these studies is that the application of motivational strategies "can WORK" (Lamb, 2017, p. 310). The importance of *context* in the appropriateness and application of any strategy cannot be overstated. This is firstly important relating to the *interpretation* of various strategies. As Lamb (2017) exemplifies, "Using classroom language sensitively"—a strategy from Dörnyei's taxonomy—has been interpreted in different contexts as requiring both more *and* less use of the target language. A similarly critical recognition is that of the dynamic interrelationships between factors relating to the "application" of any strategy, and the context into which it is "applied": the relative success of any motivational strategies employed cannot, therefore, be understood without reference to the environment in which any intervention is situated (see Ushioda, 2009).

Motivating Learner Groups

The vast majority of motivational concepts overviewed in this chapter center on *individual* conceptualizations of motivation. This is seemingly at odds with the practical reality for teachers worldwide, the vast majority of whom find themselves standing in front of learner *groups*. Group-level counterparts to individuals' personal goals, attitudes, intentions, and values are equally significant motivational antecedents. These include, for example, group roles and norms, group cohesiveness, and group leadership (Dörnyei & Murphey, 2003) (see Chapter 22). As Dörnyei and Muir (2019, p. 11) have noted, "when we discuss the learning behavior of groups of learners, motivational psychology and group dynamics converge."

Although such a focus may seem self-evident (research into the management of groups is certainly a longstanding area of inquiry across other areas of psychology; cf. Forsyth, 2019), there is only a modest body of work in this area to be found in the field of LLing (Dörnyei & Muir, 2019). Recent studies using novel methodological approaches indicate that research into group motivation is, however, (re)emerging as an area of investigation (e.g. Poupore, 2016, 2018). It may be the case that one reason for such a lacuna of study is linked to the challenges of researching and conceptualizing these issues: *Linear* approaches to understanding rooted in notions of cause and effect can offer little in explaining the *complex* relationships between the students and teacher of a class group, between this class group as a whole and aspects of its surrounding environment, nor can it adequately represent how each may evolve over time. It may not be a coincidence that the renewed focus and innovation in this area is in parallel with the growing prominence and acceptance of complexity approaches throughout the field. Such findings have substantial potential to contribute key implications for practice.

Tackling Demotivation

Thorner and Kikuchi (2019, p. 367) reflect that, compared to motivation, "Demotivation is arguably a greater issue." Demotivation concerns itself with the processes by which an individual's motivational level is "pulled" downwards—*de*motivation is thus conceptually distinct from general low motivation—by factors either *internal* or *external* to a learner (Kikuchi, 2015, p. 4). Factors that have been highlighted as demotivating include language teachers and the classroom environment and materials (external factors), and experiences of failure and loss of interest (internal factors; Sakai & Kikuchi, 2009). Critically, however, a factor may be classed as "demotivating" only when it is *perceived* as such by a learner. It may be the case, therefore, that what is perceived as *motiv*ating by one student is similarly perceived as *de*motivating by another, that a factor may be perceived as demotivating by a student one week but not the next, and differences in the factors reported as demotivating have also been identified not only *across contexts* but also as described by learners at *different language levels* (cf. Thorner & Kikuchi, 2019). A socially situated, *person-in-context* approach is therefore required (Ushioda, 2009). In considering demotivation in the context of language pedagogy, similarly important is the notion of *re*motivation: Demotivated learners may not necessarily stay as such indefinitely (Kikuchi, 2015).

Key Implications for Research

In introducing the field of LLing motivation earlier in this chapter, I noted the change witnessed in recent years linked to the broad adoption of complexity approaches to research across the field. In many respects, the current "socio-dynamic period" may itself also be one of transition. As Hiver and Papi (2019) have argued,

> This new way of thinking provides a set of powerful intellectual concepts and principles (e.g., time; self-organisation) that allow us to theorize and interpret particular phenomena or aspects of L2 motivation in new ways that are grounded in a context-dependent and dynamic view of development.
>
> *p. 118–119*

Davis and Sumara also offer a highly accessible overview of complexity and educational psychology (2006). Referencing both MacIntyre et al. (2015) and Ushioda (2009), Hiver and Papi further reflect on the fact that, "It is possible, even highly likely, that using these conceptual tools will challenge many of our existing assumptions and encourage us to reconsider research and practice in the field of L2 motivation," potentially even leading to "a deliberate rejection of certain other principles and ideas" (2019, p. 119).

Future Directions

Throughout this chapter, I have highlighted many key directions for future research as they have arisen. In this final section, I suggest a further three important concerns for future study.

Nonconscious Processes

Sherman, Gawronski, and Trope (2014, p. xi) describe *dual-process theories* as "one of the most significant developments in the history of scientific psychology." As Sherman et al. describe, "The overarching assumption of these theories is that psychological process can be divided into two distinct categories depending on whether they operate in an automatic or controlled fashion" (2014, p. xi). Throughout the cognitive revolutions in both mainstream and LLing motivation research, the centrality of human *agency* to the understanding of motivational process was foregrounded. As a consequence, a strong bias persisted, emphasizing the primacy of *conscious* motives. Undoubtedly, and paralleling the direction of research in mainstream motivational psychology, an emphasis on dual-process models as well as a raising of the profile of unconscious motives to a par with that of conscious motives is likely to become an increasingly prominent avenue of future research in the field of LLing motivation (see Al-Hoorie, 2019).

Teacher Motivation

Compared to the body of research investigating student motivation, there is a relative dearth of research investigating language *teacher* motivation across all fields of study. In educational psychology, *teacher motivation* has been investigated from many of the cognitive perspectives highlighted previously in relation to *student motivation*. In addition, there has been a growing body of work related to language teacher emotions, as situated in specific contexts and with regards to teachers' aspirations and career trajectories (see Richardson, Karabenick, & Watt, 2014). A parallel body of work can be found specific to language learning (e.g. Gkonou, Dewaele, & King, 2020), yet a more systematic program of research is needed to fully drive this agenda forwards (see Hiver, Kim, & Kim, 2018). Care is also needed in translating concepts and ideas between student and teacher motivation literatures: "there are adequate reasons to suspect that language teacher motivation differs from L2 learning motivation" (Hiver et al., 2018, p. 28). The investigation of teacher motivation is a clear area in need of further research, both in its own right and with respect to supporting student motivation.

The fact that language teachers' motivation and their pedagogy "are inextricably linked" (Dörnyei & Kubanyiova, 2014, p. 3) requires that research also explore the relationship of teacher motivation with other factors, including *student* motivation. An important avenue of related research is therefore that of the relationships and motivational synergy *between* teachers and learners. Although there is similarly limited research to date on this topic—arguably due to the indirect link between the two making these relationships different to empirically demonstrate (Dörnyei & Ryan, 2015)—complexity and other novel approaches have begun to demonstrate tangible inroads (e.g. Henry & Thorsen, 2018; Pinner, 2019). This is an area poised for a surge of research interest dedicated to exploring these issues.

Diversified Research Sites & Contexts

Significant biases can be found in the research aims and ideals of LLing motivation research. For example, Boo et al.'s (2015) detailed analysis of the field from 2005–2015 lays this truth bare: Over 70 percent of studies reviewed investigated the learning of *English*, and over 50 percent drew participants who were studying in *tertiary education*. This has significant implications for not only the generalizability of findings to other research contexts, but also with regards the generalizability of the theoretical frameworks developed in these contexts and their application elsewhere (for example, the learning of languages other than English/LOTEs; see Ushioda & Dörnyei, 2017). Well-entrenched terminology such as "second language acquisition/SLA" and "second language/L2" also brings with it challenges in its implicit assumption of monolingual learners and implications of foreign or second language learning contexts. Such legacy wording fails to recognize the extent of the multilingual, transnational norms of international mobility that are characteristic of the world in which we live (see e.g. Duff, 2015).

Bringing to the fore these issues of context similarly shines the spotlight on the need to acknowledge and address the significant power relations and inequalities present in many learning contexts (Ortega, 2018) (see Chapter 25). A well-established line of research in this respect is that of Bonny Norton's notion of *investment*, which she defines as "the socially and historically constructed relationship of learners to the target language, and their often-ambivalent desire to learn and practice it" (Norton, 2000, p. 10) (see Chapter 7). As Ushioda reflects, "motivation to learn and use a second language may be *socially constrained* rather than *socially constructed*" (2013, p. 4; emphasis added). Implications of these arguments likewise translate to implications for pedagogy; for example, the need for the development of more diversified and contextually rooted pedagogic practices. Future work must be mindful of the need to address these biases in order to continue opening up horizons.

The publication of this chapter comes at a compelling point of transition and innovation within the field of LLing motivation research. The field has opened itself up to methodological uncertainty, brought about with the broad adoption of complexity ideals (cf. Hiver & Al-Hoorie, 2016), at a time when it is similarly returning to its roots (Al-Hoorie & MacIntyre, 2020) and reassessing the arguments and assumptions then put forward (Al-Hoorie & Hiver, 2020). This throwing open of the doors has led to the emergence of novel, fascinating lines of research, including those foregrounded in this final section. When theoretical constructs are drawn from psychology and translated into other fields, such as LLing, it is imperative they are thoroughly validated in the new domain; the process is not as simple as to merely "change a few wordings" (Lou & Noels, 2019, p. 555). Yet, perhaps now more than ever, the field is equipped and ready to do so, setting the scene for motivation research to continue forging a voracious path forwards for the foreseeable years to come.

Reflection Questions

- Consider all of the issues raised throughout this chapter. Which are most relevant to understanding language learners' and teachers' motivation in your context (and why)?
- *De*motivation has been argued to be a more important topic of investigation than *moti*vation. What are key factors potentially contributing to the demotivation of learners in your teaching/learning context, and to what extent might they be under a teacher's control?
- As a field, motivation research in the context of LLing has several clear historic biases. In what ways might research specific to your context be able to contribute novel insight to the existing body of work on language learners' and teachers' motivation?

Recommended Reading

Lamb, M., Csizér, K., Henry, A., & Ryan, S. (Eds.). (2019). *The Palgrave handbook of motivation for language learning.* Palgrave Macmillan.

This extensive handbook offers a cutting edge, detailed overview of the field as a whole—it is a must read for anyone interested in exploring further any aspect of motivation in the context of language learning and teaching.

Dörnyei, Z., & Ushioda, E. (2011). *Teaching and researching motivation* (2nd ed.). Routledge.
Offering a more detailed discussion of the development of the field of LLing motivation research, this thorough narrative provides a comprehensive overview. A third edition of this book is currently in press.

Schunk, D. H., Meece, J. R., & Pintrich, P. R. (2014). *Motivation in education: Pearson new international edition: Theory, research, and applications* (4th ed.). Pearson.
This highly accessible yet thorough volume offers a comprehensive discussion of many cornerstones of educational psychology.

References

Al-Hoorie, A. (2019). Motivation and the unconscious. In M. Lamb, K. Csizér, A. Henry, & S. Ryan (Eds.) *The Palgrave handbook of motivation for language learning* (pp. 561–578). Palgrave Macmillan.
Al-Hoorie, A., & MacIntyre, P. (Eds.). (2020). *Contemporary language motivation theory: 60 years since Gardner and Lambert (1959)*. Multilingual Matters.
Atkinson, J. W. (1957). Motivational determinants of risk-taking behavior. *Psychological Review*, 64, 359–372.
Bandura, A. (1997). *Self-efficacy: The exercise of control*. W. H. Freeman.
Boo, Z., Dörnyei, Z., & Ryan, S. (2015). L2 motivation research 2005–2014: Understanding a publication surge and a changing landscape. *System*, 55, 145–157.
Christenson, S. L., Reschly, A. L., & Wylie, C. (Eds.). (2012). *Handbook of research on student engagement*. Springer.
Crookes, G., & Schmidt, R. W. (1991). Motivation: Reopening the research agenda. *Language Learning*, 41, 469–512.
Csizér, K. (2019). The L2 motivational self-system. In M. Lamb, K. Csizér, A. Henry, & S. Ryan (Eds.) *The Palgrave handbook of motivation for language learning* (pp. 71–94). Palgrave Macmillan.
Csizér, K., & Kálmán, C. S. (Eds.). (2019). Language learning experience: The neglected element in L2 motivation research (Special Issue). *Studies in Second Language Learning and Teaching*, 9(1).
Davis, B., & Sumara, D. (2006). *Complexity and education: Enquiries into learning, teaching and research*. Lawrence Erlbaum.
Deci, E. L., & Ryan, R. M. (1985). *Intrinsic motivation and self-determination in human behavior*. Plenum.
Dörnyei, Z. (1994). Motivation and motivating in the foreign language classroom. *Modern Language Journal*, 78, 273–284.
Dörnyei, Z. (2001a). *Motivational strategies in the language classroom*. Cambridge University Press.
Dörnyei, Z. (2009). The L2 motivational self system. In Z. Dörnyei & E. Ushioda (Eds.) *Motivation, language identity and the L2 self* (pp. 9–42). Multilingual Matters.
Dörnyei, Z. (2020). *Innovations and challenges in language learning motivation*. Routledge.
Dörnyei, Z., Henry, A., & Muir, C. (2016). *Motivational currents in language learning: Frameworks for focused interventions*. Routledge.
Dörnyei, Z., & Kubanyiova, M. (2014). *Motivating learners, motivating teachers: Building vision in the language classroom*. Cambridge University Press.
Dörnyei, Z., MacIntyre, P., & Henry, A. (Eds.). (2015). *Motivational dynamics in language learning*. Multilingual Matters.
Dörnyei, Z., & Muir, C. (2019). Creating a motivating classroom environment. In X. A. Gao (Ed.) *Second handbook of English language teaching*. Springer.
Dörnyei, Z., & Murphey, T. (2003). *Group dynamics in the language classroom*. Cambridge University Press.
Dörnyei. Z., & Ryan, S. (2015). *The psychology of the language learner revisited*. Routledge.
Dörnyei, Z., & Ushioda, E. (2011). *Teaching and researching motivation* (2nd ed.). Routledge.
Duff, P. A. (2015). Transnationalism, multilingualism, and identity. *Annual Review of Applied Linguistics*, 35, 57–80.
Eccles, J. S. (2005). Subjective task value and the Eccles et al. model of achievement-related choices. In A. J. Elliot & C. S. Dweck (Eds.) *Handbook of competence and motivation* (pp. 105–121). Guilford Press.
Forsyth, D. (2019). *Group dynamics* (7th ed.). Cengage Learning.

Gardner, R. C. (1985) *Social psychology and second language learning: The role of attitudes and motivation*. Edward Arnold.

Gardner, R. C. (2010). *Motivation and second language acquisition: The socio-educational model*. Peter Lang.

Gardner, R. C. (2019). The socio-educational model of second language acquisition. In M. Lamb, K. Csizér, A. Henry, & S. Ryan (Eds.) *The Palgrave handbook of motivation for language learning* (pp. 19–38). Palgrave Macmillan.

Gardner, R. C., & Lambert, W. E. (1959). Motivational variables in second-language acquisition. *Canadian Journal of Psychology*, *13*(4), 266–272.

Gkonou, C., Dewaele, J-M., & King, J. (2020). *The emotional rollercoaster of language teaching*. Multilingual Matters.

Henry, A. (2019). Directed motivational currents: Extending the theory of L2 vision. In M. Lamb, K. Csizér, A. Henry, & S. Ryan (Eds.) *The Palgrave handbook of motivation for language learning* (pp. 139–162). Palgrave Macmillan.

Henry, A., & Davydenko, S. (2020). Thriving? Or surviving? An approach-avoidance perspective on adult language learners' motivation. *The Modern Language Journal*, *104*(2), 363–380.

Henry, A., & Thorsen, C. (2018). Teacher-student relationships and L2 motivation. *Modern Language Journal*, *102*(1), 218–241.

Hidi, K. A., & Renninger, K. A. (2019). Introduction: Motivation and its relation to learning. In K. A. Renninger & S. E. Hidi (Eds.) *The Cambridge Handbook of Motivation and Learning* (pp. 1–14). Cambridge University Press.

Higgins, E. T. (1987). Self-discrepancy: A theory relating self and affect. *Psychological Review*, *94*, 319–340.

Higgins, E. T. (1998). Promotion and prevention: Regulatory focus as a motivational principle. In M. P. Zanna (Ed.), *Advances in experimental social psychology* (Vol. 30, pp. 1–46). Academic Press.

Hiver, P., & Al-Hoorie, A. H. (2016). Putting complexity theory into practice: A dynamic ensemble for second language research. *Modern Language Journal*, *100*(4), 741–756.

Hiver, P., Al-Hoorie, A., & Mercer, S. (Eds.). (2020). *Student engagement in the language classroom*. Multilingual Matters.

Hiver, P., Kim, T.-Y., & Kim, Y. (2018). Language teacher motivation. In S. Mercer & A. Kostoulas (Eds.), *Language teacher psychology* (pp. 18–33). Multilingual Matters.

Hiver, P., & Papi, M. (2019). Complexity theory and L2 motivation. In M. Lamb, K. Csizér, A. Henry, & S. Ryan (Eds.) *The Palgrave handbook of motivation for language learning* (pp. 117–138). Palgrave Macmillan.

Kikuchi, K. (2015). *Demotivation in second language acquisition: Insights from Japan*. Multilingual Matters.

Lamb, M. (2017). The motivational dimension of language teaching. *Language Teaching*, *50*(3), 301–346.

Lamb, M., Csizér, K., Henry, A., & Ryan, S. (2019). Introduction. In M. Lamb, K. Csizér, A. Henry, & S. Ryan (Eds.) *The Palgrave handbook of motivation for language learning* (pp. 1–18). Palgrave Macmillan.

Lantolf, J. P., & Thorne, S. L. (2006). *Sociocultural theory and the genesis of second language development*. Oxford University Press.

Larsen-Freeman, D., & Cameron, L. (2008). *Complex systems and applied linguistics*. Oxford University Press.

Lou, N. M., & Noels, K. A. (2019). Language mindsets, meaning-making, and motivation. In M. Lamb, K. Csizér, A. Henry, & S. Ryan (Eds.), *The Palgrave handbook of motivation for language learning* (pp. 537–560). Palgrave Macmillan.

Markus, H., & Nurius, P. (1986). Possible selves. *American Psychologist*, *41*(9), 954–969.

Marsden, E., & Kasprowicz, R. (2017). Foreign language educators' exposure to research: Reported experiences, exposure via citations, and a proposal for action. *The Modern Language Journal*, *101*(4), 613–642.

McAdams, D. P., & Pals, J. L. (2006). A new Big Five: Fundamental principles for an integrative science of personality. *American Psychologist*, *61*, 204–217.

MacIntyre, P. D., Dörnyei, Z., & Henry, A. (2015). Hot enough to be cool: The promise of dynamic systems research. In Z. Dörnyei, P.D. MacIntyre, & A. Henry (Eds.), *Motivational dynamics in language learning* (pp. 419–429). Multilingual Matters.

MacIntyre, P. D., Gregersen, T., & Mercer, S. (Eds.). (2016). *Positive psychology in SLA*. Multilingual Matters.

Mercer, S. (2019). Language learner engagement: Setting the scene. In A. Gao (Ed.), *Second handbook of English language teaching*. Springer.

Mercer, S., & Dörnyei, Z. (2020). *Engaging language learners in contemporary classrooms*. Cambridge University Press.

Muir, C. (2020). *Directed motivational currents and language education: Exploring implications for pedagogy*. Multilingual Matters.

Noels, K. A., Lou, N. M., Lascano, D. I. V., Chaffee, K. E., Dincer, A., Zhang, Y. S. D., & Zhang, X. (2019). Self-determination theory and motivated engagement in language learning. In M. Lamb, K. Csizér, A. Henry, & S. Ryan (Eds.), *The Palgrave handbook of motivation for language learning* (pp. 95–116). Palgrave Macmillan.

Norton, B. (2000). *Identity and language learning: Gender, ethnicity and educational change*. Longman.

Ortega, L. (2018). SLA in uncertain times: Disciplinary constraints, transdisciplinary hopes. *Working Papers in Educational Linguistics*, *33*, 1–30.

Papi, M., Bondarenko, A. V., Mansouri, S., Feng, L., & Jiang, C. (2018). Rethinking L2 motivation research: The 2x2 model of L2 self-guides. *Studies in Second Language Acquisition, 42*(2), 337–361.

Pinner, R. S. (2019). *Authenticity and teacher-student motivational synergy: A narrative of language teaching*. Routledge.

Poupore, G. (2016). Measuring group work dynamics and its relation with L2 learners' task motivation and language production. *Language Teaching Research, 20*(6), 719–740.

Poupore, G. (2018). A complex systems investigation of group work dynamics in L2 interactive tasks. *The Modern Language Journal, 102,* 350–370.

Reeve, J., & Lee, W. (2019). Motivational neuroscience. In R. Ryan (Ed.) *The Oxford handbook of human motivation* (2nd ed., pp. 355–372). Oxford University Press.

Richardson, P. W., Karabenick, S. A., & Watt, H. M. G. (Eds.). (2014). *Teacher motivation: Theory and practice*. Routledge.

Rosenzweig, E. Q., Wigfield, A., & Eccles, J. S. (2019). Expectancy-value theory and its relevance for student motivation and learning. In K. A. Renninger & S. E. Hidi (Eds.), *The Cambridge handbook of motivation and learning* (pp. 617–644). Cambridge University Press.

Ryan, R. (Ed.). (2019a). *The Oxford handbook of human motivation* (2nd ed). Oxford University Press.

Ryan, R. (2019b). Inside the black box: Motivational science in the 21st century. In R. Ryan (Ed.), *The Oxford handbook of human motivation* (2nd ed., pp. 3–7). Oxford University Press.

Ryan, S. (2019). Motivation and individual differences. In M. Lamb, K. Csizér, A. Henry, & S. Ryan (Eds.), *The Palgrave handbook of motivation for language learning* (pp. 163–182). Palgrave Macmillan.

Sakai, H., & Kikuchi, K. (2009). An analysis of demotivators in the EFL classroom. *System, 37*(1), 57–69.

Schunk, D. H., Meece, J. R., & Pintrich, P. R. (2014). *Motivation in education: Pearson new international edition: Theory, research, and applications* (4th ed.). Pearson.

Seligman, M. E. P., & Csíkszentmihályi, M. (2000). Positive psychology: An introduction. *American Psychologist, 55*(1), 5–14.

Sherman, J. W., Gawronski, B., & Trope, Y. (Eds.). (2014). *Dual-process theories of the social mind*. The Guildford Press.

Sinatra, G. M., Heddy, B. C., & Lombardi, D. (2015). The challenges of defining and measuring student engagement in science. *Educational Psychologist, 50*(1), 1–13.

Storbeck, J., & Clore, G. L. (2007). On the interdependence of cognition and emotion. *Cognition and Emotion, 21*(6), 1212–1237.

Teimouri, Y. (2017). L2 selves, emotions, and motivated behaviours. *Studies in Second Language Acquisition, 39,* 681–709.

Thorner, N., & Kikuchi, K. (2019). The process of demotivation in language learning: An integrative account. In M. Lamb, K. Csizér, A. Henry, & S. Ryan (Eds.), *The Palgrave handbook of motivation for language learning* (pp. 367–388). Palgrave Macmillan.

Ushioda, E. (1994). L2 motivation as a qualitative construct. *Teanga, 14,* 76–84.

Ushioda, E. (2009). A person-in-context relational view of emergent motivation, self and identity. In Z. Dörnyei & E. Ushioda (Eds.), *Motivation, language identity and the L2 self* (pp. 215–228). Multilingual Matters.

Ushioda, E. (2013). Motivation in second language acquisition. In C. A. Chappelle (Ed.), *The encyclopedia of applied linguistics*. Blackwell Publishing.

Ushioda, E., & Dörnyei, Z. (2017). Beyond global English: Motivation to learn languages in a multicultural world (Special Issue). *Modern Language Journal, 101*(3).

Vygotsky, L. S. (1978). *Mind in society: The development of higher psychological processes*. Harvard University Press.

Weiner, B. (1992). *Human motivation: Metaphors, theories, and research*. Sage Publications.

Williams, M., & Burden, R. L. (1997). *Psychology for language teachers*. Cambridge University Press.

11
ENGAGEMENT

Hayo Reinders and Sachiko Nakamura

Engagement is one of those words (of many in the field of psychology) which every lay person intuitively feels they know what it means. Similarly, teachers "know" when a learner is engaged and when she is not, and to be called an "engaging teacher" is surely seen as a compliment. Yet, what exactly engagement is and—perhaps trickier to determine—what it is not, is not at all straightforward, as research in the last decades has shown. Where does motivation end and engagement begin? How does one measure levels of engagement? How do we encourage learner engagement? These are only some of the questions that remain to be answered and that only now are starting to be asked systematically in our field.

A few clarifications are in order in this introduction, especially for readers unfamiliar with the topic. Firstly, engagement is related to, but separate from, other psychological constructs, such as motivation, interest, and attention. At the risk of oversimplifying a longstanding discussion in the field, engagement is often considered one instantiation of motivation (see Chapter 10); the action (engagement) resulting from the drive (motivation) to learn the language. However, although useful in spurring engagement, motivation is not a prerequisite for engagement as a learner can be deeply engaged in a particularly interesting activity while not having a broader interest in or desire to learn the subject. In other words, motivation is a helpful contributor to engagement, but not a necessary one. Similarly, in general usage, words like "interest" and "enjoyment" are used as synonyms of engagement when in actual fact they are merely confluent. A learner can have an unspecific "interest" in a topic without this interest rising to the level of determined action. Similarly, a learner can enjoy an activity (e.g., watching a TV program in class), without actively engaging with it. Lastly, words like "attention" and "noticing" are related in that they refer to the psychological processes by which cognitive resources are directed towards certain stimuli. Being engaged in a learning activity may lead to a greater likelihood of noticing something, but this is not a necessary outcome.

Another clarification is needed to distinguish between engagement-in-the-moment (also referred to as "task-level engagement"), which could, for example, be measured by how actively a learner contributes to a role-play task, and engagement in learning more generally (often referred to as "student engagement"), which could be measured by attendance over time, or participation in self-access learning, or language exchanges. These two broad strands are discussed in some more detail below.

A final point to make is that the concept of engagement is not limited to learners. "Teacher engagement," as the voluntary allocation of personal resources to the tasks demanded within a particular vocational role (Christian, Garza, & Slaughter, 2011), has become an active field of inquiry

DOI: 10.4324/9780429321498-14

in recent years. Teacher effectiveness has been shown to have a major impact on learning outcomes (Hindman & Stronge, 2009) and teachers' engagement in their work is closely related to teacher effectiveness as well as job satisfaction and well-being (Bakker & Bal, 2010) (see Chapter 15). Recent years have seen the development of instruments for measuring teachers' work engagement (e.g., Klassen, Aldhafri, Mansfield, Purwanto, Siu, Wong, & Woods-McConney, 2012), which are paving the way for better exploring the interrelationships in terms of engagement of different variables (teachers, learners, parents, the wider environment) within the educational context. However, the primary focus of this chapter is on the learner. For the interested reader, we recommend Skaalvik and Skaalvik (2014).

The growing interest in all forms of engagement is perhaps not surprising when considering its role in all human endeavors, including learning. It is also not surprising when seen in light of the convergence in recent years of the cognitive, social, and affective research strands and the recognition that a more holistic, integrated view helps to improve our understanding of the language learning process. Engagement is starting to be recognized as the culmination of all the individual variables that contribute to the manifestation of learning at a particular moment, and thus a highly promising site of inquiry and worthy educational endeavor; indeed, engagement has been dubbed "the holy grail of learning" (Sinatra, Heddy, & Lombardi, 2015, p. 1). In this chapter, we will briefly review the origins of research into engagement and current definitions and operationalizations before considering its increasing role in language education practice and research.

Engagement in Psychology

Research on engagement began in the 1980s in the field of educational psychology. Interest initially arose from the desire to understand students' learning and achievement, typically with the aim of preventing student dropout and promoting school completion (Finn, 1989; Mosher & McGowan, 1985). This broader field, usually referred to as *student engagement*, is "characterized as participation in educationally effective practices, both inside and outside the classroom, which leads to a range of measurable outcomes" (Kuh, Kinzie, Buckley, Bridges, & Hayek, 2007, p. 7). This participation was also highlighted as a key concept in the seminal work by Finn (1989), whose *participation-identification model* conceptualized dropout through participation in school activities, together with identification with school—that is, a sense of belonging and valuing the school environment.

A different strand of research on student engagement emerged from the 1990s, where greater attention started to be given to the psychological components involved in engagement. Newmann (1992) defined engagement as "the student's psychological investment in and effort directed toward learning, understanding, or mastering the knowledge, skills, or crafts that academic work is intended to promote" (p. 12). He emphasized that psychological investment, which is not always observable, depicts the "inner quality of concentration and effort to learn" (Newmann, 1992, p. 13). This led to a proliferation of engagement models consisting of different sub-constructs together with a wide range of operationalizations. Table 11.1 provides selected prominent engagement models, illustrating this range. As shown, there is a general agreement across different models that engagement involves some form of behavioral and affective dimensions and that the cognitive dimension involves self-regulation or related strategy use. However, there is an overlap between the descriptions of academic and behavioral engagement, and some focus on particular types of emotions while others refer to a sense of belonging in conceptualizing affective aspects of engagement. Another notable variation can be found in the operationalizations. The contexts that engagement models concern themselves with range from the activity level (e.g., attention, concentration), to the class/school level (e.g., attendance). Consequently, there have been ongoing calls for greater conceptual clarity (Fredricks, Blumenfeld, & Paris, 2004; Philp & Duchesne, 2016). In response, researchers in the field of SLA have proposed an engagement model specific to L2 learning (e.g., Svalberg, 2009, 2017; Philp & Duchesne, 2016). In

Table 11.1 Summary of Selected Models of Engagement

Authors	Constructs of engagement	Definitions/descriptions
Appleton, Christenson, Kim, & Reschly (2006)	Academic	Time on task Credit hours toward graduation Homework completion
	Behavioral	Attendance Voluntary classroom participation Extracurricular participation Extra credit options
	Cognitive	Self-regulation Relevance of school to future aspirations Value of learning Strategizing
	Psychological	Belonging Identification with school School membership
Skinner, Furrer, Marchand, & Kindermann, (2008)	Behavioral	Action initiation Effort/Exertion Attempts/Persistence Intensity Attention/Concentration Absorption Involvement
	Emotional	Enthusiasm Interest Enjoyment Satisfaction Pride Vitality Zest
Reeve (2012)	Behavioral	On-task attention and concentration High effort High task persistence
	Emotional	Presence of task-facilitating emotions Absence of task-withdrawing emotions
	Cognitive	Use of sophisticated, deep, and personalized learning strategies Seeking conceptual understanding rather than surface knowledge Use of self-regulatory strategies
	Agentic	Proactive, intentional, and constructive contribution into the flow of the learning activity Enriching the learning activity, rather than passively receiving it as a given
Reschly & Christenson (2012)	Affective	Belonging/Identification with school School connectedness
	Cognitive	Self-regulation Relevance of school to future aspirations Value of learning
	Behavioral	Attendance Participation Behavioral incidents
	Academic	Time on task Credit hours toward graduation Homework completion rate and accuracy Class grades

the next section, we review engagement in language learning by drawing on the language learners' engagement model proposed by Philp and Duchesne (2016) as a guiding theoretical framework.

Engagement in SLA

SLA researchers have more recently begun to explore engagement in language learning, and this interest has grown rapidly in recent years. It has been increasingly acknowledged that engagement plays a key role in language learning (Dörnyei & Kormos, 2000; Mercer, 2019; Philp & Duchesne, 2016; Svalberg, 2009, 2017). For example, it is argued that engagement is an initial condition for language processing to take place; learners need to be actively involved and producing the language in order for their L2 skills to be developed (Dörnyei & Kormos, 2000). Cyclical engagement in the learning process is argued to help develop learners' *academic buoyancy*, the capacity to handle difficulties and challenges in school (Skinner & Pitzer, 2012), and buoyancy has been shown to predict L2 achievement (Yun, Hiver, & Al-Hoorie, 2018). SLA research has also shown that engagement is positively associated with intrinsically regulated motives for L2 learning (Oga-Baldwin & Nakata, 2017) and personal investment (King, Yeung, & Cai, 2019).

One key characteristic of engagement highlighted among SLA researchers is that engagement, while a psychological construct, deals with action-related elements in the learning process (Mercer, 2019; Oga-Baldwin, 2019). This feature makes engagement stand out from other affective constructs, such as motivation, which is characterized as intention and/or energy. Mercer (2019) succinctly articulates this point: "learners need to be motivated and willing to engage, but the next step is whether they actually translate that willingness into sustained active engagement" (p. 3). Another key characteristic of engagement is that it is a multidimensional construct, although there are different views about the number and types of dimensions. For example, Mercer (2019) describes engagement in terms of behavioral, affective, and cognitive dimensions, while Oga-Baldwin (2019) views engagement as consisting of behavioral, emotional, cognitive, and agentic dimensions. Svalberg (2009) proposes the type of engagement specific to a language learning context: *Engagement with language*, which depicts a cognitive, affective, and social process in which learners develop language awareness as the agent with the language being the object, as opposed to being a tool for communication. Here we focus primarily on engagement at the task level as it has been the focus of the vast majority of SLA research, and as insights into engagement at this level can be of particular use to SLA research given its action focus (Mercer, 2019). For engagement conceptualized at the class and school levels, see, e.g., Oga-Baldwin, (2019) and Reschly and Christenson (2012).

Conceptualization and Measures of Engagement in SLA

Engagement at the task level can be understood as a state of heightened attention and involvement, in which participation is reflected not only in behavior but also in manifestations of cognitive and social dimensions, as well as in affective dimensions of learners' emotions and responses to tasks (Lambert, Philp, & Nakamura, 2017; Philp & Duchesne, 2016). Behavioral engagement refers to the degree and quality of learners' participation (Philp & Duchesne, 2016). This includes learners' effort, persistence, and active involvement in learning activities (Fredricks et al., 2004; Lambert et al., 2017) as well as intensity, persistence, determination, and perseverance when faced with difficulties (Skinner & Pitzer, 2012). At the same time, the term *effort* needs clarification as it is also used to describe cognitive engagement, as in *mental effort*. When researchers use the term "effort" in describing behavioral engagement, it generally refers to the types of behaviors manifested by learners' effort such as the amount of L2 output produced or time invested in completing a task. Indicators of behavioral engagement can include responding to instructions, teachers, and peers such as in help-seeking, gazing, nodding, asking questions, and completing more work than required (Finn & Zimmer, 2012; Oga-Baldwin, 2019; Mahatmya, Lohman, Matjasko, & Farb, 2012).

Cognitive engagement encompasses sustained attention, focus, and alertness (Lambert et al., 2017; Svalberg, 2009). This dimension depicts heads-on participation, as opposed to hands-on participation (i.e., behavioral dimension). A wide range of indicators has been proposed, but some of them overlap with those of behavior engagement. For example, Helme and Clarke (2001) describe asking questions as an indicator of cognitive engagement, whereas Mahatmya et al. (2012) categorize it as behavioral engagement. Some indicators are SLA-specific. Examples include *language-related episodes*, which refer to dialogues where learners discuss the language that they are producing and question their language use, for example, through negotiation of meaning and form and self-repairs (Baralt, Gurzynski-Weiss, & Kim, 2016; Nakamura, Phung, & Reinders, in review; Phung, 2017). Other indicators are *private speech* and *exploratory talk*, the latter of which refers to learners' utterances produced for reasoning or exemplification purposes, typically articulated with phrases such as "I think" and connectors such as "because" (Lambert et al., 2017; Philp & Duchesne, 2016). Other indicators are specific to peer interaction during collaborative activities: justifying an argument, explaining, and evaluating ideas (Helme & Clarke, 2001; Philp & Duchesne, 2016).

Social engagement concerns the relationship among learners through which they interact and affiliate with each other (Lambert et al., 2017; Philp & Duchesne, 2016). Socially engaged learners "listen to one another, draw from one another's expertise and ideas, and provide feedback to one another" (Philp & Duchesne, 2016, p. 10). Such interactions can be characterized as interactive, initiating, supportive, and collaborative, and learners seek to maintain such interaction when socially engaged (Svalberg, 2009). Two points need to be noted about social engagement. The first is that the social dimension is not included in all engagement models. However, we argue that the social aspects involved in peer interaction should be foregrounded as one dimension of engagement (Philp & Duchesne, 2016; Svalberg, 2009), given the increasing emphasis on learners' collaboration in language learning underpinned by socio-cultural perspectives in SLA, and research showing peer interaction facilitating language learning (Sato & Ballinger, 2016; Swain & Watanabe, 2012). The second is that social engagement in educational psychology research has been typically described in terms of students' behaviors following (or not following) school and classroom rules. Such behaviors include coming to class on time, appropriately interacting with teachers and peers, and not distracting classroom work (Finn & Zimmer, 2012).

Affective engagement concerns "the affective nature of learners' involvement in the learning activities" (Philp & Duchesne, 2016). While some researchers use the term "emotional engagement," we opt for the term "affective" because we view this dimension as involving not only specific types of emotions but also a wide range of affective constructs. A number of affective constructs have been used to describe the affective dimension of engagement, examples of which include interest, enthusiasm, enjoyment (Skinner, Kindermann, & Furrer 2009), excitement, curiosity (Reeve, 2012), value (Mercer, 2019), purposefulness, and autonomy (Baralt et al., 2016). Negative emotions such as anxiety, boredom, frustration, fear, and anger have been used to describe emotional disengagement, or "task-withdrawing" emotions, as opposed to "task-promoting emotions" (Reeve, 2012, p. 150). Learners' subjective responses to tasks (Lambert et al., 2017; Phung, 2017) and perceived connections with task interlocutors (Philp & Duchesne, 2016) are also related to affective engagement.

A key characteristic of this multidimensional model of engagement is that these dimensions overlap, interact with each other, and can manifest themselves differently. For example, a learner spontaneously and automatically writing or speaking for purely communicative purposes can be socially engaged but may not be engaged with language (Svalberg, 2009). A study by Mercer, Talbot, and Wang (forthcoming) in fact found that learners sometimes consciously manipulate their behaviors in front of the teacher in order to feign engagement, or project superficial outward displays of engagement. This complexity in engagement points to the importance of considering different dimensions in measuring engagement.

In measuring engagement, self-report surveys have long been the most commonly used tools. This has particularly been the case in educational research. Some of the survey instruments are well-established with delineated items with strong psychometric validity, including the Student Engagement Instruments (SEI; Appleton, Christenson, Kim & Reschly, 2006), Agentic Engagement Questionnaire (AEQ; Reeve, 2013), Engagement Versus Disaffection with Learning measure (EVDL; Skinner et al., 2009), Metacognitive Strategies Questionnaire (MSQ; Wolters, 2004), and Motivated Strategies for Learning Questionnaire (MSLQ; Pintrich, Smith, Garcia, & McKeachie, 1991). These self-report instruments are typically used to elicit students' typical behavior or general beliefs within a specific school subject or at class/school levels. What is noticeable from these different tools is that they refer to different levels of engagement and different manifestations of engagement. As such, SLA researchers call for the expansion of foci and levels of granularity in assessing engagement in order to gain a fuller picture of the construct in a range of contexts (Hiver, Al-Hoorie, & Mercer, forthcoming).

TBLT studies have made methodological contributions to researching engagement at the task level. For example, researchers have examined interactional discourse and combined it with self-report and/or interviews. Behavioral engagement measures include the amount of time invested, the number of words produced, and the frequency of turn-taking during communicative tasks (Bygate & Samuda, 2009; Dörnyei & Kormos, 2000). As families of language-related episodes, private speech, and exploratory talk, occurrences of negotiation of meaning and form, self-repairs (i.e., a speaker's attempt to change what has been said), and elaborative clauses produced to expand semantic content have been used as cognitive engagement measures (Lambert et al., 2017; Nakamura et al., in review; Phung, 2017; Qiu & Lo, 2017). Backchannelling is widely used as a social engagement measure as it indicates active listening behavior as well as responsiveness and willingness to be involved in the conversation (Philp & Duchesne, 2016). Other measures include overlaps, i.e., instances of more than one speaker speaking at the same time, and turn-completions, i.e., instances of a speaker completing the other speaker's utterance (Nakamura et al., in review; Phung, 2017). Affective engagement measures have employed both qualitative and quantitative methods. Examples of the former include post-task interviews and stimulated recalls (Phung, 2017; Qiu & Lo, 2017). Examples of the latter include a questionnaire on *flow* (Egbert, 2003), referred to as all-encompassing involvement of the optimal focus, attention, enjoyment, and a sense of control, and Likert-scale items assessing specific emotions (Aubrey, 2017; Lambert et al., 2017; Nakamura et al., in review).

Antecedents of Engagement

Several factors have been suggested as antecedents of engagement. Such factors can be arranged according to hierarchical levels of contexts ranging from individual (Fredricks et al., 2004; Mercer, 2019), task (Phung, 2017; Nakamura et al., in review), class (Jang, Kim, & Reeve, 2012; Reeve, 2012), school (Finn, 1989), family (Kraft & Dougherty, 2013), and culture (Conner, 2009). Wang and Mercer (forthcoming) have recently proposed Willingness to Engage (WTE), which consists of individual, social, and contextual variables, to describe a dynamic emergent state prior to actual engagement in L2 learning opportunities. In the context of this handbook, we focus the discussion of antecedent of engagement primarily on psychological constructs. In doing so, we draw on the Self-System Model of Motivational Development (SSMMD; Connell & Wellborn, 1991; Ryan, Connell, & Deci, 1985). SSMMD is a model of positive motivational development grounded in self-determination theory and it has been widely used to explain student engagement. The model posits that individual learners have fundamental psychological needs for *autonomy*, *competence*, and *relatedness*, and that the degree to which learners perceive these needs as being met shapes how they engage in available learning opportunities. Numerous empirical findings have also supported this claim (e.g., Dincer, Yeşilyurt, & Noels, 2019; Dincer, Yeşilyurt, Noels, & Vargas Lascano, 2019; Jang et al., 2012).

Autonomy refers to the need to experience one's self as a source of action and to express the authentic self (Reeve, 2012; Skinner & Pitzer, 2012) (see Chapter 19). It has been argued that learners become more engaged when they feel more autonomous, that is, they have choice, shared decision making, and relative freedom to influence their own actions (Connell & Wellborn, 1991; Nakamura et al, in review). *Competence* refers to the need to experience oneself as effective in one's pursuits and interactions with the environment (Reeve, 2012; Skinner & Pitzer, 2012). Similarly, *mindset* concerns learners' beliefs about whether their language skills can be advanced through continuous effort and practice (a growth mindset), or whether they are viewed as fixed (a fixed mindset); (Mercer & Ryan 2010) (see Chapter 13). As such, learners holding fixed mindsets may not feel willing to invest in learning no matter how engaging tasks and materials may be (Mercer, 2015). *Relatedness* describes the basic human need for connection with others. A sense of belonging, which refers to an individual's sense of being accepted, valued, and encouraged by others (Baumeister & Leary, 1995) is similar. When individuals experience belonging, it gives them a sense of security and support. Experiencing a sense of belonging in the classroom with peers and the teacher can help increase learners' readiness and willingness to engage in learning activities (Booker, 2006; Furrer & Skinner, 2003; Hughes & Kwok, 2007).

Various layers of factors come into play in shaping the emergence and degree of learners' engagement. Teachers' instructional styles, school support, and relational climates in class are often discussed as important factors thought to influence learner engagement. At the same time, it is the learners themselves who perceive, acknowledge, and appraise all that surrounds them. The psychological constructs reviewed above indicate the importance of considering both environmental and learner factors when examining the antecedents of engagement.

Integrating Perspectives on Engagement from Psychology and SLA

At present, SLA is marked by a growing interest in learning "beyond the classroom" (Reinders & Benson, 2017). This has its heritage in approaches designed to foster learner autonomy as a language educational aim (Holec, 1979). A broad range of learner training efforts including an increased focus on the development of learning strategies, the development of self-access/independent learning centers, and the provision of language advising services, among others, are areas intended to prepare learners for and support them during time spent out of class (see Reinders, 2010 for an overview). At the same time, there is a growing interest in ecological perspectives on learning that examine multiple contexts of learning and their influence on each other, including both formal (in class) and informal domains. In general education and psychology, studies of engagement to date have by and large focused on investigations and interventions in formal contexts. Yet, there is considerable opportunity for cross-fertilization between the two domains; clearly what learners do in their lives outside of formalized education affects their engagement within the school context and vice versa. By combining the insights from holistic studies of lifelong and lifewide learning with the more fine-grained understanding of in-class engagement, it could be possible to gain a richer understanding of how experiences in the two domains are linked. In this regard, SLA can possibly lead the way given its current interest in and strong connections between language learning in and beyond the classroom.

Indeed, the present moment offers an especially opportune context for this integration to take place; in many countries, significant, large-scale movements are underway to encourage and better prepare learners for taking on greater responsibility for their own learning, both within and out-of-class, with the aim of encouraging more active involvement and participation of learner engagement. Examples of these include Thailand's Ministry of Education, which requires learners to become more autonomous, Japan's efforts to promote *active learning* across the entire educational system, and China's *College English*, the compulsory English language courses taught at universities across the country, which expects learners to take more responsibility for their education. Such movements offer considerable opportunities for observing and investigating engagement and language learning and use. SLA engagement work could thus inspire scholars of engagement from beyond the field as a model for more holistic perspectives on learners and their engagement.

Implications for Practice and Research

It is tempting to wish for immediately applicable and unambiguous recommendations to enhance learner engagement in language education, but caveats and gaps remain in our empirical and theoretical understandings of the construct in our field. As such, any recommendations must be expressed with a degree of caution. Firstly, as talk of affect is becoming more mainstream, teachers are looking for more systematic ways of valuing and supporting this key aspect of the language learning process. As indicated in the previous section, self-determination theory is prominent in engagement studies. Mercer (2019) reminds us that these are areas in which a great deal of work can be done by teachers. For example, competence can be enhanced by developing a growth mindset (Dweck, 2008), autonomy by giving learners greater responsibility over their own learning (Reinders, 2011), and relatedness by working on improving the classroom atmosphere and enhancing a sense of belonging. These are (only some of the) techniques that many teachers are familiar with and that teacher development programs can use as a starting point for a more differentiated discussion of the role of engagement.

Another development, which supports the promotion and measurement of learner engagement, is the use of digital tools, including, for example, classroom management tools like Seesaw, Socrative, and Ditto; all of which allow teachers to observe, comment on, and record student contributions to the classroom environment. Many of these help teachers to monitor engagement levels and encourage teachers to reward positive behaviors, such as when asking questions or helping another student. These are, of course, of particular benefit at a time when many teachers have had to move classes online. With the added challenge of not being able to receive visual cues in the same way as in real life, and the added issues of poor audio and general unfamiliarity of protocols and practices online, monitoring engagement is of primary concern. Teachers find themselves needing to quickly learn to use features such as virtual break-out rooms for small-group work, chatrooms for backchannelling, and polling and quizzes to check understanding and participation.

Similarly, as more dynamic, complex, and holistic views of language learning become more accepted, the multidimensional nature of engagement will, over time, lead to more refined teaching methods to recognize and enhance different aspects of engagement, both inside and outside the classroom. Although most instruments that currently exist are primarily used for research purposes, some of these may be adapted to suit diagnostic and monitoring purposes by teachers. Current instruments in use in education, such as the High School Survey of Student Engagement (ceep.indiana.edu/hssse) and the Student Engagement Instrument (checkandconnect.umn.edu/sei/default.html), will be refined and adapted to suit engagement in language learning specifically. Similarly, databases of best practices in student engagement from general education have been available since at least 2008 (Christenson, Reschly, Appleton, Berman, Spanjers, & Varro, 2008) and continue to grow. Such records offer a good starting point for teacher-researchers. Likewise, intervention programs, such as the long-established Check & Connect (Christenson & Reschly, 2010), designed as a long-term mentoring program to support student engagement in US high schools, can provide many valuable lessons for language educators.

Next, the growing recognition of the highly contextual nature of engagement means that insights gleaned from research have implications not only for teachers, but also for the broader environment in which learners operate. This means involving not only learners and teachers, but also administrators, parents, and social groups, all of whom play a significant part in the engagement process.

Future Directions

There are also opportunities afforded by new technologies, which are creating novel opportunities to measure engagement in broadly two different ways. On the one hand, there are new tools for directly observing (indicators of) engagement and, on the other hand, there are new approaches to making sense of large sets of data relating to engagement. New tools that offer promise include increasingly affordable eye-tracking devices. Whereas previously a set-up for research purposes was at least US$20,000, simple systems can now be purchased for a few hundred dollars (albeit with less fidelity). Tracking what someone is attending to can be one indicator of engagement, but it is also possible to track eye movements over a longer period of time (say a whole class) to get insight into patterns of engagement that can be related to, for example, different class activities. At present, such devices are still too large and require more set up time than is reasonable in most classrooms, but as the technology improves we are seeing basic eye tracking included in cellphones and other portable devices, which could conceivably provide data on all learners in a class. Another option is to use POV (point-of-view) cameras worn by one or more participants in the class (innovative studies exist that compare teachers' actions and attention to particular students, with students' responses). A technologically simpler example is the use of fitness watches and bands, which can record data (such as heart rate) about a learner's physiological reactions to the environment (complex and expensive brain scanning techniques like fMRI and PET scans have been used in the past, but not directly linked to engagement to the best of our knowledge). Engagement outside the classroom can be tracked through wearable devices like the Kapture wristband, which records audio at all times and saves only the audio that a learner chooses. The first author has experimented with this for the purposes of encouraging learners to record instances of, for example, a grammatical point discussed in class when interacting outside the classroom. It has also been used by both authors in initial teacher training where teachers recorded critical incidents during work placements for follow-up afterwards with their mentor or supervisor; this could be used as an indicator of emotional engagement.

The classroom itself could also record other forms of data that can be used in engagement research. For example, with the development of Internet of Things (IoT) devices, physical objects are being connected to, for example, the Internet. With a simple sensor, a seat in a classroom could record that it is occupied. By linking with a user's cellphone, the system can record whether someone attended school that day. By recording such data over longer periods of time, it is possible to detect patterns and changes therein and identify students at risk. The processes used to make sense of such data are referred to as learning analytics or educational data mining (see Reinders, 2018). Another example, already widely in use, is the analysis of data generated through interaction with online resources, such as learning management systems (LMS) or social networking sites. LMS in particular record a great deal of data about the amount of time students spend working with different resources, when, with whom, and a great deal of other user data that can be mined for research purposes as indicators of behavioral engagement. Classroom management programs like Kahoot and Ditto, mentioned above, similarly record a great deal of data about who does what in class and when and of course Zoom and other synchronous programs used for online instruction allow teachers to record all interaction in the class, both audio and video and chat comments. This data is then available for the teacher during and after the class, which has practical potential and also offers a valuable source of information for research purposes. Social interaction patterns can be investigated using social network analysis processes (Knoke & Yang, 2019) as indicators of social engagement. As more data becomes available about more aspects of learners' lives over longer periods of time, many opportunities arise to find out how learner engagement patterns develop and how this relates to other variables in learners' lives, while remaining mindful of ethical concerns. The field of engagement studies in SLA is certain to have a major influence on our understanding of language learning processes in all its idiosyncratic ways in the coming years and new technologies will facilitate that growth.

Reflection Questions

- Consider the tools discussed in the Future Direction section. Can you think of ways of using one of these tools for observing engagement among your learners either within or outside your class?

- A colleague in your department is doing interesting work on learner uptake in peer-interaction as part of a language exchange program. How could you draw on this data for your own study of engagement?
- In your context, how could engagement research contribute to enhanced learning and teaching?

Recommended Reading

Hiver, P., Mercer, S., & Al-Hoorie, A. H. (Eds.). (Forthcoming). *Engagement in the second language classroom*. Multilingual Matters.

This edited volume offers a great collection of conceptual discussions of the construct, which include definitional, theoretical, and measurement issues, as well as empirical studies showcasing a range of methodologies in varying contexts. A great place to learn about the up-to-date engagement research in SLA.

Christenson, S. L., Reschly, A. L., & Wylie, C. (Eds.). (2012). *Handbook of research on student engagement*. Springer.

This edited book offers a comprehensive view on engagement from educational psychology. Much of the work discussed in the book has benefitted SLA in advancing the research on engagement. A useful place to explore the root of engagement in learning as well as expand the knowledge of the construct.

Philp, J., & Duchesne, S. (2016). Exploring engagement in tasks in the language classroom. *Annual Review of Applied Linguistics, 36*, 50–72.

This pioneering work by Philp and Duchesne has made a substantial contribution to the advancement of engagement in SLA. It is a great place to start in conceptualizing engagement through a comprehensive discussion and illustration of engagement.

References

Appleton, J. J., Christenson, S. L., Kim, D., & Reschly, A. L. (2006). Measuring cognitive and psychological engagement: Validation of the Student Engagement Instrument. *Journal of School Psychology, 44*(5), 427–445.

Aubrey, S. (2017). Inter-cultural contact and flow in a task-based Japanese EFL classroom. *Language Teaching Research, 21*(6), 717–734.

Bakker, A. B., & Bal, P. M. (2010). Weekly work engagement and performance: A study among starting teachers. *Journal of Occupational and Organizational Psychology, 83*, 189–206.

Baralt, M., Gurzynski-Weiss, L., & Kim, Y. (2016). Engagement with language: How examining learners' affective and social engagement explains successful learner-generated attention to form. In M. Sato & S. Ballinger (Eds.), *Peer interaction and second language learning. Pedagogical potential and research agenda* (pp. 209–240). John Benjamins.

Baumeister, R. F., & Leary, M. R. (1995). The need to belong: Desire for interpersonal attachments as a fundamental human motivation. *Psychological Bulletin, 117*(3), 497–529.

Booker, K. C. (2006). School belonging and the African-American adolescent: What do we know and where should we go? *The High School Journal, 89*, 1–7.

Bygate, M., & Samuda, V. (2009). Creating pressure in task pedagogy: The joint roles of field, purpose, and engagement within the interaction approach. In A. Mackey & C. Polio (Eds.), *Multiple perspectives on interaction: Second language research in honour of Susan M. Gass* (pp. 90–116). Routledge.

Christenson, S. L., & Reschly, A. L. (2010). Check & Connect: Enhancing school completion through student engagement. In E. Doll & J. Charvat (Eds.), *Handbook of prevention science* (pp. 327–348). Routledge.

Christenson, S. L., Reschly, A. L., Appleton, J. J., Berman, S., Spanjers, D., & Varro, P. (2008). Best practices in fostering student engagement. In A. Thomas & J. Grimes (Eds.), *Best practices in school psychology V* (pp. 1099–1120). National Association of School Psychologists.

Christian, M. S., Garza, A. S., & Slaughter, J. E. (2011). Work engagement: A quantitative review and test of its relations with task and contextual performance. *Personnel Psychology, 64*, 89–136.

Connell, J. P., & Wellborn, J. G. (1991). Competence, autonomy, and relatedness: A motivational analysis of self-system processes. In M. R. Gunnar & L. A. Sroufe (Eds.), *The Minnesota Symposia on Child Psychology: Vol. 23. Self processes and development* (p. 43–77). Lawrence Erlbaum Associates.

Conner, J. O. (2009). Student engagement in an independent research project: The influence of cohort culture. *Journal of Advanced Academics, 21*(1), 8–38.

Dincer, A., Yeşilyurt, S., & Noels, K. A. (2019). Self-determined engagement in language learning: The relations among autonomy-support, psychological needs, and engagement. *Cumhuriyet Uluslararası Eğitim Dergisi, 8*(4), 1130–1147.

Dincer, A., Yeşilyurt, S., Noels, K. A., & Vargas Lascano, D. I. (2019). Self-determination and classroom engagement of EFL learners: A mixed-methods study of the self-system model of motivational development. *SAGE Open, 9*(2), 1–15.

Dörnyei, Z., & Kormos, J. (2000). The role of individual and social variable in oral task performance. *Language Teaching Research, 4,* 275–300.

Dweck, C. S. (2008). *Mindset: The new psychology of success.* Random House.

Egbert, J. (2003). A study of flow theory in the foreign language classroom. *The Modern Language Journal, 87,* 499–518.

Finn, J. D. (1989). Withdrawing from school. *Review of Educational Research, 59*(2), 117–142.

Finn, J. D., & Zimmer, K. S. (2012). Student engagement: What is it? Why does it matter? In S. L. Christenson, A. L. Reschly, & C. Wylie (Eds.), *Handbook of research on student engagement* (pp. 97–131). Springer.

Fredricks, J. A., Blumenfeld, P. C., & Paris, A. H. (2004). School engagement: Potential of the concept, state of the evidence. *Review of Educational Research, 74*(1), 59–109.

Furrer, C., & Skinner, E. (2003). Sense of relatedness as a factor in children's academic engagement and performance. *Journal of Educational Psychology, 95*(1), 148–162.

Sinatra, G. M., Heddy, B. C., & Lombardi, D. (2015). The challenges of defining and measuring student engagement in science, *Educational Psychologist, (50)*1, 1–13.

Helme, S., & Clarke, D. (2001). Identifying cognitive engagement in the mathematics classroom. *Mathematics Education Research Journal, 13,* 133–153.

Hindman, J., & Stronge, J. (2009). The $2 million decision: Teacher selection and principals' interviewing practices. *ERS Spectrum, 27,* 1–10.

Holec H. (1979). Prise en compte des besoins et apprentissage auto-dirigé. *Mélanges Pédagogiques, 10,* Université de Nancy 2: CRAPEL.

Hughes, J., & Kwok, O. M. (2007). Influence of student-teacher and parent-teacher relationships on lower achieving readers' engagement and achievement in the primary grades. *Journal of Educational Psychology, 99*(1), 39–51.

Jang, H., Kim, E. J., & Reeve, J. (2012). Longitudinal test of self-determination theory's motivation mediation model in a naturally occurring classroom context. *Journal of Educational Psychology, 104,* 1175–1188.

King, R. B., Yeung, S. S. S., & Cai, Y. (2019). Personal investment theory: A multi-faceted framework to understand second and foreign language motivation. *System, 86,* 102–123.

Klassen, R. M., Aldhafri, S., Mansfield, C. F., Purwanto, E., Siu, A. F., Wong, M. W., & Woods-McConney, A. (2012). Teachers' engagement at work: An international validation study. *The Journal of Experimental Education, 80*(4), 317–337.

Knoke, D., & Yang, S. (2019). *Social network analysis* (Vol. 154). CA, SAGE.

Kraft, M. A., & Dougherty, S. M. (2013). The effect of teacher-family communication on student engagement: Evidence from a randomized field experiment. *Journal of Research on Educational Effectiveness, 6*(3), 199–222.

Kuh, G. D., Kinzie, J., Buckley, J. A., Bridges, B. K., & Hayek, J. C. (2007). Piecing together the learner success puzzle: Research, propositions, and recommendations. *ASHE higher education report, 32*(5).

Lambert, C., Philp, J., & Nakamura, S. (2017). Learner-generated content and engagement in second language task performance. *Language Teaching Research, 21*(6), 665–680.

Mahatmya, D., Lohman, B. J., Matjasko, J. L., & Farb, A. F. (2012). Engagement across developmental periods. In S. L. Christenson, A. L. Reschly, & C. Wylie (Eds.), *Handbook of research on student engagement* (pp. 45–63). Springer.

Mercer, S. (2015). Learner agency and engagement: Believing you can, wanting to, and knowing how to. *Humanizing Language Teaching, 17*(4), 1–19.

Mercer, S. (2019). Language learner engagement: Setting the scene. In Gao, X., Davison, C., & Leung, C. (Eds.), *International Handbook of English Language Teaching.* Springer.

Mercer, S., & Ryan, S. (2010). A mindset for EFL: Learners' beliefs about the role of natural talent. *ELT Journal, 64*(4), 436–444.

Mosher, R., & McGowan, B. (1985). Assessing student engagement in secondary schools: Alternative conceptions, strategies of assessing, and instruments. *University of Wisconsin, Research and Development Center* (ERIC Document Reproduction Service No. ED 272812).

Nakamura, S., Phung, L, & Reinders, H. (2021). The effect of learner choice on L2 task engagement. *Studies in Second Language Acquisition, 43*(2), 428–441.

Newmann, F. M. (1992). *Student engagement and achievement in American secondary schools*. Teachers College Press.
Oga-Baldwin, W. Q. (2019). Acting, thinking, feeling, making, collaborating: The engagement process in foreign language learning. *System, 86*, 102–128.
Oga-Baldwin, W. L. Q., & Nakata, Y. (2017). Engagement, gender, and motivation: A predictive model for Japanese young language learners. *System, 65*, 151–163.
Philp, J., & Duchesne, S. (2016). Exploring engagement in tasks in the language classroom. *Annual Review of Applied Linguistics, 36*, 50–72.
Phung, L. (2017). Task preference, affective response, and engagement in L2 use in a US university context. *Language Teaching Research, 21*(6), 751–766.
Pintrich, P. R., Smith, D. A. F., Garcia, T., & McKeachie, W. J. (1991). *A manual for the use of the Motivated Strategies for Learning Questionnaire (MSLQ)* [Tech. Report No. 91-B-004]. Board of Regents, University of Michigan, Ann Arbor, MI.
Qiu, X., & Lo, Y. Y. (2017). Content familiarity, task repetition and Chinese EFL learners' engagement in second language use. *Language Teaching Research, 21*(6), 681–698.
Reeve, J. (2012). A self-determination theory perspective on student engagement. In S. L. Christenson, A. L. Reschly, & C. Wylie (Eds.), *Handbook of research on student engagement* (pp. 149–172). Springer.
Reeve, J. (2013). How students create motivationally supportive learning environments for themselves: The concept of agentic engagement. *Journal of Educational Psychology, 105*(3), 579–595.
Reinders, H. (2010). Towards a classroom pedagogy for learner autonomy: A framework of independent language learning skills. *Australian Journal of Teacher Education, 35*(5), 40–55.
Reinders, H. (2011). Towards an operationalisation of autonomy. In A. Ahmed, G. Cane, & M. Hanzala (Eds.), *Teaching English in multilingual contexts: Current challenges, future directions* (pp. 37–52). Cambridge Scholars Publishing.
Reinders, H. (2018). Learning analytics for language learning and teaching. *JALT CALL Journal, 14*(1), 35–44.
Reinders, H., & Benson, P. (2017). Language learning beyond the classroom: A research agenda. *Language Teaching, 50*(4), 561–578.
Reschly A. L., & Christenson S. L. (2012). Jingle, jangle, and conceptual haziness: Evolution and future directions of the engagement construct. In S. L. Christenson, A. L. Reschly, & C. Wylie (Eds.), *Handbook of research on student engagement* (pp. 3–19). Springer.
Ryan, R. M., Connell, J. P., & Deci, E. L. (1985). A motivational analysis of self-determination and self-regulation in education. In C. Ames & R. Ames (Eds.), *Research on motivation in education: The classroom milieu* (pp. 13–52). Academic.
Sato M., & Ballinger, S. (2016). Understanding peer interaction: Research synthesis and directions. In M Sato & S. Ballinger (Eds.), *Peer interaction and second language learning: Pedagogical potential and research agenda* (pp. 1–30). John Benjamins.
Skaalvik, E. M., & Skaalvik, S. (2014). Teacher self-efficacy and perceived autonomy: Relations with teacher engagement, job satisfaction, and emotional exhaustion. *Psychological Reports, 114*(1), 68–77.
Skinner, E. A., Furrer, C., Marchand, G., & Kindermann, T. (2008). Engagement and disaffection in the classroom: Part of a larger motivational dynamic? *Journal of Educational Psychology, 100*(4), 765.
Skinner, E. A., Kindermann, T. A., & Furrer, C. J. (2009). A motivational perspective on engagement and disaffection: Conceptualization and assessment of children's behavioral and emotional participation in academic activities in the classroom. *Educational and Psychological Measurement, 69*(3), 493–525.
Skinner, E. A., & Pitzer, J. R. (2012). Developmental dynamics of student engagement, coping, and everyday resilience. In S. L. Christenson, A. L. Reschly, & C. Wylie (Eds.), *Handbook of research on student engagement* (pp. 21–44). Springer.
Svalberg, A. M-L. (2009). Engagement with language: Developing a construct. *Language Awareness, 18*(3–4), 242–258.
Svalberg, A. M.-L. (2017). Researching language engagement; current trends and future directions. *Language Awareness, 27*, 21–39.
Swain, M., & Watanabe, Y. (2012). Languaging: Collaborative dialogue as a source of second language learning. *The Encyclopedia of Applied Linguistics*, 1–8.
Yun, S., Hiver, P., & Al-Hoorie, A. H. (2018). Academic buoyancy: Exploring learners' everyday resilience in the language classroom. *Studies in Second Language Acquisition, 40*(4), 805–830.
Wolters, C. A. (2004). Advancing achievement goal theory: Using goal structures and goal orientations to predict students' motivation, cognition, and achievement. *Journal of Educational Psychology, 96*, 236–250.

12
ATTITUDES AND BELIEFS

Amy S. Thompson

The chapter title, "attitudes and beliefs," represents an enormous umbrella under which many different constructs can be found both in the field of Second Language Acquisition (SLA) and in the field of psychology. This chapter unpacks these terms in the context of both disciplinary norms, illustrating the overlap and the potential for further development. The chapter starts with an overview of these terms in the field of psychology and continues to do the same in the field of SLA. In psychology, terms such as *implicit* and *explicit attitudes* are discussed, along with common data collection practices. In the section focusing on SLA, an overview of attitudes and beliefs about language learning is presented, as well as attitudes towards different languages in a variety of contexts. The chapter culminates with how psychology and SLA are integrated with regard to these terms and includes implications and potential for future research. Throughout these sections, the multifaceted nature of *attitudes* and *beliefs* unfolds. A fascinating topic in both SLA and psychology, the chapter will provide the reader with an overview of what has already been done, as well as what is yet to come.

Attitudes and Beliefs in Psychology

In psychology, there are several key terms that relate to the concepts of *attitudes* and *beliefs*; however, as *attitude* is the typical term found in the psychology literature, this section will focus on attitudes in psychology. These attitudes are oftentimes linked to what is known as *social cognition,* or "how people think about others and the social world" (Hess & Pickett, n.d., p. 2). Specifically, *attitude* is defined in psychology as a "psychological tendency that is expressed by evaluating a particular entity with some degree of favor or disfavor" (Eagly & Chaiken, 1993, p.1). There are two main types of attitudes addressed in psychological research: explicit and implicit. Explicit attitudes are those of which a person is aware and that can be documented by asking that person direct questions. An example of gathering information on explicit attitudes might be in a survey or focus group when people are asked to try two or more products and provide feedback on which they like better and why. These types of surveys are oftentimes used in market research as companies decide how to move forward with specific types of products. Two main types of survey items that can be used to measure explicit attitudes are semantic-differential scales (Osgood, Suci, & Tannenbaum, 1957) and Likert scales (Likert, 1932). A semantic-differential scale item takes a specific animate or inanimate object with two opposing adjectives on either end of the scale. For example, *cat* could be the object, and the scale could refer to *friendliness*, so an example would be as follows:

DOI: 10.4324/9780429321498-15

Please mark an X to determine your feelings about cats.

friendly X ___ ___ ___ ___ ___ unfriendly

The participant who marked an X closest to the adjective of *friendly* indicates that they believe cats are quite friendly. In SLA research, this type of semantic-differential scale was used in Gardner's (1985) Attitude Motivation Test Battery (AMTB) with several adjective pairs to evaluate attitudes towards a student's French teacher and French course.

The most common measure of explicit attitudes are Likert scale items. For such items, participants have to choose how much they strongly agree or disagree with a statement:

West Virginia is the most beautiful state in the US

Strongly disagree   1   2   3   4   5   ⑥   Strongly agree

In this case, the participant is absolutely sure that West Virginia is the most beautiful state in the US. In terms of the numbers on the scale itself, there has been some debate if Likert scale items should consist of an even or an odd number of choices. An odd number, such as a scale of seven, gives the participant the opportunity to be neutral by picking the middle number, which is useful when presenting items that might not elicit any type of specific attitude from a participant, or when a neutral option is an important piece of the point of inquiry. The danger in odd-numbered scales is that some participants might take the path of least resistance and choose primarily neutral answers throughout the questionnaire. In order to force a positive or negative choice, even-numbered scales would require participants to choose a side, so to speak, even if the answer is only slightly positive or slightly negative. In psychology research, a neutral answer might be an important insight; SLA researchers might more often look for an opinion one way or another. Thus, although some researchers do not agree, Dörnyei and Taguchi (2010) recommend even-numbered Likert-scale items to be used in SLA research.

It is the case, however, that people sometimes are not consciously aware of their attitudes or do not want to directly state their attitudes about a specific topic out of fear of being labeled negatively (i.e. sexist); thus, more subtle ways need to be used to measure these *implicit attitudes* (Fazio & Olson, 2003). In psychology, one way to measure these implicit attitudes is using reaction times (in milliseconds) when participants are asked to categorize things. For example, if someone were asked to categorize their job as "positive" or "negative," the faster the person chooses "positive" will indicate more implicit positive attitudes. The Implicit Association Test (IAT, Greenwald, McGhee, & Schwartz, 1998), the most common measure used for implicit aptitudes in psychology, is a series of tasks used to measure implicit bias, and the first study published regarding the predictive validity of the IAT was Phelps, O'Connor, Cunningham, Funayama, Gatenby, Gore, and Banaji (2000). In a meta-analysis, Greenwald, Poehlman, Uhlmann, and Banaji (2009) classified major themes examined in psychology with this test: Black versus white race, other stigmatized groups, gender/sexual orientation, consumer preferences, political preferences, personality traits, alcohol and drug use, clinical phenomena, and close relationships. Greenwald, Banaji, and Nosek (2015) found that even with statistically small effects, the "IAT measures predict societally important discrimination" (p. 559). As a counterpoint, however, Oswald, Mitchell, Blanton, Jaccard, and Tetlock (2013), via a meta-analysis of IAT studies that predict ethnic and racial discrimination, found that the IAT did not have better predictive ability than explicit measures: "This closer look at the IAT criterion studies in the domains of ethnic and racial discrimination revealed, however, that the IAT provides little insight into who will discriminate against whom, and provides no more insight than explicit measures of bias" (p. 188).

Much of the traditional work on attitudes in psychology has involved examining implicit bias within and among specific groups of people. Implications of racial discrimination and prejudice are common themes (Carr, Dweck, & Pauker, 2012; Cohrs, Kämpfe-Hargrave, & Riemann, 2012; Hackel, Looser, & Van Bavel, 2014; Kutlaca, Becker, & Radke, 2019; McConnell & Leibold, 2001; Ratner, Dotsch, Wigboldus, van Knippenberg, & Amodio, 2014). There are also publications on predicting membership to political groups (Malka, Soto, Inzlicht, & Lelkes, 2014), as well as issues surrounding globalization and xenophobia (Chen, Lam, Hui, Ng, Mak, Guan, Buchtel, Tang, & Lau, 2016; Stürmer, Benbow, Siem, Barth, Bodansky, & Lotz-Schmitt, 2013). Studies of the latter category are particularly relevant in the modern, globalized world, and also have implications for SLA research. For example, Chen et al. (2016) examine *global orientation,* operationalized as "individual differences in the process of globalization-based acculturation. It denotes individual-level psychological processes in response to globalization, comprising affective, behavioral, and cognitive responses of acculturating individuals" (p. 304). The construct has two components: *multicultural acquisition*, the promotion-focused and proactive response to globalization, and *ethnic protection*, a prevention-focused and defensive response to globalization. In this article composed of ten unique studies, it was found that multicultural acquisition is "positively correlated with the personality traits of openness to experience, extraversion, restraint, and intellect, as well as holistic thinking, multicultural ideology, promotion focus, self-esteem, self-efficacy, cross-cultural efficacy, bicultural identity integration, and liberalism" (p. 325). A correlation was also shown between developing language skills other than the L1 and positive well-being. Conversely, ethnic protection "reflects the narrowing of the cultural mind, with an ethnocentric, essentialized approach to guarding one's cultural status, adhering to behavioral ideals of local culture, and resisting multicultural environments and intercultural exchanges" (p. 326). Individuals with high levels of ethnic protection feel anxious about losing their own culture and have a more difficult time dealing with novel situations. When living in a multicultural context, the result is accumulative stress.

Attitudes and Beliefs in Second Language Acquisition (SLA)

There is substantial overlap in researching attitudes and beliefs in psychology and SLA, although there are some key differences. One of the main differences is the focus on the teaching and learning process itself in SLA research. Indeed, *beliefs* from the SLA perspective has traditionally referred to learner beliefs. It should be noted that *teacher cognition* (Borg, 2015) is a common framework used to study teacher beliefs. In the SLA context, Horwitz (1985, 1987, 1988) was the first to operationalize beliefs with regards to language learning. Horwitz (1988) introduced the Beliefs About Language Learning Inventory (BALLI); using 34 Likert-scale items, the BALLI elicits answers for a variety of different kinds of language learning beliefs. The original questionnaire was thought to measure beliefs of five different types: difficulty of language learning, foreign language aptitude (see Chapter 30), the nature of language learning, learning and communication strategies, and motivation (see Chapter 10) and expectations. However, subsequent exploratory factor analyses (EFAs) did not yield these five latent variables. For example, Thompson and Aslan (2015) found different factors, such as *fear of ambiguity*, and others. Öz (2007) also performed an EFA and found five factors, which were distinct from the original five that were proposed. As the EFAs do not lead to the same factors, it can be concluded that the beliefs of language learning vary greatly depending on the learners and the context. The BALLI, either in its original form or as a modified version, has been used to measure beliefs about learning English and languages other than English (Ariogul, Ünal, & Onursal, 2009; Diab, 2006; Kern, 1995). Other types of beliefs questionnaires have been used to measure different types of beliefs, such as the connection with confidence and experience with ESL students (Cotterall, 1995), student attitudes and beliefs about grammar instruction and error correction across languages (Loewen, Li, Fei, Thompson, Nakatsukasa, Ahn, & Chen, 2009), teacher beliefs about characteristics of an effective teacher (Bell, 2005), and teacher beliefs about instruction in the target language (Bateman, 2008). Teacher cognition (Borg, 2015) is also an approach to studying teacher beliefs. The results of these studies differed greatly depending on both context and languages involved.

A new wave of research on beliefs about language learning research was launched with the volume edited by Kalaja and Barcelos (2003), who challenged the traditional notion that beliefs were a stable construct. Barcelos and Kalaja (2011) outlined the characteristics of this updated paradigm of beliefs research, stating that beliefs are fluctuating, complex, ideologically determined, intrinsically related to other affective constructs such as emotions and self-concept, other-oriented, influenced by reflection, and related to action in complex ways (see Dörnyei & Ryan, 2015, for further details on this shift). This change in the concept of the dynamicity of beliefs coincides with a shift in individual difference research as a whole. No longer thought to be static, all individual differences of language learners are now thought to interact with various contextual elements; these interactions shape the learner and also shape the context in which the learner is situated (Mercer, 2016; Ushioda, 2009). Related to the idea of beliefs as dynamic, Dweck (2006, 2012) coined the terms *fixed mindset* and *growth mindset* (see Chapter 13). Encompassing the basic notion of beliefs, the mindset concept also includes other aspects such as *self-efficacy* (see Chapter 8) and *motivation* (see Chapter 10).

Pulling from the fields of both SLA and psychology, Gardner and colleagues have been some of the first, and most influential, researchers who have studied the effects of attitudes on language learning success. The research originated with Anglophones learning French in Canada, and thus was "directed primarily towards individuals from unilingual families learning another language largely in required language courses and was based on the assumption that such an experience could have implications for one's self-identity; hence the emphasis on social psychology variables" (Gardner, 2020, p. 5). Gardner and colleagues' focus on social psychological variables was directly influenced by Mowrer (1950), who studied first language learning. Mower's research revolved around children's motivation in learning the L1, using parents as a model. Gardner and colleagues postulated that there might be a similar link between language learners and the models they found in their language learning context, a concept influenced by Ervin (1954), who studied how older language learners never gave up all of their earlier identities, even when forming new ones (see also, Gardner, 2019). Such a connection needed to be examined by social psychological variables; thus, Gardner and colleagues expanded the concept of motivation, the primary topic under examination, to measure the following: motivational intensity, desire to learn French, and attitudes towards learning French. Three additional constructs were found to be correlated with French achievement: "integrativeness (integrative orientation, attitudes towards the French, and interest in foreign languages), attitudes towards the learning situation (French teacher evaluation and French course evaluation), and language anxiety (French class anxiety and French use anxiety)" (Gardner, 2020, p. 7). It should be noted that *attitudes* play an important role in three of the four constructs that form the socio-educational model and that these four underlying constructs (motivation, integrativeness, attitudes towards the learning situation, and language anxiety) formed the basis for the final version of the Attitude Motivation Test Battery (AMTB, Gardner, 1985). One major criticism of the model is that motivation is tied to the concept of integrativeness, which is directly informed by the desire to become closer to, or integrate with, speakers of the language in question. Arguably, those learning English for work, study, or other instrumental reasons, might not care anything about integrating with L1 English-speakers; thus, the relevance to the SE model to learning English as a global language was raised.

The response to this was Dörnyei's (2009) L2 Motivation Self System (L2MSS), which removed the connection of attitudes, motivation, and successful acquisition with a focus on possible selves: the ideal self, who a language learner wants to become, and the ought-to self, who a language learner thinks they need to become. Other types of selves have emerged in the literature, particularly a self that shows resistance to societal expatiations: the anti-ought-to self (Thompson, 2017a) or rebellious self (Lanvers, 2016). The learning experience facet of the L2MSS is the least developed (Dörnyei, 2019) and is not well defined. Thompson (2017b) describes it as the contextual factors that influence language learning, whereas Dörnyei (2019) links it to motivated learning behavior. Both interpretations could be linked to the attitudinal aspects of Gardner's (1985) model in terms of the relationship of the learner and the context. Gardner (2010) has also illustrated the relationship to the SE model and learners of global English with data that was collected in Croatia, Poland, Romania, Spain, Brazil, and Japan. Recent publications, such as Thompson (2021), also illustrate the symbiotic relationship of context and development of self with chapters on Argentina, Egypt, Turkey, Vietnam, Senegal,

Ukraine, and Estonia. No matter the motivational framework, context is emerging as a crucial piece of the puzzle.

In the field of SLA, attitudes toward specific languages in a variety of sociopolitical contexts is another visible theme in the literature; particularly prevalent is that of attitudes towards English as a global language. What follows are a few illustrative examples.

Selvi (2011) discusses various reasons for the resistance of English in Turkey. Two of the main reasons are as follows: (a) Some believe that the influx of English words is making the Turkish languages less pure, and (b) political tensions between the US and Turkey make some people want to resist English. There is also a discussion regarding the push for English-medium universities and programs, which are not necessarily done in the best interest of the students; this issue is also raised in Selvi (2020) in the context of Turkey, in Doiz, Lasagabaster, and Sierra (2011) in the context of Spain, and in Kamwangamalu (2013) in the context of Africa (sic). In other contexts, for example, in Egypt, people are grappling with how English, as the representation of a Western entity, is interacting with Islam in this modern era (Abouelhassan & Meyer, 2016). International corporations located in non-Anglophone contexts are oftentimes using English to communicate daily, such as the Russian office practices described in Gritsenko and Laletina (2016), with the belief that this makes communication more effective. In locations which have many national languages, such as Kenya (Kamwangamalu & Tovares, 2016), a common attitude towards English is that of a unifying entity. When Anglophone communities are artificially set up in non-Anglophone contexts, however, such as the example in Paraguay (Perez, 2016), the longevity is limited. Certainly, in many countries, there is an additional layer of complexity in terms of the relationship with English because of its role as a colony in the former British Empire. That being said, with the current status of English as a global language, people in most contexts recognize English as a useful tool, even when their attitudes towards English as a whole are not entirely positive. As such, attitudes towards English are multifaceted. On the one hand, English is recognized as a valuable skill in most contexts; however, negative attitudes also surface, particularly regarding the topic of English and colonialization.

The situation becomes more variable when examining attitudes of languages other than English (LOTEs) in Anglophone contexts, either with regards to the need for LOTEs in this context, or attitudes towards specific LOTEs. L1 English speakers sometimes fail to see the importance of learning languages other than English, in large part because of the misconception of English being the only language needed to succeed in work or school. Some people in these Anglophone settings are cognizant of the impact that being an L1 English speaker has on their motivation to learn LOTEs. For example, several participants in Lanvers (2012) indicated that being an English speaker makes them "lazy" (p. 162), as they can get by with only speaking English. In this same article, the participants indicate that they have a difficult time finding people to practice their LOTE with and that individuals do not expect people from the UK to be able to speak anything but English; both of these types of attitudes hamper the motivation for Anglophones to learn a LOTE. In the context of the US, some participants (Huensch & Thompson, 2017; Thompson, 2017b) expressed the pressure that they have felt NOT to study a language other than English. Specifically, one participant stated:

> I have felt strong resistance from family and co-workers to NOT study anything but English. Some of the people closest to me have made fun of my language learning both directly and indirectly. Directly I have been told that "this is America and we only need to speak English."
>
> *Thompson, 2017b, p. 496*

As such, the attitudes towards LOTEs in general are oftentimes hard to overcome; as Barnwell (2008) states, "It would be naïve to believe that foreign language education is today a central concern of the majority of Americans" (p. 237). Thus, the attitudes towards LOTEs of many Anglophones seem to be strongly influenced by the perceived lack of need of any language other than English.

On the other hand, there are some Anglophone learners who perform contrary to expectations when it comes to learning a LOTE. Other researchers (Lanvers, 2016; Thompson, 2017a; Thompson & Vásquez, 2015) talk about a type of Anglophone language learner who enjoys doing the unexpected; in this case, the unexpected is learning a language other than English. Thompson's work operationalizes this as the anti-ought-to self; conceptualized as being part of the L2MSS, a learner with a strong anti-ought-to self thrives on doing something challenging or unexpected. Lanvers terms this the rebellious self, or someone who succeeds in language learning despite expectations to the contrary. Both Thompson's and Lanvers's work describe Anglophone language learners who push back against the attitudes and beliefs of language learning of those surrounding them.

Recent studies have found that explicit instruction of either the importance of knowing a language other than English (Lanvers, Hultgren, & Gayton, 2019) or on teaching and interpreting cultural aspects of the target languages communities (Acheson, Nelson, & Luna, 2015) can change beliefs of Anglophones learning LOTEs in a positive manner. Curiously, there is not a strong link between general attitudes towards learning LOTEs and the follow-through to do so for L1 English speakers. As an illustration of this, Eddy (1980), in a nationwide survey of 962 respondents found that 75.6 percent of the participants who had studied a language answered *yes* to the question, "Do you feel that studying a foreign language was worthwhile?" For those who had not studied a language, about half indicated that they would like to do so (p. 61). Nonetheless, of those surveyed, only 30 percent had indeed studied a language at school with only 8 percent studying long enough to have "usable knowledge of it." The author concluded that "the vast majority of American citizens have virtually no knowledge of foreign languages" (p. 59). Fast forwarding about 30 years, the general positive attitude towards learning a LOTE remains. Rivers, Robinson, Harwood, and Brecht (2013) found in their 2008 survey that 80 percent agreed or strongly agreed with the statement, "Children in the United States should learn a second language fluently before they finish high school" (p. 332). However, in a different publication by the same research group (Rivers & Robinson, 2012), it was found that in 2008, only 28 percent of those surveyed indicated knowing a LOTE. Of those, less than half indicated that they spoke it "very well" (p. 372). Muchnick & Wolfe (1982) found similar results in their survey of attitudes of students learning Spanish in the US: "It seems that students find the actual learning situation very different from their reported general attitudes" (p. 279). Thus, there is a disconnect between the positive attitudes towards learning a language and the ultimate result of doing so.

Certainly, attitudes towards languages and language learning differ depending on the context, and there are several studies that cite the complexities of LOTEs in a variety of contexts; attitudes towards Kurdish in Turkey (Fernandes, 2012) or Russian in the Ukraine (Friedman, 2009, 2016) are two of the many examples of this. On this topic, the attitudes of Spanish in the context of the US is something that has been frequently discussed in the applied linguistics literature, as the relationship is a complex one.

Since the 1970s, Spanish has been the most commonly studied language in the United States at all levels of instruction (Barnwell, 2008). Although it would seem that the influx of speakers of LOTEs to the US would affect change in languages spoken, "Immigration to the United States has always been characterized by a fairly rapid adoption of English and a concomitant loss of proficiency in the language(s) of the immigrant group" (Barnwell, 2008, p. 240), with few exceptions in insular communities. Although there have been academic studies of language attrition (see Ecke, 2016, for a review), as well as evidence of attrition in pop-culture literature, (Rodriguez, 1982), Spanish continues to be omnipresent in many sectors of US society largely because of the continuous influx of Spanish-speaking immigrants.

The constant influx of Spanish-speakers is also one reason that Spanish is currently the most commonly studied LOTE in the US context. Although it is chosen to be studied because of the belief of its usefulness, much like global English, there is also a certain stigma that accompanies it. As Barnwell (2008) indicates, "if newly arrived Spanish-speakers, often undocumented aliens, are the main source for priming up the numbers of Spanish-speakers, the language will continue to be seen as that of the gardeners, home helpers, restaurant workers and so on" (p. 240, see also García & Mason, 2009). The prevalence of Spanish in blue-collar industry could also give the illusion to what Friedrich (1997) refers to as an American urban legend: Spanish is easy. Schwartz (2014) acknowledges that Spanish is familiar, even to monolinguals, and that it is "simultaneously romanticized and belittled in popular media and entertainment" (p. 164), leading to conflicting emotions and attitudes for American Anglophones (see also Pomerantz & Schwartz, 2011). Spanish is seen as useful (Thompson, 2017b), but lacks the social capitol afforded to global English.

With the range of topics within the *attitudes* and *beliefs* frameworks in SLA, the research methods are becoming increasingly diverse. The field started with measuring these constructs primarily with questionnaires, a practice which is still currently prevalent with research on these topics. However, more dynamic methods, outlined by Barcelos and Kalaja (2011), are becoming increasingly popular. Although less common than in psychology, measurements of implicit attitudes are also used in SLA research to measure topics such as attitudes towards speakers (Al-Hoorie, 2016a) and as related to motivation and achievement (Al-Hoorie, 2016b). As can be seen, the research on *attitudes* and *beliefs* in SLA is multifaceted. Stretching from beliefs about the language learning process itself to the importance of learning a LOTE in general, from personal attitudes to those generally present in different societies, and from global English to LOTEs in Anglophone contexts, there are endless possibilities of future research on these topics.

Integrating Perspectives

The exchange of ideas between SLA and psychology is mostly unilateral; SLA pulls in constructs from the psychology literature, whereas the reverse is not as common. For example, much of the survey-style research done in SLA uses Likert-scale items, and although they are not as common, some have used semantic differential scales for data collection in SLA. As described above, both of these measures originated in the field of psychology. Gardner's early work on motivation, which included a large portion of attitudes of French and of the French teacher, had a psychological foundation. The response to Gardner's work, Dörnyei's (2009) L2MSS, was also based on self research in psychology (Higgins, 1987; Markus & Nurius, 1986).

That being said, many of the researchers who are known for individual difference research in SLA, such as with the topics of attitudes and beliefs, are indeed psychologists. Considering this, it is perhaps not that the flow is primarily unidirectional; perhaps it could be considered that psychology is the broader umbrella that encases the concepts dealing with the psychology of language learning. It is also the case that SLA is a much younger field than psychology. Until recently, particularly in the North American context, there were not unique PhD programs for those who wanted to study SLA. Thus, the advanced degrees were obtained in fields such as psychology or linguistics, with the dissertation done on a topic emphasizing language learning/acquisition in some way. It is not surprising, therefore, that psychological concepts have more of an impact on the field of SLA, rather than the other way around, especially considering that psychology is a larger field with a much longer history than SLA.

This is not to say that SLA cannot influence psychology. There are topics, such as globalization and xenophobia, that frequently appear in SLA literature. For example, Yashima's (2009) concept of international posture is related to Chen et al.'s (2016) of global orientation, as are some of Ryan's (2009) categories of the Motivational Factors Questionnaire (MFQ). In terms of research methods, psychology tends to be primarily quantitatively oriented, with some exceptions in social psychology; indeed, this is how the SLA methodology tended to be at the inception of the field, particularly the sub-field of individual differences in SLA. Recently, however, there has been a shift in methodology in SLA to support qualitative or mixed-methods research. Additionally, there are increasingly diverse methodologies used in SLA that utilize the images and visualization techniques as data. The earliest forms of this type of research were exemplified by studying linguistic landscapes (Backhaus, 2006;

Shohamy & Gorter, 2009). More recently, research using visualization tools to describe multilinguals and their experiences in a variety of contexts has also emerged (Kalaja & Melo-Pfeifer, 2019; Kalaja & Pitkänen-Huhta, 2018). Examining topics that are explored in both psychology and SLA both quantitatively and qualitatively, as well as other innovative methodologies used, could expand the understanding of these constructs in both fields.

Implications for Practice and Research

The study of language attitudes has come full circle in the field of SLA and psychology. Gardner's work on motivation, which included explicit information on language attitudes, was augmented by the rise of Dörnyei's (2009) L2MSS. With an eye to conceptualizing motivation in the context of learning English as a global language (i.e. arguably fewer reasons for the desired attitude of integration with the target culture), the L2MSS focuses purely on the psychological aspects of self (ideal and ought-to selves, with other selves proposed in the literature), with little attention to the facet of the "learning experience." Indeed, Dörnyei (2019) acknowledges that the learning experience aspect of the L2MSS has all but been ignored and recommends operationalizing the learning experience as "the perceived quality of the learners' engagement with various aspects of the language learning process" (p. 26). However, others, such as Thompson (2017b), have indicated that the learning experience should be operationalized as the context where the language learning takes place, which includes the larger sociopolitical context. Temporal perspectives have also been examined in terms of context; Begić and Mercer (2017) examined temporal perspectives of language learners, finding that some participants were more past-oriented in their language domain than in their general domain. These contextual variables relate to Ushioda's (2009) person-in-context theory that proposes to analyze learners in their specific environments, and the idea of considering the specific environments of language learners and acknowledging that the elements in the environments will affect people differently (Mercer, 2016) inexorably circles back to the idea of beliefs and attitudes. Language learners are certainly affected by the beliefs and attitudes in their environments, whether it be a belief or attitude of a specific person (i.e. a parent) or those of society as a whole (i.e. Spanish is the easiest language to learn). Some learners with a strong anti-ought-to self (Thompson, 2017a) who have the wherewithal to study a language, despite resistance from those around them find their language study less affected by the attitudes and beliefs of others. However, many potential language students find themselves succumbing to the influences of others. In terms of both research and practice, it is paramount to understand the complex relationship between beliefs/attitudes, the language in question, and the multifaceted contextual variables.

Future Directions

The language learning process is affected by beliefs and attitudes insofar as these concepts affect motivation and desire to learn, as well as the behaviors that result in certain beliefs and attitudes. What students believe about the language learning process or if they believe knowing a LOTE is important will inevitably affect the success of the learning experience. As language learners are situated in a larger sociopolitical context, the attitudes and beliefs of those around them will affect their own belief systems. Certainly, future research, using qualitative, quantitative, and mixed-methods, as well as innovative methods using visualization techniques, should focus on understanding the relationship between language learning, beliefs and attitudes, and how the learning process is affected by micro and macro contexts where the learner is situated.

Reflection Questions

- What similarities do you see between attitudes towards global English in non-Anglophone contexts and attitudes towards LOTEs in Anglophone contexts? What are the differences?

- Do you think that explicit types of questions are effective in measuring attitudes towards languages/language learning/language teaching? Why or why not?
- Reflect on your own language learning process and/or teacher development. How much are you affected by the attitudes of those around you when it comes to your own experiences? Think about close relationships (teachers, friends, parents, etc.), as well as attitudes of society in general.

Recommended Reading

Chen, S. X., Lam, B. C. P., Hui, B. P. H., Ng, J. C. K., Mak, W. W. S., Guan, Y., Buchtel, E. E., Tang, W. C. S., & Lau, V. C. Y. (2016). Conceptualizing psychological processes in response to globalization: Components, antecedents, and consequences of global orientations. *Journal of Personality and Social Psychology, 110*(2), 302–331.
This study is from the field of psychology but examines a concept that is relevant to SLA: Global orientation. This manuscript is a summary of ten studies on this topic, all centering around the use of the *Global Orientations Scale (GOS)*. Two types of questions on this scale indicate either a positive or negative global orientation: "Cultural diversity is beneficial to a society." and "My own culture is much superior to other cultures." Implications of global orientation are discussed.

Gardner, R. (1985). *Social psychology and second language learning. The role of attitudes and motivation.* Edward Arnold.
This is a seminal work for both attitude and motivation work in SLA and contains deep descriptions of the foundational work on the socio-educational (SE) model. The manuscript starts with operationalization of important terms for the model, including what is meant by *attitude,* and culminates with a presentation and analysis of the SE model itself. The appendix contains all items from the AMTB, although not in a form you could administer directly, and the entire manuscript can be found on Gardner's website: publish.uwo.ca/~gardner/

Schwartz, A. (2014). Third border talk: Intersubjectivity, power negotiation and the making of race in Spanish language classrooms. *International Journal of the Sociology of Language, 2014*(227), 157–173.
This article is an excellent source for those wishing to understand more about the complex attitudes towards Spanish in the US context. Schwartz explains that Spanish is both familiar and unfamiliar, and that even those who have a positive attitude towards Spanish tend to have an "us" versus "them" mentality when it comes to the language. The delicate issues of race and linguistic identities are unpacked for the reader.

References

Abouelhassan, R. S. M., & Meyer, L. M. (2016). Economy, modernity, Islam, and English in Egypt. *World Englishes, 35*(1), 147–159.
Acheson, K., Nelson, M., & Luna, K. (2015). Measuring the impact of instruction in intercultural communication on secondary Spanish learners' attitudes and motivation. *Foreign Language Annals, 48*(2), 203–217.
Al-Hoorie, A. H. (2016a). Unconscious motivation. Part I: Implicit attitudes toward L2 speakers. *Studies in Second Language Learning and Teaching, VI*(3), 423–454.
Al-Hoorie, A. H. (2016b). Unconscious motivation. Part II: Implicit attitudes and L2 achievement. *Studies in Second Language Learning and Teaching, VI*(4), 619–649.
Ariogul, S., Ünal, D. Ç., & Onursal, I. (2009). Foreign language learners' beliefs about language learning: A study on Turkish university students. *Procedia – Social and Behavioral Sciences, 1,* 1500–1506.
Backhaus, P. (2006). *Linguistic landscapes: A comparative study of urban multilingualism in Tokyo.* Multilingual Matters.
Barcelos, A. M. F., & Kalaja, P. (2011). Introduction to beliefs about SLA revisited. *System, 39*(3), 281–289.
Barnwell, D. (2008). The status of Spanish in the United States. *Language, Culture and Curriculum, 21*(3), 235–243.
Bateman, B. E. (2008). Student teachers' attitudes and beliefs about using the target language in the classroom. *Foreign Language Annals, 41*(1), 11–28.

Begić, I., & Mercer, S. (2017). Looking back, looking forward, living in the moment: Understanding the individual temporal perspectives of secondary school EFL learners. *Innovation in Language Learning and Teaching, 11*(3), 267–281.

Bell, T. R. (2005). Behaviors and attitudes of effective foreign language teachers: Results of a questionnaire study. *Foreign Language Annals, 38*(2), 259–270.

Borg, S. (2015). *Teacher cognition and language education: Research and practice*. Bloomsbury Publishing.

Carr, P. B., Dweck, C. S., & Pauker, K. (2012). "Prejudiced" behavior without prejudice? Beliefs about the malleability of prejudice affect interracial interactions. *Journal of Personality and Social Psychology, 103*(3), 452–471.

Cohrs, J. C., Kämpfe-Hargrave, N., & Riemann, R. (2012). Individual differences in ideological attitudes and prejudice: Evidence from peer-report data. *Journal of Personality and Social Psychology, 103*(2), 343–361.

Cotterall, S. (1995). Readiness for autonomy: Investigating learner beliefs. *System, 23*(2), 195–205.

Diab, R. L. (2006). University students' beliefs about learning English and French in Lebanon. *System, 34*(1), 80–96.

Doiz, A., Lasagabaster, D., & Sierra, J. M. (2011). Internationalisation, multilingualism and English-medium instruction. *World Englishes, 30*(3), 345–359.

Dörnyei, Z. (2009). The L2 motivational self system. In Z. Dörnyei & E. Ushioda (Eds.), *Motivation, language identity and the L2 self* (pp. 9–42). Multilingual Matters.

Dörnyei, Z. (2019). Towards a better understanding of the L2 learning experience, the Cinderella of the L2 Motivational Self System. Studies in second language learning and teaching. *Studies in Second Language Learning and Teaching, 9*(1), 19–30.

Dörnyei, Z., & Ryan, S. (2015). *The psychology of the language learner revisited* (1st ed.). Routledge.

Dörnyei, Z., & Taguchi, T. (2010). *Questionnaires in second language research: Construction, administration and processing* (2nd ed.). Routledge.

Eagly, A. H., & Chaiken, S. (1993). *The psychology of attitudes*. Harcourt Brace Jovanovich College Publishers.

Ecke, P. (2016). Language attrition and theories of forgetting: A cross-disciplinary review. *International Journal of Bilingualism*.

Eddy, P. A. (1980). Foreign languages in the USA: A national survey of American attitudes and experience. *Modern Language Journal, 64*(1), 58–63.

Ervin, S. (1954). *Identification and bilingualism (mimeo)*. Harvard University.

Fazio, R. H., & Olson, M. A. (2003). Implicit measures in social cognition research: Their meaning and use. *Annual Review of Psychology, 54*(1), 297–327.

Fernandes, D. (2012). Modernity and the linguistic genocide of Kurds in Turkey. *Ijsl, 2012*(217), 75–98.

Friedman, D. A. (2009). Speaking correctly: Error correction as a language socialization practice in a Ukrainian classroom. *Applied Linguistics, 31*(3), 346–367.

Friedman, D. A. (2016). Our language: (Re)imagining communities in Ukrainian language classrooms. *Journal of Language, Identity, and Education; Philadelphia, 15*(3), 165.

Friedrich, E. (1997). Strategies for recruiting and retaining students in French classes. *Proceedings of the (1997), Southern Conference on Language Teaching*, 76–97.

García, O., & Mason, L. (2009). Where in the world is US Spanish? Creating a space of opportunity for US Latinos. In W. Harbert (Ed.), *Language and poverty* (pp. 78–101). Multilingual Matters.

Gardner, R. (2010). *Motivation and second language acquisition: The socio-educational model*. Peter Lang.

Gardner, R. C. (2019). The socio-educational model of second language acquisition. In M. Lamb, K. Csizér, A. Henry, & S. Ryan (Eds.), *The Palgrave handbook of motivation for language learning*. Palgrave Macmillan.

Gardner, R. C. (2020). Looking back and looking forward. In A. H. Al-Hoorie & P. D. MacIntyre (Eds.), *Contemporary Language Motivation Theory 60 Years Since Gardner and Lambert (1959)*. Multilingual Matters.

Greenwald, A. G., Banaji, M. R., & Nosek, B. A. (2015). Statistically small effects of the Implicit Association Test can have societally large effects. *Journal of Personality and Social Psychology, 108*(4), 553–561.

Greenwald, A. G., McGhee, D. E., & Schwartz, J. L. K. (1998). Measuring individual differences in implicit cognition: The Implicit Association Test. *Journal of Personality and Social Psychology, 74*(6), 17.

Greenwald, A. G., Poehlman, T. A., Uhlmann, E. L., & Banaji, M. R. (2009). Understanding and using the Implicit Association Test: III. Meta-analysis of predictive validity. *Journal of Personality and Social Psychology, 97*(1), 17–41.

Gritsenko, E., & Laletina, A. (2016). English in the international workplace in Russia. *World Englishes, 35*(3), 440–456.

Hackel, L. M., Looser, C. E., & Van Bavel, J. J. (2014). Group membership alters the threshold for mind perception: The role of social identity, collective identification, and intergroup threat. *Journal of Experimental Social Psychology, 52*, 15–23.

Hess, Y. D., & Pickett, C. L. (n.d.). *Social Cognition and Attitudes*. Noba. nobaproject.com/modules/social-cognition-and-attitudes

Higgins, E. T. (1987). Self-discrepancy: A theory relating self and affect. *Psychological Review, 94*(3), 319–340.

Horwitz, E. K. (1985). Using student beliefs about language learning and teaching in the foreign language methods course. *Foreign Language Annals, 18*(4), 333–340.

Horwitz, E. K. (1987). Surveying student beliefs about language learning. In A. L. Wenden & J. Rubin (Eds.), *Learner strategies in language learning* (pp. 119–129). Prentice Hall.

Horwitz, E. K. (1988). The beliefs about language learning of beginning university foreign language students. *The Modern Language Journal, 72*(3), 283–294.

Huensch, A., & Thompson, A. S. (2017). Contextualizing attitudes toward pronunciation: Foreign language learners in the United States. *Foreign Language Annals, 50*(2), 410–432.

Kalaja, P., & Barcelos, A. M. F. (Eds.). (2003). *Beliefs about SLA: New research approaches*. Springer Netherlands.

Kalaja, Paula, & Melo-Pfeifer, S. (Eds.). (2019). *Visualising multilingual lives: More than words*. Multilingual Matters.

Kalaja, P., & Pitkänen-Huhta, A. (2018). ALR special issue: Visual methods in applied language studies. *Applied Linguistics Review, 9*(2–3), 157–176.

Kamwangamalu, N. M. (2013). Effects of policy on English-medium instruction in Africa: Effects of policy on English-medium instruction in Africa. *World Englishes, 32*(3), 325–337.

Kamwangamalu, N., & Tovares, A. (2016). English in language ideologies, attitudes, and educational practices in Kenya and South Africa: English practices in Kenya and South Africa. *World Englishes, 35*(3), 421–439.

Kern, R. G. (1995). Students' and teachers' beliefs about language learning. *Foreign Language Annals, 28*(1), 71–92.

Kutlaca, M., Becker, J., & Radke, H. (2019). A hero for the outgroup, a black sheep for the ingroup: Societal perceptions of those who confront discrimination. *Journal of Experimental Social Psychology*.

Lanvers, U. (2012). "The Danish speak so many languages it's really embarrassing." The impact of L1 English on adult language students' motivation. *Innovation in Language Learning and Teaching, 6*(2), 157–175.

Lanvers, U. (2016). Lots of selves, some rebellious: Developing the self discrepancy model for language learners. *System, 60*, 79–92.

Lanvers, U., Hultgren, K., & Gayton, A. M. (2019). "People can be smarter with two languages": Changing anglophone students' attitudes to language learning through teaching linguistics. *The Language Learning Journal, 47*(1), 88–104.

Likert, R. (1932). A technique for the measurement of attitudes. *Archives of Psychology, 140*, 1–55.

Loewen, S., Li, S., Fei, F., Thompson, A., Nakatsukasa, K., Ahn, S., & Chen, X. (2009). Second language learners' beliefs about grammar instruction and error correction. *The Modern Language Journal, 93*(1), 91–104.

Malka, A., Soto, C. J., Inzlicht, M., & Lelkes, Y. (2014). Do needs for security and certainty predict cultural and economic conservatism? A cross-national analysis. *Journal of Personality and Social Psychology, 106*(6), 1031–1051.

Markus, H., & Nurius, P. (1986). Possible selves. *American Psychologist, 41*, 954–969.

McConnell, A. R., & Leibold, J. M. (2001). Relations among the Implicit Association Test, discriminatory behavior, and explicit measures of racial attitudes. *Journal of Experimental Social Psychology, 37*(5), 435–442.

Mercer, S. (2016). The contexts within me: L2 self as a complex dynamic system. In J. King (Ed.), *The dynamic interplay between context and the language learner* (pp. 11–28). Palgrave Macmillan.

Mowrer, O. H. (1950). *Learning theory and personality dynamics*. Ronald.

Muchnick, A. G., & Wolfe, D. E. (1982). Attitudes and motivations of American students of Spanish. *Canadian Modern Language Review, 38*(2), 262–281.

Osgood, C. E., Suci, G., & Tannenbaum, P. (1957). *The measurement of meaning*. University of Illinois Press.

Oswald, F. L., Mitchell, G., Blanton, H., Jaccard, J., & Tetlock, P. E. (2013). Predicting ethnic and racial discrimination: A meta-analysis of IAT criterion studies. *Journal of Personality and Social Psychology, 105*(2), 171–192.

Öz, H. (2007). Understanding metacognitive knowledge of Turkish EFL students in secondary education. *Novitas-ROYAL, 1*(2), 53–83.

Perez, D. (2016). English and language shift in Paraguay's New Australia: English and language shift in Paraguay's New Australia. *World Englishes, 35*(1), 160–176.

Phelps, E. A., O'Connor, K. J., Cunningham, W. A., Funayama, E. S., Gatenby, J. C., Gore, J. C., & Banaji, M. R. (2000). Performance on indirect measures of race evaluation predicts amygdala activation. *Journal of Cognitive Neuroscience, 12*(5), 729–738.

Pomerantz, A., & Schwartz, A. (2011). Border talk: Narratives of Spanish language encounters in the United States. *Language and Intercultural Communication, 11*(3), 176–196.

Ratner, K. G., Dotsch, R., Wigboldus, D. H. J., van Knippenberg, A., & Amodio, D. M. (2014). Visualizing minimal ingroup and outgroup faces: Implications for impressions, attitudes, and behavior. *Journal of Personality and Social Psychology, 106*(6), 897–911.

Rivers, W. P., & Robinson, J. P. (2012). The unchanging American capacity in languages other than English: Speaking and learning languages other than English, 2000–2008. *The Modern Language Journal, 96*(3), 369–379.

Rivers, W. P., Robinson, J. P., Harwood, P. G., & Brecht, R. D. (2013). Language votes: Attitudes toward foreign language policies. *Foreign Language Annals, 46*(3), 329–338.

Rodriguez, R. (1982). *Hunger of memory: The education of Richard Rodriguez*. Penguin Random House.

Ryan, S. (2009). Self and identity in L2 motivation in Japan: The ideal L2 self and Japanese learners of English. In Z. Dörnyei, & E. Ushioda (Eds.), *Motivation, Language Identity and the L2 Self* (pp. 120–143). Multilingual Matters.

Schwartz, A. (2014). Third border talk: Intersubjectivity, power negotiation and the making of race in Spanish language classrooms. *International Journal of the Sociology of Language, 2014*(227), 157–173.

Selvi, A. F. (2011). World Englishes in the Turkish sociolinguistic context. *World Englishes, 30*(2), 182–199.

Selvi, A. F. (2020). Resisting English medium instruction through digital grassroots activism. *Journal of Multilingual and Multicultural Development, 0*(0), 1–17.

Shohamy, E., & Gorter, D. (2009). *Linguistic landscape: Expanding the scenery*. Routledge.

Stürmer, S., Benbow, A. E. F., Siem, B., Barth, M., Bodansky, A. N., & Lotz-Schmitt, K. (2013). Psychological foundations of xenophilia: The role of major personality traits in predicting favorable attitudes toward cross-cultural contact and exploration. *Journal of Personality and Social Psychology, 105*(5), 832–851.

Thompson, A. S. (2017a). Don't tell me what to do! The anti-ought-to self and language learning motivation. *System, 67*, 38–49.

Thompson, A. S. (2017b). Language learning motivation in the United States: An examination of language choice and multilingualism. *The Modern Language Journal, 101*(3), 483–500.

Thompson, A. S. (2021). *The Role of Context in Language Teachers' Self Development and Motivation: Perspectives from Multilingual Settings*. Multilingual Matters.

Thompson, A. S., & Aslan, E. (2015). Multilingualism, Perceived Positive Language Interaction (PPLI), and learner beliefs: What do Turkish students believe? *International Journal of Multilingualism, 12*(3), 259–275.

Thompson, A. S., & Vásquez, C. (2015). Exploring motivational profiles through language learning narratives. *The Modern Language Journal, 99*(1), 158–174.

Ushioda, E. (2009). A person-in-context relational view of emergent motivation, self and identity. In Z. Dörnyei & E. Ushioda (Eds.), *Motivation, language identity and the L2 self* (pp. 215–228). Multilingual Matters.

Yashima, T. (2009). International posture and the ideal L2 self in the Japanese EFL context. In Z. Dörnyei & E. Ushioda (Eds.), *Motivation, language identity and the L2 self* (pp. 144–163). Multilingual Matters.

13
ATTRIBUTIONS AND MINDSETS

Xijia Zhang, Nigel Mantou Lou, Kimberly A. Noels, and Lia M. Daniels

When language learners perform well in a language test or a conversation with interlocutors, to whom do they give credit? When they fail, what or who do they think is responsible? Like all people, language learners regularly come up with reasons to explain their achievements and setbacks. Researchers in education and psychology have long been interested in understanding the role of these reasons in a meaning making system, and their effects on motivation, affect, and behavior. More specifically, researchers study the ways students attribute their success and failure, how these attributions influence students' emotions and learning outcomes, what social and psychological factors influence different attributions, and, importantly, how to help students to make more adaptive attributions (Weiner, 1986).

These issues lie at the root of attribution theory (Weiner, 1986) and mindset theory (Dweck, 2006), not only in general achievement contexts, but also specifically in the domain of language learning. Attribution theory has been used by researchers to inform their understanding about the reasons, or attributions, that students (or teachers) use to explain their success or failure in second language (L2) learning (or teaching), and how these attributions affect future efforts to learn (or teach; e.g., Dörnyei & Ryan, 2015). A related framework, mindset theory, has helped further understandings of the relation between beliefs about the nature of L2 learning ability and various aspects of L2 learning (e.g., Lou & Noels, 2016). Although these two theories have generally been investigated separately in second language acquisition (SLA) research, studies in psychology show that mindsets can influence motivated behaviors by affecting the attributions individuals make and how specific attributions such as ability and effort are interpreted (e.g., Bernecker & Job, 2019; Blackwell, Trzesniewski, & Dweck, 2007). In this chapter, we propose that the relation between attributions and mindsets in psychology can usefully be extended to better explain motivation in SLA. To this end, we start with a discussion about the definition of attributions and mindsets and their relation in psychology before talking about their integration in SLA research. We then review the attributional literature in SLA in light of the proposed relation between attributions and mindsets in SLA, so as to provide directions for future research and practice.

Attributions and Mindsets in Psychology

In this section, we will first review how attributions and mindsets are defined and studied in psychology. The definitions and empirical research of these two psychological constructs serve as the foundation for discussing them in SLA.

Attribution Theory in Psychology

Attributions are individuals' subjective explanations about why a certain outcome has occurred. There are several conceptual models of attributional processes, but Weiner's (1986) theory is most widely used in the academic achievement context. The central premise of this theory is that individuals' attributions could affect their motivated behaviors when they are engaged in similar activities in the future. As shown in Figure 13.1 (Weiner, 1986), the outcome of an act often generates emotional reactions from individuals affected by that act. If the outcome is deemed as negative, important, and/or unexpected, individuals are more likely to undertake a process known as "causal search" to try and find an explanation for the outcome.

There are infinite possible attributions, although some, like "ability, effort, task difficulty [and] luck [etc.]," are more common than others (Weiner, 1986, pp. 37–40). Weiner (1986) suggests that all explanations can be categorized along the three causal dimensions of locus, stability, and controllability. Locus refers to whether a cause is related to the person who makes the attribution. If one believes that the cause resides in themselves, it is an internal cause, and if one thinks it concerns circumstances or people separate from themselves, it is an external cause. Stability is about whether the cause may change in the future. A stable cause remains the same regardless of one's intentions and behaviors, and an unstable cause could change or be changed. Controllability is defined as whether the cause is under the control of the attribution-seeking person or other people involved in the act or the outcome. Table 13.1 depicts Weiner's model (1986, 2006) about causal dimensions associated with common attributions.

Depending on whether the outcome is positive or negative, the categorization of the attribution into these three causal dimensions will lead to specific psychological consequences. For instance,

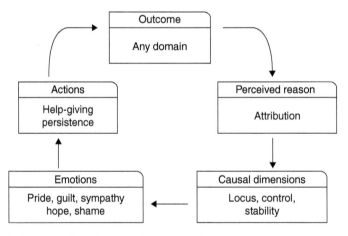

Figure 13.1 Attributional/causal search process (Weiner, 1986)

Table 13.1 Causal Dimensions with Four Common Attributions as Examples (Weiner, 1986, 2006)

Controllability \ Stability	*Locus*			
	Internal		*External*	
	Stable	Unstable	Stable	Unstable
Controllable		Effort		
Uncontrollable	Ability		Task difficulty	Luck

attributing a positive outcome to an internal cause may promote one's self-esteem and make one feel proud (e.g., Weiner, 1986, 2006), whereas attributing a negative outcome to internal and/or controllable cause may generate a sense of guilt (e.g., Weiner, 1986, 2006). These affective consequences will in turn affect individuals' future behaviors when they are faced with similar tasks (Weiner, 1986). The link among causal thinking, emotions, and behaviors proposed by attribution theory has helped researchers understand emotions such as pride, hope, helplessness, anger, sympathy, gratitude, guilt, and regret (Weiner, 1986, 2006), as well as motivated behaviors like help-giving, reactions to stigma, and achievement strivings (Weiner, 2018).

Empirical findings of attribution theory have also been extended to domains outside of psychology, including organizational behaviors, politics, and group processes (Weiner, 2018). In addition, researchers have tried to refine the original theory in order to make it more comprehensive. For example, some researchers sought to improve the theory by making more nuanced conceptual distinctions. Scherer (2018) contends that controllability could be further broken down into control and power. Control refers to how well individuals could affect the act or the outcome they are involved in, whereas power is the resource that individuals could conjure to exert control over the act or the outcome (Scherer, 2018). Distinguishing these two aspects of the controllability dimension of an attribution could help researchers in psychology better understand the link among the attribution and the emotional and/or behavioral reactions it may generate (Scherer, 2018). Apart from theoretical refinement, some researchers in psychology have entertained the possibility of utilizing neuro-science technologies like EEG to study the impact of attributions (e.g., Scherer, 2018). These developments underscore the generativity of this theory, and also point to possible avenues for research in SLA.

Mindset Theory in Psychology

Whereas attribution theory focuses on how individuals understand various causes in terms of all three dimensions of locus, stability, and controllability, mindset theory is particularly focused on the stability dimension. Each person has beliefs about whether human characteristics (e.g., intelligence, personality, and/or language aptitude) are malleable, which are termed "implicit theories" (Dweck, 2006; Dweck & Leggett, 1988) or "mindsets." Incremental theorists, or individuals with a growth mindset, regard their own aptitude (see Chapter 30) or intelligence as unstable and changeable. As a result, they seek opportunities to develop their aptitude or intelligence, and are more likely to adopt a learning or mastery goal for achievement activities. In other words, their primary goal for engaging in an activity is to develop their aptitude and/or intelligence. They see difficulties as chances to increase their aptitude and failures as temporary and as indications for a revision of strategies. They are more likely to embrace challenges, and failures may not thwart them from putting more effort into what they are doing (Dweck & Leggett, 1988).

In contrast, entity theorists, or those with a fixed mindset, think that their own aptitude or intelligence is crystalized and cannot be changed. Because they think they only have a certain amount of aptitude, in achievement activities their goal orientation shifts to demonstrating that aptitude. For these individuals, failures are regarded as indications of aptitude inadequacy. They are more likely to avoid challenges so as to avoid the risk of failure. Experiencing failure poses a threat to their self-esteem and is more likely to result in a sense of helplessness, a kind of feeling that they cannot control the outcomes of the achievement activities and they are doomed to fail (Dweck & Leggett, 1988).

As mindset theory was originally developed from children's different reactions to failures and/or difficulties in learning (Dweck, 2012), it is widely studied in the academic achievement domain (Bernecker & Job, 2019). Common research questions about mindset theory include where children's or learners' implicit theories of intelligence come from (e.g., Haimovitz & Dweck, 2016), how their mindsets affect their learning goals (e.g., Bernecker & Job, 2019), their understanding of their effort, their attributions, their learning strategies, and their actual academic performance (e.g., Blackwell et al., 2007).

Mindset theory has been expanded to encompass individuals' beliefs about not only their aptitude but also their other personal characteristics, including but not limited to personality (e.g., Bernecker & Job, 2019), willpower (e.g., Job, Walton, Bernecker, & Dweck, 2015), and interpersonal/peer relationships (e.g., Rudolph, 2010). As a result, the theory has also been used to study individuals' goals (e.g., Rudolph, 2010), attributions, and strategies (e.g., Bernecker & Job, 2019) in the interpersonal domain. This extension beyond the classroom provides the necessary broad scope to understand language learning, which can take place both within and outside the classroom, which clearly has important implications for SLA scholarship.

Attribution and Mindset in SLA

Both attribution and mindset theory have been extended to the field of SLA to help understand language learning motivation (see Chapter 10). Whereas motivational research in SLA tends to explore these two constructs separately, the definitions of attribution and mindset have shown that they are actually closely related. In this section, we will first discuss whether/how attribution and mindset have been redefined when they were introduced into SLA. Then, a conceptual model will be proposed to connect attributions and mindsets in SLA. It should be noted that, due to a lack of empirical SLA studies involving both attributions and mindsets, the model we propose here is based largely on theoretical definitions of these two constructs and some empirical research from the broader field of psychology.

Defining Attribution and Mindset in SLA

The definition of attribution in SLA is used in pretty much the same way as in psychology (Dörnyei & Ryan, 2015). For mindset, some researchers simply reframe the general mindset specifically to the language learning context (e.g., Papi, Rios, Pelt, & Ozdemir, 2019; Waller & Papi, 2017), just like how attribution is dealt with in SLA studies. Other researchers, however, define language mindset in a more nuanced way. Lou and Noels (2016, 2017) extended this general definition of language mindset and, based on qualitative studies conducted by Mercer and Ryan (2010), argued that language mindsets should be assessed with reference to three subsets of beliefs: general language intelligence beliefs (i.e., whether language intelligence is changeable), L2 aptitude beliefs (i.e., whether L2 ability is changeable), and beliefs about age sensitivity of language learning (i.e., whether there is a critical period influencing ultimate L2 learning attainment). In addition, L2 learners may hold different mindsets for different L2 learning areas such as pronunciation, speaking, and writing (Mercer & Ryan, 2010).

Attribution-Mindset Relation: Mindsets as Moderators and Antecedents of Attributions

According to the definition of attributions and mindsets, these two constructs are connected in that mindsets may moderate how attributions are categorized into different causal dimensions (e.g., Weiner, 2018) (see Figure 13.2). The clearest example of this moderation effect is for ability attribution. The essence of mindset theory concerns individuals' implicit beliefs about whether their own ability is stable or not. Those with a fixed mindset categorize ability as a stable cause, whereas those with a growth mindset categorize it as unstable (Weiner, 2018). Accordingly, students in these two groups should demonstrate very different emotional and behavioral reactions for the same attribution (i.e., ability) because they associated it with a different causal dimension (Weiner, 1986, 2006, 2018).

Specifically, in the SLA context, L2 learners with a fixed mindset and L2 learners with a growth mindset disagree on whether L2 learning aptitude is stable (e.g., Ryan & Mercer, 2012a). L2 learners with a fixed mindset hold the belief that their language learning aptitude is innate and cannot be

Attributions and Mindsets

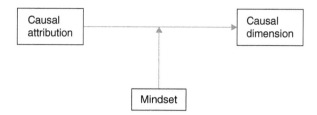

Figure 13.2 Mindset's moderation effect between attribution and causal dimension

Mindset	Cognition	Affect	Behavior
Fixed	Stable/Unchangeable –L2 aptitude is good –Effort is negative	Depressed affect –Anxiety –Fear of failure –Shame –Boredom	Maladaptive helpless pattern
Growth	Unstable/Malleable –L2 aptitude is neutral –Effort is positive	Positive affect –Hope	Adaptive mastery pattern

Figure 13.3 Mindset as causal antecedent of attributions

changed. Therefore, when they attribute their failures in language learning to their lack of aptitude, they would take it as a stable attribution and feel depressed and hopeless as they assume that their inadequate language learning aptitude would not change no matter how hard they try. In contrast, L2 learners with a growth mindset believe that their L2 learning aptitude can be improved through their effort. They see ability as an unstable attribution and work hard to promote their L2 learning aptitude. In this case, L2 learners' mindsets can be theorized to moderate how they categorize their L2 attributions into different causal dimensions.

Apart from being a moderator between attribution and causal dimensions, mindsets may also serve as a causal antecedent that could lead to attributions with different cognitive, affective, and/or behavioral consequences (e.g., Blackwell et al., 2007; Hong, Chiu, Dweck, Lin, & Wan, 1999) (see Figure 13.3). Psychological research has shown that in the academic achievement domain, learners with a growth mindset were more likely to attribute negative performance feedback to a lack of effort, and were also more likely to take remedial actions to improve their learning when they were faced with academic failures than their fixed-mindset peers (e.g., Hong et al., 1999). Likewise, in the interpersonal domain, people with a growth mindset attribute conflicts and social challenges more to situational factors, whereas people with a fixed mindset attribute these conflicts and challenges more to others' personalities (e.g., Bernecker & Job, 2019). Hence, people with a fixed mindset are generally angrier about social offenses and are also more likely to seek revenge compared with their growth-mindset counterparts (e.g., Bernecker & Job, 2019).

Based on these psychological studies, it can be proposed that in SLA settings, L2 learners with a fixed mindset may attribute their L2 learning outcomes more to L2 learning aptitude, viewed in its typical stable fashion, thereby resulting in less willingness to put effort into their L2 learning. These L2 learners believe that what one can achieve in L2 learning is largely determined by their innate L2 learning aptitude and thus it is pointless to work hard (e.g., Mercer, 2012). They assume that great effort indicates a lack of innate L2 aptitude (Mercer & Ryan, 2010) and often deem effort as negative and unnecessary (Lou & Noels, 2016, 2017). When they attribute their L2 learning outcomes to a lack of L2 learning aptitude or high learning effort, they may experience negative affect like fear of failure and in turn demonstrate maladaptive, helpless L2 learning behaviors, as they think their limited L2 aptitude cannot be developed in any way. In the meantime, if they feel that they have high L2 learning aptitude, they may feel bored and stop working hard, because they think their high L2 aptitude could easily help them master the language (see Figure 13.3).

In contrast, L2 learners with a growth mindset may attribute L2 learning outcomes more to their L2 learning efforts, an unstable cause, and be more likely to work hard to improve their L2 learning through their own effort. They regard effort and hard work as critical for mastery (e.g., Mercer & Ryan, 2010). For these L2 learners, attributing L2 learning outcomes to a lack of L2 aptitude and/or effort both suggest that they need to put more hard work into their L2 learning. Therefore, they tend to feel hopeful about their L2 learning and are more willing to try harder to make progress in their L2 learning than their fixed-mindset peers. They may not feel bored or that they have done enough because they believe that, however competent they are, there is still room for improvement (see Figure 13.3).

To sum up, attributions and mindsets are closely related. In SLA, a mindset could moderate how L2 attributions, especially L2 aptitude-related attributions, are categorized into different causal dimensions (e.g., Ryan & Mercer, 2012a). When an L2 learner with a fixed mindset lands on L2 aptitude as the cause of their L2 learning outcomes, they view it as stable and their persistence is undermined. When an L2 learner with a growth mindset lands on L2 aptitude as the cause of their L2 learning outcomes, they view it as unstable and their persistence is preserved. In addition, mindsets could work as a causal antecedent that generates L2 attributions with adaptive cognition, affect, and L2 learning behaviors (e.g., Lou & Noels, 2016, 2017; Mercer, 2012; Mercer & Ryan, 2010). L2 learners with a fixed mindset tend to make more L2 aptitude-related attributions and they hold a negative attitude toward effort—an attributional pattern resulting in more negative affect and maladaptive L2 learning behaviors. L2 learners with a growth mindset tend to make more effort-related attributions and they see effort in a positive way: An attributional pattern leading to more positive affect and adaptive L2 learning behaviors.

L2 Attributional Studies in Light of Attribution-Mindset Relation

By reflecting on theoretical definitions of attribution and mindset in SLA and by extending empirical findings about these two constructs in psychology into SLA, we have argued that attributions and mindsets can be thought of as related to each other in SLA. Specifically, we have articulated how mindset could be regarded as both (a) a moderator of how L2 learners categorize their L2 attributions into different causal dimensions and (b) a causal antecedent that results in L2 attributions with various cognitive, affective, and behavioral consequences. In this section, L2 attributional studies will be reviewed from the lens of the proposed attribution-mindset relation model specific to SLA. The intention is that the proposed attribution-mindset relation model may provide alternative explanations for some existing findings about attribution research in SLA and may in turn inspire future research and practice about L2 attribution.

Attribution Research in SLA

We conducted a systematic review of attributional SLA studies in 15 databases. The search words we used were "attribution" and "second language acquisition" or "second language learning" or "foreign language learning," etc. In total, we found 47 studies that investigated the role of attribution in SLA. Most were empirical research (44 out of 47) and three were theoretical review papers. Among the 44 empirical studies (see Appendix), 29 of them were conducted in English as a foreign language (EFL) context, 12 in foreign languages other than English (FLOE) context, and two in English as a second language (ESL) context. One study compared heritage language (HL) and non-HL learners. In terms of research method, there are 20 quantitative, 17 mixed-method, and seven qualitative studies. With regard to research design, there are 41 cross-sectional studies, one intervention study, and one quasi-experimental study. One study was categorized as both an intervention and a quasi-experimental study. Most of the quantitative data were collected using survey questionnaires. Some studies measured attributions using established scales like the Causal Dimension Scale II (e.g., McAuley, Duncan, & Russell, 1992). Other researchers developed their own scales by formulating causal statements and asking participants to rate the extent to which these statements applied to them. Qualitative data were collected through interviews, open-ended questions, and written journals. Most of the studies we reviewed analyzed both specific attributions and the causal dimensions of these attributions. In terms of data analysis, quantitative data were analyzed through mean analysis, factor analysis, correlation, *t*-test, ANOVA, multiple regression, and structural equation modeling. Qualitative data were analyzed through approaches like content analysis. Among the 44 empirical studies we found, 39 focused on L2 learners' attributions, one examined L2 teachers' attributions, and four looked at both (see Appendix).

Reflections from the Lens of Attribution-Mindset Relation in SLA

Studies about L2 learners' attributions could be divided into four categories depending on their research objectives and findings. First, there were studies that explored frequency of attributions, including those that examined L2 learners' most common attributions (e.g., Tse, 2000) and those that made intra- and interpersonal comparisons of L2 attributions (e.g., Williams & Burden, 1999). This was the most common type of study. Second, there were studies that investigated the association between L2 attributions and L2 achievement (e.g., Erten & Burden, 2014) and between L2 attributions and various cognitive and affective factors in L2 learning (e.g., Hsieh & Schallert, 2008). The third group of studies looked at antecedents of L2 attributions (e.g., Peacock, 2010). Fourth, there were studies that focused on intervention or attributional retraining (e.g., Hussein & Samad, 2005). Additionally, we briefly consider the literature on teachers' attributions in SLA. Each category of studies had some findings that could be (re)explained from the perspective of our proposed attribution-mindset relation model.

In terms of the most common attributions of L2 learners, *L2 aptitude* and *effort* were the two most frequently cited attributions of L2 learners (e.g., Williams, Burden, Poulet, & Maun, 2004). Most of these studies either only reported the frequency of each L2 attribution (e.g., Williams et al., 2004) or assumed L2 aptitude as a stable attribution (e.g., Bouchaib, Ahmadou, & Abdelkader, 2018). However, in support of our proposed attribution-mindset relation model, L2 learners did not always assume aptitude as a stable attribution; some learners thought that their L2 aptitude could be improved through practice (e.g., Nakamura, 2018). As such, attributing L2 learning failures to L2 aptitude was only "dangerous" for those who regarded their L2 aptitude as "fixed" (Seyyedrezaie, Ghonsooly, Shahriari, & Fatemi, 2016, p. 105). These findings were identified by SLA researchers as "interesting" (Nakamura, 2018, p. 567) as they contradicted traditional conclusions about ability attribution. We believe that the findings could be well explained by our proposed attribution-mindset relation model. In other words, it is possible that L2 learners in these previous studies held different mindsets, which made them categorize L2 aptitude as a stable or unstable attribution, and in turn, which influenced their effort and L2 development differently.

Under the first category of studies about L2 learners' attributions, the other subcategory involves studies that explored intra- and interpersonal differences of L2 learners' attributions (see Table 13.2) (e.g., Gobel & Mori, 2007; Williams & Burden, 1999). Some of these comparative studies generally

Table 13.2 Studies that Made Intra- and Interpersonal Comparisons of L2 Learners' Attributions

Intrapersonal comparison	*Interpersonal comparison*
• L2 success and failure (e.g., Gobel & Mori, 2007) • Different L2 learning activities (reading vs. speaking, etc.; e.g., Gobel & Mori, 2007)	• Different age groups (e.g., Williams & Burden, 1999) • Male and female learners (e.g., Tulu, 2013) • Learners of different L2s (e.g., Williams et al., 2004) • Successful and unsuccessful learners (e.g., Genç, 2016) • L2 learners from different countries (e.g., Lim, 2009) • Gifted and non-gifted L2 learners (e.g., Bain et. al., 2010) • L2 learners from different academic disciplines (e.g., Peacock, 2010) • L2 learners with different proficiency levels (elementary vs. advanced, etc.; e.g., Mohammadi & Sharififar, 2016)

provided mixed findings, which may be clarified by applying our proposed attribution-mindset relation model. For instance, in terms of L2 attributions across different age groups, Williams and Burden (1999) suggested that elder L2 learners' attributions were wider in range than their younger peers', whereas Genç (2016) indicated that age did not have an essential influence over L2 attributions. Such mixed findings apply to many comparison studies in this category, and so far not much has been done to explain these complex findings. As mindset may be a causal antecedent of L2 attributions, it is possible that L2 learners in these comparison studies held different mindsets that led to different conclusions about their L2 attributions.

As for those comparative studies that have more consensus in their conclusions, they usually did not explain why differences in L2 attributions emerged. Again, we apply our proposed attribution-mindset relation model to reconsider the findings of these studies. Specifically, research has shown that mindset may vary across different L2 learning activities (Mercer & Ryan, 2010) and between success and failure (Leith, Ward, Giacomin, Landau, Ehrlinger & Wilson, 2014). Therefore, according to the attribution-mindset relation model, the different attributions between L2 learning activities, as well as those between L2 success and failure (Gobel & Mori, 2007), may be related to L2 learners' different mindsets. Research has also shown that L2 learners with different cultural backgrounds (Ryan & Mercer, 2012b) may differ in their mindsets, which could be used to account for the different attributions among L2 learners from different countries (e.g., Lim, 2009).

The second category of studies includes a large percentage that examined the relation between attributions and L2 achievement (e.g., Erten & Burden, 2014) and a smaller proportion that focused on L2 attributions' association with various cognitive and affective variables of L2 learning (e.g., Hsieh & Kang, 2010; Hsieh & Schallert, 2008), such as self-efficacy (e.g., Hsieh & Kang, 2010), L2 learning attitude and anxiety (e.g., Bell & McCallum, 2012), self-construal, competence, and achievement goals (e.g., Luo, Hogan, Yeung, Sheng, & Aye, 2014). For studies about the relation between attributions and L2 achievement, similar to those in the first category, some found that attributing L2 learning outcomes to L2 aptitude had a positive correlation with L2 test score (e.g., Erten & Burden, 2014), whereas others found that changing from effort attribution to L2 aptitude attribution was detrimental to L2 learning (Yantraprakorn, Darasawang, & Wiriyakarun, 2018). Similarly, this inconsistency may be explained by L2 learners' mindsets. Those with a growth mindset see their L2 aptitude as changeable and when they attribute L2 learning outcomes to their aptitude, they may generally feel that they could make more progress by putting in more effort. In this case, L2 aptitude attribution may be beneficial for their L2 learning. In contrast, those with a fixed mindset see their L2 aptitude as fixed and attributing L2 learning outcomes to their aptitude may make them feel that there is nothing they could do to change their L2 aptitude or their L2 learning in general.

As a result, L2 aptitude attribution may generally result in maladaptive L2 learning behaviors and less satisfactory L2 achievement.

For studies about the association between L2 attributions and various cognitive and affective factors in L2 learning, some of their findings could be further explained using our proposed attribution-mindset relation model and others may not always hold if the proposed attribution-mindset relation is taken into account. For instance, Luo et al. (2014) found that L2 learners with a performance-avoidance goal tended to make L2 aptitude-related attributions. They were also pretty anxious and not particularly willing to work hard in their L2 learning (Luo et al., 2014). This is rather similar to L2 learners with a fixed mindset. As research has shown that variances in mindsets may lead to variances in achievement goal orientations (Murayama, Elliot, & Friedman, 2012), the above association between L2 attributions and achievement goals may actually reflect the connection between L2 attributions and mindsets. In addition, Hsieh and Schallert (2008) found that for L2 learners who were unsatisfied with their L2 test performance, attributing their self-rated failures to a lack of effort would produce a higher level of self-efficacy, as effort attribution was unstable and could provide these L2 learners with a sense that they had the competence to control their future L2 learning outcomes. According to our proposed attribution-mindset relation, this conclusion may only hold true for unsuccessful L2 learners with a growth mindset, as those with a fixed mindset tend to view effort negatively and as an indicator of low aptitude. For these unsuccessful fixed-mindset L2 learners, failing in L2 learning due to a lack of effort may mean that they need more effort to compensate for their low L2 aptitude, a belief that could be detrimental to their self-efficacy.

The third category of studies investigated antecedents of L2 learners' attributions. (e.g., Peacock, 2010). According to Peacock (2010), L2 learners' attributions may come from (a) their successful and/or unsuccessful personal L2 learning experiences; (b) verbal messages from important others like family and/or teachers; and (c) their observations of other L2 learners. Based on our proposed attribution-mindset relation model, mindset may also be a potential antecedent of L2 attributions and it may interact with the above factors to create a mutual impact on L2 attributions. For instance, for an L2 learner with a fixed mindset, experiencing repeated failures in L2 learning may further strengthen the belief that his/her L2 aptitude cannot be improved whatsoever, which in turn may result in attributions that lead to negative affect and maladaptive L2 learning behaviors.

Intervention and attributional retraining research is a fourth category (e.g., Hussein & Samad, 2005). As Hussein and Samad (2005) have pointed out, training students to answer for their own learning and to develop adaptive attributions (i.e., to attribute learning outcomes to internal, unstable, and/or controllable factors like effort) could be very difficult sometimes. That being the case, we encourage researchers to consider our proposed attribution-mindset relation model because it may be important to cultivate growth mindsets first to maximize uptake of attributional retraining.

Finally, though most attribution research we found is about L2 learners' attributions, there are also studies that looked at L2 teachers' attributions (e.g., Ghanizadeh & Ghonsooly, 2014). One study examined the influence of EFL teachers' attributions on EFL teacher burnout and self-regulation (Ghanizadeh & Ghonsooly, 2014), and four looked at both L2 teachers' and learners' attributions (Golovatch & Vanderplank, 2007; Peacock, 2010; Rojas-Barreto & Artunduaga-Cuellar, 2018; Yilmaz, 2012). Whereas the proposed attribution-mindset relation mainly focuses on L2 learners' attributions, it is possible that they could also be used to explain findings about L2 teachers' attributions in instances when traditionally stable attributions end up having adaptive outcomes.

Integration of Perspectives

We have proposed that mindsets function as both a moderator between L2 attributions and causal dimensions, and as an antecedent of L2 attributions with distinct outcomes. Our resultant attribution-mindset relation model can provide L2 researchers with a new lens from which they can reflect upon existing L2 attributional studies, especially those with mixed or complex results. The proposed attribution-mindset relation is mainly based on logical combinations of their theoretical definitions and propositions, and empirical evidence testing the model in SLA specifically is largely lacking to date. Nonetheless, the breadth of these constructs in the broad psychological literature and the applicability of the model in an ad-hoc manner to pre-existing studies gives us confidence that the model holds potential implications both for SLA research and practice. In this section, we will start by discussing implications of the proposed attribution-mindset relation for attributional research in SLA and then move on to implications for L2 teaching.

Implications for L2 Research

The attribution-mindset relation model could offer potential new directions both for research about L2 learners' mindsets and attributions, as well as those about L2 teachers' attributions and mindsets. At its most fundamental level, our proposed attribution-mindset relation model suggests that researchers should consider *both* students' L2 mindsets and their attributions. Continuing to focus on one construct to the exclusion of the other may perpetuate mis-specified models and conflicting results that prevent the field from making significant advancements. This is particularly relevant as intervention research becomes more pronounced in the field. If mindsets have the ability to influence both the selected attribution and the causal dimensions, then interventions must first ensure L2 learners have a growth mindset. Keep in mind that Lou and Noels (2016, 2017) suggested that L2 mindsets have three distinct elements, and thus this domain-specific definition should be fit into the attribution-mindset relation model in order to tailor it to future research in SLA. As for SLA teachers, researchers can apply the attribution-mindset relation model to their understanding of their learners but also to their own beliefs about teaching.

Implications for L2 Teaching

The application of our proposed attribution-mindset relation model may benefit L2 teachers by helping them tailor their teaching to support L2 learners' growth mindsets and controllable attributions. Specifically, our proposed attribution-mindset relation model indicates that changing L2 learners' mindsets has an impact on their subsequent attributions—either directly or through the dimensional categorization. As such, although both mindsets and attributions are important, teachers may first want to focus on helping their learners develop a growth mindset that allows them to see L2 aptitude as unstable and view effort positively. Alternatively, SLA teachers may use less formal messaging in their classrooms that focuses on promoting growth, praising effort rather than ability, and intra-individual standards rather than comparisons. In combination, these messages and practices can help shift L2 learners' mindsets.

With a growth mindset in place, teachers could then focus on students' attributions. The essence of most attributional retraining programs is to help L2 learners change from uncontrollable attributions to controllable ones, a shift that will be further facilitated by already holding a growth mindset. Specific attributional retraining protocols (Haynes, Perry, Stupnisky, & Daniels, 2009) will need to be adapted to the SLA context but then could help L2 learners further realize that there are things they could control in order to change these unstable causes and to achieve better L2 learning outcomes. In turn, L2 teachers will need to focus on ensuring their learners do indeed have some control over their learning. This can be accomplished through small shifts in delivery, such as allowing learners to choose a conversational partner or a writing topic.

Future Directions

Both attributions and mindsets have been researched in SLA to help understand the role of motivation in L2 learning and teaching. Despite their close theoretical relation, so far these two constructs have been investigated independently in SLA. In this chapter, we proposed an attribution-mindset relation model based on the definitions, theoretical commonalities, and existing research about these two constructs. The model indicates that mindset could (a) moderate how L2 attributions are categorized into different causal dimensions, and (b) be seen as a causal antecedent that could result in selection of L2 attributions with more adaptive cognition, affects, and behaviors in the process of L2 learning. Accordingly, incorporating mindsets into L2 attribution studies may help explain existing findings about attribution in SLA and offer new directions for L2 empirical and intervention research as well as teaching.

Reflection Questions

- How can research be conducted to better understand the associations amongst L2 learners' attributions and mindsets?
- What mindsets do I have about anguage learning and what attributions do I tend to make when I fail/succeed?
- How can I help build growth mindsets and adaptive attributions in my L2 learners?

Recommended Reading

Lou, N. M., & Noels, K. A. (2019). Language mindsets, meaning-making, and motivation. In M. Lamb, K. Csizér, A. Henry, & S. Ryan (Eds.), *The Palgrave handbook of motivation for language learning* (pp. 537–559). Palgrave Macmillan.
This book chapter reviews existing research findings about mindset theory in SLA. It discusses how attributions and mindsets are related psychological constructs. This reading provides a general understanding about how mindsets and attributions are part of a larger meaning-making system.

Hong, Y. Y., Chiu, C. Y., Dweck, C. S., Lin, D. M. S., & Wan, W. (1999). Implicit theories, attributions, and coping: A meaning system approach. *Journal of Personality and Social Psychology*, 77(3), 588–599.
This is an empirical study that investigates the relation between attributions and mindsets. Its research design and findings provide insights into how attributions and mindsets are connected. It is noteworthy that mindsets may also be termed as implicit theories in some studies.

Ryan, S., & Mercer, S. (2012a). Implicit theories: Language learning mindsets. In S. Mercer, S. Ryan, & M. Williams (Eds.), *Psychology for language learning: Insights from research, theory and practice* (pp. 74–89). Palgrave Macmillan.
This book chapter discusses the application of mindset theory into the field of SLA. Its explanation about the association between attributions and mindsets in psychology, together with a definition of language learning mindsets, offers the seminal foundation for connecting attribution and mindset theories in SLA research.

References

Bain, S. K., McCallum, R. S., Bell, S. M., Cochran, J. L., & Sawyer, S. C. (2010). Foreign language learning aptitudes, attitudes, attributions, and achievement of postsecondary students identified as gifted. *Journal of Advanced Academics*, 22(1), 130–156.
Bell, S. M., & McCallum, R. S. (2012). Do foreign language learning, cognitive, and affective variables differ as a function of exceptionality status and gender? *International Education*, 42(1), 85–106.
Bernecker, K., & Job, V. (2019). Mindset theory. In K. Sassenberg & M. L. W. Vliek (Eds.), *Social psychology in action: Evidence-based interventions from theory to practice* (pp. 179–191). Springer Nature Switzerland AG.
Blackwell, L. S., Trzesniewski, K. H., & Dweck, C. S. (2007). Implicit theories of intelligence predict achievement across an adolescent transition: A longitudinal study and an intervention. *Child Development*, 78(1), 246–263.
Bouchaib, B., Ahmadou, B., & Abdelkader, S. (2018). High school students' attributions of success in English language learning. *International Journal of Instruction*, 11(2), 89–102.

Chang, H., Windsor, A., & Helwig, L. (2017). Exposing the dynamic nature and potential role of student attribution processes on English for academic purposes achievement in higher education. *English in Australia*, 52(2), 73–81.
Demir, Y. (2017). Turkish EFL learners' attributions for success and failure in speaking English. *International Journal of Contemporary Educational Research*, 4(2), 39–47.
Dişlen Dağgöl, G. (2019). Learning climate and self-efficacy beliefs of high school students in an EFL setting. *Novitas-ROYAL (Research on Youth and Language)*, 13(1), 19–35.
Dong, Y., Stupnisky, R. H., & Berry, J. C. (2013). Multiple causal attributions: An investigation of college students learning a foreign language. *European Journal of Psychology of Education*, 28(4), 1587–1602.
Dörnyei, Z. & Ryan, S. (2015). *The psychology of the language learner revisited*. Routledge.
Dweck, C. S. (2006). *Mindset: The new psychology of success*. Random House.
Dweck, C. S. (2012). Implicit theories. In P. A. M. Van Lange, A. W. Kruglanski, & E. T. Higgins (Eds.), *Handbook of theories of social psychology* (Vol. 2, pp. 43–61). SAGE Publications Ltd.
Dweck, C. S., & Leggett, E. L. (1988). A social-cognitive approach to motivation and personality. *Psychological Review*, 95(2), 256–273.
Erler, L., & Macaro, E. (2011). Decoding ability in French as a foreign language and language learning motivation. *The Modern Language Journal*, 95(4), 496–518.
Erten, İ. H., & Burden, R. L. (2014). The relationship between academic self-concept, attributions, and L2 achievement. *System*, 42, 391–401.
Fielden, L. V., & Rico, M. (2018). Attribution theories in language learning motivation: Success in vocational English for hospitality students. *English Language Teaching*, 11(11), 44–54.
Genç, G. (2016). Attributions to success and failure in English language learning: The effects of gender, age and perceived success. *European Journal of Education Studies*, 2(12), 25–43.
Ghanizadeh, A., & Ghonsooly, B. (2014). A tripartite model of EFL teacher attributions, burnout, and self-regulation: Toward the prospects of effective teaching. *Educational Research for Policy and Practice*, 13(2), 145–166.
Gobel, P., & Mori, S. (2007). Success and failure in the EFL classroom: Exploring students' attributional beliefs in language learning. *EUROSLA Yearbook*, 7(1), 149–169.
Golovatch, Y., & Vanderplank, R. (2007). Unwitting agents: The role of adult learners' attributions of success in shaping language-learning behaviour. *Journal of Adult and Continuing Education*, 13(2), 127–155.
Gosiewska-Turek, B. (2017). The interdependence between attributions and second language attainments in secondary school students. *The Journal of Education, Culture, and Society*, 8(1), 109–124.
Graham, S. J. (2004). Giving up on modern foreign languages? Students' perceptions of learning French. *The Modern Language Journal*, 88(2), 171–191.
Haimovitz, K., & Dweck, C. S. (2016). Parents' views of failure predict children's fixed and growth intelligence mind-sets. *Psychological Science*, 27(6), 859–869.
Haynes, T. L., Perry, R. P., Stupnisky, R. H., & Daniels, L. M. (2009). A review of attributional retraining treatments: Fostering engagement and persistence in vulnerable college students. In J. C. Smart (Ed.), *Higher education: Handbook of theory and research* (Vol. 24, pp. 227–272). Springer.
Hong, Y. Y., Chiu, C. Y., Dweck, C. S., Lin, D. M. S., & Wan, W. (1999). Implicit theories, attributions, and coping: A meaning system approach. *Journal of Personality and Social Psychology*, 77(3), 588–599.
Hsieh, P. P. H., & Kang, H. S. (2010). Attribution and self-efficacy and their interrelationship in the Korean EFL context. *Language Learning*, 60(3), 606–627.
Hsieh, P. H. P., & Schallert, D. L. (2008). Implications from self-efficacy and attribution theories for an understanding of undergraduates' motivation in a foreign language course. *Contemporary Educational Psychology*, 33(4), 513–532.
Hussein, H. B., & Samad, A. A. (2005). Helping remedial students help themselves: Causal attribution and language proficiency. *The Journal of Asia TEFL*, 2(3), 49–65.
Jernigan, C. G. (2004). What do students expect to learn? The role of learner expectancies, beliefs, and attributions for success and failure in student motivation. *Current Issues in Education*, 7(4), 1–38.
Job, V., Walton, G. M., Bernecker, K., & Dweck, C. S. (2015). Implicit theories about willpower predict self-regulation and grades in everyday life. *Journal of Personality and Social Psychology*, 108(4), 637–647.
Kálmán, C., & Gutierrez Eugenio, E. (2015). Successful language learning in a corporate setting: The role of attribution theory and its relation to intrinsic and extrinsic motivation. *Studies in Second Language Learning and Teaching*, 5(4), 583–608.
Leith, S. A., Ward, C. L. P., Giacomin, M., Landau, E. S., Ehrlinger, J., & Wilson, A. E. (2014). Changing theories of change: Strategic shifting in implicit theory endorsement. *Journal of Personality and Social Psychology*, 107(4), 597–620.
Lim, H. Y. (2009). Culture, attributions, and language anxiety. *Applied Language Learning*, 19, 29–52.
Lou, N. M., & Noels, K. A. (2016). Changing language mindsets: Implications for goal orientations and responses to failure in and outside the second language classroom. *Contemporary Educational Psychology*, 46, 22–33.

Lou, N. M., & Noels, K. A. (2017). Measuring language mindsets and modeling their relations with goal orientations and emotional and behavioral responses in failure situations. *The Modern Language Journal, 101*(1), 214–243.

Luo, W., Hogan, D. J., Yeung, A. S., Sheng, Y. Z., & Aye, K. M. (2014). Attributional beliefs of Singapore students: Relations to self-construal, competence and achievement goals. *Educational Psychology, 34*(2), 154–170.

MacIntyre, P. D., & Legatto, J. J. (2011). A dynamic system approach to willingness to communicate: Developing an idiodynamic method to capture rapidly changing affect. *Applied Linguistics, 32*(2), 149–171.

McAuley, E., Duncan, T. E., & Russell, D. W. (1992). Measuring causal attributions: The revised causal dimension scale (CDSII). *Personality and Social Psychology Bulletin, 18*(5), 566–573.

Mercer, S. (2012). Dispelling the myth of the natural-born linguist. *ELT journal, 66*(1), 22–29.

Mercer, S., & Ryan, S. (2010). A mindset for EFL: Learners' beliefs about the role of natural talent. *ELT journal, 64*(4), 436–444.

Mohammadi, A., & Sharififar, M. (2016). Attributions for success and failure: Gender and language proficiency differences among Iranian EFL learners. *Theory and Practice in Language Studies, 6*(3), 518–524.

Murayama, K., Elliot, A. J., & Friedman, R. (2012). Achievement goals. In R. M. Ryan (Ed.), *The Oxford handbook of human motivation* (pp. 191–207). Oxford University Press.

Nakamura, S. (2018). How I see it: An exploratory study on attributions and emotions in L2 learning. *Studies in Second Language Learning and Teaching, 8*(3), 553–574.

Paker, T., & Özkardeş-Döğüş, A. (2017). Achievement attributions of preparatory class learners in learning English. *Journal of Language and Linguistic Studies, 13*(2), 109–135.

Papi, M., Rios, A., Pelt, H., & Ozdemir, E. (2019). Feedback-seeking behavior in language learning: Basic components and motivational antecedents. *The Modern Language Journal, 103*(1), 205–226.

Peacock, M. (2010). Attribution and learning English as a foreign language. *ELT journal, 64*(2), 184–193.

Rojas-Barreto, L. S., & Artunduaga-Cuellar, M. T. (2018). Students and teachers' causal attributions to course failure and repetition in an ELT undergraduate program. *English Language Teaching, 11*(5), 39–54.

Rudolph, K. D. (2010). Implicit theories of peer relationships. *Social Development, 19*(1), 113–129.

Ryan, S., & Mercer, S. (2012a). Implicit theories: Language learning mindsets. In S. Mercer, S. Ryan, & M. Williams (Eds.), *Psychology for language learning: Insights from research, theory and practice* (pp. 74–89). Palgrave Macmillan.

Ryan, S., & Mercer, S. (2012b). Language learning mindsets across cultural settings: English learners in Austria and Japan. *OnCUE Journal, 6*(1), 6–22.

Sahinkarakas, S. (2011). Young students' success and failure attributions in language learning. *Social Behavior and Personality, 39*(7), 879–886.

Scherer, K. R. (2018). Attribution theory: A lively legacy. *Motivation Science, 4*(1), 15–16.

Seyyedrezaie, Z. S., Ghonsooly, B., Shahriari, H., & Fatemi, H. H. (2016). A mixed methods analysis of the effect of Google Docs environment on EFL learners' writing performance and causal attributions for success and failure. *Turkish Online Journal of Distance Education, 17*(3), 90–110.

Shimbo, K. (2007). The effect of suggestion on tertiary students' attribution and self-concept. *Education Research and Perspectives, 34*(1), 179–197.

Thang, S. M., & Jaafar, N. M. (2017). The interplay between teacher-centredness and self-critical tendency among Malaysian ESL learners: New insights for the Asian context. *International Journal of Instruction, 10*(2), 161–178.

Tse, L. (2000). Student perceptions of foreign language study: A qualitative analysis of foreign language autobiographies. *The Modern Language Journal, 84*(1), 69–84.

Tulu, G. (2013). Boys' and girls' attribution of performance in learning English as a foreign language: The case of Adama high schools in Ethiopia. *Educational Research and Reviews, 8*(23), 2197–2211.

Waller, L., & Papi, M. (2017). Motivation and feedback: How implicit theories of intelligence predict L2 writers' motivation and feedback orientation. *Journal of Second Language Writing, 35*, 54–65.

Weiner, B. (1986). *An attributional theory of motivation and emotion*. Springer-Verlag.

Weiner, B. (2006). *Social motivation, justice, and the moral emotions: An attributional approach*. Lawrence Erlbaum Associates.

Weiner, B. (2018). The legacy of an attribution approach to motivation and emotion: A no-crisis zone. *Motivation Science, 4*(1), 4–14.

Wen, X. (2011). Chinese language learning motivation: A comparative study of heritage and non-heritage learners. *Heritage Language Journal, 8*(3), 333–358.

Williams, M., & Burden, R. (1999). Students' developing conceptions of themselves as language learners. *The Modern Language Journal, 83*(2), 193–201.

Williams, M., Burden, R., Poulet, G., & Maun, I. (2004). Learners' perceptions of their successes and failures in foreign language learning. *Language Learning Journal, 30*(1), 19–29.

Wu, J. (2011). An investigation and analysis of attribution preference and gender difference of non-English majors' English learning–Based on investigation of non-English majors in Tianjin Polytechnic University. *Journal of Language Teaching and Research, 2*(2), 332–337.

Yantraprakorn, P., Darasawang, P., & Wiriyakarun, P. (2018). Self-efficacy and online language learning: Causes of failure. *Journal of Language Teaching and Research, 9*(6), 1319–1329.

Yavuz, A., & Höl, D. (2017). Investigation of Turkish EFL learners' attributions on success and failure in learning English. *Journal of Language and Linguistic Studies, 13*(2), 379–396.

Yilmaz, C. (2012). An investigation into Turkish EFL students' attributions in reading comprehension. *Journal of Language Teaching and Research, 3*(5), 823–828.

Yilmaz, F., & Kahyalar, E. (2017). University students' perceptions of their failures in learning English as a foreign language. *International Journal of Languages' Education and Teaching, 5*(4), 440–449.

Zhao, L. (2015). The influence of learners' motivation and attitudes on second language teaching. *Theory and Practice in Language Studies, 5*(11), 2333–2339.

Table 13.3 Appendix: Attribution Studies in SLA research

	Year	Author(s)	Method		Context		Contact Situation	Country/region
			Design	Data	Participant			
	Year of publication		cross-sectional/ longitudinal/ intervention/ quasi-experimental	quantitative/ qualitative/ mixed	elementary (E)/ secondary (S)/ Post-secondary (PS)/adult learners (AL)/ teacher (T)		heritage language (HL)/ second language other than English (SLOE)/ English as a second language (ESL)/ foreign language other than English (FLOE)/ english as a foreign language (EFL)	country/region in which data were collected
1	1999	Williams & Burden	cross-sectional	qualitative	E & S		FLOE	England
2	2000	Tse	cross-sectional	qualitative	PS		FLOE	USA
3	2004	Williams et al.	cross-sectional	qualitative	S		FLOE	England
4		Jernigan	cross-sectional	mixed	PS (& T)[a]		FLOE	USA
5		Graham	intervention	mixed	S		FLOE	England
6	2005	Hussein & Samad	cross-sectional	quantitative	PS		EFL	Malaysia
7	2007	Gobel & Mori	cross-sectional	mixed	PS		EFL	Japan
8		Golovatch & Vanderplank	cross-sectional	mixed	AL & T		EFL	Belarus
9		Shimbo	intervention & quasi-experimental	mixed	PS		FLOE	Australia
10	2008	Hsieh & Schallert	cross-sectional	quantitative	PS		FLOE	N/A
11	2009	Lim	cross-sectional	quantitative	PS		ESL	USA
12	2010	Bain et al.	cross-sectional	quantitative	PS		FLOE	N/A
13		Peacock	cross-sectional	mixed	PS & T		EFL	China
14		Hsieh & Kang	cross-sectional	quantitative	S		EFL	South Korea
15	2011	MacIntyre & Legatto	quasi-experimental	mixed	PS		FLOE	Canada
16		Erler & Macaro	cross-sectional	quantitative	S		FLOE	England
17		Wu	cross-sectional	quantitative	PS		EFL	China
18		Wen	cross-sectional	mixed	PS		HL & FLOE	USA

(continued)

Table 13.3 Cont.

	Year	Author(s)	Method		Context	Contact Situation	Country/region
	Year of publication		Design	Data	Participant	heritage language (HL) / second language other than English (SLOE) / English as a second language (ESL) / foreign language other than English (FLOE) / english as a foreign language (EFL)	country/region in which data were collected
			cross-sectional / longitudinal / intervention / quasi-experimental	quantitative / qualitative / mixed	elementary (E) / secondary (S) / Post-secondary (PS) / adult learners (AL) / teacher (T)		
19		Sahinkarakas	cross-sectional	qualitative	E	EFL	N/A
20	2012	Bell & McCallum	cross-sectional	quantitative	PS	FLOE	USA
21		Yilmaz	cross-sectional	mixed	PS & T	EFL	Turkey
22	2013	Dong et al.	cross-sectional	quantitative	PS	FLOE	USA
23		Tulu	cross-sectional	mixed	S	EFL	Ethiopia
24	2014	Erten & Burden	cross-sectional	quantitative	E	EFL	Turkey
25		Ghanizadeh & Ghonsooly	cross-sectional	quantitative	T	EFL	Iran
26		Luo et al.	cross-sectional	quantitative	S	EFL	Singapore
27	2015	Zhao	cross-sectional	quantitative	PS	EFL	China
28		Kálmán & Gutierrez Eugenio	cross-sectional	quantitative	AL	EFL	Hungary
29	2016	Mohammadi & Sharififar	cross-sectional	quantitative	S & PS & AL	EFL	Iran
30		Seyyedrezaie et al.	cross-sectional	mixed	PS	EFL	Iran
31		Genç	cross-sectional	quantitative	PS	EFL	Turkey
32	2017	Yavuz & Höl	cross-sectional	mixed	PS	EFL	Turkey
33		Paker & Özkardeş-Döğüş	cross-sectional	mixed	PS	EFL	Turkey
34		Demir	cross-sectional	quantitative	PS	EFL	Turkey
35		Chang et al.	cross-sectional	quantitative	PS	ESL	Australia
36		Gosiewska-Turek	cross-sectional	quantitative	S	EFL	Poland
37		Thang & Jaafar	cross-sectional	mixed	PS	EFL	Malaysia

38		Yilmaz & Kahyalar	cross-sectional	qualitative	PS	EFL	Turkey
39	2018	Bouchaib et al.	cross-sectional	mixed	S	EFL	Morocco
40		Yantraprakorn et al.	cross-sectional	qualitative	S	EFL	Thailand
41		Rojas-Barreto & Artunduaga-Cuellar	cross-sectional	qualitative	PS & T	EFL	Colombia
42		Nakamura	cross-sectional	mixed	AL	EFL	Japan
43		Fielden & Rico	cross-sectional	quantitative	AL	EFL	Spain
44	2019	Dişlen Dağgöl	cross-sectional	mixed	S	EFL	Turkey

Note: [a] L2 teacher participants are listed in parentheses for studies that included both L2 learners and teachers as participants but focused on L2 learners' attributions only.

14
EMOTION

Rebecca L. Oxford

This chapter focuses on the construct of emotion. The first two sections explore emotion research and practice as it relates to psychology and Second Language Acquisition (SLA). Although the input of diverse disciplines has caused a definitional melee regarding emotion, it is also true that such disparate contributions have significantly advanced the knowledge of it. The third section considers the ways that emotion has been integrated into L2 education from psychological and SLA perspectives. The fourth section examines the implications for practice and research in L2 education. Lastly, the fifth section provides a summary of the high points; what we have learned about emotion in psychology, SLA, and cross-area integration; and future directions to consider. The chapter ends with reflection questions and an annotated recommended reading list for those who want to further pursue the topic of emotion in psychology, SLA, and L2 education.

Definitional Concerns

Because numerous disciplines have provided input into what emotion is, the field of psychology is replete with definitional issues concerning the construct of emotion, and while this poses some terminological problems, we also gain important insights. "The whole topic [of emotion] ... extends across psychology, neuroscience, psychiatry, biology, anthropology, sociology, literature, and philosophy" (Oatley, Keltner, & Jenkins, 2006). The extension of emotion across so many disciplines means that each has added its part to what psychology as a field understands about emotion. For example, from sociology, psychologists have drawn upon Hochschild's (1983) notion of emotional labor that suggests some professions are prone to displaying certain emotions to meet the requirements of a job. Social psychology has especially been important in adding ideas about self-construal (i.e., the grounds of self-definition and the extent to which the self is defined independently in individualist cultures or interdependently in collectivist cultures; see Markus & Kitayama, 1991), while SLA has added its own concept of emotional labor drawn from sociology, through psychology. Adolphs and Anderson (2018) remarked that, "the scientific study of emotions is a piecemeal and confused discipline with some ... advocating that we get rid of the word *emotion* altogether" (p. xi, emphasis in the original). Dixon (2012) called emotion "a keyword in crisis" (p. 338).

There have, however, been attempts to understand emotion by systematizing it in psychology, but this too has proven problematic as each subfield of psychology and, in some cases, specific theorists within one subfield use terms and/or definitions idiosyncratically and interchangeably. Let us start with affect. *Affect* is often used as an umbrella term (Fox, 2018), but with diverse constructs subsumed below it. Arnold and Brown (1999) named 15 elements closely tied to affect drawn from various sources: emotions, feelings, moods, emotional traits (dispositions), self-esteem, motivation (see Chapter 10), identity (see Chapter 7), interests, attitudes (see Chapter 12), values, Jungian psychological types, learning styles, stress management as a form of emotion regulation (see Chapter 17), flow, and emotion-tied humanistic teaching (see Chapter 3). By way of comparison, Gass with Behney and Plonsky (2013) seem to mention only two components of affect: emotions or feelings. Dirkx (2008) remarked that, "emotion, affect, and feeling" are "used fairly interchangeably" (p. 10). Using greater differentiation, emotion is an unconscious, brief (in seconds to minutes), dynamic, physiologically based state that occurs in response to a situation or object in the environment; and a feeling is a subjective, conscious interpretation of that emotion (Fox, 2018). If we do differentiate between emotion and feeling, there is argumentation about whether feelings are necessary to emotion. A possible resolution is that only complex emotions—aggregates of two or more (e.g., interest, inspiration, compassion, and indignation) require experiencing of corresponding feelings (Immordino-Yang & Damasio, 2007). When we use a survey or interview to ask about students' emotions, are we really assessing a feeling (i.e., the conscious interpretation of an unconscious emotion), or are we assessing unconscious emotions? The meanings of *emotional experience* and *emotional expression* might seem transparent, but the *emotional labor* concept and social-psychological self problematize these terms greatly. *Mood* is an affective state of longer duration (in hours, days, or weeks) than emotion. Mood is a broad, diffuse reaction to the general environment and is therefore not closely linked with a specific event or object (Fox, 2018). An *emotional trait* (sometimes called an *emotional habit*) is a stable disposition or predisposition to respond in a similar emotional state over time. *Action tendencies* are propensities for certain goal-directed behaviors channeled through the person's appraisal of the situation and its meaning (Sampson, 2020).

Arguably, psychology has made significant advances in our understanding of emotion, but often in separate subareas and without overall theoretical clarity. Work by Gross (2014) has stretched psychology's understanding of *emotion regulation* at the higher levels of cognition and academic sophistication. According to Gross (2014), core features of emotion regulation are: (a) activating a *goal*, either intrinsic (regulating one's own emotions), or extrinsic (regulating someone else's emotions); (b) choosing and employing relevant *strategies*, or processes, from explicit to unconscious/automatic, that can alter the emotion trajectory and thus fulfill the goal (regulation of one's or someone else's emotions); and (c) identifying the *outcome* (the emotion dynamics, as well as the emotion modulation or change caused by activating the goal and using the strategies). Gross (2014) noted that emotion regulation is part of *affective regulation*, which also includes *mood regulation* and *coping*. Gross also listed five "families" of emotion regulation: (a) situation selection, i.e., taking actions that make it more (or less) likely that one will be in a situation that might cause desirable or positive emotions; (b) situation modification, i.e., directly changing an external situation to alter its emotional impact; (c) attentional deployment, i.e., directing attention to a specific situation, including using distraction, to control emotions such as anxiety; (d) cognitive change (reframing, also known as cognitive reappraisal; see Troy, Wilhelm, Shallcross, & Mauss, 2010), i.e., modifying how one appraises an external or internal situation; and (e) response modulation, i.e., directly influencing experiential, behavioral, or physiological (deep breathing, changing heart rhythm) aspects of emotional responding.

Relatedly, theories of *emotional intelligence* (EI) in psychology have expanded our understanding of emotion. EI is the cognitive capability to use reason to comprehend and deal effectively with emotions (Oxford & Gkonou, 2020). More specifically, EI is "the ability to understand feelings in the self and others and to use these feelings as informational guides for thinking and action" (Salovey, Mayer, Caruso, & Yoo, 2011, p. 238). EI as a "hot" intelligence combines reasoning with personally significant information. This contrasts with cool intelligences, which relate to less personal knowledge (e.g., math, visual-spatial). Salovey et al. offered a four-part EI model: (a) perceiving emotions in self and others; (b) using emotions to facilitate cognition; (c) understanding emotions; and (d) managing emotions in self and others.

Furthermore, cultural and social concepts of emotion in psychology have helped clarify emotion and its operation. In social psychology, Markus and Kitayama (1991) discussed experiencing an emotion without expressing it as related to *culturally-based self-construal*. Emotional expression is often direct and intense in individualist cultures and indirect in collectivist cultures, with intense emotion expression perceived as not being culturally appropriate. A sociological construct, *emotional labor* (Hochschild, 1983), having additionally become a social-psychological construct (thanks to Markus & Kitayama, above), is now also used in education (Wang, Hall, & Taxer, 2019) and SLA (King & Ng, 2018). Emotional labor concerns both emotional expression and emotional experience. The concept began with Hochschild's (1983) sociological studies of service-industry workers, e.g., flight attendants, call-center workers, and salespeople, who must act in certain ways to fulfill expectations from the organization or society at large. Hochschild wrote about two types of acting: (a) *surface acting*, in which one alters one's emotional expression to meet institutional or societal requirements; and (b) *deep acting*, in which one works to transform one's private feelings based on "feeling rules," reflecting demands of the organization or the larger society. Either of these forms of emotional labor is stressful and can be debilitating.

Further insights from psychology as concerns our understanding of emotion address it in a more personal mode through Acceptance and Commitment Therapy or ACT (Hayes, Strosahl, & Wilson, 2011; Zegers, 2015). The premise of this theory is that individuals need not eliminate difficult feelings but rather it encourages people to learn skills by mindfully *A*ccepting a painful emotion, *C*hoosing a valued direction, and *T*aking action. ACT has much in common with hardiness, also known as existential courage (see Maddi, 2006). ACT avoids dividing the world of emotion into "positive" and "negative" valence, defined as intrinsic positive/pleasant/nonthreatening emotions versus intrinsic negative/unpleasant/threatening emotions. Instead of asserting an inherently "positive" or "negative" valence of any particular emotion, ACT lets perception of valence arise in relation to the person and context. Happiness is often considered the premier positive emotion, but it is better understood as a skill to be developed. Matthieu Ricard (2007), author of *Happiness: A Guide to Developing Life's Most Important Skill,* argued that happiness is the skill of accepting both pleasant and painful emotions. He explained that we frequently confuse real happiness with merely seeking pleasurable emotions. Ford, Lam, John, and Mauss (2018) reported that habitually accepting, rather than judging, negative emotions and thoughts was linked with greater psychological health, even after ruling out potentially confounding effects of ethnicity, gender, socioeconomic status, and severity of life stress.

Theoretical Frameworks

Viewing the complex labyrinth of emotion definitions through theoretical frameworks may help guide us through the complications that multidisciplinary contributions have provoked. For example, among emotion theories, *natural kinds* (propounded by Ekman, 1977, 1999) and *conceptual constructionist* (promoted by Barrett, 2006, 2017) were at odds for decades. Natural kinds theory suggests emotions are universal and identifiable across cultures though facial expression (Ekman, 1977). Natural kinds theory first identified six basic or discrete emotions: anger, disgust, fear, sadness, happiness, and surprise (Ekman, 1977), with contempt sometimes also included. However, Ekman (1999) increased the number of basic emotions or emotion families to 15 (amusement, anger, contempt, contentment, disgust, embarrassment, excitement, fear, guilt, pride in achievement, relief, sadness/distress, satisfaction, sensory pleasure, and shame); each with five dimensions: (a) an antecedent event; (b) a rapid, unconscious appraisal, although more conscious (extended) appraisal could occur; (c) a neural response for each emotion; (d) a distinctive, universally identifiable signal or expression[1]; and (e) a probable behavioral response. In contrast, Barrett's (2006, 2017) conceptual constructionist theory[2] is frequently termed "dimensional" because of its two key dimensions: (a) *valence* and (b) *arousal*, or degree of emotional intensity. Barrett (2017) argued that emotions are constructions, not reactions to the world (key steps in conceptual construction of emotions are as follows: (a) the person cognitively appraises inner processes and the environment, using perception, attention, memory, social factors, and language; and (b) the appraisal results in the categorization (valence and arousal) of the emotion in "core affect." The emotional experience can occur in the present moment, can reactivate a past emotion (memory), or can involve an imagined, hypothetical emotion.

Another theoretical lens used in relation to the study of emotion has been positive psychology (see Chapter 5). Martin Seligman initiated "positive psychology" in 2000, when he, as president of the American Psychological Association, decided that much of Western psychology was focusing too much on human weaknesses and that an approach centering on strengths and positive emotions would be important at the opening of the new millennium. His introduction to positive psychology (Seligman & Csíkszentmihályi, 2000) captures the spirit of the idea, which has both adherents and critics. The goal of positive psychology is to increase *flourishing* by increasing positive emotion (P), engagement (E), positive relationships (R), meaning (M), and accomplishment (A), with the acronym PERMA revealing this combination and with *well-being* as the operationalization of flourishing (Seligman, 2011). *Negative emotions* are warning signs of external irritants or threats, such as sadness being related to a thought of loss (Seligman, 2011), yet our emotional reaction is usually out of proportion to the threat. Negative emotions are "firefighting emotions" that pose "fight-or-flight" questions (Seligman, 2011, p. 66).

Seligman (2011) often praised Rational Emotive Behavior Therapy, or REBT (Bernard & Dryden, 2019; Ellis, 2003) and mentioned REBT as an important source of his own positive psychological suggestions. REBT is a successful cognitive process in which the individual realizes his or her anxiety-producing, disruptive, maladaptive assumptions (unhealthy negative beliefs), then practices changing these assumptions. Ellis (2003), who created REBT in the 1950s, noted that healthy negative assumptions and emotions, like dissatisfaction, can serve as motivators.

In contrast, but still looking through a positive psychology lens, Frederickson's (2001, 2003, 2004) studies on positive emotions resulted in the influential "broaden-and-build" theory[3], which states that *positive emotions*—happiness, curiosity, interest, pleasure, joy, and, added by Seligman (p. 17), "ecstasy, comfort, warmth, and the like"—broaden the individual's scope of awareness, build necessary skills and resources for the future, and achieve other remarkable things: trigger upward spirals toward emotional well-being, add to resilience (see Chapter 16), speed recovery from cardiac disorders related to negative emotions, and open individuals to receive and appreciate more meaning (see Frederickson's interview with Zegers, 2015). "Finding a silver lining" was the metaphor Tugade and Frederickson (2002) employed for "positive reappraisal" (p. 322), which is often needed in a stress-inducing situation where coping is necessary. As mentioned earlier, positive reappraisal is also known as "reframing" and as "cognitive reappraisal" (Troy, Wilhelm, Shallcross, & Mauss, 2010). When interviewed by Zegers (2015), Frederickson alluded to context as the only way to know whether an emotion is appropriate. She said,

> as a field, we've inherited some language in terms of calling classes of emotions positive and negative … I think that what's meant by it, is this: "If all other things were equal, would this be a wanted [emotional] state? Would you want the state to continue?"

This is a nuanced, circumspect treatment of "positive" and "negative" emotion. She also said, carefully, that positive psychology is *not* "a separate domain of psychology. It's an emphasis, a leaning, a call within psychology to also focus on positive aspects" (Zegers, 2015). Her 2015 tone is much different from Seligman's (2011) less nuanced, sometimes overwhelmingly bold pronouncements about positive psychology (see Gibbon, 2020; Miller, 2008).

When considering an extreme operationalization of positive emotion, Maslow (1970) talked about *peak experiences* as a transient but powerful moment of self-actualization (Maslow, 1970) and "a great and mystical experience, a religious experience if you wish—an illumination, a revelation, an insight … [leading to] 'the cognition of being,' … almost, you could say, a technology of happiness …" (Maslow, 1971, p. 169). Peak experiences are especially joyous, exciting, ego-transcending moments in life, involving sudden feelings of intense happiness or ecstasy, creativity, meaning, well-being, wonder, awe, love, unity, empathy, limitlessness, and timelessness. Maslow (1971) indicated that "most people, or perhaps all people, have peak experiences, or ecstasies" (p. 168). Similarly, Csíkszentmihályi (2008) depicts *flow* as complete engagement (see Chapter 11), joy, confidence, intrinsic motivation (see Chapter 10), challenge-competence balance, effortlessness, lack of self-consciousness, and a sensation of altered time. Flow occurs "when a person's body or mind is stretched to its limits in a voluntary effort to accomplish something difficult and worthwhile" (p. 3).

Another way to organize how we think about emotion is to define those that go beyond the self as opposed to those that are internalized. Emotions that usually go beyond the self include compassion, empathy, love, and gratitude. The in-depth Oxford Handbook of Compassion Science (Seppälä, Simon-Thomas, Worline, Cameron, & Doty, 2017) offers a framework for understanding studies of compassion, augmented by a book on the neuroscience of empathy and compassion (Stevens & Woodruff, 2018). The vagus nerve is the cranial nerve in the body with the widest influence, affecting speech, head positioning, digestion, the parasympathetic branch of the autonomic nervous system, and the heart, which affects compassion (Simon-Thomas, 2015; Stellar, Cohen, Oveis, & Keltner, 2015).

More than two decades ago, PolyVagal theory suggested that the vagus nerve fundamentally drives human social affiliation and since then, researchers found that the vagus nerve is implicated in empathy, sympathy, and compassion (Simon-Thomas, 2015). Krznaric (2014), Miller (2018), and Noddings (2013) discussed development of compassion, self-compassion, caring, empathy, mindfulness, and love in different contexts. Contemporary research on gratitude, infrequent until recently (Watkins, 2014), has been showing that gratitude is linked with subjective well-being, positive social relations, and resilience to trauma. Algoe (2012) described the functions of gratitude as to "find, remind, and bind" in everyday relationships, meaning that an expression of gratitude increases a benefactor's motivation to remain engaged in the relationship with the grateful person.

Untangling the web of what emotion means requires an understanding that it is at the heart of every human discipline and that each field has valuable contributions to offer. Although this makes the construct messy and sometimes perplexing, it also demonstrates its complexity and dynamism. Let us now turn our attention to how those in SLA have embraced the chaos.

Emotion in SLA

This section focuses first on the question, "How has SLA significantly advanced the knowledge of emotion?" Dörnyei and Ryan (2015) pointed out that although emotions play a crucial part in our lives, SLA scholars have largely "shunned" emotions (p. 9). Perhaps this is changing, because the cognitivist grip on SLA is relaxing a bit. Unfortunately, the same problems psychologists have about terms and definitions of emotion have spilled over into SLA. However, inroads are being made in terms of understanding more about phenomena that are related to emotion in language learning such as motivation and cognition, the role of negative and positive emotions among bilinguals and language learners, the role of EI in the attitudes and behaviors of learners, and the toll that emotional labor can take on language teachers in particular.

One area of progress in emotions in SLA is work drawing on the interconnectedness of emotion, cognition, and motivation. For instance, Schumann (1997) designed an SLA theory, the neurobiology of affect, asserting that emotion underlies most of what we consider cognition and motivation. In his theory, motivation for sustained, deep learning involves multiple neurobiological structures: the amygdala, which assigns motivational and emotional value to the experiences encountered by the learner; the orbitofrontal cortex; and body systems, such as the ANS, the endocrine system, and the musculoskeletal system. Stimulus appraisal creates a bodily state (somatic marker), communicated to the brain as a feeling, by which the learner makes learning decisions. Thus, emotion, motivation, and cognition are directly interlinked. After frequent associations between bodily states and stimulus appraisals, the bodily states become centrally represented in the brain itself, without needing to be processed in the peripheral nervous system. The stimulus appraisal system learns to recognize environmental cues predicting learner reward. The cues are relevant to needs/goals, coping potential, pleasantness, novelty, and compatibility to self and social image. Schumann illustrated the five stimulus appraisal dimensions with data from diary studies and autobiographies.

Relatedly, Dörnyei (2009) identified emotion as one of three subsystems of the "human mind," the other two being cognition and motivation. Relationships among these three subsystems are interactive, mutually influential, organic, holistic, dynamic, nonlinear, nested, self-organizing, open, and emergent. Dörnyei (2014) encouraged researchers and readers to look carefully for the salient patterns or "signature dynamics" associated with system outcomes, though he reminded us that it is impossible to generalize across situations.

Data-gathering methods in SLA—particularly narrative studies of language learning—have also offered progress toward a deeper understanding toward emotion. In them, researchers found multiple emotions, most of which were negative and potentially "narrowing" in the sense of Frederickson's psychology writings (see earlier). For example, in Pavlenko's (2006) investigation, the narratives of bilingual writers who had learned English as a second language displayed "an array of emotions," such as guilt, insecurity, anxiety, worry, sadness, and confusion (p. 5). In another study, Japanese women learning English self-identified feelings of longing, disappointment, sadness, and powerlessness, but also occasional confidence (Piller & Takahashi, 2006). In *Lost in Translation,* Hoffman (1990) explained the emotional changes and sense of dispossession that occurred when she moved with her family from Poland to Canada. In *Hunger of Memory: The Education of Richard Rodriguez,* Rodriguez (2004) portrayed emotional and social alienation from his familial linguistic and cultural identity. However, for Oxford, Pacheco Acuña, Solís Hernández, and Smith (2015) and Oxford and Cuéllar (2014), positive psychology was a backdrop for analyzing L2 learners' stories of their language development with a focus on positive emotions. These studies discovered a mix of emotions but found that positive emotions, such as interest and admiration, were more prevalent than negative emotions among bilinguals.

A negative emotion that has received considerable attention in SLA is anxiety. SLA research reveals that severe language anxiety has many "insidious" outcomes (Dewaele & MacIntyre, 2014, p. 238), such as reductions in any of the following, depending on the student: worsened cognition and achievement, lower self-confidence, reduced personal agency and sense of control, inability to express and recognize emotions, negativity toward the target language, lack of willingness to communicate, and even desire to drop language study (Gkonou, 2018; Horwitz, 2001, 2007; Horwitz & Young, 1991; MacIntyre, 2002; MacIntyre & Gregersen, 2012a).

Language anxiety has been shown not to be the mirror image of language enjoyment, as high anxiety can co-occur with high enjoyment (Dewaele & MacIntyre, 2014, 2016; Dewaele, Witney, Saito, & Dewaele, 2018), and enjoyment has been found to be more strongly related to performance than anxiety (Dewaele & Alfawzan, 2018). However, language anxiety can provide a facilitative spark of tension, alertness, focus, excitement, and resilience to language performance (e.g., Dewaele & MacIntyre, 2014; Marcos-Llinas & Juan Garau, 2009; Oxford, 2016, 2017). In addition, completely separately from language anxiety, Ellis (2003) stated that anxiety can foster realistic caution, concern, watchfulness, and ordinary self-protection. Ellis (2003) explained that anxiety is harmful when it emerges as panic, reduces coping, halts performance, and is based on irrational thinking. However, if anxiety is not too severe, it can have useful purposes.

Gregersen, MacIntyre, and Meza (2014) also added to the body of knowledge concerning anxiety in their study that involved anxiety-related changes in emotional reactions of learners of Spanish as a foreign language over a very short span of time. In a Spanish class, participants were video-recorded giving a presentation in Spanish while wearing heart monitors. High-anxiety and low-anxiety learners self-rated their anxiety many times over three-and-a-half minutes and explained their emotional reactions later in interviews. The study uncovered the utility of re-interpreting physiological cues and the value of "escape routes" to let participants remain communicatively active.

Another inroad into understanding emotion in SLA comes with how emotional intelligence (EI) theory has been used to understand differences in the attitudes and behavior of L2 learners and users. Dewaele, Petrides, and Furnham (2008) found that adult multilinguals with higher EI had lower levels of foreign language anxiety in various situations and languages. They discovered that in communication situations, such individuals, compared to individuals with lower EI, perceived themselves as more capable of (a) gauging the emotions of their interlocutor, (b) controlling their own stress, and (c) feeling confident (and hence less anxious). Other factors in lower anxiety and stronger confidence were younger age of acquisition of the foreign language, stronger socialization in that language, higher self-perceived proficiency, use of the language outside the classroom, communication with a larger network of people, and knowledge of more languages (Dewaele et al., 2008).

An additional pathway to our understanding of emotion in SLA addresses the wider social context, including power relations. Benesch (2017) perceives emotions as discursively constructed in that they do not reside exclusively within individuals but rather are constructed in the immediate classroom context and institution and are related to expansive social phenomena that involve unequal power relationships, like racism. She introduces the notion of *feeling rules* to characterize the expectations for proper feelings intrinsically present in established policies and teaching discourses. The struggle between what one actually feels and these expected feelings is what Benesch calls *emotional labor*, defined earlier. She posits that there is an opportunity to transform teachers' experiences of emotions as they may indicate inconsistencies among policies, philosophies, and personal commitments. When teachers emote, opportunities are made available for them to examine such incongruities and change policies that do not attend to the lived experiences of ELT teachers and students (Benesch, 2017).

Like the discipline of psychology, SLA has also had some difficulty in coming to terms with how emotion should be understood. Nevertheless, among other progress, the field of SLA has expanded in its grasp of the elements that interact with emotion, the role of negative and positive emotion, the part emotional intelligence plays in behavior and attitudes, and the way in which emotion is discursively and socially constructed.

Integrating Psychological and SLA Perspectives

Researchers and practitioners have integrated emotion concepts from psychology and SLA into L2 learning and teaching. Two obvious emotion concepts that have expanded from psychology are emotion regulation and emotional labor (which came into psychology from sociology). SLA scholars Gkonou and Miller (2020) built on *emotion regulation* (see Chapter 17) from psychology and demonstrated that English *teachers'* emotion regulation skills develop over time and are not merely momentary reactions to class events. Specifically, teachers were found to have developed strong emotion regulation skills after years of teaching experience and as a response to numerous moments of hardship and emotional challenges, called "critical incidents," in their careers. King and Ng (2018) reported a study about the *emotional labor* of native language English teachers who had taught in Japan for at least five years. The teachers' emotional labor was considerable. They were "cultural mediators," cognitively appraising and reappraising the cultural beliefs to manage their emotions about student silence, emotionally distancing from students when needed, and surface acting to seem entertaining, cheerful, and enthusiastic. King and Ng (2018) suggested antecedent-focused emotion regulation for these teachers: (a) modifying the situation (using instructional activities that preclude student behaviors that trigger a teacher's negative emotion); (b) deploying attention (ignoring students' trigger behaviors that disturb teachers); and (c) cognitive change (positive self-talk).

Sadly, but not surprisingly, it does not seem that SLA concepts have been integrated into psychology, nor have they caught the eye of psychologists in general. However, some insights that SLA could offer to psychology include the following: (a) the value of longitudinal, mixed methods multicase studies concerning emotions in learning and teaching the language of peace (and peaceful emotions), along with other subjects (Olivero, 2017); (b) the utility of creative research methodologies, such as the idiodynamic method (Gregersen, MacIntyre, & Meza, 2014) and retrodictive analysis (Dörnyei, 2014) for emotion research; (c) SLA-based conversation analysis and critical discourse analysis involving emotions (Oxford, 2013); (d) emotion regulation strategies as identified in SLA (Oxford & Gkonou, 2020); and (e) the discursive, socially constructed lens through which emotional labor needs to be viewed (Benesch, 2017).

Implications

This review of research and theory surrounding the study of emotions has several implications for practice and research. First, psychology, SLA, and L2 education all require greater agreement on emotion terms and definitions, because no science can continue to exist meaningfully if "anything goes" and "nobody knows." At this time, the vast confusion in terms and definitions keeps researchers from talking with each other effectively and sharing emotion-related ideas important to all three areas. One example of a need for greater agreement is the tendency to use different terms (e.g., emotions and feelings) that have different meanings as though they are interchangeable. Scholars in psychology and neuroscience have already taken the time to differentiate between emotions and feelings (see terminology and definitions in psychology earlier), and these distinctions could lead to more robust study designs, generating more meaningful study results and implications that are respected and useful across related fields. Secondly, psychology, SLA, and L2 education would advance even further if they all cooperated and attempted to draw on research from across disciplines. For instance, the working of the vagus nerve in the development of compassion and other socially affiliative emotions (Simon-Thomas, 2015) has implications for all three fields. Thirdly, it would help to identify interdisciplinary trailblazers and follow their lead, such as Immordino-Yang, whose disciplines are neuroscience, education, and complexity and who has interests in internationalism and interculturalism. Following the emotion work of such interdisciplinary scholars will help us maintain our interdisciplinary scope and could open doors to significant international and intercultural relationships in research and practice. Lastly, thinking across areas and subareas, e.g., emotion regulation, ACT, REBT, and SLA, and use of imagining/envisioning tools (Dörnyei & Kubanyiova, 2014) could be valuable.

Future Directions

Based on what we have learned about emotion in psychology and SLA, several future directions for research emerge. First, partial or full replication studies are helpful and often essential for developing and testing theories about learning-related emotions, a notoriously difficult topic because of the quicksilver nature of emotion and all the factors in learning and teaching. Anytime we do not consider at least partial replication, we are losing the chance to build and test theory in a systematic way. Second, following Sampson (2020), it seems useful to delve deep into complexity perspectives (see Chapter 4) or emotion research in L2 learning contexts. Third, using critical incident methodology involving teachers' emotions may uncover insights into dealing with teachers' lived hardships and challenges (Gkonou & Miller, 2020). The REBT distinction between healthy negative emotions (e.g., sorrow, regret, frustration) and unhealthy negative emotions (e.g., panic, depression, rage, self-hatred, and self-pity) deserves attention in relation to SLA and L2 learning (Bernard & Dryden, 2019; Ellis, 2003). Relatedly, some studies on the emotion relationships among REBT, ACT, and positive psychology could be of service to clinical and counseling psychology and to L2 education in ways so that, rather than working from a deficit perspective, individuals are empowered to make personal positive change.

Social and emotional learning (SEL) is a second direction. SEL is helping teachers and students to focus on emotions in social contexts. Pentón Herrera (2020) has devised a well-articulated, creative SEL curriculum for TESOL using the five official SEL competencies (i.e., children and adults understand and manage emotions, set and achieve positive goals, feel and show empathy for others, establish and maintain positive relationships, and make responsible decisions) from the Collaborative for Academic, Social, and Emotional Learning or CASEL (2020). SEL appears to be having a significant effect in terms of creative curricula that are widely influencing schools and students. In some countries it is called SEAL, Social Emotional and Academic Learning, using concepts from Goleman (2005) and this, too, may prove an interesting direction for future research and practice.

Another emotion-related future direction consists of *self-transcendent emotions*, such as compassion, love, empathy, and caring. Examples of study areas are science and neuroscience of compassion (Seppälä, Simon-Thomas, Worline, Cameron, & Doty, 2017; Stevens & Woodruff, 2018) and educational practices of compassion and love (Miller, 2018), empathy (Krznaric, 2014), and caring (Noddings, 2013). Knowing whether and how such emotion may be susceptible to contagion and/or synchronicity would be a value avenue for further study. Today we need and are gathering increasing information about the psychology of hate speech (Oxford, 2020), teacher anxiety (Gkonou, Dewaele, & King, 2020), and teacher emotional labor (King & Ng, 2018). Interest is deepening in the study of emotions of vulnerable groups, such as displaced elderly people and children, traumatized ethnic groups, survivors of migration caused by climate and environment, and immigrants and refugees receiving verbal and nonverbal threats or worse (Bruhn, Rees, Mohsin, Silove, & Carlsson, 2018; DeLeersnyder, Mesquita, & Sim, 2011*)*

Reflection Questions

- What is the importance of *context* for categorizing emotions by valence (pleasant or unpleasant, comfortable or painful, positive or negative), and how might context influence your perception of the arousal (intensity) of an emotion?
- Why has there been a historical clash between natural kinds and conceptual constructivism as approaches to understanding emotion? Has this clash dissipated, and if so, how?
- Which are the three to five most interesting topics in this chapter and why? How do those topics relate to your life and to either SLA or the integration of psychology or SLA into L2 education?

Recommended Readings

Bielak, J., & Mystkowska-Wiertelak, A. (2020). Language teachers' interpersonal learner-directed emotion-regulation strategies. Language Teaching Research. Online before publication.
This article describes a scenario-based emotion regulation scale, the *Managing Your Emotions (MYE) Questionnaire* (Gkonou & Oxford, in Oxford, 2017, pp. 317–333). The article describes the features of the questionnaire, its purpose in assessing emotion regulation in L2 education settings, and its use in measuring language teachers' emotional regulation. The *MYE* is also used for assessing language learners' emotion regulation. Format, scenarios, psychometric details, and flexible use are included in the article.

Gkonou, C., Daubney, M., & Dewaele, J-M. (Eds.). (2017). *New insights into language anxiety: Theory, research, and educational implications.* Multilingual Matters.
This recent book takes a fresh look at a field that was begun by Elaine Horwitz decades ago and that has burgeoned into a major area of SLA and L2 education research. The book contains chapters

written by well-known L2 anxiety experts and rising young researchers, who are already pushing language anxiety inquiry into new methodologies and areas of thought.

Gregersen, T., MacIntyre, P. D., & Meza, M. D. (2014). The motion of emotion: Idiodynamic case studies of learners' foreign language anxiety. *Modern Language Journal, 98*(2), 574–588.
This article, which I include here for its idiodynamic research methodology and fascinating results, is a readable and captivating view of a new way of looking at language anxiety. Reading it might make you run out to get a heart monitor and try out the idiodynamic method. At the very least it will convince you of the power of emotion in language learning.

Notes

1 The signal might not be observable because the person has inhibited it, or for other reasons.
2 This theory was earlier called the Conceptual Act Theory, or CAT (Barrett, 2006). The theory is now also called the *theory of constructed emotion* (Barrett, 2017).
3 See also MacIntyre & Gregersen (2012b).

References

Adolphs, R., & Anderson, D. J. (2018). *The neuroscience of emotion: A new synthesis*. Princeton University Press.
Algoe, S. B. (2012). Find, remind, and bind: The functions of gratitude in everyday relationships. *Social and Personality Psychology Compass, 6*, 455–469.
Arnold, J., & Brown, H. D. (1999). A map of the terrain. In J. Arnold (Ed.), Affect in language learning (pp. 1–24). *Affect in language learning*. Cambridge University Press.
Barrett, L. F. (2006). Are emotions natural kinds? *Perspectives on Psychological Science, 1*, 28–58.
Barrett, L. F. (2017). The theory of constructed emotions. *Social Cognitive and Affective Neuroscience, 12*(1), 1–23.
Bernard, M. E., & Dryden, W. (Eds.). (2019). *Advances in REBT*. Springer.
Benesch, S. (2017). *Emotions and English language teaching: Exploring teachers' emotion labor*. Taylor & Francis.
Bielak, J., & Mystkowska-Wiertelak, A. (2020). Language teachers' interpersonal learner-directed emotion-regulation strategies. Language Teaching Research.
Bruhn, M., Rees, S., Mohsin, M., Silove, D., & Carlsson, J. (2018). *Journal of Nervous and Mental Disorders, 206*(1), 61–68.
Collaborative for Academic, Social, and Emotional Learning (CASEL). (2020). *SEL: What are the core competencies and where are they promoted?* CASEL.
Csíkszentmihályi, M. (2008). *Flow: The psychology of optimal experience*. Harper Perennial.
Damasio, A. R. (1994). *Descartes' error: Emotion, reason, and the brain*. HarperCollins.
Damasio, A. R. (2000). *The feeling of what happens: Body, emotion, and the making of consciousness*. Vintage.
DeLeersnyder, J., Mesquita, B., & Sim, H. S. (2011). Where do my emotions belong? A study of immigrants' emotional acculturation. *Personality and Social Personality, 37*(4), 451–463.
Dewaele, J.-M., & Alfawzan, M. (2018). Does the effect of enjoyment outweigh that of anxiety in foreign language performance? *Studies in Second Language Learning and Teaching, 8*(1), 21.
Dewaele, J.-M., & MacIntyre, P. D. (2014). The two faces of Janus? Anxiety and enjoyment in the foreign language classroom. *Studies in Second Language Learning and Teaching, 4*, 237–274.
Dewaele, J.-M., & MacIntyre, P. D. (2016). Foreign language enjoyment and foreign language classroom anxiety: The right and left feet of the language learner. In P. D. MacIntyre, T. Gregersen, & S. Mercer (Eds.), *Positive psychology in SLA* (pp. 215–236). Multilingual Matters.
Dewaele, J-M., Petrides, K.V., & Furnham, A. (2008). The effects of trait emotional intelligence and sociobiographical variables on communicative anxiety and foreign language anxiety among adult multilinguals: A review and empirical investigation. *Language Learning, 58*, 911–960.
Dewaele, J-M., Witney, J., Saito, K., & Dewaele, L. (2017). Foreign language enjoyment and anxiety: The effect of teacher and learner variables. *Language Teaching Research, 22*(6).
Dirkx, J. M. (Ed.). (2008). *Adult learning and the emotional self*. Jossey-Bass.
Dixon, T. (2012). "Emotion": The history of a keyword in crisis. *Emotion Review, 4*(4), 338–344.
Dörnyei, Z. (2009). *The psychology of second language acquisition*. Oxford University Press.
Dörnyei, Z. (2014). Researching complex dynamic systems: Retrodictive qualitative modeling in the language classroom. *Language Teaching, 47*(1), 80–91.

Dörnyei, Z., & Kubanyiova, M. (2014). *Motivating teachers, motivating teachers: Building vision in the language classroom.* Cambridge University Press.
Dörnyei, Z., & Ryan, S. (2015). *The psychology of language learning revisited.* Routledge.
Durlack, J. A., Domitrovich, C. E., Weissberg, R. P., & Gullotta, T. P. (Eds.). (2016). *Handbook of social and emotional learning: Research and practice.* Guilford.
Ehrman, M. E. (1996). *Understanding second language learning difficulties.* SAGE.
Ehrman, M. E., & Dörnyei, Z. (1998). *Interpersonal dynamics in second language education: The visible and invisible classroom.* SAGE.
Erisen, C., Vasilopoulou, S., & Kentmen-Cin, C. (2020). Emotional reactions to immigration and support for EU cooperation on immigration and terrorism, *Journal of European Public Policy, 27*(6), 795–813.
Ekman, P. (1977). Facial expression and emotion. *American Psychologist, 48*(4), 384–32.
Ekman, P. (1999). Basic emotions. In T. Dalgleish & M. Power (Eds.), *Handbook of cognition and emotion* (pp. 45–60). Wiley.
Ellis, A. (2003). Early theories and practices of Rational-Emotive Behavior Therapy and how they have been augmented and revised during the last three decades. *Journal of Rational-Emotive and Cognitive-Behavior Therapy, 21*(3/4), 219–243.
Ford, B. O., Lam, P., John, O. P., & Mauss, I. B. (2018). The psychological health benefits of accepting negative emotions and thoughts: Laboratory, diary, and longitudinal evidence. *Journal of Personality and Social Psychology, 115*(6), 1075–1092.
Fox, E. (2018). Perspectives from affective science on understanding the nature of emotion. *Brain and Neurosciences Advances, 2.*
Frederickson, B. L. (2001). The role of positive emotions in positive psychology: The broaden-and-build theory of positive emotions. *American Psychologist, 56,* 218–226.
Frederickson, B. L. (2003). The value of positive emotions: The emerging science of positive psychology looks into why it's good to feel good. *American Scientist, 91,* 330–335.
Frederickson, B. L. (2004). The broaden-and-build theory of positive emotions. *Philosophical Transactions of the Royal Society of London (Biological Sciences), 359,* 1367–1377.
Gibbon, P. (2020). Martin Seligman and the rise of positive psychology. *Humanities, 41*(3).
Gkonou, C. (2018). Listening to highly anxious EFL learners through the use of narrative: Metacognitive and affective strategies for learner self-regulation. In R. L. Oxford & C. M. Amerstorfer (Eds.), *Language learning strategies and individual learner characteristics: Situating strategy use in diverse contexts* (pp. 79–97). Bloomsbury.
Gkonou, C., Daubney, M., & Dewaele, J.-M. (Eds.). (2017). *New insights into language anxiety: Theory, research and educational implications.* Multilingual Matters.
Gkonou, C., Dewaele, J-M., & King, J. (Eds.). (2020). *Language teaching: An emotional rollercoaster.* Multilingual Matters.
Gkonou, C., & Mercer, S. (2017). *Understanding emotional and social intelligence among English language teachers.* British Council.
Gkonou, C., & Miller, E. R. (2020). Critical incidents in language teachers' narratives of emotional experience. In C. Gkonou, J.-M. Dewaele, & J. King (Eds.), *The emotional rollercoaster of language teaching* (pp. 131–149). Multilingual Matters.
Gkonou, C., & Oxford, R. L. (2016). *Managing Your Emotions (MYE) Questionnaire.* University of Essex.
Goleman, D. (2005). *Emotional intelligence: Why it can matter more than IQ.* Bantam.
Gregersen, T., MacIntyre, P. D., & Meza, M. (2014). The motion of emotion: Idiodynamic case studies of learners' foreign language anxiety. *Modern Language Journal, 98*(2), 574–588.
Gross, J. J. (Ed.). (2014). *Handbook of emotion regulation.* (2nd ed.). Guilford Press.
Hochschild, A. R. (1983). *The managed heart: Commercialization of human feeling.* University of California Press.
Hoffman, E. (1990). *Lost in translation: A life in a new language.* Penguin.
Hayes, S. C., Strosahl, K., & Wilson, K. G. (2011). *Acceptance and Commitment Therapy: The process and practice of mindful change,* (2nd ed.). Guilford.
Horwitz, E. (2001). Language anxiety and achievement. *Annual Review of Applied Linguistics, 21,* 112–126.
Horwitz, E. (2007). *Words fail me: Foreign language anxiety crippling for some students* (E. Horwitz interviewed by K. Randall). University of Texas at Austin. www.utexas.edu/features/2007/language
Horwitz, E., & Young, D. J. (Eds.). (1991). *Language anxiety: From theory and research to classroom implications.* Prentice Hall.
Immordino-Yang, M. H., & Damasio, A. R. (2007). We feel, therefore we learn: The relevance of affective and social neuroscience to education. *Mind, Brain, and Education, 1*(1), 3–10.
King, J., & Ng, K-Y. S. (2018). Teacher emotions and the emotional labor of second language teaching. In. S. Mercer & A. Kostoulas (Eds.), *Language teacher psychology* (pp. 141–157). Multilingual Matters.
Krznaric, R. (2014). *Empathy: Why it matters, and how to get it.* Perigee/Penguin.

Larsen-Freeman, D. (2020). Teaching and researching grammar skills: Theory- and research-based practices. In N. Polat, T. Gregersen, & P. D. MacIntyre (Eds.), *Research-driven pedagogy: Implications of L2A theory and research for the teaching of language skills* (pp. 97–124). Routledge.

Larsen-Freeman, D., & Cameron, L. (2008). *Complex systems and applied linguistics*. Oxford University Press.

LeDoux, J. (2012). Rethinking the emotional brain. *Neuron, 73*(4), 653–676.

Lindstromberg, S., & Eyckmans, J. (2017). The particular need for replication in the quantitative study of SLA: A case study of the mnemonic effect of assonance in collocations. *Journal of the European Second Language Association, 1*(1), 126–136.

Lyubomirsky, S. (2007). *The how of happiness: a practical guide to getting the life you want*. Penguin.

MacIntyre, P. D. (2002). Motivation, anxiety, and emotion in second language acquisition. In P. Robinson (Ed.), *Individual differences and instructed language learning* (pp. 45–68). John Benjamins.

MacIntyre, P. D., & Gregersen, T. (2012a). Affect: The role of language anxiety and other emotions in language learning. In S. Mercer, S. Ryan, & M. Williams (Eds.), *Psychology for language learning* (pp. 103–118). Palgrave Macmillan.

MacIntyre, P. D., & Gregersen, T. (2012b). Emotions that facilitate language learning: The positive-broadening power of the imagination. *Studies in Second Language Learning and Teaching, 2*(2), 193–213.

MacIntyre, P. D., Gregersen, T., & Mercer, S. (2016). *Positive psychology in SLA*. Multilingual Matters.

Maddi, S. R. (2006). Hardiness: The courage to grow from stresses. *The Journal of Positive Psychology, 1*(3), 160–168.

Marcos-Llinas, M., & Juan Garau, M. (2009). Effects of language anxiety on three proficiency-level courses of Spanish as a foreign language. *Foreign Language Annals, 42*(1), 94–111.

Markus, H. R., & Kitayama, S. (1991). Culture and the self: Implications for cognition, emotion, and motivation. *Psychological Review, 98*(2), 224–255.

Maslow, A. H. (1970). *Motivation and personality*. (Rev. Ed.). Harper & Row.

Maslow, A. H. (1971). *The farther reaches of human nature*. Penguin Compass.

Mason, M. (2008). What is complexity theory and what are its implications for educational change? *Educational Philosophy and Theory, 40*(1), 35–49.

Mason, M. (2009). Making educational development and change sustainable: Insights from complexity. *International Journal of Educational Development, 29*(2), 117–124.

Miller, A. (2008). A critique of positive psychology—or "the new science of happiness." *Journal of Philosophy of Education, 42*(3–4), 591–608.

Miller, J. P. (2018). *Love and compassion: Exploring their role in education*. University of Toronto Press.

Murray, K. E., & Max, D. M. (2013). Attitudes toward unauthorized immigrants, authorized immigrants, and refugees. *Cultural Diversity and Ethnic Minority Psychology, 19*(3), 332–341.

Noddings, N. (2013). *Caring: A relational approach to ethics and moral education (2nd ed.)*. University of California Press.

Oatley, K., Keltner, D., & Jenkins, J. M. (2006). Abstract. *Understanding emotions* (2nd ed.). Blackwell Publishing.

Olivero, M. M. (2017). *Cultivating Peace via Language Teaching: Pre-Service Teachers' Beliefs and Emotions in an EFL Argentine Practicum*. Graduate Theses and Dissertations. scholarcommons.usf.edu/etd/7432

Oxford, R. L. (2013). *The language of peace: Communicating to create harmony*. Information Age Publishing.

Oxford, R. L. (2015). Emotion as the amplifier and the primary motive: Some theories of emotion with relevance to language learning. In S. Ryan & S. Mercer (Eds.), Psychology and language learning (Special Issue). *Studies in Second Language Learning and Teaching, 5*(3), 371–393.

Oxford, R. L. (2016). Toward a psychology of well-being for language learners: The "EMPATHICS" vision. In P. MacIntyre, T. Gregersen, & S. Mercer (Eds.), *Positive psychology in SLA* (pp. 10–87). Multilingual Matters.

Oxford, R. L. (2017). Anxious language learners can change their minds: Ideas and strategies from traditional psychology and positive psychology. In C. Gkonou, M. Daubney, & J-M. Dewaele (Eds.), *New insights into language anxiety: Theory, research and educational implications* (pp. 177–197). Multilingual Matters.

Oxford, R. L., & Cuéllar, L. (2014). Positive psychology in cross-cultural narratives: Mexican students discover themselves while learning Chinese. *Studies in Second Language Learning and Teaching, 4*(2), 173–203.

Oxford, R. L., & Gkonou, C. (2020). Working with the complexity of language learners' emotions and emotion regulation strategies. In R. J. Sampson & R. S. Pinner (Eds.), *Complexity perspectives on researching language learner and teacher psychology* (pp. 52–67). Multilingual Matters.

Oxford, R. L., Pacheco Acuña, G., Solís Hernández, M., & Smith, A. L. (2015). "A language is a mentality": A narrative, positive-psychological view of six learners' development of bilingualism. *System, 55*, 100–110.

Pavlenko, A. (Ed.). (2006). *Bilingual minds: Emotional experience, expression and representation*. Multilingual Matters.

Pentón Herrera, L. J. (2020). Social-emotional learning in TESOL: What, why, and how. *Journal of English Learner Education, 10*(1), Article 1.

Piller, I., & Takahashi, K. (2006). A Passion for English: desire and the language market. In A. Pavlenko (Ed.), *Bilingual minds: emotional experience, expression, and representation* (Vol. 56, pp. 59–83). Multilingual Matters.

Reeve, J. (2018). *Understanding motivation and emotion* (7th ed.). Wiley.

Ricard, M. (2007). *Happiness: A guide to developing life's most important skill*. Little Brown.
Rodriguez, R. (1983). *Hunger of memory: The education of Richard Rodriguez*. Bantam.
Salovey, P., Mayer, J. D., Caruso, D., & Yoo, S. H. (2011). The positive psychology of emotional intelligence. In S. J. Lopez & C. R. Snyder (Eds.), *The Oxford handbook of positive psychology* (pp. 237–248). Oxford University Press.
Salzberg, S. (2020). *Real change: Mindfulness to heal ourselves and the world*. Flatiron Books.
Sampson, R. J. (2020). Interacting levels and timescales in the emergence of feelings in the L2 classroom. In R. J. Sampson & R. S. Pinner (Eds.), *Complexity perspectives on researching language learner and teacher psychology* (pp. 35–51). Multilingual Matters.
Schumann, J. (1997). *The neurobiology of affect in language learning*. Blackwell.
Seligman, M. E. P. (2011). *Flourish: A visionary new understanding of happiness and well-being*. Atria/Simon & Schuster.
Seligman, M. E. P., & Csíkszentmihályi, M. (2000). Positive psychology: An introduction. *American Psychologist, 55*(1), 5–14.
Seppälä, E. M., Simon-Thomas, E., Worline, S. L., Cameron, C. D., & Doty, J. R. (Eds.). (2017). *The Oxford handbook of compassion science*. Oxford University Press.
Shrout, P. E., & Rodgers, J. L. (2018). Psychology, science, and knowledge construction: Broadening perspectives from the replication crisis. *Annual Review of Psychology, 69*, 487–510.
Simon-Thomas, E. R. (2015). Measuring compassion in the body. Greater Good Science Center. greatergood.berkeley.edu/article/item/measuring_compassion_in_the_body
Stellar, J. E., Cohen, A., Oveis, C., & Keltner, D. (2015). Affective and physiological responses to the suffering of others: Compassion and vagal activity. *Journal of Personality and Social Psychology, 108*(4), 572–585.
Stevens, L., & Woodruff, C. C. (Eds.). (2018). *The neuroscience of empathy, compassion, and self-compassion*. Academic/Elsevier.
Troy, A. S., Wilhelm, F. H., Shallcross, A. J., & Mauss, I. B. (2010). Seeing the silver lining: cognitive reappraisal ability moderates the relationship between stress and depressive symptoms. *Emotion, 10*(6), 783–795.
Tugade, M. M., & Frederickson, B. L. (2002). Positive emotions and emotional intelligence. In L. F. Barrett & P. Salovey (Eds.), *Emotions and social behavior: The wisdom in feeling: Psychological Processes in Emotional intelligence* (pp. 319–340). Guilford.
Tugade, M. M., & Frederickson, B. L. (2008). Emotional intelligence: Perspectives on education and positive psychology. *Counterpoints, 336*, 145–167.
Watkins, P. C. (2014). *Gratitude and the good life: Toward a psychology of appreciation*. Springer.
Wang, H., Hall, N. C., & Taxer, J. L. (2019). Antecedents and consequences of teachers' emotional labor: A systematic review and meta-analytic investigation. *Educational Psychology Review*, 1–36.
Zegers, H. (2015). *When negative emotions are positive*. Positive Psychology News. positivepsychologynews.com/news/hein-zegers/2015082434668

15
WELL-BEING

Kyle Read Talbot

In, *The Moral Landscape*, Harris (2010) claims that the most serious questions in life, such as those that relate to values, morality, and purpose, concern well-being. His view contends that well-being is foundational and that all other priorities a person may have are best enjoyed under the auspices of the good life. For Harris (2010), uncovering knowledge about human well-being is not a luxury; it is a fundamental necessity for both individuals and members of society. He poses the question:

> Ask yourself, if the difference between the Bad Life and the Good Life doesn't matter to a person, what could possibly matter to him? …Wouldn't any real priority be best served amid the freedom and opportunity afforded by the Good Life?
>
> *Harris, 2010, p. 18*

Harris (2010) outlines a case for why maximizing and learning about well-being should be a central concern for the individual and society, and why scientific inquiry is an essential tool in this pursuit. Many psychologists would agree. Ryan and Deci (2001), for instance, claim that how we answer the question as to what "the good life" is has substantial theoretical and practical consequences. They explain that what we learn about it and how we define it "influences our practices of government, teaching, therapy, parenting, and preaching as all such endeavors aim to change humans for the better, and thus require some vision of what 'the better' is" (p. 143). Naturally, the theoretical and pragmatic consequences of how well-being is defined and measured also have significant ramifications for educational contexts. Research suggests that enjoying positive well-being can improve educational outcomes (Gilman & Huebner, 2006) and the quality of teaching (Sammons, Day, Kington, Gu, Stobart, & Smees, 2007). Experiencing high well-being is also relevant for relationships among classroom stakeholders (Roorda, Koomen, Spilt, & Oort, 2011). Beyond the classroom, a positive sense of well-being is also important for non-educational outcomes related to schooling (Jackson, Porter, Easton, Blanchard, & Kiguel, 2020). For these and other reasons, Seligman, Ernst, Gillham, Reivich, and Linkins (2009) argue that well-being should be taught in schools "as an antidote to depression, as a vehicle for increasing life satisfaction, and as an aid to better learning and more creative thinking" (p. 295).

A focus on well-being is also beginning to take hold within second language acquisition (SLA), particularly, within the field of the psychology of language teaching and learning (PLLT) (for review, see Mercer & Ryan, 2016). This can, at least in part, be attributed to the emergence of positive psychology (PP) (see Chapter 5) as a domain of inquiry within SLA (MacIntyre, Gregersen, & Mercer, 2019a), as well as to recent calls for Positive Language Education (PLE), which involves integrating linguistic and non-linguistic well-being focused aims simultaneously (Mercer, MacIntyre, Gregersen, & Talbot, 2018).

In this chapter, I will review some of what has been learned thus far about well-being, including how it has been measured and conceptualized within psychology, as well as some of its causes and consequences. Subsequently, I will provide a brief overview of the foundation upon which explorations on well-being within SLA are built and what the implications of this are for language education. Finally, I reflect on a few possibilities about what the future may hold for well-being as a domain of inquiry in SLA.

Well-Being in Psychology
Background

Discussions of well-being extend at least as far back as classical Hellenic philosophy (Waterman, 2008), most famously in Artistole's Nichomachean Ethics (Aristotle, 1999). Psychologists have argued that explorations of human well-being had become stagnant since they were first discussed centuries ago. Hartmann (1934), for instance, suggested that, "The theory of the happy life remains at about the level where Greek philosophers left it" (p. 202). Since then, well-being has been explored within psychology and in such disciplines as philosophy, economics, political science, medicine, and business. Within psychology, it has been investigated in the domains of "personality/social, clinical, health, industrial/organization, cognitive, community, and developmental psychology, as well as human factors and behavioral neuroscience" (Disabato, Goodman, & Kashdan, 2019, p. 3) as well as community psychology and educational psychology (Martela & Sheldon, 2019).

In the last two decades, well-being has become more popular as a topic of interest within psychology because of increasing interest in PP. In 2000, Seligman and Csíkszentmihályi edited a special issue of American Psychologist; in it, they argued that research in psychology was not uncovering "knowledge of what makes life worth living" (p. 5). As such, they named and outlined a framework for the science of PP with the aim to focus on factors, conditions, and mental states related to positive functioning. Naturally, the aims of PP and its goal to explore what makes life worth living helped ignite a renewed academic focus on well-being.

Though the PP movement was influential in sparking interest in well-being, this is not to say that there was no focus in psychology or allied disciplines on well-being in between Hartmann's investigation (1934) and the beginning of the PP movement. In fact, in 1989, Ryff pointed out that:

> On a more general level, increased interest in the study of psychological well-being follows from the recognition that the field of psychology, since its inception, has devoted much more attention to human unhappiness and suffering than to the causes and consequences of positive functioning.
>
> *p. 1069*

Notably, Ryff's (1989) argument is nearly indistinguishable from the argument forwarded by Seligman and Csíkszentmihályi 11 years later.

Traditions of Well-Being Research

Well-being is notoriously difficult to define. Jayawickreme, Forgeard, and Seligman (2012) pointed out what they considered to be a major dilemma in how well-being is theorized. They explain that:

On the one hand, the study of well-being has been hampered by the multiplicity of theory (Diener, Scollon, & Lucas, 2003), leading to a blurred and overly broad definition of well-being. Focusing on a single approach, on the other hand, has led to myopia in how the term "well-being" is understood by both researchers and the general public, which the multiplicity then attempts to correct.

p. 327

Despite considerable debate, well-being has typically been conceptualized into two over-arching categories, hedonic and eudemonic well-being. Hedonic well-being is characterized by affect and evaluating one's life overall as satisfying (cf. Disabato et al., 2019), whereas eudemonic well-being is generally characterized by self-actualization, meaning in life, and purpose (Kashdan, Biswas-Diener, & King, 2008). Keyes and Annas (2009) have referred to this distinction as the difference between "feeling good" and "functioning well" (p. 197). These two lines of inquiry have been influential and have shaped how well-being has been measured and understood over time.

Defining and Measuring Well-Being

In one review, Linton, Dieppe, and Medina-Lara (2016) identified 196 independent conceptualizations of well-being and 99 distinct adult well-being measures. Linton et al. (2016) noted that one of the most referenced theories among these studies was Diener's subjective well-being (SWB), defined as "levels of pleasant affect, lack of unpleasant affect, and life satisfaction" (Diener, 1994, p, 103). SWB is the most well-known hedonic conceptualization of well-being. Diener and Ryan (2009) suggest that although SWB is subjective, it can be measured objectively in both verbal and non-verbal behavior. However, SWB is typically measured through self-report with the Satisfaction with Life Scale (SWLS) (for review, see Pavot & Diener, 2008). Other well-known measures of SWB include the Self-Anchoring Striving Scale (Cantril, 1965), Fordyce's Happiness measure (1977), and the Positive and Negative Affect Scale (PANAS) (Watson, Clark, & Tellegen 1988).

For some researchers, the focus on affective states with SWB ignored much of the philosophical and earlier psychological theories describing positive functioning (Waterman, 2008). As a result, researchers have pointed out that eudemonic well-being should also be conceptualized and measured alongside SWB (Martela & Sheldon, 2019). As such, Ryff (1989) conceptualized psychological well-being (PWB). PWB is part of the eudemonic tradition and includes six dimensions (i.e., autonomy, self-acceptance, positive relationships, personal growth, purpose in life, and environmental mastery). PWB is one of the most prominent eudemonic well-being constructs and is typically measured with the Scales of Psychological Well-Being (SPWB) (Ryff, 1989). However, there are a number of other ways in which eudemonia has been conceptualized and measured. Martela and Sheldon (2019), for instance, point out that eudemonic well-being "has been operationalized in at least 45 different ways, using measures of at least 63 different constructs" (p. 458).

Well-being has also been conceptualized as a social phenomenon. For example, Keyes's (1998) social well-being model "focused on peoples as members of a community rather than isolated individuals" (Disabato et al., 2019, p. 6). In addition to SWB, PWB, and social well-being, other notable conceptualizations of well-being exist (for a review, see Jayawickreme et al., 2012), including self-determination theory (Deci & Ryan, 1980), the capabilities approach (Nussbaum, 2003; Sen, 1992), and Maslow's hierarchy of needs (1954, 1971).

Integrative Well-Being Frameworks

Integrative frameworks for well-being have also been proposed, which combine the hedonic and eudemonic traditions. One such model was named "the engine model of well-being" (Jayawickreme et al., 2012, p. 327). This integrative model is "a framework that aims to make sense of the multiplicity of theory by organizing the constructs at hand around inputs, processes, and outcomes" (Jayawickreme et al., 2012, p. 327). Essentially, the engine model was designed in order to integrate "major perspectives on well-being in the field of psychology, economics and human development" (Jayawickreme et al., 2012, p. 338).

A second integrative model is Seligman's (2011) PERMA model. PERMA is the most well-known model of well-being generated from PP. Butler and Kern (2016) explain that the PERMA model of well-being is an acronym that "advocates that flourishing arises from five well-being pillars (positive emotion, engagement, relationships, meaning, accomplishment" (p. 2). PERMA is typically measured using the PERMA Profiler (Butler & Kern, 2016) and can be utilized in various domains, such as the workplace or within schools.

Causes and Consequences of Well-Being

Why should researchers focus on well-being? One reason is that well-being is a favorable outcome in and of itself (Campbell, 1976). A second reason to do so is that well-being relates to positive outcomes in various life domains. Diener and Ryan (2009) explain of SWB, that, "[A] growing body of evidence suggests that high well-being and life satisfaction significantly improve life within the four areas of health and longevity, work and income, social relations, and societal benefits" (p. 392; see also Lyubomirksy, King, & Diener, 2005). Diener and Ryan (2009) further suggest that in these domains, "evidence suggests that the causal arrow between these two variables moves in both directions" (p. 392). As such, it is often difficult to parse whether SWB is a cause or consequence, whether the effect is bidirectional or if it is inextricable from the event, context, behavior, or relationship itself. To illustrate one example of the bidirectional influence of well-being, in a recent study, Chen, Tian, and Huebner (2020) found that relations between in school SWB and prosocial behavior were positive, bidirectional, and stable over time in a population of 634 primary students in China.

Individual differences also impact well-being. Studies show that internal and demographic factors such as an individual's temperament, personality, or age, and external factors such as availability of material resources, social resources, and characteristics in society all can impact SWB (for a review, see Diener, Suh, Lucas, & Smith, 1999). Other relevant factors influencing this include religious affiliation, level of intelligence, education level, quality of relationships, employment status, income (for a review, see Diener & Ryan, 2009), and culture (Diener & Suh, 2000).

Similar to SWB, a growing body of eudemonic research has found correlates within several important life domains. For instance, Ryff, Singer, Dienberg Love, and Love (2004) correlated the six dimensions of PWB with favorable biomarkers (e.g., neuroendocrine regulation, lower inflammatory markers, etc.) and better sleep. PWB has also correlated with various psychological constructs, for example, emotion regulation (Gross & John, 2003), self-regulation (Simon & Durand-Bush, 2015), and Big-Five personality traits (Grant, Langan-Fox, & Anglim, 2009). Additionally, PWB has been explored in terms of its sociodemographic correlates (for review, see Ryff & Singer, 2008). One particularly relevant finding is that "PWB and educational standing are strongly positively linked, with the association being especially pronounced for personal growth and purpose in life, the two pillars of eudaimonia" (Ryff & Singer, 2008, p. 29).

Well-Being in Education

This chapter now turns to research on well-being in education. Particularly, I highlight three areas where a focus on well-being is important as it relates to educational psychology, namely, positive education (PE), PP interventions (PPIs), and positive emotions in education.

Within educational psychology, Positive Education (PE) has recently risen in prominence. Norrish (2015) defines PE as, "the bringing together of the science of positive psychology with best teaching practices, to encourage and support schools and individuals to flourish" (p. xxvii). Essentially, PE focuses on the holistic learning and teaching experience. A PE approach recognizes that well-being and academic growth are mutually reinforcing goals, and as a result, both are prioritized. In a recent study, Jackson et al. (2020) demonstrated using value-added models that students' socio-emotional development (SED) was impacted positively by promoting well-being and hard work. Their study specifically finds that "high SED value-added schools improve attendance, reduce disciplinary incidents, improve course grades, reduce the number of school-based arrests, increase high school graduation, increase four-year college going, and increase college persistence" (Jackson et al., 2020, p. 3). Studies such as this highlight how focusing on a more holistic educational experience which includes well-being and other socio-emotional skills can benefit students in both the short and long term.

One means of bringing attention to well-being in education is through the use of PP Interventions (PPIs). PPIs are intentional activities or programs which aim to bolster positive emotions, behaviors, or thoughts (Sin & Lyubomirsky, 2009). Generally, PPIs have been reported to be successful in terms of enhancing the well-being of participants (for review, see, Bolier, Haverman, Westerhof, Riper, Smit, & Bohlmeijer, 2013). Many PPIs target positive emotions, a core component of SWB and integrated well-being models. In one study, Subramaniam, Kounios, Parrish, and Jung-Beeman (2009) show how positive emotion impacts creativity and mental flexibility positively, both of which are relevant for teaching and learning. Frequently experiencing positive emotions in educational contexts has specifically been shown to be beneficial. For instance, it has been found to impact students' grades (Pekrun, Goetz, Frenzel, Barchfeld, & Perry, 2011) and their levels of engagement more generally (King, McInerney, Ganotice, & Villarosa 2015).

Well-Being in SLA

Academic explorations on well-being have a long history in psychology and allied disciplines, yet it is has only recently gained attention in SLA. While there are fewer studies explicitly investigating well-being, a number of studies exist under the SLA umbrella that are closely related to well-being. For example, the aim of PP is to help individuals flourish and to promote well-being, and, as such, studies under the PP umbrella are naturally connected to well-being. Similarly, a focus on the benefit of positive emotions for language learning is relevant as positive emotions are often a defining feature of hedonic (e.g., SWB) and integrated frameworks of well-being (e.g., PERMA). Rather than reviewing the gamut of SLA studies relevant to well-being, this paper specifically focuses on how well-being has been defined in SLA and on the limited number of empirical studies with an explicit focus on well-being. Such conceptualizations of well-being that are less overt will not be described in this chapter in the detail that they deserve. This includes constructs such as language teacher immunity (Hiver & Dörnyei; 2015; Hiver, 2017), foreign language enjoyment (Dewaele & MacIntyre, 2014), Trait Emotional Intelligence (Dewaele & Mercer, 2018) and self-determination theory (Noels, Vargas Lascano, & Saumure, 2019), all of which either have well-being components or are closely related. This chapter also does not review various PPIs (for reviews, see Dewaele, Padilla, & Lake, 2019; MacIntyre et al., 2019a).

Defining Well-Being in SLA

How has well-being been conceptualized thus far in SLA? Several studies have looked to SWB (Diener, 1994) to understand this (Gruber, Lämmerer, Hofstadler, & Mercer, 2020; Hessel, Talbot, Gruber, & Mercer, 2020; Hofstadler, Babic, Lämmerer, Mercer, & Oberdorfer, 2020a; Hofstadler, Talbot, Mercer, Lämmerer, & Mercer, 2020b; Talbot, Gruber, Lämmerer, Hofstadler, & Mercer, 2021; Talbot & Mercer, 2018). Such research has explored the relationships between positive and negative emotions, the balance between the two, and life satisfaction experienced by teachers across educational levels.

Well-being has also been conceptualized and measured in similar ways in SLA as it has been in PP. This is not surprising, as PP has had a significant impact on SLA research. For example, Seligman's (2011) well-being theory represented by the PERMA framework has often been featured within SLA (Gregersen, MacIntyre, & Ross, 2019; Gregersen, Mercer, MacIntyre, Talbot, & Banga, 2020; Helgesen, 2016; Hessel et al., 2020; MacIntyre et al., 2019b; Oxford, 2016, Oxford & Cuéllar, 2014). For instance, MacIntyre et al. (2019b) and Gregersen et al. (2020) defined and measured well-being according to PERMA because they understood well-being to be multidimensional and consisting of both hedonic and eudemonic aspects. PERMA has also been used to create classroom interventions. For example, Helgesen (2016) took cues from the PERMA model in creating ELT PPIs. These PPIs included a focus on savoring positive experiences, expressing gratitude, and complimenting others.

Another example of how PERMA has been utilized in SLA research can be found in Oxford and Cuéllar's (2014) narrative study focusing on the ups and downs of students' language learning trajectories. In using the PERMA framework in previous studies (Oxford, 2014; Oxford & Cuéllar, 2014), Oxford (2016a) found this not to be as broad, dynamic, or as interactive as she would have liked. As a result, she created her own framework to represent language learner well-being, EMPATHICS. EMPATHICS, an acronym, represents:

> E: emotion and empathy; M: meaning and motivation; P: perseverance, including resilience; A: agency and autonomy; T: time; H: habits of mind; I: intelligences; C: character strengths; and S: self-factors, especially self-efficacy.
>
> *Oxford, 2016a, p. 26*

According to Oxford (2016b), EMPATHICS "is more extensive, more grounded in the theory of complex systems, and richer in related research" than PERMA, and more specific to language learning contexts in general (p. 22).

A dynamic approach to understanding teacher well-being can also be seen in Hofstadler et al.'s (2020a) recent study and in theoretical work from Jin, Mercer, Babic, and Mairitsch (in press). Hofstadler et al. (2020a) explored how teachers' professional SWB was shaped by different layers of their ecology and how this affected their practice. The researchers analyzed teachers professional SWB through Bronfenbrenner's ecological systems theory (2009). Jin et al. (in press) also drew on Bronfenbrenner's ecological systems theory, pointing out that they view teacher well-being as an emergent quality which cannot be meaningfully understood without considering the broader context of teachers' lives. Similarly, Mercer and Talbot (2020), influenced by a view of well-being as inherently complex, theorize that well-being itself can be construed as a complex dynamic system. What seems to be a common thread in how well-being is conceptualized in SLA thus far is the acknowledgment of the importance of context and dynamism.

Empirical Research on Well-Being in SLA

A number of studies in SLA have explored teacher well-being, with comparatively fewer studies having focused on learner well-being. One study with an explicit focus on teacher well-being was conducted by Talbot and Mercer (2018), who investigated factors related to the emotional well-being (EWB) (i.e., the affective components of SWB) of 12 tertiary-level ESL/EFL teachers (four from the US, Japan, and Austria, respectively). One factor that contributed positively to all of the teacher participants' EWB was interacting with their students. For ten of the teachers, a sense of meaning and belief in the importance of their work also impacted their EWB positively. One shared stressor reported by the majority of teachers in the study (n=10) were the periods of intense temporal stress they experienced periodically throughout the year.

An explicit focus on well-being was also at the center of an experience-sampling (ESM) research project exploring the daily stressors and joys of an international sample of language teachers (n=52) through the use of a specially designed smartphone app (Gregersen et al., 2020; MacIntyre et al. 2019b). Participants in this project responded to a series of ten daily surveys gauging participants' stressors and uplifts, what was impacting their feelings, and why. In addition to daily surveys, the teachers also answered questions about their personality traits, well-being as measured by the PERMA profiler (Butler & Kern, 2016), sources of long term and chronic stress, and physical health. MacIntyre et al. (2019) specifically focused on the interactions of personality, stress, and well-being of the teachers in their sample. This study had three main findings: 1) personality is connected to teacher well-being, 2) teacher well-being is connected to stress, and 3) personality is not connected to stress.

Drawing on the same data set, Gregersen et al. (2020) took a granular look at six case study participants from the larger sample of 52. They were interested in identifying which teachers reported the highest and lowest well-being scores according to PERMA and whether qualitative differences could be found in how these groups experienced well-being and responded to stress. Their study showed that while teachers in the higher and lower well-being categories did not differ greatly in terms of their daily stressors and uplifts, the group reporting higher well-being reported experiencing significantly better physical health overall.

Several studies have also explored teachers' well-being in integrated content and language settings such as content and language integrated learning (CLIL), English medium instruction (EMI), and content-based instruction settings (CBI) (Talbot, Gruber, & Nishida, 2021). The fact that there is a conscious research effort to explore teacher well-being in such settings is not surprising. In such programs, teachers may face threats to their professional identity (Moate, 2011), and experience a shift in their roles and responsibilities (Talbot et al., 2021). Furthermore, there may be additional challenges for teachers that have difficulty expressing themselves fully in the target language or who lack training in language pedagogy (Mercer, Oberdorfer, & Saleem, 2016).

In one qualitative study, Hofstadler et al. (2020b) explored CLIL teachers' emotional well-being (EWB) at the secondary level in Austria. They pointed out that factors affecting the participants' EWB often were neither wholly positive nor negative, for example, some viewed an ad hoc implementation of CLIL as a drawback to teaching in these settings, whereas some of the teachers experienced a lack of top-down control as freeing and supportive of their autonomy. In a second qualitative study, this one a comparative analysis comparing the SWB of CLIL/EMI teachers across educational levels in Austria, Talbot et al. (2021) found that the factors affecting the participating teachers' well-being were largely comparable across educational levels, yet they pointed out that primary and secondary teachers tended to perceive more sensitivity about their social status as teachers than did teachers at the tertiary level, which affected their SWB negatively.

One quantitative contribution is Hessel et al.'s (2020) study comparing the well-being and job satisfaction of secondary CLIL (n=123) and tertiary EMI teachers (n=219) in Austria. They found that secondary CLIL teachers scored consistently lower in terms of their well-being (as measured by a modified version of the PERMA profiler) than their tertiary EMI counterparts. Interestingly, the differences between these teacher groups in terms of their job satisfaction (as measured by a modified version of the SWLS) were less pronounced.

Perhaps surprisingly, there are fewer studies focusing on language learner well-being. Two notable exceptions are Oxford (2014) and Oxford and Cuéllar (2014). In Oxford's (2014) study, she reflected on the L2 learning histories of two learners "representing extreme ends of the spectrum of learner well-being" (p. 593). She was interested in whether a modified version of the PERMA framework was useful in understanding the well-being of both learners, one of which was experiencing high well-being and was a strategic learner, and the other, who was described as experiencing relatively lower well-being and less strategic.

Oxford and Cuéllar (2014) also utilized the PERMA framework in their narrative study, which centered on five university students learning Chinese in Mexico. The narratives, focusing on the ups and downs of the student participants' language learning trajectories, showed "clear examples of the

PERMA model... albeit with a more obvious interweaving of cultural factors than found in that theory" (Oxford and Cuéllar, 2014, p. 174).

Finally, Fatemi and Asghari (2016) investigated relationships between learners' PWB and their attributional patterns in a study of 96 Iranian university students. Their study found positive and significant correlations between the students' PWB and their attributional patterns. Additionally, they showed that certain subscales from Ryff's (1989) SPWB were able to predict learners' attributions.

Integrating Psychology and SLA Perspectives

Despite the relatively short history of research on well-being in SLA, there has been a substantially growing interest in psychological factors that affect language learning and teaching more generally. The growing research interest within SLA on these factors can be at least partially explained by substantial interest in the SLA subdiscipline, the psychology of language teaching and learning (PLLT). In 2016, Mercer and Ryan described the emergence of PLLT. In it, they explain that:

> In terms of both practice and research, language education has been moving away from solely language or teaching-based models towards a greater focus on the various contributions learners make to their own learning (Breen, 2001) as evident in the shift towards more learner-centered models of learning.
>
> p. 2

While researchers have explored motivation and learner-centered work since at least the 1960s (e.g., Gardner & Lambert, 1959), PLLT has helped create an umbrella field and helped to broaden the range of constructs available within SLA, including well-being.

As well-being is a relatively newer domain of inquiry within SLA, the conceptual contributions have tended to flow from psychology to SLA. This is not to say that SLA has little to offer psychology, or that the contributions will not be bidirectional or more heavily interdisciplinary in the future. On the contrary, SLA has much to offer the study of well-being in psychology. In particular, SLA foregrounds issues related to identity (Norton, 2012), the self (Mercer & Williams, 2014), dynamics (Ellis, 2008), and culture. While these factors have been investigated in relation to well-being in psychology, they are often at the center of research in SLA.

Oxford's (2016a) work developing EMPATHICS by adapting PERMA shows how a construct from SLA has the potential to impact related disciplines. She created her own model of well-being with added dimensions, which she sees as "complex, interrelated, interacting, and evolving" (Oxford, 2016a, p. 26). Though she draws on the PERMA theory and framework generated from PP, one could imagine that her more expansive model could now act to influence psychology in the other direction.

Implications for Practice and Research

MacIntyre et al. (2019a) suggest that with PP in SLA, "We find ourselves with an open treasure chest, an *embarras de richesses* of concepts waiting to be explored" (emphasis in original) (p. 268). The same can also be said in regard to explorations on well-being within SLA. Well-being has been referred to as both an "umbrella construct" and a "meta-construct" in psychology (Abdel-Khalek, 2012; Levin & Chatters, 1998). Viewed from this perspective, its explorations within SLA will only be limited by the creativity of its researchers, stakeholders, and practitioners. In other words, its potential applications for research and practice are substantial.

One example at the theoretical level can be found in Gregersen et al.'s (2020) study highlighting connections between Gardner's (1985) integrative motive and Seligman's PERMA model. Their theoretical contribution resulted in empirically testable research propositions (e.g., "People with more positive *attitudes towards the learning situation* will show more fervent enthusiasm, assertiveness gratitude and compassion in the classroom"; Gregersen et al., 2020, p. 35). As more constructs from psychology and PP become incorporated into SLA, we can expect more novel research propositions to become available.

Another theoretical consideration is how to balance a multiplicity of theory with a unified approach to defining well-being (Disabato et al., 2019; Jayawickreme et al., 2012). A lack of definitional precision in well-being discussions may create a lack of clarity as to whether researchers mean the same thing when they refer to well-being. Disabato et al. (2019) make this point as they argue for a general unified definition of well-being for psychology. They argue that, "only by conceptually defining well-being can measures be designed to map onto the concept… researchers can [then] move towards nomological network analyses where association between well-being constructs and theoretically related constructs can be used to establish construct validity" (p. 13). They draw parallels to models of intelligence and personality to show the utility of a general construct at the top of a hierarchy with narrower constructs below. This debate is on-going in psychology and allied disciplines. Assuredly, the way in which SLA researchers address this will have significant implications for the field.

In terms of practice, educational stakeholders may consider the efficacy of implementing a PLE-like approach in their settings or implementing empirically validated PPIs in their classrooms. Mercer et al. (2018) suggest that PE initiatives could take both strong and weak forms and could be implemented in ways that do not unduly burden language educators who, in some cases, are already under significant amounts of pressure. Within SLA, MacIntyre et al. (2019a) describe examples of approaches to language education that utilize a dual-focused approach. This includes CLIL-like settings where there is a dual focus on content and language (Coyle, Hood, & Marsh, 2010). CLIL could provide a model for what a dual-strand approach to language learning and well-being may look like.

A further pragmatic consideration is to take comfort in the fact that well-being has been found to impact student achievement positively (Briner & Dewberry, 2007; Sammons et al., 2007). For teachers, simply recognizing that enjoying positive well-being can impact the classroom success of their students, and furthermore, has been shown to enhance teachers' practice and ability to teach at their full capacity, is essential and powerful knowledge (Mercer & Gregersen, 2020). From this perspective, well-being is not viewed as a triviality, but rather as the foundation of successful and effective language teaching. Of course, teachers should not focus on their own well-being only because this impacts their students and classrooms positively, with links to positive outcomes in a variety of domains (Diener & Ryan, 2009); enjoying positive well-being is a worthy aim in and of itself.

Future Directions

Although it is early, there appears to be a relative imbalance in SLA research on well-being in favor of teachers. Redressing this imbalance is likely to occur quickly but should be a consideration for SLA researchers interested in the topic. Noble, McGrath, Roffey, and Rowling (2008) point out that improving student well-being is "important for maximizing the likelihood that young people can benefit from their participation in schooling" (p. 14) and is "strongly linked to student learning" (p. 16). Although they refer to schooling, the notion applies to learners spanning a range of contexts, ages, and educational levels.

Regarding the future of research on well-being within SLA, Talbot and Mercer (2020) highlighted a number of areas where they suggested further attention is merited as it relates to language teacher well-being. Their suggestions were made with language teachers in mind; however, these suggestions could easily be adapted to apply to language learner well-being. First, they suggest that more needs to be known about the ecologies of language teacher well-being. This would include, for example, how language teacher well-being is related to teachers' personal and professional lives as well as how it is influenced by institutional factors and situated contexts. An example of this line of research can be found in Hofstadler et al.'s (2020a) study examining how the SWB of CLIL teachers in Austria; their data show how the SWB of their teacher participants was influenced by larger contextual factors, but also how their own interpretations affected this.

Additionally, the dynamics (see Chapter 4) of language learner and teacher well-being involving various timescales merit further exploration. For instance, researchers could investigate how language teacher well-being fluctuates during intensive periods throughout the course of a semester or year or how language learner well-being fluctuates during the course of a single class or task. A contemporary example can be found in research by MacIntyre, Gregersen, and Mercer (2020), who examine the coping strategies, well-being, and stressors of an international sample of language teachers in light of the COVID-19 global pandemic. Such a glimpse into the lives of language teachers during a period of instability can cast a light on how teachers adapt to difficult and more intensive periods of time. Naturally, exploring similar factors is equally important when it comes to language learners.

It is also worth exploring the relationship between well-being and teaching efficacy for teachers and self-efficacy for students. In a synthesis of 40 years of research on teacher self-efficacy, Zee and Koomen (2016) found that teaching self-efficacy "shows positive links with students' academic adjustment, patterns of teacher behavior and practices related to classroom quality, and factors underlying teachers' psychological well-being" (p. 1). In relation to students, Chan (2007) found that self-efficacy had "direct effects" on students SWB in Hong Kong. Investigating such links within language learning contexts surely would add significant value to the field. Arguably, the role of self-efficacy could be even more important in language learning and teaching contexts where FLA can be a compounding factor (Horwitz, Horwitz, & Cope, 1986).

Explorations on individual differences and their impact on well-being should also be investigated in language learning contexts. One example of such a research initiative from the psychological domain is Gross and John's (2003) study showing that the frequency with which individuals use cognitive reappraisal influences their PWB. Studies such as this have significant crossover potential when it comes to SLA. Understanding how language learner and teacher well-being is linked to personality and other individual differences such as age, gender, ability to cope, language repertoire, or socio-contextual factors will provide insight into ways that we can better support individual students and teachers in a variety of contexts.

Finally, special consideration to how well-being might be applied in special language learning contexts where refugees or other at-risk populations are being taught is needed (see Chapter 25). Because such populations are more at risk for psychological problems (Fazel, Wheeler, & Danesh, 2005), Mercer et al. (2018) suggest, "it is possible they would benefit even more for a dual strand approach to language learning that incorporates a wellbeing life skills perspective when approached in culturally sensitive ways" (p. 21).

Though we have seen the emergence of the PP movement within SLA (Dewaele et al., 2019; MacIntyre et al. 2019a), and with it, many studies related to well-being, a relatively fewer number of studies exist that focus explicitly on learner and teacher well-being. As such, there is ample space for growth and development in this domain. A positive sense of well-being is a necessary condition for both language learners and language teachers; it forms the foundation for successful teaching and successful learning and should be a central concern of educational stakeholders seeking to support learners' and teachers' development. After all, any priorities that language teachers and learners have are likely to be better served under the auspices of the good life.

Reflection Questions

- What challenges and joys do language education present for learners and teachers? Are these challenges and joys specific to language teaching, or do they also apply to education more generally?

- How can the well-being of language learners and teachers be supported at multiple levels of their ecologies?
- In what ways are language learner and language teacher well-being interconnected, and what factors impact this connection?

Recommended Reading

Jayawickreme, E., Forgeard, M. J. C., & Seligman, M. E. P. (2012). The engine of well-being. *Review of General Psychology, 16*(4), 327–342.
This article is a particularly useful starting point in helping to establish a foundation about the history of well-being, its various traditions, and how it has been defined and measured.

Dewaele, J.-M., Chen, X., Padilla, A. M., & Lake, J. (2019). The flowering of positive psychology in foreign language teaching and acquisition research. *Frontiers in Psychology, 10,* 1–13.
As the goal of PP is to bolster individual and societal well-being (Seligman, 2011), the studies reviewed by the authors relate to well-being even if the mention of this is not explicit. This article can act as a foundation for those interested in well-being, PP, and its interconnections with SLA.

Mercer, S., & Gregersen, T. (2020). *Teacher wellbeing*. Oxford University Press.
This book explains why a positive sense of well-being is helpful for language teachers personally, but is also centrally important for teachers' capacity to excel in their teaching.

References

Abdel-Khalek, A. M. (2012). Subjective well-being and religiosity: A cross-sectional study with adolescents, young and middle-aged adults. *Mental Health, Religion, & Culture, 15*(1), 39–52.
Aristotle (1999). *Nicomachean ethics* (T. Irwin, Tans, 2nd ed). Hackett Publishing Company.
Bolier, L., Haverman, M., Westerhof, G. J., Riper, H., Smit, F., & Bohlmeijer, E. (2013). Positive psychology interventions: A meta-analysis of randomized controlled studies. *BMC Public Health, 13*(1), 1–20.
Briner, R., & Dewberry, C. (2007). *Staff wellbeing is key to school success: A research study into the links between staff wellbeing and school performance*. Worklife Support.
Bronfenbrenner, U. (2009). *The ecology of human development*. Harvard University Press.
Butler, J., & Kern, M. L. (2016). The PERMA-Profiler: A brief multidimensional measure of flourishing. *International Journal of Wellbeing, 6*(3), 1–48.
Campbell, A. (1976). Subjective measures of well-being. *American Psychologist, 31*(2), 117–124.
Cantril, H. (1965). *The pattern of human concerns*. Rutgers University Press.
Chan, D. W. (2007). Positive and negative perfectionism among Chinese gifted students in Hong Kong: Their relationships to general self-efficacy and subjective well-being. *Journal for the Education of the Gifted, 31*(1), 77–102.
Chen, X., Tian, L., & Huebner, E. S. (2020). Bidirectional relations between subjective well-being in school and prosocial behavior among elementary school-aged children: A longitudinal study. *Child & Youth Care Forum, 49*(1), 77–95.
Coyle, D., Hood, P., & Marsh, D. (2010). *CLIL: Content and language integrated learning*. Cambridge University Press.
Deci, E., & Ryan, R. (1980). Self-determination theory: When mind mediates behavior. *The Journal of Mind and Behavior, 1*(1), 33–43.
Dewaele, J.-M., Chen, X., Padilla, A. M., & Lake, J. (2019). The flowering of positive psychology in foreign language teaching and acquisition research. *Frontiers in Psychology, 10,* 2128.
Dewaele, J.-M., & MacIntyre, P. D. (2014). The two faces of Janus? Anxiety and enjoyment in the foreign language classroom. *Studies in Second Language Learning and Teaching, 4*(2), 237–274.
Dewaele, J.-M., & MacIntyre, P. D. (2019) The predictive power of multicultural personality traits, learner and teacher variables on foreign languge enjoyment and anxiety. In M. Sato & S. Loewen (Eds.), *Evidence-based second language pedagogy: A collection of Instructed Second Language Acquisition studies* (pp. 263–286). Routledge.
Dewaele, J.-M., & Mercer, S. (2018). Variation in ESL/EFL teachers' attitudes towards their students. In S. Mercer & K. Achilleas (Eds.), *Language teacher psychology* (pp. 178–195). Multiligual Matters.

Dewaele, J.-M., Gkonou, C., & Mercer, S. (2018). Do ESL/EFL teachers' emotional intelligence teaching experience, proficiency and gender, affect their classroom practice? In J. de Dios Martínez Agudo (Ed.), *Emotions in second language teaching. Theory, research and teacher education* (pp. 125–141). Springer.

Diener, E. (1994) Assessing subjective well-being: Progress and opportunities. *Social Indicators Research, 31*(2), 103–157.

Diener, E., & Ryan, K. (2009). Subjective well-being: A general overview. *South African Journal of Psychology, 39*(4), 391–406.

Diener, E., Scollon, C., & Lucas, R. (2003). The evolving concept of subjective well-being: The multifaceted nature of happiness. *Advances in Cell Aging and Gerontology, 15*, 187–219.

Diener, E., & Suh, E. M. (Eds.). (2000). *Culture and subjective well-being*. MIT Press.

Diener, E., Suh, E. M., Lucas, R. E., & Smith, H. L. (1999). Subjective well-being: Three decades of progress. *Psychological Bulletin, 125*(2), 276–302.

Disabato, D., Goodman, F. R., & Kashdan, T. B. (2019). *A hierarchical framework for the measurement of well-being* [Preprint].

Ellis, N. C. (2008). The dynamics of second language emergence: Cycles of language use, language change, and language acquisition. *The Modern Language Journal, 92*(2), 232–249.

Fatemi, A. H., & Asghari, A. (2016). The role of psychological well-being on university EFL learners' attributional patterns. *Journal of Educational and Social Research, 6*(1), 189–197.

Fazel, M., Wheeler, J., & Danesh, J. (2005). Prevalence of serious mental disorder in 7000 refugees resettled in Western countries: A systematic review. *The Lancet, 365*(9467), 1309–1314.

Fordyce, M. W. (1977). Development of a program to increase personal happiness. *Journal of Counseling Psychology, 24*(6), 511–521.

Gardner, R. C. (1985). *Social psychology and second language learning: The role of attitudes and motivation*. Edward Arnold.

Gardner, R. C., & Lambert, W. E. (1959). Moticational variables in second-language acquisition. *Canadian Journal of Psychology/Revue Canadienne de Psychologie, 13*(4), 266–272.

Gilman, R., & Huebner, E. S. (2006). Characteristics of adolescents who report very high life satisfaction. *Journal of Youth and Adolescence, 35*(3), 311–319.

Grant, S., Langan-Fox, J., & Anglim, J. (2009). The Big Five traits as predictors of subjective and psychological well-being. *Psychological Reports, 105*(1), 205–231.

Gregersen, T., MacIntyre, P. D., & Ross, J. (2019). Extending Gardner's socio-educational model to learner well-being: Research propositions linking integrative motivation and the PERMA framework. In A. H. Al-Hoorie & P. D. MacIntyre (Eds.), *Contemporary language motivation theory* (pp. 17–39). Multilingual Matters.

Gregersen, T., Mercer, S., MacIntyre, P., Talbot, K. R., & Banga, C. A. (2020). Understanding language teacher wellbeing: An ESM study of daily stressors and uplifts. *Language Teaching Research*, 1–22.

Gross, J. J., & John, O. P. (2003). Individual differences in two emotion regulation processes: Implications for affect, relationships, and well-being. *Journal of Personality and Social Psychology, 85*(2), 348–362.

Gruber, M.-T., Lämmerer, A., Hofstadler, N., & Mercer, S. (2020). Flourishing or floundering? Factors contributing to CLIL primary teachers' wellbeing in Austria. *CLIL Journal of Innovation and Research in Plurilingual and Pluricultural Education, 3*(1), 19.

Harris, S. (2010). *The moral landscape: How science can determine human values*. Free Press.

Hartmann, G. W. (1934). Personality traits associated with variations in happiness. *The Journal of Abnormal and Social Psychology, 29*(2), 202–212.

Helgesen, M. (2016). Happiness in ESL/EFL: Bringing positive psychology to the classroom. In P. D. MacIntyre, T. Gregersen, & S. Mercer (Eds.), *Positive psychology in SLA* (pp. 305–323). Multilingual Matters.

Hessel, G., Talbot, K., Mercer, S., & Gruber, M.-T. (2020). The well-being and job satisfaction of secondary CLIL and tertiary EMI teachers. *Journal for the Psychology of Language Learning, 2*(2), 73–90.

Hiver, P., & Dörnyei, Z. (2015). Language teacher immunity: A double-edged sword. *Applied Linguistics, 38*(3), 1–20.

Hiver, P. (2017). Tracing the signature dynamics of language teacher immunity: A retrodictive qualitative modeling study. *The Modern Language Journal, 101*(4), 669–690.

Hofstadler, N., Babic, S., Lämmerer, A., Mercer, S., & Oberdorfer, P. (2020a). The ecology of CLIL teachers in Austria—An ecological perspective on CLIL teachers' wellbeing. *Innovation in Language Learning and Teaching*, 1–15.

Hofstadler, N., Talbot, K. R., Mercer, S., & Lämmerer, A. (2020b). The thrills and ills of CLIL. In C. Gkonou, J.-M. Dewaele, & J. King (Eds.), *The emotional rollercoaster of language teaching*. Multilingual Matters.

Horwitz, E. K., Horwitz, M. B., & Cope, J. (1986). Foreign language classroom anxiety. *The Modern Language Journal, 70*(2), 125–132.

Jackson, C. K., Porter, S., Easton, J., Blanchard, A., & Kiguel, S. (February 2020). *School effects on socio-emotional development, school-based arrests, and educational attainment* (Working Paper No. 226–0220; pp. 1–31). National Bureau of Economic Research.

Jayawickreme, E., Forgeard, M. J. C., & Seligman, M. E. P. (2012). The engine of well-being. *Review of General Psychology*, *16*(4), 327–342.

Jin, J., Mercer, S., Babic, S., & Mairitsch, A. (in press). Understanding the ecology of foreign language teacher wellbeing. In K. Budzińska & O. Majchrzak (Eds.), *Positive psychology in second and foreign language education*. Springer.

Kashdan, T. B., Biswas-Diener, R., & King, L. A. (2008). Reconsidering happiness: The costs of distinguishing between hedonics and eudaimonia. *The Journal of Positive Psychology*, *3*(4), 219–233.

King, R. B., McInerney, D. M., Ganotice, F. A., & Villarosa, J. B. (2015). Positive affect catalyzes academic engagement: Cross-sectional, longitudinal, and experimental evidence. *Learning and Individual Differences*, *39*, 64–72.

Keyes, C. L. M. (1998). Social well-being. *Social Psychology Quarterly*, *61*(2), 121–140.

Keyes, C. L. M., & Annas, J. (2009). Feeling good and functioning well: Distinctive concepts in ancient philosophy and contemporary science. *The Journal of Positive Psychology*, *4*(3), 197–201.

Levin, J. S., & Chatters, L. M. (1998). Religion, health, and psychological well-being in older adults: Findings from three national surveys. *Journal of Aging and Health*, *10*(4), 504–531.

Linton, M.-J., Dieppe, P., & Medina-Lara, A. (2016). Review of 99 self-report measures for assessing well-being in adults: Exploring dimensions of well-being and developments over time. *BMJ Open*, *6*(7), 1–16.

Lyubomirsky, S., King, L., & Diener, E. (2005). The benefits of frequent positive affect: Does happiness lead to success? *Psychological Bulletin*, *131*(6), 803–855.

MacIntyre, P. D., Gregersen, T., & Mercer, S. (2019a). Setting an agenda for positive psychology in SLA: Theory, practice, and research. *The Modern Language Journal*, *103*(1), 262–274.

MacIntyre, P. D., Gregersen, T., & Mercer, S. (2020). Language teachers' coping strategies during the Covid-19 conversion to online teaching: Correlations with stress, wellbeing and negative emotions. *System*, 1–31.

MacIntyre, P. D., Ross, J., Talbot, K., Mercer, S., Gregersen, T., & Banga, C. A. (2019b). Stressors, personality and wellbeing among language teachers. *System*, *82*, 26–38.

Martela, F., & Sheldon, K. M. (2019). Clarifying the concept of well-being: Psychological need satisfaction as the common core connecting eudaimonic and subjective well-being. *Review of General Psychology*, *23*(4), 458–474.

Maslow, A. H. (1954). The instinctoid nature of basic needs. *Journal of Personality*, *22*(3), 326–347.

Maslow, A. H. (1971). *The farther reaches of human nature*. Viking.

Mercer, S., & Gregersen, T. (2020). *Teacher wellbeing*. Oxford University Press.

Mercer, S., Oberdorfer, P., & Saleem, M. (2016). Helping language teachers to thrive: Using positive psychology to promote teachers' professional well-being. In D. Gabryś-Barker & D. Gałajda (Eds.), *Positive psychology perspectives on foreign language learning and teaching* (pp. 213–229). Springer.

Mercer, S., MacIntyre, P. D., Gregersen, T., & Talbot, K. R. (2018). Positive language education: Combining positive education and language education. *Theory and Practice of Second Language Acquisition*, *4*(2), 11–31.

Mercer, S., & Ryan, S. (2016). Stretching the boundaries: Language learning psychology. *Palgrave Communications*, *2*(1), 1–5.

Mercer, S., & Talbot, K. R. (2020). *Well-being as a complex dynamic system* [Manuscript in preparation].

Mercer, S., & Williams, M. (2014). *Multiple perspectives on the self in SLA*. Multilingual Matters.

Moate, J. M. (2011). The impact of foreign language mediated teaching on teachers' sense of professional integrity in the CLIL classroom. *European Journal of Teacher Education*, *34*(3), 333–346.

Noble, T., McGrath, H., Roffey, S., & Rowling, L. (2008). *A scoping study on student well-being*. Department of Education, Employment & Workplace Relations.

Noels, K. A., Vargas Lascano, D. I., & Saumure, K. (2019). The development of self-determination across the language course: Trajectories of motivational change and the dynamic interplay of psychological needs, orientations, and engagement. *Studies in Second Language Acquisition*, *41*(04), 821–851.

Norrish, J. M. (2015). *Positive education: The Geelong Grammar School journey*. Oxford University Press.

Norton, B. (2012). Identity and second language acquisition. In C. Chapelle (Ed.), *The encyclopedia of applied linguistics* (pp. 1–6). John Wiley & Sons, Inc.

Oxford, R. L. (2014). What we can learn about strategies, language learning, and life from two extreme cases: The role of well-being theory. *Studies in Second Language Learning and Teaching*, *4*(4), 593.

Oxford, R. L. (2016a). Toward a psychology of well-being for language learners: The "EMPATHICS" vision. In T. Gregersen, P. MacIntyre, & S. Mercer (Eds.), *Positive psychology and language learning*. Multilingual Matters.

Oxford, R. L. (2016b). Powerfully positive: Searching for a model of language learner well-being. In D. Gabryś-Barker & D. Gałajda (Eds.), *Positive psychology perspectives on foreign language learning and teaching* (pp. 21–37). Springer International Publishing.

Oxford, R. L., & Cuéllar, L. (2014). Positive psychology in cross-cultural learner narratives: Mexican students discover themselves while learning Chinese. *Studies in Second Language Learning and Teaching*, *4*(2), 173–203.

Nussbaum, M. C. (2003). Capabilities as fundamental entitlements: Sen and social justice. *Feminist Economics, 9*, 33–59.

Pavot, W., & Diener, E. (2008). The satisfaction with life scale and the emerging construct of life satisfaction. *The Journal of Positive Psychology, 3*(2), 137–152.

Pekrun, R., Goetz, T., Frenzel, A. C., Barchfeld, P., & Perry, R. P. (2011). Measuring emotions in students' learning and performance: The achievement emotions questionnaire (AEQ). *Contemporary Educational Psychology, 36*(1), 36–48.

Roorda, D. L., Koomen, H. M. Y., Spilt, J. L., & Oort, F. J. (2011). The influence of affective teacher–student relationships on students' school engagement and achievement: A meta-analytic approach. *Review of Educational Research, 81*(4), 493–529.

Ryan, R. M., & Deci, E. L. (2001). On happiness and human potentials: A review of research on hedonic and eudaimonic well-being. *Annual Review of Psychology, 52*(1), 141–166.

Ryff, C. D. (1989). Happiness is everything, or is it? Explorations on the meaning of psychological well-being. *Journal of Personality and Social Psychology, 57*(6), 1069–1081.

Ryff, C. D., & Singer, B. H. (2008). Know thyself and become what you are: A eudaimonic approach to psychological well-being. *Journal of Happiness Studies, 9*(1), 13–39.

Ryff, C. D., Singer, B. H., Dienberg Love, G., & Love, G. (2004). Positive health: Connecting well–being with biology. *Philosophical Transactions of the Royal Society of London. Series B: Biological Sciences, 359*(1449), 1383–1394.

Sammons, P., Day, C., Kington, A., Gu, Q., Stobart, G., & Smees, R. (2007). Exploring variations in teachers' work, lives and their effects on pupils: Key findings and implications from a longitudinal mixed-method study. *British Educational Research Journal, 33*(5), 681–701.

Seligman, M. E. P. (2011). *Flourish: A visionary new understanding of happiness and well-being*. Free Press.

Seligman, M. E. P., & Csíkszentmiályi, M. (Eds.) (2000). Positive psychology [Special issue]. *American Psychologist, 55*.

Seligman, M. E. P., Ernst, R. M., Gillham, J., Reivich, K., & Linkins, M. (2009). Positive education: Positive psychology and classroom interventions. *Oxford Review of Education, 35*(3), 293–311.

Sen, A. K. (1992). *Inequality reexamined*. Clarendon Press.

Simon, C. R., & Durand-Bush, N. (2015). Does self-regulation capacity predict psychological well-being in physicians? *Psychology, Health & Medicine, 20*(3), 311–321.

Sin, N. L., & Lyubomirsky, S. (2009). Enhancing well-being and alleviating depressive symptoms with positive psychology interventions: A practice-friendly meta-analysis. *Journal of Clinical Psychology, 65*(5), 467–487.

Subramaniam, K., Kounios, J., Parrish, T. B., & Jung-Beeman, M. (2009). A brain mechanism for facilitation of insight by positive affect. *Journal of Cognitive Neuroscience, 21*(3), 415–432.

Talbot, K. R., Gruber, M.-T., Lämmerer, A., Hofstadler, N., & Mercer, S. (in press). Comparatively speaking: CLIL/EMI teacher well-being at the primary, secondary and tertiary levels in Austria. In K. R. Talbot, M.-T. Gruber, & R. Nishida (Eds.), *The psychological experience of integrating language and content*. Multilingual Matters.

Talbot, K. R., Gruber, M.-T., & Nishida, R. (Eds.). (2021). *The psychological experience of integrating content and language*. Multilingual Matters.

Talbot, K. R., & Mercer, S. (2018). Exploring university ESL/EFL teachers' emotional well-being and emotional regulation in the United States, Japan and Austria. *Chinese Journal of Applied Linguistics, 41*(4), 410–432.

Talbot, K. R., & Mercer, S. (2020). Language teacher well-being [Manuscript submitted for publication]. In H. Mohebbi & C. Coombe (Eds.), *Research questions in language education: A reference guide for teachers*.

Waterman, A. S. (2008). Reconsidering happiness: A eudaimonist's perspective. *The Journal of Positive Psychology, 3*(4), 234–252.

Watson, D., Clark, L. A., & Tellegen, A. (1988). Development and validation of brief measures of positive and negative affect: The PANAS scales. *Journal of Personality and Social Psychology, 54*(6), 1063–1070.

Zee, M., & Koomen, H. M. Y. (2016). Teacher self-efficacy and its effects on classroom processes, student academic adjustment, and teacher well-being: A synthesis of 40 years of research. *Review of Educational Research, 86*(4), 981–1015.

16
RESILIENCE

Phil Hiver and Ana Clara Sánchez Solarte

One of the central tenets of developmental perspectives is that human life, and learning, is an often-unpredictable journey: In addition to moments of satisfaction and highlights of triumph, it presents challenges, disappointments, and even hardships. This is even clearer at the turn of a new decade in which increasing numbers of humans aspire to live life "on the edge," while countless others grapple with sociopolitical disadvantage, marginalization, or exclusion. Language education, arguably, mirrors these conditions. For many individuals, language learning contributes in important ways to positive self-fulfillment and engagement with the world more broadly (Hiver, Al-Hoorie, & Mercer, 2021). Equally, however, the physical and psychological energy and resources that language learning requires can be accompanied by an immense pressure to perform, the stress of high-stakes assessments, struggles to persist, and setbacks and failures along the road to language development (Yun, Hiver, & Al-Hoorie, 2018).

Because human life and learning within that lifespan features such highs and lows, a major part of growth from childhood to maturity involves building the skills to face such difficult events and circumstances. There are many general factors in psychology literature (e.g., coping, hardiness, optimism, persistence) that contribute to long-term functioning and the overcoming of odds, and, in this chapter, we explore the most prominent of these: resilience. *Resilience* is the capacity to withstand and recover from experiences of psychological adversity or to maintain effective functioning despite adverse circumstances (Masten, 2001). In this chapter, we provide an overview of the construct of resilience, beginning with definitional issues and the research that it has inspired in educational circles. We then turn to how resilience might relate specifically to language learning through a review of relevant work on the topic and examine the insights that might be integrated into our field's understanding of resilience. We then think through the lessons from resilience research for our own field, and end with some directions to realize the potential of resilience for language education in the new decade.

Resilience in Psychology

The foundations of resilience research were set in the early work (circa the 1970s and 80s) of developmental psychologists studying the origins of mental illness and behavioral problems in children raised in extreme physical, emotional, and psychological deprivation (see, e.g., Masten, Best, & Garmezy,

1990 for a review). What emerged from these researchers' work surprised them: Many high-risk children faced with extreme deprivation or threats to their development were in fact thriving in ways that defied the researchers' expectations. Several key "lessons" emerged from psychologists' ongoing work on resilience, which proved instrumental in moving the field of psychology toward positive frameworks that illustrate how human development is robust and adaptive in the face of adversity.

Lesson 1: Resilience is a Powerful Individual Capacity

Early work to define and operationalize resilience was concerned with discovering the unique characteristics that differentiate individuals who thrive when challenged with adversity from those who succumb to threatening circumstances (see Lipsitt & Demick, 2012 for one review). This exploratory work systematically described the (a) attributes of resilient individuals, (b) aspects of their relationships with significant others, and (c) characteristics of their wider social-cultural environments (see, e.g., Richardson, 2002 for a review). Emergent from this work is a clear picture of resilience as a robust adaptive capacity for individuals to maintain a positive outcome despite the occurrence of traumatic experiences—the *sustaining* aspect of resilience (Luthar, Chiccetti, & Becker, 2000)—as well as the ability of individuals to bounce back from such challenges—the *recovery* aspect of resilience (Windle, 2011).

There are two major dimensions to this understanding of resilience. The first concerns the existence of a threat or a risk: Individuals are not thought of as resilient unless they have encountered a significant risk or have had to grapple with a threat to their normal functioning. Masten (2001) calls this half of the resilience equation "demonstrable risk" (p. 228), and in the decades preceding the discovery of resilience, there was no shortage of psychology research specifying such risk factors (Chiccetti & Garmezy, 1993). The other dimension is the positive adaptation aspect, whether external (e.g., the absence of substance abuse or delinquency) or internal (e.g., psychological well-being) (Luthar et al., 2000). Resilient individuals, in this sense, are those who effectively adapt or achieve a positive outcome despite encountering a demonstrable risk or threat (Hu, Zhang, & Wang, 2015).

Lesson 2: Resilience Develops as an Adaptive and Dynamic Process in Context

Resilience researchers quickly recognized that identifying the factors that help individuals turn adversity into advantage was crucial, but also that approaching resilience as an adaptive developmental process would allow them to understand exactly how and why resilient individuals achieve this outcome of effective functioning despite traumatic events (Chiccetti, 2010). Contrary to the early paradigm of individualism, scholars realized that environments counted much more for developing resilience than initially thought, perhaps even more than individual capacity (Luthar, 2006). It soon became clear that positive adaptation resulting in resilience was a function of the person in dynamic interaction with their environment. The wave of resilience research that this understanding inspired saw psychologists begin to study resilience as a process involving a dynamic interaction of psychological and social factors in particular environments, thereby enabling individuals to successfully resolve or adapt to risks and threats (Wright, Masten, & Narayan, 2013).

This understanding of resilience is more inclusive as it proposes multiple pathways to resilience. It also sees the individual as an active participant in an adaptive developmental process in context and across time, with prior experiences and interactions shaping the organization of this protective functioning (Bonanno, 2004). Clear implications for prevention and intervention emerged from this developmental perspective. Through this focus on the mechanisms underlying resilient functioning, researchers began to study how to engineer the conditions for resilience to develop, for instance, by increasing the balance of protective factors over risk factors (Hu et al., 2015). The consensus in most current theorizing is that the development of this self-righting and steeling capacity is the result of fundamental systems for human development and adaptation operating normally, and that it can be found in every human to varying degrees at various times in one's life span (Reich, Zautra, & Hall, 2010).

Lesson 3: Resilience Depends on "Ordinary Magic"

Although there are conditions under which, arguably, no human can thrive, resilience is all around us. The design of initial studies on the development of resilience implied that successful adaptation in the face of debilitating circumstances was an extraordinary capacity, but this perspective was soon questioned when researchers realized that resilience was much more common than they first assumed (Masten, 2001). There is surprising heterogeneity in humans' adaptive response to various psychological and environmental hazards, and this can be seen, for example, in how many approaches to parenting advocate some exposure to challenges and risks as indispensable for learning to successfully navigate or counter them (Rutter, 2012). Contrary to very early work, psychologists now recognize that resilience does not require extraordinary resources, and, in most cases, arises more or less naturally from the interaction of adaptive systems that foster and protect human development and psychological recovery. The expanding research agenda for resilience emphasizes the surprisingly widespread occurrence of resilience (Chiccetti, 2010). Masten has termed this "ordinary magic" (2009) to show that resilience is the result of powerful, yet fundamental, cognitive, social, and emotional adaptive mechanisms that afford individuals with learning and problem-solving capacities, as well as the motivation to adapt and recover from hardship.

Lesson 4: Resilience is Responsive to Intervention and can be Promoted

The overarching mission of those studying resilience has always been to understand risk and protective factors well enough to intervene in ways that deliberately promote positive development (Masten, 2001). In a sense, resilience research has been the spearhead of a more positive approach to psychology that exists to engineer strengths and protective processes, and to promote competence, adaptation, and thriving. This has been realized most prominently in studies designed to identify and assess tools for developing positive resources, adaptive behavior, and gains in developmentally appropriate skills and competencies (Joyce, Shand, Tighe, Laurent, Bryant, & Harvey, 2018). Evidence has also grown that strategic timing is important, and that there may be windows of opportunity in development where the leverage for building resilience is at its highest. Another "take-away" from this body of work is the central role significant others (family members, peers, teachers, mentors) play in nurturing all the tools of resilience. Resilience, thus, relies on gaining human capital along with social capital and marshalling these both in adaptive responses to challenges and crises. From this work has emerged frameworks to define positive goals; boost assets, strengths, and outcomes; and provide strategies to reduce risk, increase resources, and mobilize adaptive systems (Masten, 2009).

Much of this work suggests reducing risk as the first lever in any intervention to develop resilience. Along with this, many see increasing assets and resources, or the effectiveness of existing resources, as crucial to counterbalancing risk factors. Finally, there is an array of powerful protective systems ranging from cognitive to emotional and individual to relational that can facilitate a resilient response to crisis or adversity (Wilkes, 2002). Resilience intervention research shows that, among other things, resilience can be deliberately formed by establishing positive attachments with nurturing and competent caregivers; initiating relationships and prosocial networks of friends and partners; seeking out supportive services from effective community institutions; building positive self-perceptions and self-efficacy (see Chapter 8); fostering active coping strategies; developing self-regulation skills (see Chapter 17) needed to be autonomous and goal-oriented; and seeking a sense of broader meaning in life (e.g., Masten & Wright, 2010; Wright et al., 2013).

As might be expected from such a vibrant topic of research that spans many subdomains of psychology, there are still unresolved questions in resilience research (Reich et al., 2010). For example, there is some debate over whether resilience constructs can be generalized and directly applied from developmental psychology to other areas of human development and learning (e.g., education), whether resilience manifests itself similarly or disparately across cultural groups and contexts, whether positive adaptation occurs across all spheres of life, or whether resilience constitutes a onetime or a continuous and cumulative phenomenon. In response to ongoing debates in this area, some scholars have highlighted the need to refine existing conceptualizations of resilience (Windle, 2011). One reason for this relates to the nature of risk and the extent of adversity: Resilience has typically been associated with acute and chronic adversities, but may also apply equally well to individuals who are faced with more routine hassles, setbacks, challenges, and pressures that are part of the ordinary course of life.

Next to one's family, school may be the most important social environment for most developing humans. Resilience, some believe, is the ultimate aim of education (Pajares, 2009), and because of their central role in children's development, educational settings have enormous potential to promote resilience. In the next section, we turn to reviewing how resilience relates specifically to language learning through a review of relevant work on the topic.

Resilience in Second Language Learning

Definitions of Resilience for L2 Learning and Use

Resilience and other positive character strengths have gained recent attention in second language learning research due to their potential to influence learners' success (MacIntyre, Gregersen, & Mercer, 2019). One of the more prominent frameworks for incorporating such insights into second language learning is Oxford's (2016b) EMPATHICS model. This framework draws explicit ties between psychology and second language learning, while providing a framework to work with constructs, such as resilience, that "positively influence language learners' achievement and proficiency" (Oxford, 2016a, p. 26). Resilience in Oxford's (2016b) EMPATHICS model is defined as the capacity to face and recover from adversity; contributing to this capacity are aspects such as self-efficacy, emotional positivity, productive goal orientations, ethics, a sense of meaning, compassionate relationships, and opportunities for participation (Oxford, 2016b). Learning how such character strengths interact, evolve, and affect each other may be key to supporting learners through their daily struggles of language learning and fostering both recovery from setbacks and continued resistance to new ones.

Others working on resilience in the field of language learning have offered their own definitions (e.g., Kim & Kim, 2017). Resilience is understood by these scholars as a multifaceted construct made up of different adaptive capacities that enable an individual to recover from hardship and succeed in spite of it. The multidimensionality of resilience in second language learning is evident when considering the individual learner factors (Chen & Padilla, 2019), teacher characteristics (Chaffee, Noels, & McEown, 2014) and teaching practices in the L2 classroom (Dunn, Bundy, & Woodrow, 2012), and the contexts of instruction (Padrón, Waxman, Brown, & Powers, 2000) and social environments (Waxman, Rivera, & Powers, 2012) that have been found to feed into it. These various studies also suggest, as with resilience from psychology more broadly, that resilience develops as a dynamic process, that it may change through time, and that it is susceptible to being altered.

Conceptually, resilience develops from major adversity or extreme threats to development during the course of language learning (Kim & Kim, 2017), a feature that differentiates it from its cognate character strengths buoyancy and hardiness. Buoyancy is more relevant to everyday problems and difficulties that interrupt learners' motivation and engagement in the learning process by threatening their self-confidence and persistence (Yun, Hiver, & Al-Hoorie, 2018). The capacity to overcome these hassles and setbacks in the course of language learning (e.g., buoyancy) can be seen as a precursor for resilience, given that the ability to face everyday nuisances can equip an individual to deal with more adverse developmental events (Yun, Hiver, & Al-Hoorie, 2018). Hardiness, by contrast, is a personality disposition that can moderate the impact of chronic stressors on mental and physical health (Maddi, 2004), for example, through positive cognitive appraisals. Hardiness, thus, precedes resilience as it improves short-term performance, uses stress as a positive force, and fosters the development of creativity and adaptivity (Maddi, 2005). The differences lie in the scope and scale: "resilience is the ability to spring back from adversity, while hardiness is the existential courage to do so" (Oxford, Acuña, Hernández, & Smith, 2015, p. 103).

Research associated with resilience in second language learning and use is twofold. The first strand of resilience research focuses on the characteristics of individuals and works to identify and describe factors that interact with resilience, and by extension to devise and implement interventions that foster resilience in L2 classroom contexts. We should note that the deliberate emphasis in this chapter is on learners, but a great deal of work has also been done with teachers (see, e.g., Hiver, 2018). In a larger sense, resilience has also been studied as part of "broader humanitarian, refugee, and development contexts" (Capstick, 2018, p. 201). One example of this is the ongoing *Language for Resilience* project spearheaded by the British Council and the United Nations (Capstick & Delaney, 2016). In these contexts, resilience is used as a lens to study how groups of language users adapt as languages either shift and disappear, or are revitalized and thrive.

Resilience in Formal L2 Learning Contexts

One line of research examines the behavior of resilient and non-resilient learners in formal instruction—specifically, English Language Learners (ELs) and their challenges in such classroom environments (Padrón et al., 2000; Rivera & Waxman, 2011; Waxman et al., 2012)—and highlights the importance of context in resilience. These studies draw on a range of data from linguistic and cultural minority students to uncover threats to the learners' resilience in these settings. Among other things, this work demonstrates that the predominant teacher-directed instructional model, characterized by mechanical drills and repetition instead of more cooperative learning, lowers resilience in ELs because it encourages a passive role and an external focus on preparing for state-mandated tests. These studies also showed that teachers are able to effectively identify resilient and non-resilient learners, but that they rarely act upon this information while adhering to such teacher-directed practices, and that teaching was more top-down even though cooperative learning was identified as an effective strategy for non-resilient students. These findings underscore the role of educators and their classroom pedagogical practices in fostering resilience among ELs.

In their study focused on identifying differences among resilient and non-resilient learners, Padrón et al. (2000) found that resilient ELs in elementary schools had a more positive perception of the learning environment, displayed more satisfaction with reading and language arts classrooms, used effective cognitive strategies more frequently, and had less difficulty with classwork than their non-resilient peers. Resilient students also had a tendency to speak the heritage language (Spanish) more frequently at home and with friends, had a more positive relationship with their teachers, and exhibited fewer problematic behaviors at school. In summarizing the findings of this line of research with Hispanic ELs, Waxman et al. (2012) observed that "while student success and failure in school is dependent upon a number of influential determinants, it appears that the classroom learning environment and students' classroom behavior are contributing factors" (p. 66) due to their strong link to resilience formation.

The joint role of the educational context and teachers in fostering or hindering L2 learner resilience is also a part of previous studies. For instance, Chaffee et al. (2014) examined the resilience of undergraduate language learners when confronted with an instructor they perceived as controlling and authoritarian, among several other factors influencing students' learning outcomes. These scholars found that working with autonomy-supportive instructors and autonomy-supportive environments resulted in positive resilience outcomes, and that language learners' strategic positive reappraisals of events and of the environment, when the instructor was controlling, supported their resilience.

Students who used positive reappraisals strategically displayed high energy towards the language class and low classroom anxiety, and reported greater self-determined motivation. This work shows that learner characteristics and the learning context can interact to foster resilience and that one can diminish the harmful effect of the other on resilience. In secondary school L3 learning, Chen and Padilla (2019) investigated the link between resilience, emotions, creativity, and motivation. Their findings indicate that positive emotions and creativity were moderately associated with resilience for additional language learning, while, not surprisingly, negative emotions were negatively related to resilience. The authors propose that promoting positive emotions and fostering a positive classroom environment in such settings strengthens the language learners' response to the challenges they encounter throughout the learning process.

The relationship between resilience and subsequent motivation for language learning has also been of interest (Kim & Kim, 2017; Kim, Kim, & Kim, 2017, 2019). These studies set out to determine the components of resilience in compulsory language classrooms and to identify its effect on L2 motivation among elementary school and undergraduate students. The authors reported that constituents of resilience include metacognitive adaptation, sociability, optimism, perseverance, and communicative efficacy (Kim, Kim, & Kim, 2019), and that resilience had an important impact on the learners' motivation. In turn, motivation and demotivation influenced the learners' L2 proficiency (see Chapter 10). In secondary school L2 English classroom settings (Kim & Kim, 2017), the resilience factors identified were happiness, empathy, sociability, persistence, and self-regulation. For these scholars, persistence emerged as the most important predictor of motivated L2 learning behavior and L2 proficiency. Interestingly, Kim, Kim, and Kim (2019) found that learners' demotivation increased with their exposure to teaching, and was influenced by unsupportive teachers in an unsupportive environment. This finding mirrors Kim and Kim's (2017) results and confirms that the context of instruction plays an important role in building resilience for language learning.

Resilience in L2 Communities

Fitzgerald (2017) and Tse (2001) position their work as part of the second strand of research and advocate the importance of maintaining and developing heritage languages (HL), while also exploring the factors that contribute to or minimize those processes in L2 communities. Tse (2001) focused on language resilience in multilingual homes across the United States in which "over 14 percent of children ages five to seventeen live in homes where languages other than English are spoken" (p. 676). These learners face a cross-generational language shift from speaking the HL at home while learning the majority language, to displaying high levels of majority-language English that corresponds with more restricted HL use at home, to having a third generation of speakers who use English exclusively due to little or no knowledge of the HL. The reality for many bi/multilinguals is one where there is a lack of validation (or deliberate marginalization) of the HL, resulting in limited opportunities to interact in it and scarce affordances for learning it, all of which undermine the HL resilience. Tse (2001) drew on language histories and showed that resilience was linked to language vitality (i.e., individuals' perceptions of the native language and its prestige), and the literacy environment (i.e., usefulness of the native language and exposure to its use at home and in the community). The support of peers, family, and institutions was also notable in helping these learners develop HL proficiency and resilience. Tse (2001) proposes that concerted efforts at the institutional level, and the provision of experiences where the HL is legitimized, are needed to foster HL resilience.

Fitzgerald (2017) echoed these views and highlighted the need for a resilience-based framework to support language vitality and revitalization in the face of maladaptive language shifts (e.g., shifting from a multilingual community to a monolingual community in a few short generations). Implied in this work is the notion that language shift and language loss are embedded in other more damaging processes (e.g., loss of land, culture, and sovereignty), and that the resilience of indigenous groups and language revitalization act as protective factors for individuals in the group. To enhance language resilience, Fitzgerald (2017) advocates immersive language education and language reclamation, both of which go beyond deliberate minority language use and involve the restoration of a community's well-being "where significant disparities otherwise exist" (p. 292). As the *Language for Resilience* project illustrates, the resilience of languages is a focal area that is unique to SLA. From this view of language resilience, language is the key to unlocking broader positive changes in a community that can result in increased well-being among members of a community and build its capacity for thriving (see Chapter 25).

Resilience Interventions with L2 Learners

The body of research we have reviewed above is a constant reminder that resilience is not merely a quality that some lucky students have to help them navigate the challenges of language learning. Instead, resilience is a dynamic capacity susceptible to growth and enhancement through deliberate action in educational environments. Research on resilience interventions with L2 learners is still rare. Notable interventions used to enhance resilience among language learners include strategies related to storytelling (Nguyen, Stanley, Stanley, & Wang, 2015) and immersive drama (Dunn, Bundy, & Woodrow, 2012). Storytelling is a deliberate technique that can foster the resilience of foreign language learners in new international settings who must deal with particular challenges as part of their experience abroad (Nguyen et al., 2015). Adult L2 learners who used storytelling found that it contributed to their sensemaking in novel social and cultural contexts and led to resilience among those adults who adopted this strategy. Ultimately, it seems that the process of remembering childhood stories and prior experiences of overcoming challenges and adverse circumstances indeed helped adult learners cope with the challenges associated with their ongoing L2 learning.

Resilience transcends the classroom walls because language and the capacity to persist in learning can have a more profound and more sustained impact on people's lives. This is seen, for example, in interventions that incorporate language learning as part of a broader humanitarian response (Capstick, 2018). Dunn et al. (2012) report how drama pedagogy has been used to foster the resilience of recently arrived refugee children in Australia. Language lessons in this setting were structured around a character who did not speak English, but wanted to communicate with the children. The narrative elements of the drama, supported by rich visuals and digital technology, enhanced the learners' opportunities for contextualized vocabulary learning, spurred interaction in the L2 through various modalities, and reinforced prior L2 learning. The researchers also reported that because of this drama intervention, an enjoyable atmosphere was created in the classroom and even reluctant students were more willing to participate in the lesson and achieve their L2 learning goals (Dunn et al., 2012).

There is still too little intervention work in the field to offer a systematic review. At this stage, however, it is clear that resilient learners draw on a clear sense of purpose, are goal-oriented and autonomous, display social competence and adaptive problem-solving skills, and as a result are more satisfied with their classroom learning experiences and have a stronger academic self-concept. As a general takeaway, we feel that not only is there tremendous potential for future resilience intervention work with L2 learners, but also that L2 teachers are important agents in promoting learners' resilience through their instructional practices, their attitudes towards learners, and their actual interactions with students (Waxman, Gray, & Padrón, 2003).

Resilience and Language Teachers

A final body of research has connected the life, work, and experience of language teachers by examining the contextual realities of classroom practice and exploring ways to maximize language teacher psychological well-being, effectiveness, and self-reliance (Hiver, 2017; MacIntyre, Ross, Talbot, Gregersen, Mercer & Banga, 2019). Teacher resilience offers a way to investigate the attitudes and behaviors of language teachers within the context of their work and professional lives, and sheds light on how they maintain their commitment, motivation, and engagement (Hiver, 2018; Hiver & Dörnyei, 2017). In the context of teaching, resilience is "the capacity to maintain equilibrium" in the face of adversity while using all the resources available in a productive way to achieve learning success with students (Gu & Day, 2013). Resilient teachers have high self-efficacy (see Chapter 8) and use active coping strategies, possess the meta-cognition and self-regulation skills (see Chapter 17) needed to be autonomous (see Chapter 19) and goal-oriented, are altruistic and possess a sense of purpose in life, and have positive self-perceptions and an optimistic disposition (Mansfield, Beltman, Broadley, & Wetherby-Fell, 2016). Additionally, they build positive relationships with competent and nurturing colleagues and superiors, seek out friends and partners who are supportive, and use the support and attachment of social networks in their professional lives. A variety of personal and social or professional factors can enhance or inhibit the extent to which teachers acquire these resilient qualities, and as teacher resilience manifests itself in response to situational demands it can develop and change continuously with emerging conditions or contexts (Kostoulas & Lämmerer, 2018).

While the research on language teacher resilience is still just taking off, the broader implication from this research is that teacher resilience plays an important role in maximizing students' well-being, progress, and achievement (Mercer, Oberdorfer, & Saleem, 2016). Research into academic resilience has shown that the capacity for resilience in students is linked to prosocial behavior and peer acceptance (see Chapter 25), school attendance, class participation and perseverance, self-efficacy, motivation and aspirations, and ultimately, long-term academic success (see, e.g., Hiver, 2018). Because the teacher is the hub of a classroom, their resilience can be defining, and students cannot be expected to develop resilience if their teachers do not exhibit this ability themselves. Educators who want their students to develop the capacity to successfully adjust to challenging circumstances and overcome setbacks and failures must first develop resilience themselves (Hiver, 2017).

Integration

While work on resilience in education and language learning cannot come close to the sheer quantity of resilience research in various domains of psychology, the definitions and frameworks for understanding resilience from psychology have been well integrated into language learning and teaching. Insights that have not yet found cross-discipline transfer are those related to the scale and target of study, as well as the scope of resilience as unitary and focused or systemic and cross-cutting in nature. First, when speaking about resilience in groups or communities versus the individuals that make them up, the issue of scale must be dealt with. Resilience work in language education so far has remained focused on the individual. However, because much of language learning and use occurs relationally and in groups, there are also more collective forms of resilience worth investigating. Resilient groups are not necessarily made of resilient individuals when those individuals are viewed in isolation. Instead, a highly resilient group or community may be one that is robust and adaptive in spite of the significant vulnerability of some of its members. This is a notion that is perhaps implicit in the language learning work on the topic but that has not yet been integrated into a clear understanding of individual-level resilience versus collective resilience. The capacity to maintain current stability (i.e., robustness) and the capacity to transform part of current functioning (i.e., adaptability) in a group or at the collective level is qualitatively different when thinking about those same categories in the individual. Scaling up the level of granularity in resilience thinking may result in trade-offs (e.g., less exclusive focus on the individual), but it is also likely to result in empowering marginalized groups, instituting new ethical structures of responsibility, and promoting social justice in language learning and use.

Second, the field of language learning has taken its cues from early waves of resilience research in psychology in treating resilience as unitary rather than as a systemic phenomenon (i.e., a property of an integrated system), and in focusing on the individual agent who has resilience rather than seeing the concepts of transformation and adaptability as cutting across societies and institutions and meeting the needs of such organizational equilibrium. Increasingly, resilience has come be understood holistically as part of a system—a collection of connected parts interacting together to form a state or outcome, or to produce some behavior (see, e.g., Ungar, 2012 for a detailed introduction). For instance, in this day and age, there is no shortage of media concern about resilient cities and communities that are able to rebound from natural disasters, resilient economies that can resist a spectrum of changes and crises, or resilient ecosystems that can maintain stability and recover their initial equilibrium. The ideas of resistance, stability, and adaptation would benefit from this more holistic lens and would recalibrate work in the field of language learning around this idea of resilience as an integrated property of complex adaptive systems—taking time, context, and proactive agency into account.

Implications for Practice and Research

The nature of resilience and its potential value for L2 learners' and their success in language learning and use underscore the need to be deliberate in searching for ways to link resilience to practice. Studies we reviewed above indicate three high-leverage strands that might be used to address this need: institutions, teachers, and targeted intervention strategies.

We suggested earlier that resilience is a relational construct, which implies that resilience development requires more than well-meaning effort from individual teachers. First and foremost, the implication of this is that schools, classrooms, and their structures play an active role in creating a resilience-conducive environment by endorsing policies that minimize learners' exposure to risks and provide the professional support teachers need to promote students' resources for resilience. The inclusion of resilience building in L2 learning curricula can be augmented by involving families and communities to increase protective factors (e.g., interpersonal relationships). In addition, institutions can engineer the conditions for more bottom-up and emergent resilience development by fostering warm, respectful connections between students, teachers, and parents; by communicating and enabling realistic, consistent expectations for behavior and performance; and by mobilizing resources that maximize the benefits of supportive learning environments and classroom practices.

Second, teachers also play a pivotal role in simultaneously helping students tackle their L2 learning tasks and facilitating resilience (see Chapter 21). From deliberately reducing unnecessary stressors for learners, to encouraging learners to accept and reframe challenges, to giving them the opportunity to experience success and meaningful rapport within the classroom, teachers are in a powerful position to shape their L2 learners' trajectory and resources to face adverse situations. Given the prominence of teachers' roles in developing resilience, a more proactive stance may be needed to effectively identify resilient and non-resilient students, deliberately attempt to intervene by limiting or preventing risks to them, and introduce changes in the L2 classroom structure that provide accommodations for learners developing resilience. Practices that have proven effective in enhancing learning opportunities among at-risk students include providing relevant constructive feedback, conveying clear goals and expectations, adopting a culturally and linguistically responsive stance to instruction, and ensuring that teachers can develop and model their own resilience for learners.

Third, L2 classrooms offer enough flexibility in their content and organization to include tasks infused with components of resilience. Targeted intervention strategies such as drama and storytelling can be effectively implemented in L2 lessons to take a dual resilience-building and language-development approach with various language learners and users at different levels. Drama, for instance, affords learners the opportunity to distance themselves from the characters being played while using them to create stories, practice language in context, strengthen their competence in the language, and share engaging experiences. Storytelling may also assist learners in affirming their identity as they step back and reframe their learning experience so far. L2 learners can articulate milestones in their language development process and acknowledge strategies used in the past to bounce back. What these targeted strategies have in common is their non-threatening quality, while still being used deliberately to engineer resilience through language classroom activities.

With regard to implications for research, we can also think of three broad issues to guide more detailed questions or programs of research. First, the field would need to establish whether resilience for L2 learning exists as a special case of this generalized protective factor or if it is a genuinely domain-specific strength. This has implications for the tools, measurements, and frameworks used in resilience research, as was once the case with other constructs (e.g., L2 aptitude, L2 anxiety) that are known to have language learning-specific dimensions. Future work will need to tackle this empirical question and the downstream implications of whether or not there is a substantive difference in risk factors, protective factors, and developmental mechanisms for the field of language learning.

Second, the dynamic and context-dependent nature of resilience is widely recognized, and researchers will need to consider how resilience can be studied in ways that do justice to its situated and dynamic nature (see e.g., Hiver & Al-Hoorie, 2020). This has implications for research designs and models for explaining empirical findings. For instance, if resilience is being studied as a collective, societal, or institutional phenomenon, then a group level design may be appropriate. However, if it is the individual and how they develop and deploy resilience that concerns us, we would need an individual design. Depending on the purpose of the research too, we could imagine studies that are confirmatory or exploratory, and adopt a qualitative, quantitative, or mixed and multimethod approach.

Finally, given what we have said about the potential for further intervention work with individuals and communities of language learning and use, the field will need to work to establish what constitutes empirically sound and ecologically effective resilience intervention. Particularly, if resilience is something that emerges as part of adaptation in the course of ordinary development, the role of teachers and others in deliberately trying to engineer that outcome for learners is open to question. Because no consensual methodological training framework exists to guide the application of such a language resilience program, it would also have to be responsive to the contextual demands of each particular setting and to the needs of the individual learners or community of language use.

Future Directions

As we have hinted earlier, one future direction for our field would be to recalibrate the focus of resilience on communities and institutions (i.e., not exclusively on individuals) by taking a more systemic perspective. Systems research is informed by complexity and dynamic systems theory (CDST) and has begun to permeate much of the field (Hiver & Al-Hoorie, 2020) (see Chapter 4). Anything can be studied as part of a complex adaptive system; systems are subject-neutral. Studying resilience using insights from this framework of complex adaptive systems (e.g., Kostoulas & Lämmerer, 2018) will bring time, context, and proactive agency into sharper focus, and enable the field of language learning to rethink success and failure, conceive of responsiveness to feedback in new, more holistic ways, aim for transformative learning and sustainability, and equip learners to embrace change and maximize cycles of adaptability. Adopting a systemic lens will also allow the field to pursue a second future direction, namely, to focus on how language learning can develop language competence while simultaneously enhancing learners' resilience. This will be especially important in settings where multilingualism coincides with conflict of one sort or another, and where language learners for one reason or another (e.g., minority language users in a monolingual society) also experience disadvantage, marginalization, or exclusion (Capstick, 2018).

Many studies outside our field have examined the benefits of resilience training among various specific groups of people (see, e.g., Joyce et al., 2018 for a review). To this list, in a few years' time, we imagine being able to add language learners. While the training programs in fields outside of language education typically share the common aim of enhancing resilience or resilience resources, they tend to differ greatly in terms of content, delivery, and length. The future direction we would advocate is to take an embedded approach in which resilience training is interwoven *with* or embedded *in* language education. Poorly designed language education can erode or accelerate the erosion of learners' resilience. Consequently, the guiding principles or objectives for such language education programs would be to enhance the robustness of learners' functioning in and through language and build their adaptive capacity by channeling language education as a pathway to resilience and well-being (e.g., MacIntyre et al., 2019a). In addition to externally-directed interventions, more self-organized forms of development are part of resilience building as well. As work outside of language education shows, resilience can be driven by internal growth mechanisms, provided learners are presented with the necessary environmental conditions and psychological resources to draw on for this transformational process. Consequently, a major agenda for future work, in addition to studying ways to overtly engineer resilience, will be to uncover how to enable and accelerate learners' active resilience formation in particular environments.

Reflection Questions

- The twenty-first century is marked by transnational mobility, growing multilingualism and cross-cultural interactions, and rising global civic literacy and activism. Against the backdrop of these developments, how do individuals' experiences of language learning and use contribute (or not) to learners' resilience?
- Resilience is thought to arise more or less naturally from the interaction of adaptive recovery systems that foster and protect individual or group development, which Ann Masten terms "ordinary magic." Within this surprisingly common process, what is the contribution of teachers, caretakers, and peers? What role might language learning and use with these relationally important individuals play in this process?
- Taking a more holistic "systemic" perspective, how can groups, classrooms, communities, and institutions that are part of language education help foster learners' language development while simultaneously enhancing their resilience?

Recommended Reading

Gillham, J., Abenavoli, R., Brunwasser, S., Linkins, M., Reivich, K., & Seligman, M. (2013). Resilience education. In S. David, I. Boniwell, & A. Conley Ayers (Eds.), *The Oxford handbook of happiness* (pp. 609–630). Oxford University Press.
The authors of this chapter advance the argument that schools have the responsibility not only of educating learners from the neck up, but also of preparing fully-functioning and resilient individuals. They propose that resilience education is indispensable in contemporary societies where the number of children exposed to adversity in some form (violence, poverty, mental health issues, neglect, emotional or physical abuse) is steadily increasing. Their chapter explores how resilience education is relevant to all students, applicable to a range of challenges, and consistent with the broader aims of educational systems worldwide.

Masten, A. (2001). Ordinary magic: Resilience processes in development. *American Psychologist, 56*, 227–238.
In her seminal article on the topic (cited nearly 9,000 times), Ann Masten defines and traces the genesis of resilience research, highlighting the extent to which resilience has influenced the rest of psychology. She examines conclusions drawn from existing resilience research and its contribution to an integrative understanding of human adaptivity. She proposes understanding resilience as an adaptive system and looking at multiple facets of human development in tandem to push the area forward. This article is a good start for newcomers.

Rutter, M. (2012). Resilience as a dynamic concept. *Development and Psychopathology, 24*, 335–344.
In this review article, Michael Rutter examines nine features that characterize resilience research as distinctive from other overlapping areas of psychology research. He outlines the ways in which resilience research builds on and contributes to knowledge in developmental psychology and associated subdomains of psychology. This article is a good in-depth read for researchers interested in empirical issues related to resilience.

References

Bonanno, G. (2004). Loss, trauma, and human resilience: Have we underestimated the human capacity to thrive after extremely aversive events? *American Psychologist, 59*, 20–28.
Capstick, T. (2018). Key concepts in ELT: Resilience. *ELT Journal, 7*(2), 210–213.
Capstick, T., & Delaney, M. (2016). *Language for resilience: The role of language in enhancing the resilience of Syrian refugees and host communities.* British Council.
Chaffee, K. E., Noels, K. A., & McEown, M. S. (2014). Learning from authoritarian teachers: Controlling the situation or controlling yourself can sustain motivation. *Studies in Second Language Learning and Teaching, 4*(2), 355–387.
Chen, X., & Padilla, A. M. (2019). Emotions and creativity as predictors of resilience among L3 learners in the Chinese educational context. *Current Psychology*, 1–11.
Chiccetti, D. (2010). Resilience under conditions of extreme stress: A multilevel perspective. *World Psychiatry, 9*, 145–154.
Chiccetti, D., & Garmezy, N. (1993). Prospects and promises in the study of resilience. *Development and Psychopathology, 5*, 497–502.
Dunn, J., Bundy, P., & Woodrow, N. (2012). Combining drama pedagogy with digital technologies to support the language learning needs of newly arrived refugee children: A classroom case study. *Research in Drama Education: The Journal of Applied Theatre and Performance, 17*(4), 477–499.
Fitzgerald, C. M. (2017). Understanding language vitality and reclamation as resilience: A framework for language endangerment and "loss" (Commentary on Mufwene). *Language, 93*(4), 280–297.
Gu, Q., & Day, C. (2013). Challenges to teacher resilience: Conditions count. *British Educational Research Journal, 39*, 22–44.
Hiver, P. (2017). Tracing the signature dynamics of language teacher immunity: A retrodictive qualitative modeling study. *The Modern Language Journal, 101*(4), 669–699.
Hiver, P. (2018). Teachstrong: The power of teacher resilience for L2 practitioners. In S. Mercer, & A. Kostoulas (Eds.), *Language teacher psychology* (pp. 231–246). Multilingual Matters.
Hiver, P., & Al-Hoorie, A. H. (2020). *Research methods for complexity theory in applied linguistics.* Multilingual Matters.
Hiver, P., & Dörnyei, Z. (2017). Language teacher immunity: A double-edged sword. *Applied Linguistics, 38*(3), 405–423.
Hiver, P., Al-Hoorie, A. H., & Mercer, S. (Eds.) (2021). *Student engagement in the language classroom.* Multilingual Matters.
Hu, T., Zhang, D., & Wang, J. (2015). A meta-analysis of the trait resilience and mental health. *Personality and Individual Differences, 76*, 18–27.
Joyce, S., Shand, F., Tighe, J., Laurent, S. J., Bryant, R. A., & Harvey, S. B. (2018). Road to resilience: A systematic review and meta-analysis of resilience training programmes and interventions. *BMJ Open, 8*(6).
Kim, T.Y., & Kim, Y. K. (2017). The impact of resilience on L2 learners' motivated behavior and proficiency in L2 learning. *Educational Studies, 43*(1), 1–15.
Kim, T.Y., Kim, Y., & Kim, J.Y. (2017). Structural relationship between L2 learning (de)motivation, resilience, and L2 proficiency among Korean college students. *The Asia-Pacific Education Researcher, 26*(6), 397–406.
Kim, T.Y., Kim, Y., & Kim, J.Y. (2019). Role of resilience in (de)motivation and second language proficiency: Cases of Korean Elementary School Students. *Journal of Psycholinguistic Research, 48*(2), 371–389.
Kostoulas, A., & Lämmerer, A. (2018). Making the transition into teacher education: Resilience as a process of growth. In S. Mercer & A. Kostoulas (Eds.), *Language teacher psychology* (pp. 247–263). Multilingual Matters.
Lipsitt, L., & Demick, J. (2012). Theory and measurement of resilience: Views from development. In M. Ungar (Ed.), *The social ecology of resilience: A handbook of theory and practice* (pp. 43–52). Springer.
Luthar, S. (2006). Resilience in development: A synthesis of research across five decades. In D. Chiccetti & D. Cohen (Eds.), *Developmental psychopathology* (2nd ed., Vol. 3, pp. 739–795). John Wiley.
Luthar, S., Chiccetti, D., & Becker, B. (2000). The construct of resilience: A critical evaluation and guidelines for future work. *Child Development, 71*(3), 543–562.

MacIntyre, P. D., Gregersen, T., & Mercer, S. (2019a). Setting an agenda for positive psychology in SLA: Theory, practice, and research. *The Modern Language Journal, 103*, 262–274.

MacIntyre, P. D., Ross, J., Talbot, K., Gregersen, T., Mercer, S., & Banga, C. A. (2019b). Stressors, personality and wellbeing among language teachers. *System, 82*, 26–38.

Maddi, S. (2004). Hardiness: An operationalization of existential courage. *Journal of Humanistic Psychology, 44*, 279–298.

Maddi, S. (2005). On hardiness and other pathways to resilience. *American Psychologist, 60*, 261–262.

Mansfield, C., Beltman, S., Broadley, T., & Wetherby-Fell, N. (2016). Building resilience in teacher education: An evidenced informed framework. *Teaching and Teacher Education, 54*, 77–87.

Masten, A. (2001). Ordinary magic: Resilience processes in development. *American Psychologist, 56*, 227–238.

Masten, A. (2009). Ordinary magic: Lessons from research on resilience in human development. *Education Canada, 49*(3), 28–33.

Masten, A., Best, K., & Garmezy, N. (1990). Resilience and development: Contributions from the study of children who overcome adversity. *Development and Psychopathology, 2*, 425–444.

Masten, A. S., & Wright, M. O. (2010). Resilience over the lifespan: Developmental perspectives on resistance, recovery, and transformation. In J.W. Reich, A.J. Zautra, & J.S. Hall (Eds.), *Handbook of adult resilience* (pp. 213–237). Guilford.

Mercer, S., Oberdorfer, P., & Saleem, M. (2016). Helping language teachers to thrive: Using positive psychology to promote teachers' professional well-being. In D. Gabryś-Barker & D. Gałajda (Eds.), *Positive psychology perspectives on foreign language learning and teaching* (pp. 213–232). Springer.

Nguyen, K., Stanley, N., Stanley, L., & Wang, Y. (2015). Resilience in language learners and the relationship to storytelling. *Cogent Education, 2*(1), 991160.

Oxford, R. (2016a). Powerfully positive: Searching for a model of language learner well-being. In D. Gabryś-Barker & D. Gałajda. (Eds.), *Positive psychology perspectives on foreign language learning and teaching* (pp. 21–37). Springer.

Oxford, R. (2016b). Toward a psychology of well-being for language learners: The EMPATHICS vision. In P.D. MacIntyre, T. Gregersen, & S. Mercer (Eds.), *Positive psychology in SLA* (pp. 10–87). Multilingual Matters.

Oxford, R., Acuña, G. P., Hernández, M. S., & Smith, A. L. (2015). "A language is a mentality": A narrative, positive-psychological view of six learners' development of bilingualism. *System, 55*, 100–110.

Padrón, Y. N., Waxman, H., Brown, A. P., & Powers, R. A. (2000). Improving classroom instruction and student learning for resilient and non-resilient English language learners.

Pajares, F. (2009). Toward a positive psychology of academic motivation: The role of self-efficacy beliefs. In R. Gilman, E.S. Huebner, & M.J. Furlong (Eds.), *Handbook of positive psychology in schools* (pp. 149–160). Routledge.

Reich, J., Zautra, A., & Hall, J. S. (Eds.). (2010). *Handbook of adult resilience.* Guilford Press.

Richardson, G. (2002). The metatheory of resilience and resiliency. *Journal of Clinical Psychology, 58*, 307–321.

Rivera, H. H., & Waxman, H. C. (2011). Resilient and nonresilient Hispanic English language learners' attitudes toward their classroom learning environment in mathematics. *Journal of Education for Students Placed at Risk, 16*(3), 185–200.

Rutter, M. (2012). Resilience: Causal pathways and social ecology. In M. Ungar (Ed.), *The social ecology of resilience: A handbook of theory and practice* (pp. 33–42). Springer.

Tse, L. (2001). Resisting and reversing language shift: Heritage-language resilience among U.S. native biliterates. *Harvard Educational Review, 71*(4), 676–709.

Waxman, H. C., Gray, J. P., & Padron, Y. N. (2003). *Review of research on educational resilience.* Center for Research on Education, Diversity, and Excellence.

Waxman, H. C., Rivera, H., & Powers, R. (2012). English language learners' educational resilience and classroom learning environment. *Educational Research Quarterly, 35*(4), 53–72.

Ungar, M. (2012). Social ecologies and their contribution to resilience. In M. Ungar (Ed.), *The social ecology of resilience: A handbook of theory and practice* (pp. 13–31). Springer.

Wilkes, G. (2002). Introduction: A second generation of resilience research. *Journal of Clinical Psychology, 58*(3), 229–232.

Windle, G. (2011). What is resilience? A review and concept analysis. *Reviews in Clinical Gerontology, 21*(2), 152–169.

Wright, M. O., Masten, A. S, & Narayan, A. J. (2013). Resilience processes in development: Four waves of research on positive adaptation in the context of adversity. In S. Goldstein & R.B. Brooks (Eds.), *Handbook of resilience in children* (2nd ed., pp. 15–37). Springer.

Yun, S., Hiver, P., & Al-Hoorie, A. H. (2018). Academic buoyancy: Exploring learners' everyday resilience in the language classroom. *Studies in Second Language Acquisition, 40*(4), 805–830.

17
SELF-REGULATION

Isobel Kai-Hui Wang

The capacity to self-regulate has long been considered one of the most important qualities that people need to possess (Forgas, Baumeister, & Tice, 2009; Zimmerman, 2000). Self-regulation plays a crucial role in affecting people's performance in a wide range of areas, such as education, health, and in the workplace (Seker, 2016; Zeidner, Boekaerts, & Pintrich, 2000). The construct of self-regulation has been conceptualized from various psychological perspectives. More recently, it has also been gaining recognition in the field of second language acquisition (SLA). This chapter examines self-regulation from both psychological and SLA perspectives. It begins by considering how to conceptualize the construct from a psychological perspective with a particular focus on core essential features of self-regulation. Then, I take a closer look at the construct within SLA and explain the processes involved in self-regulated language learning on the basis of two leading models of strategic self-regulation. The construct of self-regulation is explored by reviewing empirical studies that explore its relationship with other variables, L2 learners' experiences of self-regulated learning beyond the classroom, as well as interventions for promoting self-regulation. The next section seeks possible synergies between the two perspectives in order to further our current understanding of self-regulation in language learning. The chapter concludes with a discussion of the main research and practical implications.

Self-Regulation in Psychology

Definitions

The construct of self-regulation has been defined from diverse theoretical perspectives in various fields of psychology, such as social psychology, educational psychology, clinical health psychology, and developmental psychology, leading to a diversity of definitions (Zeidner et al., 2000). Problems in identifying self-regulation have been further compounded by its interchangeable use with other related terms in the literature (e.g., self-control, self-management, and self-regulated learning). Hence, as with other constructs, such as "strategies" and "motivation," it also suffers from definitional fuzziness and a degree of theoretical incoherence. It is not possible to reach a consensual definition of the construct accepted by all. Instead, I have chosen to provide a series of essential features of self-regulation as they appear in psychology. First, the self is one of the essential features of self-regulation. Forgas et al. (2009, p. 4) stress that "self-regulation is regulation of the self by the self." In other words, it focuses on human agency. The authors viewed *the capacity for change* as another key ingredient of self-regulation. To achieve self-regulation, an individual agent must be able to change in response to a changing circumstance/environment. In order to enhance our understanding of self-regulation, the self should not be viewed in isolation; rather, it is socioculturally embedded, for example, evaluating one's actions in relation to external norms and expectations (Crafa, 2015; Jackson, Mackenzie, & Hobfoll, 2000). Self-regulation emphasizes the active role that the self/agent plays in regulating one's thoughts, feelings, and actions in accordance with the social context.

Often, self-regulation involves individuals' conscious, deliberate efforts to pursue goals (Hagger, Wood, Stiff, & Chatzisarantis, 2010; Koole, 2009). This points to two important features of the construct—consciousness and goal-oriented behavior (see Chapter 18). Firstly, with regard to the degree of consciousness involved in self-regulation, much of the literature on the construct suggests that self-regulation is unlikely to occur at the unconscious level without any conscious awareness and effortful attempts from the individual (e.g., Aarts, 2007; Baumeister & Alquist, 2009; Oettingen & Gollwitzer, 2009). However, other researchers also argue that self-regulation cannot be completely separated from unconscious activities and consciousness has manifested in varying degrees in the whole self-regulation processes. Recently, there has been a growing recognition of the role of subconsciousness or unconsciousness in motivating human action (e.g., Aarts & Custers, 2012; Boo, Dörnyei, & Ryan, 2015; Thrash, Wadsworth, Sim, Wan, & Everidge, 2019). In particular, unconscious cognitive processes play a pertinent role in forming an intention or decision to act. It has been noted that it is possible to generate and sustain the motivation of people's thinking and action in the absence of conscious awareness, since they can be primed by contextual as well as behavioral information to acquire intrinsic reward value, and this prepares and regulates their behavior (Aarts & Custers, 2012).

Secondly, another feature of self-regulation is the focus on goal-oriented behavior. Goal-directed behavior consists of both goal setting (i.e., forming goal intentions and framing goals) and behavioral implementation of goal intentions. On the one hand, goals or intentions are a key concept in models of self-regulation since they motivate, shape, and guide cognition and actions over time and across situations and play a major role in organizing beliefs, thoughts, and behavior into meaningful changes (Crafa, 2015; Freund & Hennecke, 2015). On the other hand, there is considerable evidence that self-regulatory processes contribute to goal setting and pursuit. For example, according to Oettingen and Gollwitzer (2009), regulating both thought (e.g., making plans) and emotions (e.g., channeling positive emotions) (see Chapter 14) can help people form strong goal commitments and enhance their chances of successful goal completion. Therefore, it is clear that the relation between self-regulation and goal-directed behavior is reciprocal. People's goal-oriented behavior adds a dynamic feature to self-regulation and this encourages us to consider more dynamic interactions between the two factors; for example, how do people regulate when adjusting to changes in goals (Brandtstädter, 2009) or when dealing with the interaction of proximal and distal goals over time (Neal, Ballard, & Vancouver, 2017)?

There has been a growing agreement that self-regulation should be described as a multidimensional construct rather than a singular internal state or trait. Self-regulation has been viewed as a broad construct comprising motivational, affective, cognitive, and social components that adjust individuals' attention, emotions, and behavior to changing personal and environmental conditions (Bassett, Denham, Wyatt, & Warren-Khot, 2012; Zeidner et al., 2000). Firstly, motivation is viewed as a core component of self-regulation. Researchers have shown the important roles of motivational resources for effective self-regulation, such as willpower and impulse strength (Friese, Wänke, & Hofmann, 2009), and self-enhancement and self-protection (Sedikides, 2009). Regulating powerful motives and impulses is also recognized as the most challenging task for self-regulation (Forgas et al., 2009). With regard to the role of affective mechanisms in self-regulation, anticipated emotions appear to promote self-regulation through directing behavior towards desired goals. However, negative emotions (e.g., emotional distress) can impair self-regulation by making people narrow the temporal focus, ignore relevant information, and become insensitive to probabilities (Tice, 2009). A self-regulated activity also relies on a variety of higher-order cognitive processes, such as reasoning, conditioning, and problem solving (Oettingen & Gollwitzer, 2009; Wäenke & Hofmann, 2009). Furthermore, self-regulation is not only an intrapersonal process, but also it exists within people's social lives, depending on social systems, social institutions, and interpersonal contexts (Fitzsimons & Finkel, 2010) (see Chapter 24). As such, self-regulation is related to various motivational, affective, cognitive, and social processes.

A further feature of self-regulation is metacognition. It is defined as "thinking about thinking" (Miller, Kessel, & Flavell, 1970, p. 613). The construct is considered to involve both knowledge about cognition and the use of metacognitive strategies—also referred to as metacognitive regulation (Oxford, 2017). Metacognition plays an important part in self-regulation, since strategies shaped by metacognitive knowledge, such as strategies for monitoring and evaluating, help to direct and enhance self-regulation (Winne, 2017). Although self-regulation is closely related to metacognition, both constructs have distinct characteristics. Metacognition has a clear cognitive orientation and its emphasis is on the strategic control of cognitive processes, while self-regulation constitutes the relatively complex interaction of behavior, cognition, emotion, motivation, and social environment (for more on the distinctions and associations between these two terms, see Dinsmore, Alexander, & Loughlin, 2008).

A number of key features of self-regulation have been identified in this section and include:

1. Self-regulation has varying degrees of consciousness. It can be conscious, sub-conscious, or even unconscious.
2. Self-regulation is goal oriented.
3. Self-regulation is a higher-order construct which comprises motivational, affective, cognitive, and social components.
4. Self-regulation requires metacognition.

Models in Education

The concept of self-regulated learning (Schunk & Zimmerman, 2008; Zimmerman, 1986, 1989) was developed to gain a better understanding of the learning process as well as academic performance from a self-regulatory perspective. According to Zimmerman (2001), self-regulated learning refers to learning that results from students' self-generated thoughts, feelings, and actions toward the achievement of their learning goals. It has been noted that self-regulated learning involves elements of both self-regulation (e.g., self-regulatory strategies) and metacognition (e.g., knowledge about cognition) within academic domains (Dinsmore et al., 2008; Winne, 2017). It also emphasizes the active role of the learner in participating metacognitively, motivationally, and behaviorally in their own learning process.

Drawing from a social cognitive perspective, Zimmerman (2000) developed a self-regulated learning model which contains three cyclical and recursive phases: forethought, performance or volitional control, and self-reflection processes. The *forethought* phase refers to two influential processes prior to learners' efforts to act and set the stage for it: task analysis (including goal setting and strategic planning) and managing self-motivational beliefs, especially self-efficacy, outcome expectations, intrinsic interest, and goal orientation. During the *performance* or *volitional control* phase, learners actively engage in the processes that help them improve their attention and action, involving self-controlling their learning processes (such as imagery and attention focusing) and self-observing their learning progress (including self-monitoring and self-recording). The self-reflection phase involves processes that take place after the performance phase and that are affected by the learner's reaction to their previous performance, including self-judging and self-reacting to their performances. The learner is likely to return to the forethought phase, then forming a self-regulatory cycle. Zimmerman (2001) stresses that a self-regulated learner must proactively initiate and regulate their own learning processes; however, learners may not self-regulate during all their experiences. He identifies different factors which can cause learners to fail at self-regulating their learning. For example, very young children cannot formally self-regulate their learning due to their inability to be aware of a situation from another person's point of view (or egocentrism) and the fact that they cannot use language covertly to seek social support, as well as their lack of metacognitive knowledge and abilities (de la Fuente & Lozano, 2010; Whitebread & Pino Pasternak, 2013). As children get older, they develop their capacity to self-regulate their learning during their school years, but they can still experience failures or difficulties in self-regulation for reasons such as low self-efficacy beliefs, a lack of consideration of outcome expectations, unrealistic goals, negative self-evaluation of competences, and insufficient motivation. This means that learners can vary considerably in their abilities to self-regulate their learning.

Teachers can play an important role in developing learners' self-regulatory competence. Schunk and Zimmerman's (1997, 2007) model describes the social origin of self-regulation and shows four levels of development in self-regulatory competence. The first two levels (i.e., observational and emulative) depend on social factors. Novice learners start by learning and developing new skills and strategies from "social modelling, teaching, task structuring, and encouragement" (Schunk, 2001, p. 135). Subsequently, the next two levels (i.e., self-controlled and self-regulated) rely on self-sources, and enable learners to internalize the skill or strategy being learned and develop their own repertoire of skills and strategies that are appropriate to themselves and their own learning contexts. The model suggests that the processes of acquiring self-regulated skills are primarily social. Schunk (2001) further argues that social influences continue to play a role in learners' strategy development at the two more advanced levels, even though self-controlled and self-regulated learners make use of social sources less frequently.

As we have seen in this section, both models contribute to our understanding of self-regulated learning from a social cognitive perspective. Elements of Zimmerman's model (2000) suggest the conditions from which self-regulation emerges, the motivation to self-regulate, and key variables that foster self-regulated learning (such as self-efficacy, attitudes, values, and goals). The self-regulatory competence development model of Schunk and Zimmerman (1997, 2007) highlights the socially constructed rather than self-generated nature of self-regulated learning and explains how students' self-regulatory strategies can be developed by means of social support and assistance. The two models reveal the benefits of interventions designed to promote students' self-regulated learning and offer useful insights into the implementation procedures of interventions (for more educational applications of Zimmerman's model, see Bembenutty, Cleary, & Kitsantas, 2013).

Empirical Studies of Self-Regulated Learning

There has been an established body of research in both psychology and educational psychology looking at the effect of self-regulated learning in students' achievement and its various pedagogical benefits. For example, Mega, Ronconi, and de Beni (2014) conducted a questionnaire study consisting of 5,805 undergraduate students to explore what made a good student. Their findings showed that level of self-regulation was a powerful predictor of academic achievement and the influence of self-regulation on academic achievement also depended on the interplay between students' emotions and motivation. In particular, to be successful, students need to manage their emotions and sustain positive emotions, which are crucial to the metacognitive and motivational regulation of learning. Regarding the positive relations between self-regulated learning and academic achievement, Ahmed, van der Werf, Kuyper, and Minnaert (2013) highlighted the importance of self-regulatory interventions for improving students' learning performance, and they suggested that interventions designed to cultivate students' positive emotions could also enhance their self-regulated learning. In line with the value of self-regulated learning, intervention studies have been conducted aiming at developing students' ability to apply self-regulated learning to manage their learning autonomously. Stoeger and Ziegler (2010), for example, examined the effectiveness of a training program on primary school pupils' self-regulated learning and also determined whether differences in training effects would occur among four different ability groups. They found that except for self-reflection of learning and willingness to invest effort, all the participants were able to benefit equally from the training program across the four ability groups. With regard to their self-regulation of learning and willingness to invest effort, the strongest training effect showed up in the second lowest ability group. The explanation given by the authors was that the difficulty level of the tasks was at an optimal level for the pupils in this group, which contributed to greater amounts of learning effort or preparation after class. In Sontag and Stoeger's study (2015), they also suggested that even highly intelligent students were able to benefit from explicit instruction in self-regulated learning, although it is often assumed that high-achieving students do not need training in self-regulated learning and learning strategies. They highlighted both the short-term and long-term effects of the explicit instruction on learning behavior and performance across all levels. It would appear that despite students' individual or group differences in self-regulated learning, the research studies reviewed above suggest that self-regulation interventions or strategy-based instruction can make a difference in student performance.

Self-Regulation in SLA

Models of Self-Regulated Learning in SLA

Self-regulation in SLA refers to the processes in which the learner proactively controls the cognitive, emotional, motivational, and behavioral aspects of their language learning (Kormos & Csizér, 2014). In L2 learning, Dörnyei and Ryan (2015) view self-regulation as a dynamic, multidimensional concept which is closely linked to strategic capacity, intent, and language learning behavior. It plays a crucial role in understanding the psychology of the L2 learner and their actions. Dörnyei (2005) raised a fundamental criticism of the concept of language learning strategies (LLSs) due to "the absence of a tight definition" (p. 188), and thus he proposed re-conceptualizing self-regulation in SLA in order to contribute to a broader understanding of LLSs. Tseng, Dörnyei, and Schmitt (2006) developed a taxonomy of self-regulation consisting of five facets: *commitment control*, which regulates the learners' goal commitment; *metacognitive control*, which focuses on the monitoring and managing of concentration; *satiation control*, which assists learners in eliminating boredom; *emotion control*, which helps to manage emotions and generate positive emotions; and *environmental control*, which helps learners to manage environmental influences in order to achieve difficult goals.

In the light of Dörnyei's criticism about LLSs and his conceptualization of self-regulation, some scholars (e.g., Gao, 2006; Ranalli, 2012; Rose, 2012) argued that Dörnyei's (2005) model of self-regulation is compatible with the notion of learning strategies since they merely represent different approaches to measuring the same event. "Self-regulation is looking at the initial driving forces, while learning strategies examine the outcome of these forces" (Rose, 2012, p. 95). They have attempted to integrate two notions together rather than replacing the concept of learner strategies completely with that of self-regulation. In order to reach a more complete understanding of L2 learning strategies, Oxford (2011) proposes a model of strategic language learning that incorporates self-regulation concepts from both cognitive and sociocultural perspectives, named the *Strategic Self-regulation (S^2R) model of language learning*. In the S^2R model, Oxford (2011) provides a broader definition of LLSs and defines *self-regulated L2 learning strategies* as "deliberate, goal-directed attempts to manage and control efforts to learning the L2" (p. 12). Based on her previous taxonomy of LLSs (Oxford, 1990), the S^2R model includes not only three major dimensions of L2 learning (i.e., cognitive, affective, and sociocultural-interactive), but a new component, named *metastrategies*. Metastrategies includes three sub-categories: *metacognitive strategies*, *metaaffective strategies*, and *metasociocultural-interactive strategies*. Metastrategies and the three dimensions do not exist in isolation; rather, metastrategies guide the use of cognitive, affective, and sociocultural-interactive strategies. The concept of metastrategies emphasizes the role of self-regulation in the process of strategic language learning because it enables the learner to control and manage not only cognition, but also affective states and the social environment. Oxford (2011) further suggests six types of metaknowledge underlying metastrategies to explain the learner's strategic self-regulated learning: *person knowledge, group or culture knowledge, task knowledge, whole-process knowledge, strategy knowledge,* and *conditional knowledge.* This model shifts the focus from the product (learner strategy) to the L2 learning process (learners' capacity for self-regulation, such as capacity for metacognition, for combining strategies effectively in any given situation), and from the quantity of strategy use to the quality of strategy use. Compared with Zimmerman's (2000) model of self-regulated learning, Oxford's (2011) model places a greater emphasis on the metacognitive dimension of L2 learning and strategies, although both models represent the multifaceted nature of self-regulation. In addition, Zimmerman's model shifts the emphasis from processes of self-regulation at a macro level (i.e., metacognitive control of learning in general) to a more micro level, looking at processes of self-regulation at a particular task level. In contrast, Oxford's S²R model is concerned with not only the task level, but also the whole process of language learning.

In addition to Oxford's S²R model, Rose (2010, 2012) followed a similar direction and constructed another model which combines elements of cognitive and memory strategies from SLA and language cognition theory and self-regulation theory. Rose (2010) developed a model of self-regulation based on his study of learning strategies of L2 students learning Japanese. The unique feature of this model is that it highlights the breakdown of self-regulation and illustrates casual relationships between the four categories of self-regulation (i.e., commitment control, emotional control, satiation control, and metacognitive control). Firstly, the model takes into account language learners' learning commitments in relation to their language goals and beliefs. He found that a lack of short-term goals and a lack of belief of one's own progress affected commitment control. A breakdown in emotional control in terms of self-criticism and stress can lead to re-assessment of commitments and also influences learners' ability to control their goal commitment. In addition, the model shows that a breakdown in metacognitive control in terms of the regulation of procrastination leads to issues of negative emotion. A breakdown in satiation control in terms of the regulation of boredom can further influence learners' desire to achieve a goal, leading to a breakdown in metacognitive control. Rose and his colleagues (Rose, Briggs, Sergio, & Ivanova-Slavianskaia, 2018) suggest that language learners can encounter a variety of difficulties in managing commitments and controlling emotion, boredom, and procrastination if they regulate their language learning ineffectively. The model provides a further insight into the difficulties that L2 learners experienced in their learning processes that a traditional LLS framework may not reveal. It also addresses more complex relationships between categories of self-regulation than presented in previous models of self-regulation (e.g., Dörnyei, 2005; Oxford, 2011).

Empirical Studies of Self-Regulated Learning in SLA

In SLA, researchers have typically focused on examining the interconnections among motivation, self-regulation, and autonomy. For example, Kormos and Csizér (2014) claimed that the broad sense of self-regulation, motivation, and autonomy is difficult to operationalize in research contexts within SLA due to their overlaps. In order to make them more easily operationalized in research, they defined motivation as consisting of goals, future self-guides, and intended learning effort, while motivational factors in relation to control were subsumed under self-regulation. Self-regulation was understood as a strategy that L2 learners use to control language learning, in which they focused on one aspect of learner autonomy, named "autonomous learning behavior" (i.e., independent use of language learning resources, see also Benson, 2001). In their study, research findings showed that the motivational factors such as learning goals associated with the international status of English, instrumental orientation, and positive self-related beliefs, were the precursors to the use of effective self-regulatory strategies. The motivational factors (e.g., strong international and instrumental orientations and positive self-image) contributed to autonomous learning behavior through the mediation of self-regulation strategies, especially efficient management of time and boredom.

Effective self-regulatory strategies are perhaps especially important in language learning beyond the classroom, since they enable the learner to fully exploit learning affordances outside of class (Kormos & Csizér, 2014). The importance of effective self-regulation in language learning beyond the classroom is increasingly acknowledged in the literature. In a study involving an online questionnaire and semi-structured interviews in Hong Kong, Lai and Gu (2011) explored university students' experiences of self-regulated L2 learning by means of technology. They found that most of the L2 participants engaged with technology to regulate their learning experiences, but there is considerable variation in the way learners use technological resources to regulate their learning. The variation was attributed to both contextual variables (e.g., the length of study) and personal variables (e.g., digital literacy, metacognitive strategies for managing online learning, preparation for communication with native speakers, and learning beliefs). As a result of their research, they suggest that teachers' support for effective technology use beyond the classroom needs to be integrated into the language curriculum. Training in metacognitive knowledge about technology-enhanced language learning should also be provided to foster learners' self-regulation outside the classroom.

The roles of other motivational variables have been also acknowledged in research on self-regulation in language learning. In a study exploring the influence of intrinsic variables on self-regulated language learning, Tsuda and Nakata (2013) administered a 45-item questionnaire consisting of learners' cognitive, behavioral, and affective aspects to 1076 Japanese senior high school EFL students. The analysis of the survey data allowed the creation of four distinct profiles of students and follow-up interviews with six students of each profile type were further conducted. The results revealed the complex interplay of L2 learners' internal variables affecting their self-regulation in language learning, including self-efficacy, self-motivation and willingness to communicate (WTC), intrinsic value, metacognition, and cognitive strategies. The researchers highlighted the important role of teachers in transforming students into self-regulated learners and they suggested that teachers should provide learners with individualized support and guidance (e.g., moment-to-moment elicitation and responding in the classroom and providing feedback to students' reflective journals), taking into account learner characteristics, readiness, and background.

Some researchers have investigated the effects of gender on self-regulation in language learning. Tseng, Liu, and Nix (2017), for example, conducted a questionnaire study consisting of 1,037 EFL students studying in seven high schools in Taiwan, and showed that gender exerts a substantial influence on the students' self-regulatory capacity in language learning. They found that, overall, female students had better self-regulatory control than their counterparts. In particular, female students had a higher level of control over emotion, awareness, and boredom aspects in language learning than male students. Studenska (2011), in a Polish study with 194 female and 186 male EFL students across different school levels, indicated that gender was a more significant factor affecting the students' self-regulation in language learning than their education level. In order to close the gender gap in their self-regulatory capacity, Tseng et al. (2017) suggested that the explicit development of self-regulatory strategies appears to be essential for male students and relevant self-regulation educational programs should be implemented to develop their knowledge and skills as to self-regulation in their language learning.

Another research area that has been looked at is self-regulation's relationship with L2 learners' proficiency levels. In Rose and Harbon's study (2013), the researchers elicited the voice from 12 learners of Japanese across different proficiency levels through conducting a series of interviews over a one-year timeline in order to enrich the understanding of learners' self-regulation in *kanji* learning (i.e., one of the Japanese writing systems containing adopted Chinese characters). Interview data showed that higher-proficiency participants were more likely to set long-terms goals for vocabulary size than lower-proficiency participants, but the participants at higher levels of language proficiency tended to have greater difficulty in fulfilling their commitments with learning. Compared with lower-proficiency learners, higher-proficiency learners also reported a greater challenge in controlling emotions such as frustration and self-criticism. In addition, participants with higher proficiency tended to experience challenges in controlling boredom and a lack of satisfaction and interest in *kanji* learning more frequently than lower-proficiency students. With regard to implications for language instructors, the researchers highlighted the importance of setting more realistic, achievable, and believable goals. In order to avoid the breakdown of self-regulation in language learning, they suggested that language instructors can discuss the difficulty of language learning from the beginning stages and assist learners in setting both realistic short- and long-term learning goals according to their different proficiency levels and use a systematic way to track their learning progress over time.

In addition to L2 learners' internal variables, some studies have examined the relationship between self-regulation in language learning and social-cultural variables. Kormos and Kiddle (2013), in a study of 740 Chilean secondary school students belonging to different social classes, found that L2 learners' immediate environment (i.e., their family and friends) and their broader socio-economic context play an important role in influencing their self-regulatory behavior, especially in terms of goal setting (see Chapter 18), attitude formation (see Chapter 12), self-efficacy beliefs (see Chapter 8), and the effort and persistence in learning English as a foreign language. In particular, there was a difference in self-regulation between upper-middle and upper-class students on the one hand and lower- and lower middle-class students on the other hand. This socio-economic divide among the students was explained by both instructional (e.g., outdated methods of teaching and limited or no use of technology in teaching) and contextual factors (e.g., lack of learning resources and no access to the modern technological developments and information technology). The findings of this study underscore the continuing need to invest in the training of English teachers in rural areas and to create educational opportunities for students from lower socioeconomic backgrounds to learn English beyond the classroom (see also Lamb, 2012). A case study by Jang and Iddings (2010) conducted with two immigrant Korean learners of English revealed that the development of their self-regulatory capacity was intertwined with social-contextual factors, such as L2 learners' previous and new linguistic, social, and cultural experiences, participation in English-related practices, and socially mediated resources (i.e., L1 and L2). In relation to practice, the researchers suggest that student sojourners need both L1 and L2 as a mediational tool to help them to develop from a passive receiver of knowledge and skills to a self-regulated agent in the process of language learning.

The general picture that emerges from the research highlights the complex nature of self-regulated learning, reflecting the various relationships between self-regulation and a plethora of variables involved in language learning, including motivational, individual, and sociocultural variables.

Integrating Perspectives

Both psychological and SLA perspectives have examined self-regulation as related to other aspects of learner psychology (e.g., motivation, autonomy, and strategies). However, the two perspectives also provide unique insights into self-regulation. The field of psychology highlights the role played by the individual in regulating thoughts, feelings, and actions, and it remains focused on cognitive, metacognitive, motivational, and behavioral processes. In order to explain success in learning, there have been various attempts at understanding learners' internal characteristics and individual variation in the use of self-regulatory strategies (e.g., Bidjerano & Dai, 2007; Zimmerman & Schunk, 2011). In SLA research, researchers have tended to draw more attention to the social rather than the psychological side of self-regulated learning. Research efforts have been made to explore how strategies for self-regulating L2 learning can develop from participation in cultural-specific activities (e.g., Gao, 2010; Graham & Macaro, 2008). Scholars in SLA have also acknowledged the importance of effective self-regulation in language learning beyond the classroom owing to the expansion of modern learning technology and digital learning resources, and have paid special attention to the out-of-class experiences of self-regulated language learning across different cultural contexts and student populations (Kormos & Csizér, 2014; Lai & Gu, 2011). In addition, SLA researchers have become increasingly concerned with the dynamic nature of self-regulation and its temporal and situational variation (Dörnyei & Ryan, 2015). Both perspectives have made unique contributions in helping us to understand self-regulation. The two perspectives can complement each other, and an integrative approach is encouraged, in an effort to achieve a more holistic, complex, and dynamic understanding of self-regulation.

Implications for Practice and Research

Self-regulatory capacity is crucial to the quality and ultimate success of language learning within and beyond classrooms. The benefits and roles of explicit strategy-based instruction in the development of self-regulation in language learning have been explored in a number of studies (see Chang, 2005; Chamot & Harris, 2019). For example, one study, by Lam (2015a), investigated how explicit strategy instruction can promote self-regulated learning in the EFL writing classrooms in Hong Kong. The strategy instruction focused on personal knowledge (i.e., motivation and self-concept), task knowledge (i.e., text knowledge and concern for audience), and strategy knowledge (i.e., planning, organizing, and evaluating), and it was integrated into the regular 15-week process-oriented writing course. The results revealed that the explicit strategy instruction improved individual writers' self-regulated learning and metacognitive knowledge. The researcher concluded that explicit strategy instruction, especially containing sufficient knowledge in planning and evaluating writing processes, could help L2 writers to become more self-regulated.

Another pedagogical strategy to promote self-regulation has been through portfolio assessment. For example, a study Mak and Wong (2018) conducted with two teachers and their students from two primary schools in Hong Kong found that students considered portfolio assessment as an effective activity to help them become self-regulated learners. In particular, Lam (2015b) explored the effects of feedback in portfolio assessment on self-regulated learning by examining two specific writing classrooms in Hong Kong. The researcher suggested that provision of feedback at four levels (i.e., task, process, self-regulation, and self) tended to enhance L2 writers' self-regulatory capacity. This points to the key role of feedback provision and learner engagement with feedback. Graham and Macaro (2008) also encouraged language teachers to provide feedback not only on their students' performance in language learning tasks (in this case, L2 listening tasks), but also on their strategy use in terms of how their strategies could be orchestrated effectively in order to help them achieve their control of learning. In this study, the researchers highlight the long-term benefits of incorporating a strong metacognitive element in teacher feedback on strategy use for learners regarding their capacity to regulate their learning and beliefs about learning.

The majority of studies reviewed in this chapter show that researchers tend to heavily rely on questionnaires to examine the relationship between self-regulation and other variables. However, more recently, researchers (e.g., Rose et al., 2018; Wang, 2018) have increasingly recognized the potential contribution of qualitative approaches in order to capture the richness and complexity of strategic self-regulation in a more contextualized and dynamic manner. Calls have been issued for researchers to use multiple methods (Ben-Eliyahu & Bernacki, 2015; Jang & Iddings, 2010; Oxford, 2011) to produce a fuller account of self-regulated processes. For example, research might utilize case studies, classroom observations, self-report, and interviews as a means to explore the complex, situated nature of self-regulatory processes in context (Jang & Iddings, 2010), and the employment of a mix of self-report surveys and semi-structured interviews could be used to examine the processes of self-regulated learning from a more holistic, dynamic perspective (Lai & Gu, 2011; Tsuda & Nakata, 2013) (see Chapter 4).

Future Directions

Comparatively, there is less work on self-regulation in SLA than in psychology to date. There are a number of possible reasons for this, including the dominance of work on strategies and autonomy in

SLA, which overlaps considerably with self-regulation. The construct has clear roots in psychology. It is also difficult for L2 researchers and teachers to adequately measure and operationalize self-regulation in language learning since it can entail not only conscious control of the learning process but also unconscious processing. However, SLA has potentially unique characteristics, including the strong connection between formalized learning and learning beyond the classroom, in which self-regulation may play an especially pertinent role. The more students can regulate and control their cognition, affect, and behavior in the language learning process, the more likely it is that they can manage their learning efficiently and develop their language ability (Teng & Zhang, 2016). Although their learning can benefit from classroom instruction, access to formal instruction is often restricted by time, space, and pace. Given the growth of the Internet and mobile technologies for expanding learners' affordances for learning beyond the classroom, we can expect a growth in studies exploring this interface.

Further research may also develop a better understanding of how self-regulation relates to a number of other variables, such as striving (e.g., self-enhancement) and interest, and may consider the importance of self-regulated strategies for positive beliefs, thinking, and emotions in L2 learning. More research is needed to understand the complexity and dynamism of self-regulatory processes. Indeed, a valuable lens for this could be complex dynamic systems theory, which is enjoying considerable attention within language learning psychology (e.g., Dörnyei, MacIntyre, & Henry, 2015; Dörnyei & Ryan, 2015; Oxford, 2017). If such a perspective is taken, it suggests that the typical self-report questionnaires of data collection for self-regulated learning in psychology can only take us so far. Here, SLA has a typically much broader repertoire of research tools and approaches to draw than is usually the case in psychology. It would be interesting for researchers to investigate L2 learners' self-regulatory capacity or strategies at different proficiencies and the role of self-regulatory strategies in further developing their proficiency.

From a lifelong learning perspective, the ultimate goal of teaching is to help students become self-regulated learners. This chapter invites the reader to reconsider the significant role of self-regulation in stimulating, sustaining, and expanding learning efforts. Both psychological and SLA perspectives can add important contributions to our understanding of self-regulated learning, and more integrated approaches could offer rich vistas for exploring this construct, along with a range of diverse and varied research methodologies.

Reflection Questions

- What do you think are the essential features of self-regulation in language learning?
- What ideas can you gain from this chapter for integrating the instruction of self-regulated strategies into a regular language course?
- What are some of the challenges for teachers developing L2 learners' self-regulatory capacity beyond the classroom? What other ways can you think of to help teachers promote the development of self-regulation in language learning?

Recommended Reading

Vohs, K. D., & Baumeister, R. F. (2016). *Handbook of self-regulation: research, theory, and applications* (3rd ed.). The Guilford Press.
This handbook provides a comprehensive, multidisciplinary overview of theories, models, and research findings on self-regulation.

Oxford, R. L. (2017). *Teaching and researching language learning strategies: Self-regulation in context* (2nd ed.). Routledge.
This book situates language learning strategies in a broader context of self-regulation and makes a great attempt to explore the concept of "strategic self-regulation" from both cognitive and sociocultural perspectives. It also provides rich insights into different types of strategy-based instruction for the development of self-regulation in language learning.

Schunk, D. H., & Greene, J. A. (2018). *Handbook of self-regulation of learning and performance* (2nd ed.). Routledge.
This book provides an invaluable overview of theoretical principles of self-regulation in educational settings and incorporates research findings into practice. It gives rich and critical accounts of research methods for assessing self-regulated learning as well as self-regulatory training with elementary and secondary students.

References

Aarts, H. (2007). On the emergence of human goal pursuit: The nonconscious regulation and motivation of goals. *Social and Personality Psychology Compass, 1*, 183–201.
Aarts, H., & Custers, R. (2012). Unconscious goal pursuit: Nonconscious goal regulations and motivation. In R. M. Ryan (Ed.), *The Oxford handbook of human motivation* (pp. 232–247). Oxford University Press.
Ahmed, W., van der Werf, G., Kuyper, H., & Minnaert, A. (2013). Emotions, self-regulated learning, achievement in mathematics: A growth curve analysis. *Journal of Educational Psychology, 105*, 150–161.
Bassett, H. H., Denham, S., Wyatt, T. M., & Warren-Khot, H. K. (2012). Refining the preschool self-regulation assessment for use in preschool classrooms. *Infant and Child Development, 21*(6), 596–616.
Baumeister, R. F., & Alquist, J. L. (2009). Is there a downside to good self-control? *Self and Identity, 8*, 115–130.
Bembenutty, H., Cleary, T., & Kitsantas, A., (2013). *Applications of self-regulated learning applied across diverse disciplines: A tribute to Barry J. Zimmerman.* Information Age Publishing.
Ben-Eliyahu, A., & Bernacki, M. L. (2015). Addressing complexities in self-regulated learning: A focus on contextual factors, contingencies, and dynamic relations. *Metacognition and Learning, 10*, 1–13.
Benson, P. (2001). *Teaching and researching autonomy in language learning.* Longman.
Bidjerano, T., & Dai, D. Y. (2007). The relationship between the big-five model of personality and self-regulated learning strategies. *Learning and Individual Differences, 17*(1), 69–81.
Boo, Z., Dörnyei, Z., & Ryan, S. (2015). L2 motivation research 2005–2014: Understanding a publication surge and a changing landscape. *System, 55*, 145–157.
Brandtstädter, J. (2009). Goal pursuit and goal adjustment: Self-regulation and intentional self-development in changing developmental contexts. *Advances in Life Course Research, 14*, 52–62.
Chamot, A. U., & Harris, V. (2019) *Learning strategy instruction in the language classroom: Issues and implementation.* Multilingual Matters.
Chang, M. M. (2005). Applying self-regulated learning strategies in a web-based instruction: An investigation of motivation perception. *Computer Assisted Language Learning, 18*(3), 217–230.
Crafa, D. (2015). Development of self-regulation during early childhood across cultures: A systems perspective. In J. Wright (Ed.), *International encyclopaedia of social and behavioural sciences* (2nd ed.) (pp. 553–556). Elsevier.
de la Fuente, J., & Lozano, A. (2010). Assessing self-regulated learning in early childhood education: Difficulties, needs, and prospects. *Psicothema, 22*(2), 278–283.
Dinsmore, D. L., Alexander, P. A., & Loughlin, S. M. (2008). Focusing the conceptual lens on metacognition, self-regulation, and self-regulated learning. *Educational Psychology Review, 20*(4), 391–409.
Dörnyei, Z. (2005). *The psychology of the language learner: Individual differences in second language acquisition.* Erlbaum.
Dörnyei, Z., MacIntyre, P. D., & Henry, A. (Eds.). (2015). *Motivational dynamics in language learning.* Multilingual Matters.
Dörnyei, Z., & Ryan, S. (2015). *The psychology of the second language learner revisited.* Routledge.
Fitzsimons, G. M., & Finkel, E. J. (2010). Interpersonal influences on self-regulation. *Current Directions in Psychological Science, 19*, 101–105.
Forgas, J. P., Baumeister, R. F., & Tice, D. M. (2009). The psychology of self-regulation: An introductory review. In J. P. Forgas, R. F. Baumeister, & D. M. Tice (Eds.), *The psychology of self-regulation: Cognitive, affective, and motivational processes* (pp. 1–17). Psychology Press.

Freund, A. M., & Hennecke, M. (2015). Self-regulation in adulthood. In J. Wright (Ed.), *International encyclopedia of social and behavioral sciences* (2nd ed., pp. 557–562). Elsevier.

Friese, M., Wänke, M., & Hofmann, W. (2009). Unscrambling self-regulatory behavior determination: The interplay of impulse strength, reflective processes, and control resources. In J. P. Forgas, R. F. Baumeister, & D. M. Tice (Eds.), *The psychology of self-regulation: Cognitive, affective, and motivational processes* (pp. 53–72). Psychology Press.

Gao, X. S. (2006). Understanding changes in Chinese students' uses of learning strategies in China and Britain: A socio-cultural re-interpretation. *System, 34*(1), 55–67.

Gao, X. S. (2010). *Strategic language learning: The roles of agency and context*. Multilingual Matters.

Graham, S., & Macaro, E. (2008). Strategy instruction in listening for lower-intermediate learners of French. *Language Learning, 58*, 747–783.

Hagger, M. S., Wood, C., Stiff, C., & Chatzisarantis, N. L. D. (2010). Self-regulation and self-control in exercise: The strength-energy model. *International Review of Sport and Exercise Psychology, 3*, 62–86.

Jackson, T., MacKenzie, J., & Hobfoll, S. E. (2000). Communal aspects of self-regulation. In M. Boekaerts, P. R. Pintrich, & M. Zeidner (Eds.), *Handbook of self-regulation* (pp. 275–300). Academic Press.

Jang, E-Y., & Iddings, A. C. D. (2010). The social genesis of self-regulation: The case of two Korean adolescents learning English as a second language. *Mind, Culture, and Activity: An International Journal, 17*, 350–366.

Koole, S. L. (2009). Does emotion regulation help or hurt self-regulation? In J. P. Forgas, R. F. Baumeister, & D. M. Tice (Eds.), *The psychology of self-regulation: Cognitive, affective, and motivational processes* (pp. 217–231). Psychology Press.

Kormos, J., & Csizér, K. (2014). The interaction of motivation, self-regulatory strategies, and autonomous learning behaviour in different learner groups. *TESOL Quarterly, 48*(2), 275–299.

Kormos, J., & Kiddle, T. (2013). The role of socio-economic factors in motivation to learn English as a foreign language: The case of Chile. *System, 41*, 399–412.

Lai, C., & Gu, M. (2011). Self-regulated out of class language learning with technology. *Computer Assisted Language Learning, 24*, 317–335.

Lam, R. (2015a). Understanding EFL students' development of self-regulated learning in a process-oriented writing course. *TESOL Journal, 6*(3), 527–553.

Lam, R. (2015b). Feedback about self-regulation: Does it remain an "unfinished business" in portfolio assessment of writing? *TESOL Quarterly, 49*(2), 402–413.

Lamb, M. (2012). A self-system perspective on young adolescents' motivation to learn English in urban and rural setting. *Language Learning, 62*, 997–1023.

Mak, P., & Wong, K. M. (2018). Self-regulation through portfolio assessment in writing classrooms. *ELT Journal, 72*(1), 49–61.

Mega, C., Ronconi, L., & de Beni, R. (2014). What makes a good student? How emotions, self-regulated learning, and motivation contribute to academic achievement. *Journal of Educational Psychology, 106*(1), 121–131.

Miller, P. H., Kessel, F. S., & Flavell, J. H. (1970). Thinking about people thinking about people thinking about…: A study of social–cognitive development. *Child Development, 41*, 613–623.

Neal, A., Vancouver, J. B., & Ballard, T. (2017). Dynamic self-regulation and multiple-goal pursuit. *Annual Review of Organizational Psychology and Organizational Behavior, 4*(1), 401–423.

Oettingen, G., & Gollwitzer, P. M. (2009). Making goal pursuit effective: Expectancy-dependent goal setting and planned goal striving. In J. P. Forgas, R. F. Baumeister, & D. M. Tice (Eds.), *The psychology of self-regulation: Cognitive, affective, and motivational processes* (pp. 127–146). Psychology Press.

Oxford, R. L. (1990). *Language learning strategies: What every teacher should know*. Newbury House.

Oxford, R. L. (2011). *Teaching and researching language learning strategies*. Longman.

Pintrich, P. R. (2000). The role of goal orientation in self-regulated learning. In M. Boekaerts, P. R. Pintrich, & M. Zeidner (Eds.), *Handbook of self-regulation, research, and applications* (pp. 451–502). Academic Press.

Ranalli, J. (2012). Alternative models of self-regulation and implications for L2 strategy research. *Studies in Self-Access Learning Journal, 3*(4), 357–376.

Rose, H. (2010). *Kanji learning of Japanese language learners on a year-long study exchange program at a Japanese university: An investigation of strategy use, motivation control and self-regulation* [Doctoral dissertation, The University of Sydney]. Academia. www.academia.edu/446999/Kanji_learning_Strategies_Motivation_control_and_self-regulation

Rose, H. (2012). Reconceptualizing strategic learning in the face of self-regulation: Throwing language learning strategies out with the bathwater. *Applied Linguistics, 33*, 92–98.

Rose, H. L., Briggs, J. G., Boggs, J. A., Sergio, L., & Ivanova-Slavianskaia, N. (2018). A systematic review of language learner strategy research in the face of self-regulation. *System, 72*, 151–163.

Rose, H., & Harbon, L. (2013). Self-regulation in second language learning: An investigation of the learning task. *Foreign Language Annals, 46*(1), 96–107.

Schunk, D. (2001). Social cognitive theory and self-regulated learning. In B. J. Zimmerman & D. H. Schunk (Eds.), *Self-regulated learning and academic achievement: Theoretical perspectives* (pp. 125–151). Lawrence Erlbaum.

Schunk, D. H., & Zimmerman, B. J. (1997). Social origins of self-regulatory competence. *Educational Psychologist, 32*(4), 195–208.

Schunk, D. H., & Zimmerman, B. J. (2007). Influencing children's self-efficacy and self-regulation of reading and writing through modeling. *Reading & Writing Quarterly, 23,* 7–25.

Schunk, D. H., & Zimmerman, B. J. (Eds.). (2008). *Motivation and self-regulated learning: Theory, research, and applications.* Lawrence Erlbaum Associates Publishers.

Sedikides, C. (2009). On self-protection and self-enhancement regulation: The role of self-improvement and social norms. In J. P. Forgas, R. F. Baumeister, & D. M. Tice (Eds.), *The psychology of self-regulation: Cognitive, affective, and motivational processes* (pp. 73–92). Psychology Press.

Seker, M. (2016). The use of self-regulation strategies by foreign language learners and its role in language achievement. *Language Teaching Research, 20*(5), 600–618.

Sontag, C., & Stoeger, H. (2015). Can highly intelligent and high achieving students benefit from training in SRL in a regular classroom context? *Learning and Individual Differences, 41,* 43–53.

Stoeger, H., & Ziegler, A. (2010). Do pupils with differing cognitive abilities benefit similarly from a self-regulated learning training program? *Gifted Education International, 26,* 110–123.

Studenska, A. (2011). Educational level, gender and foreign language learning self-regulation difficulty. *Procedia—Social and Behavioral Sciences, 29,* 1349–1358.

Teng, L. S., & Zhang, L. J. (2016). A questionnaire-based validation of multidimensional models of self-regulated learning strategies. *The Modern Language Journal, 100*(3), 674–701.

Thrash, T., Wadsworth, L. M., Sim, Y. Y., Wan, X., & Everidge, C. E. (2019). Implicit-explicit motive congruence and moderating factors. In R. M. Ryan (Ed.), *The Oxford handbook of human motivation* (2nd ed., pp. 187–204). Oxford University Press.

Tice, D. M. (2009). How emotions affect self-regulation. In J. P. Forgas, R. F. Baumeister, & D. M. Tice (Eds.), *The psychology of self-regulation: Cognitive, affective, and motivational processes* (pp. 201–216). Psychology Press.

Tseng, W. T., Dörnyei, Z., & Schmitt, N. (2006). A new approach to assessing strategic learning: The case of self-regulation in vocabulary acquisition. *Applied Linguistics, 27,* 78–102.

Tseng, W. T., Liu, H., & Nix, J. M. L. (2017). Self-regulation in language learning: Scale validation and gender effects. *Perceptual and Motor Skills, 124*(2), 531–548.

Tsuda, A., & Nakata, Y. (2013). Exploring self-regulation in language learning: A study of Japanese high school EFL students. *Innovation in Language Learning and Teaching, 7,* 72–88.

Wang, I. K.-H. (2018) *Learning vocabulary strategically in a study abroad context.* Palgrave Macmillan.

Whitebread, D., & Pino Pasternak, D. (2013). Video analysis of self-regulated learning in social and naturalistic contexts: The case of preschool and primary school children. In S. Volet & M. Vaurus (Eds.), *Interpersonal regulation of learning and motivation: Methodological advances* (pp. 14–44). Springer.

Winne, P. H. (2017). Cognition and metacognition in self-regulated learning. In D. Schunk & J. Greene (Eds.), *Handbook of self-regulation of learning and performance* (2nd ed., pp. 36–47). Routledge.

Zeidner, M., Boekaerts, M., & Pintrich, P. R. (2000). Self-regulation: Directions and challenges for future research. In M. Boekaerts, P. R. Pintrich, & M. Zeidner (Eds.), *Handbook of self-regulation* (pp. 750–768). Academic Press.

Zimmerman, B. J. (1986). Development of self-regulated learning: Which are the key subprocesses? *Contemporary Educational Psychology, 16,* 307–313.

Zimmerman, B. J. (1989). A social cognitive view of self-regulated academic learning. *Journal of Educational Psychology, 81*(3), 329–339.

Zimmerman, B. J. (2000). Attaining self-regulation: A social cognitive perspective. In M. Boekaerts, P. R. Pintrich, & M. Zeidner (Eds.), *Handbook of self-regulation* (pp. 13–39). Academic Press.

Zimmerman, B. J. (2001). Theories of self-regulated learning and academic achievement: An overview and analysis. In B. J. Zimmerman & D. H. Schunk (Eds.), *Self-regulated learning and academic achievement: Theoretical perspectives* (pp. 1–37). Lawrence Erlbaum.

Zimmerman, B. J., & Schunk, D. H. (Eds.). (2011). *Handbook of self-regulation of learning and performance.* Routledge.

18
VISION AND GOAL SELF-CONCORDANCE

Alastair Henry

Introduction

Why is it that some people thrive on the process of acquiring another language, and maintain momentum in their learning, while others struggle to keep on track and fail to achieve proficiency? Why is it that some people willingly engage in time-consuming activities, learning the conjugations of irregular verbs, while others find it hard to keep focused? For William James (1842–1910), one of the founding figures in modern psychology, answers may lie in the processes in which people weigh up different possibilities for action and, once settled upon, how an action can become visually imprinted in the mind. Discussing human will in his classic work *The Principles of Psychology* (1890/1983), James uses his own reluctance to rise from bed on a cold winter's morning as an example of how vision prompts action. Arriving at a point where other possibilities (staying in bed) begin to recede from his mind, James describes how thoughts of the things needing to be accomplished during the day become the focal point of his attention, and force him into action (getting up). The spur for this or any other path of action, James maintains, is the *image* conjured in the mind. As he argues, "the essential achievement of the will, in short, when it is most 'voluntary,' is to ATTEND to a difficult object and hold it fast before the mind" (James 1890/1983, p. 1166; see also Cross & Markus, 1990; Hunt, 2007).

Focusing on *vision*—the mental images of objects held "fast before the mind"—and on *goals* that have a deeper personal meaning, this chapter discusses their roles in shaping L2 learning behavior. Drawing on work in mainstream and L2 psychology, it examines the ways in which vision can generate and sustain focused energy, and highlights the potentially positive effects of learning goals that resonate with personal interests, values, and beliefs.

Vision and Goal Self-Concordance in Psychology

Vision

Vision is the recasting of bodily sensations (sight, sound, smell, touch, etc.) as images in the mind (Robertson, 2002). True to the adage that "a picture is worth a thousand words," research shows that compared with verbal thoughts, mental images are perceived as more "real" (Mathews, Ridgeway, & Holmes, 2013). Visionary images can elicit stronger emotions than the verbal processing of similar content, and it is for this reason that visual imagery is sometimes described as a "weak" or "noisy" form of perception (Pearson, Naserlaris, Holmes, & Kosslyn, 2015, p. 590). Evidence from neuroimaging supports these ideas, the brain structures underlying mental imagery being strikingly similar to those that underlie actual perception (Kosslyn, Ganis, & Thompson, 2001).

Mental representations recalled from memory enable the individual "to *re-experience* a version of the original stimulus or some novel combination of stimuli" without a need for direct sensory input (Pearson et al., 2015, p. 590, emphasis added). However, visionary capacity is not limited to mental play-backs. As Holmes and her colleagues have shown, mental imagery can also enable people to *pre-experience* future events and activities (Holmes, Blackwell, Burnett Heyes, Renner, & Raes, 2016; Holmes, Lang, & Shah, 2009). Thus, as James ponders on the advantages of leaving the warmth and comfort of his bed, the image of himself sitting at his desk might enable him to *re-experience* the pleasure of writing. Equally, the same image might also trigger the *pre-experiencing* of a future event—the pleasure of grappling with a philosophical problem or constructing a convincing argument. In the psychology of the imagination, the re-experiencing and the pre-experiencing of an event each constitutes a particular form of *mental time travel* (Michaelian, Klein, & Szpunar, 2016).

Although the pre-experiencing of a future event will often involve visual imagery (Holmes et al., 2009), aspects of a future experience can also be mediated through other sensory modalities (Pearson et al., 2015). One of the most common forms of *pre-experiencing* involves the conversations people imagine will take place at a particular time, or in particular circumstances (Pearson, Deeprose, Wallace-Hadrill, Heyes, & Holmes, 2013). Equally, in acts of *re-experiencing*, people can mentally rerun previous discussions and arguments, imagining what they might, or could have said (Taylor, Pham, Rivkin, & Armor, 1998). In both re-experiencing and pre-experiencing, the *valence* attaching to the event or activity—whether it is pleasant or unpleasant—is part of the experience. In pre-experiencing, anticipation of the emotional consequences of future action influences current behavior, with various studies showing how anticipated emotions impact decision-making and goal-directed actions (Renner, Murphy, Ji, Manly, & Holmes, 2019; Sandberg & Conner, 2008; Schacter, Addis, Hassabis, Martin, Spreng, & Szpunar, 2012).

In educational contexts, prominent work examining mental imagery and student outcomes has involved applications of the theory of *possible selves* (Markus & Nurius, 1986). Possible selves are mental representations of the self in the future. They involve tangible images and senses, and are represented in a similar imaginary and semantic state as the "here-and-now" self. The elicitation of possible selves involves projecting into the future in a manner in which planning is combined with fantasy. It involves the trying out of possibilities, and the trying on of identities (Segal, 2006). Markus and Nurius (1986) identify three types of possible self: those that the individual would like to become (*an ideal self*), those that the individual is afraid of becoming (*the feared self*), and those that the individual could become (*an expected, or likely, self*). Beyond its descriptive validity, the importance of Markus and Nurius's theory lies in providing a means through which interventions focusing on behavioral change can be carried out. In educational psychology, successful interventions based on possible selves are widely reported (Dunkel & Kerpelman, 2006). In a meta-analytic review of motivational interventions, Lazowski and Hulleman (2016) found that possible self-based studies reported positive effects, the average effect size for interventions being 0.49. While this mean was lower than for interventions based on self-determination and attribution theories ($d = 0.7, 0.54$ respectively), it was higher than interventions based on expectancy–value and achievement goal theories ($d = 0.39, 0.38$ respectively).

However, while these studies support the idea that mental imagery influences goal-directed behavior (see also Rawolle, Schultheiss, Strasser, & Kehr, 2017; Ruvolo & Markus, 1992; Sherman et al., 1981), there are also studies that have failed to find positive effects of mental images involving possible futures. Indeed, some studies have shown that positive fantasies can have negative effects on motivated behavior (Kappes & Oettingen, 2011; Oettingen & Mayer, 2002; Oettingen, Pak, & Schnetter, 2001). As Oettingen and her colleagues (2001) have argued, if a positive fantasy about the future is not contrasted with current reality, and if it lacks anchoring in the present, it may predict less effort and can prevent the person from successfully overcoming obstacles. Indulging in fantasies about positive futures may not result in positive outcomes if, that is, mental imagery does not also contain visions of the *process* of getting there. Positive fantasies about the future can have the effect that people embellish the path that can take them there. They can put an overly positive slant on the challenges and sacrifices likely to be involved and be encouraged "to mentally enjoy the desired future in the here and now" (Oettingen et al., 2001, p. 737). In order for goal-focused behavior to be triggered, Oettingen and colleagues argue, it is necessary to visually position the desired future in the context of representations of current obstacles. This process involves *mental contrasting*, and is an issue to which we will return later in the chapter.

Another factor that seems likely to impact the effectiveness of mental imagery in spurring goal-directed action is the degree to which a conjured image aligns with the person's identity. In recent research on the effects of mental imagery on motivation, Rawolle and colleagues (2018) have suggested that it may be that only certain types of future vision affect behavior. Mental images effective in prompting action, they argue, are those that involve picture-like representations of a desirable (positive) future that is relevant to the person's identity. The importance of *identity-relevance* lies in the fact that mental images pertaining to an identity that the person desires to achieve represent an instantiation or embodiment of that identity. This has the effect that implicit motives—those that are subconsciously generated—become aroused. Here, it is important to recognize that psychological processing is regarded as taking two distinct forms: unintentional, uncontrollable, unconscious (but efficient) forms (so-called Type 1 processes), and intentional, controllable, conscious (but inefficient) forms (Type 2 processes) (Melnikoff & Bargh, 2018). When mental imagery is identity-relevant, implicit motives are triggered. Efficient (Type 1) processing is facilitated, and motivational energy is enhanced (Rawolle et al., 2018).

Goal Self-Concordance

Parallel to theorizing on the motivational influences of identity-relevant mental imagery, research in mainstream psychology has also examined the effects of pursuing goals that have deeper personal significance. Goals specify and steer behavior. They enable a marshalling of energy, and promote self-regulation (Sheldon, 2014). In their theory of *goal self-concordance,* Sheldon and Elliot (1998, 1999) argue that goals that are connected to the self in some important way function to enhance and sustain motivational energy. An extension of Deci and Ryan's (1985) theory of self-determination (SDT), self-concordance indexes the degree of personal ownership that people experience in relation to a self-generated goal. As is well recognized, not all goals are created equal (Ryan, Sheldon, Kasser, & Deci, 1996). Nor are all personal goals "personal" (Sheldon & Elliot, 1998, p. 555). Thus, even if a goal is self-determined, it does not follow that it will be experienced as fully autonomous and self-integrated. For a goal to be genuinely "owned" by an individual, in addition to being self-determined, it needs also to represent an abiding belief and a person's authentic interests. Goals that have a deeper personal meaning, that align with a person's identity in a self-affirming sense, and which are generally congruent with aspects of personality, can be understood as being high in self-concordance.

Goal self-concordance has been shown to have enduring influences on behavior. It predicts sustained effort and increased goal-attainment (Sheldon & Elliot, 1998, 1999). When behavior is guided by a self-concordant goal, the impulsive attraction to goal-disruptive temptations decreases. This means that goal pursuit is perceived as obstructed by fewer obstacles (Milyavskaya, Inzlicht, Hope, & Koestner, 2015). Goal self-concordance has also been demonstrated to enhance the positive effects that goal-attainment can have on well-being. Compared to goals that lack self-concordance, self-concordant goals generate greater satisfaction and increased well-being (Sheldon & Houser-Marko, 2001). For these reasons—and because they are linked with positive personality traits and futures that are growth-promoting and personally expressive (Waterman, 2013)—self-concordant goals typically align with projects that are personally meaningful, and with change that the person wants to achieve (Sheldon, 2014).

While all personal goals involve representations of the future, the extent to which they trigger future-situated imagery can vary (Miller & Brickman, 2004). For goals that are desired in a stronger sense, mental representations of the goal will include the positive valence of the desired state. The combined mental representation of the goal and its effects—what goal achievement feels like—plays an important role in the conscious and nonconscious motivational processes that underpin goal pursuit (Carver & Scheier, 1981; Custers & Aarts, 2005). A goal that is central to a person's identity and which is pursued out of conviction rather than obligation can be mentally represented in a manner that includes feelings of satisfaction, fulfillment, and well-being. Seen this way, self-concordant goals function as a "type of self-concept" and can serve to direct much of people's behavior (Sheldon & Elliot, 1999, p. 485).

Nonconscious processes not only guide behavior, they are also implicated in goal-selection. In research exploring the reasons for selecting self-concordant goals, Sheldon and colleagues (2019) argue that when people decide whether or not to adopt a goal that is objectively congruent with a core aspect of identity, there is "a signal that can communicate that congruence to them; namely, the fact that congruent goals *feel* like they would be interesting and meaningful to pursue, rather than being a burden or a drag" (Sheldon, Prentice, & Osin, 2019, p. 127, emphasis added). The intuition that a goal is personally valuable and worth pursuing has the effect of triggering emotional and motivational knowledge within the domain of automatic, image-based cognition. Thus, as Sheldon and colleagues (2019) suggest, it may be "the imagery based imagining of the self in situated goal pursuits" that facilitates decision-making when selecting and pursuing self-concordant goals (p. 128).

Vision and Goal Self-Concordance Combined

One research strand where vision and goal self-concordance have been studied as integrated dimensions in behavior-steering processes is work on *episodic future thinking* (D'Argembeau, 2016, 2020). A particular form of mental time travel (Michaelian, Klein, & Szpunar, 2016), episodic future thinking refers to the simulation of future events expected to occur in one's life. Episodic future thinking involves "pre-experiencing" the future in ways that enable the individual to imagine what it is like to be in a particular situation, and to envision the settings, people, and interactions.

A key idea in episodic future thinking is that it is not enough that an image is representationally elaborate for it to influence behavior. To steer behavior effectively, it needs also to be linked to a personally important goal. Research into the connections between event representations and self-concordant goals has yielded interesting findings. In a study by Ernst, Philippe, and D'Argembeau (2018), goal self-concordance was shown to facilitate the imagining of future events, and to enhance the "realness" of a mental image. When a future event was connected with a self-concordant goal, there was a stronger sense of pre-experiencing, and a firmer belief that the event would actually occur. Compared to future events associated with non-concordant goals (goals that, although self-determined, lack deeper personal meaning), events associated with self-concordant goals were rated as better fulfilling the basic psychological needs of autonomy, competence, and relatedness. Events associated with self-concordant goals were also more closely integrated with identity motives (self-esteem, distinctiveness, belonging, efficacy, and meaning). The emotional loading of a self-concordant event was also greater, as was the emotional intensity of future thoughts.

Vision and Goal Self-Concordance in SLA

Vision

Vision lies at the root of the central constructs of Dörnyei's (2009) L2 Motivational Self System (L2MSS). In accordance with Higgins' (1987) theory of self-discrepancy, self-guides are theorized to steer the learner's behavior in a positive direction by reducing gaps with current self-conceptions.

Both of the system's self-guides have visionary components. While the *ideal L2 self* (the "best-case" scenario) involves mental projections of self-images of the L2 speaker/user the person would like to become, the *ought-to L2 self* involves mental representations of the L2 speaker/user that the person feels they are expected to become (see Dörnyei, 2020a, and Papi, Bondarenko, Mansouri, Feng, & Jiang, 2019, for detailed discussions).

The L2MSS has been employed in countless studies in settings around the globe (Boo, Dörnyei, & Ryan, 2015). In a meta-analytic study (Al-Hoorie, 2018), the ideal and ought-to L2 selves were found to be significant predictors of intended effort (see also Muir, this volume). One group of studies has specifically focused on the effects of vision, and the relationship of visionary modalities to the L2MSS self-guides. In a sample of secondary school Chinese students, Dörnyei and Chan (2013) found significant associations between visual perceptual style and the L2MSS self-guides (an association that was accentuated when other sensory variables were also included), and between the self-guides and criterion measures. In a large-scale stratified sample of over 10,000 Chinese learners of English, and using the measures of vision developed by Dörnyei and Chan (2013) plus additional scales, You, Dörnyei, and Csizér (2016) found engagement in mental imagery to be positively correlated with the L2MSS self-guides, which in turn were correlated with the criterion variable of intended effort. In a theoretical replication of this study by Hiver and Al-Hoorie (2020), strong positive correlations between visual style and the ideal L2 self, and between the ideal L2 self and intended effort were also found. However, in an alternative model where grades were the criterion, these correlations were substantially weaker. Moreover, effects for the ought-to L2 self, which were weak in the original model, were non-existent in the revised model.

In addition to survey-based research pointing to the importance of vision and visualization capacity in generating motivation for language learning, studies have also demonstrated the effects of visionary-based interventions in L2 classrooms (see Vlaeva & Dörnyei, in press, for a discussion). In a series of early intervention studies, promising results were found (see Mackay, 2019). While these studies drew on vision-development programs from mainstream psychology, in a series of "second generation" studies, researchers have applied Dörnyei and Kubanyiova's (2014) multi-stage program of visionary training for language learning, implementing it in robust quasi-experimental designs (see e.g., Busse, Cenoz, Dalmann, & Rogge, 2020; Safdari, 2019; Sato, 2020; Sato & Lara, 2019). In this program (see also Hadfield & Dörnyei, 2013), visualization techniques and strategy training comprise six discrete components: (a) *creating the vision* (support in constructing L2 imagery), (b) *strengthening the vision* (support in developing elaborated L2 selves), (c) *substantiating the vision* (support in calibrating L2 selves with realistic expectations of success), (d) *transforming the vision into action* (support in creating action plans for self-realization), (e) *keeping the vision alive* (providing opportunities for regular activation of L2 self-images), and (f) *counterbalancing the vision* (prompting reflection on the consequences of not achieving a desired L2 self).

In a study with third grade students in a German setting, and based on material developed by Hadfield and Dörnyei (2013), Busse and colleagues (2020) carried out an intervention designed to promote ideal language-speaking selves. As part of the intervention, students engaged in an affective-experiential activity that involved a dream journey during which different languages could be auditorily experienced. Assessed on a scale measuring idealized visions of being a person who would speak many languages, students in the intervention group scored higher in post-test measurements than those in the control group.

In a Chilean study of university learners of English, Sato and Lara (2019) carried out a vision-based intervention where classroom communicative activities were integrated with the imagery techniques and visual stimuli in Dörnyei and Kubanyiova's (2014) vision-enhancing program. For students in the intervention group, the ideal L2 self was positively affected (see also Sato, 2020 for a study that generated similar findings). In another study using Dörnyei and Kubanyiova's program, Safdari (2019) obtained corresponding results. Similarly to Sato and Lara's study, Iranian EFL learners in an intervention group received a six-step program that included activities designed to enhance vision and imagination. Following the intervention, measurements revealed increases in the strength of participants' imagery capacity and their ideal L2 self. Intended effort also improved. Notable in these studies, however, is that the ought-to L2 self remained unaffected by the interventions. Given these findings, and the recent application of regulatory focus theory to the L2MSS model (Papi et al., 2019), the conceptualization and operationalization of the ought-to L2 self is likely to be the subject of much future work.

In a novel study in a Japanese setting, Munezane (2015) explored the effects of visualization and goal-setting on a different criterion variable: willingness to communicate. In Munezane's study, two intervention conditions were incorporated. In one intervention group participants worked with visualization techniques, while in the other visualization was combined with goal-setting activities. Here, students considered what they wanted to achieve in their lives, and how learning English fitted with these goals. The results showed that when visualization was combined with goal-setting, effects on WTC were significantly enhanced. This was true not only in comparison with the control group, but also in relation to the visualization-only group.

Goal Self-Concordance

While there is an abundance of work on vision in SLA, there is hardly any research exploring L2 learners' goals (McEown & Oga-Baldwin, 2019). In this respect, Munezane's study constitutes a notable exception. One area where research into the qualities of learners' goals has taken place is in the development of the theory of Directed Motivational Currents (DMCs) (Dörnyei, Henry, & Muir, 2016; see also Muir, this volume). A DMC is a construct that captures a powerful form of motivation that arises whenever a goal of significant personal importance is matched with a structured pathway of action. In a DMC, the energy generated in goal pursuit is amplified so that goal-oriented actions become automatized, and an intensive endeavor is experienced as effortless and pleasurable. Although the constituents of DMCs have recognizable counterparts in mainstream psychology, and involve well-established motivational processes, a DMC is different from other types of motivated behavior. While the type of regulation characteristic of good students—dedication, commitment, and focus—are manifestly observable, in a DMC there is no need for conscious regulation. This is because the overarching goal is an integrated dimension of the individual's identity. This has the effect that engaging in goal-directed activities becomes an automatic part of life, and that activities which in normal circumstances might be experienced as tedious or resource-intensive, feel effortless and generate feelings of satisfaction and fulfillment.

There is now an accumulating body of empirical work where DMCs have been investigated (Henry, 2019; Muir, this volume). While particular elements of the theory have been emphasized in different studies, the investigation of goal self-concordance is prominent in many (see e.g., Ibrahim, 2016; Selçuk & Erten, 2017; Zarrinabadi & Tavakoli, 2016). In a study examining the experiences of adult language learners in Sweden, Henry, Davydenko, and Dörnyei (2015) highlighted how the goal of developing L2 skills was highly self-concordant. For the three women in this study, becoming proficient in Swedish was driven by the desire to integrate into the communities in which they lived. Pointing to how the fusing together of a self-concordant goal and a desired future identity (becoming an established and worthy member of society) could set in motion an intense and enduring flow of goal-directed energy, the study highlights the importance of examining L2 vision in the context of learners' goals. It also points to the potential importance of constructs—such as episodic future thinking (D'Argembeau, 2016, 2020)—where personal goals and mental representations of desired future states are conceptually integrated (Henry, 2020).

As we have seen, self-concordant goals are aligned with endeavors that are personally meaningful. Compared to goals that are self-determined, but which lack self-concordance, they generate greater satisfaction and enhanced well-being (Sheldon & Houser-Marko, 2001). In a study investigating the patterns of regulation associated with self-concordant and non-concordant goals, Henry and Davydenko (2020) showed how differences in the qualities of participants' goals were associated with different learning experiences. For participants who pursued goals that were self-concordant, the development of L2 skills corresponded with patterns of thriving. For these participants, pleasure, satisfaction, and well-being were more generally characteristic of their learning experiences. However, for participants whose goals lacked self-concordance, learning was not only effortful, but was associated with negative emotions such as worry, fear, and stress.

Integrating Psychology and SLA Perspectives

While research into learners' goals is only just beginning in L2 psychology (McEown & Oga-Baldwin, 2019), vision has generated a substantial body of work (Henry, 2019). Despite the extensive use of identity-based theories of motivation, conceptual transfer between L2 and mainstream psychology remains largely unidirectional. It is clear, however, that ideas also have the potential to travel in the opposite direction. Here, a noteworthy example is Kubanyiova's work on language teacher possible selves, which has had impact in mainstream education, with a chapter on the topic appearing in a volume of the Routledge *Research into Higher Education* series (Kubanyiova, 2018). Dörnyei's (2020a) work developing understandings of L2 perseverance is another area where research exploring L2 vision has received the attention of mainstream scholars. Here, an article on long-term motivation is included in the *Advances in Motivational Science* series edited by Andrew Elliot (Dörnyei & Henry, in press).

Because L2 learning is by nature a long-term endeavor, conceptualization of the mechanisms through which perseverance is generated means that work on L2 vision can provide insights that are valuable to mainstream psychology. In addition to the L2MSS and the DMC construct, Dörnyei's identification of *self-concordant vision* has particular relevance (Dörnyei, 2020a). In developing this concept, Dörnyei draws on Adler's (1981) theory of momentum and the identification of behavior that is purposefully directed to goal accomplishment, and which is characterized by "an accelerated rhythm and intensity" (p. 13).

In educational and sports psychology, there is now a growing interest in momentum and the ways in which high-intensity motivational behavior develops and is sustained over time (Markman & Guenther, 2007; Vallerand, Colavecchio, & Pelletier, 1988). In the theory of psychological momentum, previous experiences of success (or failure) in a particular task/domain form a context promoting the likelihood of future successes (or failures). As Hubbard (2017, p. 52) explains, psychological momentum "can be positive (current success or victory is believed to increase the likelihood of subsequent success or victory) or negative (current failure or defeat is believed to increase the likelihood of subsequent failure or defeat)". What is important to note is that anticipation of the outcomes of future actions is underpinned by processes of momentum, with similar types of momentum effect being observed in varying activities, and across various timescales (Den Hartigh, Van Geert, Van Yperen, Cox, & Gernigon, 2016; Hubbard, 2015).

In Adler's (1981) conceptualization of momentum, the long-term goal and the vision of its accomplishment are tightly intermeshed. Arguing that "goal-oriented behaviour is key to momentum," Adler explains how "the vision of a goal, arising from any of several spheres, serves as the central inspiration that binds and impels the entire vortex of subsequent behavior" (1981, p. 53). Buttressed by Adler's identification of how momentum emerges when an overarching goal that steers behavior is visualized in mental imagery, Dörnyei (2020a) identifies *self-concordant vision* as the signum of enduring motivational capacity, and the primary characteristic of long-term motivation. As he explains:

> ...vision becomes particularly relevant when future self-images are fused with self-concordance. When one visualises scenarios that are closely aligned with one's deepest feelings, values and aspirations, these identity-relevant visionary images–or 'self-concordant visions'–have long-lasting motivational capacity
>
> p. 138

In any long-term activity, self-concordant vision generates momentum by channeling the person's focus. By visualizing the goal together with the means of accomplishment, self-concordant vision facilitates persistence in that competing activities lack similar attraction. Even when interruptions do occur, having a self-concordant vision means that the image of oneself engaged in activities which represent an aimed-for future outcome can brace against the "motivational pull" of a competing activity. Thus, having a self-concordant vision enables the person to rapidly return into a flow of energy following an interruption (Dörnyei, 2020a; Dörnyei & Henry, in press).

Implications for Practice and Research

Implications for Practice

Because L2 learning involves developing (and changing) identities, activities encompassing different types of mental projection form an important part of teaching practice (Arnold, 1999; Arnold, Puchta, & Rinvolucri, 2007). A growing body of work now points to the value of mental imagery in L2 learning, adding to the list of domains in human life in which vision functions as a motivational resource–business management (Kouzes & Posner, 2017), psychotherapy (Singer, 2006), and theology (Dörnyei, 2020b), to name but a few. Moreover, emerging evidence indicates that technological innovations can enhance this potential (Adolphs et al., 2018). In the same way that visionary training has been shown to bolster focus and motivation, explorations of the ways in which students' L2 goals might "fit" with aspects of identity—for example as an L2 speaker or a multilingual person—may also provide a means of generating positive responses to learning in focused interventions.

As we have seen in this chapter, not all goals are self-concordant. Not all goals generate the type of endurance that L2 learning often requires. Indeed, people can devote inordinate amounts of time to pursuing learning goals that may not be optimally aligned with aspects of identity and personality (if, indeed, they are aligned at all). Choosing the "right" goal is therefore a decision of some importance. However, identifying self-appropriate goals is no easy matter. It is a skill that needs to be actively developed (Sheldon et al., 2019).

In situations where L2 learning involves choice (between languages on offer, methods of learning or, for that matter, whether to embark on the process in the first place), there can be value in exploring *goal appropriateness*. Consideration of goal-fit can improve the choices people make. As Sheldon and colleagues (2019) explain, although it can be very difficult for people to objectively identify goals that are "right" for them, "it may be easier for people to know how they *feel* about what they *think* they want, or think they *might* want" (p. 127, original emphasis).

For L2 students, accessing intuitions relating to long-term aspirations can help in identifying goals that are—or which could become—personally meaningful. Students can be supported in uncovering underlying preferences and helped in setting L2 learning goals that accord more closely with who they are as individuals. At the outset of a program of study, goal exploration could be directed to misconceptions about language learning (for example about the centrality of grammar, and the ways in which languages are taught and acquired). In this light, teachers and study counselors could support students in focusing on aspects of language learning—for example developing intercultural and multilingual skills—that might provide a closer fit with personally important values and beliefs.

Implications for research

Although not widely investigated, the idea that goal quality can affect the power of mental imagery is certainly not new. In the context of possible selves, Oyserman, Bybee, Terry, and Hart-Johnson (2004) explain how the impact that a possible self has on behavior can depend on the extent to which it represents a personally important goal. According to Hoyle and Sherrill (2006), possible selves can relate to goals that are self-*defining*, as well as goals that are merely self-*enhancing*. Although a self-enhancing goal can generate positive feelings about the self, it may not have immediate and direct relevance for focused behavior. A goal that is self-defining, on the other hand, is likely to generate more consistently strategic forms of regulation.

In much of her work, Markus has focused on the role of possible selves in generating growth and longer-term behavioral change (see, e.g., Wurf & Markus, 1991). In particular, the degree to which the image of a future self connects with one or more of the individual's *self-schema* is regarded as highly important. Self-schema are domains of the self in which a person is deeply invested. As Stein and Markus (1996) have suggested, possible selves are expected to function effectively insofar as they are connected with a currently important self-schema:

> One source of variability among possible selves is the extent to which they are tied to an existing current self-schema. Some possible selves are closely tied to a current self-schema such that they represent an extension or elaboration of the self in the domain. Others have little or no connection to the current self-definition. Possible selves function most effectively to motivate goal-directed behavior when they are closely tied to established current self-schemas.
>
> *pp. 366-367*

Bringing these arguments together, it would appear that while *all* possible selves *can* have an influence on behavior, those with the potential to have the strongest impact represent goals that are *self-relevant* and, to some extent, *self-defining*. Harking back to James's (1890/1983) seminal theorizing, Cross and Markus (1990) argue that while possible selves allow the person to sustain a vision of the future, "it is when the desired end state is made self-relevant or is personalized that it is most easily *held before the mind*" (p. 731, emphasis added).

Yet, there are further ways in which possible selves that represent self-relevant goals can be understood to influence behavior. In a recent study, Oyserman, Destin, and Novin (2015) found that positive and negative future identities were motivational only to the extent that they fitted with the way that the *context* was experienced. Goal-directed behavior, they argue, is augmented when a future self is imagined "in a valenced way that is relevant to the immediate context" (p. 184). It follows, therefore, that a focus on positive outcomes can function as a general strategy to the degree that the learning context is "success-likely." However, in situations that are "success-*un*likely"—and where goals may lack self-relevance—an ideal self may not have great motivational potential. In such situations, the cuing of an undesired possible self may be more likely to generate focused learning behaviors (Oyserman, Destin, & Novin, 2015).

Returning to the previous discussions of self-discrepancy (Higgins, 1987) and mental contrasting (Oettingen et al., 2001), it would appear that for visions of future L2 situations to be optimally effective in generating goal-focused action, assemblages of mental imagery need to meet a number of requirements. The image of an ideal L2 self is likely to be most effective if: (i) it relates to a goal that has a degree of self-concordance; (ii) it is more generally activated in positively valenced, success-likely contexts; (iii) it encompasses a broad range of situational components, including the relationship to the current L2 self; and (iv) it encapsulates perceptions of the processes and pathways leading to goal accomplishment.

While the importance of these issues was flagged in Dörnyei's (2009) original theorizing, and in MacIntyre and colleagues' prescient critiques in conjunction with the launch of the L2MSS (MacIntyre, Mackinnon, & Clément, 2009a, 2009b), it is notable how few studies have engaged with conceptualizations of the *imagery content* of the L2 self-guides, the manner in which images of future L2 use are *represented* in the learner's imagination (i.e. self-construal), and the extent to which L2 self-guides might encompass *process imagery* relating to routes and obstacles. Along with studies investigating the interconnectedness of imagery and learning goals (Henry, 2020, in press), these are areas that would benefit greatly from future research.

Future Directions

This chapter began by asking why it is that some people thrive on the process of learning another language, whereas others can struggle to keep on track, and why it is that some people derive satisfaction from mundane activities, while others are easily distracted. Together with many of the other psychological concepts in this "Constructs" section of the handbook, theories of goal self-concordance (Sheldon, 2014) and episodic future thinking (D'Argembeau, 2016, 2020) can provide keys in understanding why some people maintain momentum in L2 learning, and why others falter (Henry, 2020). However, in common with concepts such as personality (Dewaele, this volume) and resilience (Hiver & Sanchez Solarte, this volume), questions arise about how these constructs can be usefully used in L2 research.

While imagery-focused interventions demonstrate the positive benefits of capacity-building (e.g., Busse et al., 2020; Munezane, 2015; Safdari, 2019; Sato, in press; Sato & Lara, 2019; Vlaeva & Dörnyei, in press), and while research from mainstream psychology testifies to the motivational and emotional advantages of having/choosing goals that are strong in self-concordance (Sheldon & Elliot, 1998, 1999; Sheldon & Houser-Marko, 2001; Sheldon et al., 2019), in employing these constructs in empirical work there is an inherent risk of "blaming the victim"; "if only L2 learners could see skills development as more personally fulfilling, and could imagine their L2-speaking futures in a more positive light, they might be able to generate greater enthusiasm for study." Furthermore, the value of these constructs needs to be carefully assessed in relation to situations where language learning is not an endeavor freely entered into, but, as in migration situations, takes place in contexts of social duress (Ortega, 2018).

In considering the effects that research with a focus on mental imagery might have on the people who take part in a study, and the ways in which they can be positioned in research outputs, Henderson, Bathmaker, and Stevenson (2018) pose the question, "what questions…. can we ask about what students imagine, without implicitly suggesting what they *should* imagine?" (p. 4, original emphasis). Moreover, when research focuses on abandoned or unimagined possible selves, it becomes necessary to ask the question as to what extent analyses can (or should) "move beyond the tendency to situate such absence in the failures and deficits of individuals, rather than in the structures that shape them?" (p. 4). These are important questions. In continued work with L2 vision and goal self-concordance, they raise methodological and ethical issues that researchers will need to carefully address.

Reflection questions

- Given the interrelatedness of ideal selves and self-concordant goals, what challenges are presented when operationalizing the constructs in research designs?
- What ethical issues should researchers take into consideration when inviting participants to imagine future selves, and to explore goal appropriateness?
- So far, self-concordant goals have only been examined in relation to the behaviors of language *learners*. What potential does the construct have for investigating the motivations and goals of language *teachers*?

Recommended Reading

Markman, K. D., Klein, W. M. P., & Suhr, J. A. (Eds.). (2008). *Handbook of Imagination and Mental Simulation*. Routledge.
This handbook provides a comprehensive survey of theories of human imagination.

Robertson, I. (2002). *The mind's eye: An essential guide to boosting your mental power*. Bantam Books.
This book offers an excellent overview of the range of psychological domains where imagery is implicated and provides insights valuable to a range of areas within SLA.

Dörnyei, Z., & Kubanyiova, M. (2014). *Motivating learners, motivating teachers: Building vision in the language classroom*. Cambridge University Press.
This award-winning monograph describes how vision can be used as a motivational resource in language classrooms, and sets out a program of visionary training.

References

Adler, P. (1981). *Momentum: A theory of social action*. Sage.
Adolphs, S., Clark, L., Dörnyei, Z., Glover, T., Henry, A., Muir, C., et al. (2018). Digital innovations in L2 motivation: Harnessing the power of the ideal L2 self. *System 78*, 173–185.
Al-Hoorie, A. H. (2018). The L2 motivational self system: A meta-analysis. *Studies in Second Language Learning and Teaching, 8*, 721–754.
Arnold, J. (Ed.). (1999). *Affect in language learning*. Cambridge University Press.
Arnold, J., Puchta, H., & Rinvolucri, M. (2007). *Imagine that! Mental imagery in the EFL classroom*. Cambridge University Press.
Boo, Z., Dörnyei, Z., & Ryan, S. (2015). L2 motivation research 2005–2014: Understanding a publication surge and a changing landscape. *System, 55*, 145–157.
Busse, V., Cenoz, J., Dalmann, N., & Rogge, F. (2020). Addressing linguistic diversity in the language classroom in a resource-oriented way: An intervention study with primary school children. *Language Learning 70, 2*, 382–419.
Carver, C. S., & Scheier, M. F. (1981). *Attention and self-regulation: A control-theory approach to human behavior*. Springer.
Cross, S. E., & Markus, H. R. (1990). The willful self. *Personality and Social Psychology Bulletin, 16*, 726–742.
Custers, R., & Aarts, H. (2005). Positive affect as implicit motivator: On the nonconscious operation of behavioral goals. *Journal of Personality and Social Psychology, 89*(2), 129–142.
D'Argembeau, A. (2016). The role of personal goals in future-oriented mental time travel. In K. Michaelian, S. B. Klein, & K K. Szpunar (eds.), *Seeing the future: Theoretical perspectives on future-oriented mental time travel* (pp. 199–214). Oxford: Oxford University Press.
D'Argembeau, A. (2020). Imagination and self-referential thinking. In A. Abraham (ed.). *The Cambridge handbook of the imagination* (pp. 354–372). Cambridge University Press.
Deci, E. L., & Ryan, R. M. (1985). *Intrinsic motivation and self-determination in human behavior*. Plenum.
Den Hartigh, R. J., Van Geert, P. L., Van Yperen, N. W., Cox, R. F., & Gernigon, C. (2016). Psychological momentum during and across sports matches: Evidence for interconnected time scales. *Journal of Sport & Exercise Psychology, 38*, 82–92.
Dörnyei, Z. (2009). The L2 motivational self system. In Z. Dörnyei & E. Ushioda (Eds.), *Motivation, language identity and the L2 self* (pp. 9–42). Multilingual Matters.
Dörnyei, Z. (2020a). *Innovations and challenges in language learning motivation*. Routledge.
Dörnyei, Z. (2020b). *Vision, mental imagery and the Christian life: Insights from science and Scripture*. Routledge.
Dörnyei, Z., & Chan, L. (2013). Motivation and vision: An analysis of future L2 self images, sensory styles, and imagery capacity across two target languages. *Language Learning, 63, 3*, 437–462.
Dörnyei, Z., & Henry, A. (in press). Accounting for long-term motivation and sustained motivated learning: Motivational currents, self-concordant vision, and persistence in language learning. In A. J. Elliot (ed.), Advances in Motivation Science, Vol. 9. Academic Press.
Dörnyei, Z., Henry, A., & Muir, C. (2016). *Motivational currents in language learning: Frameworks for focused interventions*. Routledge.
Dörnyei, Z., & Kubanyiova, M. (2014). *Motivating learners, motivating teachers: Building vision in the language classroom*. Cambridge University Press.
Dunkel, C., & Kerpelman, J. (2006). *Possible selves: Theory, research and applications*. Nova Science.
Ernst, A., Philippe, F. L., & D'Argembeau, A. (2018). Wanting or having to: The influence of goal self-concordance on the representation of personal future events. *Consciousness and Cognition, 66*, 26–39.
Hadfield, J., & Dörnyei, Z. (2013). *Motivating learning*. Longman.
Henderson, H., Stevenson, J., & Bathmaker, A. M. (2018). *Possible selves in higher education*. Routledge.
Henry, A. (2019). Directed motivational currents: Extending the theory of L2 vision. In M. Lamb, K. Csizér, A. Henry, & S. Ryan (Eds.), *The Palgrave handbook of motivation for language learning* (pp. 139–161). Palgrave Macmillan.

Henry, A. (2020). Possible selves and personal goals: What can we learn from episodic future thinking? *Eurasian Journal of Applied Linguistics, 6*(3), 481–500.

Henry, A. (in press). Goal self-concordance and motivational sustainability. In A. H. Al-Hoorie & F. Szabó (Eds.), *Researching language learning motivation: A concise guide*. Bloomsbury.

Henry, A., & Davydenko, S. (2020). Thriving? Or surviving? An approach–avoidance perspective on adult language learners' motivation. *The Modern Language Journal 104*(2).

Henry, A., Davydenko, S., & Dörnyei, Z. (2015). The anatomy of Directed Motivational Currents: Exploring intense and enduring periods of L2 motivation. *The Modern Language Journal, 99*(2), 329–345.

Higgins, E. T. (1987). Self-discrepancy: A theory relating self and affect. *Psychological Review, 94*, 319–340.

Hiver, P., & Al-Hoorie, A. H. (2020). Reexamining the role of vision in second language motivation: A preregistered conceptual replication of You, Dörnyei, and Csizér (2016). *Language Learning, 70*(1), 48–102.

Holmes, E. A., Blackwell, S. E., Burnett Heyes, S., Renner, F., & Raes, F. (2016). Mental imagery in depression: Phenomenology, potential mechanisms, and treatment implications. *Annual Review of Clinical Psychology, 12*, 249–280.

Holmes, E. A., Lang, T. J., & Shah, D. M. (2009). Developing interpretation bias modification as a "cognitive vaccine" for depressed mood: Imagining positive events makes you feel better than thinking about them verbally. *Journal of Abnormal Psychology, 118*, 76–88.

Hoyle, R. H., & Sherrill, M. R. (2006). Future orientation in the self-system: Possible selves, self-regulation, and behavior. *Journal of Personality, 74*, 1673–1696.

Hubbard, T. L. (2015). The varieties of momentum-like experience. *Psychological Bulletin, 141*, 1081–1119.

Hubbard, T. L. (2017). Toward a general theory of momentum-like effects. *Behavioural Processes, 141*, 50–66.

Hunt, M. (2007). *The story of psychology*. Anchor Books.

Ibrahim, Z. (2016). Affect in directed motivational currents: Positive emotionality in longterm L2 engagement. In P. MacIntyre, T. Gregersen, & S. Mercer (Eds.), *Positive psychology in second language acquisition* (pp. 258–281). Multilingual Matters.

James, W. (1890/1983). *The principles of psychology*. Harvard University Press.

Kappes, H. B., & Oettingen, G. (2011). Positive fantasies about idealized futures sap energy. *Journal of Experimental Social Psychology, 47*, 719–729.

Kosslyn, S. M., Ganis, G., & Thompson, W. L. (2001). Neural foundations of imagery. *Nature Reviews Neuroscience, 2*, 635–642.

Kouzes, J. M., & Posner, B. Z. (2017). *The leadership challenge: How to make extraordinary things happen in organisations* (6th ed.). Wiley.

Kubanyiova, M. (2018). A discursive approach to understanding the role of educators' possible selves in widening students' participation in classroom interaction: language teachers' sense making as "acts of imagination." In H. Henderson, J. Stevenson, & A.M. Bathmaker (Eds.), *Possible selves in higher education* (pp. 59–77). Routledge.

Lazowski, R. A., & Hulleman, C. S. (2016). Motivation interventions in education: A meta-analytic review. *Review of Educational Research, 86*, 602–640.

Mackay, J. (2019). An ideal second language self intervention: Development of possible selves in an English as a Foreign Language classroom context. *System 81*, 50–62.

MacIntyre, P. D., Mackinnon, S. P., & Clément, R. (2009a). The baby, the bathwater, and the future of language learning motivation research. In Z. Dörnyei & E. Ushioda (Eds.), *Motivation, language identity and the L2 Self* (pp. 43–65). Multilingual Matters.

MacIntyre, P. D., Mackinnon, S. P., & Clément, R. (2009b). Toward the development of a scale to assess possible selves as a source of language learning motivation. In Z. Dörnyei & E. Ushioda (Eds.), *Motivation, language identity and the L2 Self* (pp. 193–214). Multilingual Matters.

Markman, K. D., & Guenther, C. L. (2007). Psychological momentum: Intuitive physics and naïve beliefs. *Personal and Social Psychological Bulletin, 33*, 800–812.

Markus, H. R., & Nurius, P. (1986). Possible selves. *American Psychologist, 41*, 954–969.

Mathews, A., Ridgeway, V., & Holmes, E. A. (2013). Feels like the real thing: Imagery is both more realistic and emotional than verbal thought. *Cognition & Emotion, 27*(2), 217–229.

McEwon, M. S., & Oga-Baldwin, W. L. Q. (2019). Self-determination for all language learners: New applications for formal language education. *System 86*, 102–124.

Melnikoff, D. E., & Bargh, J. A. (2018). The mythical number two. *Trends in Cognitive Sciences, 22*, 280–293.

Michaelian, K., Klein, S. B., & Szpunar, K. K. (Eds.). (2016). The past, the present, and the future of future-oriented mental time travel: Editors' introduction (pp. 1–22). Oxford University Press.

Miller, R. B., & Brickman, S. J. (2004). A model of future-oriented motivation and self-regulation. *Educational Psychology Review, 16*, 9–33.

Milyavskaya, M., Inzlicht, M., Hope, N., & Koestner, R. (2015). Saying "no" to temptation: Want-to motivation improves self-regulation by reducing temptation rather than by increasing self-control. *Journal of Personality and Social Psychology, 109*, 677–693.

Munezane, Y. (2015). Enhancing willingness to communicate: Relative effects of visualization and goal setting. *The Modern Language Journal, 99*, 175–191.

Oettingen, G., & Mayer, D. (2002). The motivating function of thinking about the future: Expectations versus fantasies. *Journal of Personality and Social Psychology, 83*, 1198–1212.

Oettingen, G., Pak, H., & Schnetter, K. (2001). Self-regulation of goal setting: Turning free fantasies about the future into binding goals. *Journal of Personality and Social Psychology, 80*, 736–753.

Ortega, L. (2018). SLA in uncertain times: Disciplinary constraints, transdisciplinary hopes. *Working Papers in Educational Linguistics, 33*, 1–30.

Oyserman, D., Destin, M., & Novin, S. (2015). The context-sensitive future self: Possible selves motivate in context, not otherwise. *Self and Identity, 14*, 173–188.

Oyserman, D., Bybee, D., Terry, K., & Hart-Johnson, T. (2004). Possible selves as roadmaps. *Journal of Research in Personality, 38*, 130–149.

Papi, M., Bondarenko, A. V., Mansouri, S., Feng, L., & Jiang, C. (2019). Rethinking L2 motivation research: The 2X2 model of L2 self-guides. *Studies in Second Language Acquisition 41*, 337–361.

Pearson, D. G., Deeprose, C., Wallace-Hadrill, S. M. A., Heyes, S. B., & Holmes, E. A. (2013). Assessing mental imagery in clinical psychology: A review of imagery measures and a guiding framework. *Clinical Psychology Review, 33*, 1–23.

Pearson, J., Naselaris, T., Holmes, E. A., & Kosslyn, S. M. (2015). Mental imagery: Functional mechanisms and clinical applications. *Trends in Cognitive Sciences, 19*, 590–602.

Rawolle, M., Schultheiss, O. C., Strasser, A., & Kehr, H. M. (2017). The motivating power of visionary images: Effects on motivation, affect, and behavior. *Journal of Personality, 85*, 769–781.

Renner, F., Murphy, F. C., Ji, J. L., Manly, T., & Holmes, E. A. (2019). Mental imagery as a "motivational amplifier" to promote activities. *Behaviour Research and Therapy, 114*, 51–59.

Robertson, I. (2002). *The mind's eye: An essential guide to boosting your mental power*. Bantam Books.

Ruvolo, A. P., & Markus, H. R. (1992). Possible selves and performance: The power of self-relevant imagery. *Social Cognition, 10*, 95–124.

Ryan, R. M., Sheldon, K. M., Kasser, T., & Deci, E. L. (1996). All goals are not created equal: The relation of goal content and regulatory styles to mental health. In J. A. Bargh & P. M. Gollwitzer (Eds.), *The psychology of action: Linking cognition and motivation to behavior* (pp. 7–26). The Guilford Press.

Safdari, S. (2019). Operationalizing L2 motivational self system: Improving EFL learners' motivation through a vision enhancement program. *Language Teaching Research, 25*, 282–305.

Sato, M. (in press). Generating a roadmap for possible selves via a vision intervention: Motivation and classroom behavior. *TESOL Quarterly*.

Sato, M., & Lara, P. (2019). Interaction vision intervention to increase second language motivation: A classroom study. In M. Sato & S. Loewen (Eds.), *Evidence-based second language pedagogy: A collection of instructed second language acquisition studies* (pp. 287–313). Routledge.

Sandberg, T., & Conner, M. (2008). Anticipated regret as an additional predictor in the theory of planned behaviour: A meta-analysis. *British Journal of Social Psychology, 47*, 589–606.

Schacter, D. L., Addis, D. R., Hassabis, D., Martin, V. C., Spreng, R. N., & Szpunar, K. K. (2012). The future of memory: Remembering, imagining, and the brain. *Neuron, 76*, 677–694.

Segal, H. G. (2006) Possible selves, fantasy distortion, and the anticipated life history: Exploring the role of imagination in social cognition. In C. Dunkel and J. Kerpelman (Eds.) *Possible selves: Theory, research and applications* (pp. 79–96). Nova Science.

Selçuk, Ö., & Erten, H. (2017). A display of patterns of change in learners' motivation: Dynamics perspective. *Novitas-ROYAL (Research on Youth and Language), 11*, 128–141.

Sheldon, K. M. (2014). Becoming oneself: The central role of self-concordant goal selection. *Personality and Social Psychology Review, 18*, 349–365.

Sheldon, K. M., & Elliot, A. J. (1998). Not all personal goals are personal: Comparing autonomous and controlled reasons for goals as predictors of effort and attainment. *Personality and Social Psychology Bulletin, 24*, 546–557.

Sheldon, K. M., & Elliot, A. J. (1999). Goal striving, need satisfaction, and longitudinal well-being: The self-concordance model. *Journal of Personality and Social Psychology, 76*, 482–497.

Sheldon, K. M., & Houser-Marko, L. (2001). Self-concordance, goal attainment, and the pursuit of happiness: Can there be an upward spiral? *Journal of Personality and Social Psychology, 80*, 152–165.

Sheldon, K. M., Prentice, M., & Osin, E. (2019). Rightly crossing the Rubicon: Evaluating goal self-concordance prior to selection helps people choose more intrinsic goals. *Journal of Research in Personality, 79*, 119–129.

Sherman, S. J., Skov, R. B., Hervitz, E. F., & Stock, C. B. (1981). The effects of explaining hypothetical future events: From possibility to actuality and beyond. *Journal of Experimental Social Psychology, 17*, 142–158.
Singer, J. L. (2006). *Imagery in psychotherapy*. American Psychological Association.
Stein, K. F., & Markus, H. R. (1996). The role of the self in behavioral change. *Journal of Psychotherapy Integration, 6*, 349–384.
Taylor, S. E., Pham, L. B., Rivkin, I. D., & Armor, D. A. (1998). Harnessing the imagination: Mental simulation, self-regulation, and coping. *American Psychologist, 53*, 429–439.
Vallerand, R. J., Colavecchio, P. G., & Pelletier, L. G., 1988. Psychological momentum andperformance differences: a preliminary test of the antecedents-consequencespsychological momentum model. *Journal of Sport and Exercise Psychology, 10*, 92–108.
Vlaeva, D. & Dörnyei, Z. (in press). Vision enhancement and language learning: A critical analysis of vision-building in an English for Academic Purposes programme. *Language Teaching Research*.
Waterman, A. (Ed.). (2012). *The best within us: Positive psychology perspectives on eudaimonic functioning*. American Psychological Association.
Wurf, E., & Markus, H. R. (1991). Possible selves and the psychology of personal growth. In D. J. Ozer, J. M. Healy Jr., & A. J. Stewart (Eds.), *Perspectives in Personality* (Vol. 3, pp. 39–62). Kingsley.
You, C. J., & Dörnyei, Z. (2016). Language learning motivation in China: Results of a large-scale stratified survey. *Applied Linguistics, 37*(4), 495–516.
Zarrinabadi, N., & Tavakoli, M. (2017). Exploring motivational surges among Iranian EFL teacher trainees: Directed motivational currents in focus. *TESOL Quarterly, 51*, 155–166.

19
AUTONOMY AND AGENCY

Paula Kalaja and Maria Ruohotie-Lyhty

This volume is about Psychology of Language Learning and Teaching (PLLT), and the two constructs to be discussed in this chapter, learner and/or teacher autonomy and agency, seem to be treated differently in previous reviews of the field. Even in an updated review of L2 learner psychology, Dörnyei and Ryan (2015) mention only briefly the first construct, i.e., *autonomy* viewing it as one individual difference (ID). In contrast, in *Exploring Psychology in Language Learning and Teaching*, Williams, Mercer, and Ryan (2016) review only the second construct, i.e., *agency* in relation to aspects of self-regulation, including learning strategies and styles. In a review of individual (L2 learner) *social* differences, Duff (2017) discusses agency, in addition to identities, communities, and trajectories, or with reference "to larger social constructs, groups, histories, boundaries, and ideologies that are also discursively invoked and (re)produced in social settings" (p. 380). Most recently, in *Language teacher psychology*, edited by Mercer and Kostoulas (2018), autonomy and agency are discussed in a few chapters, but only in passing. Interestingly, three of the recent reviews focus on L2 learners, and just one on L2 teachers, pointing to a general bias towards research on L2 learning rather than teaching in applied linguistics.

In this chapter, we review autonomy and agency as related to L2 learner and teacher psychology. We discuss the significance of the two constructs in understanding the personal, yet socially mediated nature of L2 learning and teaching processes. The two constructs are first discussed *separately*, but we conclude the chapter by noting the close connections that the constructs turn out to have.

Autonomy

The Construct in Psychology

The term autonomy comes from Greek: auto meaning "self" and nomos meaning "rule or law," that is, "a state that is self-ruled or -governed," and related terms abound, including self-instruction, self-regulation, independent learning, self-access learning, and self-directed learning. Psychology and education seem to be the main disciplines that have influenced developments in fostering (and doing research) on autonomy in SLA. Of the different schools of psychology, autonomy has been addressed especially within *social psychology* (and positive psychology): Autonomy is claimed to be an important *psychological need*. It "represents a sense of volition, or the feeling of doing something by one's own decision or initiative" (Ryan & Sapp, 2007, p. 90). When individuals behave autonomously, they feel better and perform better. In contrast, if they lack autonomy, they may lose interest and not feel well.

More specifically, within Self-Determination Theory (launched by Ryan and Deci, 2000), autonomy is viewed in relation to another two psychological needs: 1) competence (or the need to be effective in dealing with the environment), and 2) relatedness (or the need to have close and affectionate relationships with others). Autonomy can be viewed either as a fairly stable personal trait or as a state related to motivation (which in turn can be intrinsic or extrinsic); and in the latter case, it can vary from one situation to another or from moment to moment (Legault, 2018, p. 2). The experience of autonomy is always subjective, and is dependent on: (a) the perceived locus of causality (being either internal or external), (b) a sense of volition, and (c) perceived choice (Reeve, 2014, pp. 141–169). To satisfy the need of individuals for autonomy, contexts are needed that "facilitate the development and satiation of the need for autonomy by offering choice and opportunity for self-direction. They nurture inner motivational resources, offer explanations and rationales, and use informational language rather than directives or commands" (Legault, 2018, p. 2).

Of the experts in education (for a comprehensive review, see Benson, 2011, pp. 26–57), school reformists over the past few centuries from Rousseau to Dewey, Freire, and Rogers have called for greater freedom in learning. Secondly, adult educationalists have advocated for greater flexibility in organizing teaching for their specific groups of learners, namely, adults. Thirdly, psychologists have launched new ideas, including constructivist and sociocultural theories (see Chapter 2) and experiential learning, in which learners should be viewed as active and agentive participants responsible for their learning (instead of passive recipients of teaching). As a result, teachers' roles also must shift within such approaches: from transmitters of information to facilitators of learning. In addition, philosophers, since Kant (from the eighteenth century), have been emphasizing the free will of individuals and being rational when making decisions, and more recently post-modernists have raised some important points, being critical of the assumed essentialist nature of phenomena. Finally, language educationalists have also launched some new L2 teaching approaches over the past few decades, including communicative, humanistic, and task-based approaches. These have increased interest in fostering autonomy—initially that of learners, but more recently that of teachers, too, in SLA (or more broadly in L2 learning and teaching or *L2 education*).

The Construct in SLA

In SLA, *autonomy* has traditionally (and briefly) been defined as "the capacity to take control of one's learning" (Benson, 2011, p. 2). The fostering of autonomy in SLA (or applied linguistics) grew out of the need in 1970s Europe to ensure opportunities for adult learners (with families and jobs) to continue learning L2s possibly after compulsory education: They needed greater flexibility in organizing their studies. To cater for their special needs, self-access learning centers were set up in different countries. Initially, the focus was on fostering the autonomy of learners and only more recently on that of teachers.

By now autonomy has been researched for some 40 years in the field. Research on it originated in Europe but has since spread to all levels of language education and to different parts of the world, arriving most recently in Africa as the last continent to engage with autonomy in language teaching (for details, see Chik, Naoki, & Smith, 2016).

To understand the nature of autonomy in SLA, we draw on three key reviews, namely, an extensive book-length account by Benson (2011) (an update from 2001), and articles by Benson (2006) and Lamb (2017). In SLA, autonomy, especially that of learners, has been widely advocated and researched for a number of reasons (Borg & Al-Busaidi, 2012, p. 3): (a) [learner] autonomy improves the quality of L2 learning; (b) it makes studying possible not only in the classroom but also out of the classroom; (c) it makes life-long learning possible; (d) it is a human right; and (e) it promotes democracy in societies. A comprehensive bibliography maintained for some years by an AILA Special Interest Group contained over 1,200 entries on (learner and/or teacher) autonomy, and since then research on the topic has continued flourishing.

Over the years, there have been attempts to characterize *[learner] autonomy* either by compiling shorter or longer *lists of features* that it is claimed to comprise or not to comprise (the idea being to challenge possible misconceptions of the construct), or by providing concise definitions of it. Table 19.1 illustrates how the definitions have evolved over time.

The definitions in Table 19.1 are listed from the earliest and most widely cited to some more recent ones to indicate how understandings of autonomy have evolved over the past few decades, depending on different background theories or perspectives. Autonomy can either be looked as an attribute of the learner or that of the learning context and/or environment. As an attribute of the learner, it can be viewed as something the learner is born with (*ability*) or as something that can be developed, if needed

Table 19.1 Definitions of Autonomy

Type of definition Focus	Sample definitions
Cognitive definition (informed by cognitive psychology) *Attribute of the learner (= **personal** autonomy): ability / capacity to control; willingness; independence*	"…the ability to take charge of one's own learning … To take charge of one's own learning is to have, and to hold, the responsibility for all the decisions concerning all aspects of this learning, i.e. • determining the objectives • defining the contents and progressions • selecting methods and techniques to be used • monitoring the procedure of acquisition … (rhythm, time, place, etc.) • evaluating what has been acquired." (Holec, 1981, p. 3) "The basis of learner autonomy is that the learner accepts responsibility for his or her learning. This acceptance has both socio-affective and cognitive implications: it entails at once a positive attitude to learning and the development of a capacity to reflect on the content and process of learning with a view to bringing them as far as possible under conscious control." (Little, 1995, p. 175)
Socio-cognitive definition (informed, e.g., by social constructivism, sociocultural theory, situated learning) *A capacity of the learner that can be developed in social contexts; interdependence; collaboration / negotiation; affordances and constraints*	"… concerned with the expression and exploration of a learner's own meanings and purposes, facilitated by a process of negotiation and mediation in an atmosphere of genuine dialogue and collegiality." (Huang, 2006, cited in Teng, 2018, p. 4) "the competence to develop as a self-determined, socially responsible and critically aware participant in (and beyond) educational environments, within a vision of education as (inter)personal empowerment and social transformation" (Jiménez Raya, Lamb, & Vieira, 2017, cited in Vieira, 2018, p. 164; note: this definition applies not only to learners but also to *teachers*)
Systemic definition (informed, e.g., by ecology, complexity) *A system consisting of parts that interact*	"a complex socio-cognitive system, subject to internal and external constraints, which manifests itself in different degrees of independence and control of one's own learning process. It involves capacities, abilities, attitudes, willingness, decision making, choices, planning, actions, and assessment either as a language learner or as a communicator inside or outside the classroom. As a complex system it is dynamic, chaotic, unpredictable, non-linear, adaptive, open, self-organizing, and sensitive to initial conditions and feedback" (Paiva 2006, cited in Murray, & Lamb, 2018b, p. 11, in the chapter manuscript)

(*capacity*). Control, in turn, can involve three dimensions of learning: (a) self-management, (b) cognitive processes, and (c) content; or more specifically: where, when, how, what, how much, and why learn an L2? Yet another way of describing autonomy is to talk about a learner's ability, desire, and freedom to choose (instead of taking control over) (Huang & Benson, 2013, pp. 7–11). Interestingly, the more recent definitions emphasize that autonomy is an outcome of negotiation and cooperation of learners with the teacher involved in the learning situation and results in the empowerment and social transformation of both parties (see, e.g., Murray, 2014). This rather highlights their *inter*dependence than independence and, thus, the social nature of the construct. In addition, some definitions stress the systemic nature of autonomy, and, therefore, its complexity and dynamicity as a construct. Over the years, some more critical voices have been raised, too (reviewed in Benson, 2006, 2011, pp. 23–25). Initially, the ESSENTIALIST nature of (learner) autonomy was challenged, and more recently it has been suggested that autonomy involves communities and networks of people (i.e., not just the learner and/or the teacher) located in specific spaces, or places and times (Murray & Lamb, 2018).

Implications for Practice and Research

Over the past few decades, the various ways of fostering (learner) autonomy and doing research on the construct can be grouped under six approaches (Table 19.2), based on the reviews by Benson (2006, 2011, pp. 121–198) and Lamb (2017).

As is evident from Table 19.2, *learner autonomy* has been fostered in a variety of contexts: in the classroom, outside the classroom, and, most recently, virtually/online. Overall, the approaches have had two aims: (a) to provide learners with opportunities to make decisions about the ways they would like to study more independently, and (b) to provide learners with opportunities for self-directed learning. The means (or practices) of reaching the first aim (or independent learning) have focused on learner *external* factors (e.g., self-management). In contrast, the means to reach the second aim

Table 19.2 Approaches to Promote Autonomy in Language Learning and Teaching/Language Education

Approaches to promote autonomy	Practices/Applications
Resource-based approach	Self-access, tandem learning, distance learning, self-instruction, out-of-class learning, including study abroad
Technology-based approach	Computer-assisted language learning (CALL) with its various phases over the past few decades; mobile-assisted language learning (MALL)
Learner-based approach	Giving advice or training, e.g., in the use of learning strategies or techniques; or fostering learner development (e.g., manuals, sessions, courses)
Classroom-based approach	Planning and implementing classroom learning; evaluating classroom learning, including self-assessment, e.g., DIALANG, an online diagnostic language assessment system for 14 European languages, developed at the University of Lancaster, UK
Curriculum-based approach	Applying process syllabi, e.g., Autonomous Learning Modules (ALMS), developed at the University of Helsinki, Finland, with sessions on: reflecting on past language learning experiences; raising awareness of language learning strategies and use of these; conducting a needs analysis; setting goals and making plans for future
Teacher-based approach	Organizing, advising, and counselling for learners, and providing them with technical and psycho-social support (with consequent changes in traditional teacher roles); (re)organizing language teacher education to promote learner and/or teacher autonomy; advancing teacher autonomy in other respects, too, regarding teachers' professional development in general

(or autonomous learning) have focused on learner *internal* factors, including self-awareness, self-regulation (see Chapter 17), learning strategies, beliefs (see Chapter 12) or metacognitive knowledge, and motivation (see Chapter 10). Research on learner autonomy has addressed any of these in the contexts/environments outlined in Table 19.2.

Initially, the role of teachers seems to have been only secondary in enabling learner autonomy. More recently, the fostering of autonomy has been viewed as a joint effort by learners and teachers (for a general framework of promoting pedagogy for autonomy in language education, see Jiménez Raya, Lamb, & Vieira, 2017). Thus, it is now recognized that the fostering of *teacher autonomy* can be an aim in itself regarding teachers' own professional development over careers of some 40 years (starting from teacher education), and, as such, it is worth fostering and doing research on. More specifically, it has been suggested that teacher autonomy be viewed as a transitional process of one of three types, depending on the role(s) teachers take on: (a) when being involved in their learners' efforts to learn L2s, (b) when developing themselves as professionals, and (c) when maintaining their professional freedom (Benson & Huang, 2008), and so the focus of studies can vary. Recently, autonomy has been linked to a number of other constructs adopted from (positive) psychology (see Chapter 5), such as professional well-being (see Chapter 15) and positive emotions (see, e.g., Gabryś-Barker & Gałajda, 2016; Gkonou, Dewaele, & King, 2020) (see Chapter 14).

Future Directions

Research on (learner) autonomy has typically been conducted on the initiative of a teacher or groups of teachers working in their specific educational contexts (possibly as a result of curriculum revisions) and with their specific groups of students. Basically, the studies have sought to find out: (a) how autonomous their students are currently in their efforts to learn L2s; (b) how the teachers themselves have attempted to foster the autonomy of their learners and with what effects; and (c) how autonomy is related to the L2 learning outcomes of their students (for details, see, e.g., Benson, 2011, pp. 201–239). Furthermore, the studies can be characterized as being for the most part *action research* in nature, the idea being to find solutions to everyday real problems and bring about immediate changes in practices (for a recent collection of articles along these lines, see Ludwig, Pinter, van de Poehl, Smits, Tassinari, & Ruelens, 2018). To complement the previous reviews cited so far, we compiled a list of some highlights in the field published more recently (Table 19.3), pointing to further directions in theory, practice, and research in fostering learner and/or teacher autonomy.

The selected highlights (most reporting more than one study) point to further and further possibilities of fostering autonomy, though still mainly that of learners, expanding contexts from regular L2 classrooms to CLIL classrooms (and beyond), illustrating ways of raising awareness of issues related to autonomy by administering a questionnaire, and diversifying theorizing in the field and its research methodologies (in addition, for a recent textbook on *action research*, see Digilitaş & Griffiths, 2017, and for another on *case studies*, see Jiménez, Raya, & Vieira, 2015).

One of the most recent collections that we reviewed is entitled *Space, place, and autonomy in language learning* (Murray & Lamb, 2018). It stands out from those found in Table 19.3 in a number of respects: It broadens autonomy to apply to any speaker of more than one language or *multilinguals*; it replaces contexts with the notion of *spaces* being transformed into meaningful *places* for L2 learning (and being of three types: physical, virtual, or metaphorical, including curriculums); it views autonomy in such terms as struggle and resistance; it is interdisciplinary in its theoretical starting points; and, finally, it uses a variety of research methodologies (including ethnography). Overall, the volume sheds "fresh light on the definition and nature of autonomy as a political, collectivist construct, interwoven in space/place with communities and networks rather than individuals as the basic unit, thus extending critical versions of autonomy in language learning," as is noted by two of its contributors (Lamb & Vodicka, 2018, p. 10). In our opinion, this volume is bound to take autonomy and its research to yet unexplored roads in the years to come.

Table 19.3 New Directions in Research on Autonomy: Some Recent Highlights (of the Length of Full Books or Edited Collections) Pointing to New Directions in Research on Autonomy

Recent publications	Focus: learner/L and/or teacher/T	Context	Main contents
Díaz-Vera (2011)	L autonomy	Virtual	Exploring applications of mobile-assisted L2 learning (MALL)
Everhard & Murphy (2015)	L autonomy	Classroom	Exploring three types of assessment
Murray & Fujishima (2015)	L autonomy	Out-of-classroom	Setting up L(anguage)-cafés to practice the use of L2s; narratives
Barnard & Li (2016)	L autonomy	Teacher education	Studying L2 teachers' beliefs about L autonomy, case studies, questionnaire (complemented with interviews and discussions), replications/adaptations of Borg and Al-Busaidi (2012)
Cappellini, Lewis, & Rivens Mompean (2017)	L autonomy	Virtual	Exploring further applications of computer-assisted L2 learning (CALL), Web 2.0 (or Stage 3 in CALL developments)
Jiménez Raya, Ramos, Javier, & Tassinari (2017)	L/T autonomy	Higher education	University students and teachers, teacher trainees
Little, Dam, & Legenhausen (2017)	L autonomy	Classroom	L2 teaching of learners of mixed abilities (basic education, Denmark); logbooks and posters (longitudinal design); and immigrants (university, Ireland)
Maschmeier (2019)	L autonomy	Classroom	Expanding classroom contexts into language and content integrated learning (CLIL), Germany
Ludwig & Mynard (2018)	L autonomy	Higher education	Advising, university students

Agency

The Construct in Psychology

The word *agency* is a derivation of Latin *agentem*, meaning "effective, powerful," and it is used in social and educational sciences as well as in SLA to describe individuals' capacity to affect their environment. At the core of the construct of agency is the idea of learners as active participants in their learning process rather than as passive receivers of outside input. This power to act is, however, always considered in connection to existing conditions and affordances surrounding the individual. As a construct, it is, thus, a *relational* phenomenon.

Agency is an interdisciplinary construct used in many socially oriented research traditions such as anthropology (Ahearn, 2001; Holland, Lachicotte, Skinner, & Cain, 2001) and sociology (Archer, 2003; Giddens, 1984). It became relevant in psychology with the rise of socially oriented theories and research approaches, including sociocultural theories (Vygotsky, 1978) and social cognitive theory (Bandura, 1998). Compared to behavioristic theories that assume learning to be a reactive process, these theories imply an active subject who observes, processes, and relates to the environment. In attempts to define agency in psychology, the later work of Albert Bandura has been especially influential. Accordingly, *agency* can be defined "to intentionally make things happen by one's action" (Bandura, 2001, p. 2). In this line of thought, agency is shaped by an individual's perceived efficacy, intentionality, forethought, self-reactiveness, and self-reflectiveness (Bandura, 2001). This person-centered perception of the construct is further complicated by the socioculturally and ecologically oriented studies that emphasize the socially constructed character of agency (Wertsch, Tulviste, & Hagstrom, 1993). Agency is seen as a phenomenon that is necessarily dependent on both the individual and his or her social environment, as "the socioculturally mediated capacity to act" (Ahearn, 2001, p. 112).

Agency in SLA

Agency has been brought into the field of SLA through a number of "theoretical" doorways, including sociocognitive theory, performativity, sociocultural theory (see Chapter 2), as well as complex dynamic systems theory (Larsen-Freeman, 2019) (see Chapter 4). In SLA, the definitions of agency have benefited both from research in psychology as well as related research in other disciplines, such as sociology, anthropology, and education. Studies have rarely relied solely on one definition, rather they have often drawn on several approaches to agency. The adoption of the construct of agency in SLA has been closely related to the social turn in understanding L2 learning and, in this sense, SLA has followed the pathway evident in psychological research of the construct. While both the individual and the social aspects of agency have been recognized from the beginning, the discussion around the inside-out emphasis (Bandura, 2001) and the outside-in emphasis (Wertsch et al., 1993) of the construct continues to divide different approaches. Table 19.4 provides an overview of some influential definitions of agency in SLA. The selected examples do not offer an all-encompassing perspective of existing theoretical approaches to agency in SLA and exclude, e.g., post-structuralism, critical realism,

Table 19.4 Definitions of Agency

Type of definition Focus	Sample definitions
Socio-cognitive approach *Capability to influence one's functioning: self-efficacy, intentionality*	"To intentionally make things happen by one's action" (Bandura, 2001, p. 2)
Socio-cultural approach *A socially mediated capacity: mediation, co-construction*	"a relationship that is constantly co-constructed and renegotiated with those around the individual and with the society at large" (Lantolf & Pavlenko, 2001, p. 148)
Dialogical approach *A personally experienced phenomenon: time, space, and embodiment*	"a dialogical, or relational, phenomenon that needs to be examined both as subjectively experienced and as collectively emergent" (Dufva & Aro, 2016, p. 38)
Sociologically-oriented ecological approach (informed by Emirbayer & Mische, 1998) *A situated and temporal achievement: temporality, relationality*	"a temporal and situated achievement, which is the outcome of the interplay of iterational, practical-evaluative, and projective dimensions" (Kayi-Aydar, 2015, p. 12; Priestley, Biesta, Philippou, & Robinson, 2015, p. 29)
Psychologically-oriented ecological approach (informed by van Lier, 2008) *A contextually enacted way of being: affordances, systemic perspective*	"a contextually enacted way of being in the world" (van Lier, 2008, p. 163)
Complex dynamic systems approach *A complex dynamic system: nonlinearity, complexity*	"a complex, dynamic system composed of a multitude of interrelated components" (Mercer, 2011, p. 435)

and positioning theory. The selected definitions are, however, representative of the many key phenomena related to agency in SLA.

These six different definitions of agency do not necessarily contradict each other but provide complementary perspectives on the phenomenon. The first important feature linked to the construct of agency present in Table 19.4 is the idea of *intentionality* that is raised by several reviews of the construct in SLA (Kayi-Aydar, 2019; Mercer, 2012; Teng, 2018). When defining agency in this way, the individual's possibility of affecting his or her environment becomes the central feature of the construct. This also aligns with some sociologically informed approaches that focus on the individual's capacity to act otherwise (Giddens, 1984).

Another important feature in understanding the construct of agency in SLA is its *social character*. Although this perspective features in all different definitions of the construct, it has been especially emphasized in socioculturally oriented studies of the phenomenon. This perspective foregrounds the social character of agency and shifts the focus away from individual intention to co-construction and co-negotiation of agency in a particular setting (Lantolf & Thorne, 2006). Although this perspective does not necessarily contradict the idea of an intentional subject, it does break the tight bond between agency and voluntariness. It also highlights the outside-in character of agency, especially in terms of interpsychologically constructed learning processes (Reunamo & Nurmilaakso, 2007; Vygotsky, 1978). This perspective also strongly contradicts the idea of agency as a "property" of an individual (Morita, 2004, p. 590). Another characteristic related to agency by socioculturally oriented SLA is the idea of *mediation*. In this regard, L2 learners and teachers are not directly connected to their environment, but this relationship, and thus agency, is mediated through material and psychological tools and other people in a particular environment.

In contrast to the sociocultural approaches, dialogical and sociologically oriented ecological approaches shift the emphasis again to more person-centered perspectives on the phenomenon. To highlight the affective and emotional aspects of agency (Sullivan & McCarthy, 2004), a dialogic approach focuses on the individual's experiences of agency and the personal ways of constructing the relationship with the social environment. Agency is perceived in relation to the life-course of an individual, and agency emerges from his or her previous experiences and future aspirations in a specific social context. This perspective is typical of the ecological approach informed by sociological theorists (Emirbayer & Mische, 1998).

Some of the latest approaches have paid attention to the *systemic* character of agency. These include the complex dynamic systems approach (Mercer, 2011) and the psychologically oriented ecological approach (van Lier, 2008). The psychologically oriented ecological approach is informed especially by the work of Gibson (1982). Accordingly, *affordances* mean individual possibilities for action (such as participating, negotiating, or resisting) that exist in particular physical, social, and symbolic environments (van Lier, 2010, p. 4). These approaches have sought to avoid dichotomizing the parts of a system and looked at the systems forming agency as a whole. The differences between these two approaches lie in the ways in which change is understood as part of the system. Whereas the complexity approach has highlighted the inherent instability of any system (Larsen-Freeman, 2007) and, therefore, the unpredictable nature of human agency in any particular instance, the ecological approach has opted for patterns and formations of habits that can lead to seemingly stable agency in particular conditions (van Lier, 2010). Typically for these approaches, agency has been perceived as either "through participation and action, or indeed through deliberate nonparticipation or non-action." (Mercer, 2012, p. 42). These definitions of agency are possible only from the systemic perspective where agency is not directly connected to observable changes in the activity of an individual, but to changes in the system.

Implications for Practice and Research

Compared to research on autonomy, the construct of agency is a relative newcomer to SLA, being introduced along with the sociocultural approaches in the late 1990s. Although the history of the

Table 19.5 Types of Research on Agency in L2 Learning and Teaching/L2 Education

Types of research on agency in SLA	Practices/applications
L2 learner agency	Learners as active agents inside or outside the classroom, and online (Gkonou, 2015; Kalaja, Alanen, Palviainen, & Dufva, 2011; Skinnari, 2014; van Lier 2008; Walker, 2018)
L2 learner/teacher agency and identity construction	Learners/teachers choosing, using, and refusing available resources in the construction of their identities (Kayi-Aydar, 2015; Pappa, 2018; Ruohotie-Lyhty, 2013)
Experience of L2 learner/teacher agency	Different environments affecting the experience of agency (Aro, 2016; Kitade, 2015; Muller, 2015))
Supporting L2 learner agency	Creating pedagogical tools and environments to support agency (Moate & Ruohotie-Lyhty, 2014)
Agency and L2 learning	Investigating the relationship between learner agency and language learning (García, 2015)

study of the construct is short, the large number of studies adopting the construct in recent years seems to highlight the importance of this construct in understanding L2 learning and teaching. Table 19.5 presents some of the main types of studies using agency as a key construct and the practical perspectives that these have offered to L2 learning and teaching.

Based on the existing research, it is possible to draw some important implications for practice and research in SLA. Firstly, agency has been important in affording a perspective on the active role of learners in their L2 learning both in the classroom and outside it (Larsen-Freeman, 2019). As a theoretical construct, it has made it possible to recognize different forms of participation in the classroom and the significance of this participation for L2 learning. Secondly, the studies focusing on individual agency in the development of identities have also pointed out the significance of existing affordances for the ways in which language learners can develop their identities. Along with studies on the experiences of agency, they have helped to identify crucial elements of positive L2 learning and teaching environments, such as providing space for different learning and teaching styles inside and beyond the classroom (Kayi-Aydar, 2015). The studies have also helped to identify some of the problems that are typical of classroom contexts in supporting pupils' development. For example, the study by Aro (2016) showed how pupils' agency as language learners was curtailed by institutional beliefs about good language learning that recognized only written assignments and school-based activities as valuable language learning activities. Finally, these studies on language learners have also provided knowledge needed to create environments that offer learners possibilities for active participation and positive identity development. These studies can further contribute to creating better L2 learning practices.

Compared to L2 learner agency, research on L2 teacher agency has until now covered less ground (White, 2018). However, the few existing studies illustrate the applicability of the construct on L2 teachers as well. The studies focusing on teachers' professional development have shown the close connection of agency and L2 teacher identity (Kitade, 2015; Ruohotie-Lyhty, 2013). In addition, they have provided a more thorough view of the complex interplay between the environment and the individual, thus providing a useful theoretical tool for a variety of studies adopting a more systemic perspective to L2 teaching.

Future Directions

In analyzing the existing research on L2 learner and teacher agency, it is possible to state that some research methods have been used frequently when researching the construct, whereas some others have until recently received little attention. Many of the studies up to now have relied on methods such as interviews, autobiographical essays, learning histories, visual means of self-expression, and other narrative methods in studying learner and teacher agency. All these methods enable a perspective on the experiential and personal dimensions of agency that have been the focus of these studies. However, research on agency could benefit from greater attention to classroom realities. This would be especially important to gain insights into the second important dimension of human agency, that of *observable behaviors* (Mercer, 2011, p. 42). In addition, research on agency could benefit from studies that would be truly *longitudinal* to trace the development of agency (experience) over longer periods of time (i.e., over years).

To complement the review above, we wish to summarize five recent major publications on agency in SLA (Table 19.6), pointing to further directions in theory, practice, and research on agency.

The selected highlights represent some of the most recent book-length publications on L2 agency and illustrate some potentially novel research designs to explore the construct, including *ethnographic* and *action-research* studies as well as *longitudinal* studies. Methodologically they exploit some new types of data, such as visual narratives, observation, and diary entries. They also provide insights into the relationship of agency to various other constructs such as emotions, identities, and beliefs pointing to more holistic research approaches (Kalaja, Barcelos, Aro, & Ruohotie-Lyhty, 2016) and expand the field of study to some new groups beyond the classroom, such as immigrant adults (Miller, 2014). In the book edited by Kayi-Aydar et al. (2018), two studies also point to some possible new research topics in the field, such as agency emerging in human and non-human interaction (Zotzmann, 2018), or the relation between a teacher's positioning and his or her actual performance in the classroom (Back, 2018). The book also provides new insights into L2 teacher agency, which has until recently been less studied in the field.

Table 19.6 Some Recent Highlights (of the Length of Full Books or Edited Collections) Pointing to New Directions in Research on Agency

Recent publications	Focus: learner/L and/or teacher/T	Context	Main contents
Gao (2010)	L agency	Higher education	Interplay between conditions and agency in university L2 learning; ethnography
Miller (2014)	L agency	Professional life	Discursive co-construction of L agency of adult immigrants; interviews
Deters, Gao, Miller, & Vitanova (2015)	L agency	Classroom	Theoretical, analytical and pedagogical perspectives on L agency in various socio-political contexts; various research methods including (auto) ethnography, interviews and diary entries
Kalaja, Barcelos, Aro, & Ruohotie-Lyhty (2016)	L/T agency	Classroom, higher education and professional life	L and T agency experiences in relation to other constructs, including beliefs and identities (and emotions); longitudinal studies; interviews, visual narratives
Kayi-Aydar, Gao, Miller, Varghese, & Vitanova (2019)	T agency	Classroom and adult education	Agency in different contexts; various research methods including non-participant observation, interviews and document analysis

Integrating Perspectives on Both Constructs

Compared to agency, autonomy has had a much longer history in SLA (or L2 education), and it has been researched much more widely, yet still with a heavy emphasis on learners. It is only more recently with the introduction of sociocultural theory that the two constructs have begun to be discussed together (Benson, 2006, 2011, pp. 45–49), and, most recently and interestingly, in relation to learner and/or teacher *identity* (Benson & Cooker, 2013; Huang, 2013; Huang & Benson, 2013; Teng, 2018) (see Chapter 7). As noted by Benson (2006, p. 30), "agency can perhaps be viewed as a point of origin for the development of autonomy, while identity might be viewed as one of its more important outcomes." These developments have resulted in viewing learners and teachers as *human beings* or individuals with agency (instead of processors and providers of input, for example) and in more challenging research designs, pointing to even more complex relationships among the constructs involved in L2 learning and teaching.

The study of the two constructs of autonomy and agency in SLA has had its roots in socio-cognitive or socio-cultural psychological research and it has lessons to learn from psychology, especially from its more recent schools, such as positive psychology. These have widened the frameworks within which the two constructs could be viewed as interacting with constructs not considered until very recently, including *all* emotions (not just anxiety), well-being, resilience, and enjoyment. In addition, psychology could set the standards to increase the rigor in conducting quantitative studies in SLA and its two constructs and in applying sophisticated statistical procedures. Until recently, research on autonomy and agency in SLA has focused (narrowly) on the two parties involved in learning and teaching L2s, namely, learners and teachers. It is only very recently that the focus has been widened to any user of more than one language (i.e., multilinguals).

On the other hand, psychology could learn from research in SLA (or Applied Linguistics) to appreciate the possibly greater variety in research methodologies used these days in doing research on autonomy and agency, including various types of qualitative or mixes research methodologies and innovation in types of data collected. For example, psychologists could consider making use of narratives (in various modes), observations, and diaries (in addition to interviews) subjected to various kinds of analyses (narrative, discursive, ethnographic or content analysis) to gain deeper insights or more unexpected research findings in comparison to decontextualized generalizations of quantitative studies. These methodologies allow access to phenomena that is subjectively experienced to be approached from the perspective of insiders. In addition, these methodologies could make it possible to be more sensitive to the dynamics or interplay of various constructs in specific contexts. It is only recently that psychology, especially positive psychology, has begun to widen its focus to L2 learners and teachers. The number of publications has been on the increase since the late 2010s, which is indeed a positive development.

To conclude, we would like to highlight the significance of the two constructs, autonomy and agency, for future developments in SLA. Depending on the definitions, it is possible to regard autonomy and agency either as overlapping constructs or, as we would like to suggest, as constructs that *complement* each other. Whereas research on agency has focused on contextually enacted ways of participating, research on autonomy has focused on the developing degree of independence and control of that participation. In our opinion, these complementary perspectives are both necessary in providing insights into the complex interplay between the individual and social context. Here we have attempted to develop practical solutions for better L2 learning practices in different environments, and importantly, as put by Lamb (2017, p. 184) "to sustain plurilingualism and multilingualism in the twenty-first century," considering the ever globalizing world of ours.

Reflection Questions

- In your opinion, which of the definitions of *autonomy* and *agency* (reviewed in Sections 2.2 and 3.2) best describe your own experiences of L2 learning/teaching?

- In which ways have you been agentive in your L2 learning/teaching process(es)? Consider these over your career as an L2 learner/teacher.
- In your opinion, which kind of affordances could support the development of L2 learner/teacher autonomy?

Recommended Reading

Little, D., Dam, L., & Legenhausen, L. (2017). *Language learner autonomy: Theory, practice and research*. Multilingual Matters.

This is the first collection of truly hands-on reports on attempts to foster L2 learner autonomy in basic education (with different kinds of students) and in tertiary education (with immigrant students), partly carried out over years (i.e., being longitudinal) and with indeed impressive learning outcomes.

Deters, P., Gao, X. (A.), Miller, E. R., & Vitanova, G. (Eds.) (2015). *Theorizing and analyzing agency in second language learning: Interdisciplinary approaches*. Multilingual Matters.

This is a collection of chapters on learner agency in different socio-political contexts and across different age groups; it includes both theoretical and empirical perspectives on learner agency.

Teng, M. F. (2018). *Autonomy, agency, and identity in teaching English as a foreign language*. Springer.

This monograph, one of the first to link three constructs (i.e., autonomy, agency, and identity construction) in the context of L2 learning and teaching, reports findings of a series of studies with L2 learners and teachers based on their life stories.

References

Ahearn, L. M. (2001). Language and agency. *Annual Review of Anthropology, 30*(1), 109–137.
Archer, M. S., & Archer, M. S. (2003). *Structure, agency and the internal conversation*. Cambridge University Press.
Aro, M. (2016). In action and inaction: English learners authoring their agency. In P. Kalaja, A. M. F. Barcelos, M. Aro, & M. Ruohotie-Lyhty (Eds.), *Beliefs, agency and identity in foreign language learning and teaching* (pp. 48–65). Palgrave Macmillan.
Back, M. (2018). World language teachers performing and positioning agency in classroom target language use. In H. Kayi-Aydar, X. (A.) Gao, E. R. Miller, M. Varghese, & G. Vitanova (Eds.), *Theorizing and analyzing language teacher agency* (pp. 101–120). Multilingual Matters.
Bandura, A. (1998). Exercise of agency in personal and social change. In E. Sanavio (Ed.), *Behavior and cognitive therapy today* (pp. 1–29). Pergamon.
Bandura, A. (2001). Social cognitive theory: An agentic perspective. *Annual Review of Psychology, 52*(1), 1–26.
Barnard; R., & Li, J. (Eds.). (2016). *Language learner autonomy: Teachers' beliefs and practices in Asian contexts*. IDP Education.
Benson, P. (2006). Autonomy in language teaching and learning. *Language Teaching, 40*, 21–40.
Benson, P. (2011). *Teaching and researching autonomy* (2nd revised ed.). Routledge.
Benson, P., & Cooker, L. (Eds.). (2013). *The applied linguistic individual: Sociocultural approaches to identity, agency and autonomy*. Equinox.
Benson, P., & Huang, J. (2008). Autonomy in the transition from language learning to foreign language teaching. *DELTA, 24*, 421–439.
Borg, S., & Al-Busaidi, S. (2012). *Learner autonomy: English language teachers' beliefs and practices*. ELT Research Paper 12–7. British Council.
Cappellini, M., Lewis, T., & Rivens Mompean, A. (Eds.). (2017). *Learner autonomy and Web 2.0*. Equinox.
Chik, A., Naoki, A., & Smith, R. (Eds.). (2016). *Autonomy in language learning and teaching: New research agendas*. Palgrave Macmillan.
Deters, P., Gao, X. (A.), Miller, E. R., & Vitanova, G. (Eds.). (2015). *Theorizing and analyzing agency in second language learning: Interdisciplinary approaches*. Multilingual Matters.
Díaz-Vera, J. (Ed.). (2011). *Left to my own devices: Learner autonomy and mobile-assisted language learning*. Emerald.
Digilitaş, K., & Griffiths, C. (Eds.). (2017). *Developing language teacher autonomy through action research*. Palgrave Macmillan.

Dörnyei, Z., & Ryan, S. (2015). *The psychology of the language learner revisited*. Routledge.

Duff, P. A. (2017). Social dimensions and differences in instructed SLA. In S. Loewen, & M. Sato (Eds.), *The Routledge handbook of instructed second language acquisition* (pp. 379–395). Routledge.

Dufva, H., & Aro, M. (2015). Dialogical view on language learners' agency: Connecting intrapersonal with interpersonal. In P. Deters, X. (A.) Gao, E. R. Miller, & G. Vitanova (Eds.), *Theorizing and analyzing agency in second language learning: Interdisciplinary approaches* (pp. 37–53). Multilingual Matters.

Emirbayer, M., & Mische, A. (1998). What is agency? *American Journal of Sociology, 103*(4), 962–1023.

Gabryś-Barker, D., & Gałajda, D. (Eds.) (2016). *Positive psychology perspectives on foreign language learning and teaching*. Springer.

Everhard, C. J., & Murphy, L. (Eds.). (2015). *Assessment and autonomy in language learning*.

Gao, X. (2010). *Strategic language learning: The roles of agency and context*. Multilingual Matters.

García, P. N. (2015). Verbalizing in the second language classroom: Exploring the role of agency in the internalization of grammatical categories. In P. Deters, X. (A.) Gao, E. R. Miller, & G. Vitanova (Eds.), *Theorizing and analyzing agency in second language learning: Interdisciplinary approaches* (pp. 213–231). Multilingual Matters.

Gibson, J. J. (1982). Notes on affordances. In E. Reed, & R. Jones (Eds.), *Reasons for realism: The selected essays of James J. Gibson* (pp. 401–418). Erlbaum.

Giddens, A. (1984). *The constitution of society: Outline of the theory of structuration*. Polity.

Gkonou, C. (2015). Agency, anxiety and activity: Understanding the classroom behavior of EFL learners. In P. Deters, X. (A.) Gao, E. R. Miller, & G. Vitanova (Eds.), *Theorizing and analyzing agency in second language learning: Interdisciplinary approaches* (pp. 195–212). Multilingual Matters.

Gkonou, C., Dewaele, J.-M., & King, J. (Eds.) (2020). *The emotional rollercoaster of language teaching*. Multilingual Matters.

Holec, H. (1981). *Autonomy in foreign language learning*. Pergamon.

Holland, D. C., Lachicotte Jr., W., Skinner, D., & Cain, C. (2001). *Identity and agency in cultural worlds*. Harvard University Press.

Huang, J. (2013). *Autonomy, agency and identity in foreign language learning and teaching*. Peter Lang.

Huang, J., & Benson, P. (2013). Autonomy, agency and identity in foreign and second language education. *Chinese Journal of Applied Linguistics, 36*(1), 7–28.

Jiménez Raya, M., & Vieira, F. (2015). *Enhancing autonomy in language education: A case-based approach to teacher and learner development*. Walter de Gruyter.

Jiménez Raya, M., Lamb, T., & Vieira, F. (2017). *Mapping learner autonomy in language education: A framework for learner and teacher development*. Peter Lang.

Jiménez Raya, M., Ramos, M., Javier, J., & Tassinari, M. G. (Eds.). (2017). *Learner and teacher autonomy in higher education: Perspectives from modern language teaching*. Peter Lang.

Kalaja, P., Alanen, R., Palviainen, Å., & Dufva, H. (2011). From milk cartons to English roommates: Context and agency in L2 learning beyond the classroom. In P. Benson, & H. Reinders (Eds.), *Beyond the classroom* (pp. 47–58). Palgrave Macmillan,

Kalaja, P., Barcelos, A. M. F., Aro, M., & Ruohotie-Lyhty, M. (2016). *Beliefs, agency and identity in foreign language learning and teaching*. Palgrave Macmillan.

Kayi-Aydar, H. (2015). Teacher agency, positioning, and English language learners: Voices of pre-service classroom teachers. *Teaching and Teacher Education, 45*, 94–103.

Kayi-Aydar, H. (2019). A language teacher's agency in the development of her professional identities: A narrative case study. *Journal of Latinos and Education, 18*(1), 4–18.

Kayi-Aydar, H., Gao, X. (A.), Miller, E. R., Varghese, M., & Vitanova, G. (Eds.). (2019). *Theorizing and analyzing language teacher agency*. Multilingual Matters.

Kitade, K. (2015). Second language teacher development through CALL practice: The emergence of teachers' agency. *CALICO journal, 32*(3), 396–425.

Lamb, T. (2017). Knowledge about language and learner autonomy. In J. Cenoz, D. Gorter, & S. May, (Eds.), *Language awareness and multilingualism* (3rd revised ed., pp. 173–186). Springer.

Lamb, T., & Vodicka, G. (2018). Collective autonomy in multilingual spaces in superdiverse urban contexts: Interdisciplinary perspectives. In G. Murray & T. Lamb (Eds.), *Space, place and autonomy in language learning* (pp. 9–28). Routledge.

Lantolf, J., & Pavlenko, A. (2001). Second language activity theory: Understanding second language learners as people. In M. Breen (Ed.), *Learner contributions to language learning: New directions in research* (pp. 141–158). Routledge.

Lantolf, J. P., & Thorne, S. L. (2006). *Sociocultural theory and the genesis of second language development*. Oxford University Press.

Larsen-Freeman, D. (2007). On the complementarity of chaos/complexity theory and dynamic systems theory in understanding the second language acquisition process. *Bilingualism: Language and cognition, 10*(1), 35–37.

Larsen-Freeman, D. (2019). On language learner agency: A complex dynamic systems theory perspective. *The Modern Language Journal, 103*, 61–79.

Legault, L. (2018). The need for autonomy. In V. Zeigler-Hill & T. K. Schakelford (Eds.), *Encyclopedia of personality and individual differences* (pp. 1–3). Springer.

Little, D. (1995). Learning as dialogue: The dependence of learner autonomy on teacher autonomy. *System, 3*(2), 173–182.

Little, D., Dam, L., & Legenhausen, L. (2017). *Language learner autonomy: Theory, practice and research*. Multilingual Matters.

Ludwig, C., & Mynard, J. (Eds.). (2018). *Autonomy in language learning: Advising in action*. Candlin & Mynard.

Ludwig, C., Pinter, A., van de Poehl, K., Smits, T., Tassinari, M. G., & Ruelens, E. (Eds.). (2018). *Fostering learner autonomy: Learners, teachers and researchers in action*. Candlin & Mynard.

Maschmeier, F. (2019). *Learner autonomy in the CLIL classroom*. Peter Lang.

Mercer, S. (2011). Understanding learner agency as a complex dynamic system. *System, 39*(4), 427–436.

Mercer, S. (2012). The complexity of learner agency. *Apples: Journal of Applied Language Studies, 6*(2), 41–59.

Mercer, S., & Kostoulas, A. (Eds.). (2018). *Language teacher psychology*. Multilingual Matters.

Miller, E. R. (2014). *The language of adult immigrants: Agency in the making*. Multilingual Matters.

Moate, J., & Ruohotie-Lyhty, M. (2014). Identity, agency and community: Reconsidering the pedagogic responsibilities of teacher education. *British Journal of Educational Studies, 62*(3), 249–264.

Morita, N. 2004. Negotiating participation and identity in second language academic communities. *TESOL Quarterly, 38*(4), 573–603.

Muller, T. (2015). Critical discourse analysis in a medical English course: Examining learner agency through student written reflections. P. Deters, X. (A.) Gao, E. R. Miller, & G. Vitanova (Eds.), *Theorizing and analyzing agency in second language learning: Interdisciplinary approaches* (pp. 232–251). Multilingual Matters.

Murray, G. (Ed.). (2014). *Social dimensions of autonomy in language learning*. Palgrave Macmillan.

Murray, G., & Fujishima, N. (Eds.). (2015). *Social spaces for language learning: Stories from the L-café*. Palgrave Macmillan.

Murray, G., & Lamb, T. (Eds.). (2018). *Space, place and autonomy in language learning*. Routledge.

Murray, G., & Lamb, T. (2018b). Space, place, autonomy and the road not yet taken. In G. Murray & T. Lamb (Eds.), *Space, place and autonomy in language learning* (pp. 249–262). Routledge.

Pappa, S. (2018). *"You've got the color, but you don't have the shades": Primary education CLIL teachers' identity negotiation within the Finnish context*. Jyväskylä Studies in Education, Psychology and Social Research (nro 619).

Priestley, M., Biesta, G. J. J., Philippou, S., & Robinson, S. (2015). The teacher and the curriculum: Exploring teacher agency. In D. Wise, L. Hayward, & J. Pandya (Eds.), *The SAGE handbook of curriculum, pedagogy and assessment* (pp. 187–201). Sage.

Reeve, J. (2014). *Understanding motivation and emotion*. Wiley.

Reunamo, J., & Nurmilaakso, M. (2007). Vygotsky and agency in language development. *European Early Childhood Education Research Journal, 15*(3), 313–327.

Ruohotie-Lyhty, M. (2013). Struggling for a professional identity: Two newly qualified language teachers' identity narratives during the first years at work. *Teaching and Teacher Education, 30*, 120–129.

Ryan, R. M., & Deci, E. L. (2000). Self-determination theory and the facilitation of intrinsic motivation, social development, and well-being. *American Psychologist, 55*, 68–78.

Ryan, R. M., & Sapp, A. R. (2007). In K. D. Wohs, & R. F. Baumeister (Eds.), *Encyclopedia of social psychology* (pp. 90–91). Sage.

Skinnari, K. (2014). Silence and resistance as experiences and presentations of pupil agency in Finnish elementary school English lessons. *Apples: Journal of Applied Language Studies, 8*(1), 47–64.

Sullivan, P., & McCarthy, J. (2004). Toward a dialogical perspective on agency. *Journal for the Theory of Social Behaviour, 34*(3), 291–309.

Teng, M. F. (2018). *Autonomy, agency, and identity in teaching English as a foreign language*. Springer.

van Lier, L. (2008). Agency in the classroom: Sociocultural theory and the teaching of second languages. In J. P. Lantolf & M. E. Poehner (Eds.), *Sociocultural theory and the teaching of second languages* (pp. 163–186). Equinox.

van Lier, L. (2010). The ecology of language learning: Practice to theory, theory to practice. *Procedia-Social and Behavioral Sciences, 3*, 2–6.

Vieira, F. (2018). Developing professional autonomy as … writing with a broken pencil. In C. J. Everhard, & J. Mynard (Eds.), *Autonomy in language learning: Opening a can of worms* (pp. 164–170). Candlin & Mynard.

Vygotsky, L. (1978). *Mind in society. The development of higher psychological processes*. Harvard University Press.

Walker, U. (2018). Translanguaging: Affordances for collaborative language learning. *New Zealand Studies in Applied Linguistics, 24*(1), 18–40.

Wertsch, J.V., Tulviste, P., & Hagstrom, F. (1993). A sociocultural approach to agency. In E. A. Forman, N. Minick, & C. A. Stone (Eds.), *Contexts for learning: Sociocultural dynamics in children's development* (pp. 336–356). Oxford University Press.

White, C. (2018). Language teacher agency. In S. Mercer, & A. Kostoulas (Eds.), *Language teacher psychology* (pp. 196–210). Multilingual Matters.

Williams, M., Mercer, S., & Ryan, S. (2016). *Exploring psychology in language learning and teaching*. Oxford University Press.

Zotzman, K. (2018). Language teacher agency: A critical realist perspective. In H. Kayi-Aydar, X. (A.) Gao, E. R. Miller, M. Varghese, & G. Vitanova (Eds.), *Theorizing and analyzing language teacher agency* (pp. 199–216). Multilingual Matters.

20
WILLINGNESS TO COMMUNICATE IN AN L2

Tomoko Yashima

Introduction

Willingness to communicate (WTC) is a psychological construct that was originally postulated by US communication researchers but that thrived in SLA research. While the original concept of WTC was developed as a personality-based orientation toward communication in a culture where reticence is not highly regarded, once adapted to communication in an L2, it captured the attention of researchers and practitioners as a universally relevant construct.

It is generally acknowledged that to develop L2 competence, learners need to use the language, but L2 learners do not necessarily enter into communication even though they may possess sufficient competence (MacIntyre, 2007). Under the influence of the Usage-based Model (e.g., Tomasello, 2003), language development is seen as "the constant adaptation and enactment of language-using patterns in the service of meaning-making in response to the affordances that emerge in a dynamic communicative situation" (Larsen-Freeman & Cameron, 2008, p. 158). In other words, we learn a language by using it. L2 WTC, or readiness to communicate in an L2, therefore, captures an important aspect of learner affect that facilitates learning.

Furthermore, if a fundamental objective of L2 teaching and learning is communication with different linguistic and cultural groups, L2 WTC can be the cornerstone that facilitates motivation (See Chapter xx) toward that goal.

In this chapter, I first present the definition of this construct as used in communication and SLA studies in two brief sections. Following these is a main section titled Integration and Development, where research into L2 WTC is reviewed extensively and the history and current state of the construct are presented. Two more sections follow, where I discuss implications for practice and future directions for research, leading up to reflection questions and recommended readings.

Willingness to Communicate in Psychology and Communication Studies

Willingness to communicate (WTC) is a psychological construct developed in the field of communication as a personality-based "disposition toward approaching or avoiding the initiation of communication" (McCroskey, 1992, p. 17). The concept builds on the accumulated studies of speech anxiety and communication apprehension. Based on the assumption that individuals exhibit regular communication tendencies while their behavior is largely dependent on situations, researchers developed a scale for measuring the probability of engaging in communication when given a choice, comprising four communication situations: speaking in dyads, in small groups, in meetings, and publicly, with three types of receivers: strangers, acquaintances, and friends (McCroskey, 1992; McCroskey & Richmond, 1987, 1990). These studies also attempted to identify antecedents of WTC and found negative correlations with introversion and communication apprehension and positive correlations with perceived competence.

While McCroskey and Richmond (1990) claim WTC was a construct relevant to North American culture, where in general terms, "the more a person communicates up to a very extreme, the more positively a person is evaluated" (p. 20), a cross-cultural study by Barraclough, Christophel, and McCroskey (1988) showed that US and Australian students exhibited a similar tendency in communication. Studies also found that WTC scores could predict actual communication. For example, Chan and McCroskey (1987) showed that college students with high WTC scores participated more in class than those with lower scores. However, since these early studies, little follow-up work in L1 WTC has been conducted to my knowledge in the fields of communication or psychology.

Willingness to Communicate in SLA

In SLA, social psychological research, which started in the 1960s in Canada, highlighted attitudes toward an L2 community and motivation to learn the language to communicate with the L2 group (e.g., Gardner, 1985; Gardner & MacIntyre, 1993). Given this trend, the adaption of WTC to L2 research was a natural development. Adapting McCroskey's (1992) construct of WTC in an L2 (L2 WTC) in their path analyses, MacIntyre and associates demonstrated that a number of individual variables, including extroversion/introversion, anxiety, perceived competence, integrativeness, and motivation influence a learner's tendency to communicate in the L2 (e.g., MacIntyre & Charos, 1996; MacIntyre & Clément, 1996).

L2 WTC is not simply a transfer from L1 WTC postulated as a stable individual trait. Rather, it is far more complex, not only because variation in L2 competence across individuals is much greater than in L1 competence, but also because attitudes toward the target language and culture and the motivation to learn the L2 (among other factors) affect how much each learner is willing to communicate with the target population (MacIntyre, Dörnyei, Clément, & Noels, 1998). Noting that L2 learners do not necessarily turn into L2 communicators, these researchers proposed that L2 WTC should be a goal of L2 teaching. These ideas were integrated into a heuristic pyramid-shaped model they presented. The model comprises six layers with L2 use in the top layer (at the apex) and L2 WTC in the layer immediately below, and other variables placed in lower layers converging to L2 WTC, seen as a psychological state immediately before the learner uses the language at a given moment. In the third layer from the top are situated variables: desire to communicate with a specific person, and state communication self-confidence. These two are regarded as having immediate influence on L2 WTC. Of the six layers, the three bottom layers house more enduring variables, including personality, intergroup climate, intergroup motivation, and L2 self-confidence. The idea is that the closer to the top, the more immediate and situated the influences, while further down, the influence is more remote/indirect, yet more enduring.

Thus, L2 WTC is regarded as a situated concept and is defined as "a readiness to enter into discourse at a specific time with a specific person or persons, using an L2" when free to do so (MacIntyre et al., 1998, p. 547). At this point, the concept diverges somewhat from the original personality-based trait-like construct, even though personality (See Chapter xx) is regarded as one of the enduring variables that affect situated L2 WTC. Nevertheless, in psychological terms, both trait and state L2 WTC have been the target of research ever since, as I discuss in the next section.

Integration and Development

After the L2 WTC model was presented in the seminal paper (MacIntyre et al., 1998), it rapidly captured the attention of researchers in SLA, where it was seen as having important applications and major relevance, especially in light of the dominant communicative teaching paradigm. The concept of L2 WTC suggested by the researchers using the model is an integration of psychology, communication, and SLA, and is an attempt to integrate intergroup variables that affect communication in different groups with psychological variables related to SLA, including motivation, self-confidence, and linguistic competence. The model stimulated further research in L2 WTC, which I review here by featuring two characteristics of L2 WTC research: a) research conducted across a wide range of cultural and learning contexts, and b) methodological exploration capturing trait, state, and situated or dynamic WTC.

L2 WTC Research Across Cultural Contexts

Since around 2000, research conducted across contexts has accumulated. In Canada, MacIntyre and associates carried out a range of studies of WTC in French as an L2, focusing on situational influences (e.g., in-class vs. out of class, immersion vs. non-immersion) (Baker & MacIntyre, 2000; MacIntyre, Baker, Clément, & Donovan, 2002; MacIntyre, Baker, Clément, & Conrod, 2001), to which I will return in my discussion of learning situations. Subsequently, a number of empirical studies inspired by the model have been conducted in various parts of the world, including Japan with Japanese EFL learners of English (Yashima, 2002; Yashima, Zenuk-Nishide, & Shimizu, 2004), China (Peng & Woodrow, 2010, with Chinese EFL learners), New Zealand (Cao & Philp, 2006, with mostly Asian learners of English), and the US (Kang, 2005, with Korean ESL students). While earlier studies frequently involved Asian learners, more recently, work has been conducted in Europe, including the UK (Gallagher, 2013, with Chinese-speaking students), Belgium (Denies, Yashima, & Janssen, 2015 with Flemish learners of French), and Poland (Pawlak & Mystkowska-Wiertelak, 2015; Pawlak, Mystkowska-Wiertelak, & Bielak, 2016, with Polish EFL learners), as well as in Iran (Ghonsooly, Khajavy, & Asadpour, 2012; Khajavy, Ghonsooly, Fatemi, & Choi, 2016, with Iranian EFL learners), and Turkey (Bektas- Cetinkaya, 2005; Öz, Demirezen, & Pourfeiz, 2015 with Turkish EFL learners). The fact that L2 WTC research now covers many parts of the globe reflects the universal concern of SLA researchers and educators for encouraging learners to communicate.

L2 WTC research conducted across cultural contexts often raises additional factors that may influence WTC and that researchers found relevant in each context. For example, Yashima (2002) proposed *international posture* as relevant in EFL contexts, that is, attitudes toward an international community, readiness to work overseas, openness toward different cultural groups, and interest in foreign affairs, arguing that these reflect the reality of EFL contexts such as Japan, where "intergroup attitudes" in the sense of integrativeness are not clearly formed or are relevant without many opportunities for direct intergroup interactions. Studies using Structural Equation Modeling (SEM) found that international posture enhances not only motivation to learn English but also WTC with people around the globe using English.

Through an examination of Chinese culture, Wen and Clément (2003) identified Confucian cultural heritage, other-directedness, and submissive approaches to learning and proposed that several variables be added to the WTC model. These include group cohesiveness (or motivation to remain in the group), teacher support, and inhibited monitoring (or the tendency to monitor one's behavior), among others. Peng and Woodrow (2010) also noted covert cultural (e.g., Confucian) influence on WTC in Chinese EFL learners. To capture this culturally structured feature, Peng and Woodrow focused on a learner belief or learners' value judgments about how to learn English as well as appropriate behavior in the classroom. They also included culturally featured items to elicit such learner beliefs, e.g., "The student who always speaks up in class will be loathed by other classmates." The study found that these beliefs negatively influenced the learners' WTC inside the class. In addition, WTC-promoting beliefs with lower endorsement of traditional, grammar-translation approaches were confirmed in their SEM study as influencing communication confidence, which in turn was the single strongest predictor of WTC in English. In a study of Thai ESL learners in Australia (Pattapong, 2010), two cultural norms affecting L2 WTC were identified: a) the desire to establish a network of relationships, and b) the need to maintain the hierarchical system. As shown here, cultural features are often zoomed in to explain silence or fewer turns by Asian learners. While we should avoid essentializing Asian culture, cultural influence is a theme that recurrently emerges through the analyses of empirical data (see reviews by Shao & Gao, 2016, and Yashima, 2019).

From an ecological perspective, taking into account classroom learning contexts, Peng and Woodrow (2010) included a construct called *classroom environment*, which encompasses teacher support, student cohesiveness, and task orientation. They found that high appraisal of the classroom environment predicted L2 WTC. This variable was also included in Khajavy et al.'s (2016) Iranian study and was found to be the strongest predictor of WTC in English. Noting that group work is an integral part of communicative EFL classrooms, Fushino (2010) reported that beliefs about the value of group work predicted L2 WTC in such learning situations.

L2 WTC Research Across Learning Contexts

Other studies have examined the influence of different teaching and learning contexts on WTC. In a comparison of immersion and non-immersion contexts (Baker & MacIntyre, 2000), immersion students showed lower communication apprehension, greater perceived competence, higher WTC, and more frequent communication in French. These researchers also found that anxiety correlates with L2 WTC more strongly than perceived competence in an immersion context, while the opposite is true of a non-immersion context. Their explanation for this finding rests on differences in communication experiences and L2 competence. With relatively less developed communicative competence, non-immersion students' L2 WTC is more strongly affected by perceived competence. On the other hand, with abundant communication opportunities, immersion students generally achieve higher levels of competence but feel greater pressure to meet higher performance standards, thus experiencing increased anxiety. This finding is supported by studies conducted in EFL contexts, showing that perceived competence correlated more strongly with L2 WTC than did language anxiety (Khajavy et al., 2016; Peng & Woodrow, 2010; Yashima, 2002; Yashima et al., 2004), thus exhibiting the same tendency as the non-immersion context in Canada.

MacIntyre et al. (2001) compared L2 WTC inside and outside the French immersion classroom and how this relates to learning orientations, including travel, gaining knowledge, friendship with francophone individuals, and job-related and school achievement. All these orientations were positively correlated with inside- and outside-classroom L2 WTC. No notable differences were found between the two settings. Denies et al. (2015) investigated WTC in French as an L2 in Flemish learners both in- and outside of the classroom. In using French in naturalistic settings outside of the classroom, the role of integrativeness decreased while anxiety played a larger role. The study also found that classroom WTC predicts WTC outside of the classroom.

Yashima and Zenuk-Nishide (2008) compared two at-home Content and Language Integrated Learning (CLIL) contexts with study abroad contexts and found that frequency of communication increased most dramatically in the study abroad group followed by a class with longer CLIL class time. The group with the least amount of CLIL exposure showed the least amount of change. Freiermuth and Jarrel (2006) compared Japanese learners' face-to-face and online (computer-mediated) communication and found that online chatting enhanced WTC more than face-to-face interactions, which tend to increase anxiety. Lee and Hsieh (2019) compared the relationship between affective variables (L2 self-confidence, L2 anxiety, L2 motivation, and grit) and WTC in in-class, out-of-class, and digital contexts with Taiwanese EFL learners. They found that lack of L2 anxiety was a significant predictor of L2 WTC in non-digital environments but not in the digital setting. The researchers concluded that modern learners may find the digital context more comfortable for communication.

Methodological Exploration in WTC Research

One interesting feature of WTC research is the diversification and exploration of research methods, from early quantitative research mostly focusing on trait-like WTC as a psychological construct to qualitative as well as (some) mixed-methods research concerned with classroom-related situated factors and new approaches to capturing the dynamics of L2 WTC. Earlier research inspired by the WTC concept mainly examined more enduring, trait-like variables, often using, adapting, and translating the original WTC scales developed by McCroskey and Richmond (1987). More often than not, Structural Equation Modeling (SEM) was employed in these studies to confirm the relevance of many of the enduring factors, including intergroup attitudes, communicative competence, and L2 self-confidence (or perceived competence and anxiety separately), influencing L2 WTC (e.g., Clément, Baker, & MacIntyre, 2003; Denies et al., 2015; Öz et al., 2015; Peng & Woodrow, 2010; Yashima, 2002; Yashima et al., 2004). These studies helped form a general picture of how psychological variables interrelate and affect learners' stable tendency to communicate in the L2, or trait-like WTC. In addition, scales measuring L2 WTC in classrooms have been developed (e.g., MacIntyre et al., 2001; Weaver, 2005) in order to achieve a better fit with instructed learning contexts.

A meta-analysis of quantitative WTC studies (Elahi Shirvan, Khajavy, MacIntyre, & Taherian (2019) focusing on 22 studies comprising 60 effective sizes published between 2000 and 2015 reported perceived communicative competence, language anxiety, and motivation as three high-evidence correlates of L2 WTC (with mean correlations of $r = .48$, $r = -.29$, $r = .37$, respectively). Although some studies have reported that L2 WTC predicts L2 use (Denies et al., 2015; MacIntyre & Charos, 1996; Yashima et al., 2004) and others included objectively measured L2 proficiency in the investigation (e.g., Denies et al., 2015; Yashima, 2002), the link between L2 WTC, its actual use, and proficiency is yet to be explored.

To address the context-specific needs of teachers as they assist learners and find out why some learners are willing to talk in classrooms while others are not, research into WTC has taken a qualitative turn, which MacIntyre et al. (1998) in fact intended with their definition of L2 WTC as the "readiness to enter into discourse at a specific time with a specific person or persons." Since around 2005, an increasing number of such studies have spotlighted the situated nature of L2 WTC as it emerges in interactions. These studies have revealed a number of factors influencing participants' state WTC. Through an experiment using dyads of Korean learners of English and native speakers, Kang (2005) found that the decision to communicate in a particular situation is mediated by three psychological variables: security, excitement, and responsibility. Security refers to feeling free of fear in L2 communication, a condition shaped mainly by relative familiarity among interlocutors as well as with the topic. Excitement is "a feeling of elation about the act of talking" (p. 284). Finally, responsibility is felt typically when the learners themselves introduce the topic or when the topic is one the participants are knowledgeable about. Kang also created a model summarizing these processes. Cao and Philp (2006) assessed situational WTC in Asian and European students studying English in Australia using a behavior categorization scheme they developed in three different interactional situations in classrooms (pair work, group work, and whole class). They also found that WTC levels differ substantially across interactional situations. Based on classroom observations and interviews, Cao and Philp identified group size, self-confidence, knowledge of the topic, familiarity with interlocutors, and interlocutor participation in the conversation as factors that had the greatest impact on frequency of self-initiated communication.

Further research taking situated approaches followed, identifying a number of psychological, linguistic, social, and contextual factors (e.g., Cao, 2011, 2014; de Saint Léger & Storch, 2009; Eddy-U., 2015; Freiermuth & Jarrel, 2006; Pattapong, 2010; MacIntyre, Burns, & Jessome, 2011;

Mystkowska-Wiertelak & Pawlak, 2017; Peng, 2012, 2014; Peng, Zhang, & Chen, 2017; Yu, 2015; Zarrinabadi, 2014; Zhong, 2013). To focus on situated WTC, researchers need to move away from self-report questionnaires assessing trait-like WTC. Cao (2014) used the observation scheme developed earlier by Cao and Philp (2006), in which situated WTC is operationalized in terms of the number of self-selected turns (e.g., volunteering an answer, asking the teacher a question, or responding to an opinion). Using stimulated recall interviews and analyses of journal entries, Cao revealed that situational WTC in the classroom results from the interdependence of individual characteristics (self-confidence, emotion), linguistic factors (e.g., L2 proficiency), and learner-external or environmental factors (e.g., topic, task type, interlocutor, teacher).

MacIntyre et al. (2011) asked French immersion students to write about situations in which they were most or least willing to communicate in the L2. Through the qualitative analyses of these self-reports, the researchers demonstrated that subtle differences in communication contexts can quickly change a learner's affective state from willingness to unwillingness to communicate. As an attempt to capture WTC as constructed in interactions with interlocutors, Yu (2015) investigated how Chinese EFL learners' WTC is influenced by a paired partner's WTC level. She compared interactions in pairs matched by trait WTC level and those in unmatched pairs and found that the number of turns and words recorded by low-WTC individuals did not improve when they were paired up with peers with higher WTC.

An interesting recent trend includes a focus on teacher roles. Zarrinabadi (2014) used a focused essay technique to explore how teachers influence students' WTC. The findings indicate that teachers' giving a longer wait time, delaying error correction, and giving greater freedom to choose the topic should enhance learners' WTC. Peng et al. (2017) analyzed two teaching scenarios using a multi-modal discourse analysis approach to demonstrate that teachers' use of semiotic resources, including language, gesture, and gaze influence students' WTC as well as classroom participation.

Zhang, Beckmann, and Beckmann's (2018) recent review of 35 articles (including some reviewed in this chapter) on situational antecedents contributing to variation in L2 WTC report a multitude of situational variables along with measures used to identify them. These include: a) classroom variables such as task and activity type, topic for discussion, mode of instruction (pair, group, or whole-class), group size, and atmosphere; b) teacher variables, including teacher support, teaching styles, classroom management, teachers' attitudes, and error correction; c) interlocutor variables, including mutual familiarity, relative language proficiency, personality, and cooperation; and d) learner psychology such as self-confidence, anxiety, interest in the topic and activity, and perception of teachers and classmates (among others). Zhang et al. (2018) proposed classifying these variables into objective situational features and subjective perception of such features and presenting a framework of situational antecedents in which the former influences WTC through the latter.

Methodologically, to capture objective situational features, a direct comparison of groups of different features (e.g., Baker & MacIntyre, 2000, for immersion/non-immersion) or the same learners in terms of different features was made (e.g., Cao & Philp, 2006; Zhong, 2013, for instructional modes). For perceived situational characteristics or to elicit learners' perspectives, interviews, questionnaires, and essays and journals have been used. However, classroom observation is needed to capture what actually happens. While class observation has been used for assessing the frequency of communication (Cao & Philp, 2006; Yashima, MacIntyre, & Ikeda, 2018; Zhong, 2013), it has also been used in combination with stimulated recall interviews in many studies (e.g., Cao & Philp, 2006; Pawlak & Mystkowska-Wiertelak, 2015). Stimulated recall interviews have been used widely and effectively to connect objectively observable features and learner psychology. Discourse analysis has also proved useful in examining what triggers (or inhibits) turns (Yashima, Ikeda, & Nakahira, 2016) in the flow of conversation, but Peng et al.'s (2017) study goes beyond linguistic analysis. To examine what actions taken by teachers result in higher WTC in learners, teachers' non-verbal behaviors were analyzed using multi-modal discourse analysis. Typically, most studies combine several of these techniques.

As shown above, growing interest in situated WTC has resulted in a growing number of publications using multi-methods to capture situational variables that affect L2 WTC as the emergent state of readiness to talk.

Recent Developments in Capturing Dynamics and Complexity

A notable trend coinciding with the situated approach is the influence of Complex Dynamic Systems Theory (CDST; Dörnyei, MacIntyre, & Henry, 2015) (See Chapter xx) and the development of research methods designed to capture the emergent, dynamic nature of WTC. MacIntyre and Legatto's (2011) study used such a framework to focus on the dynamic, moment-to-moment state of WTC through on-going observation and real-time assessment. The researchers developed a computerized idiodynamic method in which learners rate their level of WTC on a scale shown on the computer screen while watching the immediate playback of their performance on the same screen. Subsequently, the learners offer explanations for each fluctuation in WTC while watching the video again and looking at the printout of the WTC graph. This laboratory study involving six female students demonstrated that WTC fluctuated dramatically over the few minutes during which the participants were interviewed about eight pre-selected topics. While each participant exhibited unique reactions to the task, consistent patterns were also observed, including a decline in WTC while discussing supposedly less familiar topics. Searching memory for lexis was found to be a key factor in lowering WTC.

Pawlak et al. (2016) as well as Mystkowska-Wiertelak and Pawlak (2017) applied a similar approach in classrooms. Working in pairs or groups, Polish EFL learners recorded their WTC every five minutes on a grid with scales, revealing fluctuation in individual and group-level WTC during the class period. Participants' responses to open-ended questions and the teacher's record of activities were analyzed to identify contextual and individual variables that might account for the fluctuation. In Pawlak and Mystkowska-Wiertelak (2015), WTC in four pairs of learners conversing in English was self-recorded on a grid every 30 seconds, followed by stimulated recall interviews that revealed the influence of a number of variables. Graphs with two lines representing each pair's individual WTC fluctuation showed no consistent patterns across pairs, while participants' WTC tended to be higher while they were presenting ideas and decreased while they listened, particularly when they did not understand their partners.

Wood (2016) used the idiodynamic method to capture relations between objectively measured fluency and self-rated WTC. Such influences are found to go both ways, revealing cases of high WTC leading to high fluency and low WTC leading to low fluency, as well as low fluency leading to low WTC. In the latter case, cognitive struggles with forming ideas and vocabulary retrieval led to lower WTC. Bernales (2016) approached the dynamics of WTC focusing on learners' cognition leading to speech. The researcher analyzed the gap between what learners planned to articulate and what they actually articulated in the classroom in a German as a Foreign Language context. The results revealed that links between predicted and actual participation developed progressively over 15 weeks, which the researcher attributed to a combination of factors, including classroom norms, teacher expectations, and learner motivation.

Some studies illuminate complexity in addition to dynamics, featuring, for example, multi-level nested systems and time scales, as suggested by Larsen-Freeman and Cameron (2008) for CDST-informed classroom research frameworks. Khajavy, MacIntyre, and Barabadi (in print) used doubly latent multilevel analysis to examine the influence of affective variables on WTC at two levels: classroom and individuals, involving 1,528 secondary school students from 65 different classrooms in Iran. Their findings indicate positive emotions (See Chapter xx) such as enjoyment increased WTC at both student and classroom levels, while anxiety reduced WTC only at the individual level. Yashima et al. (2018) attempted to capture trait-like and state (See Chapter xx) WTC as operating on different timescales, while focusing on individual and group-level WTC as nested systems. For trait WTC, they used traditional questionnaires, while for situated WTC, they observed the class interactions and counted the number of self-selected turns. Within a nested-system framework, this study also paid attention to the communication behavior of individuals as well as that of the group, with findings indicating that individual learners contribute to constructing group-level communication behavior, which simultaneously influences the way these individuals communicate. The researchers noted that with a few exceptions (Cao, 2014; Cao & Philp, 2006), empirical research thus far has mostly focused on either enduring/trait-like or situated/contextual L2 WTC, which were originally theorized as complementary (MacIntyre et al., 1998). Their study was an attempt to address this gap.

Thus, many methods have been employed to capture the nature of L2 WTC. However, a challenge remains regarding how to operationalize situated WTC. Unlike trait-like WTC, for which traditional psychometric scales have been developed, situated WTC has been operationalized to date either through frequent, real-time self-assessment on scales (e.g., MacIntyre & Legatto, 2011) or as the frequency of self-selected turns (as well as other-selected turns and hand-raising that did not result in turns) observed in classrooms and coded by the researchers (e.g., Cao & Philp, 2006). Nevertheless the accumulated research has shown how WTC can change momentarily in classrooms and how various factors intertwine to change the dynamics. What we see here is the development of research in L2 WTC as a construct relevant to language learning, reflecting keen pedagogical interest among SLA researchers and practitioners.

Implications for Practice and Research

We have gained a great many insights regarding the variety of factors that make L2 learners more willing to communicate in classrooms and other interactional situations. As reviewed in the previous section, a number of situated antecedents has been identified, mostly in qualitative studies, and teachers can use this information to design effective L2 classrooms. Suggestions include giving learners autonomy in choices of discussion topics, changing modes of instruction from teacher-centered to collaborative, implementing planned pair or group formations, enhancing supportive teacher roles, and avoiding immediate error correction, to name a few. The dynamic view of WTC as fluctuating radically during a class or even during a task is a feature L2 teaching professionals should keep in mind. In particular, interlocutor influence seems vital. Since in pair or group conversations this influence is mutual, preparing students to be good conversational partners is imperative because positive as well as negative affect can be infectious. Further, some interventional studies have been conducted in which a training or instruction method is specifically designed to enhance WTC. For example, Munezane (2015) compared CLIL classes under different experimental conditions (vision enhancing vs. visionary plus goal setting activity) with a control group. She found that the visualization plus goal-setting condition led to significantly greater improvement in L2 WTC than the other two conditions. A similar experimental study using visualization and goal-setting training was conducted by Al-Murtadha (2019) with secondary school EFL learners in rural Yemen. The study found that the experimental group's WTC increased significantly as a result of the intervention. Al-Murtadha discusses the effectiveness of the intervention in helping learners connect their ideal self to the imagined future of the community, drawing on Norton's (2000) identity study.

We also have information about the differential influence of psychological variables as antecedents of WTC depending on teaching or learning contexts, including immersion, non-immersion, or EFL; digital vs. face-to-face; and in-class vs. natural societal contexts. This information could be used in designing courses and curriculum. Finally, Elahi Shirvanet et al.'s (2019) meta-analysis showed that the highest correlates are found between perceived communication competence and WTC in an L2, confirming our understanding that boosting self-confidence (See Chapter xx) is of paramount importance.

As reviewed in the previous section, L2 WTC research has gained momentum and led to a number of innovative methods that reflect researchers' enthusiasm for capturing the emerging nature of WTC in classrooms. Yet, there is still plenty of room for progress. First, more research on relations between L2 WTC and language proficiency is needed. To my knowledge, only a handful of studies (e.g., Denies et al., 2015; Yashima, 2002) have investigated this link. From an SLA perspective, a vital question is whether enhancing WTC will lead to improved linguistic competence. Studies might explore this link in different contexts and thus illuminate the process of how language is learned through willingness to use it. Finally, more interventional classroom studies are called for, examining different instruction methods designed to stimulate WTC along with assessments of their long-term influence in- and outside of the classroom. Ideally, these should include more studies of WTC involving languages other than English (LOTE).

WTC should be a goal of L2 instruction not only because it has the potential to trigger acquisition but also because it motivates people to take part in intergroup relations (See Chapter xx). Research into this aspect remains limited except for investigations of relations between integrativeness as representing intergroup motivation and WTC (e.g., Denies et al. 2015). WTC studies can illuminate intergroup situations, as did Abu-Rabia (1998) in a study of motivation among Arab learners of Hebrew.

Future Directions

WTC research has come a long way over a relatively short period of some 20 years. We have come to understand an individual's L2 WTC as it triggers communication at a specific moment and as a convergence of influences of various learner-internal and learner-external factors interacting in a complex manner. Further, while some recent studies focus on WTC beyond the individual as constructed socially in pairs or groups, others attempt to capture both individual and collective communication behavior. Because communication is fundamentally social in the sense that a person always needs someone else to communicate with, this constitutes an important future direction of WTC research. It also means that it becomes necessary to find ways to reconcile WTC as an individual characteristic and communication as a hyper-individual phenomenon.

Positive psychology (See Chapter xx) also has the potential to suggest a new direction in WTC research. Based on Peterson's (2006) definition of positive psychology as "the scientific study of what goes right in life" (p. 4), MacIntyre, Gregersen, and Mercer (2019) acknowledge the need for an "evidence-based evaluation of claims about positive development and interventions that are likely to facilitate it" (p. 263). Although many learners struggle to communicate in an L2, a process often accompanied by negative emotions, they also express the joy of communicating, for example, when they learn something they did not know about their classmates (Toyoda, Yashima, & Aubrey, forthcoming). In Kang (2005), learners experienced excitement about communication with interlocutors from different cultural backgrounds. These examples remind us of Gudykunst's (1991) theory of communication as a process of anxiety and uncertainty reduction, in other words a process of expanding what we share with others. Given substantial interlocutor effect on WTC, promoting supportive, cooperative approaches to communication, for example, in pair or group work, can create a globally pro-communicative atmosphere. In this sense, enhanced L2 WTC should be accompanied by increasing positive emotions such as enjoyment, engagement (See Chapter xx), and excitement, which in turn should result in a positive classroom atmosphere and heightened well-being for teachers and learners.

Reflection Questions

1) In cultures where it is not necessarily the case that "the more a person communicates up to a very extreme, the more positively a person is evaluated" (McCroskey & Richmond, 1990 p. 20), how do teachers create a new norm for heightening WTC in an L2? Or, is it right to impose such a norm?

2) Should L2 WTC research seek evidence linking emotion and linguistic gain in order to have a stronger connection with mainstream SLA and to be more informative as regards L2 teaching?
3) How can research in positive psychology be applied to L2 WTC research?

Recommended reading

MacIntyre, P. D., Dörnyei, Z., Clément, R., & Noels, K. A. (1998). Conceptualizing willingness to communicate in an L2: A situational model of L2 confidence and affiliation. *Modern Language Journal, 82*, 545–562.
This seminal paper, which triggered L2 WTC research in SLA, will be useful for those who are new to this construct. The paper presents the WTC model, which emerged from brainstorming between the four authors on situated WTC at a particular time with particular interlocutors. A detailed discussion of each variable included in the model is presented.

Peng, J. E. (2014). *Willingness to communicate in the Chinese EFL university classroom: An ecological perspective*. Bristol: Multilingual Matters.
This book reports a mixed-methods research approach following an extensive literature review based on the author's doctoral dissertation. It comprises a quantitative study, or the "Big Picture," which investigates interrelationships between variables using SEM, and a qualitative study conducted from an ecological perspective, or a "Situated Lens," capturing fluctuations over time and situations through four multiple-case studies.

Yashima, T., MacIntyre, P., & Ikeda, M. (2018). Situated willingness to communicate in an L2: Interplay of individual characteristics and context. *Language Teaching Research, 22*, 115–137.
This paper reports a study guided by CDST frameworks, namely nested systems and timescales. Nested systems were employed to examine L2 WTC in individual learners and the group (class) constituted by these learners as they interacted with each other. Situated and enduring WTC are regarded as operating on different timescales. The study is an attempt to use a CDST perspective in providing a fuller understanding of the concept.

References

Abu-Rabia, S. (1998). The learning of Hebrew by Israeli Arab students in Israel. *Journal of Social Psychology, 138*, 331–341.
Al-Murtadha, M. (2019). Enhancing EFL learners' willingness to communicate with visualization and goal-setting activities. *TESOL Quarterly, 53*, 133–157.
Baker, S. C., & MacIntyre, P. D. (2000). The role of gender and immersion in communication and second language orientation. *Language Learning, 50*, 311–341.
Barraclough, R. A., Christophel, D. M., & McCroskey, J. C. (1988). Willingness to communicate: A cross-cultural investigation. *Communication Research Reports, 5*, 187–192.
Bektas-Cetinkaya, Y. (2005). Turkish college students' willingness to communicate in English as a foreign language. Unpublished doctoral dissertation, Ohio State University.
Bernales, C. (2016). Towards a comprehensive concept of willingness to communicate: Learners' predicted and self-reported participation in the foreign language classroom. *System, 56*, 1–12.
Cao, Y. (2011). Investigating situational willingness to communicate within second language classrooms from an ecological perspective. *System, 39*, 468–479.
Cao, Y. (2014). A sociocognitive perspective on second language classroom willingness to communicate. *TESOL Quarterly, 48*, 789–814.
Cao, Y., & Philp, J. (2006). Interactional context and willingness to communicate: A comparison of behavior in class, group, and dyadic interaction. *System, 34*, 480–493.
Chan, B., & McCroskey, J. C. (1987). The WTC scale as a predictor of classroom participation. *Communication Research Reports, 4*, 47–50.
Clément, R., Baker, S. C., & MacIntyre, P. D. (2003). Willingness to communicate in a second language: The effects of context, norms, and validity. *Journal of Language and Social Psychology, 22*, 190–209.

Denies, K., Yashima, T., & Janssen, R. (2015). Classroom versus societal willingness to communicate: Investigating French as a second language in Flanders. *Modern Language Journal, 99*, 718–739.

de Saint Léger & Storch, N. (2009). Learners' perceptions and attitudes: Implications for willingness to communicate in an L2 classroom. *System, 37*, 269–285.

Dörnyei, Z., MacIntyre, P. D., & Henry, A. (Eds.). (2015). *Motivational dynamics in language learning*. Bristol: Multilingual Matters.

Eddy-U, M. (2015). Motivation for participation or non-participation in group tasks: A dynamic systems model of task-situated willingness to communicate. *System, 50*, 43–55.

Elahi Shirvan, M., Khajavy, G. H., MacIntyre, P. D., & Taherian, T. (2019). A meta-analysis of L2 willingness to communicate and its three high-evidence correlates, *Journal of Psycholinguistic Research, 48*, 1241–1267.

Freiermuth, M., & Jarrell, D. (2006). Willingness to communicate: Can online chat help? *International Journal of Applied Linguistics, 16*, 190–213.

Fushino, K. (2010). Causal relationships between communication confidence, beliefs about group work, and willingness to communicate in foreign language group work. *TESOL Quarterly, 44*, 700–724.

Gallagher, H. C. (2013). Willingness to communicate and cross-cultural adaptation: L2 communication and acculturative stress as transaction. *Applied Linguistics, 34*, 53–73.

Gardner, R. C. (1985). *Social psychology and second language learning: The role of attitudes and motivation*. London: Arnold.

Gardner, R. C., & MacIntyre, P. D. (1993). On a measurement of affective variables in second language learning. *Language Learning, 43*, 157–194.

Ghonsooly, B., Khajavy, G. H., & Asadpour, S. F. (2012). Willingness to communicate in English among Iranian non-English major university students. *Journal of Language and Social Psychology, 31*, 197–211.

Gudykunst, W. E. (1991). *Bridging differences: Effective intergroup communication*. Newbury Park, CA: Sage.

Kang, D. M. (2014). The effects of study-abroad experiences on EFL learners' willingness to communicate, speaking abilities, and participation in classroom interaction. *System, 42*, 319–332.

Kang, S. J. (2005). Dynamic emergence of situational willingness to communicate in a second language. *System, 33*, 277–292.

Khajavy, G. H., Ghonsooly, B., Fatemi, A. H., & Choi, C. W. (2016). Willingness to communicate in English: A microsystem model in the Iranian EFL classroom context. *TESOL Quarterly, 50*, 154–180.

Khajavy, G. H., MacIntyre, P. D., & Barabadi, E. (in print). Role of the emotions and classroom environment in willingness to communicate: Applying doubly latent multilevel analysis in second language acquisition. *Studies in Second Language Acquisition*.

Larsen-Freeman, D., & Cameron, L. (2008). *Complex systems and applied linguistics*. New York: Oxford University Press.

Lee, J. S., & Hsieh, J. C. (2019). Affective variables and willingness to communicate of EFL learners in in-class, out-of-class, and digital contexts. *System, 82*, 63–73.

MacIntyre, P. D. (2007). Willingness to communicate in the second language: Understanding the decision to speak as a volitional process. *The Modern Language Journal, 91*, 564–576.

MacIntyre, P. D., Baker, S. C., Clément, R., & Conrod, S. (2001). Willingness to communicate, social support, and language-learning orientations of immersion students. *Studies in Second Language Acquisition, 23*, 369–388.

MacIntyre, P. D., Baker, S. C., Clément, R., & Donovan, L. A. (2002). Sex and age effects on willingness to communicate, anxiety, perceived competence, and L2 motivation among junior high school French immersion students. *Language Learning, 52*, 537–564.

MacIntyre, P. D., Burns, C., & Jessome, A. (2011). Ambivalence about communicating in a second language: A qualitative study of French immersion students' willingness to communicate. *Modern Language Journal, 95*, 81–96.

MacIntyre, P. D., & Charos, C. (1996). Personality, attitudes, and affect as predictors of second language communication. *Journal of Language and Social Psychology, 15*, 3–26.

MacIntyre, P. D., & Clément, R. (1996, August). A model of willingness to communicate in a second language: The concept, its antecedents, and implications. Paper presented at the 11th World Congress of Applied Linguistics, Jyväskylä, Finland.

MacIntyre, P. D., Dörnyei, Z., Clément, R., & Noels, K. A. (1998). Conceptualizing willingness to communicate in an L2: A situational model of L2 confidence and affiliation. *Modern Language Journal, 82*, 545–562.

MacIntyre, P. D., Gregersen, T., & Mercer, S. (2019). Setting an agenda for positive psychology in SLA: Theory, practice, and research. *Modern Language Journal, 103*, 262–274.

MacIntyre, P. D., & Legatto, J. J. (2011). A dynamic system approach to willingness to communicate: Developing an idiodynamic method to capture rapidly changing affect. *Applied Linguistics, 32*, 149–171.

McCroskey, J. C. (1992). Reliability and validity of the willingness to communicate scale. *Communication Quarterly, 40*, 16–25.

McCroskey, J. C., & Richmond, V. P. (1987). Willingness to communicate. In J. C. McCroskey, & J. A. Daly (Eds.), *Personality and interpersonal communication* (pp. 129–156). Newbury Park, CA: Sage.

McCroskey, J. C., & Richmond, V. P. (1990). Willingness to communicate: A cognitive view. In M. Both-Butterfield (Ed.), *Communication, cognition, and anxiety* (pp. 19–37). Newbury Park, CA: Sage.

Munezane, Y. (2015). Enhancing willingness to communicate: Relative effects of visualization and goal setting. *The Modern Language Journal, 99*, 1, 175–191.

Mystkowska-Wiertelak, A., & Pawlak, M. (2017). *Willingness to communicate in instructed second language acquisition: Combining a macro- and microperspective.* Bristol: Multilingual Matters.

Norton, B. (2000). *Identity and language learning: Gender, ethnicity, and educational change.* London: Longman.

Öz, H., Demirezen, M., & Pourfeiz, J. (2015). Willingness to communicate of EFL learners in Turkish context. *Learning and Individual Differences, 37*, 269–275.

Pattapong, K. (2010). Willingness to communicate in a second language: A qualitative study of issues affecting Thai EFL learners from students' and teachers' point of view. Unpublished doctoral dissertation, University of Sydney.

Pawlak, M., & Mystkowska-Wiertelak, A. (2015). Investigating the dynamic nature of classroom willingness to communicate. *System, 50*, 1–9.

Pawlak, M., Mystkowska-Wiertelak, A., & Bielak, J. (2016). Investigating the nature of L2 willingness to communicate (WTC): A micro-perspective. *Language Teaching Research, 20*, 654–671.

Peng, J. E. (2012). Towards an ecological understanding of willingness to communicate in EFL classrooms in China. *System, 40*, 203–213.

Peng, J. E. (2014). *Willingness to communicate in the Chinese EFL university classroom: An ecological perspective.* Bristol: Multilingual Matters.

Peng, J. E., & Woodrow, L, (2010). Willingness to communicate in English: A model in the Chinese EFL classroom context. *Language Learning, 60*, 834–876.

Peng, J. E., Zhang, L., & Chen, Y. (2017). The mediation of multimodal affordances on willingness to communicate in the English as a foreign language classroom. *TESOL Quarterly, 51*, 302–331.

Peterson, C. (2006). *A primer in positive psychology.* New York: Oxford University Press.

Shao, Q., & Gao, X. (2016). Reticence and willingness to communicate (WTC) of East Asian language learners. *System, 63*, 115–120.

Tomasello, M. (2003). *Constructing a language.* Harvard University Press.

Toyoda, J., Yashima, T., & Aubrey, S. (forthcoming). Enhancing situational willingness to communicate in novice EFL learners through task-based learning, *JALT Journal*.

Weaver, C. (2005). Using the Rasch model to develop a measure of second language learners' willingness to communicate within a language classroom. *Journal of Applied Measurement, 6*, 396–415.

Wen, W. P., & Clément, R. (2003). A Chinese conceptualization of willingness to communicate in ESL. *Language, Culture, and Curriculum, 16*, 18–38.

Wood, D. (2016). Willingness to communicate and second language speech fluency: An idiodynamic investigation. *System, 60*, 11–28.

Yashima, T. (2002). Willingness to communicate in a second language: The Japanese EFL context. *The Modern Language Journal, 86*, 54–66.

Yashima, T. (2019). L2 motivation and willingness to communicate. In M. Lamb, K. Csizér, A. Henry, & S. Ryan (Eds.), *The Palgrave handbook of motivation for language learning* (pp. 203–224). Cham, Switzerland: Palgrave Macmillan.

Yashima, T., Ikeda, M., & Nakahira, S. (2016). Talk and silence in an EFL classroom: Interplay of learners and context. In J. King, (Ed.), *The dynamic interplay between context and the learner* (pp. 104–126.) Basingstoke: Palgrave Macmillan.

Yashima, T., MacIntyre, P., & Ikeda, M. (2018). Situated willingness to communicate in an L2: Interplay of individual characteristics and context. *Language Teaching Research, 22*, 115–137.

Yashima, T., & Zenuk-Nishide, L. (2008). The impact of learning contexts on proficiency, attitudes, and L2 communication: Creating an imagined international community. *System, 36*, 566–585.

Yashima, T., Zenuk-Nishide, L., & Shimizu, K. (2004). The influence of attitudes and affect on willingness to communicate and second language communication. *Language Learning, 54*, 119–152.

Yu, M. (2015). An examination of the dynamic feature of WTC through dyadic group interaction. *System, 55*, 11–20.

Zarrinabadi, N. (2014). Communicating in a second language: Investigating the effect of teacher[s] on learners' willingness to communicate. *System, 42*, 288–295.

Zhang, J., Beckmann, N., & Beckmann, J. F. (2018). To talk or not to talk: A review of situational antecedents of willingness to communicate in the second language classroom. *System, 72*, 226–239.

Zhong, Q. M. (2013). Understanding Chinese learners' willingness to communicate in a New Zealand ESL classroom. *System, 41*, 740–751.

PART 3

Groups and Communities

21
TEACHER-LEARNER RELATIONSHIPS

Christina Gkonou

The relationship between teachers and learners is perhaps the most important relationship in the school context, given that, on average, teachers and learners spend six and a half hours per day at school for at least 180 days throughout the year (OECD, 2014). In other words, teachers and students spend much of their time together at school, interacting with each other, and this relationship is pertinent across all educational settings. For such interaction to result in positive teaching and learning outcomes, it should take place within healthy interpersonal relationships in which teachers and learners communicate effectively with each other, feelings and thoughts are expressed, and concerns about progress are openly shared. In this chapter, I discuss the conceptualization of teacher-learner relationships in psychology and second language acquisition (SLA), the integration of insights from these two fields, and implications that can be drawn for language teacher practice and research. I conclude the chapter by reflecting on possible future directions and suggesting useful external sources for readers who wish to find out more about this topic.

Teacher-Learner Relationships in Psychology

For many, the term "teacher-learner relationship" is self-explanatory. In fact, previous writings on teacher-learner relationships do not even begin with a definition of the term but move straight to relationship qualities and the impact of positive and healthy interpersonal relationships on learners' academic achievement and teachers' professional—and even personal—well-being (see Chapter 15). However, providing a comprehensive definition of the term will facilitate understandings of both the theoretical underpinnings of teacher-learner relationships and the implications for practice and research presented later in the chapter. For such a definition of teacher-learner relationships, I draw on Wubbels, Brekelmans, den Brok, Wijsman, Mainhard, and van Tartwijk (2014), who define them as "the generalized interpersonal meaning students and teachers attach to their interactions with each other" (p. 364). These interactions could be considered the building blocks of the relationship between a teacher and a learner because they happen on a daily basis, multiple times throughout the day.

Nevertheless, such interactions are important not just for their high frequency of occurrence but also the ways in which they take place and are interpreted by each member that participates in the interaction. As Wubbels and Brekelmans (2005) explain, individuals function within a communicative system in the presence of others and it is almost impossible to "*not communicate* when in the presence of someone else" (p. 7; italics in the original) as this could lead to different—and often wrong—interpretations of one's silence (e.g., ignoring others, showing indifference toward others, devaluing the question). The cognitive processes that take place when one interprets and evaluates patterns of interaction and relatedness as they emerge from repeated interpersonal experiences with a specific individual produce relational schemata (Baldwin, 1992). As relationships are formed on the basis of repeated interactions with the same people, relational schemata enable individuals to distinguish between a positive relationship filled with "affection, warmth, and open communication" (Pianta, 2001, p. 11) and a hostile relationship, even at the early stages of its relationship building, as well as predict behavior in future encounters. In all cases, relationships affect all those involved.

The human proclivity to relate and connect with others has been highlighted in a number of different theories within psychology. According to the self-determination theory of motivation (Deci & Ryan, 1985, 2012; Ryan & Deci, 2000), individuals work toward meeting three basic psychological needs: autonomy, which refers to the desire to act as an independent agent, taking on tasks and responsibilities to fulfill them; relatedness, which is defined as the willingness to interact with others, supporting and caring for them; and competence, which is needed to produce desired outcomes, rise to challenges, and feel that something new has been learned and mastered. The second need, relatedness, manifests in teacher-learner relationships.

Additionally, interpersonal theory (Horowitz & Strack, 2011) has also shown that human behavior is best understood along two dimensions: agency and communion. In exercising agency, individuals are able to control the interaction and act independently. In communion with others, they also show affection toward them. Both agency and communion encompass a set of other constructs that pertain to human relationships. For example, communion can contain proximity, empathy, and care, whereas agency often entails power, influence, and hierarchy or authority. With respect to teacher-learner relationships in particular, hierarchical structures normally apply, as the two participants in the relationship (i.e., the teacher and the learner) are not typically of equal standing, with the teacher usually being the one who has the power and is able to direct and decide how a lesson will take place, even in learner-centered contexts.

In his ecosystems model, Bronfenbrenner (1979) also explained how a child—and in principle every individual—can develop through reciprocal interactions with others in their immediate social settings. The developing person exists in a microsystem, the most immediate social context, and is influenced by other people surrounding them both at the micro- and the mesosystem (i.e., the bridge between settings in which a person participates or has participated). In addition, the developing person has control over interactions that are happening in the micro- and mesosystem but not in the exo- and macrosystem. This is because the developing person is unlikely to enter the exo- and macrosystem, which respectively refer to the interrelatedness among settings in which the developing person may never enter and the overarching ideological and organizational patterns of social institutions (e.g., governmental bodies) that shape a particular culture. It is worth noting, however, that ecological environments stretch beyond the boundaries of the immediate setting that surrounds a developing person, and for this reason events and changes that take place in the distant settings (i.e., exo- and macrosystem) can potentially influence what happens in the person's immediate setting—that is, their microsystem. The theory highlights the value of healthy interpersonal relationships and the fact that these relationships are more prominent than the environment in which they develop, since "a powerful and positive relationship may have the power to overcome the impacts of even the most damaging environment, and even a positive environment may be insufficient to support positive development in the absence of warm and loving relationships" (Hayes, O'Toole, & Halpenny, 2017, p. 44).

Within educational psychology, insights drawn from the above theorizations of teacher-learner relationships have informed a considerable body of empirical research, showing that both teachers and learners can benefit from positive relationships. Specifically, positive teacher-learner relationships promote teacher professional longevity (Day & Gu, 2010; O'Connor, 2008; Veldman, van Tartwijk, Brekelmans, & Wubbels, 2013), positive teacher identities (Chhuon & Wallace, 2014), and reduce the levels of work-related stress among teachers (Chang, 2009; Friedman, 2006; Hargreaves, 2000; Jennings & Greenberg, 2009; Yoon, 2002). Minimizing teacher stress is particularly important as high-quality interpersonal relationships with learners help cultivate teacher well-being, which is related by extension to successful teaching (Rimm-Kaufman & Hamre, 2010). With respect to learners, a relationship with their teacher characterized by emotional warmth and a consideration of their needs contributes to school-related happiness (Chu, Saucier, & Hafner, 2010; Suldo, Shaffer, & Riley, 2008; Tian, Tian, & Huebner, 2016), higher learner investment (Furrer & Skinner, 2003; Hughes, Luo, Kwok, & Loyd, 2008), and positive socio-emotional development and competence (McCormick & O'Connor, 2015). Substantial research also reveals that good teacher-student relationships protect students with behavioral problems or those from lower socio-economic backgrounds from school failure (Froiland, Worrell, & Oh, 2019; Ladd & Burgess, 2001; McCormick, O'Connor, Cappella, & McClowry, 2013; Niehaus, Rudasill, & Rakes, 2012; O'Connor, Dearing, & Collins, 2011). Hattie's (2009) meta-analytic study of educational factors that positively influence learning also reveals that teacher-learner relationships figure high on the list (i.e., at place 11 in a list of 138 key factors that influence learning). Hattie (2012) specifically mentions care, trust, cooperation, respect, and team skills as key determinants of healthy teacher-learner relationships and of a positive classroom climate.

Additionally, specific teacher practices and characteristics also help to mediate close teacher-learner relationships. Research in educational psychology has shown that teachers who tend to involve their students in classroom decision-making and embrace their individual differences are more likely to increase learner engagement and their students' positive attitudes toward their class (Daniels & Perry, 2003). Also, teachers who are emotionally supportive of their learners and show sensitivity to their feelings and personal difficulties are better able to help their students to achieve their goals and perform better at school (Hamre & Pianta, 2005). On the contrary, teachers who show negativity, for example through sarcastic comments on learners' performance or frustration and anger, create negative relationships, which are usually stressful for both learners and teachers (Jennings & Greenberg, 2009; Lisonbee, Mize, Payne, & Granger, 2008; O'Connor, Collins, & Supplee, 2012). The Model for Interpersonal Teacher Behavior has also revealed that both the type and quality of teacher-learner relationships are largely determined by the dimensions of teacher influence and teacher proximity, leading to eight possible types of teacher behavior: leading, helpful/friendly, understanding, giving students responsibility and freedom, uncertain, dissatisfied, admonishing, and strict (Wubbels & Brekelmans, 2005). Although some of the above types of teacher behavior, such as the admonishing or strict teacher, may seem somewhat unwelcome—or, at least, they look less desirable than the friendly teacher, for instance—they still have the potential to facilitate the formation of quality teacher-learner relationships. Research has shown that different teacher leadership styles and degrees of control (e.g., a laissez-faire vs. a more controlling attitude) can lead to positive interpersonal relationships, which develop through either controlling or autonomy-supportive teacher behaviors, or even a combination of such behaviors depending on the aims and stages of the lesson, the dynamics of the class, and general classroom management (Reeve, 2006, 2009).

Teacher-Learner Relationships in SLA

Within SLA, empirical research into teacher-learner relationships is scarce despite recent acknowledgements that the field seems to be undergoing a relational turn (Mercer, 2016). The closest concept to relationships discussed within SLA is perhaps group dynamics (Dörnyei & Murphey, 2003) (see Chapter 22). Group dynamics refers to the relationships among individuals in the classroom which can be either positive or negative depending on the group atmosphere and the extent to which members of the group bond. Given the fundamentally social and interpersonal nature of language learning and teaching, understanding groups helps teachers to develop appropriate classroom management strategies, design materials that foster communication and interaction, and set group norms—all of which contribute toward more successful learning and teaching. Past experiences can have a fundamental effect on the behaviors, attitudes, and social interactions among members of a group (Murphey, Falout, Fukuda, & Fukuda, 2012). Such past experiences can often be detrimental to one's learning but redressed by helpful practices with respect to group dynamics from present teachers and positive classroom experiences. Just as past experiences working in different groups can influence current attitudes toward group work, groups that have worked together successfully are more likely to become members of another cohesive, well-formed group in the future.

Although SLA research has mainly focused on group dynamics as the closest concept to teacher-learner relationships, there is a small set of empirical studies concentrating, as such, on teacher-learner relationships in language classrooms, stemming from three different datasets. The first is from Gkonou and Mercer's (2017) multi-phase project on English language teachers' emotional and social intelligence. Through a series of classroom observations and in-depth, stimulated-recall interviews with three highly socio-emotionally competent teachers in the UK and three in Austria, the authors concluded that the participating teachers were striving for quality interpersonal relationships in their classrooms that were characterized by four main relationship qualities: empathy, (mutual bidirectional) respect, trust, and responsiveness. While within these relationships teachers valued honesty and harmony, they felt that discipline and "temporary disharmony" were also necessary (ibid, p. 18). Positive interpersonal relationships were also bidirectional in that they influenced learner achievement (i.e., teachers' effect on learners) and teacher professional well-being (i.e., learners' effect on teachers).

Strategies for enacting the characteristics of quality teacher-learner relationships, mainly associated with effective classroom management, were also explored in Gkonou and Mercer (2017). These included learning and using students' names (and encouraging learners to do so too), "cold calling" by name to involve everyone, knowing about and showing sensitivity to learners' backgrounds and past experiences, using non-verbals, exploiting classroom space and sitting close to students, using (often self-deprecating) humor and welcoming humor from students, making use of the first language (L1) for interpersonal reasons, and using set routines. Teacher-learner relationships were further mediated by contextual factors such as the physical design and layout of classrooms, the length of time over which a relationship between teachers and learners may develop, and the role of leadership within an institution (for example, through support from the headteacher).

In a second publication from the same dataset, Gkonou and Mercer (2018) explored the relational beliefs and practices of the above-mentioned teachers by additionally looking at teachers' views of the relationships among their learners and extending their study to also include relationships beyond the classroom such as with significant others both at a professional (e.g., colleagues) and personal (e.g., partners) level. The study showed that teachers' relationships with learners, amongst learners, and between teachers and peers/family members elevated the quality of classroom teaching, interactions, and problem solving. It should be noted that in both studies, the participants were highly emotionally and socially intelligent teachers. This should not, however, mean that teachers who might score lower on scales that measure emotional and/or social intelligence are not sensitive to the interpersonal dynamics of language classrooms and cannot develop their skills in fostering positive relationships with their learners.

The second dataset emerged from an interview-based study with two highly experienced secondary-school teachers in Austria (Mercer & Gkonou, 2020), who expressed difficulty in being caring and friendly, yet firm when needed. Evidence suggested that although investing in relationships with learners was stressful and required both time and effort on the part of the teachers, at the same time it generated positivity. Teachers reported experiencing higher job satisfaction as a result of their good relationships with their learners and appreciated more the importance of helping their learners to develop their interpersonal, relationship-building skills. In addition, the teachers highlighted the importance of sharing personal experiences with learners and investing in the process of getting to know each other better. The latter finding was also substantiated by Miller and Gkonou (2018) in a third set of data. In their study, the authors looked at emotions and associated agentic behavior of English language teachers working in Higher Education Institutions in the US and the UK. Among different points discussed during in-depth interviews, participants were asked which aspect of their teaching they enjoy the most. Nearly unanimously teachers said that they enjoyed interacting with their students and highlighted how relationships and caring for their students helped them to gain emotional rewards as teachers experienced happiness, enjoyment, enthusiasm, positivity, and satisfaction. Through the process of nurturing good relationships with their learners, teachers were able to know their learners better and improve their teaching practices, which they saw as an essential part of their own cycle of development. Additionally, their teaching-as-caring approach (Wentzel, 2015), which was not, however, without stress and instances of masking their true feelings, helped them to find purpose in teaching.

Integrating Perspectives from Psychology and SLA

The above sections have offered an overview of theories and research into teacher-learner relationships in psychology and SLA. Specifically, the need to relate with others, which forms an integral component of self-determination theory, has been discussed within SLA and with respect to the interface between relationships, motivation, and engagement (see, e.g., Noels, Chaffee, Lou, & Dincer, 2016; Noels, Vargas Lascano, & Saumure, 2019). For example, second language (L2) motivation (see Chapter 10) researchers have used it as a framework to better understand what motivates language learners and how they could persist with their studies (Gardner, 2020). It is important to take stock of this body of research and examine more ways of how self-determination and, subsequently, motivation are interconnected with L2 teacher-learner relationships. The nested ecosystems model has also been integrated into language learning and teaching and, in particular, in conceptualizations of L2 willingness to communicate (Peng, 2012) and language learner anxiety (Gkonou, 2017). Although the model underscores the key role of environment in forming quality interpersonal relationships, it has not yet been applied as such to empirical investigations of teacher-learner relationships within SLA. Additionally, the concepts of emotional and social intelligence, which have laid the foundations for interdisciplinary research with highly emotionally and socially intelligent English language teachers (Gkonou & Mercer, 2017, 2018; Mercer & Gkonou, 2016), helped to better understand how emotionally and socially intelligent teachers in particular manage their classrooms and how consciously they attend to building positive relationships with their students in class. Although teacher-learner relationships were not intended as the main research focus of these projects, the fact that they emerged so prominently in the findings is a clear indication that psychological constructs such as emotional intelligence could be integrated into SLA research on social relationships in the classroom. It would be worth examining the emotional and social intelligence of both learners and teachers, given that both groups form part of a relationship, and how each group constructs or experiences the relationship. This could move beyond individual relationships and extend to groups or networks of relationships (Mercer, 2015) to further inform group dynamics research within SLA.

Although insights from SLA research have not yet been drawn for psychology with regard to teacher-learner relationships per se, there is potential. Within educational psychology, for instance, one possible suggestion concerns approaching classroom relationships more holistically by taking into account the whole environment of teachers. Research within SLA has revealed that in order to improve their relationships with their learners and thus boost the effectiveness of teaching and learning, teachers often turn to colleagues and partners for advice and to share any painful emotions they might be experiencing (e.g., Gkonou & Mercer, 2018). Thus, to better understand and improve teacher-learner relationships, it would be worthwhile taking into account the interactions between teachers and significant others at both the professional and personal level. Lastly, what language and how language can be used to construct relationships could be examined within educational and social psychology and within the wider context of human relationships.

Implications for Practice and Research

Although the importance of teacher-learner relationships is well documented in previous research, the relational strategies teachers can use and their role in fostering quality interpersonal relationships in actual practice is still somewhat unclear. Therefore, I will discuss implications for practice along three key dimensions. The first one refers to the process of getting to know students, which includes knowing their personal interests and difficulties with language/learning as well as their personalities, personal experiences, and background. Knowing about interests, strengths, and weaknesses gives teachers useful insights into topics of personal relevance for their learners and better understanding of ways to help learners achieve their potential at school. Familiarity with learners' personalities also facilitates differentiated instruction and helps teachers tailor their approach toward different learners and potential learning opportunities that may prove successful (Dewaele, 2012). For example, a shy learner could benefit from a private, one-to-one tutorial with the teacher, whereas an easily distracted learner would benefit from a variety of instructional strategies and more frequent breaks.

The second dimension concerns the importance of teachers showing learners that they care by providing clear, explicit, and realistic expectations, constructive and meaningful feedback on accomplishments and improvements, and a sense that these actions are taken because teachers want their learners to do well (Wentzel, 1997). Consistency and fairness in conveying such messages is critical. Another important dimension of teacher-learner relationships concerns dealing with difficult students and challenging behaviors. For teachers, this requires a higher level of emotional work and a more careful approach toward students (Gkonou & Miller, 2020), such as using positive discourse, noticing and talking about positive actions students take, and expending effort in helping them develop trust in the teacher.

The third dimension is about creating a positive classroom atmosphere, which will enhance teacher-learner relationships and enable relationships among students to flourish. The latter is equally important to teacher-learner relationships. A set of relational strategies for supporting this dimension includes using humor, creating a sense of community among classroom members to increase confidence in discussing learning-related concerns openly and honestly, building fun into classroom activities, using names, making the link between content taught in class and personally relevant experiences, and overall offering emotional support when necessary (see Gkonou & Mercer, 2017, for strategies within SLA; also, Roffey, 2011; Wentzel, 2010, for strategies within general education).

Furthermore, previous studies have specifically looked at the extent to which teacher-learner relationships correlate with academic achievement (Furrer & Skinner, 2003; Hamre & Pianta, 2001; McCormick & O'Connor, 2015) and particular psychological constructs such as stress, burnout, and happiness, among others (Chang, 2009; Hargreaves, 2000; Jennings & Greenberg, 2009). Although these studies have contributed toward establishing teacher-learner relationships as key in contemporary education, there is still much that we do not know about classroom interpersonal relationships. Adopting a more contextual view of relationships and studying them in tandem with—and not in isolation from—specific teacher behaviors and classroom management techniques is a promising research avenue. In other words, more empirical studies on how relationships are created, sustained, and fostered in actual classrooms are needed, given the inherent complexity of relationships and the inherently complex nature of language classrooms. For example, this could entail lesson observations and follow-ups, stimulated-recall interviews with teachers and learners to take into account both perspectives, and studies could seek to elucidate how relationships are formed at the classroom level, both between the teacher and an individual student, and amongst learners. Additionally, as relationships are dynamic (Newberry, 2010; O'Connor, 2010) and take time to build and establish (Davis, 2003; O'Connor et al., 2011), researchers could consider employing longitudinal research designs, which extend beyond one school year and look specifically at how developmental transitions for learners (e.g., from elementary to secondary school and through adolescence) affect relationships. For instance, the teachers in the Gkonou and Mercer (2017) study commented that having a relationship over a number of years enables quality relationships to grow and helps both parties to become familiar with each other and know what to expect. Teacher-learner relationships can also have a long-lasting influence, especially on learners and as learners move to next stages in education. For instance, kindergarten children who are close to their teachers usually develop stronger social skills and avoid conflict as they go through primary school and enter high school (Berry & O'Connor, 2009).

Future Directions

The topic of teacher-student relationships should be central in psychology, education, and SLA because of its link to improved teaching and student outcomes (Bingham & Sidorkin, 2010; Roffey, 2011). This points to the need for pre-service and in-service teacher education programs to include a component in their curricula that explicitly considers the teacher-student relationship. In this context, accounts of teachers who have positive and potentially less positive relationships with their students could be studied—along with information about their influence on teachers and learners—and lesson observations could be conducted with a focus on relationship behaviors. Learning about other teachers' success stories is beneficial for fellow teachers; and even others' identified struggles often function as starting points for enhancing continuous professional development. Teachers should also be explicitly taught how to teach with emotional and social intelligence as both competencies contribute toward positive relationships with their learners. Subsequently, through a stronger focus on emotional and social intelligence and through group dynamics work in the classroom, teachers can teach positive relationship skills to their learners, which can boost the teacher-learner and the learner-learner relationship. Additionally, it is important to encourage teachers to make use of student and parent feedback, collected through surveys or informal conversations, to evaluate the extent to which their relationship-building techniques have an impact on the lives of their students and how they have also contributed toward their own personal progress as practitioners. The effect of such revised professional development syllabi on teaching and learning outcomes could also be examined through empirical research projects and specifically pre- and post-tests, interspersed with carefully designed interventions.

Another fruitful future direction for research into teacher-learner relationships concerns taking into consideration a broader range of geographical locations, demographics, class sizes, and the various reasons why students are learning a language—all of which naturally influence how teachers relate to their learners and vice versa. In particular, future endeavors within SLA could concentrate on different levels of education (e.g., primary school, secondary school, post-secondary education); urban and rural settings; schools in English-speaking countries with high proportions of students with English as an additional language, which could result into somewhat less homogeneous student cohorts in terms of the different languages spoken within one specific class; high-performing and less well-performing schools according to national standards; schools where large classes are the norm rather than the exception. SLA research that specifically focuses on teachers with differential levels of experience such as newly qualified teachers and teachers who have been in the profession for a long time. Finally, given that previous SLA research has primarily employed cross-sectional designs, further longitudinal attempts following suggestions offered in the previous section could look at how relationships are fostered between teachers and students who have retained the same teacher for the subsequent year; or what happens when the classroom dynamics change because of a new teacher or new student members and relationships are presumably affected.

Reflection Questions

- What relational strategies and practices do you find effective in cultivating positive and healthy interpersonal relationships among teachers and students in language classrooms?
- How could the process of fostering good teacher-learner relationships be best explored through classroom observations?

- In what ways do you feel that the contextual specificities of language classrooms potentially affect teacher-learner relationships?

Recommended Reading

Bingham, C., & Sidorkin, A. M. (Eds). (2010). *No education without relation*. Peter Lang.

This edited collection discusses a new approach to education based on interpersonal relationships, which is called "the pedagogy of relation." The book focuses on understanding how human relationships work—in everyday life but in actual classrooms too—and how such understandings are perhaps more important to reach than centering mainly on teaching methods, materials, and curricula in trying to improve learning and teaching conditions and achieving excellence.

Gkonou, C., & Mercer, S. (2017). *Understanding emotional and social intelligence among English language teachers*. British Council.

This publication reports on a funded research project on socio-emotional competencies among English language teachers across the globe and also specifically within the authors' working contexts. It underlines the importance of emotional and social intelligence in managing language classrooms effectively, handling students' and teachers' own emotions carefully, and promoting positive social relationships among all classroom members. The implications for practice and teacher education presented at the end of the report are drawn on the basis of the project's empirical research findings.

Roffey, S. (2011). *Changing behaviour in schools: Promoting positive relationships and wellbeing*. Thousand Oaks, CA: Sage.

This book presents examples of specific strategies for promoting positive, pro-social and collaborative behavior within relationships in the classroom, the school, and beyond. Through an overview of previous writings, case studies, and activities, it tackles aspects such as belongingness, increasing learner engagement and participation, and working together with and re-engaging challenging students or students who have been marginalized.

References

Baldwin, M. W. (1992). Relational schemas and the processing of social information. *Psychological Bulletin, 112*(3), 461–484.
Berry, D., & O'Connor, E. (2009). Behavioral risk, teacher-child relationships, and social skill development across middle childhood: A child-by-environment analysis of change. *Journal of Applied Developmental Psychology, 31*(1), 1–14.
Bingham, C., & Sidorkin, A. M. (Eds). (2010). *No education without relation*. Peter Lang.
Bronfenbrenner, U. (1979). *The ecology of human development: Experiments by nature and design*. Harvard University Press.
Chang, M. L. (2009). An appraisal perspective of teacher burnout: Examining the emotional work of teachers. *Educational Psychology Review, 21*(3), 193–218.
Chhuon, V., & Wallace, T. L. (2014). Creating connectedness through being known: Fulfilling the need to belong in U.S. high schools. *Youth & Society, 46*(3), 379–401.
Chu, P., Saucier, D., & Hafner, E. (2010). Meta-analysis of the relationships between social support and well-being in children and adolescents. *Journal of Social and Clinical Psychology, 29*(6), 624–645.
Daniels, D. H., & Perry, K. E. (2003). "Learner-centered" according to children. *Theory into Practice, 42*(2), 102–108.
Davis, H. A. (2003). Conceptualizing the role and influence of student-teacher relationships on children's social and cognitive development. *Educational Psychologist, 38*(4), 207–234.
Day, C., & Gu, Q. (2010). *The new lives of teachers*. Routledge.
Deci, E. L., & Ryan, R. M. (1985). *Intrinsic motivation and self-determination in human behaviour*. Plenum.
Deci, E. L., & Ryan, R. M. (2012). Motivation, personality, and development within embedded social contexts: An overview of self-determination theory. In R. M. Ryan (Ed.), *Oxford handbook of human motivation* (pp. 85–107). Oxford University Press.

Dewaele, J.-M. (2012). Personality: Personality traits as independent and dependent variables. In S. Mercer, S. Ryan & M. Williams (Eds.), *Psychology for language learning: Insights from research, theory and practice* (pp. 42–58). Palgrave Macmillan.

Dörnyei, Z., & Murphey, T. (2003). *Group dynamics in the language classroom.* Cambridge University Press.

Friedman, I. A. (2006). Classroom management and teacher stress and burnout. In C. M. Evertson & C. S. Weinstein (Eds.), *Handbook of classroom management: Research, practice, and contemporary issues* (pp. 925–944). Lawrence Erlbaum Associates.

Froiland, J. M., Worrell, F. C., & Oh, H. (2019). Teacher-student relationships, psychological need satisfaction, and happiness among diverse students. *Psychology in the Schools, 56*(5), 856–870.

Furrer, C., & Skinner, E. (2003). Sense of relatedness as a factor in children's academic engagement and performance. *Journal of Educational Psychology, 95*(1), 148–162.

Gardner, R. C. (2020). Looking back and looking forward. In A. H. Al-Hoorie & P. D. MacIntyre (Eds.), *Contemporary language motivation theory: 60 years since Gardner and Lambert (1959)* (pp. 5–14). Multilingual Matters.

Gkonou, C. (2017). Towards an ecological understanding of language anxiety. In C. Gkonou, M. Daubney, & J.-M. Dewaele (Eds.), *New insights into language anxiety: Theory, research and educational implications* (pp. 135–155). Multilingual Matters.

Gkonou, C., & Mercer, S. (2017). *Understanding emotional and social intelligence among English language teachers.* British Council.

Gkonou, C., & Mercer, S. (2018). The relational beliefs and practices of highly socio-emotionally competent teachers. In Mercer, S., & Kostoulas, A. (Eds.), *Language teacher psychology* (pp. 158–177). Multilingual Matters.

Gkonou, C., & Miller, E. R. (2020). An exploration of language teacher reflection, emotion labor and emotional capital. *TESOL Quarterly.* Early online view.

Hamre, B. K., & Pianta, R. C. (2001). Early teacher-child relationships and the trajectory of children's school outcomes through eighth grade. *Child Development, 72*(2), 625–638.

Hamre, B. K., & Pianta, R. C. (2005). Can instructional and emotional support in the first-grade classroom make a difference for children at risk of school failure? *Child Development, 76*(5), 949–967.

Hargreaves, A. (2000). Mixed emotions: Teachers' perceptions of their interactions with students. *Teaching and Teacher Education, 16*(8), 811–826.

Hattie, J. (2009). *Visible learning: A synthesis of over 800 meta-analyses relating to achievement.* Routledge.

Hattie, J. (2012). *Visible learning for teachers: Maximizing impact on learning.* Routledge.

Hayes, N., O'Toole, L., & Halpenny, A. N. (2017). *Introducing Bronfenbrenner: A guide for practitioner and students in early years education.* Routledge.

Horowitz, L. M., & Strack, S. (2011). *Handbook of interpersonal psychology: Theory, research, assessment, and therapeutic interventions.* John Wiley & Sons.

Hughes, J. N., Luo, W., Kwok, O., & Loyd, L. (2008). Teacher-student support, effortful engagement, and achievement: A three-year longitudinal study. *Journal of Educational Psychology, 100*(1), 1–14.

Jennings, P. A., & Greenberg, M. T. (2009). The prosocial classroom: Teacher social and emotional competence in relation to student and classroom outcomes. *Review of Educational Research, 79*(1), 491–525.

Ladd, G. W., & Burgess, K. B. (2001). Do relational risks and protective factors moderate the linkages between childhood aggression and early psychological and school adjustment? *Child Development, 72*(5), 1579–1601.

Lisonbee, J., Mize, J., Payne, A. L., & Granger, D. (2008). Children's cortisol and the quality of teacher-child relationships in child care. *Child Development, 79*(6), 1818–1832.

McCormick, M. P., & O'Connor, E. E. (2015). Teacher-child relationship quality and academic achievement in elementary school: Does gender matter? *Journal of Educational Psychology, 107*(2), 502–516.

McCormick, M. P., O'Connor, E. E., Cappella, E., & McClowry, S. G. (2013). Teacher-child relationships and academic achievement: A multilevel 149 propensity score model approach. *Journal of School Psychology, 51*(5), 611–624.

Mercer, S. (2015). Social network analysis and complex dynamic systems. In Z. Dörnyei, P. D. MacIntyre, & A. Henry (Eds.), *Motivational dynamics in language learning* (pp. 73–82). Multilingual Matters.

Mercer, S. (2016). Seeing the world through your eyes: Empathy in language learning and teaching. In P. D. MacIntyre, T. Gregersen, & S. Mercer (Eds.), *Positive psychology in second language acquisition* (pp. 91–111). Multilingual Matters.

Mercer, S., & Gkonou, C. (2017). Teaching with heart and soul. In T. Gregersen & P. D. MacIntyre (Eds.), *Innovative practices in language teacher education: Spanning the spectrum from intra- to inter-personal professional development* (pp. 103–124). Springer.

Mercer, S., & Gkonou, C. (2020). Relationships and good language teachers. In C. Griffiths & Z. Tajeddin (Eds.), *Lessons from good language teachers* (pp. 164–174). Cambridge University Press.

Miller, E. R., & Gkonou, C. (2018). Language teacher agency, emotion labor and emotional rewards in tertiary-level English language programs. Special Issue of *System* on "Interdisciplinarity in Language Teacher Agency: Theoretical and Analytical Explorations," *79*, 49–59.

Murphey, T., Falout, J., Fukuda, Y., & Fukuda, T. (2012). Group dynamics: Collaborative agency in present communities of imagination. In S. Mercer, S. Ryan & M. Williams (Eds.), *Psychology for language learning: Insights from research, theory and practice* (pp. 220–283). Palgrave Macmillan.

Newberry, M. (2010). Identified phases in the building and maintaining of positive teacher–student relationships. *Teaching and Teacher Education, 26*(8), 1695–1703.

Niehaus, K., Rudasill, K. M., & Rakes, C. R. (2012). A longitudinal study of school connectedness and academic outcomes across sixth grade. *Journal of School Psychology 50*(4), 443–460.

Noels, K. A., Chaffee, K. E., Lou, N. M., & Dincer, A. (2016). Self-determination, engagement, and identity in learning German: Some directions in the psychology of language learning motivation. *Fremdsprachen Lehren und Lernen, 45*(2), 12–29.

Noels, K. A., Vargas Lascano, D. I., & Saumure, K. (2019). The development of self-determination across the language course: Trajectories of motivational change and the dynamic interplay of psychological needs, orientations, and engagement. Studies in Second Language Acquisition, *41*(4), 821–851.

O'Connor, K. E. (2008). "You choose to care": Teachers, emotions and professional identity. *Teaching and Teacher Education, 24*(1), 117–126.

O'Connor, K. E. (2010). Teacher-child relationships as dynamic systems. *Journal of School Psychology, 48*(3), 187–218.

O'Connor, K. E., Dearing, E., & Collins, B. A. (2011). Teacher-child relationship and behavior problem trajectories in elementary school. *American Educational Research Journal, 48*(1), 120–162.

O'Connor, E. E., Collins, B. A., & Supplee, L. (2012). Behavior problems in late childhood: The roles of early maternal attachment and teacher-child relationship trajectories. *Attachment & Human Development, 14*(3), 265–288.

OECD (2014). Indicator D1: How much time do students spend in the classroom? In *Education at a Glance 2014: OECD Indicators*. OECD Publishing. www.oecd.org/education/education-at-a-glance-2014-indicators-by-chapter.htm

Peng, J.-E. (2012). Towards an ecological understanding of willingness to communicate in EFL classrooms in China. *System, 40*(2), 203–213.

Pianta, R. C. (2001). *Student-teacher relationship scale: Professional manual*. Psychological Assessment Resources.

Reeve, J. (2006). Teachers as facilitators: What autonomy-supportive teachers do and why their students benefit. *The Elementary School Journal, 106*(3), 225–236.

Reeve, J. (2009). Why teachers adopt a controlling motivating style toward students and how they can become more autonomy supportive. *Educational Psychologist, 44*(3), 159–175.

Rimm-Kaufman, S. E., & Hamre, B. (2010). The role of psychological and developmental science in efforts to improve teacher quality. *Teacher College Record, 112*(12), 2988–3023.

Roffey, S. (2011). *Changing behaviour in schools: Promoting positive relationships and wellbeing*. Sage.

Ryan, R. M., & Deci, E. L. (2000). Self-determination theory and the facilitation of intrinsic motivation, social development, and well-being. *American Psychologist, 55*(1), 68–78.

Suldo, S. M., Shaffer, E. J., & Riley, K. N. (2008). A social-cognitive-behavioral model of academic predictors of adolescents' life satisfaction. *School Psychology Quarterly, 23*(1), 56–69.

Tian, L., Tian, Q., & Huebner, E. S. (2016). School-related social support and adolescents' school-related subjective well-being: The mediating role of basic psychological needs satisfaction at school. *Social Indicators Research, 128*, 105–129.

Veldman, I., van Tartwijk, J., Brekelmans, M., & Wubbels, T. (2013). Job satisfaction and teacher–student relationships across the teaching career: Four case studies. *Teaching and Teacher Education, 32*, 55–65.

Wentzel, K. R. (1997). Student motivation in middle school: The role of perceived pedagogical caring. *Journal of Educational Psychology, 89*(3), 411–419.

Wentzel, K. (2010). Students' relationships with teachers. In J. L. Meece & J. S. Eccles (Eds.), *Handbook of research on schools, schooling, and human development* (pp. 75–91). Routledge.

Wentzel, K. R. (2015). *Teacher-student relationships, motivation, and competence at school*. Routledge.

Wubbels, T., & Brekelmans, M. (2005). Two decades of research on teacher-student relationships in class. *International Journal of Educational Research, 43*, 6–24.

Wubbels, T., Brekelmans, M., den Brok, P., Wijsman, L., Mainhard, T., & van Tartwijk, J. (2014). Teacher-student relationships and classroom management. In E. T. Emmer, E. Sabornie, C. Evertson, & C. Weinstein (Eds.), *Handbook of classroom management: Research, practice, and contemporary issues* (pp. 363–386). Routledge.

Yoon, J. S. (2002). Teacher characteristics as predictors of teacher-student relationships: Stress, negative affect, and self-efficacy. *Social Behavior & Personality: An International Journal, 30*(5), 485–493.

22
GROUP DYNAMICS

Tim Murphey, Yoshifumi Fukada, Tetsuya Fukuda, and Joseph Falout

Current pedagogies of second language acquisition (SLA) presuppose that working in groups enhances language learning. Groups provide a context for meaningful language exchange, assist individual-level learning through scaffolding, and motivate learning within and between groups. Although often described in the literature, rarely are assumptions about group-level language learning effects tested by methodical studies based upon investigation, observation, or intervention (Fukada, Falout, Fukuda, & Murphey, 2019). Group-level language learning variables from psychology were made widely accessible to SLA by Dörnyei and Murphey (2003), notably: group formation stages, inter-member relationships, group norms, group cohesion, spatial organization, leadership styles, member roles, and group conflict. Unfortunately, since its publication nearly two decades ago, few papers have appeared that take on these or other group dynamics variables as a primary focus for formal research (Fukada et al., 2019). This chapter will first look historically at group dynamics research, mainly from the field of psychology, before explaining how this knowledge has been applied in SLA thus far. Suggestions for more integration between the fields will conclude the chapter, along with implications for teaching practices and SLA research.

Group Dynamics in Psychology

Groups are "two or more individuals who are connected by and within social relationships" (Forsyth, 2019, p. 3) and have long been researched in psychology. Groups can be categorized at different levels. For example, sociologist Cooley (1909) called small, intimate associates (e.g., families, close friends, and cliques) *primary groups* and less intimate groups formed in public settings (e.g., colleagues at workplace, people in sports clubs, and congregations at churches) *secondary groups*. Most groups can also be categorized into either one of two types: "*emergent groups*, which come into existence spontaneously when individuals join together in the same physical location or gradually over time as individuals find themselves repeatedly interacting with the same subset of individuals" or "*planned groups*, which are deliberately formed by their members or an external authority for some purpose" (Forsyth, 2019, pp. 13–14).

Grouping together is an omnipresent social phenomenon that began to be academically studied by social psychologists in the 1940s, with the term *group dynamics*, coined by psychologist Kurt Lewin. Lewin defected to the US in 1933 and founded the Research Center for Group Dynamics at Massachusetts Institute of Technology in 1945. Group dynamics was formally defined in 1969 by social psychologists Cartwright and Zander as the "field of inquiry dedicated to advancing knowledge about the nature of groups, the laws of their development, and their interrelations with individuals, other groups, and larger institutions" (1969, p. 7).

Group Affiliation

Consciously or unconsciously, people choose to belong to groups for different reasons. Personal needs include: *need for affiliation* (Hill, 2009), *intimacy* (McAdams, 1995), *power or controlling others* (Fodor, 2009), and *social support* (Gleason & Iida, 2015). *Personal beliefs about groups* (Karau & Elsaid, 2009) and our *positive or negative past experiences in different types of groups* (e.g., Reining, Horowitz, & Whittenburg, 2011) can also determine the groups people join. One's gender also makes a difference in that women tend to be higher in relationality, and women's values, attitudes, and outlooks more often tend to promote the establishment as well as the maintenance of connecting with others (Gore & Cross, 2006).

Situational or environmental determinants also play a role in determining group affiliation. For instance, physical closeness promotes group-forming and similarities in values, beliefs, and interests (Newcomb, 1963). Additionally, bonding between people is strengthened when certain traits, skills, or abilities that one lacks are complemented by those in others (Miller, 2015). People tend to join and stay in groups that bring them maximum value or rewards in which the costs to them are minimal (Blau, 1964; Homans, 1961). Lastly, social psychologist Brewer (2012) posited the *optimal distinctiveness theory*, which states that people participating in groups are most satisfied when their seemingly opposing collectivist- and individualist-oriented traits can both be maintained at an optimal level. In other words, their needs to belong to groups and to act autonomously are both well-met.

Group Dynamic Stages

People do not always participate optimally in groups, however, especially considering that groups can evolve and dissolve in five stages: (a) forming, (b) storming, (c) norming, (d) performing, and (e) adjourning (Tuckman, 1965; Tuckman & Jensen, 1977). In many cases, groups as a whole and the individuals within them go back and forth through these stages irregularly throughout their existence (e.g., see the case introduced in McGrew, Bilotta, and Deeney, 1999).

Among these dynamic group processes, storming, a stage that many groups undergo, is characterized by experiences of conflict, doubt, hesitancy, and stress among group members. The three types of conflict, *task conflict, process conflict*, and *relationship conflict*, can be caused by the free riding of one or more members. Free riding, the act of getting credit for a group's achievement without engaging in its work, is a mean-spirited problem since it is contagious (Komorita & Parks, 1994), and "humans are equipped with the mental apparatus needed to detect free riders" (Forsyth, 2019, p. 419). Solutions to in-group conflicts lie in six possibilities: negotiation, understanding, cooperative tactics, forgiveness, composure, and third party's mediation (Forsyth, 2019).

After overcoming the storming and norming stages with the establishment of a *group structure* (e.g., roles and norms), groups can reach the performing stage and settle there until naturally adjourning. At the performing stage, groups are expected to have established *group cohesion*, which relates reciprocally with performance (Forsyth, 2019). Cohesion is a "lubricant" which "minimizes the friction due to the human 'grit' in the system" (Mullen & Copper, 1994, p. 213). As such, "group cohesion can lay claim to being group dynamics' most theoretically important concept" (Forsyth, 2019, p. 127).

Leadership, Followers, and Power in Groups

The psychology of group dynamics also provides insight on leadership. Since effective leadership potentially increases group productivity, leadership is treated as one of the key subjects in group dynamics studies in psychology. There are three types of leadership—autocratic (the leader acts as a dictator), democratic (the leader becomes more of a collaborator, and the members also assume some authority and responsibility in different aspects of group work), and laissez-faire (the leader allows members to act without much supervision). Autocratic and democratic leadership stimulate increased productivity, although it can decrease when the autocratic leader is not present. Meanwhile, democratic leadership can be more effective in strengthening group cohesion (Lewin, Lippitt, & White, 1939) and raising group members' satisfaction levels (Stogdill, 1974), although it may not have the same positive impact on their productivity (Miller & Monge, 1986). Furthermore, effective leadership differs depending on the situation of the group: Employees in small groups who were required to interact often with other workers and their supervisor and to be highly interdependent showed positive attitudes with democratic leadership, while employees in large work groups who had fewer opportunities of interacting with other workers and their supervisors tended to be highly independent and showed more positive attitudes toward authoritarian leadership (Vroom & Mann, 1960). Just as there are different types of leaders, there are also different types of followers (Kelley, 2008): (a) the sheep, who "are passive and look to the leader to do the thinking for them and to motivate them" (p. 7); (b) the yes-people, followers who "are positive, always on the leader's side, but still looking to the leader for the thinking, the direction, the vision" (p. 7); (c) the alienated who "think for themselves, but have a lot of negative energy" (p. 7); (d) the pragmatics who "sit on the fence and see which way the wind blows" and "once they see where things are headed, they'll get on board" (pp. 7–8) and; (e) the star followers who "think for themselves, are very active, and have very positive energy" (p. 8).

Other insights from psychology on interpersonal relations within groups concern power dynamics among members, such as from psychologists French and Raven (1959), who stated, "our theory of social influence and power is limited to influence on the person, P, produced by a social agent, O, where O can be either another person, a role, a norm, a group, or a part of a group" (p. 590). Thus, a person in a group, a portion of the group, and the group as a whole, as well as a role or a norm established within the group itself, can possess power. More specifically, French and Raven (1959) explained that power generated within groups can be categorized into six types: (a) *reward power* (the power to distribute impersonal rewards—material resources like promotions and wage raise—and personal rewards—positive interpersonal reinforcements like smiles and praise); (b) *coercive power* (the power to make punishments or threats); (c) *legitimate power* (the power to make the person follow orders); (d) *referent power* (the power to be identified, attracted, or respected); (e) *expert power* (the power based on superior skills or abilities); and (f) *information power* (the power based on the possession of valuable information).

Social Environments

In addition, the surrounding social and physical environment exerts power on groups. Lewin (1951) conceived the external social environment as a mechanism that is indispensable in explaining group dynamics. He put forward the following formula to explain that the observable behavior (B) is a function of the person (P) and the environment (E) (p. 97).

$B = f(P, E)$
B = Behavior, P = Person, E = Environment

The formula denotes that the mechanisms of group dynamics cannot be fully explained without taking into account the group's situated or surrounding environment (social, political, physical, health-related, etc.). The sub-field that studies the interaction of the two components, groups and the surrounding environment, is called *group ecology* (Forsyth, 2019, p. 481). Cabanac (2006), for example, analyzed students in classrooms and other groups, and discovered that visually attractive spaces positively affected their performance. Also, Augustin, Frankel, and Coleman (2009) found that physical features which stimulate or provoke positive emotions (e.g., music, furnishings, decorations, and lighting) promote positive group dynamics such as increased cohesion, improved communication, greater productivity, and reduced absenteeism.

In addition, other factors like temperature and surrounding noise are also found to affect group work (Forsyth, 2019). Furthermore, Sommer (1969) argued that seating arrangements also affect group dynamics since they determine the ways that the members interact (see Chapter 24). For example, *sociopetal spaces* arrange people facing toward each other, promoting eye contact, verbal communication, and intimacy, whereas *sociofugal spaces* arrange people facing away from each other, preventing such social cues from being noticed. A meta-analysis (Wannarka & Ruhl, 2008) of studies from educational psychology showed that row-and-column seating (a sociofugal arrangement) was the least effective for tasks requiring cooperative behaviors, but useful for tasks requiring independent concentration, and effective for disruptive classes requiring classroom management. However, the meta-analysis noted that seating patterns and group dynamics cannot be generalized for all kinds of task goals and purposes and all types of students. For example, one study (Gifford & Gallagher, 1985) found that high-defensive students participated more in peer group conversations in a sociofugal seating arrangement, whereas low-defensive students participated more in a sociopetal seating arrangement.

Identifying and Belonging to Groups

Interpersonal interactions among members within a group affect their perceptions of the group itself and their roles within it, which in turn affects whole-group dynamic processes. For example, individuals can perceive *social identity* (Forsyth, 2019) (see Chapter 7) in relation to other members and the culture of the group. Group culture is one that "once a group has learned to hold common assumptions, the resulting automatic patterns of perceiving, thinking, feeling, and behaving provide meaning, stability, and comfort" (Schein, 1990, p. 111). Through nurturing social identities as well as group culture, the members can become one united entity. Members' sense of a group as a group is called *entitativity*, and Campbell (1958), who coined the term, defined it as "The degree of having the nature of an entity, of having real existence" (p. 17) (see Crawford & Salaman, 2012 for more information). A simpler term would be *groupiness* (Forsyth, 2019, p. 16).

People can also nurture their self-esteem by belonging to groups on the collective level. The self-esteem that is based on one's relationships with other group members or by having membership in the group is known as *collective self-esteem*, which correlates positively with one's personal sense of self-esteem (Crocker & Luhtanen, 1990). Collective school efficacy (Bandura, 1997) is associated with belonging, bonding, and being (identifying) with groups larger than the classroom.

A sense of belonging denotes a human need, physiologically, in that exclusion from others causes emotional pain felt equivalently to physical pain caused by injury (MacDonald & Leary, 2005). Being isolated for a long time can create psychological disorders (de Sousa, Spray, Sellwood, & Bentall, 2015). In Maslow's (1970) hierarchy of human needs, there are five levels of human needs: physiological needs, safety needs, belonging and love needs, esteem, and self-actualization. In other words, belonging to groups was conceptualized as a prerequisite to realizing one's potential. It was Baumeister and Leary's (1995) belongingness hypothesis that first established the concept of belonging with a large amount of scientific evidence. Supported by many studies in psychology and other areas, Baumeister and Leary concluded that human beings are fundamentally motivated to belong and that people seek frequent, positive interactions in the context of long-term, caring relationships.

In educational psychology, school belonging has been discussed extensively in academic journals since the 1980s. At the time of this writing, the literature on school belonging has been summarized in three papers in journals (Allen, Kern, Vella-Brodick, Hattie, & Waters, 2016; Korpershoek, Canrinus, Fokkens-Bruinsma, & de Boer, 2019; Slaten, Ferguson, Allen, Brodick, & Waters, 2016), one report issued by an American governmental agency (Centers for Disease Control and Prevention, 2009), and one book dedicated to this topic (Allen & Kern, 2017). These papers differ a little in their conceptualization of school belonging and their approach to the issues concerning school belonging, but the importance of human relationships is commonly stressed. For example, the Centers for Disease Control and Prevention (2009) argue that students can feel connections when they are supported by adults, belong to a positive peer group, feel that school is important, and have a good physical environment and psychological climate. School belonging is also associated with academic motivation. According to the meta-analysis conducted by Korpershoek et al. (2019), school belonging and academic motivation were correlated at .30. From these studies, it can be said that school belonging generally works positively in learning.

Similarly, psychologists discovered the positive impact of groups on people's working as well as learning. In a century-old seminal study, Triplett (1898) investigated how people's work performance changes when they work individually or with others by analyzing bicycle races (in which research participants race individually, with other racers, or with a motor-driven cycle pacemaker) and a simple reel-turning task (in which participants work on the task alone or in pairs). Through a comparative analysis, he discovered that people working on tasks perform better when working together than alone. The presence of others to elicit better performance than that done alone is known as "*dynamogenic factors*" (Triplett, 1898, p. 516). Forsyth (2019) called this phenomenon *social facilitation*. In contrast, social facilitation potentiates *social loafing*, which is defined as, "the reduction of individual efforts due to the social presence of others" (Williams, Harkins, & Latané, 1981, p. 303) Five practical antidotes for social loafing are offered (Forsyth, 2019): (a) increase group members' identifiability by evaluating each member, (b) minimize free riding, (c) set clear goals for the group task, (d) increase involvement in group work, and (e) increase identification with the group.

Research Methodologies

Carl Rogers commented about graduate psychology students, but this could easily apply to students learning languages and their desire to help others learn or not:

> Certainly, in a number of departments the relationships between students and faculty is remote and impersonal... In some departments where there is heavy stress on evaluation, student A will not give help to student B because any improvement in B's showing will automatically put A lower "on the curve." This seems to be a vicious sort of attitude for a professional person who will later be expected to be a part of a scientific or professional team.
>
> *Rogers, 1969, p. 183*

Indeed, when evaluation positions students against each other, it can negatively affect all students. Rather, encouraging individuals to help each other inspires them to develop themselves, their fields of research, and their humanity.

Various research methods have been applied to research group dynamics in the field of psychology. Groups have been studied from different perspectives, including criteria such as age, gender, ethnicity, economics, motivation, behavior, systems, cognition, ecology, and biology (Forsyth, 2019). Group dynamics-related data have been derived both qualitatively and quantitatively, with three basic research methods frequently adopted: case studies, correlational studies, and experimental studies. These selected aspects of group dynamics were developed within the field of psychology but could relevantly be applied in SLA.

Group Dynamics in SLA

The study of group dynamics is important for both the administrators of language programs and language teachers because although the content of a language learning program is often decided by administrators, it is in the dynamic interaction of teachers and students in classrooms where content is presented and teaching is implemented that success is decided. The process of language learning can only fully be understood when it is explored through the meanings that emerge from learner interactions. Concepts from group dynamics that appear in SLA studies include *group norms, group cohesiveness*, and other group-dynamics-related concepts such as *group framing of motivation, near peer role models (NPRMs), nonverbal behaviors, circular seating, critical participatory looping (CPL), ideal classmates priming (ICP), school belonging,* and *communities of practice (CoPs)*.

Group Norms, Cohesion, and Motivation

Chang (2010) examined group norms and group cohesiveness among 152 university English students in Taiwan through a survey. The results showed that both group norms and group cohesiveness were significantly related with autonomous behaviors, such as learners' identifying their own strengths and setting their own goals, and with self-efficacy, such as feeling capable with their English abilities. The results indicated that group norms and group cohesiveness enhance positive group dynamics and are associated with autonomous behaviors and self-efficacy, which in turn influence learners' motivation to learn a language.

Group framing of motivation is defined as the "bonding, socializing, and identifying with each other's stories, present conditions, and futures [that has] a unifying influence upon [students'] individual identities and motivation" (Fukuda, Fukada, Falout, & Murphey, 2012, p. 382). This conceptualizes how language learners influence and bond with each other in a group by sharing their past histories, present feelings, and future aspirations regarding language learning. When learners share their lives' stories (narrative-bonding) and open up their lives to each other, it is also necessary to describe individual learner's motivations by referring to the potential influences from the group. To investigate this phenomenon, Fukada, Murphey, Falout, and Fukuda (2017) used survey data from 1351 students in four universities in Japan for a three-year panel study. After only one semester, quantitative data indicated that students overall had stronger measurements of and increased connections among their past, present, and future L2 motivations. Meanwhile, qualitative data demonstrated that students attributed these individual-level motivational increases mainly to collaborative engagement in learning and a sense of belonging to the classroom community. These results suggest that language learners in groups can experience positive motivational transformations together through a collective psychological shift, pointing toward feelings of collective efficacy (Bandura, 1997).

The Near-Peers, Non-Verbals, and Critical-Loopers

Social learning theory in psychology stresses that learning occurs through observation and imitation of the actions of models seen by learners in their environments, such as parents and peers (Bandura, 1986). Based on this theory, the concept of near-peer role models (NPRMs) came about (Murphey, 1998). NPRMs are defined as "peers who are close to one's social, professional, and/or age level, and whom one may respect and admire" (Murphey & Arao, 2001). The concept of NPRMs is especially useful for pedagogy. Students within a classroom group could perceive some of their classmates as their NPRMs; then their NPRMs could have a positive impact on their learning styles, strategies, performance, engagement, and participation, as well as on their agency, motivation, and eventually on their learning achievement. Dörnyei and Murphey (2003) described three ways of promoting students' becoming each other's NPRMs within the classroom, although certainly many more exist. First, in newslettering, students can be inspired by reading their anonymous classmates' comments or voices in newsletters, such as how they were able to change their attitude or performance in the classroom in more positive ways. Second, in topical videos, students can change their perceptions or beliefs on English learning by watching student peers' interviews in which the student interviewees share some significant messages such as "unnecessity of worrying too much about making mistakes in English," "merits of setting goals in learning English," "pleasure of speaking English," and "possibility of Japanese becoming good English speakers" (Ogawa & Murphey, 2012, pp. 121–128). Third, in language learning histories, students write their own English learning histories, and share them with each other. By reading other students' English learning histories, they can be aware of how their student peers went through the same hardships with similar desires and needs. Knowing how their peers overcame hardships, they can be aware of the possible choices they can make. Students' becoming each other's NPRMs can promote positive group dynamics within the classroom. See Muir (2018) for a motivational-based overview of NPRMs.

Group's nonverbal behavior can become an extremely important addition to comfortable group dynamics (Gregersen & MacIntyre, 2017). Letting students know that they are continually communicating nonverbally and that they always have an impact, positive or negative, on those around them can help them to become more consciously and unconsciously eager contributors to positive group dynamics. Simply smiling, nodding, and showing others that the learner is willing to listen encourages people around the learner to talk, both in and out of class, and thus naturally learners are more likely to become each other's NPRMs. Such prosocial learning behaviors can be curbed or remain latent, however, if students are placed in row-and-column seating, due to restrictions upon exchanges of nonverbal communication inherent within sociofugal spaces. In contrast, circular seating arrangements are ideal for language classrooms because:

> Proximity, face-to-face orientation, and eye contact afforded by the circle creates an all-includable social action zone for the whole class. Time spent in the action zone fosters empathy, respect, and trust among potentially all class members. In this environment, students can feel a sense of belonging, which provides a safe base to expand their imaginations about what can be possibly said and done in the world, while finding their own voices to express themselves and their own values to take action. These conditions allow for acceptance of others and community-based affirmations of each member to flourish, verbally and nonverbally, which provides growth in individual self-direction and well-being.
>
> *Falout, 2014, p. 295*

The concept of critical participatory looping (CPL) (Murphey & Falout, 2010) refers to an action-research-based pedagogy by which a teacher first collects opinions, ideas, or insights from students individually, gathering either quantitative or qualitative data, or both. Next, the teacher collates the student responses as they are or as analyzed and represented in tables, making sure distinguishing personal information is deleted. Then the teacher returns or "loops back" these data to a whole-class group. Students reflect upon their own generated data individually or in small groups (and perhaps later as a whole-class group). Then students are invited to respond to the teacher, allowing for their critical analyses and their own voices to be heard by the teacher first, and if published, by a wider society later (i.e., looping forward). The looping cycle may continue and studies using it (such as ideal classmates studies) have shown CPL positively influences whole-class group learning, awareness-raising, and growing together.

Ideal Classmates

The concept of ideal classmates came as a response to the concept of an ideal L2 self in SLA (Dörnyei, 2009), which itself was inspired by possible selves theory in psychology (Markus & Nurius, 1986). The use in SLA assumes that each language learner potentially generates ideal future self-images related to their TL, and that the clarity and strength of the images positively influence language learner motivation (Dörnyei, 2009) (see Chapter 10). However, Japanese EFL education is an environment in which English is rarely used by most students (King, 2013). Thus, many students are inhibited in imagining their future selves, particularly, their ideal L2 selves. Therefore, Murphey, Falout, Fukuda, and Fukada (2014) began to investigate the influences of ideal classmates priming (ICP) on learner motivation. For ICP, the procedure combines generating and sharing ideal classmates images among class-groups—using CPL (Murphey & Falout, 2010)—with a Present Community of Imagination (PCOIz)-based motivational model and instruments to measure past selves, present investments both in and out of class (separately), and future selves (expected or possible selves, as opposed to ideal selves) (see Murphey, Falout, Fukada, & Fukuda, 2012 for details of the PCOIz-based motivational model and instruments).

The ICP procedure begins with each student receiving the prompt, "Please describe a group of classmates that you could learn English well with. What would you all do to help each other learn better and more enjoyably?" The EFL students were also encouraged to discuss and share their ideal L2 classmate images in different class activities in the medium of their TL, English, or their native language, Japanese. A coding of the open-ended answers to the prompt categorized these ideal classmates images into 16 descriptors of prosocial learning support, including those that were later rated by the students themselves as the top four: explicitly teaching language features to each other; talking actively with many conversation partners; being patient, accepting, and encouraging with yourself and others as you interact; and showing passion and enthusiasm for learning. Based on the 16 descriptors, another survey was administered, and the analysis showed that the more the students thought their classmates acted like their ideal L2 classmates, the more they themselves acted like ideal L2 classmates. This phenomenon is called *reciprocal idealizing* (for details, see Murphey et al., 2014).

School Belonging

As previously reviewed, belonging has been extensively discussed in psychology and educational psychology, but not much has been examined in SLA. Recently, however, the relationship between school belonging and L2 motivation was investigated by Fukuda (2020), who employed a mixed methods design to examine how school belonging and L2 motivation interact during the first year for 540 university students in Japan. In the quantitative analysis, Rasch analysis and growth curve modeling revealed that school belonging could be a reliable psychological construct among L2 learners, that school belonging and L2 motivation are related in their initial levels and their development, and that the changes in the interactions between belonging and motivation over time are predicted by which school students attend. The qualitative data analysis from written responses and interviews supported the findings in the quantitative analyses. This mixed methods study implies the potential of researching group dynamics with school as a dependent variable in the context of language learning.

Communities of Practice

Another version of group dynamics that has become very popular in the last 20 years is Wenger's concept of communities of practice (CoPs; Wenger, 1998). Daniel Hooper (2020, p. 108) concisely summarized the field in applying the concept to groups of students in a self-access learning center (SALC):

> CoPs are "groups of people who share a concern of passion for something they do and learn how to do it better as they interact regularly" (Wenger-Trayner & Wenger-Trayner 2015:1). Lave and Wenger's (1991) ubiquitous theoretical framework has been applied over the last 28 years to a plethora of varied settings in sociology, education and business (Wenger-Trayner & Wenger-Trayner 2015), where it has been used to explore conceptions of identity, learning and how we interact with the world at large. The CoP model, it could be argued, is well suited to the field of language learning due to its relatedness with well-established Vygotskian and Deweyian theories of learning (Wenger, 1998). Furthermore, a number of influential studies in the areas of academic socialization in English as a second

language (ESL) contexts (Morita, 2004), non-participation in language classrooms (Norton, 2001) and learner identity (Toohey, 1998) were conducted with the CoP literature as a key theoretical underpinning.

Due to its focus on issues of identity, accessibility, interdependence, and self-sustainability among members of a learning community (Wenger, 1998; Wenger et al. 2002), it was not surprising to us that studies on learning within self-access centers had often turned to the CoP model as a viable theoretical framework (Gillies, 2010; Noguchi, 2015).

Hooper 2020, p. 108

One major characteristic of CoPs is the possibility for varying levels of member participation and the idea of *legitimate peripheral participation*: "Peripheral participation is about being located in the social world. Changing locations and perspectives are part of actors' learning trajectories, developing identities, and forms of membership" (Lave & Wenger, 1991:36).

Envisioning groups of students in schools as belonging to communities of practice (CoPs) allows teachers to understand better how each student may participate to different degrees because of the individual affordances that students perceive themselves possessing at different times. Letting them all know that they all have legitimate peripheral participation opens the door to more varied responses of engagement and learning.

Wenger et al. (2002) elaborated on their concept, proposing three levels of participation: the core group, the active group, and the peripheral group, with participants shifting periodically from one to the other as they naturally engage and disengage throughout classes and their lives. Hooper (2020) provides multiple examples of students who are brought into the SALC communities at first through legitimate peripheral participation though soon after find themselves as "exemplars" to be followed by other students and acted as NPRMs.

Research Methodologies

Other studies on group dynamics in SLA have been conducted either quantitatively or qualitatively or both. A quantitative study in SLA from Matsubara (2007) hypothesized group dynamics as comprising four sub-concepts: attitude towards group work, attitude towards the structure of the group, preference for a student-centered approach, and group cohesion. The statistical analyses found that her 18-item group dynamics questionnaire validated the four sub-concepts as hypothesized and that preference for a student-centered approach was significantly associated with students' willingness to communicate.

Using journals and interviews, Vosburg (2017) collected qualitative data on how learners perceived groups and discovered three main themes. First, the native speakers recruited for the group, called language guides, had a positive influence on L2 motivation. Second, lack of common interests in the group negatively influenced L2 motivation. Third, different levels of motivation among learners also had a negative impact on motivation. In another qualitative study Gałajda (2012), through keeping a journal on what went on in her classes while implementing activities to enhance group dynamics, discovered that interactions among learners can be enhanced by the teacher's reflected actions impacted by journaling.

Mixed methods designs combining qualitative and quantitative approaches have been used to investigate groups of language learners as well. Research from Kozaki and Ross (2011) and Sasaki, Kozaki, and Ross (2017) found that L2 classes can have group norms that influence how much students aspire to in their future careers. Their research implies that groups of students larger than a class, such as their entire school, might explain other individual differences, such as L2 motivation.

To sum up, although the history of group dynamics in SLA is shorter than in psychology, group dynamics seems to have been more reconceptualized in the context of language learning by theorists. Many empirical studies have been conducted using diverse methodologies.

Integrating Psychology and SLA Perspectives

Some group dynamics-related concepts or theories that were originally developed within the field of psychology have been readily adopted into the field of SLA (e.g., stages of group formation, group cohesion, group structure, group norms or roles, etc.). However, the opposite seems not to have happened much yet. Although there is a somewhat limited body of research, group dynamics research conducted in SLA could provide the field of psychology, and especially general education, insights into several possible applications of pedagogical inquiry. For example, the concepts of near-peer role models (NPRMs; Murphey & Arao, 2001), nonverbal behavior (Gregersen & MacIntyre, 2017), critical participatory looping (CPL; Murphey & Falout, 2010), and ideal classmates priming (ICP) (Murphey et al., 2014) could be adapted from SLA to enhance general education and mainstream psychological research regarding group dynamics and society. At the same time, teachers and researchers in SLA would be able to understand group-based learning processes better by adopting more group dynamic concepts developed in psychology as well as in SLA both in and out of their language classes.

Implications for Practice

Of the three types of leadership in SLA mentioned earlier—autocratic, democratic, and laissez-faire—it is usually assumed that the leader in the language classroom is the instructor who manages the classroom (Dörnyei & Murphey, 2003; Williams, Mercer, & Ryan, 2015). However, democratic leadership implies sharing the classroom decisions with the students, which is unfortunately seldom talked about.

In the field of psychology, democratic leadership (Lewin et al., 1939) was introduced more than 80 years ago. This type of leadership has also been addressed in SLA. Naturally emerging leaders or officially assigned leaders are discussed in Dörnyei and Murphey (2003), and there have been waves of student-centered teaching practices that contend that teachers can be led by and collaborate with students, inspired partially by Rogers's (1969) client-centered therapy. If democratic leadership is truly applied, the whole class (i.e., teacher and students both) can take on leadership roles. However, in reality, encouraging each individual student to lead or to be agentive in managing the class or creating better learning environments is not an easy task. Not only the instructor but learners taking the course need practical know-how for developing a positive learning atmosphere inside the classroom and for taking leadership and control over their own learning. The act of sharing classroom decisions and trajectories opens up dialogical possibilities and the assuming of more control by students, which Freire (1970) proposed long ago: "Banking education resists dialogue; problem-posing education regards dialogue as indispensable to the act of cognition which unveils reality" (p. 71).

The authors of this chapter suggest students in a classroom share their ideal L2 classmates images as a way of promoting shared democratic leadership, agency, a positive learning atmosphere, class engagement, language-mediated social interactions, individual L2-learning motivation, and an ideal L2 group (Fukuda, Fukada, Falout, & Murphey, 2021). The authors' research on ideal classmates shows that the more each student feels that his or her classmates act like ideal L2 classmates, the more the individual student acts like an ideal classmate (Murphey et al., 2014). Although it may be challenging for a teacher alone to create positive group dynamics, when a class comes together to express and appraise each other's ideals for prosocial language learning engagement, students start taking charge together of their own learning, feel a sense of belonging among themselves, and commit to doing their best to help their classmates learn.

Implications for Research

When researchers in the fields of psychology as well as sociology started researching groups, they faced one big question—that is, whether they should conduct their research focusing on the individuals within the group or the group as a whole. However, according to Forsyth (2019), "the debate between individual-level and group-level approaches waned, in time, as theorists developed stronger models for understanding group-level process" (p. 35). One of the models was Lewin's field theory, based on his formula, $B = f(P, E)$, which was introduced earlier in this chapter. Each members' behavior influences their degree of belongingness and the group's situated environment. Another model was the multilevel perspective suggested by Hackman and his colleagues (Allmendinger, Hackman, & Lehman, 1996; Hackman, 2003), which indicates the significance of analyzing groups at different levels; Micro-, Meso-, and Macro-levels. These two models showed that we need to analyze groups holistically at different levels, focusing on the related factors or aspects: the individual members, the group itself, and the group's situated environment or the group's relations with other groups, institutions, and communities.

SLA researchers seem to be moving in the same direction as psychologists by their adoption of holistic approaches and perspectives in their research, particularly the ecological approach (van Lier, 2007) and the complex dynamic system approach (Larsen-Freeman, 2008) (see Chapter 4). Mercer (2015) proposed that social interaction of individuals and groups in language learning, including classroom group dynamics, be examined through the lens of social network theory in the context of a dynamic systems approach. One notable difference, however, is that Forsyth (2019) introduces only one statistical test, the correlational coefficient test, as a principle way of analyzing groups at multi or holistic levels. In the field of SLA, a handful of researchers have started analyzing language-learning groups with other statistical modeling such as structural equation modeling (SEM) and Rasch modeling, both of which enable researchers to see causal relationships among multiple related factors statistically (see Fukada et al., 2019, for further discussion). For both psychologists and applied linguists, achieving a holistic or multilevel analysis of groups is not a straightforward task. Therefore, researchers would do well to consider exploring novel and cutting-edge quantitative, qualitative, and mix-method approaches to investigating group dynamics mechanisms and phenomena.

Future Directions

Psychological processes of group dynamics have been described in some depth in social psychology, but language learning psychology has only limited research in such processes. Meanwhile, most research in SLA rests upon assumptions that L2 learners will be learning best from situated, lived, and imagined groups inside and outside the language classroom. With so much pedagogy based on socially-oriented, cooperative learning, SLA needs more research dedicated to studying how group-based psycho-social mechanisms can affect language learning. One path for future research is to take the previously explained group dynamics phenomena and theories from psychology and explore how they fit into SLA contexts. Such an approach could validate, invalidate, or even augment and contribute to understandings in group dynamics, too. Another path for SLA research could involve expanding unexplored or unexplained issues from the group dynamics field in psychology. For example, Forsyth (2019) mentions the biopsychosocial approach as promising, yet it remains uninvestigated. The biopsychosocial approach would envision an even wider range of factors upon group dynamics than previously considered, such as group-based physiological mechanisms. Interpersonal behaviors that have hard-to-perceive social cues or more subtle manifestations are equally worth considering, such as the role civility plays for groups in business (e.g., Porath, 2016) or selflessness, mindfulness, and compassion for teamwork in sports (e.g., Jackson & Delehanty, 1995), which can also be of great relevance in language learning classrooms. Gaining knowledge in areas such as these could help teachers create physically and mentally healthier social learning environments for developing the well-being of students, not to mention that of teachers (Mercer & Gregersen, 2020), who play a significant role in classroom group dynamics. With so much important work yet to do, the future of language learning group dynamics is indeed very promising.

Reflection Questions

- From your experiences, what do you believe makes students, teachers, and researchers join groups in language learning and stay in these groups?
- What are some of the group norms and cohesion characteristics that would be attractive to you in language education? Then imagine you are one of your students and answer as they would. Then compare the lists.
- Think of a group you worked with in the past that worked effectively, and another group that did not seem to work so effectively. Write a paragraph describing each group and compare them. How are these groups different and what can you learn from the comparison?

Recommended Readings

Forsyth, D. R. (2019). *Group dynamics* (7th ed.). Cengage Learning.
This book provides comprehensive theories, concepts, and research findings related to group dynamics as explicated within the field of psychology.

Porath, C. (2016). *Mastering civility: A manifesto for the workplace*. New Grand Central Publishing.
This book concentrates on how employees in business settings who act respectfully toward each other increase both productivity and values (revenues and relationships) within their institution. This is recommended for teachers who wish to create a cohesively exciting work environment in which to learn and grow, as well as respectful classroom environments.

Hari, J. (2018). *Lost connections: Uncovering the real causes of depression—and the unexpected solutions*. Bloomsbury Publishing.
This book explains the ways people become depressed by losing connections with other people, nature, meaningfulness, etc., and it provides valuable insights for reconnecting with them again.

References

Allen, K., & Kern, M. L. (2017). *School belonging in adolescents: Theory, research and practice*. Springer.
Allen, K., Kern, M. L., Vella-Brodrick, D., Hattie, J., & Waters, L. (2016). What schools need to know about fostering school belonging: A meta-analysis. *Educational Psychology Review, 30*(1), 1–34.
Allmendinger, J., Hackman, J. R., & Lehman, E. V. (1996). Life and work in symphony orchestras. *Musical Quarterly, 80*, 194–219.
Augustin, S., Frankel, N., & Coleman, C. (2009). *Place advantage: Applied psychology for interior architecture*. John Wiley & Sons.
Bandura, A. (1986). *Social foundations of thought and action: A social cognition theory*. Prentice Hall.
Bandura, A. (1997). *Self-efficacy: The exercise of control*. WH Freeman & Co.
Baumeister, R. F., & Leary, M. R. (1995). The need to belong: Desire for interpersonal attachments as a fundamental human motivation. *Psychological Bulletin, 117*(3), 497–528.
Blau, P. (1964). *Exchange and power in social life*. John Wiley & Sons.
Brewer, M. B. (2012). Optimal distinctiveness theory: Its history and development. In P. A. M. Van, A. Lange, W. Kruglansk, & E. T. Higgins (Eds.), *Handbook of theories of social psychology* (Vol. 2, pp. 81–98). Sage.
Cabanac, M. (2006). Pleasure and joy, and their role in human life. In D. Clements-Croome (Ed.), *Creating the productive workplace* (2nd ed., pp. 3–13). Taylor & Francis.
Campbell, D. T. (1958). Common fate, similarity, and other indices of the status of aggregates of persons as social entities. *Behavioral Science, 3*(1), 14–25.
Cartwright, D., & Zander, A. (1969). *Group dynamics* (3rd ed.). Harper Row.
Centers for Disease Control and Prevention. (2009). *School connectedness: Strategies for increasing protective factors among youth*. Department of Health and Human Services.
Chang, L.Y. (2010). Group processes and EFL learners' motivation: A study of group dynamics in EFL classrooms. *TESOL Quarterly, 44*(1), 129–154.
Cooley, C. H. (1909). *Social organization: A study of the larger mind*. Charles Scribner's Sons.

Crawford, M. T., & Salaman, L. (2012). Entitativity, identity and fulfilment of psychological needs. *Journal of Experimental Social Psychology, 48*, 726–730.
Crocker, J., & Luhtanen, R. (1990). Collective self-esteem and ingroup bias. *Journal of Personality and Social Psychology, 58*, 60–67.
de Sousa, P., Spray, A., Sellwood, W., & Bentall, R. P. (2015). "No man is an island." Testing the specific role of social isolation in formal thought disorder. *Psychiatry Research, 230*(2), 304–313.
Dörnyei, Z. (2009). The L2 Motivational Self System. In Z. Dörnyei & E. Ushioda (Eds.), *Motivation, language identity and the L2 self* (pp. 9–42). Multilingual Matters.
Dörnyei, Z., & Murphey, T. (2003). *Group dynamics in the language classroom*. Cambridge University Press.
Falout, J. (2014). Circular seating arrangements: Approaching the social crux in language classrooms. *Studies in Second Language Learning and Teaching, 4*(2), 275–300.
Fodor, E. M. (2009). Power motivation. In M. R. Leary, & R. H. Hoyle (Eds.), *Handbook of individual differences in social behavior* (pp. 426–440). Guilford Press.
Forsyth, D. R. (2019). *Group dynamics* (7th ed.). Cengage Learning.
Freire, P. (1970). *Pedagogy of the oppressed*. Continuum.
French, J. R. P., Jr., & Raven, B. (1959). The base of social power. In D. Cartwright (Ed.), *Studies in social power* (pp. 259–269). Institute for Social Research.
Fukada, Y., Falout, J., Fukada, T., & Murphey, T. (2019). Motivational group dynamics in SLA: The interpersonal interaction imperative. In M. Lamb, K. Csizér, A. Henry & S. Ryan (Eds.), *The Palgrave handbook of motivation for language learning* (pp. 307–325). Palgrave Macmillan.
Fukada, Y., Murphey, T., Falout, J., & Fukada, T. (2017). Essential motivational group dynamics: A 3-year panel study. In R. Breeze, & C. S. Guinda (Eds.), *Essential competencies for English-medium university teaching* (pp. 249–266). Springer.
Fukada, T. (2020). *School belonging and L2 motivation of first-year students at four Japanese universities* (Publication No. 28027020) [Doctoral dissertation, Temple University]. ProQuest Dissertations and Theses Global.
Fukada, T., Fukada, Y., Falout, J., & Murphey, T. (2012). Holistic timing and group framing of motivation. In A. Stewart & N. Sonda (Eds.), *JALT2011 Conference Proceedings* (pp. 380–391). JALT.
Fukada, T., Fukada, Y., Falout, J., & Murphey, T. (2021). How ideal classmates priming increases EFL classroom prosocial engagement. In P. Hiver, A. H. Al-Hoorie, & S. Mercer (Eds.), *Student engagement in the language classroom* (pp. 182–201). Multilingual Matters.
Gałajda, D. (2012). Variability of group processes. Facilitating group dynamics in a FL classroom. In E. Piechurska-Kuciel, & L. Piasecka (Eds.), *Variability and stability in foreign and second language learning contexts* (pp. 198–219). Cambridge Scholars Publishing.
Gifford, R., & Gallagher, M. B. (1985). Sociability: Personality, social context, and physical setting. *Journal of Personality and Social Psychology 48*(4), 1015–1023.
Gilles, H. (2010). Listening to the learner: A qualitative investigation of motivation for embracing our avoiding the use of self-access centers. *Studies in Self Access Learning Journal 1*(3), 189–211.
Gleason, M. E., & Iida, M. (2015). Social support. In M. Mikulincer, P. R. Shaver, J. A. Simpson & J. F. Dovidio (Eds.), *APA handbook of personality and social psychology: Interpersonal relations* (pp. 351–370). American Psychological Association.
Gore, J. S., & Cross, S. E. (2006). Pursuing goals for us: Relationally autonomous reasons in long-term goal pursuit. *Journal of Personality and Social Psychology, 90*(5), 848–861.
Gregersen, T., & MacIntyre, P. (2017). *Optimizing language learners' nonverbal behavior*. Multilingual Matters.
Hackman, J. R. (2003). Learning more by crossing levels: Evidence from airplanes, hospitals, and orchestras. *Journal of Organizational Behavior, 24*, 905–922.
Hari, J. (2018). *Lost connections: Uncovering the real causes of depression–and the unexpected solutions*. Bloomsbury.
Hill, C. A. (2009). Affiliation motivation. In M. R. Leary & R. H. Hoyle (Eds.), *Handbook of individual differences in social behavior* (pp. 410–425). Guilford Press.
Homans, G. C. (1961). *Social behavior: Its elementary forms*. Harcourt Brace.
Hooper, D. (2020). Understanding communities of practice in a social language learning space. In J. Mynard, M. Burke, D. Hooper, B. Kushida, P. Lyon, R. Sampson, & P. Taw (Eds.), *Dynamics of a social language learning community: Beliefs, membership, and identity* (pp. 108–124). Multilingual Matters.
Jackson, P., & Delehanty, H. (1995). *Sacred hoops: Spiritual lessons of a hardwood warrior*. Hyperion.
Karau, S. J., & Elsaid, A. M. M. (2009). Individual differences in beliefs about groups. *Group Dynamics: Theory, Research, and Practice, 13*(1), 1–13.
Kelley, R. E. (2008). Rethinking followership. In R. E. Riggio, I. Chaleff, & J. Lipman-Blumen (Eds.), *The art of followership: How great followers create great leaders and organizations* (pp. 5–16). Jossey-Bass.
King, J. (2013). Silence in the second language classrooms of Japanese universities. *Applied Linguistics, 34*(3), 325–343.
Komorita, S. S., & Parks, C. D. (1994). *Social dilemmas*. Brown & Benchmark.

Korpershoek, H., Canrinus, E. T., Fokkens-Bruinsma, M., & de Boer, H. (2019). The relationships between school belonging and students' motivational, social-emotional, behavioural, and academic outcomes in secondary education: A meta-analytic review. *Research Papers in Education, 34*, 1–40.
Kozaki, Y., & Ross, S. J. (2011). Contextual dynamics in foreign language learning motivation. *Language Learning, 61*(4), 1328–1354.
Larsen-Freeman, D. (2008). *Complex systems and applied linguistics*. Oxford University Press.
Lave, J., & Wenger, E. (1991). *Situated learning: Legitimate peripheral participation*. Cambridge University Press.
Lewin, K. (1951). *Field theory in social science: Selected theoretical papers*. Harper & Row.
Lewin, K., Lippitt, R., & White, R. K. (1939). Patterns of aggressive behavior in experimentally created "social climates." *The Journal of Social Psychology, 10*(2), 269–299.
MacDonald, G., & Leary, M. R. (2005). Why does social exclusion hurt? The relationship between social and physical pain. *Psychological Bulletin, 131*, 202–223.
Markus, H., & Nurius, P. (1986). Possible selves. *American Psychologist, 41*(9), 954–969.
Maslow, A. H. (1970). *Motivation and Personality* (2nd ed.). Harper & Row.
Matsubara, K. (2007). Classroom group dynamics and motivation in the EFL context. In K. Bradford-Watts (Ed.), *JALT2006 Conference Proceedings* (pp. 209–220). JALT.
McAdams, D. P. (1995). What do we know when we know a person? *Journal of Personality, 63*(3), 365–396.
McGrew, J. F., Bilotta, J. G., & Deeney, J. M. (1999). Software team formation and decay: Extending the standard model for small groups. *Small Group Research, 30*(2), 209–234.
Mercer, S. (2015). Social network analysis and complex dynamic systems. In Z. Dörnyei, P. D. MacIntyre, & A. Henry (Eds.), *Motivational dynamics in language learning* (pp. 73–82).
Mercer, S., & Gregersen, T. (2020). *Teacher wellbeing*. Oxford University Press.
Miller, K. I., & Monge, P. R. (1986). Participation, satisfaction, and productivity: A meta-analytic review. *Academy of Management Journal, 29*(4), 727–753.
Miller, R. S. (2015). *Intimate Relationships* (7th ed.). McGraw-Hill.
Morita, N. (2004). Negotiating participation and identity in second language academic communities. *TESOL Quarterly 38*(4), 573–603.
Muir, C. (2018). *Motivational aspects of using near peers as role models*. Part of the Cambridge Papers in ELT series. Cambridge University Press.
Mullen, B., & Copper, C. (1994). The relation between group cohesiveness and performance: An integration. *Psychological Bulletin, 115*(2), 210–227.
Murphey, T. (1998). Motivating students with near peer role models. In B. Visgatis (Ed.), *Proceedings of the JALT 1997 International Conference on Language Teaching and Learning*. (pp. 201–206). JALT.
Murphey, T., & Arao, H. (2001). Reported belief changes through near peer role modeling. *Tesl-Ej, 5*(3), 1–15.
Murphey, T., & Falout, J. (2010). Critical participatory looping: Dialogic member checking with whole classes. *TESOL Quarterly, 44*(4), 811–821.
Murphey, T., Falout, J., Fukada, Y., & Fukuda, T. (2012). Group dynamics: Collaborative agency in present communities of imagination. In S. Mercer, S. Ryan, & M. Williams (Eds.), *Psychology for language learning: Insights from research, theory and practice* (pp. 220–238). Palgrave Macmillan.
Murphey, T., Falout, J., Fukuda, T., & Fukada, Y. (2014). Socio-dynamic motivating through idealizing classmates. *System, 45*, 242–253.
Newcomb, T. M. (1963). Stabilities underlying changes in interpersonal attraction. *The Journal of Abnormal and Social Psychology, 66*(4), 376–386.
Noguchi, J. (2015). "I'm a SALCer": Influences of identity upon fear of making mistakes. *Studies in Self Access Learning Journal 6*(2), 163–175.
Norton, B. (2001). Non-participation, imagined communities and the language learning classroom. In M. P. Breen (Ed.), *Learner contributions to language learning: New directions in research* (pp. 151–171). Longman.
Ogawa, H., & Murphey, T. (2012). Using Video Recorded Interviews to Provide Near Peer Role Models for Language Learning. *JACET Journal 55*, 121–128.
Porath, C. (2016). *Mastering civility: A manifesto for the workplace*. Grand Central Publishing.
Reinig, B. A., Horowitz, I., & Whittenburg, G. E. (2011). A longitudinal analysis of satisfaction with group work. *Group Decision and Negotiation, 20*(2), 215–237.
Rogers, C. R. (1969). *Freedom to learn: A view of what education might become*. C. E. Merrill Publishing Co.
Sasaki, M., Kozaki, Y., & Ross, S. J. (2017). The impact of normative environments on learner motivation and L2 reading ability growth. *The Modern Language Journal, 101*(1), 163–178.
Schein, E. H. (1990). Organizational culture. *American Psychologist, 45*(2), 109–119.
Slaten, C., Ferguson, J., Allen, K. A., Brodrick, D. V., & Waters, L. (2016). School belonging: A review of the history, current trends, and future directions. *The Educational and Developmental Psychologist, 33*(1), 1–15.
Sommer, R. (1969). *Personal space*. Prentice Hall.
Stogdill, R. M. (1974). *Handbook of leadership: A survey of theory and research*. Free Press.

Toohey, K. (1998). Breaking them up, taking them away; ESL students in grade 1. *TESOL Quarterly, 32*(1), 61–84.

Triplett, N. (1898). The dynamogenic factors in pacemaking and competition. *The American Journal of Psychology, 9*(4), 507–533.

Tuckman, B. W. (1965). Developmental sequence in small groups. *Psychological Bulletin, 63*(6), 384–399.

Tuckman, B. W., & Jensen, M. A. C. (1977). Stages of small-group development revisited. *Group & Organization Studies, 2*(4), 419–427.

van Lier, L. (2007). *The ecology of semiotics of language learning: A sociocultural perspective*. Kluwer Academic Publishers.

Vosburg, D. (2017). The effects of group dynamics on language learning and use in an MMOG. *CALICO Journal, 34*(1), 58–74.

Vroom, V. H., & Mann, F. C. (1960). Leader authoritarianism and employee attitudes. *Personnel Psychology, 13*, 125–140.

Wannarka, R., & Ruhl, K. (2008). Seating arrangements that promote positive academic and behavioural outcomes: A review of empirical research. *Support for Learning, 23*(2), 89–93.

Wenger, E. (1998). *Communities of practice: Learning, meaning and identity*. Cambridge University Press.

Wenger, E., McDermott, R., & Snyder, W. M. (2002). *Cultivating communities of practice: A guide to managing knowledge*. Harvard Business School Press.

Wenger-Trayner, E., & Wenger-Trayner, B. (2015). *Communities of practice: A brief introduction*. wenger-trayner.com/introduction-to-communities-of-practice/

Williams, K., Harkins, S. G., & Latané, B. (1981). Identifiability as a deterrent to social loafing: Two cheering experiments. *Journal of Personality and Social Psychology, 40*(2), 303–311.

Williams, M., Mercer, S., & Ryan, S. (2015). *Exploring psychology in language learning and teaching*. Oxford University Press.

23
CULTURE AND INTERCULTURAL COMMUNICATION

Tony Johnstone Young, Sara Ganassin, and Alina Schartner

Culture is one of the most important but most contested concepts in the social sciences (see, for example, Byram, 1997, 2009; Ganassin, 2020; Holliday, 2013; Schartner & Young, 2020). Any consideration of the "social" aspects of the psychology of Second Language Acquisition (SLA), therefore, needs to think about how culture can be understood and how it can be conveyed in teaching and in research. Intercultural Communication is one way of framing the negotiation of meaning between people from different groups and backgrounds. It is a construct which has been highly influential, at least since the 1990s, in studying SLA as a social, interactional phenomenon (Young, Sachdev, & Seedhouse, 2009).

This chapter unpacks ideas of how culture is understood and how it is approached. It explores how culture can be acquired through language learning, and summarizes different perspectives on the complex interrelationships between language and culture. It then discusses how perspectives may be integrated into the pedagogical practice of language through notions of intercultural communication and competence.

Psychological Perspectives on Culture and Intercultural Communication

As scholars, we identify with an interest in applied linguistics and intercultural communication. We do not describe ourselves as psychologists, but we do draw on ideas from social psychology to inform our approach to research. Our relationship to psychology sits in an ecumenical position between broadly positivist orientations and more critical, interpretivist orientations. We draw both on recent social psychological perspectives and on critical cultural theoretical positions. From this position, we attempt to mitigate some of the weaknesses, as we see them, apparent in both orientations, while drawing on the explanatory potentials of both in order to understand SLA as intercultural communication.

Across the disciplinary field of psychology, and the social sciences more generally, ideas of what cultures are and how the notion of culture itself can be framed and approached sit at the fault-line between broadly positivist ontologies and those of a critical, interpretivist nature (Schartner & Young, 2020). Where a researcher stands in relation to these ontologies determines their whole approach to questions of how people think, for example, about teaching and learning languages.

Positivist approaches are derived from the natural sciences and an objectivist, natural science ontological orientation. These begin with assumptions that social categories like "gender," "ethnicity," "personality type," and, crucially, "culture(s)" can be isolated for research, and that they are sufficiently stable to be observed. Interpretivist approaches, in contrast, are rooted in constructivist ontologies.

These hold that such categories can only properly be considered as social constructions formed from the perceptions and actions of social actors (Bryman, 2016)—that they have no objective social reality. At either end of this continuum sit, firstly, approaches to intercultural communication in cross-cultural psychology and the social psychology of language and communication at the positivist end (see, for example, Giles, Bonilla, & Speer, 2012). At the interpretivist end of the spectrum sit epistemologies rooted in postcolonial and critical cultural theory (see, for example, Hall, 2016; Holliday, 1999, 2016). The latter have been particularly influential in many recent approaches to SLA and applied linguistic research into teaching and learning languages.

A criticism of an objectivist ontological stance is that individual and cultural identities can tend to be reified and so made into observable entities separate from and independent of social actors (Lukács, 2000). They can also be essentialized—that is, approached as located "inside" individuals, a product of cognition rooted in the processes of socialization and enculturation (Sercombe & Young, 2011). From such a perspective, cultural identity is framed as a characteristic of a person that tends to be absolute, relatively static, and to some extent objectively knowable (Benwell & Stokoe, 2006). This can foster a tendency to directly equate nationality with cultural predispositions (e.g., Holliday, 1999), resulting in research rooted in assumptions that suggest, or even directly imply, that "(a) Culture = (a) Nation = (an) Independent Variable" (Young, 2016). Figures such as Geert Hofstede, highly influential in social psychological intercultural studies, operate from this stance. From this position, communication with people from different cultural groups is influenced by core cultural values, indexical for different nationalities or for people from different multinational regions. Such a stance has done much to inform theory, research, and practice in international marketing, management, and human resources, but much less so in informing approaches to SLA.

The critical, interpretivist stance in intercultural studies tends to position itself as directly oppositional to the positivist stance identified above, characterizing it as a dominant epistemology that needs to be challenged and, ideally, refuted for its tendency to cultural over-simplification, reductionism, and stereotyping (Young, Handford, & Schartner, 2017). It approaches cultural identities as emergent, dynamic, dialogically constructed, and multiple. Such a position has been particularly influential in applied linguistics over recent years, particularly where this disciplinary area focuses on real-time, most usually spoken, social interaction. It informs much of the work of key lingua-cultural scholars such as Claire Kramsch (1998), Adrian Holliday (1999, 2013), and Ingrid Piller (2011).

An interpretivist approach may well account for the observed realities of real-life, real-time interaction with more accuracy than its positivist equivalent. It may even be more ethically focused in its explicit resistance to and rejection of outgroup stereotyping and "othering." However, the practical, applied benefits of such an approach are harder to discern. This may explain the ongoing influence outside the interpretivist research community of more objectivist perspectives on the intercultural in organizational policy and practice in international management and business studies (Young et al., 2017; Zhu, Handford, & Young, 2017).

Overall, intercultural scholars propose different theorizations of the concept of culture. Most acknowledge that it should be dealt with criticality and seen as "something one does" during people's processes of meaning-making rather than "something you belong to or live with" (Kramsch & Zhu, 2016, p. 41). Pinning down the concept of "X culture" presents risks of essentialization, such as equating a culture with a particular nation or ethnic group in a static, unproblematized manner (see also Ganassin, 2020). Alternatively, culture can be understood as the expression of meanings, values, and behaviors that are never stable and are always changing and evolving, conforming more closely to the critical, interpretivist position we outline above (see Pavlenko & Blackledge, 2004).

SLA Perspectives on Culture and Intercultural Communication

We approach SLA from a primarily social perspective rather than as an individual cognitive process. Consequently, ideas of culture and intercultural communication are central to our way of framing processes of SLA by individuals. As we have seen, most theoreticians of culture and social identity would affirm that culture is a complex and contested entity. To some extent, it comprises sets of symbolic systems, including acquired knowledge, norms, values, beliefs, language, art, and customs, as well as habits and skills learned by members of a given society or group (Hamers & Blanc, 2000; Shiraev & Levy, 2004). In attempting to frame a consensual position relevant to language learning and teaching, Corbett (2012) characterizes culture in terms of everyday practices, understood with reference to normative attitudes and beliefs negotiated by groups whose interactions are conditioned by particular forms of social organization.

It is possible to isolate two general ways of understanding what culture is across the arts and social sciences, whether it is seen as oral or written, highbrow or popular, specific and relating to special events or relating to everyday life and practices (Kramsch, 1995; Kramsch & Sullivan, 1996). The first way of approaching culture is largely derived from the study of the arts and humanities. This has tended to focus on the way a social group represents itself and others through its material productions. These include art, music and literature, social institutions or practices of everyday life, and the mechanisms of their preservation and reproduction through history. This view can be summarized as culture as the human-made part of our environment (Kramsch & Sullivan, 1996). A second way of understanding culture is largely derived from the contributions of social scientists, especially social psychologists, anthropologists, ethnographers, and sociologists. Here culture refers to the attitudes and beliefs and the ways of thinking, behaving, and remembering shared by members of a community (Nostrand, 1989; Steinmetz, Bush, & Joseph-Goldfarb, 1994). This definition reflects the perception that certain beliefs, values, and perceptions commonly held by members of a community are often submerged below the surface of consciousness. Examples of this include Hall and Hall's (1990) metaphor of the cultural iceberg where the "visible" aspects of a culture are a relatively small part of its whole. Also, within this broad approach is the idea that "culture" refers to widely-shared ideals, values, and formations and uses of categories that tend to become unconsciously accepted as normal and "right or correct" (Brislin, 1990, p. 11) by those who identify themselves as members of a cultural group. Such beliefs, values, and perceptions may include notions of beauty or modesty, incentives to work or to conform to group norms, and theories of mental and physical health (Fennes & Hapgood, 1997; Hall & Hall, 1990). Crucially for people interested in SLA, they also include what and how people should teach and learn languages (Hinkel, 1999; Hofstede, 1986; Young & Sachdev, 2011).

According to Taft (1977, p. 130), in order to become a member of a particular society a child must be "enculturated to the particular ways and general style of life that constitutes its culture, and as a consequence become culturally competent." In other words, a child must acquire the means by which their behavior becomes meaningful to other members of his or her primary society, and by which he or she is able to ascribe meaning to other members' behavior. In short, "the child must learn how 'to mean' and to communicate" (Hamers & Blanc, 2000, p. 204). Language acquisition is central to this primary enculturation. It is also broadly accepted that the level of consciousness of this acquired primary cultural identity varies. The "submerging" of values and perceptions below the level of consciousness means that the very existence of a culturally informed milieu may not be noticed by those who are part of it, in the same way that a fish does not perceive the water it swims in (Kramsch, 1993). However, if values and assumptions are brought to greater consciousness and challenged in some way—through contact with a different set of cultural values and assumptions, for example—then it is possible that a cultural identity may be felt more keenly and asserted more strongly by an individual or group (Sachdev & Bourhis, 1990, 2001).

Such challenges to culturally derived values and assumptions may happen when a person is learning another language. There is a considerable body of research going back to the 1970s relating acculturation to *second* language settings. Here, a language is learned in a context where learners are assumed to be in direct and regular contact with the other community or its products (such as in Canada, e.g., Gardner, 1988; Gardner & Lambert, 1972; Gardner & MacIntyre, 1991, 1993; Gardner & Tremblay, 1994). Until recently, comparatively little research had addressed issues of acculturation in *foreign* language settings, where contact with the speakers of the language being learned is infrequent, virtual, or indirect (Dörnyei, 2001), although interest in this area is on the increase (Young et al., 2009; see also Schartner & Young 2020).

Language and Culture

A language is part of a culture and a culture is part of a language; the two are intricately interwoven such that one cannot separate the two without losing the significance of either.

Brown, 1987, p. 123

It is generally accepted that the interrelationship between language and culture is strong but complex (Lave & Wenger, 1991; Whorf, 1956). So, for example, along with values, beliefs, and behavioral norms, language is a component of culture. Unlike other components of culture, however, language interacts with it in different ways, because language is both a transmitter of culture and an important tool for the internalization of the cultural by the individual. Language is also a shaper of culture, an agentive entity, whereby cultural representations are shaped by the language used to express them (Fennes & Hapgood, 1997; Hinkel, 1999; Oxford & Anderson, 1995).

The link between language and culture is generally accepted as inextricable, with language being central to cultural identity. So, although approaches to questions of what constitutes competent communication between cultures may vary, *linguistic* competence is seen by most as a key element (e.g., Alred & Byram, 2002; Byram, 1997; Martin, 1993). However, in the long history of empirical research into inter- and cross-cultural communication (for reviews see Hall, 2002; Martin, Nakayama, & Carbaugh, 2012), linguistic competence has tended to be downplayed until relatively recently, usually viewed as a possible supporting factor in acquiring intercultural competence (Byram, 1997; Sercu, 2002). In a similar way, research into language learning and teaching has tended to downplay the importance of culture. Fantini (1995) describes the situation like this:

> With rare exceptions… interculturalists often overlook (or leave to language teachers) the task of developing language competence, just as language teachers overlook (or leave to interculturalists) the task of developing intercultural abilities, despite wide acknowledgement that language and culture are dimensions of each other, interrelated and inseparable.
>
> pp. 144–145

Until relatively recently, little empirical research had addressed the key issue of the extent to which culture is actually taught in foreign language courses. Where culture and cultural difference was touched upon at all, attention tended to focus on a visible, human-made view of culture and cultural difference, despite criticisms of this approach in terms of its superficiality (e.g., Atkinson, 1999). This approach has often taken the form of examinations of the different distinctive foods, dress, and festivals of the nation/culture whose language is the target for learners (Hall & Hall, 1990; Kramsch, 1993). It may also involve students learning about the main institutions and history of a country, complemented by "an intuitive selection of representations of everyday life" (Byram, 1997, p. 9). The literary products of the society may also be studied, most usually texts from what is regarded as the canon of great literature of that society. While some sociocultural information may be derived from these, this is generally, at most, a secondary learning aim (Hinkel, 1999; Kramsch, 1993).

Recent theoretical approaches to the teaching of culture in language programs have therefore put a far greater emphasis on the need for an exploration of what might be characterized as the *deeper* aspect of cultural difference (Byram & Feng, 2004; Stugielska & Piatkowska, 2017). This generally refers to the acquisition of sociocultural and sociolinguistic skills and knowledge with which to understand and then approach difference. Such an approach involves exposure to the beliefs, values, and perceptions shared by a cultural group whose language is being studied, as well as to the products (literary or otherwise) and the practices of that society. Such exploration has the explicit aim of the acquisition of intercultural communicative competence, without which, it is argued, a learner of a language will always be positioned as "an incomplete native speaker" and so a deficient user of the language (Byram, 1997, p. 19).

Integrating Perspectives: Intercultural Communication

Intercultural communication scholars draw on a rich diversity of approaches to conceptualize "culture" and to understand the relationship between culture and language in the context of language learning and teaching (Ganassin, 2020). The intercultural dimension of language and culture learning and teaching is highly relevant to the psychology of SLA. It has the potential to underpin the ecumenical position vis-à-vis some of the questions about the nature of culture and identity we discussed above. In this section, we demonstrate how key concepts in intercultural communication research combine both psychological and SLA-relevant perspectives and how they can offer a fruitful integrated perspective for work in this area. We focus on four main concepts: culture, language, intercultural competence, and intercultural communicative competence.

Reconceptualizing Culture

SLA research, historically, tended to focus on language knowledge and language skills with little concern for the relationship between language and culture. As a consequence, perhaps, little attention has been paid to the concept of "culture" itself. A notable exception is represented by the work of Ushioda (2009), who is highly critical of how research into motivation to learn other languages often conflates context with national setting. She and others draw on Holliday's (1999) concept of "small culture" to argue about the importance of (cultural) variation at the local and individual level. This conceptualization has, arguably, been one of the most influential in intercultural communication and applied linguistics studies for more than twenty years.

Holliday (2013) understands culture as a process, defining "small culture formation" as "the everyday business of engaging with and creating culture" (p. 56). In his work, he distinguishes two concepts of culture in applied linguistics: a "large" culture concept, which refers to ethnic national or international groups, and a "small" culture concept, which addresses the ways in which individuals come together on a daily basis to seek affiliation with particular social groups (e.g., neighborhoods, professional groups) often of a transient nature (Holliday, 1999). Such a perspective mirrors that of SLA scholars and psychologists with an interest in ecological perceptions on SLA (see Haugen, 2001).

According to Holliday (1999), a "large culture" concept focuses on notions of nation, center, and periphery, and conforms broadly to the positivist "received" idea we discuss above. A "small culture" concept focuses on activities within the group, rather than on the nature of the group itself, as is strongly informed by critical, interpretivist epistemologies. As groups are constructed through human interaction, they can form, develop, change, and break up, and their nature can be transient (Amadasi & Holliday, 2018). Individuals can subscribe to different, sometimes even conflicting and competing, discourses of culture, which all contribute to construction of their own identity (Holliday, 2010, 2013).

The distinction between large and small culture is also associated with a different approach to the study of culture itself (Holliday, 2016). A "small culture approach" stresses the need to observe and interpret interaction of people in real life with a focus on their individual experiences, rather than on the "essence" of specific cultures, such as essential features of ethnic national and international groups as a "large culture approach" suggests. A "small culture" approach to culture resonates with Ushioda's (2009) "person-in-context" with focus on learners' individual history, backgrounds, experiences, and the multiple macro- and micro-contexts they are part of.

Language

As discussed in the first part of this chapter, in the field of language learning and teaching, the relationship between language and culture has been variously articulated, and they are seen as either inseparable or connected but separable in some respects (Ganassin, 2020; Kohler, 2015). The work of Claire Kramsch (1993, 1998, 2003) reflects contemporary views of language and culture as inextricably interrelated. According to Kramsch (1998), the purpose of culture teaching is to help students to understand why the speakers of two different languages act and react the way they do, whether in fictional texts or in social encounters, and what the consequences of these insights may mean for the learner. Kramsch supports the view that language and culture are inseparable, and that culture is a feature of language itself. She does not attempt to differentiate language and culture in general and in relation to language teaching, but she identifies three ways in which they are bound together (Kramsch, 1998). Firstly, language expresses cultural reality: Language acts as a means for people to express not only facts and ideas but also their attitudes. Secondly, language embodies cultural reality: People give meaning to their experience through communication; through language, they also create experience and meanings understandable to the group they are part of. Thirdly, language symbolizes cultural reality: People view their language as a symbol of their social identity (Kramsch, 1998).

The extent and nature of the link between language and culture has been the subject of considerable debate in relation to language teaching and learning. A view of their inextricable interrelationship has been characterized as, for example, overly simplistic and problematic. Damen (2003) argues that language can be taught and learnt as a code with its own rules, while, in contrast, culture is dynamic, contextual, and involves different stages of acculturation.

Such a distinction is important for language teachers and for SLA research as it implies that teachers need to both develop specialized knowledge of language and culture as "systems" and to engage in some way in "acculturation" processes. The focus on "target cultures" as an object of teaching and learning is problematic in that it places learners and, it should be added, teachers, as external to processes of learning and teaching. Instead, an ICC approach to language teaching places learners as actively involved in the "other" culture as they use language to "decenter" from their own perspective and they are changed in the process (Kohler, 2015).

ICC scholars have tried to provide guidance to language teachers on how to deal with the challenges of intercultural language teaching in the classroom. For example, Liddicoat, Scarino, Papademetre, and Kohler (2003, p. 43) designed a principle-based approach based on the assumption that "intercultural language learning involves the fusing of language, culture and learning into a single educative process." In this perspective, intercultural language teaching is not just a teaching method, or a way of "doing teaching," but an actual integrated orientation towards language, culture, and learning. As much as students, teachers are asked to engage in a constant process of critical reflection, which involves a concern for their own identity and their own framing of the languages and cultures that they teach (Papademetre & Scarino, 2000).

Risager (2005, 2007) developed the work of Damen (2003) by attempting to bring greater precision in the theorization of the interface of language and culture. To facilitate this, she introduced the concept of linguaculture (or languaculture). According to Risager (2005, p. 190), "[t]here are dimensions of culture that are bound to a specific language (languaculture), and there are dimensions that are not, for instance musical traditions or architectural styles." She also argues that the relationship between language and culture includes two levels, the "generic" and the "differential" sense (Risager, 2005). At the generic level, language and culture are inseparable and they can be understood as general human phenomena with two variants: psychological/cognitive phenomena and social phenomena. The differential level enables us to distinguish between different languages and different cultural phenomena (e.g., specific forms of cultural knowledge and cultural practices associated with specific languages). Drawing on the work of Agar (1994) and others, Risager uses the concept of linguaculture (or languaculture) to understand the interface between language and culture at the differential level as a "concept that may offer us the opportunity to theorize deconnections and reconnections between language and culture as a result of migration and other processes of globalisation" (Risager, 2005, p. 190).

As we have seen, in the field of ICC the relationship between language and culture has been variously articulated. Within this diversity, there is a shared understanding that an ICC approach to language learning and teaching places the relationship between language and culture at the center of any learning process because culture is always present when we use language (Liddicoat, 2004). Communication is the ultimate goal of intercultural language learning and teaching. However, communication should not be seen only in terms of structure and lexis, but, as we shall see in the next part of this chapter, in terms of intercultural competence.

Intercultural Competence

We turn now to how intercultural theory has attempted to explain and explore the interrelationships of language and culture in SLA. The concept of intercultural competence (IC) refers to "the appropriate and effective management of interaction between people who, to some degree or another, represent different or divergent affective, cognitive, and behavioral orientations to the world" (Spitzberg & Changnon, 2009, p. 7). Barrett, Byram, Lázár, Mompoint-Gaillard, and Philippou (2013) follow Kramsch (1998) in extending this definition and arguing that intercultural competence is a combination of attitudes, knowledge, understanding, and skills applied in intercultural encounters, sites where people infused with different cultures and worldviews can negotiate cultural and social identifications and representation. Intercultural competence allows intercultural communicators to understand and respect individuals that they perceive to have different cultural affiliations; to respond appropriately, effectively, and respectfully when interacting and communicating with such individuals; to establish positive and constructive relationships with such people; and to understand themselves and their own multiple cultural affiliations through encounters with cultural "difference" (Barrett et al., 2013). Essentially, teaching and learning languages is all about effectively managing intercultural encounters.

Intercultural encounters, which Kramsch (1998) defines as sites where people infused with different cultures and world views can negotiate social and cultural identifications and representations, play a key role in intercultural language teaching and learning. Liddicoat (2004) maintains that to work most effectively, language learning needs to allow opportunities for learners to reflect on their own language and culture. At the same time, learners and teachers are asked to decenter from their own language and culture and to consider how their own identities might shape their encounters with "the other."

Over the past 25 years, a number of models of ICC have been developed. Here, we focus on the work of Michael Byram and on his ICC model (1997, 2009). Unlike other ICC models (for example, Deardorff, 2006, 2009), Byram's is explicitly linguacultural and was developed in and for the context of language teaching and learning, and so is the most relevant for those interested in SLA. Spitzberg and Changnon (2009) categorize the model as a co-orientational model, as it sees the ability of interlocutors to reach mutual understanding and a shared level of worldviews as fundamental to initiating and sustaining ICC. The model, developed in the context of foreign language learning and teaching, is premised on the view that intercultural communicative competence requires linguistic, sociolinguistic, and discourse competence in a foreign language.

Byram (1997, 2009) emphasizes the importance of engaging through a foreign language in intercultural communication and interaction with interlocutors with different culturally influenced values, beliefs, and assumptions. The model is constructed around five *savoirs* or factors in intercultural communication that reflect skills, knowledge, attitudes, and behaviors. These are:

- *Savoir être* (intercultural attitudes): The ability to see the world from the perspective of an outsider who might have a different set of values and beliefs. Curiosity and openness are central to this savoir, which assumes an ability to suspend disbelief towards individuals' own and other cultures.
- *Savoirs* (knowledge): Not primarily knowledge about a specific culture, but rather knowledge of how social groups and identities function and what is involved. It focuses on social groups in one's own culture as well on social groups in other cultures and on general interaction processes.
- *Savoir comprendre* (skills of interpreting and relating): The ability to interpret symbols and events of other cultures and to relate such interpretation to one's own culture and experience. It advocates the importance for learners to acquire the skills of finding out new knowledge and integrating it with knowledge(s) they already have.
- *Savoir apprendre/faire* (skills of discovery and interaction): The ability to acquire new knowledge of a culture and cultural practices and the ability to operate knowledge, attitudes, and skills in real-time communication and interaction.
- *Savoir s'engager* (critical cultural awareness): This concept is central to the model (Byram, 2009). It involves not only critical thinking but also social transformation through critical self-reflection, intercultural dialogue, and action (Holmes, 2014). Critical cultural awareness is the ability to interpret, evaluate, and negotiate perspectives, practices, and products in one's own and others' cultures. It highlights the importance for teachers not to try to change learners' values, but to develop their awareness of how such values might influence their interactions with others.

The model has attracted considerable critique (see Byram 2012, 2014 for a comprehensive discussion). Criticisms have included a perceived Eurocentrism, and a lack of explanation of how the *savoirs* work together (Risager, 2007). Some have also identified a lack of clear articulation of the linguistic dimension of intercultural competence (Liddicoat et al., 2003). Another possible shortcoming is the lack of acknowledgment of the affective component of ICC (Borghetti, 2017). Yet, despite its limitations, the model has been highly influential since its first presentation, and has had a considerable influence on language research, policy, and practice around the world. It is highly relevant to language learning because it articulates the multifaceted nature of ICC in the language learner experience and it is useful for making sense of learners' ICC development. It relates closely to work investigating psychological constructs such as willingness to communicate (see Chapter 20) in a second or foreign language (MacIntyre, Clément, Dörnyei, & Noels, 1998). Parallels can also be drawn between Byram's concept of ICC and Yashima's (2002, 2009) work on international posture (IP), which is concerned with "an interest in foreign affairs, willingness to go overseas to study or work, readiness to interact with intercultural partners, and a nonethnocentric attitude toward different cultures" (Yashima, 2002, p. 57).

Additionally, Byram (1997; 2009) challenges "native speaker" models of language learning in which learners are judged by native-speaker standards. Instead, he emphasizes the importance of engaging, through a foreign language, in intercultural communication and interaction with interlocutors with different culturally influenced values, beliefs, and assumptions. He calls this being an "intercultural speaker," an individual possessing, or at least attempting to operate, the five *savoirs*. In Byram's words,

> [Individuals] may also be called upon not only to establish a relationship between their own social identities and those of their interlocutors, but also to act as mediator between people of different origins and identities. It is this function of establishing relationships, managing dysfunctions and mediating which distinguishes an "intercultural speaker," and makes them different from a native speaker.
>
> Byram, 1997, p. 38

Implications for Practice and Research

Employing an intercultural approach implies moving beyond fixed understandings of language and culture to focus on how they are constructed by individuals in social interaction as they engage in "intercultural encounters." We therefore invite researchers to go beyond the idea of intercultural encounters as experiences that individuals have had with someone from a different country or language group, arguing instead that intercultural encounters can be experienced with others within the same wider ethnic background, country, or "large culture" (Holliday, 1999, 2013).

An "intercultural approach" to language learning research and practice also invites us to rethink the roles and language-aspirations of both learners and teachers. It has implications for foreign language teacher education, which, we argue, should take full account of the complexities inherent in cultural difference and its negotiation through SLA. Second language teachers can and perhaps should be seen as (intercultural) mediators as much as experts in lexis and grammar (Crozet & Liddicoat, 1999; Kohler, 2015). Similarly, the notion of learners negotiating SLA also requires rethinking and reconceptualization. The "native speaker model" is a problematic conceptualization for both teachers and learners, yet still retains considerable power and reach in terms of language policy and pedagogic modeling (see, for example, Young & Walsh, 2010). Models and targets for language learners which take account of cultural complexity and of issues of multiplicity of intersectional identities are likely to take better account of people as acquirers of second languages. Language learning will also then align more closely to individual and social realities than "culture simple" ideas of static and fixed cultures and cultural identities. Insights from SLA research and from social psychology both serve to reinforce the idea of the central value and importance of ICC in the actual effective use of language.

Future Directions

Intercultural communication is likely to retain a central position in SLA research and language policymaking into the medium term. This centrality will be motivated by ongoing processes of globalization and associated mobilities—despite global shocks such as the COVID-19 pandemic. More than 190 million people currently live outside their country of origin (Swing, 2010), and intercultural communication research that looks at the lived experience of migration and related language acquisition by people on the move will play a key role in enhancing understandings. Up until very recently, research in the area has focused on privileged groups—students in well-resourced educational systems on the global North and businesspeople, for example. There is considerable scope for this focus to shift onto the experiences of less privileged groups of migrants and sojourners, including the many people displaced through conflict or economic hardship, migrant workers, and those seeking asylum or refuge. For an example of how this might be done, see the work conducted by the authors and others as part of the *Critical Skills for Life and Work* project, a European Commission-funded project designed to help displaced people reintegrate into the workplace (CSLW, 2019; Ganassin & Young, 2020). Similarly, intercultural research has often been grounded in hegemonic global languages, principally English (MacDonald & O'Regan, 2012). The range of languages addressed within intercultural communication research can and should be expanded to reflect the linguistic diversity of "intercultural" contexts and interactions.

Other key issues for future research in intercultural communication center on ideas of identity and language. For example, the social cohesion of multiethnic, multi-religion, and multilingual states has intercultural communication, intercultural citizenship, and people's sense of themselves in relation to others and to social structures such as the state at its very core (see Chapter 7). How "diversity" is constituted and managed through discourse in both microcosmic and macrocosmic contexts—so in every sphere, from the analysis of conversations to how language policy is devised, presented, and implemented nationally and transnationally—is likely to be of great value to researchers with an interest in psychology and SLA. Relatedly, the relationship between multiculturalism as a lived phenomenon and as a policy driver and language as it is used in different contexts is likely to be a very rich research environment into the foreseeable future. Language classrooms as "small cultures" may be an interesting line of enquiry. The idea of "Communities of Practice" (see Lave, 1997; Lave & Wenger, 1991) also retains its relevance for anyone interested in how people cooperate to teach and learn languages and could also inform future investigations in SLA.

Reflection Questions

- What complexities are involved in asking a stranger where they are from and why might this be a difficult question to answer?
- How are ideas of culture and intercultural communication dealt with in public discourse—for example by politicians in different socio-political contexts?
- How might Holliday's "small cultures" concept work in the context of classroom language learning?

Recommended Reading

Byram, M. S. (2008). *From foreign language education to education for intercultural citizenship*. Multilingual Matters.

Byram (2008) is a collection of essays that analyze the evolution of theory of intercultural competence and its relationship to education for citizenship. The book is particularly significant because it argues that foreign language education should include educational objectives which are similar, ultimately, to those of education for citizenship. The book does so by analyzing the concepts of intercultural competence—including the notion of the "intercultural speaker"—by discussing the ways in which language education policy develops, and by comparing the theories and purposes of foreign language education and education for citizenship. This book and Byram's (1997) monograph remain seminal in understanding how intercultural communicative competence can be understood and approached in SLA. They are highly relevant to researchers as well as to language educators.

Holliday, A. R. (2013). *Understanding intercultural communication: Negotiating a grammar of culture*. Routledge.

This book addresses key issues in intercultural communication including:

- the positive contribution of people from diverse cultural backgrounds
- the politics of Self and Other, which promote negative stereotyping
- the basis for a bottom-up approach to globalization in which periphery cultural realities can gain voice and ownership

This book is relevant in terms of presenting theory in intercultural communication, offering pedagogical approaches to the study of culture and identity, and in terms of proposing a methodological framework with which to research them. It also offers a framework for analysis, which will make it a useful resource for undergraduate and postgraduate students studying intercultural communication from a critical, interpretivist stance, and for professionals in the field.

Atkinson, D. (1999). TESOL and Culture. *TESOL Quarterly, 33*(4), 625–654.

This was an excellent survey of thinking at the time about the "cultural turn" in applied linguistics and remains highly relevant today. The article attempts to define an "ecumenical" position on vexed questions of the nature of culture and intercultural communication in English language teaching and learning, drawing together thinking from social psychology, anthropology, and applied linguistics. It has relevance for SLA research beyond the acquisition of the English language.

References

Agar, M. (1994). *Language shock, understanding the culture of conversation*. William Morrow.
Alred, A., & Bryman, M. (2002). Becoming an intercultural mediator: A longitudinal study of residence abroad. *Journal of Multilingual and Multicultural Development, 23*(5), 339–325.
Amadasi, S., & Holliday, R. J. (2018). "I already have a culture": Negotiating competing grand and personal narratives in interview conversations with new study abroad arrivals. *Language and Intercultural Communication, 18*(2), 241–256.
Atkinson, D. (1999). TESOL and Culture. *TESOL Quarterly, 33*(4), 625–654.
Barrett, M., Byram, M., Lázár, I., Mompoint-Gaillard, P., & Philippou, S. (2013). *Developing intercultural competence through education*. Council of Europe Publishing.
Benwell, B., & Stokoe, E., (2006). *Discourse and identity*. Edinburgh University.
Borghetti, C. (2017, July). Is there really a need for assessing intercultural competence? Some ethical issues. *Journal of Intercultural Communication, 44*. immi.se/intercultural/nr44/borghetti.html
Brislin, R. W. (Ed.). (1990). *Applied cross-cultural psychology*. Sage.
Brown, H. D. (1987). *Principles of language learning and teaching* (2nd Ed.). Prentice Hall.
Bryman, A. (2016). *Social research methods* (5th Ed.). Oxford University Press.
Byram, M. (1997). *Teaching and assessing intercultural communicative competence*. Multilingual Matters.
Byram, M. (2009). Intercultural competence in foreign languages: The intercultural speaker and the pedagogy of foreign language education. In D. Deardorff (Ed.), *The SAGE handbook of intercultural competence* (pp. 321–332). Sage.
Byram, M. (2012). *Re-visiting intercultural communicative competence* [Paper presentation]. Cultnet 2012, School of Education, Durham University, England.
Byram, M. (2014). Twenty-five years on—from cultural studies to intercultural citizenship. *Language, Culture and Curriculum, 27*(3), 209–225.
Byram, M., & Feng, A. (2004). Culture and language learning: Teaching, research and scholarship. *Language Teaching, 37*, 149–68.
Corbett, J. (2012). *Discourse and intercultural language education* [Plenary presentation]. British Association for Applied Linguistics Special Interest Group in Intercultural Communication Annual Seminar, Nottingham Trent University, Nottingham, U.K.
Crozet, C., & Liddicoat, A. J. (1999a). The challenge of intercultural language teaching: Engaging with culture in the classroom. In J. Lo Bianco, A. J. Liddicoat, & C. Crozet (Eds.), *Striving for the third place: Intercultural competence through language competence* (pp. 113–126). Language Australia.
CSLW. (2019). *Developing the professional intercultural communicative competence of highly skilled refugees*. Critical Skills for Life and Work. Retrieved March 26, 2020, from cslw.eu/
Damen, L. (2003). Closing the language and culture gap: An international communication perspective. In D. L. Lange and M. R. Paige (Eds.), *Culture as the Core: Perspective on Culture Teaching and Learning* (pp. 71–88). Information Age Publishing.
Deardorff, D. K. (2006). Identification and assessment of intercultural competence as a student outcome of internationalization. *Journal of Studies in International Education, 10*(3), 241–266.
Deardorff, D. (Ed.). (2009). *The SAGE handbook of intercultural competence*. Sage.
Dörnyei, Z. (2001). *Teaching and researching motivation*. Pearson.
Fantini, A. E. (1995). Introduction—Language, culture and world view: Exploring the nexus. *International Journal of Intercultural Relations Special Issue, 19*(2), 143–153.
Fennes, H., & Hapgood, K. (1997). *Intercultural learning in the classroom*. Cassell.
Ganassin, S. (2020). *Language, culture and identity in two Chinese community schools. More than one way of being Chinese?* Multilingual Matters.
Ganassin, S., & Young, T. J. (2020). From surviving to thriving: "success stories" of highly skilled refugees in the UK. *Language and Intercultural Communication, 20*(2), 125–140.
Gardner, R. C., & Lambert, W. E. (1972). *Attitudes and motivation in second language learning*. Newbury House.
Gardner, R. C., & MacIntyre, P. D. (1991). An investigation of instrumental motivation in language study: Who says it isn't effective? *Studies in Second Language Acquisition, 13*, 57–72.
Gardner, R. C., & MacIntyre, P. D. (1993). A student's contribution to second language learning. Part II: Affective Variables. *Language Teaching, 26*, 1–11.
Gardner, R. C., & Tremblay, P. F. (1994). On motivation: Measurement and conceptual considerations. *Modern language Journal, 78*, 524–527.

Gardner, R. C. (1988). The socio-educational model of second language acquisition: assumptions, findings and issues. *Language Learning, 38*, 101–126.

Giles, H., Bonilla, D., & Speer, R. B. (2012). Acculturating intergroup vitalities, accommodation and contact. In J. Jackson (Ed.) *The Routledge handbook of language and intercultural communication* (pp. 244–260). Routledge.

Hall, E. T., & Hall, M. R. (1990). *Understanding cultural differences*. Intercultural Press.

Hall, J. K. (2002). *Teaching and researching language and culture*. Pearson.

Hall, S. (2016). *Cultural studies 1983: A theoretical history*. In J. Slack & L. Grossberg (Eds.). Duke University Press.

Hamers, J. F., & Blanc, M. H. A. (2000). *Biliguality and bilingualism* (2nd ed.). Cambridge University Press.

Haugen, E. (2001). The ecology of language. In A. Fill & P. Muhlhausler (Eds.). *The ecolinguistics reader*. Continuum.

Hinkel, E. (Ed.). (1999). *Culture in second language teaching and learning*. Cambridge University Press.

Hofstede, G. (1986). Cultural differences in teaching and learning. *International Journal of Intercultural Relations, 10*, 301–320.

Holliday, A. R. (1999). Small cultures. *Applied Linguistics, 20*(2), 237–26.

Holliday, A. R. (2010). Complexity in cultural identity. *Language and Intercultural Communication, 10*(2), 165–177.

Holliday, A. R. (2013). *Understanding intercultural communication: Negotiating a grammar of culture*. Routledge.

Holliday, A. R. (2016). Studying culture. In Zhu, H. (Ed.), *Research methods in intercultural communication: A practical guide* (pp. 23–36). Wiley-Blackwell.

Holmes, P. (2014). Intercultural dialogue: Challenges to theory, practice and research. *Language and Intercultural Communication, 14*, 1–6.

Swing, W. L. (2010). Let's invest now for tomorrow's migration. In J.-P. Chauzy, J. Pandya, C. Lom, N. Piñeiro, & J. Bloch (Eds.), *Migration* (Winter 2010, p. 3). International Organization for Migration.

Koehler, M. (2015). *Teachers as mediators in the foreign language classroom*. Multilingual Matters.

Kramsch, C. (1993). *Context and culture in language teaching*. Oxford University Press.

Kramsch, C. (1995). The cultural component of language teaching. *Language, Culture and Curriculum, 8*(2), 83–92.

Kramsch, C. (1998). *Language and culture*. Oxford University Press.

Kramsch, C. (2003). Teaching language along the cultural faultline. In D. L. Lange & R. M. Paige (Eds.), *Culture as the core: Perspectives on culture in second language learning* (pp. 19–36). Information Age Publishing.

Kramsch, C., & Hua, Z. (2016). Language, culture and language teaching. In G. Hall (Ed.), *Routledge handbook of English language teaching* (pp. 38–50). Routledge.

Kramsch, C., & Sullivan, P. (1996). Appropriate pedagogy. *ELT Journal, 50*(3), 199–212.

Lave, J. (1997). Learning, apprenticeship and social practice. *Nordisk Pedagogik, 17*, 140–51.

Lave, J., & Wenger, E. (1991). *Situated learning: Legitimate peripheral participation*. Cambridge University Press.

Liddicoat, A. J. (2004). Intercultural language teaching: Principles for practice. *New Zealand Language Teacher, 30*, 17–24.

Liddicoat, A. J., Scarino, A., Papademetre, L., & Kohler, M. (2003). *Report on intercultural language learning*. Department of Education, Science and Training.

Lukács, G. (2000). *History and class consciousness: Studies in Marxist dialectics*. The MIT Press.

MacDonald, M. N., & O'Regan, J. P. (2012). A global agenda for intercultural communication research and practice. In J. Jackson (Ed.), *The Routledge handbook of language and intercultural communication* (pp. 553–567). Routledge.

MacIntyre, P., Clément, R., Dörnyei, Z., & Noels, K. (1998). Conceptualizing willingness to communicate in a L2: A situational model of L2 confidence and affiliation. *The Modern Language Journal, 82*(4), 545–562.

Martin, J. N., Nakayama, T. K., & Carbaugh, D. (2012). The history and development of the study of intercultural communication and applied linguistics. In D. Norman (Ed.), *The Routledge Handbook of Language and Intercultural Communication* (pp. 17–36). Routledge.

Martin, J. N. (1993). Intercultural communication competence: A review. In R. L. Wiseman & J. Koestler (Eds.), *Intercultural communication competence*. Sage.

Nostrand, H. L. (1989). Authentic texts-cultural authenticity: An editorial. *Modern Language Journal, 73*(1), 5–18.

Oxford, R. L., & Anderson, N. J. (1995). A crosscultural view of learning styles. *Language Teaching, 28*, 201–215.

Papademetre, L., & Scarino, A. (2000). *Integrating culture learning in the languages classroom: A multi-perspective conceptual journey for teachers*. Language Australia.

Pavlenko, A., & Blackledge, A. (2004). Introduction: New theoretical approaches to the study of negotiation of identity in multilingual contexts. In A. Pavlenko & A. Blackledge (Eds.), *Negotiation of identities in multilingual contexts* (pp. 1–33). Multilingual Matters.

Piller, I. (2011). *Intercultural communication: A critical introduction*. Edinburgh University Press.

Risager, K. (2005). Languaculture as a key concept in language and culture teaching. In B. Preisler, A. Fabricius, H. Haberland, S. Kjærbeck, & K. Risager (Eds.), *The consequences of mobility* (pp. 185–196). Roskilde University, Department of Language and Culture.

Risager, K. (2007). *Language and culture pedagogy: From a national to a transnational paradigm*. Multilingual Matters.

Sachdev, I., & Bourhis, R. Y. (2001). Multilingual communication. In W. P. Robinson & H. Giles (Eds.), *The new handbook of language and social psychology*. John Wiley.

Sachdev, I., & Bourhis, R. Y. (1990). Language and social identification. In D. Abrams & M. Hogg (Eds.), *Social identity theory: Constructive and critical advances* (pp. 101–124). Harvester-Wheatsheaf.

Schartner, A., & Young, T. J. (2020). *Intercultural Transitions in Higher Education*. Edinburgh University Press.

Sercombe, P. G., & Young, T. J. (2011). Culture and cognition in the study of intercultural communication. In V. Cook & B. Bassetti (Eds.), *Language and bilingual cognition*, (pp. 529–542). New York Psychology Press.

Sercu, L. (2002). Autonomous learning and the acquisition of intercultural communicative competence: Some implications for course development. *Language, Culture and Curriculum, 15*(1), 61–74.

Shiraev, E., & Levy, D. (2004) *Cross cultural psychology: Critical thinking and contemporary applications*. Pearson.

Spitzberg, B. H., & Changnon, G. (2009). Conceptualizing intercultural competence. In D. K. Deardorff (Ed.), *The Sage handbook of intercultural competence* (pp. 2–52). Sage.

Steinmetz, D. L., Bush, K. A., & Joseph-Goldfarb, N. (1994). Integrating ESL and Lakota Indian culture. *TESOL Journal 3*, 12–14.

Stugielska, A., & Piatkowska, K. (2017). Turning constructionist intercultural communicative competence and complex systems theory into praxis. *Journal of Intercultural Research, Issue 43*.

Taft, R. (1977). Coping with unfamiliar cultures. In N. Warren (Ed.), *Studies in cross-cultural psychology* (Vol. 1). Academic Press.

Ushioda, E. (2009). *A person-in-context relational view of emergent motivation, self and identity*. In Z. Dörnyei, Z. & E. Ushioda (Eds.), *Motivation, language identity and the L2 self. Second language acquisition series* (pp. 215–228). Multilingual Matters.

Whorf, B. L. (1956). The relation of habitual thought and behaviour to language. In H. Zhu (Ed.), *The language and intercultural reader* (pp. 19–34). Routledge.

Yashima, T. (2002). Willingness to communicate in a second language: The Japanese EFL context. *The Modern Language Journal, 86*(1), 54–66.

Yashima, T. (2009). International posture and the ideal L2 self in the Japanese EFL context. In Z. Dörnyei & E. Ushioda (Eds.), *Motivation, language identity and the L2 self. Second language acquisition series* (pp. 144–163). Multilingual Matters.

Young, T. J. (2016). "Intercultural research and internationalisation in higher education." *Internationalisation of Higher education: Developing values-based intercultural research approaches* [Keynote]. Newton Fund Researcher Links Workshop, Bangkok, Thailand.

Young, T. J., Handford, M., & Schartner, A. (2017). Introduction: The internationalising university: An intercultural endeavour? *Journal of Multilingual and Multicultural Development (Special Issue), 38*(3), 189–191.

Young, T. J., Sachdev, I., & Seedhouse, P. (2009). Teaching and learning culture on English language programmes: A critical review of the recent empirical literature. *International Journal of Innovation in Language Learning and Teaching, 3*(2), 149–169.

Young, T. J., & Sachdev, I. (2011). Intercultural communicative competence: Exploring English language teachers' beliefs and practices. *Language Awareness, 20*(2), 81–98.

Young, T. J., & Walsh, S. (2010). Which English? Whose English? An investigation of "non-native" speaking teaches' beliefs about target varieties. *Language, Culture and Curriculum, 23*(2), 123–137.

Zhu, H., Handford, M., & Young, T. J. (2017). Framing interculturality: A corpus-based analysis of online promotional discourse of higher education intercultural communication courses. *Journal of Multilingual and Multicultural Development, 38*(3), 283–300.

24
SOCIAL INTERACTION

Jim King and Sam Morris

The language classroom is a social crucible in which learners are expected to interact with each other and their teacher during the course of lessons, not only engaging in such activities as question and answer sessions, discussions, role plays, dialogues, and so on, but also building and navigating interpersonal relationships with those around them. Affective factors play a particularly important role in these interactions, partly because classroom exchanges tend to be public and partly because learners must negotiate them using the slightly shaky linguistic code that comes with transitioning from an L1 to an L2 self. For educators in general, and language teachers especially, interaction and communicating with learners forms an essential element of the teaching and learning process, with teachers being just as open to emotional experiences during these exchanges as students. Underlining the complexity of social interaction in educational settings, we believe there exists a dynamic interplay between context and learner/teacher-internal psychological factors (see King, 2015). With this in mind, the current chapter discusses the affective side of social interaction in language classrooms by exploring the issue via discussion of two pertinent areas: Firstly, the inhibition and silent reticence of learners, and secondly, teachers' emotions (see Chapter 14) and their in-class emotional displays. These two sub-themes provide an ideal springboard from which to discuss social interaction from a psychological viewpoint because they provide fertile ground on which to discuss how an individual's internal psychological processes and related classroom behaviors are intimately linked to the nature of the learning situation and their co-participants in that setting.

Social Interaction in Psychology

Psychologically derived definitions of social interaction tend to be quite broad in scope, reflecting the myriad and intricate ways in which human beings connect, communicate, and respond to each other. For example, the American Psychological Association defines social interaction as being "any process that involves reciprocal stimulation or response between two or more individuals. These can range from the first encounters between parent and offspring to complex interactions with multiple individuals in adult life" (APA Dictionary of Psychology, n.d.). How these countless exchanges are structured is important in psychological research, and so attention is paid to how status, social roles, and norms of behavior help shape language and communication during social interactions. From developmental psychology studies exploring how mother-infant interactions function in social-emotional development (see Bornstein & Tamis-LeMonda, 2001) to geriatric psychology research looking at how the elderly can stave off cognitive impairment through engaging in group leisure activities (e.g., Iizuka, Suzuki, Ogawa, Kobayashi-Cuya, Kobayashi, Inagaki, Sugiyama, Awata, Takebayashi, & Fujiwara, 2019), social interaction represents an important construct for consideration in a wide variety of psychology's sub-fields. Unsurprisingly, it is within social psychology that the concept has garnered most attention.

With its emphasis on how interpersonal and group relationships influence human behavior and attitudes, social psychology focuses on a number of key issues related to social interaction that are highly relevant to researchers seeking a better understanding of the nature of communication and the progress of learning that takes place within education settings. An early and highly influential example is Goffman's (1967) work on face (the public self-image one presents to others when interacting), which demonstrated how so much of what occurs in social interaction happens "below the surface" and is governed by implicit understandings, unacknowledged rituals, and covert symbolic messages. Related topics include impression management (see Leary, 1995), interpersonal perception (see Hall, Mast, & West, 2016), and nonverbal communication (see Kostic & Chadee, 2015). Research into social interaction within the social psychological tradition draws on ideas from these areas and others to explore issues such as how accurately individuals are able to perceive feelings and emotions in others and how unspoken nonverbal cues (e.g., facial expressions, gestures, body posture) and paralinguistic elements of voice (e.g., pitch, volume, speech rate, pausing) play a critical role in influencing social behavior and enabling successful interaction.

Social Interaction in SLA

Though it is rarely explicitly defined within the field of SLA, social interaction typically refers to "the conversations that learners participate in" (Gass & Mackey, 2014, p. 183), or the "meaningful ways" that people interconnect when learning languages (Oxford, 1997, p. 444). These definitions, which are equally as broad as those found in general psychology, have informed research into a wide range of interactional modes, including, but not limited to, face-to-face interactions (e.g., Ohta, 2000) computer-based interactions (e.g., Warschauer, 1997), and interactions between learners and texts (e.g., Devitt, 1997).

Research into social interaction in SLA has a long history, coming to prominence in the 1980s and 1990s through so-called "interactionist approaches," which advocated that learners need sufficient amounts of input provided at an appropriate level (e.g., Krashen, 1982) alongside output affording learners the opportunity to notice language features and negotiate meaning (e.g., Swain, 2005), both of which are mediated through social interaction (Gass & Mackey, 2014; Long, 1996; Mackey, Abbuhl, & Gass, 2012). This work was founded on the theories of Russian developmental psychologist Lev Vygotsky, particularly on his notion of the "zone of proximal development" (see Chapter 2) (Vygotsky, 1978): the metaphorical gap between what a learner can do alone and what they can do in collaboration with more able peers. Within this space, Vygotsky argued that learners can be supported to move developmental functions from an interpsychological (between people) plane, to an intrapsychological (within person) plane, and this support can be exemplified in L2 education by the use of teacher and peer-led scaffolding and feedback prior to and during social interactions (Lantolf & Thorne, 2006). Interactionist approaches have had a powerful impact on language teaching, particularly on communicative language methodologies, and there is now substantial evidence that social interaction supports the acquisition of vocabulary and grammatical items if sufficient level-appropriate input and output is provided (e.g., Ellis, 1994; Gass & Mackey, 2014; Mackey et al., 2012).

While these cognitive approaches (see Chapter 1) have been highly influential, they have also been criticized for failing to fully account for the social dimension of learning (e.g., Batstone, 2010; Breen, 1985; Hall, 1995). As Breen (1985) observed more than 30 years ago, a language classroom "is an arena of subjective and intersubjective realities which are worked out, changed, and maintained. *And these realities are not trivial background to the tasks of teaching and learning a language*" (p. 142, emphasis in original). It is increasingly recognized, therefore, that there is a dynamic interplay between context and psychological factors (see King, 2015), meaning that internal components such as beliefs, motivations, and emotions, as well as external components such as relationships (see Chapter 21), task types, and institutional moods, have a controlling impact on the quality and quantity of social interactions that learners and teachers are likely to engage in. Consequently, while social interactions in SLA may be viewed as any interplay between two or more invested parties during the act of learning a language, it must be recognized that these interplays are influenced by, and simultaneously influence, a myriad of contextual factors across time.

Social Interaction and Learner Silence

Meaningful oral interaction in the target language is crucial if learners want to make progress in acquiring a second language. A good deal of research has been done in recent years on spoken aspects of learner discourse recognizing that social and cognitive factors are complexly intertwined in this process of acquisition (e.g., Atkinson, 2011; Cao & Philp, 2006; Sato, 2017). It therefore follows that educators can gain useful insights from investigations that look at how context and learner-internal factors dynamically interplay, resulting in some learners who avoid target language talk and remain silent during learning tasks. These insights can help educators to adapt their pedagogy and organize interactions in their classrooms more productively in order to facilitate learning. Studies by King and his colleagues into the silent behavior of Japanese learners of English (e.g., King 2013a, 2013b, 2014; King & Smith, 2017; King, Yashima, Humphries, Aubrey, & Ikeda, 2020) provide a good example of this type of research, demonstrating how the public sphere of the language classroom represents an *emotional danger zone* for students concerned about social evaluation, with negative affect working to inhibit the oral performance of these learners. Socio-cultural values and norms influence an individual's feelings of anxiety in social situations (Heinrichs, Rapee, Alden, Bögels, Hofmann, Ja Oh, & Sakano, 2006; Rapee, Kim, Wang, Liu, Hofmann, Chen, Oh, Bögels, Arman, Heinrichs, & Alden, 2011; Stein, 2009), and this appears to be especially true in Japan, with its enculturated notion of an ever-watching "other" (Greer, 2000) and where reserved and socially reticent behavior in public settings tends to be positively regarded. King (2014) highlights that in such a context, rather than being entirely separate phenomena, social anxiety (fear of evaluation by others during social interactions) forms a key element of foreign language anxiety.

As part of a mixed-methods, multi-site study into the classroom silences of Japanese learners of English, King (2013a) interviewed a diverse sample of reticent students and asked them to describe their feelings when called upon to interact in English in the public realm of the classroom. Interviewees repeatedly made use of the word *hazukashii* (embarrassment) or its derivatives in their responses to describe feelings of social discomfiture. Satoshi's testimony is typical of how many of the study's interviewees felt whilst lessons were in progress:

> I worry about what the people around me think of me. If I made a mistake with a simple task- like everybody- um everybody knows the answer so say there's twenty-five students and if I make a mistake when all of those twenty-five people know the answer, then they would think "Ah, this guy is stupid." ((laughs))…I worry about my pronunciation, and the combination of words, if they're in the right order or not… I don't have confidence in my answer, then I really don't like what people around me might be thinking of me… and that's embarrassing.
>
> *King, 2013a, p. 114*

The hypersensitivity to peer reactions experienced by Satoshi and anxiously silent students like him leads to an increase in self-focused attention aimed at monitoring how one appears to others on a moment-to-moment basis. With this attention-draining preoccupation with self-focused image and impression management (Leary, 1995) comes a reluctance to draw any further unwelcome attention from peers that may result from speaking out during class. With concentration directed inwards, anxious learners experiencing social-evaluative thoughts will have fewer attention resources available for lesson content as it arises and this attentional shift makes active oral participation all the more difficult to achieve (King & Smith, 2017).

Negative affect during the social interaction of language classes is a dynamic phenomenon influenced not only by the learner's fluctuating mental characteristics and cognitions but also by various immediate contextual factors. These factors might include, for example, the nature of the learning task and familiarity with the task, the number of peers present, the level of rapport with teacher and peers, and so on. Language learning is facilitated by collaboration and cooperation amongst students (McCafferty, Jacobs, & Iddings, 2006), and so examining the dynamics of particular groups (see Dörnyei & Murphey, 2003; Forsyth, 2009) (see Chapter 22) and how these influence interpersonal relationships amongst learners is a particularly fruitful avenue of inquiry for researchers interested in social interaction and student reticence. A good illustration of this is the way in which one or two dominant cliques can have the power to stymie good interpersonal relations within a class, inhibiting and silencing other students. King (2013a) describes one such clique he observed over the course of a series of English lessons at a private, foreign languages-orientated university in Japan. This all-female, eight-strong group made no attempt to mix with other students, dominating and setting the tone for the class by responding to others' mistakes with sniggering derision. When interviewed, one member of the clique revealed members actively collaborated not to respond to the teachers prompts, describing their behavior as "kind of like teamwork, ((laughs)) teamwork to make silence… there was an atmosphere where everyone was cooperating not to raise their hand" (King, 2013a, p. 118).

Closely related to the issue of cliques is silence as an aspect of power and status. Interpersonal and intergroup status disparities work to influence whether people decide to speak or not, with those in subordinate positions being more likely to keep quiet (Jaworski, 1993; King & Aono, 2017). Peer-to-peer exchanges aside, implicit power differences are present within all staff-student interactions, and this is particularly noteworthy for educators working in societies that have a particularistic orientation towards social relationships that are relatively accepting of status inequalities. While some may find it inhibiting to interact with someone of a perceived superior status, it should also be remembered that an individual's silence can carry illocutionary force (Saville-Troike, 1985) and the avoidance of talk during staff-student interactions may in some cases be employed as a means of emotional management by the learner in order to communicate a message without the potential loss of face that an overt verbal interaction could bring. Examples of this kind of use of silence can be found in Gilmore's (1985) description of the stylized sulking of US high school students and in King's (2013a) account of a class of high proficiency learners of English who passively protested against their new instructor's teaching methods by refusing to speak during lessons.

Social Interactions and Emotions

A key contextual factor involved in social interactions is the emotion that individuals experience. Emotions are both a product of interactions (a single interaction can cause a gamut of emotions, both positive and negative), and also a catalyst for interactions. Language anxiety, as has already been discussed, can be a particularly potent inhibitor of a learner's inclination for engaging with others, yet research in the positive psychology tradition suggests that the opposite is true for experiences of emotions like joy and excitement, which may free students to step out of their comfort zones (Dewaele & MacIntyre, 2014, 2016). A Chinese participant in Gao (2007), for example, who had long struggled to resolve lingering emotions from the laborious exam-oriented learning expected of him throughout university, reported that it was positive interactions with fellow language learners in a relaxed setting which were the key to helping him remove his "self-imposed shackles of achievement"

(p. 266). Emotional experiences of any kind are unique subjective experiences, but they are equally afforded and constrained by the wider context, and can change over time (King & Ng, 2018). This means that the same incident may be interpreted in different ways by the same individual under different contextual circumstances (Dewaele & MacIntyre, 2014, 2016). An example of this is the case of NM as detailed by Dewaele and Macintyre (2014). NM made a mistake in her foreign language class and felt a strong sense of embarrassment when she was teased by the teacher (who seemingly had meant the teasing as a form of rapport-building humor). Over time, the teacher's repeated teasing of mistakes led NM to reinterpret this situation in a more positive light, and she later came to enjoy such interactions.

As this case makes clear, teachers are key players in the classroom, and increasingly attention is being paid to their side of emotional experiences in social interactions. Unsurprisingly, social interactions with students are the cause of significant amounts of both positive and negative emotions, with positive emotions most frequently reported during interactions where there is a clear sense of mutual rapport and respect (Cowie, 2011; Li & Rawal, 2018; Littleton, 2018; Talbot & Mercer, 2018), and negative emotions reported during challenging interactions, such as when relationships between the teacher and student are strained, or when students do not live up to expectations (Littleton, 2018; Morris, 2019; Morris & King, 2018; Smith & King, 2018). Like students, teachers can experience multiple emotions from a single interaction, often directed both towards students and towards themselves, and these are fluid; it is not uncommon for strong negative emotions that have been directed at students to morph into feelings of guilt or disappointment directed back towards the teacher (Morris & King, 2018).

An important consideration of emotional experiences in social interactions is that students and teachers are not unwitting participants. Individuals have a significant amount of agentive control over their emotions and displays which can be exercised through emotion regulation strategies (Gross, 2014). These strategies can target various facets of the emotional experience, such as an individual's interpretation of a given circumstance (known as cognitive change strategies), or the outward display of an emotion to others (known as response modulation strategies). Research into the emotion regulation strategies that students employ to manage their learning is rare, though increasing, and researchers are beginning to consider how emotion regulation strategies can help students to better manage the quality of their social interactions (e.g., Oxford, 2017; Bielak & Mystkowska-Wiertelak, 2020). Work in this area suggests that students can be trained to increase the positivity of their experiences, for example, by improving their ability to engage with rewarding social interactions, or by supporting them to reflect on negative social interactions in a more positive light (e.g., Oxford, 2017).

Teachers are also being studied to understand how they employ their emotions during social interactions to manage their classrooms, build relationships, embody their identities, and protect their well-being (e.g., Morris & King, 2018, 2020; Talbot & Mercer, 2018). To take well-being as an example, while negative emotions arising from interactions can have a detrimental effect on language teachers, teachers can counteract this through the emotion regulation strategy of *cognitive reappraisal* (Gross, 2014). When employing this strategy, teachers modify the way that they view an emotional stressor to give them a new perspective on a situation. Language teachers have repeatedly noted that learning more about a student's social circumstances and becoming empathetic to their difficulties helps them to reduce negative emotions during interactions (Li & Rawal, 2018; Morris & King, 2020), which may have important positive net effects for long-term well-being.

Integrating Perspectives from Psychology and SLA

Given the broad interpretations of social interaction offered in both general psychology and SLA, we have already seen much integration between the two fields. This fact is both unsurprising and reassuring given that the communicative classroom in particular relies so heavily on social interaction. That said, concepts of self-regulation during social interactions that have long been studied in social psychology such as face, interpersonal perception, and impression management, are only now beginning to find a footing in SLA. An example of this is the work being done in the field of language teachers' emotional labor, the set of implicit and explicit "feeling rules" that govern teachers' emotional interactions in the classroom (e.g., Benesch, 2017; Gkonou & Miller, 2017; King, 2016; King & Ng, 2018; Yarwood, 2020). Emotional labor is attracting attention for its ability to illustrate how teachers' experiences, training, and interpretations of larger sociocultural and political climates are manifested in their notions of professionalism, identity, and ideas of best classroom practice. While in a broad sense language teachers tend to feel a responsibility to accentuate positive emotions and hide negative emotions in social interactions (King, 2016; Li & Rawal, 2018; Morris & King, 2020), feeling rules are highly contextually dependent, so that the question of what emotions should be displayed at any moment is wed to such factors as the teacher's relationships with the interlocutors, the instrumental goals they are trying to achieve, the contents being taught, the teacher's notions of their professional self, and the momentary behavior of students (Morris & King, 2020). An illustrative example of how teachers' negative emotions might be displayed during social interactions has been highlighted in testimony from a teacher in Morris and King (2020). Emma, an experienced teacher working at a Japanese university, described the seriousness of the topic under discussion as being a salient factor in her decision to display her true feelings of anger in the classroom. In the incident in question, the class was watching a video on the sexualization of women in the media. Emma reported that she felt an obligation to her students to "get passionate" (p. 205) about the topic as a form of emotional modeling. In other words, she felt that members of her passive class, who were possibly adhering to typical Japanese feeling rules precluding them from exhibiting strong emotions (Matsumoto, Seung Hee, & Fontaine, 2008; Safdar, Friedlmeier, Matsumoto, Yoo, Kwantes, Kakai, & Shigemasu, 2009), needed to understand that intense emotional responses to this kind of topic were common and, in her eyes, appropriate.

While students are not subject to emotional labor in its traditional sense (emotional labor refers to the act of meeting feeling rules in an employment context) they are required to follow implicit socio-cultural interaction rules in their classroom, and continuing work in this area has the potential to reveal much about the socio-affective nature of their interactions. Kidd (2016), for example, has explored how young Japanese learners use communication strategies and emotional displays within social interactions to preserve face within the confines of the cultural norms of their local context. Kidd's work indicates that the enactment of student identities in social interactions may very well be misconstrued or misunderstood by teachers from dissimilar backgrounds, with potentially devastating results for learning. The same holds true when teachers lack familiarity with the implicit socio-cultural interaction rules surrounding what is appropriate oral participation within the context in which they teach (see Thorp, 1991). Misinterpreting student reticence merely as uncooperativeness can potentially sour staff-student relationships and make learning through collaboration and productive social interaction much less likely.

Work in these exciting growth areas helps to highlight that social interactions in the language classroom are conducted within a dynamic and complex emotional sphere, informed by the individual and shared histories of its participants, who are managing their emotions in line with structural and cultural norms on a moment-by-moment basis. The continued integration of perspectives from both psychology and SLA will, we believe, continue to reveal to us recommendations for best practice so that the quality of social interactions for learners and teachers can be maximized.

Implications for Practice and Research

As Glaser and her colleagues (Glaser, Kupetz, and You, 2019) rightly point out, research into language teaching is increasingly placing emphasis on learning as a social accomplishment, focusing on the social interaction which takes place between teachers and learners and amongst learners themselves within the language classroom. These empirical studies can provide pre- and in-service teacher education programs with valuable insights about interactional processes, highlighting to educators that interaction is not just about language use, but also includes non-vocal elements of communication as well. In light of this, below we discuss some pedagogical implications of learner silence, suggesting strategies for educators aimed at improving social interaction and communication amongst learners, before turning our attention to the implications of social interaction from the affective perspective of teachers' in-class emotions and emotional displays.

As a starting point for dealing with the negative affect associated with silent language learners trying to minimize their social interactions in the classroom, we suggest educators consider how they can effectively manipulate the group dynamics within their classrooms, particularly at the beginning of courses, to reduce the social evaluative aspects of language anxiety and foster good interpersonal relationships within the group. Dörnyei and Murphey (2003) highlight how *acceptance* (non-judgmental, positive regard) within a class group can be encouraged through the use of activities that involve learners exchanging genuine information about themselves but on topics which avoid too much self-disclosure. Contact and proximity play an important role in encouraging good interpersonal dynamics and so small-group/pair membership should be changed frequently and seating arrangements manipulated in order to facilitate communication and avoid cliques forming. Rather than being solely silence-inducing, status differences can actually be advantageous if teachers give careful consideration to student leadership within groups. Studies by Leeming (2019) and Yashima, Nakahira and Ikeda (2016) have demonstrated that strong student leadership during small-group work is related to an absence of student silence and a better balance of participation amongst group members during interactional tasks. Hence, with careful encouragement from teachers, effective student leaders have the potential to facilitate social interaction amongst group and class members.

If encountering a silent episode when interacting with a learner, we advise educators to pay careful attention to the contextual features of the interaction and consider whether the learner might be employing silence to convey a message of some sort. Not all silences are detrimental to learning and they can in some circumstances be used as an interactional resource (Harumi, 2020), for example, by providing space for processing and reflection during an extended pause. Research into teacher silent wait time (the period between a teacher's elicitation and a learner response or subsequent teacher utterance) suggests that by increasing their tolerance to silence and extending wait time, educators can improve learner response rates and the quality of responses (Shrum, 1984) and can even shift classroom discourse out of a rigid initiation-response-feedback (IRF) pattern into more learner-driven phases (Smith & King, 2017). With the aid of training, moments of silence might also provide teachers with the opportunity to discern whether an individual is suffering from anxiety by paying close attention to the student's nonverbal cues accompanying the silent episode (see Gregersen, 2007; Gregersen, MacIntyre & Olson, 2017). Such an approach highlights the fact that social interaction in the language classroom is not just concerned with vocal communication, it also comprises nonverbal, paralinguistic elements and kinetic/bodily behaviors.

Teachers' Classroom Emotions: Implications for Trainers and Researchers

Most language teachers' pre- and in-service training does not pay adequate attention to emotions. Yet, our discussion of the emotional exchanges occurring in social interactions has shown that teachers are able to influence their emotional displays to motivate, teach, and care for their students. Emotional output can have both a positive and negative impact, and teachers could benefit from reflecting on their emotional choices and be open and aware to the influence that these might have on students. As was also mentioned, teachers are able to manage their emotions through emotion regulation strategies. Since cognitive appraisal seems to be a particularly effective way for teachers to take control of their emotional stressors (Li & Rawal, 2018; Morris & King, 2020), trainers and institutions should support and encourage teachers to learn as much as possible about their students, their previous classroom learning experiences, and the role of the target language in their lives.

Future Directions

The arrival of the emotional turn in SLA (White, 2018) means that the future of research on the affective dimension of social interaction seems bright. That said, a significant challenge will be in combining the perspectives of teachers and students. With a few exceptions, research has tended to isolate the teacher from the student and vice-versa, the student from the teacher. This can lead to data formed of rather subjective voices. As we have discussed in this chapter, the emotions of teachers and students and their silent behaviors are so inexorably linked that it does not serve our interests to deal with them separately, and research addressing dual perspectives would be most welcome.

Researching the silence that occurs in classrooms is a challenge because of its inherently ambiguous nature and because silent behavior often operates at a level below an individual's consciousness (Smith & King, 2020). While investigations to date have tended to focus on East Asian EFL contexts, it should be emphasized that reticent learners exist in every culture. There is therefore a need to broaden enquiry into other settings in order to gain a better understanding of the complexities behind why some language learners do not engage in interactive tasks. Mixed methodologies are most likely to achieve a fine-grained analysis of silent episodes which take into account learner-internal and external factors. As for emotions, research methods investigating this dimension of social interactions have leaned heavily towards qualitative interviewing, and there exists only a limited number of studies which have adopted more objective approaches through observations or quantitative methods (e.g., Gkonou & Mercer 2017; Morris & King 2020). Much more could be done to assess the universality of teachers' emotional experiences in social interactions through, for example, quantitative surveys or assessment. Given the highly contextual nature of social interaction practices, we also anticipate more locally-situated studies, and look forward to inquiries investigating how teachers negotiate their emotional output in multicultural classrooms. Just like work into classroom silence, we suspect that mixed-methods research and approaches which take into account the complex and temporally dynamic nature of the classroom ecology (such as those based on dynamic systems theory) are likely to be most successful.

Reflection Questions

- As has been noted in this chapter, the classroom environment can inspire and inhibit productive social interactions. How might teachers manage their classrooms to encourage the amount of positive social interactions that students engage in?
- The chapter discusses language learner silence in relation to social inhibition. Have you ever felt anxious in a learning situation? If yes, why do you think this was and how did your anxiety influence your classroom behavior?
- Reflect on the emotions that you display when you teach or the emotions displayed by one of your teachers: Can you think of a time when these emotions have caused difficulties in class? What could you/your teacher have done differently?

Recommended Reading

Forgas, J. P. (1985). *Interpersonal behaviour: The psychology of social interaction*. Pergamon Press.
The social psychologist Forgas has published extensively on affect in social interaction, focusing on such topics as social cognition, emotional intelligence, and interpersonal and intergroup perspectives

on the self. Although not the newest of his books, the above title is a very readable introduction to the psychology of social interaction.

King, J., Yashima, T., Humphries, S., Aubrey, S., & Ikeda, M. (2020). Silence and anxiety in the English-medium classroom of Japanese universities: A longitudinal intervention study. In J. King & S. Harumi (Eds.), *East Asian perspectives on silence in English language education* (pp. 60–79). Multilingual Matters.
This chapter describes a project which aimed to tackle non-participatory learner silence through a multi-strategy intervention focusing on three interrelated areas: learners' anxiety coping strategies, the improvement of interpersonal dynamics and social collaboration among students, and encouragement to engage in target language interaction. The study demonstrates how affect-orientated intervention activities taking place both inside and outside of the classroom can influence learner inhibition and oral participation patterns.

Morris, S., & King, J. (2020). Emotion regulation amongst university EFL teachers in Japan: The dynamic interplay between context and emotional behaviour. In C. Gkonou, J-M. Dewaele, & J. King (Eds.), *The emotional rollercoaster of language teaching* (pp. 193–210). Multilingual Matters.
In this chapter we illustrate the socially dynamic nature of teacher emotions that arise during interactions with students. The study reveals various ways in which teachers attempt to regulate their own and their students' emotions in order to achieve pedagogical goals and gain psychological well-being.

References

APA Dictionary of Psychology. (n.d.) *Social interaction*. dictionary.apa.org/social-interactions
Atkinson, D. (2011). A sociocognitive approach to second language acquisition: How mind, body, and world work together in learning additional languages. In D. Atkinson (Ed.), *Alternative approaches to second language acquisition* (pp. 143–166). Routledge.
Batstone, R. (2010). Issues and options in sociocognition. In R. Batstone (Ed.), *Sociocognitive perspectives on language use and language learning* (pp. 3–23). Oxford University Press.
Benesch, S. (2017). *Emotions and English language teaching: Exploring teachers' emotional labor*. Routledge.
Bielak, J., & Mystkowska-Wiertelak, A. (2020). Investigating language learners' emotion-regulation strategies with the help of the vignette methodology. *System*, 90, 102208.
Bornstein, M. H., & Tamis-LeMonda, C. S. (2001). *Mother-infant interaction*. In G. Bremner & A. Fogel (Eds.), *Blackwell handbook of infant development*. *(Volume 7 of Blackwell handbooks of developmental psychology)* (pp. 269–295). Blackwell.
Breen, M. P. (1985). The social context for language learning—A neglected situation? *Studies in Second Language Acquisition*, 7(2), 135–158.
Cao, Y., & Philp, J. (2006). Interactional context and willingness to communicate: A comparison of behavior in whole class, group and dyadic interaction. *System*, 34(4), 480–493.
Cowie, N. (2011). Emotions that experienced English as a Foreign Language (EFL) teachers feel about their students, their colleagues and their work. *Teaching and Teacher Education*, 27(1), 235–242.
Dewaele, J.-M., & MacIntyre, P. (2014). The two faces of Janus? Anxiety and enjoyment in the foreign language classroom. *Studies in Second Language Learning and Teaching*, 4(2), 237–274.
Dewaele, J.-M., & MacIntyre, P. D. (2016). Foreign language enjoyment and foreign language classroom anxiety: The right and left feet of the language learner. In P. D. MacIntyre, T. Gregersen, & S. Mercer (Eds.), *Positive Psychology in SLA*. Multilingual Matters.
Devitt, S. (1997). Interacting with authentic texts: Multilayered processes. *Modern Language Journal*, 81(4), 457–469.
Dörnyei, Z., & Murphey, T. (2003). *Group dynamics in the language classroom*. Cambridge University Press.
Ellis, R. (1994). *The study of second language acquisition*. Oxford University Press.
Forsyth, D. R. (2009). *Group dynamics* (5th ed.). Wadsworth, Cengage Learning.
Gao, X. (2007). A tale of Blue Rain Café: A study on the online narrative construction about a community of English learners on the Chinese mainland. *System*, 35(2), 259–270.
Gass, S. M., & Mackey, A. (2014). *Input, interaction and output in second language acquisition*. Routledge.
Gilmore, P. (1985). Silence and sulking: Emotional displays in the classroom. In D. Tannen & M. Saville-Troike (Eds.), *Perspectives on silence* (pp. 139–162). Ablex.

Gkonou, C., & Mercer, S. (2017). Understanding emotional and social intelligence among English language teachers. In *ELT Research Papers 17.03*. British Council.

Gkonou, C., & Miller, E. R. (2017). Caring and emotional labour: Language teachers' engagement with anxious learners in private language school classrooms. *Language Teaching Research, 23*(3), 372–387.

Gkonou, C., Dewaele, J.-M., & King, J. (Eds.). (2020). *The emotional rollercoaster of language teaching*. Multilingual Matters.

Glaser, K., Kupetz, M., & You, H. J. (2019). "Embracing social interaction in the L2 classroom: Perspectives for language teacher education"—an introduction. *Classroom Discourse, 10*(1), 1–9.

Goffman, E. (1967). On facework: An analysis of ritual elements in social interaction. In E. Goffman, *Interaction ritual: Essays on face-to-face behavior* (pp. 5–33). Doubleday Anchor.

Greer, D. L. (2000). "The eyes of hito": A Japanese cultural monitor of behavior in the communicative language classroom. *JALT Journal, 22*(1), 183–195.

Gregersen, T. (2007). Breaking the code of silence: A study of teachers' nonverbal decoding accuracy of foreign language anxiety. *Language Teaching Research, 11*(2), 209–221.

Gregersen, T., MacIntyre, P., & Olson, T. (2017). Do you see what I feel? An idiodynamic assessment of expert and peer's reading of nonverbal language anxiety cues. In C. Gkonou, M. Daubney, & J-M. Dewaele (Eds.), *New insights into language Anxiety: Theory, research and educational implications* (pp. 110–134). Multilingual Matters.

Gross, J. J. (2014). Emotion regulation: Conceptual and empirical foundations. In J. J. Gross (Ed.), *Handbook of emotion regulation* (2nd ed., pp. 3–22). The Guilford Press.

Hall, J. A., Mast, M. S., & West, T. V. (Eds.). (2016). *The social psychology of perceiving others accurately*. Cambridge University Press.

Hall, J. K. (1995). (Re)creating our worlds with words: A sociohistorical perspective of face-to-face interaction. *Applied Linguistics, 16*(2), 206–232.

Harumi, S. (2020). Approaches to interacting with classroom silence: The role of teacher talk. In J. King & S. Harumi (Eds.), *East Asian perspectives on silence in English language education* (pp. 37–59). Multilingual Matters.

Heinrichs, N., Rapee, R. M., Alden, L. A., Bögels, S., Hofmann, S. G., Ja Oh, K., & Sakano, Y. (2006). Cultural differences in perceived social norms and social anxiety. *Behaviour Research and Therapy, 44*(8), 1187–1197.

Iizuka, A., Suzuki, H., Ogawa, S., Kobayashi-Cuya, K. E., Kobayashi, M., Inagaki, H., Sugiyama, M., Awata, S., Takebayashi, T., & Fujiwara, Y. (2019). Does social interaction influence the effect of cognitive intervention program? A randomized controlled trial using Go game. *International Journal of Geriatric Psychiatry, 34*(2), 324–332.

Jaworski, A. (1993). *The power of silence: Social and pragmatic perspectives*. Sage.

Kidd, J. A., (2016). *Face and enactment of identities in the L2 classroom*. Multilingual Matters.

King, J. (2013a). *Silence in the second language classroom*. Palgrave Macmillan.

King, J. (2013b). Silence in the second language classrooms of Japanese universities. *Applied Linguistics, 34*(3), 325–343.

King, J. (2014). Fear of the true self: Social anxiety and the silent behaviour of Japanese learners of English. In: K. Csizér & M. Magid (Eds.), *The impact of self-concept on language learning* (pp. 232–249). Multilingual Matters.

King, J. (2016). "It's time, put on the smile, it's time!": The emotional labour of second language teaching within a Japanese university. In C. Gkonou, D. Tatzl, & S. Mercer (Eds.), *New directions in language learning psychology* (pp. 97–112). Springer.

King, J. (Ed.). (2015). *The dynamic interplay between context and the language learner*. Palgrave Macmillan.

King, J., & Aono, A. (2017). Talk, silence and anxiety during one-to-one tutorials: A cross-cultural comparative study of Japan and UK undergraduates' tolerance of silence. *Asia Pacific Education Review, 18*(4), 489–499.

King, J., & Ng, K.-Y. S. (2018). Teacher emotions and the emotional labour of second language teaching. In S. Mercer & A. Kostoulas (Eds.), *Language teacher psychology* (pp. 141–157). Multilingual Matters.

King, J., & Smith, L. (2017). Social anxiety and silence in Japan's tertiary foreign language classrooms. In C. Gkonou, M. Daubney, & J-M. Dewaele (Eds.), *New insights into language anxiety: Theory, research and educational implications* (pp. 91–109). Multilingual Matters.

King, J., Yashima, T., Humphries, S., Aubrey, S., & Ikeda, M. (2020). Silence and anxiety in the English-medium classroom of Japanese universities: A longitudinal intervention study. In J. King & S. Harumi (Eds.), *East Asian perspectives on silence in English language education* (pp. 60–79). Multilingual Matters.

Kostic, A., & Chadee, D. (Eds.). (2015). *The social psychology of nonverbal communication*. Palgrave Macmillan.

Krashen, S. (1982). *Principles and practice in second language acquisition*. Pergamon Press.

Lantolf, J. P., & Thorne, S. L. (2006). *Sociocultural theory and the genesis of second language development*. Oxford University Press.

Leary, M. R. (1995). *Self-presentation: Impression management and interpersonal behavior*. Brown & Benchmark.

Leeming, P. (2019). Emergent leadership and group interaction in the task-based language classroom. *TESOL Quarterly, 53*(3), 768–793.

Li, W., & Rawal, H. (2018). Waning and waxing of love: Unpacking layers of teacher emotion. *Chinese Journal of Applied Linguistics, 41*(4), 550–569.

Littleton, A. (2018). Emotion regulation strategies of kindergarten ESL teachers in Japan: An interview-based survey. *The Language Learning Journal*, 1–16.

Long, M. (1996). The role of the linguistic environment in second language acquisition. In W. Ritchie & T. Bhatia (Eds.), *Handbook of second language acquisition* (pp. 413–468). Academic Press.

Mackey, A., Abbuhl, R., & Gass, S. M. (2012). Interactionist approach. In S. M. Gass & A. Mackey (Eds.), *The Routledge handbook of second language acquisition* (pp. 7–23). Routledge.

Matsumoto, D., Seung Hee, Y., & Fontaine, J. (2008). Mapping expressive differences around the world: The relationship between emotional display rules and individualism versus collectivism. *Journal of Cross-Cultural Psychology, 39*(1), 55–74.

McCafferty, S. G., Jacobs, G. M., & Iddings, A. C. D. (Eds.). (2006). *Cooperative learning and second language teaching.* Cambridge University Press.

Morris, S. (2019). The frustration regulation journal: A reflective framework for educators. *Relay Journal, 2*(2), 294–305.

Morris, S., & King, J. (2018). Teacher frustration and emotion regulation in university language teaching. *Chinese Journal of Applied Linguistics, 41*(4), 433–452.

Morris, S., & King, J. (2020). Emotion regulation amongst university EFL teachers in Japan: The dynamic interplay between context and emotional behaviour. In C. Gkonou, J.-M. Dewaele, & J. King, (Eds.), *The emotional rollercoaster of language teaching* (pp. 193–210). Multilingual Matters.

Ohta, A. S. (2000). Rethinking interaction in SLA: Developmentally appropriate assistance in the zone of proximal development and the acquisition of L2 grammar. In J. P. Lantolf (Ed.), *Sociocultural theory and second language learning* (pp. 51–78). Oxford University Press.

Oxford, R. L. (1997). Cooperative learning, collaborative learning, and interaction: Three communicative strands in the language classroom. *Modern Language Journal, 81*(4), 443–456.

Oxford, R. L. (2017a). *Teaching and researching language learning strategies: Self-regulation in context* (2nd ed.). Taylor & Francis Group.

Rapee, R. M., Kim, J., Wang, J., Liu, X., Hofmann, S. G., Chen, J., Oh, K. Y., Bögels, S. M., Arman, S., Heinrichs, N., & Alden, L. E. (2011). Perceived impact of socially anxious behaviors on individuals' lives in Western and East Asian countries. *Behavior Therapy, 42*(3), 485–492.

Safdar, S., Friedlmeier, W., Matsumoto, D., Yoo, S. H., Kwantes, C. T., Kakai, H., & Shigemasu, E. (2009). Variations of emotional display rules within and across cultures: A comparison between Canada, USA, and Japan. *Canadian Journal of Behavioural Science / Revue canadienne des sciences du comportement, 41*(1), 1–10.

Sato, M. (2017). Interaction mindsets, interactional behaviors, and L2 development: An affective-social-cognitive model. *Language Learning, 67*(2), 249–283.

Saville-Troike, M. (1985). The place of silence in an integrated theory of communication. In D. Tannen & M. Saville-Troike (Eds.), *Perspectives on silence* (pp. 3–18). Ablex.

Shrum, J. L. (1984). Wait-time and student performance level in second language classrooms. *Journal of Classroom Interaction, 20*(1), 29–35.

Smith, L., & King, J. (2017). A dynamic systems approach to wait time in the second language classroom. *System, 68*, 1–14.

Smith, L., & King, J. (2018). Silence in the foreign language classroom: The emotional challenges for L2 teachers. In J. D. Martinez Agudo (Ed.), *Emotions in second language teaching* (pp. 323–340). Springer.

Smith, L., & King, J. (2020). Researching the complexity of silence in second-language classrooms. In R. J. Sampson & R. S. Pinner (Eds.), Complexity perspectives on researching language learner and teacher psychology (pp. 86–102). Multilingual Matters.

Stein, D. J. (2009.) Social anxiety disorder in the West and in the East. *Annals of Clinical Psychology, 21*(2), 109–117.

Swain, M. (2005). The output hypothesis: Theory and research. In E. Hinkel (Ed.), *Handbook of second language teaching and research* (pp. 471–484). Lawrence Erlbaum.

Talbot, K., & Mercer, S. (2018). Exploring university ESL/EFL teachers' emotional well-being and emotional regulation in the United States, Japan and Austria. *Chinese Journal of Applied Linguistics, 41*(4), 410–432.

Thorp, D. (1991). Confused encounters: Differing expectations in the EAP classroom. *ELT Journal, 45*(2), 108–118.

Vygotsky, L. S. (1978). *Mind in society: The development of higher psychological processes.* Harvard University Press.

Warschauer, M. (1997). Computer-mediated collaborative learning: Theory and practice. *Modern Language Journal, 81*(4), 470–481.

White, C. (2018). The emotional turn in applied linguistics and TESOL: Significance, challenges and prospects. In J. D. Martinez Agudo (Ed.), *Emotions in second language teaching* (pp. 19–34). Springer.

Yarwood, A. (2020). Emotional labour in the eikaiwa classroom. In D. Hooper & N. Hashimoto (Eds.), *Teacher narratives from the Eikaiwa classroom: Moving beyond "McEnglish"* (pp. 82–93). Candlin & Mynard ePublishing.

Yashima, T., Ikeda, M., & Nakahira, S. (2016). Talk and silence in an EFL classroom: Interplay of learners and context. In J. King (Ed.), *The dynamic interplay between context and the learner* (pp. 104–126). Palgrave Macmillan.

25
PROSOCIAL BEHAVIOR AND SOCIAL JUSTICE

M. Matilde Olivero

Although the debate whether humans are capable of authentic altruism has been fuming for decades, research on social psychology indicates that humans can indeed engage in prosocial behavior and that this notion has an established history in the field. As many forms of injustice keep occurring worldwide and language classrooms become more multicultural, the interest in prosociality and social justice in the field of second language acquisition (SLA) has increased in the last decade. What leads people to be willing to help others or to avoid providing assistance? How does prosocial behavior relate to social justice? How has this construct been addressed in psychology and the field of SLA? Can prosocial behavior be promoted in language education? The purpose of the current chapter is to offer answers to such questions. The chapter starts with a review of the literature on prosocial behavior within the discipline of social psychology. More specifically, it refers to the traditional and recent perspectives to the study of prosociality, including why people engage (or not) in prosocial actions across groups with special attention to prosocial behavior with respect to social justice. Next, it discusses how prosociality has been theorized and explored within the field of SLA and describes empathy, altruism, and gratitude, which are three closely related constructs. This section also refers to transformative approaches that can be incorporated in language education to cultivate favorable prosocial behaviors for building social justice. Then the chapter briefly explains how both the fields of psychology and SLA can inform each other to help better understand the phenomenon of prosociality. Subsequently, important implications both for research and practice are presented, followed by potential future directions to be taken in the field of SLA.

Prosocial Behavior in Psychology
Research Traditions and Latest Trends

Research on social psychology documents that humans have a strong capacity to act prosocially and that the study of prosocial behaviors has a long investigative history (Dovidio, 1984; Dovidio & Banfield, 2001; Dovidio, Gaertner, & Abad-Merino, 2017). As Stürmer and Snyder (2010) argue, prosociality has been a topic of great interest partly because it aims at addressing important philosophical matters, such as humans' virtues and capability of genuine altruism. Moreover, the interest in studying prosocial behaviors has been related to addressing social goals and problems—that is, understanding when and why people tend to act prosocially (or not) might help to come up with ways to promote a variety of prosocial actions that contribute to the well-being of individuals and to building social harmony and justice (Stürmer & Snyder, 2010).

Auné, Blum, Abal, Lozzia, and Horacio (2014) define prosocial behavior as "a complex phenomenon which involves individual actions based on beliefs and feelings, and which describes the way these individuals are oriented towards the others when engaging in solidarity behaviours" (p. 23). Prosocial behavior is situated within a particular context and involves psychological aspects, such as thoughts, emotions, and behaviors, and social aspects, which relate to culture (Arias, 2015; Diazgranados, 2014; Martí-Vilar, 2010). According to Martí Vilar, Serrano Pastor, and González Sala (2019), people should engage in prosocial actions in order to transform society and make it more cohesive, cooperative, and based on positive interpersonal relations. In Bhogal and Farrelly's (2019) words, "the human capacity to cooperate, to help, and to share resources with others, contributes to the success of our socially motivated species, and in part, facilitates our ability to live harmoniously in large social groups" (p. 939).

The study of prosocial behavior arose in the 1960s and 70s and has been framed within different theoretical lenses, including psychology, biology, and philosophy, among others (Bhogal & Farrelly, 2019). Regarding the history of helping within social psychology, theory and research on prosocial behavior has developed separately from research on intergroup relationships (Stürmer & Snyder, 2010). In the 1960s, traditional research on prosocial behavior focused on helping between individuals instead of members of groups (Iyer & Leach, 2010). Years later, researchers started to explore the ways in which individual level processes are influenced by processes at the group level. However, research on intergroup relations has traditionally ignored prosocial actions and has mainly focused on negative intergroup behaviors, including discrimination, prejudice, and conflict (Dovidio, Gaertner, & Abad-Merino, 2017).

By the 80s, research on prosocial behavior and on intergroup relations started integrating perspectives, which led, for example, to the study of volunteerism. The study of volunteerism across groups has served to question the belief that intergroup behavior is based on hostile competition. As Stürmer and Snyder (2010) argue, although acts of prosocial behavior across groups might occur less frequently than among members of the same group, they do in fact occur as cooperation with other groups, and mutual support is crucial for the well-being of groups and of a just society.

Prosocial Behavior Across Groups

According to psychology research, aspects related to uncertainty and prejudice between and among groups might prevent people from helping out-group members (Wright & Richard, 2010). As the needs of out-group members tend to be less known than the needs of in-group members, intergroup interactions tend to involve greater uncertainty than the same interactions within a group. For example, advantaged group members may be uncertain about the needs of disadvantaged out-group members, which might be due to experiencing anxiety provoked by cross-groups interactions, and having prejudice towards out-groups, among other aspects. However, when advantaged group members become aware of the injustice suffered by disadvantaged out-groups, they can experience empathy and unsettling emotions that can lead advantaged group members to take responsibility and engage in prosocial behaviors (Iyer, Leach, & Crosby, 2003; Powell, Branscombe, & Schmitt 2005).

Research also indicates that people tend to provide assistance to those with whom they feel they share similarities (Dovidio, Piliavin, Schroeder, & Penner, 2017). Due to this, the promotion of cross-group helping often involves strategies that aim at minimizing group differences and emphasizing perceptions of similarity. Wit and Kerr (2002), for example, showed that cooperation between groups occurred with more frequency when members thought of themselves as one common group instead of different sub groups (see Chapter 23). By the same token, Buchan, Brewer, Grimalda, Wilson, Fatas, and Foddy (2011) indicated that assistance between people from different cultural groups involved their ability to develop a common group identity (see Chapter 7). Recent research has also shown that people with higher social and emotional intelligence (Afolabi 2013; Kaltwasser, Hildebrandt, Wilhelm, & Sommer, 2017) are more likely to engage in prosocial behaviors as they tend to be mindful of themselves and sensitive to others' needs.

The Role of Affect

In general, research has not paid enough attention to the specific psychological processes that might influence advantaged groups to engage in prosocial behavior conducive to fostering social justice (Iyer & Leach, 2010). It has been shown, for example, that specific emotions (see Chapter 14), such as anger, guilt, and empathy can boost advantaged groups' motivation (see Chapter 10) to help disadvantaged groups. Appraisal theorists (Frijda, 1986; Roseman, Wiest, & Swartz, 1994) explain that each emotion leads to different forms of responses and action regarding a situation. Anger has been conceptualized as a high arousal emotion that often motivates individuals for confrontation action. This emotion leads group members to take personal and political action necessary to achieve social justice. Moreover, individuals' guilt about other people's unjust actions is associated with the need to improve the situation and help those suffering from injustice. Also, sympathy is an emotion that relates to having a positive orientation towards those in unprivileged situations, thereby leading to prosocial actions. Similarly, Hoffman (2000) argues that empathy is related to moral principles and therefore is fundamental to the foundations of justice. Closely linked to empathy is gratitude. Gulliford, Morgan, Hemming, and Abbott (2019) explain that gratitude involves moral motivations and reinforcement, which implies that receiving benefits from others has a contagion effect and encourages people to perform acts of kindness. At the same time, receiving messages of gratitude for our acts of kindness strengthens positive actions, thereby increasing the probability of them being replicated in the future.

Prosocial Behavior in SLA

The Contribution of Positive Psychology

Positive psychology (see Chapter 5) in SLA focuses on the strengths that enable language learners and teachers to flourish individually and in their communities (MacIntyre, Gregersen, & Mercer, 2016). Fredrickson's (2003) research has indicated that being able to have positive interactions and social connections can lead to greater well-being. In view of this, empathy, altruism, and gratitude have been addressed in the field of SLA in the last decade.

In recent years, influenced by the "social turn" in SLA (Block, 2003), researchers became interested in how human beings participate in their communities and how they relate to others. In this light, the construct of empathy has gained special attention. Howe (2013) defines empathy as "an effective reaction to the emotions of another; the cognitive act of adopting another's perspective; a cognitively based understanding of other people; and the communication of such an understanding" (p. 14). Similarly, according to Mercer (2016), empathy implies having the intention and making the effort to understand other people's emotions and thoughts, which influences our relationships with others. People with higher emotional intelligence, defined as "the ability to understand feelings in the self and others and to use these feelings as informational guides for thinking and action" (Salovey, Mayer, Caruso, & Yoo, 2012, p. 238), are known to have greater empathy. Emotional intelligence has also gained popularity in the field of SLA as it has been shown, among other aspects, to help regulate emotions, improve relationships, and increase awareness and appreciation of other cultures (Gkonou & Mercer, 2017).

Affective empathy, cognitive empathy, and compassion are the three components of empathy (Mercer, 2016). When people are compassionate, it is more likely that they will engage in prosocial behaviors because they are concerned and touched by the difficulties of others (Howe, 2013;

Krznaric, 2014). According to Krznaric (2014), compassion is central for building empathy in society as it can help generate important transformations as well as give true meaning to our lives.

Empathy can be enhanced through reflection, which can consequently lead to action. It has been demonstrated that biological differences as well as personal and social experiences have an impact on empathy (Howe, 2013). The contextual nature of this construct implies that having had previous experiences with empathy is crucial for a person to be empathetic. As empathy is essential for human interaction and meaningful communication, it is paramount to develop it in the language classroom. Being a competent language user involves the capacity to listen mindfully, understand others' perspectives, and accept differences with no judgment—all aspects related to empathy (Mercer, 2016). Current approaches to language learning highlight the importance of integrating the intercultural dimension. In this respect, ethnocultural empathy plays a crucial role. Ethnocultural empathy implies being able to understand the perspectives of someone from a different sociocultural background, as well as appreciate and understand their feelings. All of these abilities facilitate interacting with speakers from other cultures positively and enhance language learning (Gkonou, Olivero, & Oxford, 2020). Language learners should be offered opportunities to develop empathy, while they develop competence in the different language skills, in order to understand and accept other ways of being, thinking, and feeling in this world. That is, sequences of positive psychology-based activities can be integrated into the regular language curriculum to help learners become aware of the importance of empathy as well as to learn to empathize with others.

Naturally, if teachers are to develop empathy among their students, they themselves should be able to understand learners' perspectives and listen with kindness and without pre-judgment so as to build a safe environment where learners are given opportunities to flourish. In this light, language teacher education courses can incorporate activities intended to help future teachers be empathic and cultivate empathy in their own classroom contexts (For ideas and activities to cultivate empathy in language education see Gkonou, Olivero, & Oxford, 2020; Mercer, 2016; Olivero, 2017; Olivero & Harrison, 2020; Olivero & Oxford, 2019; Oxford, 2017).

As Oxford (2013) explains, neuroscience research indicates that human brains are neurologically predisposed for altruism. Neuroscientists have also observed that acts of altruism produce pleasure (Vedantam, 2007), and that although people tend to help those they care about more, help can also occur among strangers. Gregersen, MacIntyre, and Meza (2016) explain that acts of empathy tend to stimulate motivation for altruism, in part due to our reactions upon observing someone in need of help and realizing we can provide such help. Engaging in altruistic behaviors is also said to lead towards a stronger sense of bonding and community, which has been shown to increase happiness. Altruism plays an important role in language learning as it can help learners have a greater sense of purpose by finding meaning in what they learn. For example, when language learners are involved in altruism, they communicate in the target language and develop linguistic competence while simultaneously connecting with others in a deep, humane way. Such purposeful communication can lead to greater willingness to communicate (Gregersen, MacIntyre, & Meza 2016), which is an important factor in developing communicative competence in the foreign language. Moreover, it is known that engaging in acts of kindness increases positive emotions and motivation, which are constructs that play a key role in facilitating language learning (MacIntyre & Gregersen, 2012). Additionally, when learners engage in acts of altruism with people from different cultures, they can learn from an embodied perspective to appreciate and understand other peoples' realities, which is the main goal of embracing an intercultural approach in the language classroom. Helping others who might be in need can enable learners to become aware of social injustices and contribute to building a more just world. As mentioned earlier in this chapter, performing acts of kindness for others may motivate the recipients of such acts to be grateful and kind in turn (Gulliford, Morgan, Hemming, & Abbott, 2019). (For ideas and activities to foster altruism in language education, see Gregersen, MacIntyre, & Meza 2016; Olivero & Oxford, 2019).

Gratitude has a close relationship with empathy and altruism. According to Peterson (2006), "counting your blessings on a regular basis makes you happier and more content with life" (p. 38). Similarly, Lyubomirsky (2008) argues that expressing gratitude increases happiness in several ways, as it leads a person to savor positive life events, raises one's self-esteem, and helps regulate one's stress. In language education, it becomes particularly significant to cater for such aspects, as self-esteem and emotion regulation are known to have a direct impact on the process and the outcomes of learning and teaching a foreign language (Kostoulas & Lämmerer, 2020; Oxford, 2016). Language learners can express what they are grateful for either in written or spoken language, read texts about how gratitude influences people's happiness, give thanks to their peers and teachers, among other ideas. In this way, learners are given opportunities to practice the different language skills and focus on specific lexicogrammar while increasing their well-being, which would make the process of language learning purposeful and joyful. Moreover, being grateful and expressing gratitude enhances moral behavior, boosts positive relationships, and helps people have a greater sense of community, which are fundamental aspects in human interaction (the basis of language education) and also in building harmony and justice. (For ideas and activities to develop gratitude in language education, see Fresacher, 2016; Helgesen, 2016; Gregersen, MacIntyre, Finegan, Talbot, & Claman, 2014; Gregersen & MacIntyre, 2020; Olivero & Harrison, 2020).

The Contribution of Transformative Approaches

In SLA, prosocial behaviors can also be fostered through transformative approaches, including holistic education, contemplative practices, and experiential learning. Holistic education involves focusing on the whole person by developing the different aspects of the self (Miller, Nigh, Binder, Novak, & Crowell, 2018). Although holistic learning has been long established in the field (Stevick, 1990), recently there has been an increased interest in revitalizing holistic learning due to its great potential for developing communicative competence and enhancing teacher development, as well as for contributing to social transformation (Amerstorfer, 2020; Medley, 2016; Olivero & Harrison, 2020; Olivero & Oxford, 2019; Oxford, 2013; 2014; 2017; Oxford, Olivero, & Gregersen, in press). Addressing prosocial behaviors in the language classroom through holistic approaches helps learners find meaning in what they learn. Having a deep purpose for learning a language tends to influence learners' beliefs about learning, their motivation and engagement to learn the language, and their willingness to take risks and overcome obstacles, which are all constructs that have shown to be predictors of the acquisition of a second language (Oxford, 2016). Likewise, holistic learning has been shown to help pre-service teachers have a transformative and more pleasant experience during their practicum (Olivero, 2017).

Similarly, contemplative practices aim at developing the whole person through self-reflection with the purpose of fostering peace, love, and justice (Lin, Culham, & Edwards, 2019). It has been demonstrated that contemplation influences learners and future teachers in positive ways, including greater ethical attitude (Culham, 2013) and moral intelligence (Wei & Wei, 2013), which are fundamental characteristics for developing emotions and prosocial actions that contribute to societal harmony. Common techniques in contemplative practices include reflective writing, active listening, developing a mindful attitude, cultivating empathy, visualizing, and meditating. In language education, the inclusion of contemplative techniques has shown to help boost pre-service teachers' confidence about teaching (Olivero, 2017), increase learners' positive emotions (MacIntyre & Gregersen, 2012) and motivation (Dörnyei & Kubanyiova, 2014), reduce foreign language anxiety (Franco, Mañas, Cangas, & Gallego, 2010; Schlesiger, 1995), improve performance in exams (Scida & Jones, 2017), and facilitate listening comprehension skills (Arnold, 2011).

Experiential learning involves learning through reflection on experience (Kolb, 1984). Experiential tasks enhance learning as they allow learners to experiment with and reflect on concrete ideas (Legutke & Schocker-v. Ditfurth, 2009). For example, learners and future teachers would be able to learn about the importance of empathy and altruism to foster social justice while working on activities in which they have the opportunity to empathize with others or perform acts of kindness to strangers and reflect on their impact. This way of working has the potential to facilitate learners' transformation of their beliefs, emotions, and actions and to make the learning and teaching of the language more relevant and memorable. Experiential learning aimed at fostering prosociality in the language classroom can range from specific activities to be carried out in the classroom to service learning projects.

An approach that integrates the three learning modes described above with the purpose of developing prosocial behaviors to foster social justice and peace is the Language of Peace Approach (LPA) (Oxford, 2013). Peace in the LPA is conceived as *positive peace* and involves intergroup harmony, positive relationships, supportive social systems, human rights, and constructive conflict resolution (Galtung, 1996; Groff, 2008). The LPA considers that peace is multidimensional, encompassing six intertwined dimensions, including inner peace (peace within the person); interpersonal peace (peace between individuals); intergroup peace (peace between or among groups); intercultural peace (peace among cultures); international peace (peace between nations); and ecological peace (peace between people and the environment). The cultivation of inner peace is fundamental for acting prosocially to contribute to social transformation (Lin, 2013). Although empathy and altruism are more directly associated with peace in the interpersonal, intergroup, intercultural, and international dimensions, in order to experience and expand peace in the outer dimensions, it is crucial to develop inner peace (Oxford, 2013; Olivero, 2017). For example, it might be hard to develop compassion for others if there is no self-compassion. Moreover, deep inner reflection is necessary in order to become conscious of social injustice and of the feelings it provokes, which might in turn lead to taking action and helping those in need.

The LPA is an optimal approach to use in language education as it weaves the teaching of peace and social consciousness into language instruction. Peacebuilding activities can be used to develop different language skills and to focus on lexis, grammar, pragmatics or pronunciation, while building peace and social harmony. In language teacher education, peacebuilding activities can be used to help future teachers develop the necessary competencies (Gkonou, Olivero, & Oxford, 2020) to foster peace and social justice when they start teaching. Studies that have incorporated peacebuilding activities in the language classroom have shown that inner, interpersonal, and intergroup peace activities led learners to be empathetic and more willing to help each other, which had an impact on cooperative learning and improved classroom climate (Amerstorfer, 2020; Olivero & Oxford, 2019). In language teacher education, peacebuilding activities have facilitated teacher development and helped future teachers have a more pleasant practicum experience (Olivero, 2017). For example, inner peace activities enabled pre-service teachers to reframe negative thoughts and consequently modify unpleasant emotions, resulting in more optimism and confidence. Other activities served to develop empathy, which helped pre-service teachers have better rapport with their students. It is important to note that as the LPA integrates the holistic, contemplative, and experiential learning modes, it shares the potentials for language learning and teaching and for promoting prosocial behaviors that have been mentioned earlier in this section.

Critical approaches to language learning are also powerful for developing prosocial behaviors to foster peace and social justice. The language classroom is an optimal place to reflect on issues of peace, human rights, citizenship, and the environment and to learn to challenge the status quo (Hastings & Jacob, 2016; Ortega, 2019). Likewise, Kruger (2012) states that the teaching of a foreign language should help recognize diversity and problematize the use of language that conveys bias and emphasizes inequity and forms of injustice. Similarly, Lourdes Ortega (2018) argues that the teaching of foreign languages should, among other aspects, help build justice by teaching learners to appreciate diversity, dispel stereotypes, and become conscious of what privilege and vulnerability imply and how these relate to their identity as learners and to the specific foreign language(s) they learn. Also, within the field of language education, Mahalingappa, Rodriguez, and Polat (2020) state that in order to achieve social justice there should not be structural violence, which is violence that grows from oppression, discrimination, and inequity in terms of life chances and possibilities (Galtung, 1969). Through social justice pedagogies, teachers can prepare learners to work collectively through concrete actions to deal with societal problems (Grant & Sleeter, 2006). Social justice pedagogies consider social action to be fundamental, and thus value prosocial behaviors intended to advocate for those in underprivileged situations.

Integrating Perspectives

This chapter has explained that current research perspectives on intergroup relations in the field of social psychology arose from the dissatisfaction with traditional perspectives, which focused merely on negative intergroup behaviors (Dovidio, Gaertner, & Abad-Merino, 2017). That is, current researchers in psychology have sought to focus on what leads individuals to engage in prosociality across groups rather than focusing only on negative behaviors between groups, such as prejudice or discrimination. Under the influence of positive psychology theories, the field of SLA in the last decade has also started to pay attention to how learners' strengths and virtues, including prosocial behaviors, contribute to the well-being of individuals and communities (MacIntyre & Mercer, 2014). As it can be observed, SLA has been inspired by the field of psychology in taking a positive-oriented approach to try to understand prosociality and how it contributes to social harmony. In addition, SLA has been strongly influenced by social theories, thereby leading to an increased interest in the social dimensions of the language to explore how language users interact in this diverse globalized world.

This chapter has also helped confirm the potential that the field of SLA has in enlightening the field of psychology with respect to the role that language plays in prosocial behavior. Among the variables that influence whether an individual is willing to help a member of an outside group, the language spoken by members of each group might play a significant role. Language is intrinsically related to aspects of the self, including identity, beliefs, and emotions that can lead people to act prosocially (or not) towards social justice. Language is a powerful tool that can enhance communities and prevent conflict (Capstick & Delaney, 2016; Oxford, 2013) or separate communities and be a source of dispute.

As language education involves various aspects of the self and their psychologies (Mercer, Macintyre, Gregersen, & Talbot, 2018), it becomes reasonable to study certain phenomena through an interdisciplinary lens. In light of this, the study of prosociality in language education can benefit from the use of combined perspectives within the fields of SLA and psychology as it would allow for a better understanding of the multifaceted nature of prosociality and how it can contribute to social justice.

Implications for Practice and Research

This chapter highlights the need to embrace transformative approaches in language education that stimulate prosocial behavior conducive to social justice. The last few years have seen an increased interest in holistic, contemplative, and experiential learning modes in language education as they have the potential of both enhancing the learning and teaching of language and of cultivating important human values necessary for prosocial actions (Hastings & Jacob, 2016; Olivero & Harrison, 2020; Olivero & Oxford, 2019; Ortega, 2019; Oxford, 2017; Oxford, Gregersen, & Olivero, 2018; Yang, 2015). For example, the chapter explained that transformative learning modes tend to have an impact on constructs that play an important role in the acquisition of a second language. At the same time, contemplative and holistic learning modes are known to develop ethical and moral intelligence, which are crucial for engaging in prosocial actions to foster societal justice. Moreover, transformative approaches allow for the integration of the intercultural dimension of the language, which is a core element in current approaches to language teaching. Also, it is known that prosocial behaviors can be best enhanced through reflection. Through experiential activities that involve contemplative techniques, language teachers can offer meaningful opportunities for language practice in combination with deep reflection on beliefs and emotions to create the optimal conditions for prosocial behaviors to develop.

The literature reviewed in this chapter also reflects the need to integrate transformative approaches in language teacher education. If we are to include approaches in the language classroom that are intended to cultivate prosociality, it is crucial that language teachers develop the necessary competencies. In this light, Gkonou, Olivero, and Oxford (2020) argue that teachers should develop four related competencies, including ethnocultural empathy, intercultural understanding, cognitive flexibility, and emotion self-regulation. Language teachers should be given systematic opportunities during their teacher education programs or professional development courses to embody and reflect upon prosociality.

As it was explained in this chapter, prosocial behavior involves both psychological and social aspects (Arias 2015; Diazgranados, 2014; Martí-Vilar 2010) and is situated within a particular context (Auné et al., 2014). The nature of prosociality implies that it should be explored in particular contexts in order to see the specific beliefs and emotions that lead people to engage in prosocial actions to build social justice, and the ways in which cultural aspects and contextual factors might influence such behaviors. Moreover, it has been mentioned that empathy leads to acting prosocially. Given the strong influence of empathy in prosociality, more studies in SLA should explore not only how empathy influences the learning and teaching of a second language, but also how it contributes to social justice. In this light, Ortega (2018) highlights the need to elaborate social justice goals in the field of SLA while investigating the constructs that help explain the relationships between language learning and individual differences. She argues that the field of SLA should help understand how language learning can build capacity for social justice.

Future Directions

In the last decade, the field of SLA has advanced in incorporating theories and approaches to enhance prosociality leading to social justice and in studying their impact. An increasing body of research has helped build the foundations and laid a promising path towards a social justice agenda for the years to come.

This chapter explained that both cognitive and social aspects play a fundamental role in prosociality. Given this, cognitive and social constructs must be explored jointly in the field of SLA as they can allow for a more nuanced understanding of what makes people engage in prosocial behavior as well as the impact of prosocial actions in building social justice. Ortega (2018) has recently claimed that the field of SLA should also include new constructs and questions that explicitly address social justice matters while investigating the processes involved in second language acquisition. For example, studies should consider constructs such as cosmopolitanism, empathy, and xenophilia. An agenda that addresses social justice aspects would help further the understanding of the complex relationships between language learning and variables such as globalization, poverty, conflict, privilege, and power, among others. Moreover, new directions in SLA should consider the importance of exploring the specific psychological processes that lead people to engage in prosocial actions. For example, affect plays a key role in participation in collective action and more specifically, emotions such as empathy, gratitude, and anger can boost people's motivation to provide assistance. Although some of these emotions have been explored in the field of SLA to explain learner and teacher well-being, more studies should focus on how such emotions might stimulate prosocial behavior conducive to social justice. Studies framed within social psychology could help fill this gap. Finally, an agenda that focuses on social justice matters should involve the incorporation of research designs that seem most appropriate. Given that prosocial behavior is situated, interpretative research designs, such as phenomenological and case studies seem optimal for understanding how and when people engage (or not) in prosocial actions. Also, based on what Ortega (2018) suggests, the use of nested levels of analysis might be suitable to help understand the interaction between the different psychological and social variables involved in prosociality.

Reflection Questions

- Based on the chapter, what are the transformative approaches that can be incorporated in language education in order to enhance prosocial behavior conducive to social justice? What do you think might be the challenges of incorporating such approaches in the regular classroom curriculum?
- Given that investigating the social domains of language learning and teaching has been at its peak for two decades in the field of SLA, why do you think that prosocial behavior with respect to social justice is still considered a fertile area for further investigation?
- In what ways can prosociality be best explored in the field of SLA in order to understand how it contributes to social justice?

Recommended Reading

Hastings, C., & Jacob, L. (Eds.). (2016). *Social justice in English language teaching*. Annapolis Junction, MD: TESOL Press.
This collection of papers is intended to raise awareness on the issue of social injustices and to inspire ESL educators to address this in their own contexts. Each chapter reflects the unfavorable situations that English language learners often suffer from and highlights the essential role that language educators have in advocating for their needs.

MacIntyre, P. D., Gregersen, T., & Mercer, S. (Eds.). (2016). *Positive psychology in SLA*. Multilingual Matters.
This pioneering work focuses on positive psychology in SLA, the scientific study of what makes people and communities flourish and experience well-being. The chapters focus on aspects related to positive psychology theories and address important implications for practice and research in language education. The authors offer innovative teaching ideas to integrate positive psychology-based activities in language education, as well as the best approaches to explore positive psychology constructs in SLA.

Oxford, R., Olivero, M. M., Harrison, M., & Gregersen, T. (Eds.). (2020). *Peacebuilding in language education. Innovations in theory and practice*. Multilingual matters.
This anthology fills a significant gap by explaining how language education can contribute to the building of peace. Based on a multidimensional peace model encompassing inner and outer dimensions of peace, this cutting-edge work focuses on peacebuilding theories and practical implications with innovative ideas for the classroom.

References

Afolabi, O. (2013). Roles of personality types, emotional intelligence and gender differences on prosocial behavior. *Psychological Thought, 6*(1), 124–139.
Amerstorfer, C. (2020). Learners' inner peace and interpersonal peace in innovative L2 teaching. In R. L. Oxford, M. M. Olivero, M. Harrison, & T. Gregersen (Eds.), *Peacebuilding in language education. Innovations in theory and practice*. Multilingual matters.
Arias, W. (2015). Conducta prosocial y psicología positiva. *Avances en Psicología, 23*(1), 37–47.
Arnold, J. (2011). Seeing through listening comprehension exam anxiety. *TESOL Quarterly, 34*(4), 777–786.

Auné, S. F., Blum, D., Abal, J. P., Lozzia, G. S., & Horacio, F. A. (2014). La conducta prosocial: Estado actual de la investigación. *Perspectivas en Psicología, 11*(2), 21–33.
Bhogal, M. S., & Farrelly, D. (2019). The psychology of prosocial behavior: An introduction to a special issue. *Current Psychology, 38*, 910–911.
Block, D. (2003). *The social turn in second language acquisition.* Edinburgh University Press.
Buchan, N. R., Brewer, M., Grimalda, G., Wilson, R. K., Fatas, E., & Foddy, M. (2011). Global social identity and global cooperation. *Psychological Science, 22*, 821–828.
Capstick, T., & Delaney, M. (2016). Language for resilience: The role of language in enhancing the resilience of Syrian refugees and host communities. The British Council.
Culham, T. (2013). Exploring unconscious embodied ethical transformation: Perspectives from Daoist body-mind contemplative practices. In J. Lin, R. L. Oxford, & E. J. Brantmeier (Eds.), *Re-envisioning higher education: Embodied pathways to wisdom and social transformation* (pp. 33–56). Information Age Publishing.
Diazgranados, S. (2014). Asociación entre los ambientes escolares y las actitudes de apoyo hacia la violencia en estudiantes colombianos. *Revista Colombiana de Educación, 66*, 175–202.
Dörnyei, Z., & Kubanyiova, M. (2014). *Motivating learners, motivating teachers. Building vision in the language classroom.* Cambridge University Press.
Dovidio, J. F. (1984). Helping behavior and altruism: An empirical and conceptual overview. *Advances in Experimental Social Psychology, 17*, 361–427.
Dovidio, J., & Banfield, J. (2015). Prosocial behavior and empathy. *International encyclopedia of the social & behavioral sciences.*
Dovidio, J. F., Gaertner, S. L., & Abad-Merino, S. (2017). Helping behavior and subtle discrimination. In E. vaan Leewen & H. Hafezka (Eds.), *Intergroup helping* (pp. 30–22). Springer.
Dovidio, J., Piliavin, J., Schroeder, D., & Penner, L. (2017). *The social psychology of prosocial behavior.* Psychology Press.
Franco, C., Mañas, I., Cangas, A. J., & Gallego, J. (2010). The applications of mindfulness with students of secondary school: Results on the academic performance, self-concept and anxiety. *Knowledge Management, Information Systems, E-Learning, and Sustainability Research, Communications in Computer and Information Science, 111*, 83–97.
Fresacher, C. (2016). Why and how to use positive psychology activities in the second language classroom. In P. D. MacIntyre, T. Gregersen, & S. Mercer (Eds.), *Positive psychology in SLA* (pp. 344–358). Multilingual Matters.
Fredrickson, B. L. (2003). The value of positive emotions: The emergence science of positive psychology looks into why it's good to feel good. *American Scientist, 91*(4), 330–335.
Frijda, N. H. (1986). *Studies in emotion and social interaction. The emotions.* Cambridge University Press.
Galtung, J. (1969). Violence, peace, and peace research. *Journal of Peace Research, 6*(3), 167–191.
Galtung, J. (1996). *Peace by peaceful means.* Sage.
Gkonou, C., & Mercer, S. (2017). *Understanding social and emotional intelligence among English language teachers.* British Council.
Gkonou, C., Olivero, M. M., & Oxford, R. L. (2020). Empowering language teachers to be influential peacebuilders: Knowledge, competencies and activities. In R. L. Oxford, M. M. Olivero, M. Harrison, & T. Gregersen (Eds.), *Peacebuilding in language education. Innovations in theory and practice.* Multilingual matters.
Grant, C. A., & Sleeter, C. E. (2006). *Turning on learning: Five approaches for multicultural teaching plans for race, class, gender and disability.* Wiley/Jossey-Bass.
Gregersen, T., MacIntyre, P. D., Finegan, K. H., Talbot, K. R., & Claman, S. L. (2014). Examining emotional intelligence within the context of positive psychology interventions. *Studies in Second Language Learning and Teaching 4*(2), 327–353.
Gregersen, T., MacIntyre, P. D., & Meza, M. (2016). Positive psychology exercises build social capital for language learners: Preliminary evidence. In P. D. MacIntyre, T. Gregersen, & S. Mercer (Eds.), *Positive psychology in SLA* (pp. 147–167). Multilingual Matters.
Gregersen, T., & MacIntyre, P. D. (2020). Acting locally to integrate positive psychology and peace: Practical applications for language teaching and learning. In R. L. Oxford, M. M. Olivero, M. Harrison, & T. Gregersen (Eds.), *Peacebuilding in language education. Innovations in theory and practice.* Multilingual matters.
Groff, L. (2008). Contributions of different cultural-religious traditions to different aspects of peace–leading to a holistic, integrative view of peace for a 21st century interdependent world. *Transcultural Future Magazine 7*(1).
Gulliford, L., Morgan, B., Hemming, E., & Abbott, J. (2019). Gratitude, self-monitoring and social intelligence: A prosocial relationship? *Current Psychology, 38*, 1021–1032.
Hastings, C., & Jacob, L. (Eds.). (2016). *Social justice in English language teaching.* TESOL Press.
Helgesen, M. (2016). Happiness in ESL: Bringing positive psychology to the classroom. In P. D. MacIntyre, T. Gregersen, & S. Mercer (Eds.), *Positive psychology in SLA* (pp. 305–323). Multilingual Matters.
Hoffman, M. L. (2000). *Empathy and moral development.* Cambridge University Press.
Howe, D. (2013). *Empathy: What it is and why it matters.* Palgrave Macmillan.

Iyer, A., Leach, C. W., & Crosby, F. J. (2003). White guilt and racial compensation: The benefits and limits of self-focus. *Personality and Social Psychology Bulletin, 29*, 117–129.

Iyer, A., & Leach, C. W. (2010). Helping disadvantaged out-groups challenge unjust inequality: The role of group-based emotions. In S. Stürmer & S. Snyder (Eds.), *The psychology of prosocial behavior* (pp. 337–353). Wiley-Blackwell.

Kaltwasser, L., Hildebrandt, A., Wilhelm, O., & Sommer, W. (2017). On the relationship of emotional abilities and prosocial behavior. *Evolution and Human Behavior, 38*(3), 298–308.

Kolb, D. (1984). *Experiential learning*. Prentice Hall.

Kostoulas, A., & Lämmerer, A. (2020). Resilience in language teaching: Adaptive and maladaptive outcomes in pre-service teachers. In C. Gkonou, J. M. Dewaele, & J. King (Eds.), *The emotional rollercoaster of language teaching* (pp. 206–247). Multilingual Matters.

Krznaric, R. (2014). *Empathy: A handbook for revolution*. Random House.

Kruger, F. (2012). The role of TESOL in educating for peace. *Journal of Peace Education, 9*(1), 17–30.

Legutke, M. K., & Schocker-v. Ditfurth, M. (2009). School-based experience. In A. Burns & J. C. Richards (Eds.), *The Cambridge guide to second language teacher education* (pp. 209–217). Cambridge University Press.

Lin, J. (2013). Education for transformation and an expanded self: Paradigm shift for wisdom education. In J. Lin, R. L. Oxford, & E. J. Brantmeier (Eds.), *Re-envisioning higher education: Embodied pathways to wisdom and social transformation* (pp. 23–32). Information Age Publishing.

Lin, J., Culham, T., & Edwards, S. (Eds.). (2019). *Contemplative pedagogies for transformative teaching, learning, and being*. Information Age Publishing.

Lyubomirsky, S. (2008). *The how of happiness. A scientific approach to getting the life you want*. Penguin.

MacIntyre, P. D., & Gregersen, T. (2012). Emotions that facilitate language learning: The positive-broadening power of the imagination. *Studies in Second Language Learning and Teaching, 2*(2), 193–213.

MacIntyre, P. D., Gregersen, T., & Mercer, S. (Eds.). (2016). *Positive psychology in SLA*. Multilingual Matters.

MacIntyre, P. D., & Mercer, S. (2014). Introducing positive psychology to SLA. *Studies in Second Language Learning and Teaching, 4*(2), 153–172.

Mahalingappa, L., Rodriguez, T. L., & Polat, N. (2020). Promoting peace through social justice pedagogies for students from immigrant Muslim communities: Using critical language awareness in second language classrooms. In R. L. Oxford, M. M. Olivero, M. Harrison, & T. Gregersen (Eds.), *Peacebuilding in language education. Innovations in theory and practice*. Multilingual matters.

Martí-Vilar, M. (2010). *Razonamiento moral y prosocialidad*. CCS.

Martí-Vilar, M., Serrano Pastor, L., & González Sala, F. (2019). Emotional, cultural and cognitive variables of prosocial behavior. *Current Psychology, 38*, 912–919.

Medley, R. M. (2016). Tension and harmony: Language teaching as a peacebuilding endeavor. In C. Hastings & L. Jacob (Eds.), *Social justice in English language teaching* (pp. 49–66). TESOL Press.

Mercer, S. (2016). Seeing the world through your eyes: Empathy in language learning and teaching. In P. D. MacIntyre, T. Gregersen, & S. Mercer (Eds.), *Positive Psychology in SLA* (pp. 91–111). Multilingual Matters.

Mercer, S., MacIntyre, P. D., Gregersen, T., & Talbot, K. (2018). Positive language education: Combining positive education and language education. *Theory and Practice of Second Language Acquisition 4*(2), 11–31.

Miller, J. P., Nigh, K., Binder, M. J., Novak, B., & Crowell, S. (Eds.). (2018). *International handbook of holistic education*. Routledge.

Olivero, M. M. (2017). *Cultivating peace via language teaching: Pre-service beliefs and emotions in an Argentine EFL practicum* [Unpublished dissertation]. University of South Florida.

Olivero, M. M., & Harrison, M. (2020). Peacebuilding through classroom activities: Inner, interpersonal, intergroup, intercultural, international, and ecological peace. In R. L. Oxford, M. M. Olivero, M. Harrison, & T. Gregersen (Eds.), *Peacebuilding in language education. Innovations in theory and practice*. Multilingual matters.

Olivero, M. M., & Oxford, R. L. (2019). Educating for peace: Implementing and assessing transformative, multi-dimensional peace language activities designed for future teachers and their students. In L. Walid Lofty & C. Toffolo (Eds.), *Promoting peace through practice, academia, and the arts* (pp. 184–206). IGI Global.

Ortega, L. (2018). *Understanding vulnerability and privilege in multilingualism: What can the psychology of language learning offer?* PPL3: 3rd International Psychology of Language Learning Conference, Waseda University, Tokyo, June 7–10.

Ortega, Y. (2019). Peacebuilding and social justice in English as a foreign language: Classroom experiences from a Colombian high school. In E.A Mikulec, S. Bhatawadekar, C. T. Mcgivern, & P. Chamness (Eds.), *Readings in language studies, Volume 7: Intersections of peace and language studies* (Vol 7, pp. 63–90). International Society for Language Studies.

Oxford, R. L. (2013). *The language of peace: Communicating to create harmony*. Peace Education Series, Information Age Publishing.

Oxford, R. L. (Ed). (2014). *Understanding peace cultures*. Peace Education Series, Information Age Publishing.

Oxford, R. L. (2016). Toward a psychology of well-being for language learners: The "EMPATHICS" vision. In P. D. MacIntyre, T. Gregersen, & S. Mercer (Eds.), *Positive psychology in SLA* (pp. 10–87). Multilingual Matters.

Oxford, R. L. (2017). Peace through understanding: Peace activities as innovations in language teacher education. In T. Gregersen and P. D. MacIntyre (Eds.), *Innovative practices in language teacher education: Spanning the spectrum from intra- to inter-personal professional development* (pp.125–163). Springer.

Oxford, R. L., Olivero, M., & Gregersen, T. (2018). The interplay of language and peace education: The Language of Peace Approach in peace communication, linguistic analysis, and multimethod research. In the Special Issue (A. Curtis, Ed.), From Peace Language to Peace Linguistics, *TESL Reporter 51*(2), 10–33.

Oxford, R., Olivero, M. M., & Gregersen, T. (in press). Promoting peacebuilding through teaching language and culture from the humanities perspective. In N. Johnson (Ed.) *Engaging the humanities in education for peace: Edited volume on the role and contributions of the humanities to peace studies.* Information Age Publishing.

Peterson, C. (2006). *A primer in positive psychology.* Oxford University Press.

Powell, A. A., Branscombe, N. R., & Schmitt, M. T. (2005). Inequality as ingroup privilege: The impact of group focus on collective guilt and interracial attitudes. *Personality and Social Psychology Bulletin, 31*, 508–521.

Roseman, I. J., Wiest, C., & Swartz, T. S. (1994). Phenomenology, behaviors, and goals differentiate discrete emotions. *Journal of Personality and Social Psychology, 67*, 206–221.

Salovey, P., Mayer, J. D., Caruso, D., & Yoo, S. H. (2012). The positive psychology of emotional intelligence. *The Oxford handbook of positive psychology* (2nd Ed.).

Scida, E. E., & Jones, E. (2017). The impact of contemplative practices on foreign language anxiety and learning. *Studies in Second Language Learning and Teaching, 7*(4), 57–599.

Schlesiger, H. (1995). *The effectiveness of anxiety reduction techniques in the foreign language classroom* [Unpublished doctoral dissertation]. University of Texas.

Stevick, E. (1990). *Humanism in language teaching: A critical perspective.* Oxford University Press.

Stürmer, S., & Snyder, M. (2010). The psychological study of group processes and intergroup relations in prosocial behavior: Past, present, future. In S. Stürmer & S. Snyder (Eds.), *The psychology of prosocial behavior* (pp. 3–11). Willey-Blackwell.

Stürmer, S., & Snyder, M. (2010). Helping "Us" versus "Them": Towards a group-level theory of helping and altruism within and across group boundaries. In S. Stürmer & S. Snyder (Eds.), *The psychology of prosocial behavior* (pp. 33–58). Willey-Blackwell.

Wei, Y., & Wei, M. (2013). Developing moral intelligence. Global, networked, and embodied approaches. J. Lin, R. L. Oxford, & E. J. Brantmeier (Eds.), *Re-envisioning higher education: Embodied pathways to wisdom and social transformation* (pp. 57–73). Information Age Publishing.

Wit, A. P., & Kerr, N. L. (2002). "Me versus just us versus us all" categorization and cooperation in nested social dilemmas. *Journal of Personality and Social Psychology, 83*, 616–637.

Wright, S. C., & Richard, N. T. (2010). Cross-group helping: Perspectives on why and why not. In S. Stürmer & S. Snyder (Eds.), *The psychology of prosocial behavior* (pp. 311–335). Willey-Blackwell.

Vedantam, S. (2007, May 28). If it feels good to be good, it might be only natural. Washington Post. www.pressreader.com/usa/the washingtonpost/20070528/281509336759530

PART 4

Myths, Debates, and Disagreements

26
TRAIT AND STATE PERSPECTIVES OF INDIVIDUAL DIFFERENCE RESEARCH

Kata Csizér and Ágnes Albert

Research into second/foreign language (L2) learning has been long interested in the question as to why some students learn L2(s) more quickly than others do. This observation has given way to individual difference (ID) research with the aim of explaining the roots of these differences. As learning an additional/foreign language is a long and difficult process and learning itself might impact the role/effects of these variables, we cannot assume that these ID variables do not change over time, even though very often these variables are considered to be relatively stable traits that students possess. Although contextual and temporal variation of these variables has been increasingly acknowledged (which has given rise to the state perspective of these variables), there is a lack of systematic analysis of the trait and state perspectives in our field. This is even more curious as various psychological theories have informed second/foreign language learning research in general and ID research in particular (Dörnyei, 2009; Dörnyei & Ryan, 2015), and in the field of psychology the trait/state—or in other words person/situation—debate is one of the fundamental dichotomies, similar to the nature/nurture conundrum.

In what follows, we provide a summary of the trait/state conundrum by first outlining the most important considerations from psychology. Next, we summarize the trait/state perspective in applied linguistics by outlining the research efforts in relation to four ID variables: anxiety, motivation (see Chapter 10), aptitude (see Chapter 30), and creativity. The reason these ID variables were selected was because they represent different aspects of the trait/state debate by relating to temporal and contextual changes in different ways. By arguing for the integration of the state and trait perspectives in single designs, we provide implications for future practice and research as well as some recommended readings.

Trait and State Perspectives in Psychology

The fundamental question in connection with the trait and state debate in psychology concerns the primary determinants of human behavior: Are stable dispositions responsible for making a person more likely to act in a certain way, or are they the characteristic features of a situation which shape the individual's behavior? These seemingly opposing aspects are the focus of different areas of psychology; for example, personality psychology studies the stable dispositions called traits, whereas social psychology is more concerned with the effect different situations have on an individual's behavior, and in this sense, the particular state a person is in.

DOI: 10.4324/9780429321498-31

In psychology, the term disposition is used to label temporally stable tendencies of behavior, while "dispositions that characterize the personality of an individual are called personality dispositions or personality traits" (Asendorpf, 2009, p. 43). According to Allport (1937), the temporal stability of traits is ensured by their capacity "to render many stimuli functionally equivalent, and to initiate and guide consistent (equivalent) forms of adaptive behavior" (p. 295). As a result, a trait in personality psychology has come to be seen as "an internal psychological disposition that remains largely unchanged throughout the lifespan and determines differences between individuals" (Chamorro-Premuzic, 2011, p. 29). Therefore, a trait seems to represent a temporally stable tendency to act in a certain way across different situations, and it is found relatively stable throughout the lifespan. For example, extraverted individuals are likely to enjoy being the center of attention, and they are generally apt at navigating social situations regardless of their age. Moreover, traits represent continuums along which the population is normally distributed, which makes them different from personality types, seen as categories that a person either fits into or not in an all or nothing fashion (Chamorro-Premuzic, 2011).

Although thinkers as early as the ancient Greeks such as Hippocrates and Galen were already concerned with describing basic personality types whose traits are in some ways overlapping with modern taxonomies (Chamorro-Premuzic, 2011), it was Allport and Odbert (1936) who first attempted to taxonomize all the distinguishable psychological traits that characterize humans. They took on board Galton's (as cited in Deary, 2009) suggestion claiming that the fundamental traits of human personality will be represented in natural languages and collected and categorized close to 18,000 such terms (Allport & Odbert, 1936). It was the introduction of statistical methods like correlation and factor analysis by Cattel and Eysenck that made the reduction of this enormous number possible (as cited in Dumont, 2010). Consequently, trait models today typically contain two (see Eysenck, 1967; Gray, 1991), three (see Eysenck & Eysenck, 1985), or five (see McCrae & Costa, 2008, Norman, 1963) traits. The most popular among these currently seems to be the Big Five model (McCrae & Costa, 2008), which comprises neuroticism, extraversion, openness to experience, agreeableness, and conscientiousness (see Chapter 9).

However, besides personality traits, the current state of any individual, including cognitive, affective, and behavioral correlates, is also influenced by the situation or context they are in: "States refer to sporadic or ephemeral acts or behaviours lasting perhaps no longer than a few hours, or even occasional moods such as joy or anger" (Chamorro-Premuzic, 2011, p. 36). Although the powerful influence of situational forces has been demonstrated by several famous experiments of social-psychology, like Milgram's (1963) experiment on obedience to authority figures or the Stanford prison experiment (Zimbardo, Haney, Banks & Jaffe, 1971), "still missing is any technology for defining, for characterizing, or measuring them" (Wagerman & Funder, 2009, p. 28). Two immediate problems seem to be that of boundaries, concerning the exact points a situation starts and ends, and perspective, relating to the different viewpoints of the participants of the situation. Wagerman and Funder argue that identifying and describing important dimensions of situations could enhance a closer cooperation between personality and social psychology (Swann & Seyle, 2005) by making it possible that the situational effects are conceptualized along the same kind of general variables that are offered by the concept of traits.

Although the trait and state interpretations appear to be clearly opposing in what they identify as major determinants of human behavior (and trait theory has been profusely criticized by researchers pointing out inconsistencies of behavior across different situations) (Mischel, 1968, 1973; Shweder, 1975), studies show that personality traits do seem to have consistency both across situations (Epstein, 1977; Funder, 2001) and over the lifespan (Costa, McCrae, & Arenberg, 1980; Helson & Moane, 1987; Measelle, John, Ablow, Cowan, & Cowan, 2005). Moreover, it seems that the debate is no longer ongoing in psychology, as Brody (1988) argued "a trait psychology emphasizing extremely general dispositions can coexist with an individual difference psychology that emphasizes narrower commonalities and even with an individual difference psychology that deals with the parameters that determine performance on a single task" (p. 31). The disagreement actually appears somewhat artificially generated, even in retrospect, as one of the founding fathers of the area, Allport (1937) himself, clearly stated:

> A specific act is always the product of many determinants, not only of lasting sets, but of momentary pressures in the person and in the situation. It is only the repeated occurrence of acts having the same significance (equivalence of response) following upon a definable range of stimuli having the same personal significance (equivalence of stimuli) that makes necessary the inference of traits and personal dispositions.
>
> *p. 374*

While arguing for the concept of traits, Allport also made it clear that the effect of situations on the individual's current state cannot be ignored, thus clearly acknowledging the effect of contextual factors.

Trait and State Perspectives in Applied Linguistics

Applied linguistics is an interdisciplinary field with several different traditions and varied research approaches and methods, within which a wide range of individual difference variables are studied. Out of this large pool, we selected four ID variables because we think that the trait and state debate is reflected differently in each of them. In the case of anxiety, the trait/state distinction was apparent and openly acknowledged from early on, and researchers within our field opted for the middle ground, exploiting the advantages of both approaches. As regards motivation and aptitude, although in the past the trait interpretation of these constructs was dominant, situational aspects and the role of context are currently gaining more emphasis. This change is a result of new research methodologies being introduced to the study of motivation, while in the case of language aptitude the call for change arrived from advances at the theoretical level. Creativity, which used to be a neglected ID variable but whose popularity seems to be on the rise, is clearly interpreted as a trait in our field, and although there have been some empirical studies conducted on what might be seen as its state counterpart, flow, the state and trait interpretations have no interface in this case.

Language Learning Anxiety

When considering the trait and state dichotomy within the field of applied linguistics, the most obvious example to come to mind is the case of anxiety. Anxiety is an individual difference variable where the trait and state distinction was apparent from relatively early on within the field of psychology (Cattell, 1966). Spielberger (1983), the creator of the famous State-Trait Anxiety Inventory (STAI), made it very clear that in the case of anxiety, one term is used to refer to two different constructs: (1) "A complex emotional reaction or state that varies in intensity and fluctuates over time as a function of the intrapsychic or situational stresses that impinge upon an individual" (Spielberger, Gonzalez-Reigosa, Martinez-Urrutia, Natalicio, L. & Natalicio, D., 1971, p. 146); and (2) "Anxiety-proneness as a personality trait" (p. 146). In this sense, the first interpretation refers to an emotional state that arises in a specific situation or context, whereas the second describes temporally stable dispositions of an individual to feel and act in a certain way, and in this sense, it is closely related to the personality trait of neuroticism (Eysenck & Eysenck, 1985; McCrae & Costa, 2008).

A third approach that can be applied in studying anxiety is the so-called situation specific approach. According to MacIntyre and Gardner (1991), situation-specific anxiety "can be seen as trait anxiety measures limited to a given context" (p. 90). This means that individuals' anxiety reactions are measured in well-defined situations, like exams or foreign language classes. This approach seems to compensate for certain shortcomings of the trait approach with regard to the fact that situations differ greatly in their potential to evoke anxiety, and although individuals characterized by a higher level of trait anxiety are likely to exhibit higher levels of anxiety in a stressful situation (Spielberger, 1983), people differ greatly with regard to which situations and contexts they interpret as stressful for them. The advantage of the situation-specific approach over studying the exact moment of testing—that is, state anxiety—is that it allows certain generalizations which are not possible when considering one particular instance only.

The situation-specific approach is the one that has been adopted when studying anxiety experienced by language learners. Horwitz, Horwitz, and Cope (1986), authors of arguably the most widely used foreign language anxiety test, the Foreign Language Classroom Anxiety Scale (FLCAS), claim that foreign language anxiety is a separate and distinct phenomenon, which is particular to the foreign language classroom scenario. In the situation-specific approach, after providing a clearly defined context, respondents can be asked about those particular aspects of the situation which make them anxious. Horwitz et al. (1986) claimed that since the language learning process involves performance evaluation, performance anxieties are relevant to its conceptualization. Therefore, they argued that communication apprehension (McCroskey, 1977), fear of negative evaluation (Watson & Friend, 1969), and test anxiety (Sarason, 1980) all contribute to the foreign language anxiety experienced by language learners.

Recent publications discussing foreign language anxiety (see for example Gkonou, Daubney, & Dewaele, 2017; Gregersen, 2020) no longer address the state and trait dichotomy, but they tend to argue for a dynamic approach where anxiety is considered as one of the many factors which play a role during language learning, viewing it as a process and also emphasizing the temporal changes that are inherent in it. One such example is Gregersen, MacIntyre, and Meza's (2014) study that used the idiodynamic method to observe six pre-service teachers giving a classroom presentation in Spanish, their L2. Data deriving from different (physiological, idiodynamic, interview, and self-report survey) sources captured the moment to moment fluctuations in anxiety experienced by the participants, which raises questions about the stability of anxiety even within one particular situation or context. A less fine-grained but much longer time frame was investigated by Piniel and Csizér (2015), who studied the relationship of anxiety and motivation over the length of a 14-week L2 academic writing course using a variety of techniques. They were able to show the presence of different trajectories over time among learners associated with different profiles of anxiety and motivation, pointing to benefits of viewing anxiety from a dynamic systems perspective. The reason why the study of anxiety would benefit from the complex dynamic systems approach, according to MacIntyre (2017), is that "anxiety is influenced by internal physiological processes, cognition, and emotional states along with the demands of the situation and the presence of other people, among other things, considered over multiple timescales" (p. 27–28), suggesting that once the cross-sectional view is abandoned and time is introduced as a factor, it might render the exclusive use of situation-specific approaches inadequate.

Language Learning Motivation

Research into language learning motivation is concerned with the investigation of the amount of energy and effort students are willing to invest into learning an additional language (Dörnyei, 2001). Despite the fact that Brophy (1987) in his definition of L2 motivation distinguished between trait and state motivation (the former being more enduring, the latter seen as activity-related), L2 motivation theories until the end of the 1990s had not acknowledged important elements, such as time and context, in L2 motivational processes that would have made the investigation of state motivation possible. Accordingly, classic L2 motivation studies used cross-sectional survey designs to investigate students' motivation as this design offered a relatively cost-effective way to collect large amounts of data that allowed highly sophisticated multivariate statistical analyses, leading to a deep understanding of the intricate relationships among various motivational variables (e.g., Gardner, 1985; Dörnyei, Csizér, and

Németh, 2006). These studies, by definition, investigated the trait motivation of students and provided no insight into how L2 motivation might change over time in various learning contexts. Even when time was acknowledged as influencing motivation, such large time scales were selected (months or years) that it made the investigation of state motivation unrealistic (Gardner, Masgoret, Tennant, & Mihic, 2004). Accordingly, most empirical studies up until rather recently operationalized L2 motivation as part of large-scale cross-sectional studies and thus treated it as a characteristic personality trait measured to influence self-reported intended effort types of constructs. Even when classroom related aspects of L2 motivation such as task motivation were mapped, no differentiation was made between trait and state motivation (Dörnyei, 2001). State motivation cannot be investigated without adding time and context as variables in L2 motivation research designs and without theoretical frameworks to differentiate between trait and state motivation. The first theories related to the process (i.e. acknowledging temporal changes) of motivation have been proposed by Ushioda (1998, 2001) and Dörnyei (2000, 2001; Dörnyei & Ottó, 1998). Based on interview data, Ushioda established how L2 motivation fluctuated over time from being impacted by past experiences to being directed towards future goals. In a different light, Dörnyei and his colleague operationalized the different phases of learning being shaped by various motivational influences. These theories gave way to interest in the complex dynamic system theory (CDST, See Chapter 4), in which time and context became defining variables to be included in L2 motivation research. Dörnyei, MacIntyre, and Henry's (2015) edited volume on the dynamic nature of L2 motivation not only included a separate chapter on time but also had several studies dealing with L2 motivation as a state. De Bot (2015) argued that motivation should be researched from the point of view of different timescales as motivation to learn a foreign language can vary from one moment to another and may be influenced by different types of motivation on different timescales. Long term motivation may come from career plans, shorter term motivation from the wish to pass an exam, an even shorter term motivation from expressing a view in class (p. 36).

Some studies indeed juxtaposed L2 motivation's enduring nature, i.e., being a personality trait against its changing nature, and investigated it in a highly situated way for its state characteristics. Pawlak (2012) illustrated group-level changes in L2 motivation by asking students to indicate their level of L2 motivation for every five minutes in various lessons resulting in patterns of motivation with various levels of complexity. The changes in motivation were explained by a number of interacting external and internal reasons including topics, tasks, novelty, goals, group dynamics, and learner characteristics. Wening, Dörnyei, and de Bot (2014) measured motivation in five minute intervals for several lessons and showed how four students' motivation fluctuated in different ways during those lessons. These changes were explained by contextual and temporal issues, but the researchers also added that there were unexplainable changes as well. MacIntyre and Serroul (2015) decided to further narrow down the timescale for their investigation and employed second-by-second measurements to assess the motivation of participants during a number of different communication tasks. Their results revealed that state motivation was influenced by task difficulty in terms of topics and demand on vocabulary and there was individual difference in the volatility of state motivation, as well. Similarities among these studies not only include the fact that the contextual and temporal nature of L2 motivation was investigated using timescales of five minutes or shorter to investigate state motivation, but also the fact that these studies all used CDST as the theoretical underpinning for their investigations and employed multiple research instruments to collect data. The scarcity of similar studies might be explained by the demanding nature of these studies: Operationalization processes are not only notoriously difficult in CDST but researchers also have to juggle multiple instruments in order to measure state motivation in a reliable and valid way.

Language Learning Aptitude

Language learning aptitude has been traditionally considered and conceptualized as one of the quintessential traits affecting the rate of progress of individuals in L2 learning. Aptitude is a complex construct subsuming several independent abilities. Its classic definition provided by Carroll and Sapon explains that aptitude concerns "basic abilities that are essential to facilitate foreign language learning" (Carroll & Sapon, 1959, p. 14). More recently, Robinson pointed out that "aptitude is characterized as strengths individual learners have—relative to their population—in the cognitive abilities [which] information processing draws on during L2 learning and performance in various contexts and at different stages" (Robinson, 2005, p. 46). Despite the fact that a number of psychometrically reliable measures have been developed (e.g., MLAT, Caroll & Sapon, 1959; PLAB, Pimsleur, 1966; LLAMA, Meara, 2005), researchers called our attention to the fact that aptitude as a trait might not be stable over certain measures. Such examples include Skehan's (1989) observation that learners might score differently across the various dimensions of the aptitude tests, as well as Carroll's (1990) hypothesis that the execution of different tasks might relate to aspects of aptitude in different ways. In addition, both age (DeKeyser, 2000) and level of proficiency (Robinson, 2005) might affect learners' aptitude. All these results point to the fact that certain parts of aptitude should be regarded more as state than trait. Accordingly, Robinson (2002) conceptualizes aptitude complexes that describe the combination of a number of different cognitive abilities that need to be matched to foreign language teaching instructions. In other words, the contexts of teaching (e.g., implicit, incidental, and explicit) need to be taken into account when students' aptitude is assessed or researched. Still, at this point the extent to which the characteristic features of these contextual variables will actually shape the composite measure we call aptitude is unclear.

The idea of the "malleability" of aptitude leads to the consideration of the dynamic conceptualization of aptitude (Dörnyei & Ryan, 2015, p. 43) based on the argument that we cannot treat something as a dynamically changing entity unless it is conceptualized that way. The fact that aptitude has been considered as a trait is only an issue of conceptualization and can be overcome by developing a dynamic measure (CANAL-FT, Grigorenko, Sternberg, & Ehrman, 2000). The importance of this dynamic conceptualization of aptitude lies in the fact that more state-related pieces of information might emerge from research. As Dörnyei and Ryan (2015) concluded "an increasing willingness to entertain dynamic conceptualizations of aptitude—for example in the manner reflected in the CANAL-FT—could be empowering for learners and could potentially revitalize aptitude research by making it more attractive to classroom practitioners" (p. 70).

Creativity

Although, apart from scarce attempts (Albert & Kormos, 2004; Ghonsooly & Showqi, 2012; Karimpour & Chopoghlou, 2014; Naghadeh, 2013; Ottó, 1998; Smith, 2013), creativity has not been a frequently researched individual difference variable within applied linguistics in the past, its growing popularity is well reflected by the recent publication of a number of books on this topic in our field (Jones, 2015; Jones & Richards, 2015; Li, 2019; Maley & Kiss, 2017). Creativity is a term that is notoriously difficult to define; however, there seems to be some consensus about three key conditions for defining an act as creative: novelty, quality, and relevance (Kaufman & Sternberg, 2010, p. xiii). Difficulties in defining the term partly arise from the fact that, with regard to creativity, different aspects or facets can be emphasized, as seen in the labeling of the four (or more recently six) P's of creativity: process, product, person, place, persuasion, or potential (Kozbelt, Beghetto, & Runco, 2010, p. 24). Most of the studies conducted within our field adopted the interpretation where creativity is viewed from the perspective of the person, and in these studies creativity is typically conceptualized as the functioning of divergent thinking, a cognitive operation that is considered as a stable tendency to act in a certain way—that is, a trait. Divergent thinking has been hypothesized to be in the background of creativity since the publication of Guilford's (1968) Structure of Intellect model, and it has four facets: fluency, or the ability to produce a large number of ideas; flexibility, or the ability to produce a wide variety of ideas; originality, or the ability to produce unusual ideas; and elaboration, the ability to develop or embellish ideas to produce many details (Baer, 1993). The typically cross-sectional, correlational studies were able to establish moderate links between different aspects of divergent thinking and global measures of language proficiency (Ghonsooly & Showqi, 2012; Ottó, 1998; Smith, 2013) and some specific task performance measures (Albert & Kormos, 2004; Karimpour & Chopoghlou, 2014; Naghadeh, 2013).

When considering the state of creativity—that is the process of creation—a different term might come to mind: flow, which describes "a subjective state that people report when they are completely involved in something to the point of forgetting time, fatigue, and everything else but the activity itself" (Csíkszentmihályi, Abuhamdeh, & Nakamura, 2005, p. 600). The concept of flow was born when Getzels and Csíkszentmihályi (1976) set out to study the creative process and individual's subjective experience while being involved in it. Later, the scope of investigation broadened to include all kinds of intrinsically motivated, autotelic activities, and intended to shed light on the individuals' momentary states while experiencing such activities. In this sense, flow is a broader concept than creativity, but it is also clearly one where the state interpretation dominates. This is well reflected by the unique measurement method that was developed to capture flow, the experience sampling method (ESM) (Csíkszentmihályi, Larson, & Prescott, 1977). In studies using ESM, respondents are equipped with electronic devices like pagers or cell phones, and they are invited to answer questions regarding their momentary experiences every time they receive a signal. With the help of this technique, several self-reports are gathered daily at random time intervals, capturing a random sample of subjective experiences over an extended period of time. However, because of the demanding nature of this method, state-focused questionnaires are increasingly widespread in studying flow. Consequently, flow studies within our field (Aubrey, 2017a, 2017b; Czimmermann & Piniel, 2016; Egbert, 2003; Piniel & Albert, 2017) have all used questionnaires, as well. The above-mentioned cross-sectional studies were able to demonstrate that learners experienced flow during language learning and that there were links between learners' flow experiences reported in questionnaires and certain features of the tasks they were performing.

In the field of psychology, there are more and more theories promoting a system's view of creativity (Csíkszentmihályi, 1988; Sawyer, 2006) and ESM (Csíkszentmihályi et al., 1977) appears to be a suitable method for studying the temporal aspect. However, state and trait interpretations currently have no interface within applied linguistics in the case of this construct. This is probably the result of the limited number of studies on the one hand, and the prevalence of cross-sectional, correlational methods on the other. Although examining how creativity affects the language learning process over time would certainly deepen our understanding of its effects, carrying out such a study would definitely pose serious feasibility issues.

Conclusions and Implications for Future Research

Based on the discussion above, we would like to argue that the trait/state dichotomy should rather be considered as trait and state perspectives as both of them inform language learning processes in their own unique ways. Stable dispositions and constantly changing states can be reconciled to some extent when adopting a situation-specific approach. The stability that well-defined situations offer could be utilized in cross-sectional designs. If, however, time is introduced as a factor, a more complex approach might be needed. It seems that currently CDST might offer the best way for integrating the trait and state perspectives by offering a theoretical background to studies.

Future research studies should emphasize longitudinal designs to uncover possible changes in state characteristics by including an interactional approach between the trait and state perspectives. This means that we need to keep aspects of cross-sectional designs in consideration as they can provide a basis of comparison for situation-specific changes. An example of an idea for such a study would be to follow a group of learners over two school years with four instances of cross-sectional questionnaire surveys mapping some of their ID variables and their changes over time. During this time, situation-specific data could be collected from the same learners linking their language output, for example, to the state measures of said ID variables. Finally, the comparison of the matched datasets could be analyzed and results could offer both generalizable and transferable conclusions.

Reflection Questions

- Select an ID construct either from the ones discussed in our chapter or a different one. Think about how you would characterize yourself along this variable, considering it as a trait. Then think of specific instances when you either acted in line with or in opposition with your trait. What does this suggest about the consistency of behavior?
- Does the situation-specific approach offer a solution to the trait/state dichotomy? Why or why not?
- What research methodological approaches would you consider when investigating the interaction of any two ID variables? How would you set out to research trait and state perspectives simultaneously?

Recommended Reading

Dörnyei, Z. (2019). Psychology and language learning: The past, the present and the future. *Journal for the Psychology of Language Learning, 1,* 27–41.
This article provides a possible framework to research issues taking into account psychological approaches in applied linguistics. It does not discuss the trait/state dichotomy but rather it presents current challenges in the field and provides insight into the investigation of trait and state variables.

Larsen, R. J., Buss, D. M., King, D. D., & Ensley, C. E. (2017). *Personality psychology: Domains of knowledge about human nature.* McGraw Hill.
This volume offers a comprehensive overview of trait psychology, including discussions of trait taxonomies, measurement issues, and changes over time. Besides discussing trait psychology in detail, different chapters also address the person/situation interaction, offering the reader a deeper understanding of these concepts within the field of psychology

Lowie, W. M., & Verspoor, M. H. (2019). Individual differences and the ergodicity problem. *Language Learning, 69*(S1), 184–206.
This article illustrates exceptionally well how to put the individual back into ID research. Changes and interactions of L2 motivation and aptitude are researched. The authors explain how similar learners exhibit different learning trajectories.

Note. The writing of this chapter was supported by the NKFIH–129149 research grant.

References

Albert, A., & Kormos, J. (2004). Creativity and narrative task performance: An exploratory study. *Language Learning, 54,* 227–310.
Allport, G. W. (1937). *Personality: A psychological interpretation.* Henry Holt and Company.
Allport, G. W., & Odbert, H. S. (1936). Trait-names: A psycho-lexical study. *Psychological monographs, 47*(1), i–171.
Asendorpf, J. B. (2009). Personality: Traits and situations. In P. J. Corr & G. Matthews (Eds.), *The Cambridge handbook of personality psychology* (pp. 43–53). Cambridge University Press.
Aubrey, S. (2017a). Inter-cultural contact and flow in a task-based Japanese EFL classroom. *Language Teaching Research, 21*(6), 717–734.
Aubrey, S. (2017b). Measuring flow in the EFL classroom: Learners' perceptions of inter- and intra-cultural task-based interactions. *TESOL Quarterly, 51*(3), 661–692.
Baer, J. (1993). *Creativity and divergent thinking: A task specific approach.* Lawrence Erlbaum.
Brody, N. (1988). *Personality: In search of individuality.* Academic Press.

Brophy, J. (1987). Synthesis of research on strategies for motivating students to learn. *Educational Leadership, 45,* 40–48.

Cattell, R. B. (1966). Patterns of change: Measurement in relation to state dimension, trait change, lability, and process concepts. In J. R. Nesselroade & R. B. Cattell (Eds.), *Handbook of multivariate experimental psychology* (pp. 355–402). Springer Science & Business Media.

Carroll, J. B. (1990). Cognitive abilities in foreign language aptitude: Then and now. In T. Parry & C. Stansfield (Eds.), *Language aptitude reconsidered* (pp. 11–29). Prentice-Hall Regents.

Caroll, J. M., & Sapon, S. M. (1959). *Modern language aptitude test.* Psychological Corporation.

Chamorro-Premuzic, T. (2011). *Personality and individual differences* (2nd ed.). BPS Blackwell.

Costa, P. T., Jr., McCrae, R. R., & Arenberg, D. (1980). Enduring dispositions in adult males. *Journal of Personality and Social Psychology, 38,* 793–800.

Csíkszentmihályi, M. (1988). Society, culture, and person: A systems view of creativity. In R. J. Sternberg (Ed.), *The nature of creativity: Contemporary psychological perspectives* (pp. 325–228). Cambridge University Press.

Csíkszentmihályi, M., Abuhamdeh, S., & Nakamura, J. (2005). Flow. In A. Elliot & C. Dweck (Eds.), *Handbook of competence and motivation* (pp. 598–623). The Guilford Press.

Csíkszentmihályi, M., Larson, R., & Prescott, S. (1977). The ecology of adolescent activity and experience. *Journal of Youth and Adolescence, 6*(3), 281–294.

Czimmermann, É., & Piniel, K. (2016). Advanced language learners' experiences of flow in the Hungarian EFL classroom. In P. D. MacIntyre, T. Gregersen, & S. Mercer (Eds.), *Positive psychology in SLA* (pp. 193–214). Multilingual Matters.

de Bot, K. (2015). Rates of change: Time scales in second language development. In Z. Dörnyei, P. D. MacIntyre, & A. Henry (Eds.), *Motivational dynamics in language learning* (pp. 29–37). Multilingual Matters.

Deary, I. J. (2009). The trait approach to personality. In P. J. Corr & G. Matthews (Eds.), *The Cambridge handbook of personality psychology* (pp. 89–109). Cambridge University Press.

DeKeyser, R. M. (2000). The robustness of critical period effects in second language acquisition. *Studies in Second Language Acquisition, 22,* 499–533.

Dörnyei, Z. (2000). Motivation in action: Toward a process-oriented conceptualisation of student motivation. *British Journal of Educational Psychology, 70,* 519–538.

Dörnyei, Z. (2001). *Teaching and researching motivation.* Longman.

Dörnyei, Z. (2009). *The psychology of second language acquisition.* Oxford University Press.

Dörnyei, Z., & Ottó, I. (1998). Motivation in action: A process model of L2 motivation. *Working Papers in Applied Linguistics (Thames Valley University, London), 47,* 173–210.

Dörnyei, Z., Csizér, K., & Németh, N. (2006). *Motivation, language attitudes and globalisation: A Hungarian perspective.* Multilingual Matters.

Dörnyei. Z., MacIntyre, P., & Henry, A. (Eds.) (2015). *Motivational dynamics in language learning.* Multilingual Matters.

Dörnyei. Z., & Ryan, S. (2015). *The psychology of the language learner revisited.* Routledge.

Dumont, F. (2010). *A history of personality psychology: Theory, science, and research from Hellenism to the twenty-first century.* Cambridge University Press.

Egbert, J. (2003). A study of flow theory in the foreign language classroom. *The Modern Language Journal, 87,* 499–518.

Epstein, S. (1977). Traits are alive and well. In D. Magnusson & N. S. Endler (Eds.), *Personality at the crossroads: Current issues in interactional psychology* (pp. 83–98). Erlbaum.

Eysenck, H. J. (1967). *The biological basis of personality.* Charles C. Thomas.

Eysenck, H. J., & Eysenck, M. W. (1985). *Personality and individual differences.* Plenum Press.

Funder, O. C. (2001). Personality. *Annual Review of Psychology, 52,* 197–221.

Gardner, R. C. (1985). *Social psychology and second language learning: The role of attitudes and motivation.* Edward Arnold.

Gardner, R. C., Masgoret, A. M., Tennant, J., & Mihic, L. (2004). Integrative motivation: Changes during a year long intermediate level language course. *Language Learning, 54,* 1–34.

Getzels, J. W., & Csikszentmihalyi, M. (1976). *The creative vision: A longitudinal study of problem finding in art.* Wiley Interscience.

Ghonsooly, B., & Showqi, S. (2012). The effects of foreign language learning on creativity. *English Language Teaching, 5,* 161–167.

Gkonou, C., Daubney, M., & Dewaele, J. M. (Eds.). (2017). *New insights into language anxiety: Theory, research and educational implications.* Multilingual Matters.

Gray, J. A. (1991). Neural systems, emotion, and personality. In J. Madden (Ed.), *Neurobiology of learning, emotion, and affect* (pp. 273–306). Raven Press.

Gregersen, T. (2020). Dynamic properties of language anxiety. *Studies in Second Language Learning and Teaching, 10*(1), 6–87.

Gregersen, T., MacIntyre, P. D., & Meza, M. D. (2014). The motion of emotion: Idiodynamic case studies of learners' foreign language anxiety. *The Modern Language Journal, 98*(2), 574–588.

Grigorenko, E. L., Sternberg, R. J., & Ehrman, M. E. (2000). A theory based approach to the measurement of foreign language learning ability: The Canal-F theory and test. *The Modern Language Journal, 84*(3), 390–405.

Guilford, J. P. (1968). *Intelligence, creativity and their educational implications.* Robert R. Knapp.

Helson, R., & Moane, G. (1987). Personality changes in women from college to midlife. *Journal of Personality and Social Psychology, 53,* 176–186.

Horwitz, E. K., Horwitz, M. B., & Cope, J. (1986). Foreign language classroom anxiety. *The Modern Language Journal, 70,* 125–132.

Jones, R. H. (Ed.). (2015). *The Routledge handbook of language and creativity.* Routledge.

Jones, R. H., & Richards, J. C. (2015). *Creativity in language teaching: Perspectives from research and practice.* Routledge.

Karimpour, S., & Chopoghlou, M. A. M. (2014). The relationship between creativity and Iranian EFL learners' speaking skill. *Journal of Educational and Management Studies, 4*(4), 877–888.

Kaufman, J. C., & Sternberg, R. J. (2010). Preface. In J. C. Kaufman & R. J. Sternberg (Eds.), *The Cambridge handbook of creativity* (pp xiii–xv). Cambridge University Press.

Kozbelt, A., Beghetto, R. A., & Runco, M. A. (2010). Theories of creativity. In J. C. Kaufman & R. J. Sternberg (Eds.), *The Cambridge handbook of creativity* (pp 20–73). Cambridge University Press.

Li, L. (Ed.). (2019). *Thinking skills and creativity in second language education: Case studies from international perspectives.* Routledge.

MacIntyre, P. D. (2017). An overview of language anxiety research and trends in its development. In C. Gkonou, M. Daubney, & J. M. Dewaele (Eds.). (2017). *New insights into language anxiety: Theory, research and educational implications* (pp. 11–30). Multilingual Matters.

MacIntyre, P. D., & Gardner, R. C. (1991). Methods and results in the study of anxiety and language learning: A review of the literature. *Language learning, 41*(1), 85–117.

MacIntyre, P. D., & Serroul, A. (2015). Motivation on a per-second timescale: Examining approach-avoidance motivation during L2 task performance. In Z. Dörnyei, P. D. MacIntyre, & A. Henry (eds), *Motivational dynamics in language learning* (pp. 109–138). Multilingual Matters.

Maley, A., & Kiss, T. (2017). *Creativity and English language teaching: From inspiration to implementation.* Springer.

McCrae, R. R., & Costa, P. T. (2008). A five-factor theory of personality. In O. P. John, R. W. Robins, & L. A. Pervin (Eds.), *Handbook of personality: Theory and research* (3rd ed.) (pp. 159–181). The Guilford Press.

McCroskey, J. C. (1977). Oral communication apprehension: A summary of recent theory and research. *Human communication research, 4*(1), 78–96.

Meara, P. (2005). *Llama language aptitude tests: The manual.* Retrieved from www.lognostics.co.uk/tools/llama/llama_manual.pdf

Measelle, J. R., John, O. P., Ablow, J. C., Cowan, P. A., & Cowan, C. P. (2005). Can children provide coherent, stable, and valid self-reports on the Big Five dimensions? A longitudinal study from ages 5 to 7. *Journal of Personality and Social Psychology, 89,* 90–106.

Milgram, S. (1963). Behavioral study of obedience. *The Journal of Abnormal and Social Psychology, 67*(4), 371–378.

Mischel, W. (1968). *Personality and assessment.* Wiley.

Mischel, W. (1973). Toward a cognitive social learning reconceptualization of personality. *Psychological Review, 80,* 252–283.

Naghadeh, S. A. (2013). The relationship between creativity and Iranian EFL learners' narrative writing performance. *The Iranian EFL Journal, 54*(2), 180–206.

Norman, W. T. (1963). Toward an adequate taxonomy of personality attributes: Replicated factor structure in peer nomination personality ratings. *Journal of Abnormal and Social Psychology, 66,* 574–583.

Otto, I. (1998). The relationship between individual differences in learner creativity and language learning success. *TESOL Quarterly, 32*(4), 763–773.

Pawlak, M. (2012). The dynamic nature of motivation in language learning: A classroom perspective. *Studies in Second Language Learning and Teaching, 2,* 249–278.

Pimsleur, P. (1966). *Pimsleur language aptitude battery.* Second Language Testing Foundation.

Piniel, K., & Albert, Á. (2017). L2 motivation and self-efficacy's link to language learners' flow and anti-flow experiences in the classroom. In S. Letica Krevelj & R. Geld (Eds.), *UZRT 2016 Empirical studies in applied linguistics* (pp. 90–103). FF Press.

Piniel, K., & Csizér, K. (2015) Changes in motivation, anxiety and self-efficacy during the course of an academic writing seminar. In Z. Dörnyei, P. D. MacIntyre, & A. Henry (Eds.), *Motivational dynamics in language learning* (pp. 164–194). Multilingual Matters.

Robinson, P. (2002). Learning conditions, aptitude complexes and SLA: A framework for research and pedagogy. In P. Robinson (Ed.), *Individual differences and instructed language learning* (pp. 113–133). John Benjamins.

Robinson, P. (2005). Aptitude and second language acquisition. *Annual Review of Applied Linguistics, 25,* 46–73.

Sarason, I. G. (1980). *Test anxiety: Theory, research, and applications*. Lawrence Erlbaum Assoc, Inc.
Sawyer, R. K. (2006). *Explaining creativity: The science of human innovation*. Oxford University Press.
Shweder, R. A. (1975). How relevant is an individual difference theory of personality? *Journal of Personality, 43*, 455–484.
Skehan, P. (1989). *Individual differences in second-language learning*. Edward Arnold.
Spielberger, C. D. (1983). *Manual for the state-trait anxiety inventory* (Form Y). Consulting Psychologists Press.
Spielberger, C. D., Gonzalez-Reigosa, F., Martinez-Urrutia, A., Natalicio, L., & Natalicio, D. S. (1971). Development of the Spanish edition of the state-trait anxiety inventory. *Interamerican Journal of psychology, 5*(3–4), 145–158.
Smith, C. A. (2013). Student creativity and language performance. In N. Sonda & A. Krause (Eds.), *JALT 2012 conference proceedings* (pp. 285–297). JALT.
Swann, W. B., & Seyle, C. (2005). Personality psychology's comeback and its emerging symbiosis with social psychology. *Personality and Social Psychology Bulletin, 31*(2), 155–165.
Ushioda, E. (1998). Effective motivational thinking: A cognitive theoretical approach to the study of language learning motivation. In E. A. Soler & V. C. Espurz (Eds.), *Current issues in English language methodology* (pp. 77–89). Universitat Jaume I.
Ushioda, E. (2001). Language learning at university: Exploring the role of motivational thinking. In Z. Dörnyei, & R. Schmidt (Eds.), *Motivation and second language acquisition* (Technical Report # 23, pp. 93–125). University of Hawai'i, Second Language Teaching & Curriculum Center.
Wagerman, S. A., & Funder, D. C. (2009). Personality psychology of situations. In P. J. Corr & G. Matthews (Eds.), *The Cambridge handbook of personality psychology* (pp. 27–42). Cambridge University Press.
Waninge, F., Dörnyei, Z., & de Bot, K. (2014). Motivational dynamics in language learning: Change, stability and context. *The Modern Language Journal, 98*, 704–723.
Watson, D., & Friend, R. (1969). Measurement of social-evaluative anxiety. *Journal of consulting and clinical psychology, 33*(4), 448–457.
Zimbardo, P. G., Haney, C., Banks, W. C., & Jaffe, D. (1971). *The Stanford prison experiment*. Zimbardo, Incorporated.

27
THE SOCIAL/COGNITIVE SPLIT

Anne Feryok

Second language learning and teaching is distinguished from other teaching and learning by its object, language, but what is language? Although various people have looked at language from different perspectives, this chapter will view language as social actions or practices that are culturally transmitted. Furthermore, because of our brains' coordination of psycholinguistic and neurolinguistic functions that enable us to produce and comprehend, language is also physiological. Finally, because language expresses meaning, language is psychological.

The social practices of teaching and learning are facilitated through language and exemplify how human beings have worked together in groups for millennia. Communication through language has enabled our species to change the world to suit us, so that it is as social as it is material. Our remarkable accomplishments are attributable to our cognition, which distinguishes us from other species. Equally, human achievement can be accredited to social learning, which also differentiates us from other species. The difference between these two attributions is the social/cognitive split, which is fundamentally about psychology and language. Tomasello (1999), a developmental, comparative, and evolutionary psychologist, argues that language, cognition, and social and cultural practices are inextricably intertwined.

However, the sum of the social and the cognitive dimensions do not equal the totality of human psychology. The third aspect that underlies both of them, the physical—behavior, brain, world—provides evidence that we have human cognition and sociality. A physical brain inside a physical body that operates in a physical world are three necessary precursors of both cognitive and social approaches. So, if the social and cognitive approaches share this foundation, what is the split?

The social/cognitive split exists because diverse fields of study make different assumptions concerning the nature of human beings and their activity. The assumptions cognitive and social researchers make differ in terms of ontology (what the relevant phenomena are) and epistemology (how the phenomena are known).

In the cognitive perspective (see Chapter 1), researchers assume that the mind and/or brain holds the answers to their research questions. Since these processes cannot be directly viewed or measured, researchers postulate and then investigate by means of something measurable, which typically involves experimentation. The aim of statistical analysis in such studies is to be able to make claims about relationships that are generalizable—situation and context do not matter much, if at all.

In the social perspective, researchers assume that human interaction (see Chapter 24) and its social outcomes hold the answers to their research questions. These outcomes include socially mediated processes such as learning, constructs such as motivation, and structures such as class. Researchers propose constructs that are represented in or emerge from the production of discourse, from linguistic discourse to larger social discourses. Linguistic discourse is direct evidence of interaction and processes such as language learning. However, it may be only indirect evidence of a construct such as motivation for language learning. Interpretation of the data matters, but crucially, so does the situation and context in which the data were generated, making it difficult to generalize.

These differences are why social and cognitive research studies that appear to be about the same thing may be aimed at different phenomena that are explained by different theories and researched by different methods (Firth & Wagner, 1997). The split largely reflects the fact that second language acquisition (SLA) is a relatively recent discipline that developed by drawing on theories from other fields, and as such, the split is inherited.

The next two sections take a historical approach to show why the social/cognitive split arose. As the older and more established discipline, psychology has influenced SLA, which has also been influenced by applied linguistics and linguistics. It therefore makes sense to present psychology first, so its contributions can be referred to in the section on SLA. Subsequently, the relevant contributions of linguistics and applied linguistics will be examined.

Perspectives in Psychology

This section begins with a historical orientation to psychology, and then separately considers the cognitive and social approaches.

Historical Background

Many traditional academic disciplines began in philosophy and gradually became differentiated into separate disciplines. Psychology, the study of mind/brain in relationship to behavior and environment, developed into a separate discipline over the sixteenth and nineteenth centuries. Textbooks often describe this historical development as if it involved three stages: introspection, behaviorism, and cognitive psychology—which leaves out many other types of psychology (Costall, 2006). The three-stage history assumes that psychology is a science about cognition. Besides ignoring emotion and conation, it ignores psychology in the humanities, which disregards the social dimension. So, what are the key reasons as to why psychology split into the cognitive and social approaches?

The social/cognitive split is usually attributed to seventeenth-century philosopher Descartes. Descartes played a formative role in psychology because of his use of introspection. By introspecting on the deceptiveness of his senses, Descartes deduced that he must have a mind in order to be misled by his senses. He further deduced that since he was able to make that deduction, that mind was distinct from, and superior to, the body, by virtue of rational cognition. Descartes was also a natural philosopher (scientist) and believed that scientific theories should be deduced and subjected to doubt.

Deductive science was challenged when Francis Bacon articulated the scientific method in 1620, which had a profound impact on the natural sciences (Rees, 2002). It also influenced how psychology developed because it led the philosopher-psychologist, Christian Wulff, to propose two types of psychology: metaphysical psychology, which used deduction and introspection (as Descartes had done, although Wulff disagreed with his dualism); and scientific psychology, which examined physiological functions (such as sensation) through experimentation (Leary, 1982).

Both approaches to psychology were criticized by the eighteenth-century philosopher, Kant. He argued that neither introspection from philosophy nor experimentation from the natural sciences were suitable methods for psychology. Instead, he proposed that psychology was part of anthropology, and that it should be based on empirical data about patterns of human life (Brook, 2020). Kant helped separate psychology methodologically from philosophy, and in doing so methodologically disconnected it from science. Consequently, he pointed psychology in two directions: as a natural science and as a human science. Psychology began as an academic discipline with two aims.

Kant believed that humans do not respond to a real world of things (which we cannot know directly), but to our sense perceptions, which are mediated and organized by the mind and lead us to infer the real world. This view influenced the physician, philosopher, and psychologist, von Helmholtz, who also believed that the brain (note the shift from *mind*) mediated sense perceptions as a basis for inferring the world. However, he hypothesized that it was not an innate process, but a matter of previous sensory experiences and unconscious associations (associationism). The only way to know who was right was through experimentation (Hohwy, 2013). This associationism line of research, conducted with his assistant, Wilhelm Wundt, provided a great deal of knowledge about how the neural system works—evidence that still informs the widespread view of how the brain works. Wundt established an experimental laboratory and institute dedicated to psychology at the University of Leipzig in 1879. He defined psychology as a mental science and approached it through structuralism, which analyzes the mind or brain into parts and studies them separately in order to understand the whole (Hedman, 2017). Wundt proposed the theory of psychophysical parallelism, which explicates how the physical world develops through conscious associations of perceptions and how, as associations are repeated, they become habitual and unconscious. However, both perceptions and psychological associations continue to simultaneously occur (Kim, 2016).

According to Wundt, two processes—one physical, one psychological—exist parallel to each other. By dissociating these two processes, psychologists focused on different processes that eventually became different types of psychology. One was focused on physical processes; the other was focused on psychological processes. This dissociation sometimes involved the idea that one process is fundamentally the same as, or can be explained by, the other process, which is known as reductionism.

Physical processes were researched through experimental methods. One direction led to physiological psychology and focused on underlying processes, such as the musculoskeletal and neuronal systems, hence the branch of neuroscience (O'Donohue & Kitchener, 1998). Another direction led to behavioral psychology, the study of observable behavior in response to environmental stimuli, conditioning, and learning (O'Donohue & Kitchener, 1998). No mental processes are involved in behaviorism; whatever appears mental is reduced to behavior. Behavioral psychology dominated during the early and middle twentieth century, and its many types still powerfully influence psychology today.

Psychological processes were also researched through introspection. Wundt considered introspection to be merely a means of collecting data (Hedman, 2017). Others used introspection to emphasize the intentionality of subjective experience as always focused on *something*. That something can be our experience, including our psychology. It is quite literally *insight*—sight into—our experience, including reflective understanding, reasoning, and the self-regulation of conation and emotion. This understanding of introspection eventually became phenomenology.

When behaviorism and introspectionism are combined, behavior is considered to be the subjective experience of a whole person, and this synthesis resulted in the rise of Gestalt psychology. One branch developed in a social direction, and it is discussed below. If so many branches of psychology existed, why did cognition become the prevailing focus?

Cognitive Approach in Psychology

The cognitive revolution was an interdisciplinary effort sparked by computing and artificial intelligence in the late 1940s that comprises two core assumptions. One is that cognition is literally or metaphorically representational (mental symbols that represent physical reality). The other is that cognition is computational (mechanical procedures that always result in correct outcomes). Chomsky's (1959) theoretical linguistics contributed to linking these two assumptions by positing that language was an innate cognitive capacity to develop a representational system—a universal grammar that could generate all real grammars (hence the name generative grammar). He worked at developing a formal (mathematical or logical) means of representing this grammar, which made it compatible with computational processing.

The cognitive revolution led to the development of cognitive psychology. One popular textbook defines it "as aiming to understand human cognition by observing the behavior of people performing various cognitive tasks" (Eysenck & Keane, 2015, p. 1). It identifies "attention, perception, learning, memory, language, problem solving, reasoning and thinking" (p. 1) as cognitive and explains the function of cognition as orienting us to our environment and enabling us to make decisions about our actions.

The idea that agents such as human beings act within environments had been emphasized in cybernetics, the field that led to robotics, computer science, and artificial intelligence. Cybernetics is about the communication of information and control of behavior in animals, human beings, and machines in their environments (Ashby, 1957; Weiner, 1965). Several psychologists were inspired by this idea, including Neisser (1967), who had initially embraced the cognitive revolution, but became disenchanted by it and eventually developed an ecological psychology (Neisser, 1997).

More recently, the agent-environment idea has become a challenge to the representational and computational assumptions of the cognitive revolution in 4E (embodied, embedded, enacted, extended) cognition. Drawing on pragmatic, functionalist, ecological, and Gestalt psychological theories, 4E cognition is (a) dependent on a body, (b) embedded in the environment that the body depends on, (c) enacted in the environment that the body engages with, and (d) extended in the tools it uses beyond its body. Cognition is shaped and structured by dynamic interactions between the brain, body, and both the physical and social environments (Newen, De Bruin, & Gallagher, 2018). 4E cognition can be considered an integrated perspective that transcends the social/cognitive split.

Social Approaches

The social approach draws on the tradition of psychology as a humanities discipline—a human science. Like the cognitive approach, it begins in response both to Kant's philosophical critiques and to his proposal that psychology should be part of anthropology.

Inspired by Kant's work, Dilthey developed a foundation for empirical human sciences by distinguishing them from experimental natural sciences. Unlike Kant and other philosophers, Dilthey included emotion and conation alongside cognition (Teo, 2005), describing an individual as a psychophysical whole (Dilthey, 1894/1977). His aim for psychology was the description and analysis of consciousness as a nexus of the *lived experience* of individuals in their environments (Ash, 1998). The product of the interaction between an individual and the environment was called a Gestalt (Dilthey, 1894/1977), a unified internal structure reflecting individual experience in its historical and social context (Teo, 2005) that cannot be completely explained by analyzing and explaining its parts.

Dilthey agreed with Kant that introspection was inadequate and proposed a type of hermeneutics, or interpretation through objectification—the idea that the products of human culture, such as language, myths, laws, and institutions, were objective outcomes of human consciousness (Tool, 2014. The objective outcomes were empirical data that could be associated with the psychology of individuals within their historical, cultural, and social contexts (Dilthey, 1894/1977). Dilthey's method involved detailed first-person descriptions of familiar experiences (actions, thoughts, and feelings), and careful interpretation of these experiences in comparison to their social and linguistic contexts. Towards the end of his life, Dilthey considered how the mind objectified itself through language (Redding, 1982), a direction that suggests the relevance of interactional, discourse, and narrative analysis. His work influenced both phenomenology and Gestalt psychology, which in turn influenced 4E cognition.

One prominent Gestalt psychologist, Köhler, described a Gestalt as a relationship between internal brain processes and subjective experiences of external reality (Ash, 1998). The brain process and the experience are functionally equivalent in their form and structure. In other words, a Gestalt is not a symbolic representation or a computation. Gestalt psychology contributed to the influential work of Gibson (1979) on the direct perception of the environment and its affordances, which has contributed to ecological approaches.

Kurt Lewin developed this idea into field theory, the totality of dynamic possibilities in the environment and in the person, which interact. Lewin (1939) described behavior as a function of a person and experience—a whole person response to a situation, irreducible to individual sensations or stimuli, as opposed to what behaviorists do. Lewin influenced the Soviet psychologist Vygotsky (1896–1934), who sought to overcome the split in psychology by objectively explaining subjective consciousness. Vygotsky (1986) explained consciousness as the internalization of socially mediated processes through human interaction in the languages and cultures that emerge among people. Later, Lewin influenced the anthropologist Bateson (1972), who also drew on the cybernetic idea of agent-environment systems to develop an ecological approach to psychology that influenced humanistic psychology.

Humanistic psychology (see Chapter 3), also holistic, focuses on self-actualization, the basic drive of an organism to develop its capacities as fully as possible (Maslow, 1964; Rogers, 1959) and supports the notion that human beings are holistic, social, self-aware, autonomous, and intentional (Bugenthal, 1964). The idea that human psychology is best treated holistically also appears in narrative psychology. Bruner (1986, 1991) argues that our experience in its context is organized by narrative.

Bandura (1986) also argues for both social explanations of cognition and brain processes using an experimental approach. His social cognitive theory integrates both functional (or cognitive) consciousness and phenomenal (or social) consciousness and expands psychology beyond a mere neurological account of cognition. He argued that psychology should "advance understanding of the integrated biopsychosocial nature of humans" (Bandura, 2001, p. 18), indicating that psychology is an integral part of being human and needs to incorporate constructive collaboration across disciplinary boundaries.

Perspectives in SLA

The social/cognitive split in SLA has been influenced by linguistics and psychology. First, I provide historical background and then outline cognitive and social approaches to SLA.

Historical Background

Like psychology, linguistics was also split between two traditions before being declared a science. In the eighteenth and nineteenth centuries, linguistics from an anthropological approach was represented by Hamman, his student Herder, and Humboldt, who argued linguistics and culture were tightly intertwined, which contributed to the ideas of linguistic relativity and linguistic diversity.

Saussure, who established linguistics as a science in the late nineteenth century, criticized the lack of methodological clarity in empirical work and proposed that languages were autonomous systems, social institutions, and semiotic systems. Saussure's focus on autonomous systems led to structural linguistics, which, along with behavioral psychology, influenced the early efforts to develop a scientific basis for SLA.

Three other linguistic developments in the mid-twentieth century also influenced SLA. The first two contributed to social approaches. The Prague School, focusing on the functions of language instead of the structures, was complemented by increasing interest in interaction and was influenced by the sociological approach of ethnomethodology (Goffman, 1959). Ethnomethodology examines how conversational processes influence social interaction, and it contributed to the new disciplines of pragmatics and sociolinguistics. Functional linguistics and ethnomethodology led to discourse analysis and conversation analysis, which have strongly influenced social approaches to SLA (Firth & Wagner, 1997).

The third development was cognitive. Chomsky laid the groundwork for cognitive approaches by revolutionizing linguistics with a formal, rule-based, universal, and generative grammar. SLA was directly influenced by Chomsky's (1959) idea that the capacity for language was innate because its grammar was innate.

Cognitive Approaches

Generative grammar influenced SLA in two ways (Ellis, 2008). First, it directly created a basis for theoretically driven hypotheses that could be scientifically investigated within the cognitive sciences. Second, through its influence on cognitive psychology and first language acquisition, it indirectly influenced the direction of early SLA with the idea that first language acquisition was not a learned behavior, but an innate mental process. This evolution in first language acquisition research also influenced SLA.

These theoretical changes led to a major shift in how language was taught. Teaching moved from practicing language expressions and structures to exposing learners to comprehensible input, as reflected in Krashen's Input Hypothesis (1982). However, this method resulted in learners making many errors, since opportunities for language interaction or grammar instruction were limited to nonexistent. This outcome led to Long's (1983) Interaction Hypothesis which proposed that miscommunication in interaction offered opportunities for negotiation of meaning, therefore facilitating language acquisition. This hypothesis included, but did not highlight, the role of language production, leading to Swain's (1985) Comprehensible Output Hypothesis, which stated that by producing language, learners were pushed to shift from focusing on meaning to focusing on form so that their interlocutors would understand them.

These hypotheses underlie the dominant model in SLA, the interaction approach (Gass & Mackey, 2015), also known as the input-interaction-output (IIO) model (Block, 2003). In this approach, advocates argue that language learning occurs when learners notice the differences between their own language production and that of their interlocutors. Both exposure to meaningful input and opportunities for communicative interaction, in which feedback on output may occur, are necessary conditions for learning.

The interaction approach draws on its own extensive body of empirical research that links interaction and learning through research in cognitive psychology. This nexus has led to SLA research on noticing, working memory, and attention. Atkinson (2011) refers to Doughty and Long's (2003) argument for SLA being a cognitive science, explicitly embracing the study of mind and language through representation and computation. The influence of cognitive approaches has become so pervasive that it is often assumed to underlie studies that do not define themselves in any particular theoretical framework.

Cognitive science approaches do not necessarily share the assumptions of cognitive psychology. Cognitive linguistics, for example, focuses on the reciprocal influence of language and concepts by examining linguistic factors, conceptual structures, and cognitive constraints. Lakoff and Johnson (1980) argued that language is constituted by conceptual metaphors based on embodied experiences, and the field has since embraced the other Es of 4E cognition. SLA studies examine the influence of first language conceptual metaphors in SLA (Robinson & Ellis, 2008; Tyler, 2012).

Emergentist theories (MacWhinney & O'Grady, 2015) assume that language emerges from the interaction of simpler nonlinguistic factors. One emergentist theorist, N. Ellis (2019), has argued for a non-Cartesian cognitive science. He charted the shift in cognitive science from information processing to nonrepresentational 4E cognition. Embodiment is linked to cognitive linguistics because linguistic features and structures are modeled on physical experience and are embedded in ecological systems to which people adapt their activities. Cognitive structures emerge from adaptive activity and are reinforced and reshaped by enculturation, such as social learning and tool development. These cognitive structures are literally spread across people who communicate with each other, meaning that cognition is extended or distributed across people and the products they have developed. This account transcends the social/cognitive split because social processes are part of cognition.

Social Approaches

In the cognitive approach, social variables are, at most, indirect influences on the acquisitional process (R. Ellis, 2008). The social approach does not frame the social as a variable, but as the basis of human existence and the explanation of cognition. An increasing number of theorists and researchers has begun to consider more seriously this idea, which has led to a split between those using cognitive approaches (who believed multiple approaches would detract from building a single scientific cognitive SLA theory), and those using socially oriented approaches (who argued for theoretical pluralism) (Block, 2003).

This debate came to a head in 1997 when, in their introduction to a special issue, Firth and Wagner (1997) announced the social/cognitive split. They criticized learner discourse studies on communication strategies and input-modification, describing them as "individualistic and mechanistic" (p. 285) because of the cognitive approach of researchers. They argued that research should include social approaches with more data types, contexts, and analyses—a more balanced approach that they posited would contribute to "the evolution of a holistic, bio-social SLA" (p. 297).

Many of the social approaches that emerged in the 1980s and 1990s typically drew on sociology, including critical theory, practice theory, and poststructuralism. Although traditional sociological identity categories (e.g., class, gender, ethnicity) are still used, more recent research focuses on agency, individual subjectivity, identity, and investment (as opposed to motivation), all of which might be addressed psychologically. However, doing so would shift the focus away from individual subjectivity in relation to social structures, ideology, and power. While many studies use psychologically influenced interpretative research methods like those Dilthey advocated, others use narratives, based on assumptions that Bruner articulated.

Second language socialization (SLS), which began in the 1990s, explicitly embraced a synthesizing perspective that included psychology (Duff, 2007). Using sociolinguistic constructs such as indexicality and sociocultural constructs like communities of practice, SLS focuses on how ideologies, norms, and values are learned in communities through participation, for example, expert-novice interactions (Poole, 1992). Although SLS draws deeply on anthropology, including its use of ethnographic methods, Watson-Gegeo (2004) described it as interdisciplinary because it also draws on fields such as psychology, child language acquisition, and cognitive science.

Finally, the groundwork for an ecological approach was laid by van Lier (1996), who drew on Bateson (1972) and Gibson (1979). Besides focusing on how theory, research, and practice are related, van Lier (1996) focused on the social and ethical dimensions of language education, as illustrated by classroom discourse. His work drew on psychology through Vygotsky and the American pragmatists Peirce and Dewey, as well as other philosophers and social theorists. Van Lier's ideas would later be more thoroughly explored using semiotics and the ecological metaphor (van Lier, 2004). In many ways, van Lier's work encompasses the multiple directions and theoretical origins of socially-oriented SLA, yet is also directly grounded in and applicable to SLLT.

Other SLA theories attempt to transcend the social/cognitive split by providing non-cognitive explanations for cognition. Vygotskian sociocultural theory (SCT) (see Chapter 2) is the most established alternative to the interaction approach, arising around the same time as the interaction hypothesis in an article (Frawley & Lantolf, 1984) that raised many of the same points that Firth and Wagner (1997) would raise more than a decade later. The mediating role of language in psychological functions—such as learning—makes SCT obviously relevant to SLA and also clearly applicable to SLLT through *praxis*, the idea that theory should be practical and practice should be theoretical (Lantolf & Poehner, 2014). SCT's research agendas are strongly pedagogical, including how learners develop control of the L2, how learners construct new knowledge, and how learners are mediated by L1 and L2 concepts (Lantolf & Thorne, 2006).

The sociocognitive approach (Atkinson, 2011), as its name indicates, integrates social and cognitive approaches. Based on 4E cognition, it examines the "completed circuits" between a brain linking a body to its environment. The core construct of this circuit is alignment—continuous adaptation to a dynamic environment—which includes interaction among people. Recently, it has taken an evolutionary perspective, holding that interaction and teaching/learning co-evolve biologically and culturally (Atkinson, 2019).

Complex adaptive/dynamic systems theory (CDST) (see Chapter 4) espoused in both psychology and SLA, is a metatheoretical approach which has vast potential for overcoming the social/cognitive split. Perhaps the most ambitious theoretical work has been the Five Graces Group (2009) account of language as a complex adaptive system, which begins, "Language has a fundamentally social function. Processes of human interaction along with domain-general cognitive processes shape the structure and knowledge of language" (p. 1). Being framed socially and cognitively, CDST invites constructive collaboration among different approaches to language and its learning and teaching processes.

Integrated Perspectives

Efforts to overcome the social/cognitive split have been made in psychology (Bandura, 2001; Bateson, 1972) and in SLA (Douglas Fir Group, 2016; Five Graces Group, 2009), with similar insights. As Bandura (2001) emphasizes, human beings are inextricably intertwined biologically, psychologically, and socially, an idea that has been advanced through extensive research agendas on the foundations of interaction in comparative and developmental psychology (Tomasello, 1999) and in linguistic and cultural anthropology (Levinson & Enfield, 2006) for decades. These disciplines have been researching everyday practices that show the centrality of interaction to human beings. The interaction at the heart of being human is the interaction that ought to be at the heart of every language classroom. Despite extensive research on and in language classrooms (Loewen, 2015; Mercer, 2016), interaction is usurped by the institutional demands of time, testing, and tradition, even by experienced and well-intentioned teachers (Feryok & Oranje, 2015). It is a praxical problem—theory and practice must work together. However much theory may postulate and research may analyze educational problems, solutions require repeated acts of political will for the common social good. This requires both cognition and social interaction. Neither exists independently of the other, and neither can be understood or researched without acknowledgement of their reciprocal influence. There is no social/cognitive split in human beings, but there is a false dichotomy between the social and cognitive dimensions in academic disciplines and research.

Implications for Practice and Research

Cognitive psychology research in areas such as perception, attention, memory, and, obviously, learning in general, are clearly relevant to teaching and learning language in particular. However, the cognitive interaction approach makes no claims about its direct application to classroom teaching and learning (Gass & Mackey, 2015). Nonetheless, much of its research has been conducted in intact classrooms, and those who do make recommendations generally support providing learners with opportunities for meaningful input, interaction, and output. Providing opportunities for interaction figures prominently in lists of principles intended to guide teachers (R. Ellis, 2005; Lightbown, 2000). The interaction approach has changed SLA, apparently for the better.

Humanistic approaches (see Chapter 3) to language teaching, based on humanistic psychology (Buhler, 1971), were popular in the 1980s and 1990s and were championed by Stevick (1990). He identified the components of humanistic psychology as feelings, social relations, responsibility, intellect, and self-actualization, and added development and participation as specifically related to humanistic language teaching. One example of humanistic language teaching is the idea that teachers, like psychotherapists, are facilitators who create the conditions for change; the client or student does the rest (Edge, 1992). Such ideas were eagerly embraced by teachers, even if not by researchers. However, development and participation are central issues in SLA. Recently, positive psychology (see Chapter 5) has emerged to revitalize many of the humanistic themes, but with the aim of scientific research agendas and pedagogical implications (MacIntyre, Gregersen, & Mercer, 2016).

Of the integrated theories that concluded the cognitive and social sections, it is not surprising that SCT demonstrates *praxis* through the pedagogical orientation of its research and theory. Implications for SLA include the need for teachers and learners to develop intersubjectivity, or a common understanding of their aims; the use of explicit instruction so that learners know how to make meaning in the target language in order to choose the meaning they wish to make; and interactional opportunities for learners to use language so that they can learn to self-regulate their choices.

The social/cognitive split is largely a theoretical split, and therefore it drives research agendas. Some research agendas have pedagogical implications, others do not; it has nothing to do with whether the research is socially, cognitively, or integratively oriented, and everything to do with the aims of the research. Instructed SLA research, for example, is a mostly cognitivist approach described as systematically manipulating learning mechanisms and conditions, yet is clearly aimed at understanding how to promote language development in instructed environments (Loewen, 2015).

But in the end, when we are *doing* learning, teaching, and even researching, we are acting in our environment socially, cognitively, and bodily. In reality, there is no social/cognitive split.

Future Directions

In a recent multi-authored article, the social/cognitive split was thoroughly examined from various perspectives, including by two authors who argued it did not exist: N. C. Ellis (Hulstijn, Young, Ortega, Bigelow, DeKeyser, Ellis, Lantolf, Mackey, & Talmy, 2014) and Lantolf (Hulstijn et al., 2014). It is perhaps interesting that N. C. Ellis is usually labeled as cognitive, and Lantolf is usually labeled as social, despite both of them regularly stating that both the social and the cognitive are necessary for language learning and development.

A recent cognitively oriented book by N. C. Ellis, Römer, and O'Donnell (2016) begins by asking, "How do we learn language while engaging in communication?" (p. 23). The authors take a broad complex adaptive systems approach, with a usage-based approach to the acquisition and processing of construction grammar in L1 and L2 users. In a special issue using a similar range of cognitive theories, editors Rebuschat, Meurers, and McEnery (2017) have included pedagogically oriented studies on second language learning. This special issue showed that cognitive approaches in SLA are relevant to pedagogy, just like instructed SLA (Loewen, 2015).

A recent special issue on transdisciplinarity edited by Duff and Byrnes (2019) includes many socially oriented articles, but also a cognitively oriented one (N. C. Ellis, 2019). As the editor's note, most of the articles are theoretical or conceptual. However, a more pedagogically oriented social approach appeared in another special issue on teachables and learnables, edited by Eskildsen and Majlesi (2018), which offered a strongly empirical approach with pedagogical implications. This approach is another future direction.

These four examples show how difficult the social/cognitive split is to overcome. Even with the best intentions, research tends to fall into one camp or the other because good research must be ontologically and methodologically aligned. The efforts of Ortega (2013), Hulstijn et al. (2014), The Douglas Fir Group (2016), and N. C. Ellis (2019) are important as they suggest that perhaps the split itself is not as important as is the exchange of ideas in an atmosphere in which everyone tries to understand each other *before* they argue with each other. This effort is, after all, the very basis of the social approach *and* the cognitive approach, which share the common purpose of understanding (a cognitive activity) ourselves (embodied human beings) while using and learning language (a social activity).

Reflection Questions

- To what extent do you feel that there is a social/cognitive split in research in SLA?
- In what ways do you feel that the social/cognitive distinction influences how we understand learning and teaching?
- To what extent has the social/cognitive split influenced your work in SLA?

Recommended Reading

Duff, P. A., & Byrnes, H. (2019). SLA across disciplinary borders. [Special Issue]. *The Modern Language Journal, 103* (Supplement).
This special issue provides a theoretical perspective on transdisciplinarity. It includes current critical commentary.

Firth, A., & Wagner, J. (1997). On discourse, communication, and (some) fundamental concepts in SLA research. [Special issue]. *The Modern Language Journal, 81*(3).
This special issue draws attention to the split. Both sides are presented, and both sides take polemical positions.

Hulstijn, J. H., Young, R. F., Ortega, L., Bigelow, M., DeKeyser, R., Ellis, N. C., Lantolf, J. P., Mackey, A., & Talmy, S. (2014). Bridging the gap: Cognitive and social approaches to research in second language learning and teaching. *Studies in Second Language Acquisition, 36*, 361–421.
This article offers a balanced presentation of the social/cognitive split. It includes critical responses to each perspective.

References

Ash, M. G. (1998). *Gestalt psychology in German culture, 1890–1967: Holism and the quest for objectivity*. Cambridge University Press.
Ashby, W. R. (1957). *An introduction to cybernetics*. Chapman & Hall.
Atkinson, D. (2011). *Alternative approaches to second language acquisition*. Routledge.
Atkinson, D. (2019). Beyond the brain: Intercorporeality and co-operative action for SLA studies. *The Modern Language Journal, 103*(4), 724–738.
Bandura, A. (1986). *Social foundations of thought and actions: a social cognitive theory*. Prentice Hall.
Bandura, A. (2001). Social cognitive theory: An agentic perspective. *Annual Review of Psychology, 52*, 1–26.
Bateson, G. (1972). Steps to an ecology of mind: Collected essays in anthropology, psychiatry, evolution, and epistemology. University of Chicago.
Block, D. (2003). *The social turn in second language acquisition*. Georgetown University Press.
Brook, A. (2020). Kant's view of the mind and consciousness of self. *The Stanford Encyclopedia of Philosophy*. plato.stanford.edu/archives/spr2020/entries/kant-mind/
Bruner, J. S. (1986). *Actual minds, possible worlds*. Harvard University Press.
Bruner, J. S. (1991). The narrative construction of reality. *Critical Inquiry, 18*, 1–21.
Buhler, C. (1971). Basic theoretical concepts of humanistic psychology. *American Psychologist, 26*, 378–386.
Bugental, J. F. T. (1964). The third force in psychology. *Journal of Humanistic Psychology, 4*, 19–25.
Chomsky, N. (1959). A review of Skinner's verbal behavior. *Language, 35*, 26–58.
Costall, A. (2006). Introspectionism and the mythical origins of scientific psychology. *Consciousness and Cognition, 15*, 634–654.
Dilthey, W. (1977). *Descriptive psychology and historical understanding*. (R. M. Zaner, Trans.) Martinus Nijhoff. (Original work published 1894)

Doughty, C. J., & Long, M. H. (Eds.). (2003). *The handbook of second language acquisition*. Blackwell.
Douglas Fir Group. (2016). A transdisciplinary framework for SLA in a multilingual world. *The Modern Language Journal, 100*(S1), 19–47.
Duff, P. A. (2007). Second language socialization as sociocultural theory: Insights and issues. *Language Teaching, 40*, 309–319.
Duff, P. A., & Byrnes, H. (2019). SLA across disciplinary borders: Introduction to the special issue. *The Modern Language Journal, 103*, 3–5.
Edge, J. (1992). Co-operative development. *ELT Journal, 46*, 62–70.
Ellis, N. C. (2019). Essentials of a theory of language cognition. *The Modern Language Journal, 103*, 39–60.
Ellis, N. C., Römer, U., & O'Donnell, M. B. (2016). Usage-based approaches to language acquisition and processing. *Cognitive and corpus investigations of construction grammar*. Wiley-Blackwell.
Ellis, R. (2005). Principles of instructed language learning. *System, 33*, 209–244.
Ellis, R. (2008). *The study of second language acquisition*. Oxford University Press.
Enfield, N. J., & Levinson, S. C. (2006). *Roots of human sociality*. Berg.
Eskildsen, S. W., & Majlesi, A. R. (2018). Learnables and teachables in second language talk: Advancing a social reconceptualization of central SLA tenets. Introduction to the Special Issue. *Modern Language Journal, 102*(Supplement), 3–10.
Eysenck, M. W., & Keane, M. T. (2015). *Cognitive psychology: A student's handbook*. Routledge.
Feryok, A., & Oranje, J. O. (2015). Adopting a cultural portfolio project in teaching German as a foreign language: Language teacher cognition as a dynamic system. *The Modern Language Journal, 99*(3), 546–564.
Firth, A., & Wagner, J. (1997). On discourse, communication, and (some) fundamental concepts in SLA research. *The Modern Language Journal, 81*, 285–300.
"Five Graces Group," Beckner, C., Blythe, R., Bybee, J., Christiansen, M. H., Croft, W., Ellis, N. C., Holland, J., Ke, J., Larsen-Freeman, D., & Schoenemann, T. (2009). Language is a complex adaptive system: Position paper. *Language Learning, 59*, 1–26.
Frawley, W., & Lantolf, J. P. (1984). Speaking as self-order: A critique of orthodox L2 research. *Studies in Second Language Acquisition, 6*, 143–159.
Gass, S. M., & Mackey, A. (2015). Input, interaction, and output in second language acquisition. In B. VanPatten & J. Williams (eds.), *Theories in second language acquisition* (2nd ed.). Routledge, 180–206.
Gibson, J. J. (1979). *The ecological approach to visual perception*. Houghton Mifflin.
Goffman, E. (1959/2002). *The presentation of self in everyday life*. Anchor.
Hedman, A. (2017). *Consciousness from a Broad Perspective*. Springer.
Hohwy, J. (2013). *The predictive mind*. Oxford University Press.
Hulstijn, J. H., Young, R. F., Ortega, L., Bigelow, M., DeKeyser, R., Ellis, N. C., Lantolf, J. P., Mackey, A., & Talmy, S. (2014). Bridging the gap: Cognitive and social approaches to research in second language learning and teaching. *Studies in Second Language Acquisition, 36*, 361–421.
Kim, A. (2016, Fall). Wilhelm Maximilian Wundt. *The Stanford encyclopedia of philosophy*.
Krashen, S. D. (1982). Principles and practice in second language acquisition. Pergamon.
Lakoff, G., & Johnson, M. (1980). *Metaphors we live by*. University of Chicago Press.
Lantolf, J. P., & Thorne, S. L. (2006). *Sociocultural theory and the sociogenesis of second language development*. Oxford University Press.
Lantolf, J. P., & Poehner, M. E. (2014). *Sociocultural theory and the pedagogical imperative in L2 education: Vygotskian praxis and the research/practice divide*. Routledge.
Leary, D. E. (1982). Immanuel Kant and the development of modern psychology. In W. R. Woodward & M. G. Ash (eds.), *The problematic science: Psychology in nineteenth-century thought* (pp. 17–42). Praeger.
Lewin, K. (1939). Field theory and experiment in social psychology: Concepts and methods. *American Journal of Sociology, 44*, 868–896.
Lightbown, P. M. (2000). Anniversary article. Classroom SLA research and second language teaching. *Applied Linguistics, 21*, 431–462.
Loewen, S. (2015). *Introduction to instructed second language acquisition*. Routledge.
Long, M. H. (1983). Native speaker/non-native speaker conversation and the negotiation of comprehensible input. *Applied Linguistics, 4*, 126–141.
MacIntyre, P., Gregersen, T., & Mercer, S. (eds.). (2016). *Positive psychology in SLA*. Multilingual Matters.
MacWhinney, B., & O'Grady, W. (eds.). (2015). *The handbook of language emergence*. John Wiley & Sons.
Maslow, A. H. (1964). Further notes of the psychology of being. *Journal of Humanistic Psychology, 4*(1), 4–58.
Mercer, S. (2016). Complexity and language teaching. In G. Hall (Ed.), *The Routledge handbook of English language teaching* (pp. 473–485). Routledge.
Neisser, U. (1967). *Cognitive psychology*. Appleton-Century-Crofts.

Neisser, U. (1997). The ecological study of memory. *Philosophical Transactions of the Royal Society of London. Series B: Biological Sciences, 352*(1362), 1697–1701.

Newen, A., De Bruin, L., & Gallagher, S. (Eds.). (2018). 4E cognition: Historical roots, key concepts, and central issues. In A. Newen, L. De Bruin, & S. Gallagher, S. (eds.). *The Oxford handbook of 4E cognition* (pp. 3–15). Oxford University Press.

O'Donohue, W., & Kitchener, R. (Eds.). (1998). *Handbook of behaviorism*. Elsevier.

Ortega, L. (2013). SLA for the 21st century: Disciplinary progress, transdisciplinary relevance, and the bi/multilingual turn. *Language Learning, 63,* 1–24.

Poole, D. (1992). Language socialization in the second language classroom. *Language Learning, 42,* 593–616.

Rebuschat, P. E., Meurers, D., & McEnery, T. (2017). Language learning research at the intersection of experimental, computational and corpus-based approaches. *Language Learning, 67*(S1), 6–13.

Redding, P. (1982). Action, language and text: Dilthey's conception of the understanding. *Philosophy & Social Criticism, 9*(2), 228–244.

Robinson, P., & Ellis, N. C. (Eds.). (2008). *Handbook of cognitive linguistics and second language acquisition.* Routledge.

Rogers, C. (1959). A theory therapy, personality and interpersonal relationships as developed in the client-centered framework. In S. Koch (Ed.), *Psychology: A study of science. Vol. 3: Formulations of the person and the social context* (pp. 184–256). McGraw Hill.

Rees, G. (2002). Reflections on the reputation of Francis Bacon's philosophy. *Huntington Library Quarterly, 65,* 379–394.

Robinson, P., & Ellis, N. C. (Eds.). (2008). *Handbook of cognitive linguistics and second language acquisition.* Routledge.

Stevick, E. (1990). *Humanism in language teaching: A critical perspective*. Oxford University Press.

Swain, M. (1985). Communicative competence Some roles of comprehensible input and comprehensible output in its development. In S. Gass & C. Madden (eds.), *Input and second language acquisition*. Newbury House.

Teo, T. (2005). *The critique of psychology: From Kant to postcolonial theory*. Springer Science & Business Media.

Tomasello, M. (1999). *The cultural origins of human cognition*. Harvard University Press.

Tool, A. (2014). William Dilthey. In J. Helin, T. Hernes, D. Hjorth & R. Holt (eds.), *The Oxford handbook of process philosophy and organization studies* (pp. 129–142). Oxford University Press.

Tyler, A. (2012). *Cognitive linguistics and second language learning: Theoretical bases and experimental evidence*. Routledge.

van Lier, L. (1996). *Interaction in the language curriculum: Awareness, autonomy and authenticity*. Longman.

van Lier, L. (2004). *The ecology and semiotics of language learning: A sociocultural perspective*. Kluwer Academic Publishers.

Vygotsky, L. S. (1986). *Thought and language*. MIT.

Watson-Gegeo, K. (2004). Mind, language, and epistemology: Toward a language socialization paradigm for SLA. *Modern Language Journal, 88,* 331–350.

Wiener, N. (1965). *Cybernetics or control and communication in the animal and the machine* (2nd ed.). MIT Press.

28
THE MIND-BODY SPLIT

Steven G. McCafferty

The mind-body split is one of those intractable problems that has been around for centuries, at least in the West. In practical terms, we experience both a mind and a body, although we seem to forget about our body when engaged in heightened mental activity (solving a math problem, day dreaming, and so on). For a professional athlete, on the other hand, it is better not to think, that is, to stay centered in the body and in the moment, although, of course, to do so actually entails the unity of mind and body. It typically does not occur to us, however, that the mind and the body can be considered as completely separate, unless we grow up in a religious or spiritual community in which explicit distinctions are drawn between mind, body, spirit, and soul. Yet, how the mind and body might be separate and influence one another at the same time is a question that has persisted in Western philosophy and psychology up until the present and has become a major focus for neuroscience, particularly with regard to the science of consciousness.

This chapter unfolds by first examining different views in philosophy and psychology that have surrounded the mind-body split from the Enlightenment up until the present, at which point the focus turns to two different perspectives within consciousness science. This is followed by a consideration of the mind-body split in language before addressing SLA practice and research directly. It is critical to first lay a foundation for how our subjective experience of the world is incorporated into language and how it has been studied linguistically and psychologically in order to establish parameters that need to be considered as central to second language learning and teaching. This section begins with a consideration of language and embodiment; that is, how the two have been separated in the use of "scientific" language but highly interrelated in the use of "everyday" language together with embodied forms of communication such as gesture, facial expression, and bodily movement. This is followed by a discussion of language in the mind and brain. The next section of the chapter focuses on implications for practice and research. The final section, which addresses future directions, argues that perhaps the most prominent theory within neuroscience with regard to the study of phenomenal consciousness, integrated information theory, offers a very different perspective on mind-body relations than that of the central theory within cognitive psychology, the global neuronal workspace hypothesis, and that there are important implications for this in relation to psychology and its application to SLA research and pedagogy.

The Mind-Body Split in Psychology

In the modern philosophical era, starting with the Enlightenment in the 1600s, René Descartes, in his famous dictum, originally stated as "*Je pense, donc je suis*" in French (I am conscious, I exist), which was later translated as "*cogito ergo sum*" in Latin (I think therefore I am), essentially stated that mind is separate from matter, although certainly he was not the first to make such an observation. However, others in the philosophical community of his time pointed out to him that if mind and body are different, then one cannot influence the other (a dualism), that both would need to be physical for such a causal interaction (Westphal, 2016, pp. 15–17). Descartes, after pondering the matter further, arrived at the conclusion that the pineal gland serves as the seat of the immortal soul, including the mind, but chose not to address how mind/soul as "substance" might influence matter as "substance." Also, Descartes (1649/2005) theorized that emotions are biological, belonging to the corporeal world of the body (matter) and so not associated with mental faculties, which, he believed, are meant to exercise control over emotions, following his dualistic stance (Fossa, Pérez, & Marcotti, 2019, p. 3).

Baruch (Benedict) Spinoza, a relatively close contemporary of Descartes, and who built his metaphysics on Descartes, viewed the mind-body problem differently, believing in the unity of God/nature, including, it is said, that God has a body (a heretical view which might have contributed to his being cast out of the synagogue). Spinoza's book, *Ethics* (1667/1980), is thought to effectively counter Descartes's dualism, although his own perspective, that ideas and objects are modifications of the same substance, has not received a particularly favorable response within philosophy for the most part. For example, Kant (1871/1997), a century later in his *Critique of Pure Reason,* argues that this aspect of Spinoza's metaphysics simply does not match "what is." However, for Spinoza, emotions and experience are very much a part of the psychology of being human in the coming together of body and mind/soul, and it is this disposition that most resonates in the present in relation to the current topic: "The idea of everything that increases or decreases, favors or represses the power of our body to work, in turn increases or decreases, favors or represses, the thinking power of our soul" (Spinoza, 1667/1980, proposition XI, p. 133, as cited in Fossa et al., 2019, p. 5).

Although the idea of phenomenal consciousness (subjectivity) had been recognized by Galileo during the Enlightenment: "I think that tastes, odors, colours and so on are no more than mere names so far as the objects in which we place them is concerned, and that they reside only in the consciousness" (Galileo,1623/1957, p. 274), the "I" in Descartes's dictum began to be addressed in Western philosophy in earnest with the advent of phenomenology, a view first promulgated by Edmund Husserl in the early 1900s, which was followed up on by others, notably Martin Heidegger and Maurice Merleau-Ponty. Husserl began by examining the structures of consciousness in relation to intentionality (the "directedness" or "aboutness" of consciousness), following one of his mentors, Franz Brentano. However, initially Husserl, like Descartes, focused on the individual and ignored both cultural-historical and embodied impacts on experience, a view which he later rectified to some extent by focusing on the "life-world" we inhabit and our experience of it as central to the structures of consciousness (Varela, Thompson, & Rosch, 1993, p. 17). Through his philosophical methodology, Husserl was able to effectively begin to explore the idea that the natural world is not the same as our experience of it, although he undertook no direct, practical study of the question.

Today, we are once again at a time in history when re-examining the mind-body split has become a major pursuit. The study of phenomenal consciousness was largely dismissed or denigrated outright by scientists until recent decades, but in the form of neurocorrelates, currently has become an industry within neuroscience, including neuropsychology. Philosophers are continuing to contribute to the study of consciousness, creating a period of relatively friendlier relations between the two disciplines, at least on this topic. However, the question of whether consciousness is physical or not has eluded neuroscience so far, although there is widespread agreement that it is associated with the brain (Revonsuo, 2017).

Physicalist Approaches to the Mind-Body Split

By the mid-1960s, cognitive scientists began to enter the digital world on a large scale, which provided another platform for anti-subjectivist views, and by the 1980s, researchers in the field had taken up a computational perspective of the mind (e.g., Fordor, 1983; Pylyshyn, 1985; Simon, 1979), focusing on the processing of information as analogous to the functions of a computer. The basic premise was (is) that the brain, the hardware, manipulates "input" (visual perception, for example) as coded bytes of symbolic information, which are then processed through symbol manipulation (the software), producing "output" (the color red). The use of "symbol" in this context refers only to disembodied, internal representations of external events and objects. However, the everyday process of human decision-making, for example, typically involves feelings, emotions, and experiences, which can result in strikingly simple and biased errors (not what computers do) (Tversky & Kahneman, 1981). More accurate/better decisions often require the opportunity to deliberate, to spend time examining an issue based not only on empirical evidence but one's feelings as well (Kahneman, 2011).

Because of its undeniable presence, phenomenal consciousness needed to be explained (or explained away) from a computational perspective. Cohen and Dennett (2011), for example, argued that phenomenal consciousness is essentially a byproduct of computational operations as carried out by neurobiological mechanisms, and as such, need only be considered as epiphenomenal, deeming phenomenal consciousness of little consequence in the overall scheme of human mental functioning (a position known as eliminativism). The leading theoretical view from this perspective within cognitive psychology is currently "the global neuronal workspace hypothesis" (see Mashour, Roelfsema, Changeux, & Dehaene, 2020 for a review), which is basically an attempt to explain how through consciousness, information is selected, interacts with other selected information, and then is globally "broadcast" back to all other relevant information, which can either stay the same or change. The extreme version of the computational approach can be found in the movie *The Matrix*, where life itself is an illusion or hallucination, a computer simulation, or at least when people are plugged into the matrix.

In relation to language development and linguistics, a leading voice for the atomistic, computational approach is represented by Noam Chomsky—his "black box" theory, the language acquisition device, which he attributed to unconscious functions in the brain as based on innate linguistic principles or "universals" (Chomsky, 1965). Furthermore, given the constraints of the theory, which focuses on how words are processed in relation to one another (syntax), the connotative dimensions of semantics were necessarily subjugated to the denotative, and semantics as a whole subordinated to syntax. For example, the English word "bachelor" would be coded as +male and −married. As such, there is no real reference to something in the world, only a symbolic representation—a necessary reduction for the purpose of computational processing (called "transduction" by Pylyshyn, 1985). This represents Claude Shannon's view of information as "bits" in the reduction of uncertainty (Tononi, 2012, p. 143). However, the validity of the external-internal correspondence of meaning can obviously be questioned. If words are associated and experienced with objects, activity, and feelings in the world, then their internal sense should not be entirely different, particularly from the perspective of embodiment (Varela et al., 1993). However, the physicalist study of consciousness has also led to other approaches within neuroscience.

Towards the end of the twentieth century, Francis Crick, co-discoverer of DNA, together with Christof Koch, in searching for a biological explanation of consciousness (the beginning of what has become the science of consciousness), identified what they called "neurocorrelates of consciousness." Koch (2012, p. 42) defines a neurocorrelate of consciousness as "the minimal neural mechanisms jointly sufficient for any one conscious precept," and provides the example of a neurosurgeon who stimulates a memory through placing an electrode on the surface of a patient's brain, which, dependent upon the location and intensity of the stimulation, can trigger the re-experience of an event, "a song last heard years before, the feeling of wanting to move a limb or the sensation of movement" (p. 44).

The formation of neurocorrelates can be studied using a magnetic scanner to record brain activity when seeing/hearing/smelling/feeling/touching/saying a given stimulus, experimentally tracking the difference in experience as well, for example, between seeing the ace of hearts (the playing card) with the ace visible and when masked (p. 46). However, this method has its limitations: There is no way to make the subjectivity of experience available for direct study. In other words, the study of neurocorrelates allows for the monitoring of neuronal activity, the tracking of where activity takes place in the brain, but cannot examine the interior view of that activity. There are "subjective measures" considered by Koch (2020, pp 17–19) as relatively shallow attempts at probing phenomenal experience. Instead, plays, novels, poetry, art, dance, and music, for example, provide more in-depth portrayals of the quale of human experience (see Edelman, 2006).

Additionally, and also starting toward the end of the twentieth century, Marcello Massimini and Gulilo Tononi (2013/2018) set out to investigate whether phenomenal consciousness could be measured in relation to neuronal activity, and if so, how. Existing tests at the time of their initial research were not up to the task. For example, fMRI scans can determine the amount of oxygen consumed by the brain, which although reliable in signifying the presence of neuronal activity, cannot discern whether neuronal activity as related to phenomenal consciousness is taking place (Massimini & Tononi, 2013/2018, p. 39). Also, use of EEG reliably indicates the shape of brain waves (delta waves during sleep, for example), but again, is not a sufficient index alone to conclude, for instance, whether a coma patient (an important medical and moral issue) is conscious in the manner we would like to address, that is, if the person we know is still "there" or not.

In order to test for the presence of phenomenal consciousness at any one time, Massimini and Tononi (2013/2018) relied on "integrated information theory" (IIT) (Tononi, 2008), as built on five essential properties of consciousness (axioms), not the brain, and as formulated on two basic assumptions: "A physical system has subjective experience to the extent that it is capable of integrating information" (Massimini & Tononi, 2013/2018, p. 63), and "each conscious experience is integrated, that is, indivisible, irreducible to its parts" (pp. 70–71). Information from this perspective is "a difference that makes a difference" and causal (Tononi 2012, pp. 346–347). Also, as Koch (2020, p. 85) points out, information on this view is "intrinsic and qualitative" as opposed to Shannon's view of information, which is "observational and extrinsic." Massimini and Tononi found that the use of transcranial magnetic stimulation as applied to the thalamocortical region of the brain (perturbation), followed by measuring the neuronal response through use of EEG, allowed them to track both the spread of neuronal activity past the immediate area of stimulation and the subsequent integration of information within the thalamocortical region as a whole (a unit of measurement, called *Phi*), satisfying both of the basic assumptions of the theory (Massimini & Tononi, 2013/2018, p. 86).

Over a period of more than 15 years of research, which included clinical trials and the fine tuning of their instruments and procedures in testing different conscious states and states of consciousness (e.g., wakefulness, drowsiness, dreaming, REM sleep, deep sleep, vegetative state), the researchers were able to determine that coma patients in which both the spreading and integration of information occurred in the thalamocortical region had a much better chance of recovering responsiveness than those who exhibited no such activity (Massimini & Tononi, 2013/2018, p. 131), taking a significant step both in terms of understanding phenomenal consciousness neurobiologically and possible clinical applications.

Moreover, within IIT, qualia are regarded as "phenomenological distinctions" that integrate to "build" any one experience, Koch (2020, p. 83) providing the example of viewing the painting, the *Mona Lisa*, in which "*Mona Lisa's* mysterious smile is one higher-order distinction within countless relations that make up the larger visual experience." However, as Koch acknowledges (p. 84), it remains a formidable task, empirically, to be able to account for the immense neurological complexity that this entails, and how a phenomenal state "feels" neurologically is something that also would need to come from future empirical research, although Koch believes that the theoretical "tools and concepts" are available to undertake such work (p. 88). However, understanding how all such information might be interconnected and integrated as causal in the process of psychological development, which would seem a possible application of the theory, is hard to fathom, although not inconceivable.

Nonphysicalist Approaches to the Mind-Body Split

The nonphysicalist perspective of consciousness focuses on examining the phenomenal properties of mind as opposed to the physical properties of the brain. The philosopher David Chalmers, in his 1996 book *The Conscious Mind*, entertains the possibility that phenomenal consciousness may prove to be a second element in the natural world that is not reducible to the physical. Chalmers is largely responsible for emphasizing the importance of quale in the study of consciousness, which he dubbed "the Hard Problem of consciousness," a designation widely used by physicalists as well. From this perspective, for example, we know that there are physical explanations for what causes pain, heat, cold, and so on, but have no such explanations for why each feels the way it does in the way that it does. In another example, if astrophysicists are able to conceptualize black holes in the universe in mathematical terms, what kinds of qualia surround the experience and how might this differ from the experience of linguistic conceptualization?

Another way to think about this point of view is provided by Nagel (1974), who asks us to consider what it is like to be a bat, that is, to understand how a bat experiences being a bat, a subjectivity that is unavailable to us. Our imaginations and abductive abilities (Peirce, 1872/1986) may be quite powerful, but there are experiential limits to imagination, we presume, although clearly, this is going to vary according to the individual and is another matter for physicalists to attend to in explaining the quale of consciousness. Furthermore, in contrast to the physicalist position, which rejects the nonphysical, nonphysicalism does not require rejection of the physical, but accepts the idea that the two can coexist. After all, we can think about what we want for dinner, that is, assess our feelings and desires, while accepting that our brain plays a significant part in facilitating the process. The extreme nonphysicalist position is the iteration of panpsychism wherein the universe itself is moving towards consciousness, that all matter has the potential for consciousness (de Chardin, 1955/2018) and the "idealist" metaphysical ontology, that matter itself is an aspect of the mental, a recent iteration of which was put forward by Bernardo Kastrup (2017).

The Mind-Body Split in SLA

Both the mind and body are necessarily incorporated into any one language in order to communicate both objective and subjective experience as culturally (interpersonally) and psychologically (intrapersonally) situated, and in this sense, SLA research and pedagogy does not involve a mind-body split, per se. However, there have been linguistic approaches, also utilized in SLA research and practice, that have emphasized grammatical structure, minimizing the subjective nature of language, as with Chomsky's attempt to stipulate universal grammar. However, other linguistic theories such as cognitive linguistics focus on meaning, which precludes any such separation.

Psychological theories applied to SLA have also varied in relation to subjectivity. As established above, cognitive psychology has been, for the most part, antithetical to embodiment, instead focusing on the processing of information (an in-the-head approach), not experience. Other perspectives, sociocognitive and sociocultural, for example, have incorporated embodiment, particularly with regard to social and environmental influences, and have included the body itself in relation to non-verbal communication and bodily influences on our thoughts and actions more generally. Moreover, neuropsychology has begun to focus on second language considerations, but within the contexts of examining what happens in the brain in connection to experimentally controlled experiences. Pedagogically, there also have been various methods and approaches to second language teaching and learning that have emphasized structure over meaning, for example, grammar translation, as well as pedagogical efforts to override this dichotomy, for example, the communicative approach.

However, as stated above, the key to both second language learning and teaching is the study of language, and in relation to phenomenal consciousness, it is critical to examine how experience at this level is manifested in language before turning to SLA and pedagogy in the following section. The first subsection below considers attempts to remove the body (subjectivity) from scientific language, and then, in contrast, how embodiment is essential to our use of "everyday" language. The next subsection considers how nonverbal forms of communication contribute to meaning-making, and the final subsection discusses language in the mind (private and inner speech) and the brain (neuropsychology).

The Subjectivity of Language

The subjectivity of language proved consternating to many intellectuals during the Enlightenment. For example, the empiricist, Francis Bacon, argued that because "words are the counters or symbols of notions or mental concepts," the wide-spread use of metaphor and other forms of figurative language as found in religious texts and everyday "folk" parlance disrupted the effort to establish scientific truth (mental representation only—the mind without the body). Instead, Bacon advocated using language in a way that portrayed "an honest interpretation of nature, a true path from sense [sensory perception] to intellect" (Bacon, 1620/1965, as cited by Olson, 1996, p. 164). Galileo and Hobbs shared similar apprehensions (Olson, 1996, p. 169), although Bacon and Galileo both wrote of "reading the Book of Nature," apparently choosing to "fight fire with fire," at least with regard to the use of this particular metaphor, which for Galileo and others involved mathematics, not language. The effort to restrict interpretation to mental schema is a highly productive aspect of meaning-making in relation to the use of "scientific" language, if not entirely successful; Johnson (2012, pp. 38–39) points out that the language of science is replete with conceptual metaphors, for example, within cognitive psychology the designation of "attention spotlights," which draws on the embodied experience of a controlling agent who both moves and focuses a spotlight in analogue fashion.

Descartes's dictum is a conventionalized philosophical form of discourse, making formal statements as logically interconnected, which in Descartes and Spinoza's time included the use of Latin as the language of logic. Moreover, dictums function as abstractions, the phenomenon of no one speaking to no one. And indeed, breaking the rules, that is, translating the French into Latin then English proved problematic. Many people reading the English version assume that Descartes was referencing only cognition as meaning "to think" and not consciousness, but the latter is also encompassed in both the French and Latin. However, it is perhaps the separation of the mental from the emotional by Descartes that has likely contributed to the interpretation that "thinking" is what he meant by what he wrote. Today, the restrictive, scientific use of language is in more than ample supply, which includes reductionism, for example Chomsky's use of the term "innate" to mean "genetically determined" (Smith & Tsimpli, 1995, p. 22), and is used across academic fields and other endeavors where meaning is meant to be confined to the realm of "interpersonal intelligent systems" (Tammerman, 2008), to the supposed exclusion of phenomenal consciousness, which is considered the purview of "everyday" language, and which often centers on the body.

Everyday language, also founded on establishing shared levels of interpretence (intersubjectivity), is meant to play a larger, social and phenomenal role in the sharing of human experience, which includes our feelings, thoughts, and interpretations as structured broadly within the bounds of the languacultural (Agar, 1994) communities that we come to inhabit. The use of conceptual metaphor, as in the example of "reading the Book of Nature," plays a particularly pivotal role in fostering shared, social understanding through language, and notably in relation to the current chapter, conceptual metaphor emphasizes embodied experience through relating the body (the source domain) to the nonphysical (the target domain), "getting a leg up" on the mind-body split. In a basic but highly productive example, Lakoff and Johnson (1980, p. 59) discuss how the preposition "in" operates metaphorically as a particle in relation to the body. At a concrete, prepositional level we can say, "Harry is in the kitchen," but we also extend this circumstance to say, metaphorically, "Harry is in love," which allows us to depict an emotional state as spatial, encompassing both mind and body in the unity of subjectivity. This expression is a culturally based rendering of a particular kind of embodied, emotional state of consciousness—romantic love.

Cognitive linguistics, or the study of how a languaculture construes meaning through linguistic form, takes a metaphorical (subjective) approach to language in general, emphasizing how meaning-making guides structure, not innate, rule-driven syntactical relationships, as in the two examples concerning Harry above. In each of these instances, there is a "figure-ground" relationship that is key to analysis from a cognitive linguistics perspective (See Langacker, 1987). The "landmark" (figure) signifies the entity that is the main reference point (Harry) and a "trajector" identifies how the figure is situated in relation to the ground (in the kitchen or in love). Additionally, "foregrounding" sets the referential stage for an utterance. For example, if someone asks "Where's Harry?", we could respond "in the kitchen," or humorously, "in love," depending on the contexts, a gathering of friends in the latter case. The "frame" also contributes to usage, for example, the word "uncle" has social, institutional, psychological, biological, and figurative meanings, in which the specifics of use are dependent on the discourse as framed by the contexts of interaction—discussing the family tree, for example. From a cognitive linguistics perspective, syntax is conjoined with semantics in formulating interpretation, embodiment playing a pivotal conceptual role in relation to both literal and subjective construal as in the second Harry example, which renders a phenomenal state of consciousness.

There are also semiotic resources (O'Halloran, 2011) in the environment that bring attention in different ways to different features of meaning and across modalities as contributing to language and communication. For example, "geosemiotics" is the study of the meaning systems by which language is located in the material world (Scollon & Scollon, 2003), and relates, for example, to how words appear on a sign—the font, the letter size, indentation, and so on, but also includes graffiti, and other representations. How content is formulated and inscribed as well as placement is part of how a languaculture/community has come to organize the world as a system of social interpretation, or how meaning is embodied socially at this level and contributes to the quale of experience. Additionally, societies assign different discourses to different places, which in some cases are constructed for events or activities (auditoriums, restaurants, theatres, swimming pools). These are all aspects of environmental meaning in relation to language use. O'Halloran (2005, 2008) emphasizes how we generate meaning by our semiotic choices (word choice, gestures, referencing things in the environment, the mention of book titles, films we have seen, and so on), which can serve to recontextualize discourse as well, providing a different vantage point or discourse frame. This approach is basically an extension of Halliday's (1978) systemic functional linguistics, which provides analyses of how we represent experience in language, emphasizing language as a social semiotic, embodied in contexts.

Language and the Body Itself

It is also true that the body itself is a physical/cultural form of meaning-making utilized for communication both with and without speech, for example, gesture, gaze, and facial expression; although it is important in relation to consciousness to emphasize the combination of the verbal and nonverbal in expression. From this perspective, the face-to-face use of language is an embodied act that is contextualized socially in what constitutes an "integrationist" as opposed to "segregationist" perspective on language (see Harris, 1998). Also, there are different communicative affordances that different modalities offer. For example, gesture (primarily movement of the arms, hands and fingers) occurs motorically in three-dimensional space, which affords the ability of direct, mimetic, iconic, and holistic representation. Additionally, gestures articulate nuances in meaning (qualia) through, for example, the rapidity of arm and hand movements, exaggeration of a gesture in space, variations in hand shape, finger articulation, and degree of muscle tension (see Kendon, 2004), all of which can contribute to meaning. Speech, on the other hand, unfolds in a linear, segment-by-segment fashion. However, it is the combination of speech and gesture (co-speech gesture) that has proven to be of most interest to the field of gesture studies, where there is recognition that the two synchronize in real time to form co-expressive units, one complementing the other in a process that is both dynamic and emergent (McNeill, 1992). Moreover, neurologically, complementary co-speech gestures have been found to increase other's comprehension in comparison to a mismatch condition, reflecting the semantic integration of co-speech gesture in the brain (Kelly, Kravitz, & Hopkins, 2004).

Facial expressions, another important dimension of nonverbal communication, are typically thought of as connected to feelings and emotions (see Chapter 14) and accompany speech and gesture as well. Darwin (1872/1965) argued that there are facial expressions found for both other animals and humans that indicate a link to evolution. Recent research corroborates his basic idea, at least in part, for "primitive" emotions—fear and disgust, for example (Griffiths, 2001). However, the degree of social sophistication across cultures and communities has led to the recognition of many more facial expressions as associated with feelings and emotions. Moreover, a limitation of many studies in the area has been the static nature of the stimuli—mostly photos. To counter this limitation, Jack, Sun, Delis, Garrod, and Schyns (2016), for example, used dynamic modeling of the facial musculature in relation to 60 emotions across two broadly based cultures, East Asian and Western, identifying four basic facial patterns (visible action units) common to both cultures, but arguing that there are cultural variances ("accents") as well. However, it is also important to note, again, that facial expression is part of a whole-body expression, which when experimentally manipulated in a mismatch condition (happy face, angry body posture, for example) is recognized as incongruent, indicating that facial expression is only one of the modalities considered in evaluating the emotional states of others (Meeren, van Heijnsbergen, & de Gelder, 2005).

Gesture, facial expressions, and so on all owe expression to movement, and with the discovery of mirror neurons in monkeys in the 1990s and then in the human brain (Gallese, Keysers, & Rizzolatti, 2004) came "simulation theory": the idea that we experience what others experience through their bodily movement, which also gives us access to other's emotional or subjective states. However, more recent research suggests that mirror neurons play a less significant role that originally predicted, that they are involved with low-level body movement discrimination, not reading the intention of others (Thompson, Bird, & Catmur, 2019). Moreover, it appears that mirror neurons are forged in sensorimotor learning. For example, there is evidence that people who are expert piano players and dancers have greater mirror neuron activity when observing others engaged in these activities than people who are not as proficient (Furukawa, Uehara, & Furuya, 2017).

Language in the Mind and Brain

Descartes's dictum, in addition to the discussion above, is a fine example of the human preoccupation with meaning-making for the self through verbal mediation—language in the mind. According to Lev Vygotsky (1934/1987), starting at around age five and up until around age seven we dialogue with ourselves; that is, we both ask and answer our own questions, mirroring the social practices that surround us as critical to psychological development, an approach to "self-talk" that has been widely confirmed (see Winsler, Fernyhough, & Montero, 2009). However, as children grow older, forms of private speech, as one might expect, are often no longer fully dialogically contextualized, instead it is that which is most salient to the speaker that reaches the surface as vocalized (what Vygotsky called the "psychological predicate"). For example, if an adult sees someone they know in the distance they might say "Oh!" but significance is registered in consciousness, private speech only an outward manifestation (McCafferty, 2018). The utterance might indicate a pleasant surprise, dismay that the person has not actually gone to where they said they would, recognition that the person had been lying, and so on, remembering that for Vygotsky, following Spinoza, thinking and affect are unified, although one might outweigh the significance of the other at any given moment. However, if others overhear someone's private speech, what is said, how it is produced linguistically, the accompanying nonverbal forms of expression, knowledge of the person, and environmental and other contextual considerations may reveal more to one person than another concerning the possible psychological origins and functions of the utterance, depending on shared knowledge, level of intersubjectivity, and so forth.

Although private speech continues to be produced throughout our lives, by age seven speech for the self "goes underground" through the process of internalization, becoming what Vygotsky (1987) called "inner speech." For Vygotsky, inner speech is the realm of phenomenal consciousness, where "sense" (*smysl*), which Vygotsky (1987, p. 276) defined as "everything in consciousness which is related to what the word expresses" as linked to the "internal structure of personality," prevails over "meaning" (*znachenie*). The overpowering aspect of sense (qualia) in consciousness is further delineated by Vygotsky (1987, p. 279) through his concept of "inner sense," which he describes as "incommensurable with the word's common meaning" (p. 279). For example, the word "soldier" for a war veteran may be embedded in life experiences in such a way that it resides in the psyche as highly individualized, despite familiarity with its use, across social contexts both with others of similar experience and society at large. Also, inner speech is close to thinking in "pure meanings" (p. 280), which entails "operat[ing] not with the word itself but with its image" (p. 262). The possible psychological materialization of these aspects of inner sense also should be apparent in relation to the example of the word "soldier" in the contexts provided.

According to Vygotsky, "Consciousness as a whole has a semantic structure. *We judge consciousness by its semantic structure, for sense the structure of consciousness, is the relation to the external world*" (1987, 137, underline and italics in original). There is, then, a dynamic, interfunctional semantic, embodied base in consciousness that develops through sociocultural activity in the cultural-historical environments we inhabit and through how we come to interpret our experiences over time in relation to personality as an aspect of psychological development, or *perezhivanie* (Vygotsky, 1994). Additionally, and in further relation to embodiment, David McNeill considers co-speech gesture integral to meaning/sense-making intrapersonally as well as interpersonally in relation to language, expanding Vygotsky's theory of meaning/sense beyond speech alone, but keeping to the basic Vygotskian premise that, "the role of linguistic signs is to *mediate* consciousness" (McNeill, 1992, p. 219, italics original).

Most of the mainstream psychological research in the study of cognitive psychology on private and inner forms of speech has not drawn a specific connection to consciousness. Rather, the focus has been on developmental functions, and inner speech has primarily been considered as "silent vocalizations." For example, McCarthy-Jones and Fernyhough (2011) devised a questionnaire measuring what they designate as dialogic inner speech, evaluative/motivational inner speech, other people (the voices of others), and condensed inner speech (the extent to which inner vocalizations are abbreviated). Experience sampling also has been employed in relation to phenomenal experience (prompting participants at random intervals to report their inward verbalizations) (see Alderson-Day & Fernyhough, 2015 for a review of studies). Additionally, inner speech has been studied as an aspect of neuropsychology, although again, primarily as inner vocalizations. Research in the area, according to Geva and Fernyhough (2019, p. 2), has included "hundreds of functional imagining studies [investigating] the neural correlates of inner speech," the findings for which suggest that "inner speech processing" takes place through the interconnection of different areas in the brain that combine as the dorsal language stream.

With specific regard to neurosemantics, reading the word "kick" was found to activate neurons in the motor area of the brain associated with the physical action (Pulvermüller, 2005), although this is dependent on semantic contexts—that is, when meaning is proximal or distal in relation to the core physical meaning (he kicked the ball vs. he was kicked out of school) (see van Dam, Rueschemeyer, Bekkering, & Lindemann, 2013). This connection has also been observed for other word-sensory combinations, for example, listening to words such as "cinnamon" or "garlic" was found to activate neurons in the olfactory cortex (González, Barros-Loscertales, Pulvermüller Meseguer, Sanjuán,

Belloch, & Ávila, 2006). Furthermore, Oosterwijk, Rotteveel, Fischer, and Hess (2009) demonstrated that having participants generate disappointment-related words led participants to stoop down more than when generating pride-related words. Rueschemeyer, van Rooij, Lindemann, Willems, and Bekkering (2010) also found that neural activation when reading the word for a physical tool, such as hammer, entails how that tool is manipulated physically as an aspect of neural semantic representation. However, concept words representing higher-level abstractions are thought to be primarily linguistically mediated (Hoffman, 2016), and so not processed directly through the senses. However, other abstract words related to emotion are thought to differ in terms of embodied experiential information (Kousta, Vigliocco, Vinson, Andrews, & Del Campo, 2011) and are found to include related facial and arm movements (Moseley, Carota, Hauk, Mohr, & Pulvermüller, 2012). There also have been studies that focus on the neurocorrelates of gesture in relation to semantics. For example, a neural connection between concrete gestures and concrete words has been observed to be stronger than that for abstract words (Levey-Drori & Henik, 2006; West & Holcomb, 2000). But as indicated above, these studies do not speak directly to the qualia of what the word "kick" actually feels like to the listener/reader in relation to the contexts provided, which is an aspect of both proprioception and affect in relation to qualia.

The area of neuropsychology that would seem closest to the concerns of Vygotsky's view of inner speech as associated with sense focuses on synesthesia, or the cross-modal phenomenon where "one attribute of a stimulus (e.g., its sound, shape, or meaning) leads to the conscious experience of an additional attribute." For example, "the word 'Philip' may taste of sour oranges, the letter A may be luminous red, a C# note on the violin may be a brown funny line extending from left to right in the lower left part of space" (Ward, 2013, p. 50). Moreover, the most common inducers of synesthesia are linguistic—letters and words, especially words in a series, and numbers as well. Additionally, synesthesia is both developmental, starting at around age six and persisting over a lifetime or acquired through loss of somatosensory input, for instance, becoming blind or deaf. The qualia that synesthetes experience is highly individualized, although there are some shared patterns, for example, single digits tend to assume darker shades as the numbers increase, although each number has a different color (p. 64). Also, there are impacts on memory, numeracy, perception, and personality that many people share (p. 51). Additionally, synesthetes also are disproportionally creative thinkers, artists, and so on (p. 67). Moreover, synesthesia can be directly associated with the body, for example the projection of colors onto the fingers when counting on them (p. 57). Also, there are spatial forms of organization that have been found to be shared by synesthetes such as the image of a calendar where the days of the month appear as numbers in a circular arrangement, reflecting a cyclical sense of the start to finish of a month (p. 64).

Whether or not, however, synesthesia is causal or epiphenomenal in relation to thinking is still under investigation. However, van Leeuwen, Singer, and Nikolić (2015) argue that synesthesia addresses the nature of the Hard Problem of consciousness in relation to the role of semantics through investigating established synesthetic associations (neurocorrelates). For example, there is a difference in semantic, synesthetic associations if a symbol that appears to lie between the letter S or the number 5 is interpreted as one or the other (Myles, Dixon, Smilek, & Merikle, 2003, cited by van Leeuwen et al. 2015, p. 3), a finding which supports the argument that concepts (a letter or number) induce different synesthetic associations ("ideasthesia"), a phenomena which is found for other conceptually based semantic networks as well, for example the cross-modal associations of color to temperature (blue for cold and red for hot) (Milán, Iborra, De Cordoba, Juarez-Ramos, Artacho, & Rubio, 2013, cited by van Leeuwen, Singer, & Nikolić, 2015, p. 4). Van Leewen et al. (2015) argue that, "synesthesia helps us to realize that semantics shape our experiences" (p. 7).

Implications for Practice and Research

Psychologically, culture (which includes artifacts and environments) together with language and the dynamic interconnections between the two, shapes our experience in relation to human activity, something that has been recognized in SLA. More particularly, how one language expresses mind-body connections may not be the way another one does, leading to differences both with regard to how concepts are construed and affective impacts (qualia) on experience, although of course the contexts of exposure of a learner, goals, motives, and a myriad of other such considerations need to be taken into account as fundamental to language teaching and learning.

For example, if students are primarily interested in the L2 for academic or other specific purposes, then the use of everyday language with regard to the connection between mind and body is usually largely excluded from classroom concerns; instead usage typically focuses on the interrelation of concepts within a specified domain of knowledge or subject matter (the scientific use of language). However, this may be an important oversight. For example, Davidko (2011) argues that the semantic constitution of scientific concepts as found in the L2 should be explored pedagogically in relation to quale to help students "personalize" meaning, providing them a more concrete, embodied (subjective) conceptualization to better facilitate learning. Davidko contends that this can be accomplished, pedagogically, in part through analysis using four categories of "quale structure": "constitutive," formal," "telic," and "agentive." An example from economics provided in the text serves as an illustration: "In order to hedge risks a cautious investor may buy an option which is called a *straddle*" (p. 86, italics original). To "straddle" as a verb is to have a leg on either side of something, for instance when riding a horse, and has the entailment of having one foot in one place and the other in another at the same time, which relates to "option" in the example. Pedagogically, discussing the embodied nature of "straddle" might help contribute to a more personal understanding of the term. Moreover, at a more macro level of quale structure, Searle (2008, p. 8) points out that our "epistemic knowledge claims" are not "established independently of ... feelings, attitudes, prejudices, preferences, and commitments," which would also seem a worthwhile avenue of exploration in L2 special purposes courses—that is, to consider how a field has come to construe guiding concepts. For example, "language acquisition" implies a mechanistic, disembodied sense as historically based on theories that emphasize nonconscious functions of the brain, whereas "language development" takes into account individual agency, environment, and so on, as well as biological predispositions. Also, note that both of these designations are conceptual metaphors.

If, on the other hand, the focus for studying/learning an L2 is to enable communication with others on an everyday basis in naturalistic contexts, then the exploration of social quale becomes essential and includes lexical and grammatical features of the L2 in relation to mind-body integration. For example, there are, of course, many conceptual metaphors that relate feelings, emotions, attitudes, dispositions, and so on that are of an embodied nature across languages, which can be classified according to various structures. For example, Long (2018), following Xu and Chen (2011), considers the "quale-sense" of verbal personification, a form of conceptual metaphor that is formulated by the mapping of a nonhuman event onto an agent. In the poetic expression, "the sky is crying," rain represents tears, an image which entails the possibility of forms of qualia such as sadness, dampness, dreariness, darkness, oppression, and so on. Long argues, pedagogically, that, "image construction is a critical conscious activity in the forming of verbal personification" (p. 65), which can be addressed through examining conceptual structure as leading to conventional understandings of quale-sense. Clearly, similar analytical approaches can be utilized for the pedagogical treatment of forms of pragmatics, nonverbal communication, geosemiotics, and other lexico-grammatical structures that entail mind-body connections in relation to phenomenal impacts.

It should also be mentioned in relation to pedagogy that there have been L2 methods that have taken embodiment into specific account in one form or another in an effort to create mind-body connections in relation to the L2. For example, Asher's (1969) "Total Physical Response" is a method based on the recognition that movement and objects are directly associated in activity and as such enacting such activity is thought to facilitate language learning, with students listening to a command and then performing an action—going to and opening a window, for example. There also was a very early attempt to embody abstract concepts through gesture, perhaps again reinforcing language learning through embodied materialization (de Radonvilliers, 1807). More recently, Gregersen and MacIntyre (2017) advocate teaching nonverbal forms of communication as related to language use, including gesture, posture, facial expression, eye behavior, and space and touch, together with discursive and other language-related features of interaction, providing classroom activities that include the production of these forms as well. Another experiential approach to L2 pedagogy, which focuses on mind-body connections in general, is advocated by Buccino and Mezzadri (2015), who suggest building student understanding by making personal connections to semantic fields within the L2 in terms of their own lived experience, which in the classroom setting involves conventional as well as individual senses of quale, for example discussing conceptualizations of "frightfulness"—fear vs. terror (p. 201).

Different manifestations of L2 dramatization also emphasize mind-body connections, offering the opportunity for learners to enact themselves as speakers of the L2 in situations that are usually bounded by the conventions of L2 language and culture. Such settings also provide a chance to reflect on the qualia that surrounds interaction. For example, in another approach to L2 teaching that emphasizes the experience that learners have in using the L2 for communication (Lilja & Piirainen-Marsh, 2019), students are first prepared for a service-learning encounter ("learning in the wild"), then after the encounter a student, back in class, narrates the event through storytelling. Next, the teacher and students watch a videorecording of the encounter and direct their focus on difficulties the student may have had during the interaction. Although not specifically mentioned as such, the example of a service-learning experience provided in the text indicates that class discussion during the last stage can focus on the qualia of L2 usage (couched in terms of "form and meaning" by the authors).

In addition to pedagogical concerns, SLA research should attend to the quale of the L2 learning experience in relation to mind-body connections as found in the L2, that is, researching the quale that learners feel/experience as surrounding a particular "everyday" conceptual metaphor, for example. Research also should extend to how immigrants or others who have relocated to another country experience living in a new language and culture. For example, some people may not feel phenomenally connected to the world around them even with advanced proficiency, as in the case of Eva Hoffman (1989, p. 107), who after emigrating from Poland and living in the US wrote with regard to her use of "inner language" that "Polish, in short time, has atrophied, shriveled from sheer uselessness. Its words don't apply to my new experiences, they're not coeval with any of the objects, or faces, or the very air I breathe;" moreover, in regard to English, "the words have not penetrated to those layers of my psyche from which a private connection could proceed."

Linguistic relativity is another area of SLA research in regard to possible changes in quale as a result of differences across languages in linguistic structure as leading to differences in how an experience is conceptualized for speech production ("thinking for speaking"). For example, Brown and Gullberg (2008) found in relation to motion events ("the ball rolled down the hill") for two different language typologies that there was a bidirectional influence on Japanese intermediate learners of English, that is, the L1 influenced the production of motion events in the L2 and the L2 influenced production of the L1, co-speech gesture playing a critical role in the evaluation of this influence. In another study concerning linguistic relativity, Boroditsky (2001) found that metaphorical spatiotemporal conceptualizations of time can also change through exposure to a different linguistic system, and as an aspect of embodiment as well. Mandarin native speakers metaphorically organize time vertically, later events being "up" and earlier events "down." English arranges time horizontally, with the past "behind" and the future "ahead." However, English speakers were shown to be able to reconceptualize time vertically after "being briefly trained to talk about time using vertical terms" (p. 19). Boroditsky concludes that language can shape and reshape patterns of abstract thought. This conclusion links to the work on synesthesia (above), that qualia can develop in relation to conceptual schemes, although in this case as associated with how a L2 organizes events in time in a way that is different from the L1.

How L2 learners' regard the quale of L2 nonverbal forms of communication also has been researched as an aspect of SLA. For example, Tian and McCafferty (2020) found that Chinese graduate students studying in the US reacted differently to their use of what they perceived as American forms of gesture, one of the four participants indicating that he was aware of imitating American interlocutor's gestures, but feeling unsettled when he found himself using them when speaking Chinese, that the frequent and expressive nature of American gestures clashed with his cultural identity as Chinese. Additionally, Ruzzene (1998) found that Italian immigrant families in Australia were concerned with "primary language erosion," which he found was counteracted, in part, through retaining L1 gestures when speaking in the L2, helping to maintain an underlying sense of L1 communicative quale. However, the experience of L2 nonverbal forms of communication remains a largely unexplored area of SLA research.

Future Directions

Integrated information theory views phenomenal experience as central to the nature of consciousness, or *The Feeling of Life Itself*, as Koch entitled his 2020 volume, and defines information as "a difference that makes a difference" which is causal in producing conscious states and states of consciousness. This is a far cry from the global neuronal workspace hypothesis, the computational theory of information processing, in which quale is epiphenomenal. This means, in relation to the current chapter, integrated information theory does not separate mind and body in the sense that human experience (subjectivity) is a key to understanding consciousness. At some point, if it is determined that both of these theories, or ones like them, prove sustainable (both have accumulated strong empirical support), keeping in mind that consciousness science is only in its relatively early stages, this would entail major implications for many aspects of research within psychology and applications to SLA.

The statement by Scollon and Scollon (1981, p. 37) that "people who speak different languages, live in different worlds, not the same world with different labels attached" is supported by the importance accorded to phenomenal experience in the scientific study of consciousness, especially when linked to language in conjunction with culture, artifacts, and environments as influencing our internal worlds. This phenomenal undergirding makes the process of learning a second or other language at the conventional level far more than an attempt to fill in pre-determined linguistic slots and heightens our awareness of the social, pragmatic, phenomenal nature of language and communication in relation to being and doing in different languacultures, whether addressing second language learning, bilingualism, multilingualism, lingua francas, codeswitching, or in emerging, extemporaneous communities, and includes physical/cultural embodiment through the use of nonverbal forms of communication (McCafferty, 2020, in press).

The study of cognitive linguistics, because it is centered on "embodied meaning" (Tyler 2012, p. 28) in "communicating our *conceptualizations of experience* and our reflections on that experience" (p. 30, italics original), is particularly well suited to the analysis of both verbal and nonverbal mind-body connections in language/communication at this specific level of concern. Additionally, systemic functional linguistics has been extended to multimodal analysis—visual, and other non-verbal sensory modalities and how they contribute to meaning-making at a social, conventional level (Young, 2011). Both of these perspectives can be expected to continue to prove fruitful in addressing SLA research and pedagogy in relation to language and embodied experience.

It is also important to continue to study SLA as leading to changes in the "quality and character of experience" (Koch, 2020, p. 46) at the level of the individual, which includes possible reconceptualizations of experience in relation to semantics and linguistic form as found for L2 studies on linguistic relativity and changes in thought and language with regard to private and inner speech as well as the possible (re)development of inner sense. This is a "big tent" view of SLA, which largely was confined to mid- to late twentieth-century views of language and psychology, although expanded at this point as our overall understanding of language and psychology continues to grow, which includes contributions from neuroscience and other areas of intellectual and practical pursuit.

Reflection Questions

- If mind and body are viewed as one, then how might this affect theories of SLA?
- If phenomenal consciousness is integral to how a language construes experience, then how is this best approached pedagogically as an aspect of teaching an L2?
- If phenomenal consciousness is vital to understanding and producing an L2, then should cognitive plasticity be explicitly addressed as an aspect of L2 teaching and learning?

Recommended Reading

Johnson, M. (2008). *The meaning of the body: Aesthetics of human understanding*. University of Chicago Press. In this philosophical volume, Johnson considers the importance of the body in human activity and psychology, extending the work started by *Metaphors We Live By*.

Koch, C. (2020). *The feeling of life itself: Why consciousness is widespread but can't be computed*. MIT Press. Koch expounds on the science of consciousness and how it differs from computational models.

Velmans, M. (2009). *Understanding consciousness*. Routledge.
This book is a comprehensive overview of the philosophical, psychological, and neuroscientific study of consciousness.

References

Agar, M. (1994). *Language shock: Understanding the culture of conversation*. Morrow.
Alderson-Day, B., & Fernyhough, C. (2015). Inner speech: development, cognitive functions, phenomenology, and neurobiology. *Psychological. Bulletin, 141*, 931–965.
Asher, J. J. (1969). The total physical response approach to second language learning. *The Modern Language Journal, 53*(1), 3–17.
Bacon, F. (1620/1965). The great instauration. In S. Warhaft (Ed.), *Francis Bacon: A selection of his works* (pp. 298–324). Macmillan.
Boroditsky, L. (2001). Does language shape thought?: Mandarin and English speakers' conceptions of time. *Cognitive psychology, 43*(1), 1–22.
Brown, A., & Gullberg, M. (2008). Bidirectional crosslinguistic influence in L1-L2 encoding of manner in speech and gesture: A study of Japanese speakers of English. *Studies in second language acquisition, 30*(2), 225–251.
Buccino, G., & Mezzadri, M. (2015). Embodied language and the process of language learning and teaching. *Emotion in Language: Theory–Research–Application, 10*, 191–208.
Chomsky, N. (1965). *Aspects of the theory of syntax*. MIT Press.
Cohen, M. A., & Dennett, D. C. (2011). Consciousness cannot be separated from function. *Trends in Cognitive Sciences, 15*(8), 358–364.
Darwin, C. (1872/1965). *The expressions of emotions in man and animals*. John Marry.
Davidko, N. (2011). A cognitive approach to teaching English for Special Purposes (ESP). *Kalbų Studijos, 18*, 82–89.
de Chardin, P. T. (1955/2018). *The phenomenon of man*. Lulu Press, Inc.
de Radonvilliers, C. (1807). *De la manière d'apprendre les langues*. Université de Lausanne.
Descartes, R. (1649/2005). *Las pasiones del alma*. Austral Básicos.
Edelman, G. (2006). *Second nature: Brain science and human knowledge*. Yale University Press.
Fodor, J. A. (1983). *The modularity of mind*. MIT press.
Fossa, P., Pérez, R. M., & Marcotti, C. M. (2019). The relationship between the inner speech and emotions: Revisiting the study of passions in psychology. *Human Arenas, 3*(2), 229–246.
Furukawa, Y., Uehara, K., & Furuya, S. (2017). Expertise-dependent motor somatotopy of music perception. *Neuroscience Letters, 650*, 97–102.
Galilei, Galileo. (1623/1957). The Assayer. Excerpt in Drake, S. (1957). *Discoveries and opinions of Galileo*. Doubleday.
Gallese, V., Keysers, C., & Rizzolatti, G., (2004). A unifying view of the basis of social cognition. *Trends Cognitive Sciences, 8*, 396–403.
Geva, S., & Fernyhough, C. (2019). A penny for your thoughts: Children's inner speech and its neuro-development. *Frontiers in Psychology, 10*(1708), 1–12.

González, J., Barros-Loscertales, A., Pulvermüller, F., Meseguer, V., Sanjuán, A., Belloch, V., & Ávila, C. (2006). Reading cinnamon activates olfactory brain regions. *NeuroImage 32*, 906–912.

Gregersen, T., & Macintyre, P. D. (2017). *Optimizing language learners' nonverbal behavior*. Multilingual Matters.

Griffiths, P. E. (2001). From adaptive heuristic to phylogenetic perspective: Some lessons from the evolutionary psychology of emotion. In Holcomb III, H. R. (Ed.), *Conceptual challenges in evolutionary psychology* (pp. 309–325). Kluwer.

Halliday, M. A. K. (1978). *Language as social semiotic: The social interpretation of language and meaning*. Edward Arnold.

Harris, R. (1998). *Introduction to integrational linguistics*. Pergamon.

Hoffman, E. (1989). *Lost in translation: A life in a new language*. Dutton.

Hoffman, P. (2016). The meaning of "life" and other abstract words: Insights from neuropsychology. *Journal of Neuropsychology, 10*(2), 317–343.

Jack, R. E., Sun, W., Delis, I., Garrod, O. G. B., & Schyns, P. G. (2016). Four not six: Revealing culturally common facial expressions of emotion. *Journal of Experimental Psychology: General, 145*(6), pp. 708–730.

Johnson, M. (2012). The meaning of the body. In Overton, W. F., Muller, U., & Newman, J. L. (Eds.), *Developmental Perspectives on Embodiment and Consciousness* (pp. 19–44). Routledge.

Kahneman, D. (2011). *Thinking, fast and slow*. Macmillan.

Kant, I. (1871/1997), *Critique of pure reason*, trans. P. Guyer and A. Wood. Cambridge University Press.

Kastrup, B. (2017). An ontological solution to the mind-body problem. *Philosophies, 2*(2), 10.

Kelly, S. D., Kravitz, C., & Hopkins, M. (2004). Neural correlates of bimodal speech and gesture comprehension. *Brain and Language, 89*, 253–260.

Kendon, A. (2004). *Gesture: Visible action as utterance*. Cambridge University Press.

Koch, C. (2020). *The feeling of life itself: Why consciousness is widespread but can't be computed*. MIT Press.

Koch, C. (2012). *Consciousness: Confessions of a romantic reductionist*. MIT Press.

Kousta, S. T., Vigliocco, G., Vinson, D. P., Andrews, M., & Del Campo, E. (2011). The representation of abstract words: Why emotion matters. *Journal of Experimental Psychology: General, 140*, 14–34.

Lakoff, G., & Johnson, M. (1980). *Metaphors we live by*. University of Chicago Press.

Langacker, R. W. (1987). *Foundations of cognitive grammar, Volume 1: Theoretical Prerequisites*. Stanford University Press.

Levy-Drori, S., & Henik, A. (2006). Concreteness and context availability in lexical decision tasks. *American Journal of Psychology 119*, 45–65.

Lilja, N., & Piirainen-Marsh, A. (2019). Connecting language classroom and the wild: Re-enactments of language use experiences. *Applied Linguistics, 40*(4), 594–623.

Long, D. (2018). Something is like somebody in some way: A quale explanation of verbal personification. *Studies, 4*(3), 65–71.

Mashour, G. A., Roelfsema, P., Changeux, J. P., & Dehaene, S. (2020). Conscious processing and the global neuronal workspace hypothesis. *Neuron, 105*(5), 776–798.

Massimini, M., & Tononi, G. (2018). *Sizing up consciousness: Towards an objective measure of the capacity for experience*. Oxford University Press.

McCarthy-Jones, S., & Fernyhough, C. (2011). The varieties of inner speech: Links between quality of inner speech and psychopathological variables in a sample of young adults. *Consciousness and Cognition, 20*(4), 1586–1593.

McCafferty, S. G. (in press). Semantic consciousness and inhabiting a languacultural community: A sociocultural approach. *Status Quaestionis, 18*.

McCafferty, S. G. (2018). Vygotsky on the consciousness and the application to second language development. In Lantolf, J. P., Poehner, M. & Swain, M. (Eds.), *The Routledge handbook of sociocultural theory and second language development* (pp. 75–88). Routledge.

McNeill, D. (1992). *Hand and mind: What gestures reveal about thought*. University of Chicago press.

Meeren, H. K., van Heijnsbergen, C. C., & de Gelder, B. (2005). Rapid perceptual integration of facial expression and emotional body language. *Proc. Natl. Acad. Sci. U.S.A. 102*, 16518–16523.

Milán, E., Iborra, O., De Cordoba, M. J., Juarez-Ramos, V., Artacho, M. A. R., & Rubio, J. L. (2013). The Kiki-Bouba effect A case of personification and ideaesthesia. *Journal of Consciousness Studies, 20*(1–2), 84–102.

Moseley, R., Carota, F., Hauk, O., Mohr, B., & Pulvermüller, F. (2012). A role for the motor system in binding abstract emotional meaning. *Cerebral Cortex, 22*, 1634–1647.

Myles, K. M., Dixon, M. J., Smilek, D., & Merikle, P. M. (2003). Seeing double: the role of meaning in alphanumeric colour synaesthesia. *Brain Cognition, 53*, 342–345.

Nagel, T. (1974). What is it like to be a bat? *The Philosophical Review, 83*(4), 435–450.

O'Halloran, K. L. (2011). Multimodal discourse analysis. In K. Hyland & B. Paltridge (Eds.), *Companion to discourse* (pp. 120–137). Continuum.

O'Halloran, K. L. (2008). Systemic functional-multimodal discourse analysis (SF-MDA): Constructing ideational meaning using language and visual imagery. *Visual Communication, 7*(4), 443–475.

O'Halloran, K. L. (2005). *Mathematical discourse: Language, symbolism and visual images*. Continuum.

Olson, D. R. (1996). *The world on paper: The conceptual and cognitive implications of writing and reading*. Cambridge University Press.
Oosterwijk, S., Rotteveel, M., Fischer, A. H., & Hess, U. (2009). Embodied emotion concepts: How generating words about pride and disappointment influences posture. *European Journal of Social Psychology, 39*, 457–466.
Peirce, C. S. (1986). *Writings of Charles S. Peirce: A chronological edition, volume 3 (1872–1878)*. Peirce Edition Project (Ed.). Indiana University Press.
Pulvermüller, F. (2005). Brain mechanisms linking language and action. *Nature Reviews Neuroscience, 6*, 576–582.
Pylyshyn, Z. W. (1985). *Computation and cognition: Toward a foundation for cognitive science*. MIT Press.
Revonsuo, A. (2017). *Foundations of consciousness*. Routledge.
Rueschemeyer, S. A., van Rooij, D., Lindemann, O., Willems, R. M., & Bekkering, H. (2010). The function of words: Distinct neural correlates for words denoting differently manipulable objects. *Journal of Cognitive Neuroscience, 22*(8), 1844–1851.
Ruzzene, N. (1998). Language experience: The forgotten dimension in cross-cultural social work? *Australian Social Work, 51*(2), 17–23.
Scollon, R., & Scollon, S. W. (2003). *Discourses in place: Language in the material world*. Routledge.
Scollon, R., & Scollon, B. P. K. (1981). *Narrative, literacy and face in interethnic communication*. Ablex.
Searle, J. R. (2008). *Philosophy in a new century: Selected essays*. Cambridge University Press.
Simon, H. A. (1979). Information processing models of cognition. *Annual Review of Psychology, 30*, 363–396.
Smith, N., & Tsimpli, I-M. (1995). *The mind of a savant: Language learning and modularity*. Basil Blackwell.
Spinoza, B. (1667/1980). *Ética demostrada según orden geométrico*. Ediciones Orbis.
Tammerman, R. (2008). Sociocultural situatedness of terminology in the life sciences: The history of splicing. In Frank, R, Dirven, R, Ziemke, T. & Bernardez, E. (Eds.), *Body, Language and Mind* Vol. 2: *Sociocultural Situatedness* (pp. 327–360).
Thompson, E. L., Bird, G., & Catmur, C. (2019). Conceptualizing and testing action understanding. *Neuroscience and Biobehavioral Reviews, 105*, 106–114.
Tian, L., & McCafferty, S. G. (2020). Chinese international students' multicultural identity and second language development: gesture awareness and use. *Language Awareness*, 1–20.
Tononi, G. (2012). *Phi: A voyage from the brain to the soul*. Pantheon Press.
Tononi, G. (2008). Consciousness as integrated information: a provisional manifesto. *The Biological Bulletin, 215*(3), 216–242.
Tversky, A., & Kahneman, D. (1981). The framing of decisions and the psychology of choice. *Science, 211*(4481), 453–458.
Tyler, A. (2012). *Cognitive linguistics and second language learning: Theoretical basics and experimental evidence*. Routledge.
van Dam, W. O., Rueschemeyer, S. A., Bekkering, H., & Lindemann, O. (2013). Embodied grounding of memory: Toward the effects of motor execution on memory consolidation. *Quarterly Journal of Experimental Psychology, 66*(12), 2310–2328.
van Leeuwen, T. M., Singer, W., & Nikolić, D. (2015). The merit of synesthesia for consciousness research. *Frontiers in Psychology, 6*, 1850.
Varela, F., Thompson, E., & Rosch, E. (1993). *The embodied mind: Cognitive science and human experience*: MIT Press.
Vygotsky, L. S. (1994). The problem of the environment. In R. van der Veer & J. Valsiner (Eds.), *The Vygotsky Reader* (pp. 338–354). Blackwell Press.
Vygotsky, L. S. (1987). Thinking and speech. In N. Minick (Translator), *The collected works of LS Vygotsky* (Vol. 1). Plenum Press.
Ward, J. (2013). Synesthesia. *The Annual Review of Psychology, 64*, 49–75.
West, W. C., & P. J. Holcomb. (2000). Imaginal, semantic, and surface-level processing of concrete and abstract words: An electrophysiological investigation. *Journal of Cognitive Neuroscience, 12*, 1024–1037.
Westphal, J. (2016). *The mind–body problem*. MIT Press.
Winsler, A., Fernyhough, C., & Montero, I. (2009). *Private speech, executive functioning, and the development of verbal self-regulation*. Cambridge University Press.
Xu S. & Chen X. (2011). Quale and quale-sense. *Modern Foreign Languages, 33*(4), 331–338.
Young, L. (2011). Systemic functional linguistics. In Simpson, J. (Ed.), *The Routledge handbook of applied linguistics* (pp. 645–657). Routledge.

29
WHAT COUNTS AS EVIDENCE?

Yasser Teimouri, Ekaterina Sudina, and Luke Plonsky

Why do people differ so much in the processes and outcomes of second language (L2) learning? The field of second language acquisition (SLA) has long since attributed such differences, at least in part, to a variety of psychological factors. In other words, psychological aspects have occupied a central stage in the studies of L2 learning (Dörnyei, 2009). For more than half a century, the field of psychology of language learning (PLL) has engaged in enhancing our knowledge about the influence of L2 learners' mental experiences, processes, thoughts, feelings, motives, and behaviors related to their L2 development (Mercer, Ryan, & Williams, 2012).

But how much do we *really* know about the psychological aspects of L2 learning? And more to the point of this chapter, how do we arrive at such knowledge? In other words, our aim in this chapter is to describe and assess the sources and quality of evidence within the quantitative domain of PLL. Unfortunately, questions of this nature have rarely surfaced in SLA. In fact, it is not uncommon for researchers to simply rely on conventions and/or to report reliability and validity evidence from other studies, for example, rather than doing so themselves. However, awareness of methodological issues is growing rapidly, thanks in part to research reviews, syntheses, and meta-analyses that have explicitly addressed study quality as one of their main research objectives (e.g., Marsden & Plonsky, 2018; Sudina, 2021; see also Gass, Loewen, & Plonsky, 2021). In this chapter, we discuss some of the key markers of the quality of evidence by drawing on relevant research in other fields. We define the quality of evidence as the amount of confidence that one can have about accuracy of the observed effects and estimates in a given study. We then narrow down our focus on survey research in SLA—one of the main research tools in the domain of PLL—and evaluate its quality of evidence compared to other research designs (e.g., experimental designs). To that end, we adopt a judicial framework to discuss key elements that enhance the quality of survey research. We end the chapter with methodological recommendations regarding the design of questionnaires as well as analyses of survey data.

What Counts as Evidence in Psychology?

What counts as evidence? Or what counts as strong evidence, or even good-enough evidence? In the realms of psychology and education, questions of this nature play a critical role in developing, improving, and delivering social, clinical, and educational services and practices. In the following sections, we will review different standards for assessing the quality of evidence that have inspired and informed evidence-based research in psychology and education, among other fields.

Initial efforts to pinpoint standards of evidence began in the field of healthcare in the late 1970s by the Canadian Task Force (Hill, Frappier-Davignon, & Morrison, 1979; Woolf, Battista, Anderson, Logan, & Wang, 1990). In an attempt to promote evidence-based clinical and health-related practices, the Canadian Task Force graded levels of evidence based on study design: Level 1: Randomized control trials (RCTs) studies were classified as good evidence; Level 2: cohort and case-control studies were regarded as fair evidence; and Level 3: expert opinions were considered as poor evidence. The task force encouraged researchers, practitioners, and review bodies to use the hierarchy of evidence in their research reviews and syntheses as the basis of health-related recommendations and policies (Atkins, Eccles, Flottorp, Guyatt, Henry, Hill, Liberati, O'Connell, Oxman, Phillips, Schünemann, Edejer, Vist, & Williams, 2004).

After these initial efforts to characterize levels of evidence, several hierarchies of evidence emerged in various disciplines, such as social policy, criminal justice, and education (e.g., Davies, Nutley, & Smith, 2000; Freiberg & Carson, 2010; Luebbe, Radcliffe, Callands, Green, & Thorn, 2007; Pring & Thomas, 2004). Although these hierarchies of evidence differed in certain dimensions, in each model study design was the key marker of the quality of evidence, with RCTs placed at or near the top and non-experimental studies (e.g., case studies and surveys) occupying the lowest levels. As an example, Bagshaw and Bellomo's (2008) hierarchy of evidence contained five levels: RCTs (Level 1); underpowered RCTs (Level 2); non-randomized observational studies (Level 3); non-randomized studies with historical controls (Level 4); and case series without controls (Level 5). In the same vein, Petticrew and Roberts's (2003) framework consisted of seven levels: systematic reviews and meta-analyses (Level 1); RCTs with definitive results (Level 2); RCTs with non-definitive results (Level 3); cohort studies (Level 4); case-control studies (Level 5); cross-sectional surveys (Level 6); and case reports (Level 7). Overall, experimental studies were assigned much greater value than observational studies when grading the quality of evidence.

Despite their extensive use in evidence-based practices in diverse fields, hierarchies of evidence based on study design have been sources of heated debates and criticism (Nutley, Powell, & Davies, 2013; Pawson, 2003; Petticrew & Roberts, 2003). One of the main criticisms of such hierarchies concerns their narrow perspective about the value of evidence. According to Pawson (2003), these hierarchies of evidence mostly ignore other important dimensions of research with direct effects on the quality of evidence. In other words, how a research design was implemented and/or how research results fit in with other similar research findings are not taken into account. Should we categorize the quality of evidence of small-scale, poorly designed RCTs as high? What about the quality of evidence coming from a set of RCTs with conflicting results? Critics also raised concerns about availability, appropriateness, and feasibility of RCTs in certain scientific domains, such as social policy, and questioned the appropriateness and feasibility of standards of evidence primarily based on research design (Atkins et al., 2004). Underlying such critique was a concern that a common standard of evidence may not be equally applicable or relevant across different substantive domains. (Similar arguments made within applied linguistics in Norris, Plonsky, Ross, & Schoonen, 2015; Plonsky, 2014.) Moreover, such hierarchies of evidence place too much value on experimental studies and may underestimate the value of well-conducted observational studies (Atkins et al., 2004; Nutley et al., 2013). Why should we consider evidence provided by a well-designed, large-scale survey as always merely fair or poor? The use of such design-based hierarchies of evidence almost necessarily excludes potentially useful evidence of both a quantitative and qualitative nature (Nutley et al., 2013).

Several attempts have been made to address the shortcomings of the traditional hierarchies of evidence based on study design. In healthcare, for instance, the GRADE (Grading of Recommendations Easement, Development, and Evaluation) system (Atkins et al., 2004), was designed as an improvement over the previous hierarchies of evidence based on design. In the GRADE system, the quality of evidence is first assessed based on study design similar to the traditional models. In the next step, however, the ratings of evidence are modified by evaluating several quality factors underlying the study. For instance, although RCTs are placed at the top of the hierarchy of evidence, five main study factors have been listed as potential sources that may reduce the quality of evidence: study limitations, the inconsistency of results, indirectness of evidence, imprecisions, and reporting bias. If an RCT has serious limitations, the quality of its evidence is downgraded accordingly. On the other hand, the quality of evidence in an observational study can be improved when (a) a large magnitude of effect exists, (b) there is a dose-response gradient, and/or (c) all plausible confounders or other biases increase researchers' confidence in the estimated effect (for a review of GRADE system, see Guyatt, Oxman, Vist, Kunz, Falck-Ytter, Alonso-Coello, & Schünemann, 2008).

In the field of social policy, some scholars argued for the need to think of evidence in terms of a matrix rather than a hierarchy of evidence. Within this perspective, first, the suitability of a research design is examined in relation to the research questions that it aims to address. Then, the quality of evidence is rated in light of the research design. For instance, if the research question concerns the degree of customers' satisfaction regarding a product or service, qualitative research, survey research, case-control studies, or cohort studies are seen as more suitable than experimental studies. As such, the quality of evidence of survey research can be rated higher than the quality of evidence of an experimental study. Multiple research organizations and institutions have used this matrix of evidence approach in systematic reviews. The EPPI-Center (Institute of Education, University College London) is a prime example of an institution that has applied a matrix of evidence approach in its methods for grading the quality of evidence. After examining the consistency and appropriacy between study design and its corresponding research questions, the EPPI-Center assesses the "weights of evidence" of each study based on three dimensions: (a) internal validity, (b) appropriateness of study method, and (c) appropriateness of samples, context, and measures. Having rated every dimension of a study, an average score of quality is computed from high to low (Peersman, Oliver, & Oakley, 1997).

What Counts as Evidence in SLA?

For decades, research in SLA has focused on collecting evidence on substantive issues underlying the processes and outcomes of L2 learning. This immense body of research, however, had largely assumed the quality of its empirical efforts and provided evidence (Plonsky, 2013). Whether or not and to what extent studies in SLA have been carried out in adherence to the standards of quality remains a largely empirical question. SLA research, however, is currently undergoing a "methodological turn" (Byrnes, 2013, p. 825) in which a growing number of L2 scholars and journal editors are paying closer attention to issues of study quality (Marsden, Thompson, & Plonsky, 2018; Plonsky, 2013, 2014). As a result of and contributing to this movement, we have seen numerous research reviews, syntheses, and meta-analyses in which research designs and methodological/reporting practices in L2 research are examined empirically (e.g., Derrick, 2016; Hu & Plonsky, 2021; Liu & Brown, 2015; Marsden et al., 2018; Plonsky, 2013, 2014; Plonsky & Gass, 2011; Wei, Hu, & Xiong, 2019). Moreover, new guidelines are being published by prominent L2 research journals (e.g., *TESOL Quarterly*; *Language Learning*) enforcing more stringent criteria for study quality.

Plonsky (2013) defined study quality as adherence to standards of rigor and transparency (Plonsky, 2013). More recently, Gass et al. (2021) expanded on this definition, adding that quality in certain types of (mostly quantitative) research is also (a) concerned with estimating the magnitude of relationships and effects (rather than simply identifying their presence or lack thereof), and (b) reproducible. Several syntheses have operationalized different angles of this definition within and across different domains of L2 research. Their individual and collective results are concerning, to say the least. Methodological issues have been revealed concerning various aspects of study design, data handling and analysis, and reporting practices. Examples of findings in this line of research include a lack of control groups, pre-testing, and delayed post-testing in experimental studies (Norris & Ortega, 2000), as well as generally small, underpowered samples (e.g., Plonsky, 2013). With respect to data collection instruments, meta-studies have observed low and unreported reliability estimates (Al-Hoorie & Vitta,

2019; Plonsky & Derrick, 2016) and numerous inconsistencies and idiosyncrasies (e.g., Marsden et al., 2018; Hu & Plonsky, 2021). Likewise, quantitative data in particular have been found to be frequently mishandled and underreported (Hu & Plonsky, 2021; Nicklin & Plonsky, 2020; Plonsky & Ghanbar, 2018). Such a lack of transparency undermines consumers' ability to appropriately interpret primary study results and, at the same time, limits the potential of meta-analyses to obtain a comprehensive understanding of the substantive domains to which any given study belongs (Plonsky, 2013).

Many of these methodological criticisms apply to research on the psychology of language learning, in particular IDs research (see Plonsky, 2011, 2019). Teimouri, Goetze, and Plonsky's (2019) meta-analysis of the relationship between L2 anxiety and achievement, for example, found a lack of reporting of descriptive statistics, insufficient information on the sources of data collection instruments, and very little piloting, among other concerns. Likewise, Sudina's (2021) methodological synthesis of study and scale quality in L2 anxiety and motivation research revealed a range of areas in need of methodological scrutiny and improvement (e.g., reporting survey response rates, providing evidence of construct and content validity of self-report questionnaires, handling missing data). With these findings in mind, and because questionnaire-based surveys are central to research in PLL (e.g., learner factors such as motivation), in the following sections, we discuss their popularity, potential limitations, and the quality of evidence in relation to other study designs and instrument types. Then, we discuss ways to increase the quality of evidence of survey research by drawing on a judicial framework used as a reference guide to interpreting survey evidence in legal contexts (e.g., courtrooms).

Quality of Evidence in Survey Research in PLL

Surveys (particularly questionnaire-based ones) have been extensively used in SLA research for gaining knowledge about language learners' (a) intended and actual language learning behaviors, (b) opinions and attitudes about certain aspects of target languages, (c) perceptions, feelings, and beliefs about certain L2-related issues, (d) knowledge of certain issues in SLA, and (e) biodata (Dörnyei & Csizér, 2012). The popularity of such tools is not without good reason. First, questionnaires and self-reports in particular are easy to develop and cost-effective to administer: One can collect a huge amount of data from many participants in a relatively short amount of time (Dörnyei & Taguchi, 2010; Phakiti, de Costa, Plonsky, & Starfield, 2018). Second, self-report questionnaires are sources of rich information: No one has more information about the psychology of language learners than language learners themselves; moreover, they have access to private information, such as thoughts and feelings that are not available to others (Robins, Norem, & Cheek, 1999). Third, self-report questionnaires are generally successful at eliciting information from the respondents. That is, respondents are usually eager to engage in self-reflective activities involving the assessment of certain aspects of themselves, such as their personality types or attitudes. Fourth, people are more diligent and careful when they rate themselves as opposed to rating others, thereby enhancing the validity of self-report questionnaires (Robins et al., 1999). Fifth, self-report questionnaires engage the respondents' identity, such as how they might think of themselves compared to others or how they should behave in social events (Hogan & Smither, 2001; Ickes, Snyder, & Garcia, 1997; Vazire & Gosling, 2004). Finally, IDs are "learner-internal" phenomena, and they do not always manifest themselves externally through observable behavior. Consequently, self-report questionnaires constitute one of the most popular means of measuring many such constructs (Ozer & Reise, 1994).

Despite numerous advantages, questionnaires also suffer from several limitations. Of significance, questionnaire responses may not accurately reflect the reality of the respondent, thus undermining the validity of the data collected. Some well-known examples of such response biases are socially desirable responding (SDR), acquiescent responding (AR), and extreme responding (ER) (Paulhus, 1991). SDR occurs when the respondent believes they are compelled to project a positive image, such as during a job interview. AR, also referred to as "acquiescence, affirmation," or "agreement bias" (DeVellis, 2017, p. 112), happens when certain respondents tend to agree with statements regardless of their content (Paulhus & Vazire, 2007). ER represents the tendency to respond in an extreme manner due to certain situational factors, such as ambiguity, emotional arousal, and rapid responding (Paulhus & Vazire, 2007). However, because of the voluntary nature of research participation, the anonymous nature of most data collection tools, and minimal risks involved in IDs research, SDR, AR, and ER may pose little threat to validity of self-report questionnaires in SLA (for a detailed review of other disadvantages of self-report questionnaires, see Dörnyei, 2010).

Considering these potential challenges, how should we rate the quality of evidence of survey-based research? As noted, traditional hierarchies of evidence based on design were criticized because they downgraded the quality of evidence of observational studies. In fact, if surveys are constructed and administered appropriately, they can be used as a source of high-quality evidence (Diamond, 2000, 2011; Dillman, 1999). For example, survey-based data produced by the US Census Bureau are mostly treated by the public and media as factual. As another example, in legal contexts, survey data are used and presented as high-quality evidence. In the US, the Federal Rule of Evidence 703 has officially admitted data collected via surveys as a type of valid evidence. For instance, in a case involving allegations of discrimination in a jury panel composition, the defense team may survey a sample of prospective jurors about their age, race, education, ethnicity, and income distribution, and present the findings to the court as evidence in favor or against the case (Diamond, 2011). In sum, we would agree with Van der Stede, Young, and Chen (2005), who argue that the strength of survey-based evidence, as with other types of tools, "centers more on how it is deployed, rather than with the method itself" (p. 656). Therefore, in order to increase the quality of the evidence of survey research, we need to pay particular attention to the key elements underlying its design and implementation.

Inspired by the use of legal standards in determining the quality of research evidence (e.g., Morgan, 1990; Smith, Snyder, Swire, Donegan, & Ross, 1983; Van der Stede et al., 2005), in the following sections we use Diamond's (2000, 2011) judicial framework to discuss some of the key factors that influence the quality of survey research and apply it to the domain of PLL. Our choice of a legal framework to evaluate the quality of survey research is rooted in the belief that legal frameworks and guidelines provide relatively stringent standards for assessing the quality of evidence. As noted by Morgan (1990), "the adversarial nature of a trial exposes the survey researcher to a very hostile environment, making anonymous journal reviewers seem very supportive in comparison" (p. 68).

Enhancing the Quality of Evidence in Survey Research in SLA

Diamond's (2000, 2011) judicial framework—published in "Reference Manual on Scientific Evidence"—is written as a reference guide on survey research for judges to assist them on how to interpret the adequacy of survey data. Because of its rigorous standards for the quality of survey research, this judicial framework has also been used in other research domains, such as marketing (e.g., Morgan, 1990; Smith et al., 1983) and accounting management (e.g., Van der Stede et al., 2005). In the following sections, we discuss the five main categories of Diamonds's (2000) framework that are closely relevant to survey research on IDs: (a) the purpose and design of the survey, (b) population definition and sampling, (c) survey questions and other research method issues, (d) accuracy of data entry, and (e) disclosure and reporting. Other elements of Diamond's judicial framework that are specific to legal matters and procedures are excluded. Of note, we will not discuss the accuracy of data entry, which covers issues regarding coding and cleaning the data (interested readers can refer to Dörnyei & Csizér, 2012, for a review of such issues).

The Purpose and Design of a Survey

The purpose of most surveys can be divided into two broad categories: description and explanation (Sudman & Blair, 1999). For a descriptive purpose, a questionnaire can be used, for instance, to profile language learning backgrounds of a group of students. Survey research can also be used for an explanatory purpose, such as examining the structural components of a motivational theory. The majority of survey studies on IDs fall under the category of explanation, with many scholars conducting surveys to test the links between various theoretical constructs (e.g., language aptitude, motivation, anxiety, self-efficacy, personality) and language learning behaviors and outcomes (for reviews, see Dewaele, 2009; Dörnyei & Ryan, 2015).

The legal framework requires that researchers state the purpose of their survey clearly and explicitly (Diamond, 2000, 2011). If the purpose of a survey is to design and obtain validity evidence for a tool intending to measure a psychological construct (e.g., self-confidence), it becomes critical that the contents of the questionnaire map onto the theoretical properties underlying the construct to be measured. A mismatch between the content of the questionnaire and its underlying theoretical properties will threaten both content and construct validity of the scale (Teimouri, 2018). For instance, the construct validity of the Foreign Language Classroom Anxiety Scale (Horwitz, Horwitz, & Cope, 1986)—the most-widely used anxiety measure in SLA (Teimouri et al., 2019)—has been questioned by several scholars (e.g., Kutuk, Putwain, Kaye, & Garrett, 2020; Shao, Pekrun, & Nicholson, 2019; Sparks & Patton, 2003). Additionally, in her systematic review of scales used to measure L2 motivation and anxiety, Sudina (2021) found that some studies employed blended scales consisting of subscales targeting distinct psychological constructs (e.g., L2 willingness to communicate [WTC], motivational variables, and anxiety). When this is the case, validity (and reliability) evidence should be obtained for each subscale separately rather than for the questionnaire overall (see Flake, Pek, & Hehman, 2017, for more).

The purpose of survey research affects not only its design and the items included in the survey but the type of statistical analyses as well. If the purpose of a survey is to determine causal relations between a set of variables, for instance, the survey might be administered repeatedly over time (i.e., longitudinal design); the researcher may also opt for a cross-sectional design to examine these same objectives by running advanced inferential statistical analyses, such as multilevel linear modeling or structural equation modeling. Overall, survey research objectives play a significant part in the design, development, and implementation of survey research and interpretation of its findings. Thus, in a well-designed survey, research objectives are clearly and explicitly stated.

Population and Sampling

In a survey study, the population is defined as the entire group of people to which the survey researcher attempts to attach an attribute based on a selected sample. The key to making such inferences is the extent to which the sample is representative of the target population. If the survey sample does not represent the population, we cannot draw any valid inferences. We can increase the representativeness of a sample by selecting the sample randomly from the target population. In a random selection of the participants (i.e., probability sampling), each member of the target population has an equal chance of being selected in the sample. In non-random (non-probability) sampling, some members of the population have a greater chance of being selected than others (Dörnyei & Csizér, 2012). In the legal framework, evidence from surveys using non-random sampling can be considered valid provided that the methods used to choose the participants are justifiable (Diamond, 2011). "We must not forget, however, that no matter how principled a nonprobability sample strives to be, the extent of generalizability in this type of sample is often negligible" (Dörnyei & Csizér, 2012, p. 81). It is recommended that survey researchers should at least try to apply random sampling techniques to some aspects of sample selection in order to minimize the likelihood of sampling error (Diamond, 2011; Van der Stede et al., 2005). For instance, researchers can use stratified random sampling—a sampling technique in which the target population is defined and divided into groups (or strata), and then a number of people from each group is selected randomly.

Another key factor that affects the quality of survey research evidence is the sample size. What is the minimum number of people to be recruited in survey research? We can answer this question based on several criteria. For instance, considering the normal distribution of the participants as the key factor in survey research, a total number of 30 people might suffice (Hatch & Lazaraton, 1991). However, this rule is not absolute because non-parametric tests can be used in situations when normal distributions are not achieved (Dörnyei, 2007, 2010). Another useful criterion for determining the size of a sample is to calculate how big a sample should be in order to reach a statistically significant level for a specific statistical analysis. For instance, if a negative correlation of −.30 to −.40 between language anxiety and achievement is expected based on the findings of past research (e.g., Teimouri et al., 2019), the researcher should calculate how many participants are needed for those correlational coefficients to reach statistical significance. Various formulas have been suggested by scholars to calculate the necessary sample size for running multiple regressions analyses, factors analyses, or structural equation modeling (e.g., Ullman, 2012). A sample size of 200–300 should, in many instances, be sufficient to reduce sample-size-based threats to internal validity for survey research in court (Morgan, 1990; Diamond, 2011).

Non-sampling errors also undermine the quality of evidence in survey research. Non-sampling errors typically fall into one of the following two categories: (a) non-response error, which happens when some of the respondents do not reply to survey questions, causing responses to be an incomplete representation of the selected sample, and (b) response error, which happens when some of the respondents respond inaccurately to survey questions. These two sources of non-sampling error have the potential to threaten the internal validity of a survey study. Put another way, they limit the extent to which observed variances in the dependent variable can be attributed to variances in the independent variable. Another important issue that undermines the internal validity of a survey study is item non-response, which occurs when the respondents do not answer particular questions in the questionnaire, thereby reducing the sample size and potentially inducing bias. In such instances, if data are missing completely at random (MCAR) or missing at random (MAR) and meet the assumption of multivariate normality, modern techniques such as multiple imputation and maximum likelihood estimation can be employed to alleviate bias; this is why they are preferred over traditional methods such as listwise or pairwise deletion (see Baraldi & Enders, 2010; Lang & Little, 2018).

To reduce the impact of non-sampling errors, the legal standards emphasize enhancing clarity of survey questions and avoiding misunderstandings by piloting the survey before administering the main study. The purpose of piloting the questionnaire should be to test both the questions and the questionnaire. According to Dörnyei and Csizér (2012), the results of a pilot test will help researchers eliminate ambiguous items, improve the clarity of item wordings, finalize the layout, dry-run the analyses to examine the expected results, and rehearse the administration procedures. Nonetheless, piloting of tools and instruments in the wider field of SLA is a rarity, as shown in several meta-analyses and methodological syntheses (e.g., Derrick, 2016; Sudina, 2021). Thus, to increase the quality of evidence of survey research, L2 scholars should pilot their self-report questionnaires using various techniques (e.g., small-scale testing; cognitive interviewing or think-aloud protocols) before the main data collection takes place.

Dependent Measures

L2 learners' behaviors play a powerful role in predicting L2 learning outcomes, and because of this, they have occupied a central role in IDs research. However, a serious limitation of this research domain is its overreliance on a handful of self-reported measures of behaviors as the main dependent criteria (e.g., L2 use, L2 WTC, intended behavior). Although these measures reflect respondents' perceptions of their L2 learning behaviors, their subjective nature might also result in measurement error due to certain biases (Birnberg, Shields, & Young, 1990; Van der Stede et al., 2005). In order to increase the quality of evidence in this regard, we advocate a multi-method approach to assessing language learning behaviors. Within this approach, observers' ratings of language learners' behaviors are used along with self-report measures of behaviors (Hofstee, 1994). Research has shown that observers who are familiar with the target participants can provide reliable and valid assessment of individuals' behaviors (McCrae & Weiss, 2007). For instance, language teachers can be used as rich sources of observational information regarding language learners' behaviors in class. In a personality study, for instance, Teimouri, Plonsky, and Tabandeh (in press) measured learners' grit—the perseverance and passion of learning a second language—by using a self-report measure, which was filled out by the students. Complementary to the self-report tool was an observational measure of grit (i.e., informant report), which was filled out by their teacher based on the students' actual behaviors in class. The correlational analyses revealed a very strong association between both measures, thus supporting the new scale's validity argument. Classmates can also be used as sources of information for an observer's ratings. For instance, each student can be asked to rate participation and contributions of other peers during a group activity—although how group dynamics might influence students' ratings should not be downplayed (e.g., Dörnyei, 1997; see also Mercer, Talbot, & Wang, 2020, for an alternate view on the realities of learner engagement in the L2 classroom).

L2 proficiency and achievement have also been used frequently as dependent variables in IDs research. Like behavioral measures, self-reported instruments of language proficiency abound in this research domain (e.g., Gardner, 2000; Kozaki & Ross, 2011; Teimouri, 2018). Although L2 learners can assess their language proficiency ability fairly accurately if sound and appropriate measures with clear descriptions are used (e.g., Li & Zhang, 2021), errors of judgment may still occur (MacIntyre, Noels, & Clement, 1997; Papi & Teimouri, 2014). Course grades and GPAs can and are often used in lieu of self-reports and standardized tests; however, such indicators should be used cautiously. The construct validity of GPAs as a measure of language achievement has been questioned because they normally represent academic achievement (Teimouri et al., 2019). Likewise, L2 scholars have advised against using course grades as measures of language achievement because they often include sources of variances not necessarily associated with proficiency, such as attendance (for a detailed review of the use of course grades in L2 research, see Brown, Plonsky, & Teimouri, 2018). We advocate a multi-method approach toward measuring L2 learners' language proficiency, which involves using both subjective and objective measures of language proficiency and achievement in order to increase the quality of evidence in IDs research.

Disclosure and Reporting

The trustworthiness of survey research is highly dependent on its comprehensive and transparent reporting practices (Diamond, 2000, 2011). As mentioned above, in his review of study quality in SLA research, Plonsky (2013, 2014) set the transparency of reporting practices as a key dimension of study quality. Numerous research reviews, syntheses, and meta-analyses have examined the reporting practices involved in L2 research (e.g., Derrick, 2016; Hu & Plonsky, 2021; Liu & Brown, 2015; Larson-Hall & Plonsky, 2015; Marsden et al., 2018; Plonsky & Gass, 2011; Sudina, 2021). The results of these reviews have identified that critical data often go unreported, which is a recurring methodological issue in L2 research. This lack of transparency is evident when it comes to piloting the instrument, reporting descriptive analyses (e.g., means, SDs), checking the assumptions, reporting and interpreting effect sizes, reporting the results of reliability analyses, dealing with missing data, and so forth.

In IDs research, one particular challenge to transparency concerns how much of the original survey data were used in the published study. Some IDs studies are part of a larger project, and full disclosure in this regard should become the norm. Other practices of transparency are related to sharing of all research materials (whenever possible) used in the study (see Marsden, Mackey, & Plonsky, 2016). Overall, a lack of transparency in research studies, including survey research, weakens our progress in the field in several ways. Unreported data restrict our understanding and interpretation of research findings at primary and secondary (i.e., meta-analytic) levels. Complete and transparent reporting practices are imperative to increasing the quality of evidence in survey research on IDs.

Integrating Perspectives

PLL has a long history in SLA research (Dörnyei, 2009; Mercer et al., 2012), and the use of self-report instruments has long-since been the backbone of this research domain. Similar to other sub-domains of SLA, researchers interested in PLL have mainly focused on substantive issues regarding the impact of various psychological factors on L2 learning; by contrast, rarely do they take a retrospective perspective toward scrutinizing their methodological practices and the quality of evidence they have produced. Questions like, "what counts as evidence?" or "how one can grade the quality of evidence?" have rarely received attention. As discussed before, traditional hierarchies of evidence based primarily on design undervalue the quality of well-designed observational studies because they ignore critical issues regarding the quality of study conduct as well as their theoretical underpinnings. We advocate in this paper, rather, for a more nuanced understanding of evidential quality that considers a wider range of considerations.

Implications for Practice and Research

Given that self-report tools arguably comprise one of the dominant data collection methods in PLL research, in this chapter, we have adopted a judicial framework to discuss some of the key elements in survey research that enhance its quality of evidence. Innovative methodological advances in designing, administering, and analyzing surveys will, we believe, enhance the quality of evidence generated in the domain of PLL. The strength of evidence determines the strength of implications for theory, practice, and future research. As such, and as a community of researchers that very much wants to contribute to these realms, we encourage researchers to continue to consider, reflect on, and seek ways to improve the quality of evidence they produce.

Future Directions

In this final section, we would like to highlight a few points that might also enhance the quality of evidence in PLL research and, consequently, lead to a more thorough understanding of the roles that psychological factors play in the complex process of L2 development and use. First, PLL research is in need of innovative techniques for measuring psychological factors. For instance, for many decades, de-contextualized, statement-like questionnaires have been the default choice in this domain, despite the existence of other questionnaire designs and formats. We recommend the addition of scenario-based questionnaires to survey-based tools. Although scenario-based questionnaires are common in certain areas of SLA (e.g., pragmatics), they have been used only scarcely in PLL research (e.g., Gkonou & Oxford, 2016; Teimouri, 2018). The use of scenario-based questionnaires allows L2 researchers to assess psychological factors in relation to the context; more importantly, a scenario-based questionnaire allows L2 researchers to examine the interactions between psychological and contextual factors, a key aspect of complex dynamic approaches to PLL in SLA (e.g., Hiver & Al-Hoorie, 2019; Larsen–Freeman & Cameron, 2008).

Along with innovations in questionnaire designs, the use of more solid and sophisticated statistical analyses of survey data will also likely increase the quality of evidence in PLL research. For instance, PLL research would benefit from moving beyond the classical test theory approaches to data analysis and apply—whether instead of or in tandem—item response theory to analyze and interpret research results. Also, currently we are witnessing the introduction of a novel statistical approach, Bayesian hypothesis testing and estimation, which casts doubts on the heretofore dominant approaches embodied by frequentist statistics and, of course, null hypothesis significance testing (e.g., Norouzian, de Miranda, & Plonsky, 2018, 2019). In a re-analysis of 418 t-test studies in L2 research using the Bayesian approach, for instance, Norouzian et al. (2019) found "insufficient evidence to reject the null hypothesis" (p. 248) in more than half of the studies (64 percent) in which the null hypothesis was already rejected because the p values fell between .01 and .05.

In closing, the purpose of this chapter was to examine and raise awareness about the quality of evidence in the domain of PLL with a particular focus on survey research relying on quantitative research strategies. As such, methodological issues pertaining to qualitative or mixed method survey designs in PLL research were beyond the scope of this chapter. We recognize that these research designs are subject to their own concerns for quality and encourage an in-depth discussion and comprehensive exploration thereof in future research. Therefore, we see this chapter as a starting point for a much-needed dialogue on the state of quality of evidence in PLL.

Reflection Questions

- How do meta-analyses in SLA in general and PLL in particular address the quality of evidence they have aggregated before generalizing their findings?
- Imagine a colleague was planning a study on one or more aspects of the psychology of language learning. What suggestions would you offer, based on this chapter, in terms of study design and instrumentation?
- What are some of the standards to enhance the quality of evidence in qualitative research?

Recommended Readings

Levant, R. F., & Hasan, N. T. (2008). Evidence-based practice in psychology. *Professional Psychology: Research and Practice, 39*(6), 658–662.
This paper provides a comprehensive review of the use of the 2005 American Psychological Association Presidential Task Force on evidence-based research in the field of psychology. The authors discuss the justifications and findings of the Task review as well as its implications in the domain of psychology.

Teimouri, Y. (2018). Differential roles of shame and guilt in L2 learning: How bad is bad? *Modern Language Journal, 102*(4), 632–652.
In this study, the author assessed how shame-proneness and guilt-proneness of L2 learners influence their L2 learning behaviors and achievement. The study offers a fine example of the development and validation of a scenario-based questionnaire to assess psychological factors in L2 learning.

Plonsky, L. (2013). Study quality in SLA: An assessment of designs, analyses, and reporting practices in quantitative L2 research. *Studies in Second Language Acquisition, 35*(4), 655–687.
This pioneering methodological synthesis examines the state of study quality in various subdomains of quantitative L2 research, offers detailed account of methodological practices across 606 primary studies, and provides empirically grounded recommendations for future research.

References

Atkins, D., Eccles, M., Flottorp, S., Guyatt, G. H., Henry, D., Hill, S., Liberati, A., O'Connell, D., Oxman, A. D., Phillips, B., Schünemann, H., Edejer, T. T., Vist, G.E., & Williams, J. W., Jr. (2004). Systems for grading the quality of evidence and the strength of recommendations I: Critical appraisal of existing approaches The GRADE Working Group. *BMC Health Services Research, 4*(1), 38.
Bagshaw, S., & Bellomo, R. (2008) The need to reform our assessment of evidence from clinical trials: A commentary. *Philosophy, Ethics, and Humanities in Medicine, 3*(23).
Baraldi, A. N., & Enders, C. K. (2010). An introduction to modern missing data analyses. *Journal of School Psychology, 48*(1), 5–37.
Birnberg, J. G., Shields, M. D., & Young, S. M. (1990). The case for multiple methods in empirical management accounting research (with an illustration from budget setting). *Journal of Management Accounting Research, 2*, 33–66.
Brown, A. V., Plonsky, L., & Teimouri, Y. (2018). The use of course grades as metrics in L2 research: A systematic review. *Foreign Language Annals, 51*(4), 763–778.

Byrnes, H. (2013). Editor's introduction. *Modern Language Journal, 97*, 105–108.
Carroll, J. B., & Sapon, S. M. (1960). *Modern language aptitude test: MLAT*. Psychological Corporation.
Davies, H. T. O., Nutley, S. M., & Smith, P. C. (Eds.). (2000). *What works? Evidence-based policy and practice in public services*. Policy Press.
Derrick, D. J. (2016). Instrument reporting practices in second language research. *TESOL Quarterly, 50*, 132–53.
DeVellis, R. F. (2017). Scale development: Theory and applications (4th ed.) Sage Publications.
Dewaele, J. M. (2009). Individual differences in second language acquisition. In W. C. Ritchie & T. K. Bhatia (Eds.), *The new handbook of second language acquisition* (pp. 623–646). Emerald Insight.
Diamond, S. S. (2000). Reference guide on survey research. In *Reference manual on scientific evidence* (2nd ed., pp. 229–276). The Federal Judicial Center.
Diamond, S. S. (2011). Reference guide on survey research. In *Reference manual on scientific evidence* (3rd ed., pp. 359–423). The National Academies Press.
Dillman, D. (1999). *Mail and internet surveys: The tailored design method*. Wiley.
Dörnyei, Z. (1997). Psychological processes in cooperative language learning: Group dynamics and motivation. *Modern Language Journal, 81*(4), 482–493.
Dörnyei, Z. (2007). *Research methods in applied linguistics*. Oxford University Press.
Dörnyei, Z. (2009). *The psychology of second language acquisition*. Oxford University Press.
Dörnyei, Z., & Czisér, K. (2012). How to design and analyze surveys in second language acquisition research. In A. Mackey & S. M. Gass (Eds.), *Research methods in second language acquisition: A practical guide* (pp. 74–94). Wiley-Blackwell.
Dörnyei, Z., & Ryan, S. (2015). *The psychology of the language learner revisited*. Routledge.
Dörnyei, Z., with Taguchi, T. (2010). *Questionnaires in second language research: Construction, administration, and processing* (2nd ed.). Routledge.
Flake, J., Pek, J., & Hehman, E. (2017). Construct validation in social and personality research: Current practice and recommendations. *Social Psychological and Personality Science, 8*, 370–378.
Freiberg, A., & Carson, W. G. (2010). The limits to evidence-based policy: Evidence, emotion and criminal Justice 1. *Australian Journal of Public Administration, 69*(2), 152–164.
Gass, S., Loewen, S., & Plonsky, L. (2021). Coming of age: the past, present, and future of quantitative SLA research. *Language Teaching, 54*(2), 245–258.
Gardner, R. C. (1960). *Motivational variables in second-language acquisition* [Doctoral dissertation, McGill University]. ProQuest Dissertations Publishing.
Gardner, R. C. (2000). Correlation, causation, motivation, and second language acquisition. *Canadian Psychology, 41*, 10–24.
Gardner, R. C., & Lambert, W. E. (1959). Motivational variables in second language acquisition. *Canadian Journal of Psychology, 13*, 266–272.
Gardner, R. C., & Lambert, W. E. (1965). Language aptitude, intelligence, and second-language achievement. *Journal of Educational Psychology, 56*(4), 191–199.
Gkonou, C., & Oxford, R. L. (2016). Questionnaire: Managing your emotions for language learning. University of Essex.
Guyatt, G. H., Oxman, A. D., Vist, G. E., Kunz, R., Falck-Ytter, Y., Alonso-Coello, P., & Schünemann, H. J. (2008). GRADE: An emerging consensus on rating quality of evidence and strength of recommendations. *BMJ, 336*(7650), 924–926.
Hatch, E. & Lazaraton, A. (1991). *The research manual: Design and statistics for applied linguistics*. Newbury House.
Heyde, A. (1977). The relationship between self-esteem and the oral production of a second language. In H. D. Brown, C. A. Yorio, & R. H. Crymes (Eds.), *On TESOL '77* (pp. 226–240). TESOL.
Hill, N., Frappier-Davignon, L., & Morrison, B. (1979). The periodic health examination. *Canadian Medical Association Journal, 121*, 1193–1254.
Hiver, P., & Al-Hoorie, A. H. (2019). *Research methods for complexity theory in applied linguistics*. Multilingual Matters.
Hofstee, W. K. (1994). Who should own the definition of personality? *European Journal of Personality, 8*(3), 149–162.
Hogan, R., & Smither, R. (2001). *Personality: Theories and applications*. Westview Press.
Horwitz, E. K., Horwitz, M. B., & Cope, J. (1986). Foreign language classroom anxiety. *The Modern Language Journal, 70*(2), 125–132.
Hu, Y., & Plonsky, L. (2021). Statistical assumptions in L2 research: A systematic review. *Second Language Research, 37*(1), 171–184.
Ickes, W., Snyder, M., & Garcia, S. (1997). Personality influences on the choice of situations. In R. Hogan, J. Johnson, & S. Briggs (Eds.), *Handbook of personality psychology* (pp. 166–198). Academic Press.
Kozaki, Y., & Ross, S. J. (2011). Contextual dynamics in foreign language learning motivation. *Language Learning, 61*(4), 1328–1354.
Kutuk, G., Putwain, D. W., Kaye, L., & Garrett, B. (2020). Development and validation of a New Multidimensional Language Class Anxiety Scale. *Journal of Psychoeducational Assessment, 38*(5), 649–658.

Lang, K. M., & Little, T. D. (2018). Principled missing data treatments. *Prevention Science, 19*(3), 284–294.

Larsen–Freeman, D., & Cameron, L. (2008). *Complex systems and applied linguistics*. Oxford University Press.

Larson-Hall, J., & Plonsky, L. (2015). Reporting and interpreting quantitative research findings: What gets reported and recommendations for the field. *Language Learning, 65*(S1), 127–159.

Li, M., & Zhang, X. (2021). A meta-analysis of self-assessment and language performance in language testing and assessment. *Language Testing, 38*(2), 189–218.

Liu, Q., & Brown, D. (2015). Methodological synthesis of research on the effectiveness of corrective feedback in L2 writing. *Journal of Second Language Writing, 30*, 66–81.

Luebbe, A. M., Radcliffe, A. M., Callands, T. A., Green, D., & Thorn, B. E. (2007). Evidence-based practice in psychology: Perceptions of graduate students in scientist–practitioner programs. *Journal of Clinical Psychology, 63*(7), 643–655.

MacIntyre, P. D., Noels, K., & Clement, R. (1997). Biases in self-ratings of second language proficiency: The role of language anxiety. *Language Learning, 47*, 265–287.

Marsden, E., & Plonsky, L. (2018). Data, open science, and methodological reform in second language acquisition research. In A. Gudmestad & A. Edmonds (Eds.), *Critical reflections on data in second language acquisition* (pp. 219–229). John Benjamins.

Marsden, E., Mackey, A., & Plonsky, L. (2016). Breadth and depth: The IRIS repository. In A. Mackey & E. Marsden (Eds.), *Advancing methodology and practice: The IRIS repository of instruments for research into second language* (pp. 1–21). Routledge.

Marsden, E., Thompson, S., & Plonsky, L. (2018). A methodological synthesis of self-paced reading in second language research. *Applied Psycholinguistics, 39*, 861–904.

McCrae, R. R., & Weiss, A. (2007). Observer ratings of personality. *Handbook of research methods in personality psychology*, 259–272.

Mercer, S., Ryan, S., & Williams, M. (Eds.). (2012). *Psychology for language learning: Insights from research, theory and practice*. Palgrave Macmillan.

Mercer, S., Talbot, K. R., & Wang, I. K.-H. (2020). Fake or real engagement—looks can be deceiving. In P. Hiver, A., Al-Hoorie, & S. Mercer (Eds.), *Student engagement in the language classroom* (pp. 143–162). Multilingual Matters.

Morgan, F. W. (1990). Judicial standards for survey research: An update and guidelines. *Journal of Marketing, 54*(1), 59–70.

Nicklin, C., & Plonsky, L. (2020). Outliers in L2 research: A synthesis and data re-analysis from self-paced reading. *Annual Review of Applied Linguistics, 40*, 26–55.

Norouzian, R., de Miranda, M. D., & Plonsky, L. (2019). A Bayesian approach to measuring evidence in L2 research: An empirical investigation. *The Modern Language Journal, 103*(1), 248–261.

Norouzian, R., de Miranda, M., & Plonsky, L. (2018). The Bayesian revolution in second language research: An applied approach. *Language Learning, 68*(4), 1032–1075.

Norris, J. M., & Ortega, L. (2000). Effectiveness of L2 instruction: A research synthesis and quantitative meta-analysis. *Language learning, 50*(3), 417–528.

Norris, J. M., Plonsky, L., Ross, S. J., & Schoonen, R. (2015). Guidelines for reporting quantitative methods and results in primary research. *Language Learning, 65*, 470–476.

Nunan, D. (1996). Issues in second language acquisition research: Examining substance and procedure. In W. C. Ritchie & T. K. Bhatia (Eds.), *The handbook of second language acquisition* (pp. 349–374). Academic Press.

Nunan, D. (1991). Methods in second language classroom-oriented research: A critical review. *Studies in Second Language Acquisition, 13*, 249–274.

Nutley, S. M., Powell, A. E., & Davies, H. (2013). *What counts as good evidence?* Alliance for Useful Evidence.

Oswald, F. L., & Plonsky, L. (2010). Meta-analysis in second language research: Choices and challenges. *Annual Review of Applied Linguistics, 30*, 85–110.

Ozer, D. J., & Reise, S. P. (1994). Personality assessment. *Annual Review of Psychology, 45*(1), 357–388.

Phakiti, A., De Costa, P., Plonsky, L., & Starfield, S. (Eds.). (2018). *The Palgrave handbook of applied linguistics research methodology*. London: Palgrave Macmillan.

Papi, M., & Teimouri, Y. (2014). Language learner motivational types: A cluster analysis study. *Language Learning, 64*, 493–525.

Paulhus, D. 1991. Measurement and control of response bias. In J. Robinson, P. R. Shaver, & L. S. Wrightsman (Eds.), *Measures of personality and social psychological attitudes, Vol. 1* (pp. 17–59). Academic Press.

Paulhus, D. L., & Vazire, S. (2007). The self-report method. *Handbook of Research Methods in Personality Psychology, 1*, 224–239.

Pawson, R. (2003). Assessing the quality of evidence in evidence-based policy: Why, how and when. *Working Paper No. 1. ESRC Research Methods Programme*. University of Manchester.

Peersman, G., Oliver, S., & Oakley, A. (1997). *EPPI-center review guidelines: data collection for the EPIC database*. EPPI-Centre Social Science Research Unit.

Petticrew, M., & Roberts, H. (2003). Evidence, hierarchies, and typologies: horses for courses. *Journal of Epidemiology & Community Health*, *57*(7), 527–529.

Plonsky, L. (2019). Recent research on language learning strategy instruction. In A. U. Chamot & V. Harris (Eds.), *Learning strategy instruction in the language classroom: Issues and implementation* (pp. 3–21). Multilingual Matters.

Plonsky, L. (2013) Study quality in SLA: An assessment of designs, analyses, and reporting practices in quantitative L2 research. *Studies in Second Language Acquisition, 35,* 655–.

Plonsky, L. (2014) Study quality in quantitative L2 research (1990–2010): A methodological synthesis and call for reform. *Modern Language Journal, 98,* 450–70.

Plonsky, L. (2015) Statistical power, p values, descriptive statistics, and effect sizes: A "back-to basics" approach to advancing quantitative methods in L2 research. In L. Plonsky (Ed.), *Approach to advancing quantitative methods in L2 research* (pp. 23–45). Routledge.

Plonsky, L. & Derrick, D. J. (2016). A meta-analysis of reliability coefficients in second language research. *Modern Language Journal, 100,* 538–553.

Plonsky, L., & Gass, S. (2011) Quantitative research methods, study quality, and outcomes: The case of interaction research. *Language Learning, 61,* 325–66.

Plonsky, L., & Oswald, F. L. (2014). How big is "big"? Interpreting effect sizes in L2 research. *Language Learning, 64*(4), 878–912.

Pring, R., & Thomas, G. (2004). *Evidence-based practice in education*. McGraw-Hill Education.

Robins, R. W., Norem, J. K., & Cheek, J. M. (1999). Naturalizing the self. *Handbook of Personality: Theory and Research, 3,* 421–447.

Rubin, J. (1975). What the "good language learner" can teach us. *TESOL Quarterly,* 41–51.

Shao, K., Pekrun, R., & Nicholson, L. J. (2019). Emotions in classroom language learning: What can we learn from achievement emotion research? *System, 86,* 102121.

Smith, J. G., Snyder, W. S., Swire, J. B., Donegan, T. J., & Ross, I. (1983). Legal standards for consumer survey research. *Journal of Advertising Research, 23,* 19–35.

Sparks, R. L., & Patton, J. (2013). Relationship of L1 skills and L2 aptitude to L2 anxiety on the Foreign Language Classroom Anxiety Scale. *Language Learning, 63,* 870–895.

Sudina, E. (2021). Study and scale quality in second language survey research, 2009–2019: The case of anxiety and motivation. *Language Learning.* Advance online publication.

Sudman, S., & Blair, E. (1999). Sampling in the twenty-first century. *Journal of the Academy of Marketing Science, 27*(2), 269–277.

Teimouri, Y. (2018). Differential roles of shame and guilt in L2 learning: How bad is bad? *The Modern Language Journal, 102*(4), 632–652.

Teimouri, Y., Goetze, J., & Plonsky, L. (2019). Second language anxiety and achievement: A meta-analysis. *Studies in Second Language Acquisition, 41*(2), 363–387.

Teimouri, Y., Plonsky, L., & Tabandeh, F. (in press). L2 grit: Passion and perseverance for second-language learning. *Language Teaching Research,* 1–26.

Ullman, J. B. (2012). Structural equation modeling. In B. G. Tabachnick & L. S. Fidell (Eds.), *Using multivariate statistics* (6th ed., pp. 681–785). Pearson/Allyn and Bacon.

Van der Stede, W. A., Young, S. M., & Chen, C. X. (2005). Assessing the quality of evidence in empirical management accounting research: The case of survey studies. *Accounting, Organizations and Society, 30*(7–8), 655–684.

Vazire, S., & Gosling, S. D. (2004). E-perceptions: Personality impressions based on personal websites. *Journal of Personality and Social Psychology, 87*(1), 123–132.

Wei, R., Hu, Y., & Xiong, J. (2019). Effect size reporting practices in applied linguistics research: A study of one major journal. *Sage Open, April-June,* 1–11.

Woolf, S. H., Battista, R. N., Anderson, G. M., Logan, A. G., & Wang, E. (1990). Assessing the clinical effectiveness of preventive maneuvers: Analytic principles and systematic methods in reviewing evidence and developing clinical practice recommendations. A report by the Canadian task force on the periodic health examination. *Journal of Clinical Epidemiology, 43*(9), 891–905.

Yashima, T. (2009). International posture and the ideal L2 self in the Japanese EFL context. *Motivation, Language Identity and The L2 Self, 86*(1), 144–163.

30
LANGUAGE APTITUDES

Zhisheng (Edward) Wen

The term language aptitude generally refers to specific abilities that allow some people to learn a foreign/second language easier, faster, and better than their peers (Carroll, 1990; Wen, 2012). Research into language aptitude in the modern era started in the late 1950s, although interest in this topic has undergone both waxing and waning days in the past six decades (Wen, Biedron, & Skehan, 2017; Wen, Biedron, Skehan, Li, & Sparks, 2019). Between the 1950s and 1960s, for example, language aptitude was in its golden era, with much of its popularity largely attributable to the pioneering work laid down by the American educational psychologist John Carroll and his associate Stanley Sapon at Harvard University during 1952–1958. The highlight of their research was the publication of the Modern Language Aptitude Test (MLAT) in 1959, which has become almost synonymous with the very concept of language aptitude itself (Wen et al., 2017). Over the years and up until today, MLAT has been widely used by government agencies (such as the FSI; Jackson & Kaplan, 2001), civil servants (Wesche, 1981), language educators and practitioners, and educational researchers (Stansfield & Reed, 2019; Stansfield & Winke, 2008).

During the 1970s and onwards, the initial enthusiasm about language aptitude in the 50s and 60s had gradually diminished and the public attitude towards the concept seemed to change considerably (Stansfield & Winke, 2008). Many people began to become skeptical about the validity of the MLAT battery and they also questioned the viability of the concept itself. Major criticisms came from different fronts (Skehan, 1998, 2012; Wen, 2012; Wen et al., 2017). To begin with, the "anti-egalitarian" nature of the aptitude test score was a big concern for many educators in that it could have negative impacts on students' self-esteem (especially if they got a low score on the aptitude tests), which could consequently stifle their motivation to continue further learning. Second, Stephen Krashen (1981) had argued that language aptitude was at its best predictive only of the conscious instructed classroom learning, but not of the more desirable naturalistic acquisition contexts. Third, language educators embracing the communicative language teaching (CLT) approach began to associate MLAT's origin in the 50s and 60s with the "old-fashioned" audio-lingual teaching method.

A direct consequence of these criticisms and other misconceptions of language aptitude was several decades of marginalized research interest and a scarce number of empirical studies on this topic. DeKeyser and Juffs (2005) once lamented the unpopularity of language aptitude as similar to that of the term "grammar" among language educators. For decades, language aptitude has been conceived as the neglected "backwater" in applied linguistics (Singleton, 2017). In contrast, the same period had witnessed growing research enthusiasm about other individual differences (IDs) factors, such as L2 learning strategies and L2 motivation (see Chapter 10). In retrospect, language aptitude research is now lagging behind all other IDs (especially L2 motivation) in terms of its theoretical conception, test developments, and pedagogical applications (Wen, 2016; Wen et al., 2017).

Towards the end of the 1990s, the situation began to improve and research enthusiasm about language aptitude managed to pick up steam again around the turn of the new millennium (Vuong & Wong, 2019). An increasing number of theoretical and empirical studies has been published in key journals and edited volumes (e.g., Granena & Long, 2013; Hyltanstam, 2018; Jackson, Granena, & Yucel, 2016; Reiterer, 2018; Wen et al., 2019). Indeed, Rod Ellis (2019) has unequivocally pointed out these new waves in his Foreword to the recent volume entitled *Language Aptitude* (Wen et al., 2019). According to Ellis, the topic of language aptitude had only covered two pages in his first edition of *Understanding Second Language Acquisition* in 1985. Then, when this monograph was updated and published again in 2015, language aptitude occupied almost seven full pages. The mere expansion in print page numbers here represents one piece of evidence that the topic of language aptitude currently stands at a central position in contemporary SLA and applied linguistics.

Indeed, as demonstrated amply in recent edited volumes on language aptitude listed above (three of them are also included in the annotated recommended readings at the end of the chapter), the concept is now garnering a resurgence of interest from the diverse fields of education, psychology, neuroscience, and SLA (e.g., Reiterer, 2018; Wen et al., 2019). In the sections that follow, I aim to trace the developments of cognitive language aptitude models and test batteries from an interdisciplinary perspective, with a view to delineating the nature, structure, and measurement of the construct. In tandem with these reviews, I also extend the current language aptitude theory to incorporate a working memory component. Put into perspective, these interdisciplinary insights culminate in an emerging consensus view of language aptitude as a multi-componential, complex, dynamic, and adaptive cognitive system that is malleable and develops with the learning experience. In light of these new insights, I call for implementing an integrated framework of language aptitude that subsumes prognostication, explanation, and application. I will close the chapter by highlighting the remaining challenges and proposing possible directions for future research.

Perspectives from Psychology

Carroll's MLAT and the Four-Factor Aptitude Model

Language aptitude in the modern era witnessed its heyday in the 1950s and 1960s, characterized by the development and use of several language aptitude tests that are still prevailing today (Spolsky, 2005). Among these, the influence of the pioneering work from the American educational psychologist John Carroll was particularly profound and far-reaching (Stansfield & Reed, 2014). For Carroll (1981), language aptitude refers to "an individual's initial state of readiness and capacity for learning a foreign language" given sufficient time and motivation. To begin with, the MLAT devised by Carroll and his associate Sapon in 1959 represents the epitome of this golden period of language aptitude research, as it has set the benchmark for all ensuing aptitude tests to measure against. More specifically, the MLAT subsumes *five* major parts:

- MLAT I: Number learning
- MLAT II: Phonetic script learning
- MLAT III: spelling clues
- MLAT IV: Words in sentences
- MLAT V: Paired associates learning

In the past six decades since its inception, MLAT has continued to be used worldwide, either in its original paper-and-pencil format (with an online format pending; Stansfield, personal

Table 30.1 Carroll's Four-Factor Aptitude Model and MLAT's Five Parts

Aptitude Components	Definitions	MLAT Parts
Phonetic coding ability	Capacity to code unfamiliar sound so that it can be retained;	MLAT I (weakly), II & III (weakly);
Grammatical sensitivity	Capacity to identify the functions that words fulfill in sentences;	MLAT IV;
Inductive language learning ability	Capacity to extrapolate from a given corpus to create new sentences;	MLAT I (weakly);
Associative memory	Capacity to form associative links in memory.	MLAT I & V.

communication), or in its adapted or translated variants in a dozen other languages such as French, Japanese, Polish, Hungarian, etc. (Stansfield & Reed, 2014, 2019).

As Carroll had recalled in his interview with Stansfield and Reed (2014), the MLAT test would be administered before an intensive language training program. Then the MLAT score initially obtained can fairly accurately predict the ultimate attainment of foreign language learning, especially for intensive training programs, with correlations sometimes reaching the 0.80-0.90 level. After 60 years, MLAT still enjoys supreme predictive validity, as indicated by a recent meta-analysis of 34 empirical studies (involving 3239 participants) published between 1963 and 2013 (Li, 2015). According to Li's study, the MLAT's predictive power stood at around 0.34, higher than the average of all aptitude tests considered as a whole, which was averaged about 0.32. Put together, these positive results from both single empirical studies and the meta-analysis are all lending strong support to MLAT's supreme predictive power, rendering the battery synonymous with the concept of language aptitude itself (Wen, 2012; Wen et al., 2017).

In addition, John Carroll (1981, 1990,) applied the statistical technique of factor analysis, which allowed him to extract and identify *four* major abilities from the enormous amount of MLAT test items. These abilities derived from MLAT included phonetic coding ability, grammatical sensitivity, language induction ability, and associative memory ability. Table 30.1 above summarizes these four components and their definitions, alongside their corresponding MLAT parts (Dörnyei & Skehan, 2003; also see Doughty, 2019; Stansfield & Reed, 2019). Overall, Carroll's MLAT and his four-factor model have laid a strong foundation for all ensuing research in language aptitude, directing, and guiding both theory construction and test development over the last 60 years (Wen et al., 2017; Wen et al., 2019).

Sparks and Ganschow's "LCDH" and Tests

Inspired by early studies of L1 reading research investigating learning difficulties, educational psychologists Richard Sparks and Lenore Ganschow (1991, 2001; also see Sparks, 1995) proposed the "Linguistic Coding Differences Hypotheses" (LCDH). As postulated by the authors, the basic premise of LCDH lies in the assumption that native language (L1) skills are essential for predicting L2 learning and that L1 ability is the foundation of L2 aptitude (Sparks & Ganschow, 2001). Like Skehan (1998), they view language as special, that is, language is qualitatively different from other domain-general cognitive skills (also see Skehan, 2019 for more details on this). In line with the tenets of the LCDH, the authors also argue that it is necessary to examine similarities and differences between languages (especially the transfer effects from morpho-syllabic languages such as Chinese to alphabetic languages such as English, and vice versa) and to include phonological measures in language aptitude tests (Sparks & Ganschow, 2001). In essence, the LCDH model by Sparks and Ganschow complements Carroll's four-factor view of language aptitude by adding an *orthographic decoding skill* that is essential for predicting L2 reading. Their model is similar to Cummins's (1979)

Linguistic Interdependence Hypothesis, that L1 and L2 have a common underlying foundation, and the Linguistic Threshold Hypothesis, that the level of L2 proficiency is moderated by one's level of attainment in L1.

In their numerous follow-up studies with secondary and postsecondary US L2 learners since the early 1990s, Sparks and Ganschow have generated extensive empirical support for the LCDH, showing that (1) L1 and L2 learning have strong relationships; (2) L2 learners exhibit differences in their L1 skills and L2 aptitude (on the MLAT); and (3) individual differences (IDs) in L1 skills and L2 aptitude are the most robust predictors of L2 achievement and proficiency. For example, in a recent factor-analytical study by Sparks and colleagues (Sparks, Patton, Ganschow, & Humbach, 2011), they have identified *four* basic components of L2 aptitude, including (1) students' L1 and L2 Phonology/Orthography skills (subsuming phonemic coding and phonological processing ability), (2) L1 and L2 language analysis skills (comprising comprehension, grammar, vocabulary, and inductive language learning), (3) students' IQ/memory skills (including L1 intelligence and L2 paired-associate learning measures), and (4) self-perceptions of L2 motivation and anxiety. Factor analysis results have suggested that these *four* components (measured by *L2* separate tests, including MLAT's five parts) combined to explain 76 percent of the variance in their ultimate oral and written L2 proficiency.

In another recent longitudinal study spanning over several years (Sparks, Patton, & Luebbers, 2019), it was found that high, average, and low-achieving US L2 learners exhibited significant overall differences on most L1 measures, i.e., reading, spelling, vocabulary, working memory, phonological short-term memory, writing, print exposure, reading attitudes, and significant between-group differences on the aforementioned L1 measures and the MLAT score. IDs in students' L1 literacy, working memory, and L2 aptitude best discriminated among students who completed three years of L2 study vs. those who discontinued L2 study after two years. Notably, students' skills in L2 achievement reflected their L1 achievement, that is to say, students who were strong in L1 reading exhibited stronger L2 reading, and vice versa.

Robert Sternberg's "CANAL-F" Model and Tests

Another group of educational psychologists, Elena Grigorenko, Robert Sternberg, and Madeline Ehrman (2000), by drawing on Sternberg's (1997) triadic conception of human intelligence (the theory of "successful intelligence" in particular), has proposed a new interpretation of language aptitude. In their conception, namely, the "Cognitive Ability for Novelty in Language Acquisition-Foreign" (shortened as the CANAL-F theory), language aptitude represents the students' *potential* for future learning of foreign languages (Grigorenko et al., 2000). In particular, the model identifies *five* knowledge acquisitional processes and particularly highlights students' ability to handle novelty and solve ambiguity in foreign language learning materials L2 learners are likely to encounter.

In line with this new conception of language aptitude, the authors have also devised a new format of aptitude test, i.e., the "Cognitive Ability for Novelty in Language Acquisition as applied to Foreign Language Test" (shortened as the CANAL-FT). The test battery was constructed based on an artificial language (Ursulu) and it contains *nine* sections that are postulated to tap into cognitive abilities such as recall and inferencing of new linguistic materials, under both immediate and delayed conditions (as cited in Dörnyei & Skehan, 2003, p. 595). According to its proponents (Sternberg & Grigorenko, 2002, p. 140), the CANAL-FT distinguishes itself from previous aptitude tests in three significant ways, i.e., by being (1) driven by cognitive theory; (2) dynamic and situational rather than static; (3) simulation-based and adaptive. Unfortunately, despite its innovative design features and great potential, CANAL-FT's validation results from empirical work (e.g., Sternberg, 2002) failed to outperform the MLAT in terms of predictive validity, although the test battery has considerable potential (Ellis, 2004).

Perspectives from SLA and Cognitive Science
Paul Meara's LLAMA Model and Tests

The LLAMA test battery was designed by the British SLA scholar Paul Meara (2005). The battery has been welcomed by a growing number of SLA researchers in recent years (Granena, 2013). Bokander and Bylund (2019) tabulated a total of 43 empirical studies that have used the LLAMA (or its predecessor LAT) as the aptitude test instrument. One major advantage of the LLAMA is its "language neutrality" principle that has guided its design of test items. Of course, it's easy accessibility and free online download (www.lognostics.co.uk/tools/llama/) plus its user-friendliness are also contributing to its growing popularity among researchers (especially when most previous language aptitude tests were classified and not easily available for public use). More specifically, the entire battery includes *four* parts, respectively known as LLAMA_B, LLAMA_D, LLAMA_E, and LLAMA_F (Rogers, Meara, Barnett-Legh, Curry, & Davie, 2017).

- LLAMA_B tests vocabulary pairing learning
- LLAMA_D examines the ability to recognize repeated pronunciation in spoken language.
- LLAMA_D can be regarded as a measure of implicit learning ability (Granena, 2013).
- LLAMA_E is adapted from the corresponding tasks of sound symbols in MLAT test questions.
- LLAMA_F is a grammatical inference test.

Recently, Granena (2013) and Rogers et al. (2016, 2017) have provided validation studies showing preliminary results about its validity. For example, Rogers (2017) pointed out that LLAMA is robust to a series of individual differences (IDs) in SLA, though suggested that the battery should consider how to improve the test items in the future to better fit young L2 learners. In another empirical study, Bokander and Bylund (2019) explored the internal validity of this test battery by inviting 350 participants to collect their LLAMA data. Data were analyzed through classic item analysis, Rasch analysis, and principal component analysis. The results indicated that only one of the four components of LLAMA (LLAMA_B) produced a score that was in good fit with the latent trait model. From this point of view, the validity of the LLAMA test battery needs to be further enhanced in the future. As its designer has recently reported, improvement and refinement efforts of the LLAMA are now underway (Rogers & Meara, personal communication).

Peter Robinson's Aptitude Complexes Model and Tests

Another SLA scholar, Peter Robinson (2005), combines the educational psychologist Richard Snow's concept of "aptitude complexes" (1994) with the "fundamental differences hypothesis" advocated by SLA scholar Bley-Vroman (1990) to propose his Aptitude Complexes/Differential Abilities model. According to Robinson (2019), aptitude is a theoretical construct, operationalized in the form of a test, which aims to predict phenomena that characterize second language acquisition (SLA), such as incidental learning, metalinguistic awareness, fossilization, and others, and the extent to which successful SLA occurs as a result.

This aptitude model conceived by Robinson was portrayed visually in a wheel shape consisting of four layers encompassing basic cognitive abilities, aptitude complexes, task aptitudes, and pragmatic/interactional traits/abilities (Robinson, 2005). In the inner circle of the wheel, the ten most basic human cognitive abilities were identified, including processing speed, pattern recognition, rote memory, phonological short-term memory, text working memory capacity, semantic priming, etc. In the second circle, these ten cognitive abilities are then combined to form *five* aptitude complexes, such as processing speed and pattern recognition combine to form "noticing the gap," phonological working memory capacity, and phonological working memory speed combine to form "memory for contingent speech," etc. In the third circle, aptitude complexes are interacting with task features and task conditions (e.g., ±planning time, or ±background knowledge), which give rise to task aptitudes. The outer circle portrays the transfer of task performance from the third circle to affect or modulate real-world interactional settings.

In essence, Robinson's aptitude model (2007, 2012) offers a blueprint describing how different clusters of cognitive abilities are combined to form integrated aptitude complexes that in turn dynamically modulate different L2 learning conditions, such as explicit instruction, incidental learning from both written and oral input, and corrective recasting of output (Stansfield & Winke, 2008). Interpreted this way, the dynamic aptitude complexes model highlights the limitations of current language aptitude tests, such as the MLAT's "developmental and situational insensitivity," and thus points to the future direction of aptitude test development. In other words, future research should aim to develop new tests of aptitude which are situationally and developmentally sensitive and can predict successful learning in different implicit, incidental, or explicit learning conditions, across the range of proficiency levels, from beginner to advanced stages of second language development (Robinson, 2019).

Skehan's Staged Model and Tests

By adopting insights from classical information processing theory in cognitive psychology, Peter Skehan (1998, 2002, 2012, 2016; Dörnyei & Skehan, 2003) has postulated *four* macro stage-based aptitude constructs that are derived from acquisitional processes in SLA. According to Skehan (1998), research into language aptitude has been to discover "whether there is a specific talent for learning languages, and if so, what the structure of such a talent might be". Skehan further pointed out that previous research in this area (up to the 1990s) seemed to have ignored the latest developments achieved in SLA. Therefore, it becomes imperative to situate aptitude theory within SLA stages of input processing, central processing, and output—and to further identify the finer-grained acquisitional processes embedded within each stage—to clarify the corresponding aptitude constructs underlying these cognitive processes.

As conceived by Skehan, for example, it can be argued that L2 learners' "phonetic coding ability" allows them to selectively process the language input, so it is most closely related to the cognitive mechanism of controlling noticing resources of linguistic input. On the other hand, the "language analytical ability" is dominantly implicated in recognizing, identifying, and coding patterns from language input materials and subsequently internalizing it as a language rule. Finally, (working) memory ability should not only store newly acquired language materials but also include retrieval and extraction of language materials that have been stored in (long-term) memory. These may implicate storing and retrieving formulaic sequences or chunks to achieve the lexicalization and automatization of language output expressions.

Recently, in his updated aptitude theory, Skehan (2016) identified ten acquisitional stages (such as input processing and segmenting, coming into focus, identifying patterns, error avoidance, etc.), and aligned them with four macro stage-based aptitude constructs (such as handling sound, handling patterns, proceduralizing, automatizing). Overall, at least two significant implications can be drawn from Skehan's stage-based aptitude model. First, the putative acquisitional processes thus aligned form a sequence, beginning with the acquisition from the input stage (of linguistic stimuli) until reaching fluent and effortless use in the output or performance stage, echoing the classic information processing model. Second, a great advantage of taking such a micro approach to analyze these acquisitional processes is to clarify how to develop new aptitude subtests in the future. In essence, the fine-grained nature of the sequence of acquisitional processes then becomes a useful means of exploring existing aptitude subtests to see where they might be located and which acquisitional processes they would be most relevant for. As such, the macro-staged aptitude model also provides a general framework for guiding future research to locate all putative acquisitional processes for which there are currently no, or only a small number of, language aptitude subtests in existing aptitude batteries (Skehan, 2016).

The HI-LAB Model and Tests

In recent years, an important development in language aptitude theory and testing has been the "High-level Language Aptitude Battery," i.e., the Hi-LAB Model and the associated tests constructed by a group of cognitive psychologists cum SLA researchers at the University of Maryland's Centre for Advanced Studies in Languages (CASL; Doughty, Campbell, Mislevy, Bunting, Bowles, & Koeth, 2010; Doughty, Jackson, & Hughes, 2015; Doughty, 2013, 2014, 2019; Linck, Hughes, Campbell, Silbert, Tare, Jackson, & Doughty, 2013). According to Hi-LAB's principal inventor, Doughty (2013, 2014, 2019), language aptitude is defined as the special talent for learning languages, and it thus constitutes a "ceiling" on ultimate attainment. In other words, when all other key factors are optimal (i.e., "all else being equal"), differences in aptitude will determine how successful an individual ultimately can be in the domain constrained by their aptitude (Doughty, 2019).

The original motivation of Hi-LAB had been to develop an aptitude battery that could serve to distinguish high-level language achievers who acquire foreign languages after the post-critical period. The "Hi-LAB" test battery consists of *13* subtests that tap into *seven* putative cognitive abilities, including both domain-general capacities (e.g., working memory functions and phonological short-term memory, etc.) and domain-specific perceptual abilities. Overall, Hi-LAB was partially emulating existing language aptitude tests (such as the MLAT) but went far beyond them by incorporating interdisciplinary insights from contemporary cognitive psychology, neuroscience, and SLA, thus achieving an impressive standard of construct validity (Wen et al., 2017).

Recent empirical validation studies have reported quite encouraging results as well (Doughty, 2014, 2019; Doughty et al., 2010, 2015). For example, Linck et al. (2013) showed that Hi-LAB could indeed distinguish a group of "high-level achievers" from a group of "normal achievers." Moreover, it was found that among the 13 subtests, three individual instruments, namely, Paired Associates, Serial Reaction Time, and Letter Span provided substantial classification information across the ultimate learning outcomes of listening, reading, and either-skill analyses. These results were interpreted by the authors as consistent with the assumption that associative memory, implicit learning, and phonological short-term memory play particularly important roles in achieving high-level attainment. In another recent validation study by Doughty (2019), it was also suggested that compared with MLAT, Hi-LAB is indeed more predictive of the learning outcomes of high-level L2 learners. Thus, the author concluded that MLAT and Hi-LAB are two complementary test batteries that could predict different aspects of basic and advanced L2 proficiency. Despite these positive results and its great potential to help promote the development of language aptitude theory and testing, Hi-LAB has been restricted to internal use only and not released to the general public.

Towards an Integrative Perspective

The P/E Model and Tests

After reviewing the research in the field of cognitive psychology on the nature, structure, and functions of the working memory construct and synthesizing the empirical studies investigating its role in SLA domains and skills in the past 30 years or so, I recently have argued to extend current language aptitude theory to incorporate a working memory perspective (Wen, 2016 & 2019; Wen & Skehan, 2011; cf. Miyake & Friedman, 1998). These efforts have culminated in an integrative perspective of the "Phonological/Executive Hypothesis" (shortened as the P/E model) concerning the working memory-SLA nexus (Wen, 2015, 2016, 2019). The P/E model builds on the theoretically motivated links delineating two key components of the working memory system, namely, Phonological Working

Memory (PWM) and Executive Working Memory (EWM) that are further fractionated into *five* component mechanisms and functions. The two key working memory components, namely, PWM and EWM, are purported to subserve to varying degrees specific domains of L2 acquisition (e.g., phonology, lexis, formulaic chunks, morpho-syntactic constructions) and sub-skills (bilingual) processing (e.g., listening, speaking, reading, writing, and interpreting, etc.). Specifically, the P/E model postulates that its phonological component, i.e., PWM, which in turn subsumes a phonological short-term store and an articulatory rehearsal mechanism, constitutes the foundation for storing, chunking, and consolidating novel phonological forms into the long-term knowledge base (cf. Ellis, 1996; Ellis & Sinclair, 1996; Martin & Ellis, 2012). In line with its domain-specific nature, PWM is purported to underpin and sustain sound-based aspects of language acquisition and representation, facilitating the chunking and consolidation of L2 pronunciation or sound imitation, lexis, or vocabulary, formulaic sequences, morpho-syntactic structures or constructions. Portrayed in this sense, PWM is equivalent to the well-established proposal of the "Language Learning Device" originally conceived in the multicomponent WM model (Baddeley, Gathercole & Papagno, 1998; Wen, 2019).

On the other hand, the "E" part of the P/E model is similar to the "central executive" component of the multi-modality model of working memory (Baddeley, 1993, 1996), or its equivalent concept of "executive attention" as advocated by Engle (2002). Specifically, EWM is purported to subsume *three* major executive functions of (memory) updating, set or task switching, and inhibitory control (Miyake & Friedman, 2012; cf. Indrarathne & Kormos, 2018). Viewed this way, EWM is likely to be more closely related to the processing demands placed upon working memory resources, which in turn coordinates or modulates cognitive processes or performance dimensions of L2 sub-skills. As such, it is postulated by the P/E model that EWM constrains selective online and offline processes implicated in L2 listening, speaking, reading, writing, and bilingual interpreting, etc. Given its constraints of resources and control of attention, EWM will exert impacts upon such cognitive processes as the noticing of corrective feedback or recasts during L2 interactions (Mackey, Philp, Egi, Fujii, & Tatsumi, 2002). Interpreted this way, EWM can be regarded as a language processing or parsing device (or a "language processor/parser"; Wen, 2019) in the language aptitude system.

In terms of measurement, the P/E model currently draws on research on the two traditional paradigms of assessment procedures in contemporary cognitive psychology (Redick, Broadway, Meier, Kuriakose, Unsworth, Kane, & Engle, 2012). To measure PWM, it is recommended to adopt a "simple" (i.e. storage-only) version of the working memory span tasks, such as the most common format of the non-word repetition span task (Gathercole, 2006; Gathercole, Willis, Baddeley, & Emslie, 1994). On the other hand, regarding measuring EWM, it is postulated by the P/E model that a "complex" storage-plus-processing working memory span task can be administered, such as the domain-specific reading span task (Daneman & Carpenter, 1980) or its domain-general variant of the operation span task (Turner & Engle, 1992). It is also acknowledged by the P/E model that a series of internal and external factors are weighing in distinctively to affect the outcomes of working memory span tasks administered to L2 learners. These potentially confounding factors range from the most significant, i.e., information types (linguistic vs. non-linguistic), the encoding modalities (listening-based vs. reading-based vs. speaking-based), to the least obvious, that is the encoding languages (L1 vs. L2). Given the perplexing nature of working memory tests and scoring procedures, further research needs to refine the hierarchical nature of these factors influencing outcomes of working memory span tasks in SLA research. (Wen, Juffs, & Winke, 2021).

Above all, empirical evidence is now accumulating pointing to the pivotal and pervasive role of working memory effects, manifested by its two key components and sub-level mechanisms or functions in second language learning processes and outcomes (Wen & Li, 2019). Empirical studies from two recent volumes (Wen et al., 2013, 2015; also see Wen, 2016), as well as recent meta-analytical studies (e.g., Linck, Osthus, Koeth, & Bunting, 2014), are all pointing to the great potential of working memory in both *predicting* and *explaining* SLA processes and ultimate attainments (Wen,

2019). For example, based on a meta-analysis of 79 empirical studies published between 1992 and 2013, Linck et al. (2014) showed that working memory has an important impact on both the process and outcome of SLA, with the coefficient standing at 0.255. Conversely, Grundy and Timmer (2017) also used a meta-analytic method to analyze 27 empirical studies and found that bilingual learners (bilinguals) have a higher working memory than their monolingual counterparts, with a correlation of 0.20 at the significant level. Thus, the close association between working memory and SLA is both theoretically and empirically established, though future research also needs to work out the directionality of their reciprocal impacts (Bialystok, 2017; Jackson, 2020). In addition, future research still needs to gauge the distinctive effects of the two working memory components, either independently or in combination, across different linguistic tasks, different learning conditions, and across different L2 developmental stages or proficiency levels. To top it all, the proposal of "working memory as language aptitude" holds great promise in *explaining* SLA, which goes far beyond previous aptitude models and tests that had focused only on predicting ultimate attainment.

Implications for Research and Practice

From these reviews, we can draw two more conclusions regarding the different language aptitude models and tests proposed in the past 60 years. First of all, due to the long period of marginalization, research in language aptitude has lagged far behind other IDs in SLA, particularly eclipsed by the blossom of L2 motivation research (Dörnyei, 2020), in all essential developments of theoretical construction, measurement procedures, and pedagogical applications. That said, given language aptitude's supreme predictive validity (on par with L2 motivation on most occasions; Skehan, 1998, 2002; only next to the age factor; Stansfield & Winke, 2008) plus its great potential to *explain* both the SLA process and the ultimate attainment, it is imperative to speed up research efforts in this line of inquiry.

Second, it should be obvious from the reviews here that interdisciplinary perspectives (e.g., education, psychology, neuroscience, and SLA; Reiterer, 2018; Wen et al., 2019) are providing complementary insights to illuminate the *nature* and *structure* of the language aptitude construct. Indeed, a big breakthrough achieved by these current cognitive models of language aptitude and their test batteries lies in their enhanced *explanatory* power rather than a moderate predictive validity. In this sense, these cognitive aptitude models in SLA (e.g., that of Skehan's and Robinson's), as opposed to their predecessors (e.g., MLAT), represent a fundamental shift of the research paradigm in current and future language aptitude research, from their previous focus on prognostication to the current pursuit of explanation, and from future endeavors to application.

Put together, the many aptitude models and test batteries reviewed here are making distinctive and unique contributions towards a deeper understanding of the nature and structure of the concept of language aptitude as well as its measurement. As I shall argue in the next section, such a re-conceptualization of language aptitude can be pushed further towards the prevailing approach of complex dynamic systems theory (CDST) currently pursued by an increasing number of SLA researchers (e.g., Gurzynski-Weiss, 2020).

Moving Towards a CDST Future?

Recent years have witnessed growing attention among SLA researchers attached to the complex dynamic systems theory (CDST) approach (see Chapter 4) as a meta-theory for tracking and interpreting L2 acquisition and development (Larsen-Freeman, 1997, 2015). Regarding a CDST lens for IDs, Dörnyei has advocated as early as 2010 to adopt this approach to research language aptitude and L2 motivation as some higher-order amalgams (e.g., the aptitude/trait complexes, interests, and possible selves), rather than separating the two IDs as discreet dispositional attributes. However, despite the remarkable progress already achieved in the CDST approach towards conceptualizing L2 motivation, and other key ID factors such as L2 willingness to communicate (WTC) (see Chapter 20) and L2 anxiety (see the recent special issue of *Studies in Second Language Teaching and Learning* guest-edited by Gurzynski-Weiss, 2020), language aptitude so far seems to have remained immune to this prevailing paradigm. In this case, it is worth exploring whether a CDST approach will be a new impetus for promoting language aptitude development in the near future. My answer is a definite "Yes"!

To begin with, since the inception of the early four-factor model by Carroll and his five-part MLAT battery, the concept of language aptitude has never been conceived as a monolithic trait or measured as such by just one single test or item. On the contrary, the construct has always been conceptualized as a cognitive system consisting of *multiple components*, which range from four to seven sub-components as evident in the interdisciplinary perspectives discussed above. In a similar vein, the construct has usually been measured by a whole set of test items (i.e., a test battery), normally consisting of four to twelve subtests. As an extension, the multi-componential nature of language aptitude also highlights the increasing importance of adopting "aptitude profiles" over that of a single "aptitude score" in the past (Doughty, 2019; Linck et al., 2013). Based on learners' aptitude profiles then, teachers can design instructional treatments to optimize language learning as well as provide individualized intervention treatment procedures (e.g., Linck et al., 2013; Gregersen & Macintyre, 2014; Vuong & Wong, 2019).

Secondly, all current aptitude models have either directly or implicitly postulated a complex and dynamic relationship among its multiple components, or between internal components and external factors, thus achieving *relational dynamics* assumed by the CDST approach. Specifically, the relational dynamics can exist either between the multiple components themselves or between aptitude constructs and L2 learning tasks or real-life situations/scenarios, which the aptitude complexes model by Robinson illustrates amply. In other words, these components of the language aptitude system are manifesting the CDST characterization of *complete interconnectedness*.

Thirdly, language aptitude scores or aptitude profiles obtained by implementing language aptitude test batteries can serve as L2 learners' *initial conditions or states* (e.g., language proficiency level at the beginning) that allow others (educators/practitioners) to predict or forecast the next developmental stage or the ultimate learning outcomes. That said, their (L2) developmental stages are often *non-linear* and sometimes are challenging to predict (*unpredictable*) given the complex and dynamic interactions between the interplaying factors within the language aptitude system. However, there are CDST research methods such as the "retrodictive qualitative modeling" (Dörnyei, 2014) which can allow researchers to trace back the reason why certain components of the system ended up in one outcome state as opposed to another.

That is to say, the CDST perspective holds great potential to reveal the richness and diverse scenarios of language aptitude interplaying with language learning conditions or contexts (incidental vs. intentional; explicit vs. implicit), specific task features, or implementation conditions (or "task aptitudes" as advocated by Robinson, 2005, 2019), thus significantly broadening and refining the scope of current aptitude-treatment interactions (ATI) designs (DeKeyser, 2019). More importantly, the CDST approach is likely to facilitate an overhaul of language aptitude, as it has pointed to the limitations of previous and current conceptions and test batteries, and thus pinpoints desirable directions for future research. From now on, language aptitude should no longer be viewed as a fixed and stable trait, but rather as a multi-dimensional attribute that is both malleable and dynamically developing with L2 learners' experience (cf. Singleton, 2017). To achieve this research goal, future research also needs to further demonstrate how language aptitude develops in terms of both short-term fluctuations and long-term trajectories.

Regarding other future directions, language aptitude researchers still need to follow the legacy left behind by the educational psychologist Richard E. Snow (1992) in his integrated framework of language aptitude that highlights three development phases of prognostication, explanation, and application (Wen, 2016; Wen et al., 2017). To begin with, the first phase of prognostication implicates developing reliable and valid aptitude tests applicable to L2 learner's diverse backgrounds (native language, age, and socio-economic status). Then, in terms of explanation, language aptitude models and tests should be able to not just predict performance and outcomes with different tasks and under different learning contexts, but also be able to explain the L2 learning process and ultimate attainments adequately. Finally, regarding applications, future language aptitude theory and tests could inform language teaching pedagogy and classroom practice, as well as facilitating the diagnosis of L2 learning difficulties (Sparks, 2019) and inform remedial or intervention treatments and procedures (Vuong & Wong, 2019).

Conclusion

Above all, it is my final hope that by adopting interdisciplinary perspectives, the expanded scope of the aptitude-treatment interaction (ATI) approach will bear more fruit, and ultimately allow us to establish an efficient and effective "personalized" learning and teaching platform (Vuong & Wong, 2019). The theoretical framework of "personalized learning" sets out to identify the most effective predictors from an array of genetic and neural behavior, as well as other aspects of individual differences (IDs) in language learning by applying state-of-the-art scientific techniques and methodologies from diverse disciplines of psychology, biology, computer modeling, and neuroscience. In this respect, some encouraging results have been reported by Patrick Wong and his interdisciplinary team at the Chinese University of Hong Kong (see Wong et al., 2017; Vuong & Wong, 2019). These results are compelling evidence demonstrating the benefits of matching up learners' biological variability with optimal teaching models and instructional methods. It is conceivable that empirical work pursuing this line of inquiry should have a bright future, and that it may constitute the ultimate goal of language aptitude research.

Therefore, interdisciplinary perspectives are shedding new light on our understanding of the concept of language aptitude, as well as its pivotal role in predicting and explaining the cognitive underpinnings of the SLA process and the likely rate or speed of ultimate success. In the future, these interdisciplinary endeavors should be further expanded to leverage insights not just from educational psychology, cognitive psychology, neuroscience, and SLA, but also from other disciplines such as anthropology and evolutionary psychology, biology and genetics, computer programming and modeling, sociology, and philosophy.

Reflective Questions

Our short tour of the major language aptitude models and test batteries in the past six decades has helped us to re-examine their developments and reflect on three fundamental issues regarding the *nature*, *structure*, and *utility* of the important cognitive construct of language aptitude in relation to second and foreign language learning and teaching.

- What is your own definition and understanding of language aptitude?
- What does language aptitude consist of?
- What kind of functions can language aptitude tests serve?

Acknowledgments

The author wishes to thank Peter Skehan and Richard Sparks for constructive comments and help with the chapter at different stages. All remaining errors and limitations are my own responsibility.

Recommended Readings

Granena, G., & Long, M. (2013). *Sensitive periods, language aptitude, and ultimate L2 attainment.* John Benjamins.
This volume presents theoretical and empirical studies reflecting on age effects, bilingualism effects, maturational constraints, and sensitive periods in SLA, the sub-components of language aptitude, and the development of new aptitude measures, as well as reviews on aptitude-treatment interactions.

Reiterer, S. M. (2018). *Exploring language aptitude: Views from psychology, the language sciences, and cognitive neuroscience.* Springer-Nature.
The chapters in this volume were mostly based on the research work from the lab led by Susanne Reiterer in their investigation of such individual difference factors as (working) memory, personality, self-concept, bilingualism and multilingualism, education, musicality, and gender. As its subtitle indicates, a distinctive feature of the volume is its multidisciplinary perspectives.

Wen, Z., Biedron, A., Skehan, P., Li, S., & Sparks, R. (Eds.) (2019). *Language aptitude: Advancing theory, testing, research and practice.* Routledge.
This recent volume covers broad issues in language aptitude theory and test developments in global contexts and covers studies investigating the role language aptitude in L2 learners of different proficiency levels ranging from intermediate learners to exceptionally gifted learners or polyglots. It does not just revisit previous aptitude models and tests but also presents innovative perspectives and empirical evidence, as well as clear pointers for future research.

References

Baddeley, A. D. (1993). Working memory or working attention? In A. D. Baddeley & L. Weiskrantz (Eds.), *Attention: Selection, awareness, and control. A tribute to Donald Broadbent* (pp. 152–170). Oxford University Press.
Baddeley, A. D. (1996). Exploring the central executive. *Quarterly Journal of Experimental Psychology, 49A,* 5–28.
Baddeley, A. D., Gathercole, S., & Papagno, C. (1998). The phonological loop as a language acquisition device. *Psychological Review, 105,* 158–173.
Bialystok E. (2017). The bilingual adaptation: How minds accommodate experience. *Psychological Bulletin, 143,* 233–262.
Bley-Vroman, R. (1990). The logical problem of foreign language learning. *Linguistic Analysis, 20,* 3–49.
Bokander, L., & Bylund, E. (2019). Probing the internal validity of the LLAMA language aptitude tests. *Language learning.*
Carroll, J. B. (1981). Twenty-five years of research on foreign language aptitude. In K. C. Diller (Ed.), *Individual differences and universals in language learning aptitude* (pp. 83–118). Newbury House.
Carroll, J. B. (1990). Cognitive abilities in foreign language aptitude: Then and now. In T. Parry & C. W. Stansfield (eds.), *Language aptitude reconsidered* (pp. 11–29). Prentice-Hall.
Carroll, J. B., & S. M. Sapon (1959/2002). *Modern Language Aptitude Test (MLAT).* The Psychological Corporation. (Reprinted in 2002).
Cummins, J. (1979). Linguistic interdependence and the educational development of bilingual children. *Review of Educational Research, 49,* 222–251.
Daneman, M., & Carpenter, P. A. (1980). Individual differences in working memory and reading. *Journal of Verbal Learning and Verbal Behaviour, 19,* 450–466.
DeKeyser, R., & A. Juffs. (2005). Cognitive considerations in L2 learning. In E. Hinkel (Ed.), *Handbook of research in second language teaching and learning* (pp. 437–454). Lawrence Erlbaum.
DeKeyser, R. (2019). The future of language aptitude research. In Wen Z., Skehan, P., Biedron, A., Li, S., & Sparks, R. (Eds.), *Language aptitude: Advancing theory, testing, research and practice* (pp. 330–342). Routledge.
Dörnyei, Z. (2010). The relationship between language aptitude and language learning motivation: Individual differences from a dynamic systems perspective. In E. Macaro (Ed.), *Continuum companion to second language acquisition* (pp. 247–267). Continuum.
Dörnyei, Z. (2020). *Innovations and challenges in language learning motivation.* Routledge.
Dörnyei, Z., & P. Skehan (2003). Individual differences in second language learning. In C. Doughty & M. H. Long (Eds.), *The handbook of second language acquisition* (pp. 589–630). Blackwell Publishing.

Doughty, C. J. (2013). Optimizing post-critical-period language learning. In G. Granena & M. H. Long (Eds.), *Sensitive periods, language aptitude, and ultimate L2 attainment* (pp. 153–175). John Benjamins.
Doughty, C. J. (2014). Assessing aptitude. In A. Kunnan (Ed.), *The companion to language assessment* (pp. 25–46). Wiley-Blackwell.
Doughty, C. J. (2019). Cognitive language aptitude. *Language Learning, 68*, 101–126.
Doughty, C. J., Campbell, S. G., Mislevy, M. A., Bunting, M. F., Bowles, A. R., & Koeth, J. T. (2010). Predicting near-native ability: The factor structure and reliability of Hi-LAB. In M. T. Prior, Y. Watanabe & S-K. Lee (Eds.), *Selected proceedings of the 2008 Second Language Research Forum* (pp. 10–31). Cascadilla Proceedings Project.
Doughty, C. J., Jackson, S., & Hughes, M. (2015, October 9). *Implementation of the high-level language aptitude battery at the Foreign Service Institute and the National Security Agency* [Paper presentation]. East Coast Organization of Language Testers Conference, Washington, D.C.
Ellis, N. C. (1996). Sequencing in SLA: Phonological memory, chunking and points of order. *Studies in Second Language Acquisition, 18*, 91–126.
Ellis, N. C., & Sinclair, S. G. (1996). Working memory in the acquisition of vocabulary and syntax: Putting language in good order. *The Quarterly Journal of Experimental Psychology, 49A*(1), 234–250.
Ellis, R. (1985, 2015). *Understanding second language acquisition*. OUP.
Ellis, R. (2004). Individual differences in second language learning. In A. Davies & C. Elder (Eds.), *The handbook of applied linguistics* (pp. 525–551). Blackwell.
Ellis, R. (2019). Foreword. In Z. Wen, P. Skehan, A. Biedron, S. Li, & R. Sparks (Eds.), *Language aptitude: Advancing theory, testing, research and practice* (pp. xv–xvii). Routledge.
Engle, R. W. (2002). Working memory capacity as executive attention. *Current Directions in Psychological Science, 11*, 19–23.
Gathercole, S. E., Willis C. S., Baddeley, A., & Emslie, H. (1994). The children's test of nonword repetition: A test of phonological working memory. *Memory, 2(2)*, 103–127.
Granena, G. (2013). Reexamining the robustness of aptitude in second language acquisition. In G. Granena, & M. Long (Eds.), *Sensitive periods, language aptitude, and ultimate L2 attainment* (pp. 179–204). John Benjamins.
Grigorenko, E. L., Sternberg, R. J., & Ehrman, M. E. (2000). A theory-based approach to the measurement of foreign language learning ability: The CANAL-F theory and test. *The Modern Language Journal, 84*, 390–405.
Grundy, J. G., & Timmer, K. (2017). Bilingualism and working memory capacity: A comprehensive meta-analysis. *Second Language Research, 33(3)*, 325–340.
Gurzynski-Weiss, L. (2020). Special issue: Investigating the dynamic nature of learner individual differences in L2 learning. *Studies in Second Language Learning and Teaching, 10*(1), 1–219.
Indrarathne, B., & Kormos, J. (2018). The role of working memory in processing L2 input: Insights from eye-tracking. *Bilingualism: Language and Cognition, 21*, 355–374.
Jackson, D. O. (2020). Working memory and second language development: A complex, dynamic future? *Studies in Second Language Learning and Teaching, 10*(1), 89–109.
Jackson, F. H., & Kaplan, M. A. (2001). Lessons learned from fifty years of theory and practice in government language teaching. In J. E. Alatis & A.-H. Tan (Eds.), *Georgetown University round table on languages and linguistics 1999: Language in our time* (pp. 71–87). Georgetown University Press.
Krashen, S. (1981). Aptitude and attitude in relation to second language acquisition and learning. In K. C. Diller (Ed.), *Individual differences and universals in language learning aptitude* (pp. 155–175). Newbury House.
Larsen-Freeman, D. (1997). Chaos/complexity science and second language acquisition. *Applied Linguistics, 26*, 141–165.
Larsen-Freeman, D. (2015). Ten "lessons" from complex dynamic systems theory: What is on offer. In Z. Dörnyei, P. MacIntyre, & A. Henry (Eds.), *Motivational dynamics in language learning* (pp. 11–19). Multilingual Matters.
Li, S. (2015). The associations between language aptitude and second language grammar acquisition: A meta-analytic review of five decades of research. *Applied Linguistics, 36(3)*, 385–408.
Linck, J. A., Hughes, M. M., Campbell, S. G., Silbert, N. H., Tare, M., Jackson, S. R., & Doughty, C. J. (2013). Hi-LAB: A new measure of aptitude for high-level language proficiency. *Language Learning, 63(3)*, 530–566.
Linck, J. A., Osthus, P., Koeth, J. T., & Bunting, M. F. (2014). Working memory and second language comprehension and production: A meta-analysis. *Psychonomic Bulletin & Review 21(4)*, 861–883.
Mackey, A., Philp, J., Egi, T., Fujii, A., & Tatsumi, T. (2002). Individual differences in working memory, noticing of interactional feedback and L2 development. In P. Robinson (Ed.), *Individual differences and second language instruction* (pp. 181–209). John Benjamins.
Martin, K. I., & Ellis, N. C. (2012). The roles of phonological STM and working memory in L2 grammar and vocabulary learning. *Studies in Second Language Acquisition, 34*(3), 379–413.
Meara, P. (2005). *LLAMA language aptitude tests*. Lognostics.

Miyake, A., & Friedman N. P. (1998). Individual differences in second language proficiency: Working memory as language aptitude. In A. F. Healey & L. J. Bourne (Eds.). *Foreign language learning: Psycholinguistic studies on training and retention* (pp. 339–364). Lawrence Erlbaum.

Miyake, A., & Friedman N. P. (2012). The nature and organization of individual differences in executive functions: Four general conclusions. *Current Directions in Psychological Science, 21(1),* 8–14.

Redick, T. S., Broadway, J. M., Meier, M. E., Kuriakose, P. S., Unsworth, N., Kane, M. J., & Engle, R. W. (2012). Measuring working memory capacity with automated complex span tasks. *European Journal of Psychological Assessment, 28,* 164–171.

Reiterer, S. M. (2018). *Exploring language aptitude: Views from psychology, the language sciences, and cognitive neuroscience.* Springer-Nature.

Robinson, P. (2005). Aptitude and second language acquisition. *Annual Review of Applied Linguistics, 25,* 46–73.

Robinson, P. (2012). Individual differences, aptitude complexes, SLA processes, and aptitude test development. In M. Pawlak (Ed.), *New perspectives on individual differences in language learning and teaching.* Springer-Verlag, 57–75.

Robinson, P. (2019). Aptitude and second language acquisition. In C. Chapelle (Ed.), *The concise encyclopedia of applied linguistics* (pp. 129–133). Blackwell.

Rogers, V., Meara, P., Aspinall, R., Fallon, L., Goss, T., Keey, E., & Thomas, R. (2016). Testing aptitude: Investigating Meara's (2005) LLAMA tests. *EUROSLA Yearbook, 16*(1), 179–210.

Rogers, V., Meara, P., Barnett-Legh, T., Curry, C., & Davie, E. (2017). Examining the LLAMA aptitude tests. *Journal of the European Second Language Association, 1(1),* 49–60.

Singleton, D. (2017). Language aptitude: Desirable trait or acquirable attribute? *Studies in Second Language Learning and Teaching,* 7(1), 89–103.

Skehan, P. (1998). *A cognitive approach to language learning.* Oxford University Press.

Skehan, P. (2002). Theorising and updating aptitude. In P. Robinson (Ed.), *Individual differences and instructed language learning* (pp. 69–94). John Benjamins.

Skehan, P. (2012). Language aptitude. In S. Gass, & Mackey, A. (Eds.), *Routledge handbook of second language acquisition* (pp. 381–395). Routledge.

Skehan, P. (2016). Foreign language aptitude, acquisitional sequences, and psycholinguistic processes. In G. Granena, D. Jackson, & Y. Yilmaz (Eds.), *Cognitive individual differences in L2 processing and acquisition* (pp. 17–40). John Benjamins.

Skehan, P. (2019). Language aptitude implicates language and cognitive skills. In Z. Wen, P. Skehan, A. Biedron, S. Li, & R. Sparks (Eds.), *Language aptitude: Advancing theory, testing, research and practice* (pp. 56–77). Routledge.

Snow, R. E. (1992). Aptitude theory: Yesterday, today, and tomorrow. *Educational Psychologist, 27,* 5–32.

Sparks, R. L. (1995). Examining the Linguistic Coding Differences Hypothesis to explain individual differences in foreign language learning. *Annals of Dyslexia, 45,* 187–219.

Sparks, R. L. (2019). Why reading is a challenge for U.S. L2 learners: The impact of cognitive, ecological, and psychological factors in L2 comprehension, *Foreign Language Annals, 52*(4), 727–743.

Sparks, R. L., & Ganschow, L. (1991). Foreign language learning difficulties: Affective or native language aptitude differences? *The Modern Language Journal, 75(1),* 3–16.

Sparks, R. L., & Ganschow, L. (2001). Aptitude for learning a foreign language. *Annual Review of Applied Linguistics, 21(1),* 90–111.

Sparks, R., Patton, J., & Luebbers, J. (2019). Individual differences in L2 achievement mirror individual differences in L1 skills and L2 aptitude: Crosslinguistic transfer of L1 to L2 skills. *Foreign Language Annals, 52*(2), 255–283.

Sparks, R. L., Patton, J., Ganschow, L., & Humbach, N. (2011). Subcomponents of L2 aptitude and L2 proficiency. *The Modern Language Journal, 95,* 253–273.

Spolsky, B. (1995). Prognostication and language aptitude testing. *Language Testing, 12,* 321–340.

Stansfield, C. W., & Reed, D. J. (2004). The story behind the Modern Language Aptitude Test: An interview with John B. Carroll (1916–2003). *Language Assessment Quarterly: An International Journal, 1,* 43–56.

Stansfield, C. W., & Reed, D. J. (2019). The MLAT at 60 years. In Z. Wen, P. Skehan, A. Biedron, S. Li, & R. Sparks (Eds.), *Language aptitude: Advancing theory, testing, research and practice* (pp. 15–32). Routledge.

Stansfield, C., & Winke, P. (2008). Testing aptitude for second language learning. In E. Shohamy & N. H. Hornberger (Eds.), *The encyclopedia of language and education* (Vol. 7, pp. 81–94). Springer Verlag.

Sternberg, R. J. (1997). *Successful intelligence.* Plume.

Sternberg, R. J. (2002) The theory of successful intelligence and its implications for language aptitude testing. In P. Robinson (Ed.), *Individual differences and instructed language Learning* (pp. 13–43). John Benjamins.

Sternberg, R., & Grigorenko, E. (2002). *Dynamic testing: The nature and measurement of learning potential.* Cambridge University Press.

Turner, M. L., & Engle R. W. (1989). Is working memory task dependent? *Journal of Memory and Language, 28,* 127–154.

Vuong, L. C., & Wong, P. C. M. (2019). From individual differences in language aptitude to personalized learning. In Z. Wen, P. Skehan, A. Biedron, S. Li, & R. Sparks (Eds.), *Language aptitude: Advancing theory, testing, research and practice* (pp. 330–342). Routledge.

Wen, Z. (2012). Foreign language aptitude. *ELT Journal, 66*(2), 233–235.

Wen, Z. (2015). Working memory in second language acquisition and processing: The Phonological/Executive model. In Z. Wen, M. B. Mota, & A. McNeill (Eds.), *Working memory in second language acquisition and processing* (pp. 41–62). Multilingual Matters.

Wen, Z. (2016). *Working memory and second language learning: Towards an integrated approach.* Multilingual Matters.

Wen, Z. (2019). Working memory as language aptitude: The Phonological/Executive Model. In Z. Wen, P. Skehan, A. Biedron, S. Li, & R. Sparks (Eds.), *Language aptitude: Advancing theory, testing, research and practice* (pp. 187–214). Routledge.

Wen, Z., Juffs, A., & Winke, P. (2021). Measuring working memory. In P. Winke & T. Brunfaut (Eds.), *The Routledge handbook of second language acquisition and testing.* Routledge.

Wen, Z., & Li, S. (2019). Working memory in L2 learning and processing. In J. Schwieter & A. Benati (Eds.), *The Cambridge handbook of language learning* (pp. 365–389). Cambridge University Press.

Wen, Z., Mota, M., & McNeill, A. (2013). Working memory and SLA: Innovations in theory and research. *Asian Journal of English Language Teaching, 23,* 1–102.

Wen, Z., Mota, M., & McNeill, M. (2015). *Working memory in second language acquisition and processing.* Multilingual Matters.

Wen, Z., Biedron, A., & P. Skehan. (2017). Foreign language aptitude theory: Yesterday, today and tomorrow. *Language Teaching, 50*(1), 1–31.

Wen, Z., Biedron, A., Skehan, P., Li, S., & Sparks, R. (Eds.). (2019). *Language aptitude: Advancing theory, testing, research and practice.* Routledge.

Wen, Z., & P. Skehan (2011). A new perspective on foreign language aptitude: Building and supporting a case for "working memory as language aptitude." *Ilha Do Desterro: A Journal of English language, literatures and cultural studies, 60,* 15–44.

Wesche, M. B. (1981). Language aptitude measures in streaming, matching students with methods, and diagnosis of learning problems. In K. C. Diller (Ed.), *Individual differences and universals in language learning aptitude* (pp. 119–154). Newbury House.

Wong, P. C. M., Vuong, L.C., & Liu, K. (2017). Personalized learning: From neurogenetics of behaviors to designing optimal language training. *Neuropsychologia, 98,* 192–200.

31
PSYCHOLOGY OF LEARNING VERSUS ACQUISITION

Miroslaw Pawlak

From its inception, second language acquisition (SLA) research has heavily drawn upon theories proposed to explain diverse phenomena in the field of psychology. After all, some early explanations of how individuals get to know a second or foreign language (L2) were based on the tenets of behaviorism, positing that the learning process proceeds by means of imitation and practice of models, which results in the formation of habits (VanPatten & Williams, 2015). The impact of psychology is also evident in research on individual differences among learners and teachers (Dörnyei & Ryan, 2015; Griffiths, 2008, 2020), as illustrated by the chapters in this handbook. Somewhat inevitably, psychological accounts of human learning have also informed theoretical positions seeking to explain how L2 knowledge develops. This is particularly visible in the discussion of whether the mastery of the target language (TL) is the outcome of *learning* or *acquisition*, influential constructs describing two alternative ways of gaining L2 knowledge put forward by Krashen (1981, 1982) in his Acquisition-Learning Hypothesis, one of the five hypotheses comprising his Monitor Theory. *Learning* describes a conscious process of acquainting oneself with relevant rules and patterns as a result of explicit instruction as well as various types of practice and corrective feedback (CF). By contrast, *acquisition* refers to a process which takes place outside awareness, involves a focus on meaning, and is driven by understanding L2 data slightly beyond learners' current level of interlanguage development. The crucial assumption is that the knowledge gained consciously does not underlie spontaneous performance and can only be used to monitor TL production when certain conditions are met (i.e., focus on accuracy, familiarity with the rule, and sufficient time).

Although this distinction was extremely influential for a while and was well-received by practitioners who saw in it a reflection of the difficulty of dealing with what Larsen-Freeman (2003, 2014) refers to as the *inert knowledge problem*, or learners' failure to use what is taught explicitly in communication, it has been subject to major modifications in the last two decades. Thus, most current debates focus on the nature and role of explicit and implicit L2 knowledge, as well as the processes leading to their development, that is, explicit and implicit L2 teaching and learning (DeKeyser, 2017; Ellis, 2009; Pawlak, 2013, 2017, 2019, 2020a). The aim of this chapter is to provide an overview of these debates, first with respect to a psychology-based perspective and then an SLA-related perspective. Subsequently, interfaces between the two will be explored, implications for teaching and research will be considered, and the way forward for future empirical investigations will be charted. Two important caveats are in order at the outset. First, although the learning-acquisition debate can be approached from diverse angles grounded in psychology, such as sociocultural theory (e.g., Lantolf,

Poehner, & Swain, 2018) (see Chapter 2) or complex dynamic systems theory (e.g., Larsen-Freeman, 2017) (see Chapter 4), the present discussion will fall back upon cognitive theories (see Chapter 1). Second, while the label *cognitive* has been used to refer to several theoretical positions, including those drawing on Universal Grammar (White, 2015) or usage-based accounts of SLA (N. Ellis & Wulff, 2015), emphasis will be placed on the view of L2 learning as gaining mastery of a complex skill (DeKeyser, 2010, 2015, 2017). However, the role of attention (Schmidt, 2001) and the cognitive-interactionist perspective (Kim, 2017) will also be taken into account.

Learning Versus Acquisition Perspectives in Psychology

The distinction between learning and acquisition, or explicit and implicit learning, can be traced back to cognitive psychology, and in particular to the work of Reber (1967), who showed that learners were able to commit to memory letter sequences based on a finite-state grammar and generalize them but were subsequently unable to verbalize the relevant rules. This demonstrated that *implicit learning*, which is unintentional and unconscious, is fundamental to cognition and underlies different spheres of individuals' functioning, such as language comprehension and production, intuitive decision-making, or social interaction (Berry & Dienes, 1993; Lewicki, 1986; Rebuschat, 2015). Hayes and Broadbent (1988, p. 251) define implicit learning as "the unselective and passive aggregation of information about the co-occurrence of environmental events and features." Research in developmental psychology has also yielded evidence that *statistical learning*, which relies on computations done on the basis of units and patterns, such as syllables or syntactic categories, can also contribute to the mastery of linguistic information without awareness (Gómez, 2021; Saffran, Aslin, & Newport, 1996). These processes can be differentiated from *explicit learning*, which is conscious in the sense that learners are asked to deliberately identify rules underlying observed patterns and verbalize them (Rebuschat, 2015). There is also evidence that although learners may be cognizant that they have acquired new knowledge, they are oblivious to the nature of this knowledge, and it is more permanent than that obtained in an intentional way (Allen & Reber, 1980; Reber, 2003; Rebuschat & Williams, 2012). What must also be emphasized at this juncture is that not all psychologists are in favor of differentiating between these two disparate learning systems. For example, Shanks (2003) argues that such a dissociation is not viable on functional neurological grounds. On the other hand, Wallach and Lebiere (2003) postulate the existence of a dual learning system based on declarative and procedural memory, and this distinction finds support in neuropsychological evidence (e.g., Hezeltine & Ivry, 2003; Paradis, 2009; Ullman, 2015).

The issues of implicit and explicit learning are inextricably linked with the concept of *attention* and the role it plays in these processes. While attention can be studied from different perspectives, the most relevant to the discussion of the psychology of learning vs. acquisition is the information-processing approach (Esterman & Rothlein, 2019; Pashler, 1998; Sanders, 1998; Sergeant, 1996). In this account, attention comes into operation at three sages: (1) *intake and processing* of auditory and visual information, where selection of what should be attended to occurs, (2) *central processing*, where decisions are made about aspects of the tasks to which limited attentional resources should be allocated and automatization can be initiated, and (3) *choosing, executing and monitoring a response* to stimuli, where effort is required to keep giving attention to the task performed (Robinson, 2003). There is disagreement about the reasons why attention needs to be selective, with some arguments centering on its limited capacity and others highlighting the necessity for action control so that the demands of a task can most effectively be satisfied (Allport, 1989; Gozli & Ansorge, 2016; Neumann, 1996). It is also unclear whether attention, which is allocated in working memory, represents a single resource (Kahneman, 1973) or a pool of multiple recourses assigned to different dimensions of a task, such as visual vs. auditory, or spatial vs. verbal (Wickens, 1992). Of crucial importance is the effort to sustain attention, which hinges on the length of the required performance and the nature of the task, and the lack of which leads to gradual deterioration of performance (Wickens, 1992). It should be added that attention is subject to voluntary control because we can choose the aspect of a task to attend to, it controls access to consciousness, and its presence is essential for the occurrence of learning. Obviously, attention can occur at different levels, such as mere registration of new stimuli or awareness, and it is the intensity and nature of rehearsal in short-term memory that determine whether implicit or explicit learning processes are activated (LaBerge, 1995; Robinson, 2003; Schmidt, 2001).

Explicit and implicit learning are believed to result in the development of *explicit* and *implicit knowledge*. While individuals are cognizant of the former and can describe it, albeit not necessarily in technical terms, the latter is knowledge without awareness and therefore it cannot be verbalized (Reber, 2003; Rebuschat, 2013). There is evidence that these types of knowledge are stored in different parts of the brain (Henke, 2010; Ullmann, 2015). It should be emphasized, however, that while explicit and implicit representation are distinct, the nature of what we learn does not necessarily remain permanent. This is because, with time, we can lose awareness of things that we learned explicitly, a good example being tying shoelaces. On the other hand, we can also become conscious of mechanisms that govern things that we learned without intention, as is the case with jogging when we make a conscious effort to assume a proper running form. The differentiation between these two types of knowledge is closely related to the distinction between *declarative knowledge* and *procedural knowledge*, which was made by psychologists well over half a century ago (Ryle, 1949). Declarative knowledge, sometimes also referred to as *knowledge THAT*, is composed of facts and events, thus comprising semantic and episodic memory, it can be consciously accessed, and it can often be verbalized. By contrast, procedural knowledge, also described as *knowledge HOW*, is manifested in actual performance, such as driving a car, skiing, or fluent L2 performance, and thus it cannot be talked about (cf. DeKeyser, 2017). Gade, Druey, Souza, and Oberauer (2014, p. 16) define the two types of knowledge as follows: "Declarative representations are objects of thought, whereas procedural representations provide (cognitive) actions to work upon these objects." There are two important issues that should be highlighted here. First, the procedural reinstatement principle posits that declarative knowledge is more quickly forgotten but at the same time more generalizable, which facilitates transfer to new contexts, whereas procedural knowledge is more durable but highly specific, which diminishes its generalizability (Healy, 2007; Lohse & Healy, 2012). Second, although explicit and implicit knowledge are often conveniently equated with declarative and procedural knowledge (Ellis, 2009a, 2009b; Loewen, 2018; Nassaji, 2017), DeKeyser (2017) points out that this is an oversimplification, not least because Chomsky's (1965) concept of linguistic competence is based on the premise that declarative knowledge is tacit. For practical purposes, however, these two distinctions are collapsed in most discussions of L2 learning, and this is also the stance embraced in this chapter.

Cognitive psychologists have also naturally been interested in the relationship between explicit/declarative and implicit/procedural knowledge, investigating, for example, whether the two types of representation develop in parallel and what their respective contributions are to the process of learning (e.g., Batterink, Reber, Neville, & Paller, 2015; Sun, Xi, Slusarz, & Matthews, 2007; Willingham, Goedert-Eschmann, 1999). Another important issue, which is of particular relevance to the current discussion, is how declarative knowledge can provide a point of departure for the emergence of procedural knowledge and its subsequent automatization. This brings us to the concept of *automaticity*, which can be described as "the speed and ease with which we carry out… tasks" (DeKeyser, 2001, p. 125). However, there is no consensus among psychologists about the nature of this construct or its defining characteristics. It is not clear, for instance, whether the process requires high speed, accuracy, effortlessness, efficiency, absence of awareness, reduced reliance on attentional resources, or task performance through single-step memory retrieval. Despite initial claims that controlled and automatic processes are dichotomous (Schneider & Shiffrin, 1977), most specialists are of the opinion that automaticity should be seen on a continuum since most of the properties are gradual in nature (cf. DeKeyser, 2001; Logan & Etherton, 1994; Moors & De Houwer, 2006). Another crucial consideration is how automatization proceeds—what processes it involves as well as the stages it follows.

For example, there exist opposing views on whether it entails solely quantitative change, reflected in speedier and more error-free performance, or qualitative change as well, which brings about restructuring of different task components (Segalowitz, 2003; Segalowitz & Segalowitz, 1993). At the same time, there is a consensus that an indispensable condition for automatization is consistent practice but also that automatized behaviors are highly skill-specific in the sense that they do not easily lend themselves to transfer from one domain to another (e.g., from comprehension to production) (Anderson, 1993).

There is no single theory accounting for the process of automatization, but, given the theme of this chapter, a focus on automatization of rules rather than on retrieval from memory of previously encountered items is warranted (Logan, 1988). This is the approach embraced by Anderson (1992, 1993) in his *adaptive control of thought (ACT) theory*, according to which automatic behavior is the outcome of a three-part process consisting of the *declarative, procedural,* and *automatic* stages. The theory states that the acquisition of a complex skill starts with declarative knowledge, which has to be consciously retrieved by means of general-purpose production rules for a particular behavior to be performed. With time, when opportunities for practice are supplied together with analogy-supporting examples, qualitative change occurs, whereby the components of declarative knowledge are incorporated into a production rule. As a result, they become proceduralized, which enables faster and more accurate execution of the required behavior. Large amounts of different types of practice are necessary to set in motion quantitative change, which is quite slow but leads to the fine-tuning of production rules and their gradual automatization, with the effect that performance no longer places heavy demands on attentional resources. ACT theory has considerably affected debates concerning the role of learning and acquisition in SLA, which will be the focus of the following section.

Learning Versus Acquisition Perspectives in SLA

Although Krashen's (1981) distinction between *learning* and *acquisition*, as well as the concepts of *learned* and *acquired knowledge* were at the center of discussions about L2 learning for a while, the bulk of current theorizing and research in SLA revolves around the dichotomy of *explicit* and *implicit knowledge*, typically seen as equivalent to *declarative* and *procedural knowledge*, and the corresponding processes of *explicit* and *implicit learning* and *teaching*. Adopting the criteria proposed by Ellis (2004, 2006, 2009a), explicit knowledge is conscious and declarative, it comprises facts about L2 (such as grammar rules) that can be verbalized, but such information is frequently imprecise and inaccurate. Although the development of explicit knowledge is not constrained by age or access to requisite syntactic operations (Pienemann & Lenzing, 2015), it can only be applied in controlled processing when learners have sufficient time to draw on relevant rules. By contrast, implicit knowledge does not involve awareness and relies on intuition, it is procedural since it operates on the basis of condition-action rules, and thus it is not available for verbal report. It is this type of knowledge that underlies spontaneous, real-time performance in L2, but its development is restricted by age and mastery of necessary processing mechanisms.

However, when characterized in this way, implicit knowledge is not attainable for teenagers and adults or learners with scarce out-of-class exposure to the TL and equally scarce opportunities for its use. This problem is exacerbated by the fact that in the vast majority of settings L2 instruction starts with explicit provision of rules which are subsequently practiced in different ways, with the effect that the point of departure is explicit or declarative knowledge (cf. DeKeyser, 2010, 2017; DeKeyser & Juffs, 2005). Therefore, DeKeyser (2017) argues that it makes more sense talk about *highly automatized knowledge*, which is so efficient, fast, and independent of attentional recourses that it can underpin fluent and largely accurate L2 performance needed in everyday communication. This solution seems to be most propitious in view of the fact that, even if implicit knowledge and highly automatized knowledge might be distinct (Suzuki & DeKeyser, 2017a), they are functionally indistinguishable in communicative interaction. Besides, despite the endeavors of researchers (e.g., Ellis,

2009), constructing valid and reliable measures of implicit knowledge represents a daunting challenge (DeKeyser, 2017; Pawlak, 2019; Rebuschat, 2013; Suzuki & DeKeyser, 2015, 2017a). Another thorny issue is the relationship between explicit and implicit knowledge, which has far-reaching ramifications for L2 learning. Krashen (1981) adopted the *non-interface* position, downright denying any role for explicit knowledge in spontaneous L2 performance. The alternative views include the *weak-interface* position (Ellis, 1997), according to which such contribution is possible if the learner has reached the requisite developmental stage, and the *strong-interface position* (DeKeyser, 2007, 2010), which posits that consciously held rules can be automatized to such an extent that they can serve as a basis for real-time performance. It is this last stance that is favored here because approaching L2 learning as the acquisition of a complex skill seems to be the most pedagogically viable, a point that will be revisited later in this chapter.

Several theories representing the cognitive perspective have attempted to explain how L2 learning takes place, suggest how different types of L2 knowledge can be developed, and propose recommendations as to what instructional techniques can assist such processes. One of them is Schmidt's (1990, 1995, 2001) *noticing hypothesis*, which is based on the assumption that successful learning of TL features in the input calls for *attention at the level of noticing*. In this view, focal attention is indispensable for the selection of forms in the linguistic data that have been detected, or non-consciously registered (Tomlin & Villa, 1994), thereby allowing conversion of input into intake, making form-meaning mappings more transparent and paving the way for cognitive comparisons. However, in the case of TL features that are redundant or non-salient, such as third-person *-s* or regular past tense *-ed* in English, intentionally focused attention at the level of understanding might be required. While Schmidt (2001) recognizes that learning can potentially occur without attention, or be largely implicit, he argues that the process is more efficient when learners attend to specific L2 forms. He writes: "Language learners who take a totally passive approach to learning, waiting patiently and depending on involuntary attentional processes to trigger automatic noticing, are likely to be slow and unsuccessful learners" (2001, pp. 23–24).

The noticing hypothesis is closely connected with the *cognitive-interactionist approach*, which led to the emergence of different variants of *focus on form*, or "spontaneous attention to linguistic forms during meaning-oriented activities" (Kim, 2017, p. 128). Of pivotal significance in this connection are Swain's (1985, 1995) *output hypothesis* and Long's (1996) *updated interaction hypothesis*. The main premise of the output hypothesis is that TL production is indispensable to bring about a move from semantic to syntactic processing. Output is believed to perform three crucial functions: (1) promoting noticing of TL features; (2) enabling hypothesis-testing; and (3) fostering conscious reflection on how the L2 operates. Special emphasis is laid on the production of *pushed output*, or utterances that are accurate, precise, and appropriate, a goal that can be achieved through the provision of CF. As regards the interaction hypothesis, it stresses the contribution of negotiation of meaning as well as form, which directs learners' selective attention to TL features and the meanings they convey. In effect, these features become more salient, learners are provided with negative feedback when they commit errors, and they can subsequently modify their utterances to eliminate these errors (Long, 1996). The CF option that is given the pride of place is a *recast*, defined as a corrective reformulation of an inaccurate utterance that preserves its intended meaning and does not put in jeopardy communicative interaction. Since corrective recasts are immediately contingent on the preceding stretch of discourse, they are believed to fit perfectly into the optimal cognitive window of opportunity, or the time, 40 seconds or so, when learners are best suited to directly compare the two versions of the original utterance and notice the gap (Doughty, 2001). On the whole, attention is seen as crucial to L2 learning in the cognitive-interactionist approach and, as seen in different interpretations of focus on form, it can be triggered by means of various techniques, including other types of CF (Loewen, 2011; Nassaji, 2015).

Particularly pertinent to the current discussion in *skill-learning theory*, which was first introduced in to SLA by Johnson (1996) but later elaborated upon and popularized by DeKeyser (1998, 2001, 2007, 2010, 2015, 2017). This theoretical position is an application of Anderson's (1983, 1993) ACT theory to the field of L2 teaching and learning, where the additional language is regarded as a complex skill, similar to many other skills. Taking the present tense form of the passive in English as an example, the initial declarative knowledge first needs to be established, which can involve the provision of rules by the teacher (i.e., deduction) or their discovery by learners (i.e., induction). This knowledge then has to be proceduralized, whereby a "program" becomes available for the execution of specific operations, such as those needed to change active sentences into passive, and this program can be applied in controlled exercises (e.g., supplying the required form of the verb or paraphrasing). Although proceduralization happens relatively rapidly, automatizing the rules for the passive to such an extent that they can be used fast, effortlessly, and accurately in communicative interaction is a lengthy and arduous process. Moreover, since automatized knowledge is highly skill-specific, practice at this stage needs to occur under conditions similar to those in which relevant rules will be employed. In this case, for such *transfer appropriate processing* (Lightbown, 1998) to be activated, learners would have to complete tasks that call for the use of the passive in spontaneous communication. Obviously, since "automaticity is not an all-or-nothing affair" (DeKeyser, 2015, p. 96), these tasks should be selected in such a way that they place gradually greater demands on attentional processes so that highly automatized knowledge of the passive can emerge and be available in various kinds of spontaneous interactions. It is thus evident that skill-learning theory embodies the strong-interface position and does not take into account learners' developmental readiness to acquire a particular TL feature. DeKeyser (2017) emphasizes, however, that the development of highly automatized knowledge does not involve gradual disappearance of explicit knowledge or its relocation to a different part of the brain, as if with a wave of a magic wand, but rather the emergence of a parallel mental representation. As he notes, "all that is claimed is that existing declarative knowledge, via practice, plays a causal role in the development of procedural knowledge" (DeKeyser, 2015, p. 103).

For reasons of space, a thorough overview of empirical evidence generated by studies grounded in these theoretical positions falls outside of the scope of this chapter. Therefore, only the most prominent lines of inquiry can be highlighted and the most important findings can be synthesized. However, before this can be done, there are some crucial issues that need to be addressed. First, since the relevant studies have examined explicit and implicit learning and teaching, a question arises regarding the definition and operationalization of these concepts. As Nassaji (2017, p. 206) elucidates, "implicit learning is often defined as learning without awareness, taking place when learners are exposed to meaning-focused input, while explicit learning is conscious, taking place mainly through explicit instruction." He writes further that "explicit instruction presents learners with clear information about certain grammar rules and how they work whereas implicit instruction does not attempt to make to make learners aware of what they are supposed to learn" (p. 209). The main problem is, however, that explicitness and implicitness represent a continuum rather than a dichotomy. For instance, a recast and a clarification request are typically viewed as more implicit forms of CF but the negative evidence carried by the latter is more salient as it requires output modification. On the other hand, explicit teaching is not confined to rule provision and it can involve different types of controlled and communicative practice, some of which will be more explicit than others (Ellis, 1997; Loewen, 2011; Nassaji & Fotos, 2011; Pawlak, 2014). It is also highly doubtful that in contexts where TL features are overtly introduced and practiced, it would at all be feasible to conceal completely from learners the pedagogical purpose of an activity or task, thus making it truly implicit. All of this casts serious doubt on the assumption that implicit instruction always stimulates implicit learning processes and contributes to implicit knowledge, whereas the effect of explicit learning and teaching might not be confined to expanding explicit knowledge if its delayed effects are considered (Larsen-Freeman, 2003). Second, it should be stressed that the measures of L2 knowledge used in different studies vary widely, and not all of these studies attempt to tap into explicit/declarative and implicit/procedural/highly automatized knowledge, let alone their productive and receptive dimensions. Even when measures of these types of knowledge are included, they are often operationalized in a diversity of ways (e.g., oral production tasks, oral elicited imitation, or eye-tracking for implicit knowledge and untimed grammaticality judgment tests or controlled grammar exercises for explicit knowledge) (Loewen, 2018; Pawlak, 2019; Suzuki & DeKeyser, 2017a). This indicates that the results of different studies may be to some extent a function of assessment tools used—they are not comparable and they should be taken with circumspection.

The pertinent empirical investigations can be divided into three main strands: (a) those comparing the effects of explicit and implicit instruction, (b) those that examine the impact of different types of instruction on explicit and implicit knowledge, also taking account of the role mediating variables, and (c) those that investigate the contribution of different ways in which practice is implemented. When it comes to the first category, the results of research syntheses and meta-analyses demonstrate that although both types of intervention are effective, explicit instruction produces greater and more permanent gains (e.g., Goo, Granena, Yilmaz, & Novella, 2015; Norris & Ortega, 2000; Spada & Tomita, 2010). However, such overviews focus on a mixed bag of studies which operationalize instructional options in different ways, use diverse tasks to tap into performance, and often include outcome measures that favor explicit knowledge (Nassaji, 2017). The conclusion that explicit teaching is more efficacious is largely corroborated by studies that compare the relative effectiveness of specific instructional options. It has been shown, for example, that output-inducing, more explicit feedback types, such as prompts (e.g., clarification requests or metalinguistic clues) are superior to input-providing, more implicit CF options, such as recasts (e.g., Ellis, 2017; Lyster & Saito, 2010; Nassaji, 2015). Additionally, it was found that more salient variants of input enhancement (e.g., using bolding or coloring to make the targeted feature stand out) are more effective than less salient ones, particularly if they are accompanied by metalinguistic explanation (e.g., LaBrozzi, 2016; Indrarathne & Kormos, 2017). What needs to be emphasized is the role of mediating variables, in particular individual difference (ID) factors, such as working memory (e.g., Goo, 2016) or learning styles (Rassaei, 2015). With respect to research on the impact of different instructional options on the growth of explicit and implicit knowledge, there is evidence that explicit instruction, operationalized in different ways, can lead to the development of the latter. These beneficial effects, however, are moderated, among others, by the difficulty of the TL feature, the length of the treatment, or learners' L1 (e.g., Andringa, de Glopper, & Hacquebord, 2011; Ellis, 2002; Spada & Tomita, 2010). By contrast, implicit instruction has been shown to primarily affect implicit knowledge (e.g., Godfroid, 2015). Finally, the studies investigating the value of practice have demonstrated that it can lead to a decrease in error rate and reaction time (e.g., Rodgers, 2011), a shift in the location of brain activity (e.g., Morgan-Short, Sanz, Steinhauer, & Ullman, 2010), or enhanced fluency as a result of task repetition (e.g., de Jong & Perfetti, 2011). There is also evidence for the role of skill-specificity of practice and the occurrence of transfer-appropriate processing (e.g., Spada, Jessop, Tomita, Suzuki, & Valeo, 2014), as well as unclear effects of distributed and massed practice (e.g. Suzuki & DeKeyser, 2017b).

Integrating Perspectives

As can be seen from the preceding discussion, SLA theorists and researchers have drawn quite heavily on the developments in cognitive psychology. This is mainly evident in the adoption of the crucial distinction between explicit/declarative knowledge and implicit/procedural/highly automatized knowledge. Over the last twenty years, this distinction has effectively replaced the dichotomy of learned and acquired knowledge (Krashen, 1981), and has allowed specialists to move beyond the appealing but somewhat intuitive concepts of learning and acquisition and focus instead on the constructs of explicit and implicit learning, which are perceived as more scientifically sound. Another example of the impact of psychology on SLA is the position that an additional language is yet another complex skill and the consequent application of Anderson's (1983, 1992) ACT theory to explaining the processes involved in L2 learning. SLA specialists have also adopted the information-processing model of attention and have attempted to design optimal ways of getting learners to attend to TL features in the input without compromising the communicative nature of the interaction. The theoretical positions deriving from psychology have provided an impulse for increasingly more sophisticated studies that have investigated, among other things, the effects of different types of instruction, including different CF options, on the development of explicit and implicit knowledge, explored the role of practice in diverse learning conditions on the automatization of L2 knowledge, and yielded evidence for the role of transfer-appropriate processing. Moreover, the measures of L2 knowledge have become more and more advanced, with some researchers incorporating tools employed in psychological experiments, such as eye tracking or electrophysiological (ERP) measures.

Despite the evident interfaces, one can hardly avoid the impression that the integration of constructs and procedures originating in psychology is for the most part superficial and selective, focusing on elements that are seen as most relevant to SLA. However, while researchers should follow the latest developments in psychology, such as new research designs and tools used for tapping into explicit and implicit learning processes as well as related representations, we should keep in mind that language acquisition is far more complex than learning artificial grammars or some other complex systems, and it transpires in real-life contexts rather than laboratory conditions. In other words, the bulk of research on instructed second language acquisition (ISLA) is conducted in real classrooms and takes the form of quasi-experimental designs, where random assignment of participants to control and experimental groups is not feasible and it is impossible to fully control for extraneous variables. By the same token, the use of sophisticated measures of implicit or highly automatized knowledge is difficult to fathom in such contexts. It might in fact make little sense to use such instruments in situations where the main goal is to determine whether instruction allows learners to use the targeted features in spontaneous communication in contrast to controlled conditions, and thus the main focus is on automatized knowledge (cf. Pawlak, 2019).

The empirical investigations in the domain of SLA do not seem to have affected research in psychology in any tangible way, and thus the transfer of constructs, models, theories or data-collection procedures has largely been a one-way street. This is perhaps not surprising in view of the fact that specialists examining L2 learning and teaching have set their sights on different branches of psychology to inform their research endeavors and not the other way around. When we consider the empirical evidence discussed in this chapter, however, there are two areas on which cognitive psychologists could potentially draw to be better able interpret the findings of their own experiments. One is the burgeoning research on the effectiveness of more and less implicit instructional options, including the provision of CF, and the other are research projects exploring the moderating role of ID variables. The former can help make the operationalization of explicit and implicit learning in psychological experiments more nuanced, while the latter, even though still limited in scope in the field of SLA itself (Pawlak, 2017), can aid interpretation of the differential effects of various learning modes on explicit and implicit knowledge.

Implications for Practice and Research

The foregoing discussion can serve as a basis for some implications for L2 instruction as well as research into the role of learning and acquisition or, to use more current terminology, explicit and implicit learning. With respect to teaching, much depends on the specific context but, at least in foreign language settings, a logical solution is to embrace the strong-interface position, as embodied in skill-learning theory (DeKeyser, 2015). This is because most learners simply do not have sufficient exposure to the TL to be able to learn it implicitly; most of them are past the critical period, which precludes harnessing implicit learning; and L2 instruction typically starts with explicit knowledge anyway (cf. DeKeyser, 2017; DeKeyser & Juffs, 2005). Therefore, it seems warranted, at least in the initial stages, to follow a structural syllabus and the presentation-practice-production (PPP) procedure as this allows gradual proceduralization and automatization of TL structures. However, several important caveats are in order. First, the last element in the sequence (i.e., production) should be given much more weight than is usually the case so that learners can really have a chance to automatize the rules taught. Second, learners should have the opportunity to employ the targeted features in real-time processing required by communicative interaction as only in this way can we ensure transfer-appropriate processing (Lightbown, 2008). Third, for this to happen, L2 grammar teaching has to be viewed in terms of sequences of lessons rather than single classes, with the production phase being considerably extended over time with a view to supporting automatization. Fourth, proceduralization and automatization of L2 rules can be facilitated by the provision of CF, which should be direct and explicit in the case of the former and somewhat more implicit in the case of the latter. Fifth, at more advanced stages, a gradual shift can be engineered to a task-based syllabus, where learners are mainly engaged in message conveyance but their attention is drawn to problematic features by means of proactive (e.g., questions regarding TL forms to be used) and reactive (i.e., the use of various kinds of CF) focus on form (Loewen, 2011). Sixth, the transition from declarative to procedural and automatized knowledge can be assisted by the employment of suitable grammar learning strategies (Pawlak, 2013, 2020b).

Moving on to research, the most important lesson perhaps is that researchers conducting pedagogically oriented, classroom-based studies should be content with measures of highly automatized knowledge, such as tasks requiring the use of specific TL forms in communication, rather than pure measures of implicit knowledge, which are exceedingly difficult to come by (DeKeyser, 2017). Although laboratory research can surely generate important insights, much more useful from a pedagogical perspective are studies undertaken in real classrooms because they have greater ecological validity and can show us what works in real life. There is also room for investigations that examine the effect of constellations of instructional options rather than focus on comparisons of selected techniques, since this reflects the realities of classroom-based instruction. Finally, much more attention should be given to the role of mediating variables, and in particular ID factors, with emphasis on those that can actually be managed by practitioners (e.g., anxiety, beliefs, strategies) rather than such that might be theoretically interesting but also hardly amenable to intervention in everyday teaching (e.g., working memory).

Future Directions

Whatever the specific labels used, the distinction between learning and acquisition is crucial to research into L2 instruction and actual classroom practices. The main reason for this is that the bulk of L2 instruction starts with rule explanation or discovery and the crucial issue is what steps should be taken to expedite the employment of such rules in communication. Although there is copious empirical evidence that different types of instruction are effective and that the right kind of practice aided by appropriate feedback can lead to the automatization of TL rules, this evidence is still patchy and thus there is a need for further research in this area. Such research should focus in particular on how different techniques can be combined to facilitate the proceduralization and automatization of declarative knowledge, also taking into account the mediating role of ID factors, the properties of the TL features taught, and contextual realities. It would also be ideal if interfaces between research in psychology and SLA were to become more consistent, mutual, and pronounced as this would definitely enhance our understanding of how different learning conditions can spur the development of different types of L2 knowledge. Such understanding in turn would make it possible to offer concrete recommendations on how to overcome the inert knowledge problem (Larsen-Freeman, 2003) and make sure that learners can use the TL features they are taught in spontaneous interaction.

Reflection Questions

- How realistic do you think it is for teachers to adopt the non-interface position?

- From your experience, can you think of three examples of tasks that would allow automatization of the knowledge of the past unreal conditional in English?
- What grammar learning strategies can help proceduralization and automatization of explicit knowledge?

Recommended Reading

DeKeyser, R. (2015). Skill-acquisition theory. In B. VanPatten & J. Williams (Eds.), *Theories in second language acquisition* (2nd ed., pp. 94–122). Routledge.
This chapter provides a concise overview of the principles of skill-learning theory that is largely domain-neutral but also touches upon the explicit-implicit debate in SLA.

Nassaji, H. (2017). Grammar acquisition. In S. Loewen & M. Sato (Eds.), *The Routledge handbook of instructed second language acquisition* (pp. 205–223). Routledge.
The chapter offers a useful overview of the key areas of research into grammar teaching, with a special emphasis on the role of different instructional options in the development of explicit and implicit L2 knowledge. Pedagogical recommendations and directions for future research are also offered.

Rebuschat, P. (2013). Measuring implicit and explicit knowledge in second language research. *Language Learning, 63,* 595–626.
This article presents three measures that have been used in psychological research to tap into explicit and implicit knowledge, and which can be useful for SLA specialists, that is, retrospective verbal reports, direct and indirect tests, and subjective measures.

References

Allen, R., & Reber, A. S. (1980). Very long term memory for tacit knowledge. *Cognition, 8,* 175–185.
Allport, D. A. (1989). Visual attention. In M, Posner (Ed.), *Foundations of cognitive science* (pp. 631–682). MIT Press.
Anderson, J. R. (1983). *The architecture of cognition*. Harvard University Press.
Anderson, J. R. (1992). Automaticity and the SACT theory. *American Journal of Psychology, 105,* 165–180.
Anderson, J. R. (1993). *Rules of the mind*. Lawrence Erlbaum.
Andringa, S., de Glopper, K., & Hacquebord, H. (2011). Effect of explicit and implicit instruction on free written response task performance. *Language Learning, 13,* 67–80.
Batterink, L. J., Reber, P. J., Neville, H. J., & Paller, K. A. (2015). Implicit and explicit contributions to statistical learning. *Journal of Memory and Language,* 83, 62–78.
Berry, D. C., & Dienes, Z. (1993). *Essays in cognitive psychology. Implicit learning: Theoretical and empirical issues.* Lawrence Erlbaum.
Chomsky, N. (1965). *Aspects of the theory of syntax*. MIT Press.
De Jong, N., & Perfetti, C. A. (2011). Fluency training in the ESL classroom: An experimental study of fluency development and proceduralization. *Language Learning, 62,* 533–568.
DeKeyser, R. M. (1998). Beyond focus on form: Cognitive perspectives on learning and practicing second language grammar. In C. J. Doughty & J. Williams (Eds.), *Focus on form in classroom second language acquisition* (pp. 42–63). Cambridge University Press.
DeKeyser, R. (2001). Automaticity and automatization. In P. Robinson (Ed.), *Cognition and second language instruction* (pp. 125–151). Cambridge University Press.
DeKeyser, R. (2007). The future of practice. In R. DeKeyser (Ed.), *Practice in a second language: Perspectives from applied linguistics and cognitive psychology* (pp. 287–304). Cambridge University Press.
DeKeyser, R. (2010). Cognitive-psychological processes in second language learning. In M. H. Long & C. J. Doughty (Eds.), *The handbook of language teaching* (pp. 117–138). Wiley-Blackwell.
DeKeyser, R. (2015). Skill-acquisition theory. In B. VanPatten & J. Williams (Eds.), *Theories in second language acquisition* (2nd ed., pp. 94–122). Routledge.
DeKeyser, R. (2017). Knowledge and skill in SLA. In S. Loewen & M. Sato (Eds.), *The Routledge handbook of instructed second language acquisition* (pp. 15–32). Routledge.
DeKeyser, R., & Juffs, A. (2005). Cognitive considerations in L2 learning. In E. Hinkel (Ed.), *Handbook of research in second language teaching and learning* (pp. 437–454). Lawrence Erlbaum.

Doughty, C. J. (2001). Cognitive underpinnings of focus on form. In P. Robinson (Ed.), *Cognition and second language instruction* (pp. 206–257). Cambridge University Press.
Dörnyei, Z., & Ryan, S. (2015). *The psychology of the language learner revisited*. Routledge.
Ellis, N. C., & Wulff. S. (2015). Usage-based approaches to SLA. In B. VanPatten & J. Williams (Eds.), *Theories in second language acquisition* (2nd ed., pp. 75–93). Routledge.
Ellis, R. (1997). *SLA research and language teaching*. Oxford University Press.
Ellis, R. (2002). Does form-focused instruction affect the acquisition of implicit knowledge? A review of the research. *Studies in Second Language Acquisition, 24,* 223–236.
Ellis, R. (2004). The definition and measurement of explicit knowledge. *Language Learning, 54,* 227–275.
Ellis, R. (2006). Modeling learning difficulty and second language proficiency: The differential contributions of implicit and explicit knowledge. *Applied Linguistics, 27,* 431–463.
Ellis, R. (2009a). Implicit and explicit learning, knowledge and instruction. In R. Ellis, S. Loewen, C. Elder, R. Erlam, J. Philp, & H. Reinders (Eds.), *Implicit and explicit knowledge in second language learning, testing and teaching* (pp. 3–25). Multilingual Matters.
Ellis, R. (2009b). Measuring implicit and explicit knowledge of a second language. In R. Ellis, S. Loewen, C. Elder, R. Erlam, J. Philp, & H. Reinders (Eds.), *Implicit and explicit knowledge in second language learning, testing and teaching* (pp. 31–64). Multilingual Matters.
Ellis, R. (2017). Oral corrective feedback in L2 classrooms: What we know so far. In H. Nassaji & E. Kartchava (Eds.), *Corrective feedback in second language teaching and learning* (pp. 3–18). Routledge.
Gade, M., Druey, M. D., Souza, A. S., & Oberauer, K. (2014). Interference within and between declarative and procedural representations in working memory. *Journal of Memory and Language, 76,* 174–194.
Godfroid, A. (2015). The effects of implicit instruction on implicit and explicit knowledge development. *Studies in Second Language Acquisition, 38,* 177–215.
Gómez, R. (2012). Statistical learning in infant language development. In G. Gaskell (Ed.), *The Oxford handbook of psycholinguistics*. Oxford University Press.
Goo, J. (2016). Corrective feedback and working memory capacity in interaction-driven L2 learning. *Studies in Second Language Acquisition, 34,* 445–474.
Goo, J., Granena, G., Yilmaz, Y., & Novella, M. (2015). Implicit and explicit instruction in L2 learning: Norris & Ortega (2000) revisited. In P. Rebuschat (Ed.). *Implicit and explicit learning of languages* (pp. 443–482). John Benjamins.
Gozli, D. G., & Ansorge, U. (2016) Action selection as a guide for visual attention. *Visual Cognition, 24,* 38–50.
Griffiths, C. (2008). *Lessons from good language learners*. Cambridge University Press.
Griffiths, C. (2020). *Lessons from good language teachers*. Cambridge University Press.
Hayes, N. A., & Broadbent, D. E. (1988). Two models of learning for interactive tasks. *Cognition, 28,* 249–276.
Hazeltine, E., & Ivry, R. (2003). Neural structures that support implicit sequence learning. In L. Jimenez (Ed.), *Attention and implicit learning* (pp. 71–108). John Benjamins.
Healy, A. F. (2007). Transfer: Specificity and generality. In H. L. Roediger III, Y. Dudai, & S. M. Fitzpatrick (Eds.), *Science of memory: Concepts* (pp. 271–275). University Press.
Henke, K. (2010). A model of memory systems based on processing modes rather than consciousness. *Nature Reviews Neuroscience, 11,* 523–532.
Indrarathne, B., & Kormos, J. (2017). Attentional processing of input in explicit and implicit conditions: An eye-tracking study. *Studies in Second Language Acquisition, 39,* 401–430.
Johnson, K. (1996). *Language teaching and skill learning*. Blackwell.
Kahneman, D. (1973). *Attention and effort*. Prentice Hall.
Kim, Y. (2017). Cognitive-interactionist approaches to L2 instruction. In S. Loewen & M. Sato (Eds.), *The Routledge handbook of instructed second language acquisition* (pp. 126–145). Routledge.
Krashen, S. D. (1981). *Second language acquisition and second language learning*. Pergamon.
Krashen, S. D. (1982). *Principles and practice in second language acquisition*. Pergamon.
LaBrozzi, R. M. (2016). The effects of textual enhancement type on L2 form recognition and reading comprehension in Spanish. *Language Teaching Research, 20,* 75–91.
Lantolf, J. P., Poehner, M. E., & Swain, M. (2018). Introduction. In J. P. Lantolf, M. E. Poehner, & M. Swain (Eds.), *The Routledge handbook of sociocultural theory and second language development* (pp. 1–20).
Larsen-Freeman, D. (2003). *Teaching language: From grammar to grammaring*. Thomson & Heinle.
Larsen-Freeman, D. (2014). Research into practice: Grammar learning and teaching. *Language Teaching, 48,* 263–280.
Larsen-Freeman, D. (2017). Complexity theory: The lessons continue. In L. Ortega & Z. Han (Eds.), *Complexity theory ad language development: In celebration of Diane Larsen-Freeman* (pp. 11–50). John Benjamins.
LaBerge, D. (1995). *Attentional processing: The brain's art of mindfulness*. Harvard University Press.
Lewicki, P. (1986). *Nonconscious social information processing*. Academic Press.

Lightbown, P. M. (2008). Transfer appropriate processing as s model for classroom second language acquisition In Z. Han (Ed.), *Understanding second language process* (pp. 27–44). Multilingual Matters.
Loewen, S. (2011). Focus on form. In E. Hinkel (Ed.), *Handbook of research in second language teaching and learning: Volume II* (pp. 576–592). Routledge.
Loewen. S. (2018). Instructed second language acquisition. In A. Phakiti A., P. De Costa, L. Plonsky, & S. Starfield (Eds.), *The Palgrave handbook of applied linguistics research methodology* (pp. 663–680). Palgrave Macmillan.
Logan, G. D. (1988). Towards an instance theory of automatization. *Psychological Review, 95,* 492–527.
Logan, G. D., & Etherton, J. L. (1994). What is learned during automatization? The role of attention in constructing an instance. *Journal of Experimental Psychology: Learning, Memory and Cognition, 20,* 1022–1050.
Lohse, K. R., & Healy, A. F. (2012). Exploring the contributions of declarative and procedural information to training: A test of the procedural reinstatement principle. *Journal of Applied Research in Memory and Cognition, 1,* 65–72.
Long, M. H. (1996). The role of the linguistic environment in second language acquisition. In W. C. Ritchie & T. K. Bhatia (Eds.), *Handbook of second language acquisition* (pp. 413–468). Academic Press.
Lyster, R., & Saito, K. (2010). Oral feedback in classroom SLA: A meta-analysis. *Studies in Second Language Acquisition, 32,* 265–302.
Moors, A., & De Houwer, J. (2006). Automaticity: A theoretical and conceptual analysis. *Psychological Bulletin, 132,* 297–326.
Morgan-Short, K., Sanz, C., Steinhauer, K., & Ullman, M. T. (2010). Second language acquisition of gender agreement in explicit and implicit training conditions. An event-related potential study. *Language Learning, 60,* 154–193.
Nassaji, H. (2015). *The interactional feedback dimension in instructed second language learning. Linking theory, research, and practice.* Bloomsbury.
Nassaji, H. (2017). Grammar acquisition. In S. Loewen & M. Sato (Eds.), *The Routledge handbook of instructed second language acquisition* (pp. 205–223). Routledge.
Nassaji, H., & Fotos, S. (2011). *Teaching grammar in second language classrooms: Integrating form-focused instruction in communicative context.* Routledge.
Neumann, O. (1996). Theories of attention. In O. Neumann & A. Sanders (Eds.), *Handbook of perception and action* (pp. 389–446). Academic Press.
Norris, J. M., & Ortega, L. (2000). Effectiveness of L2 instruction: A research synthesis and quantitative meta-analysis. *Language Learning, 50,* 417–528.
Paradis, M. (2009). *Declarative and procedural determinants of second languages.* John Benjamins.
Pashler, H. (1998). Introduction. In H. Pashler (Ed.), *Attention* (pp. 1–11). Psychology Press.
Pawlak, M. (2013). Principles of instructed language learning revisited: Guidelines for effective grammar teaching in the foreign language classroom. In K. Droździał-Szelest & M. Pawlak (Eds.), *Psycholinguistic and sociolinguistic perspectives on second language learning and teaching: Studies in honor of Waldemar Marton* (pp. 199–220). Springer.
Pawlak, M. (2014). *Error correction in the foreign language classroom: Reconsidering the issues.* Springer.
Pawlak, M. (2017). Individual differences variables as mediating influences on success and failure in form-focused instruction. In E. Piechurska-Kuciel & M. Szyszka (Eds.). *At the crossroads: Challenges of foreign language learning* (pp. 75–92). Springer.
Pawlak, M. (2019). Tapping the distinction between explicit and implicit knowledge: Methodological issues. In B. Lewandowska-Tomaszczyk (Ed.), *Contacts & contrasts in educational contexts and translation* (pp. 45–60). Springer Nature.
Pawlak, M. (2020a). Grammar and good language teachers. In C. Griffiths & T. Tajeddin (Eds.), *Grammar and good language teachers* (pp. 219–231). Cambridge University Press.
Pawlak, M. (2020b). Grammar learning strategies as a key to mastering second language grammar: A research agenda. *Language Teaching, 53,* 358–370.
Pienemann, M., & Lenzing, A. (2015). Processability theory. In B. VanPatten & J. Williams (Eds.), *Theories in second language acquisition* (2nd ed., pp. 159–179). Routledge.
Rassaei, E. (2015). Recasts, field dependence-independence cognitive style, and L2 development. *Language Teaching Research, 19,* 499–518.
Reber, A. S. (1967). Implicit learning of artificial grammars. *Journal of Verbal Learning & Verbal Behavior, 6*(6), 855–863.
Reber, A. S. (2003). Implicit learning. In L. Nadel (Ed.), *Encyclopedia of cognitive science* (Vol 2, pp. 486–491). Macmillan.
Rebuschat, P. (2013). Measuring implicit and explicit knowledge in second language research. *Language Learning, 63,* 595–626.
Rebuschat, P. (2015). Introduction: Implicit ad explicit learning of languages. In P. Rebuschat (Ed.), *Implicit and explicit learning of languages* (pp. xiii–xxii). John Benjamins.

Rebuschat, P., & Williams, J. N. (2012). Implicit and explicit knowledge in second language acquisition. *Applied Psycholinguistics, 33,* 829–856.

Robinson, P. (2003). Attention and memory during SLA. In C. J. Doughty & M. H. Long (Eds.), *The handbook of second language acquisition* (pp. 631–678). Blackwell.

Rodgers, D. M. (2011). The automatization of verb morphology in instructed second language acquisition. *IRAL, 49,* 295–319.

Ryle, G. (1949). *The concept of mind.* Hutchinson.

Saffran, J. R., Aslin, R. N., & Newport, E. L. (1996). Statistical learning by 8-month-old infants. *Science, 274,* 1926–1928.

Sanders, A. F. (1998). *Elements of human performance: Reaction processes and attention in human skill.* Lawrence Erlbaum.

Schmidt, R. (2001). Attention. In P. Robinson (Ed.), *Cognition and second language instruction* (pp. 3–32). Cambridge University Press.

Schmidt, R. (1990). The role of consciousness in second language learning. *Applied Linguistics, 11,* 17–46.

Schmidt, R. (1995). Consciousness and foreign language learning: A tutorial on the role of attention and awareness in learning. In R. Schmidt (ed.) *Attention and awareness in foreign language learning* (pp. 1–63). University of Hawaii Second Language Teaching and Curriculum Center.

Schneider, W., & Shiffrin, R. M. (1977). Controlled and automatic human information processing I: Detection, search, and attention. *Psychological Review, 84,* 1–66.

Segalowitz, N. (2003). Automaticity. In C. J. Doughty & M. H. Long (Eds.), *The handbook of second language acquisition* (pp. 382–408). Blackwell.

Segalowitz, N. S., & Segalowitz, S. J. (1993). Skilled performance, practice, and the differentiation of speed-up from automatization effects: Evidence from second language word recognition. *Applied Psycholinguistics, 14*(3), 369–385.

Sergeant, J. (1996). A theory of attention: An information-processing perspective. In L. Reid & N. A. Krasnegor (Eds.), *Attention and executive function* (pp. 57–69). Paul H. Brookes.

Shanks, D. (2003). Attention and awareness in "implicit" sequence learning. In L. Jimenez (Ed.), *Attention and implicit learning* (pp. 11–42). John Benjamins.

Spada, N., Jessop, L., Tomita, Y., Suzuki, W., & Valeo, A. (2014). Isolated and integrated focus on form instruction: Effects on different types of L2 knowledge. *Language Teaching Research, 18,* 453–473.

Spada, N., & Tomita, Y. (2010). Interactions between type of instruction and type of language feature: A meta-analysis. *Language Learning, 60,* 263–308.

Sun, R., Xi, Z., Slusarz, P., & Matthews, R. (2007). The interaction of implicit learning, explicit hypothesis testing learning and implicit-to-explicit knowledge extraction. *Neural Networks, 20,* 34–47.

Suzuki, Y., & DeKeyser, R. (2015). Comparing elicited imitation and word monitoring as measures of implicit knowledge. *Language Learning, 65,* 860–895.

Suzuki, Y., & DeKeyser, R. (2017a). The interface of explicit and implicit knowledge in a second language: Insights from individual differences in cognitive aptitudes. *Language Learning, 67,* 747–790.

Suzuki, Y., & DeKeyser, R. (2017). Effects of distributed practice on the proceduralization of morphology. *Language Teaching Research, 21,* 166–188.

Swain, M. (1985). Communicative competence: Some roles of comprehensible input and comprehensible output in its development. In S. M. Gass & C. G. Madden (Eds.), *Input in second language acquisition* (pp. 235–253). Newbury House.

Swain, M. (1995). Three functions of output in second language learning. In G. Cook & B. Seidlhofer (Eds.), *Principles and practice in applied linguistics. Studies in honor of H. G. Widdowson* (pp. 125–144). Oxford University Press.

Tomlin, R., & Villa, V. (1994). Attention in cognitive science and second language acquisition. *Studies in Second Language Acquisition, 16,* 183–203.

Ullman, M. T. (2015). The declarative/procedural model. In B. VanPatten & J. Williams (Eds.), *Theories in second language acquisition* (2nd ed., pp. 135–158). Routledge.

VanPatten, B., & Williams, J. (2015). Early theories in SLA. In B. VanPatten & J. Williams (Eds.), *Theories in second language acquisition* (2nd ed., pp. 17–33). Routledge.

Wallach, D., & Lebiere, C. (2003). Implicit and explicit learning in a unified architecture of cognition. In L. Jimenez (Ed.), *Attention and implicit learning* (pp. 215–252). John Benjamins.

White, L. (2015). Linguistic theory, Universal Grammar, and second language acquisition. In B. VanPatten & J. Williams (Eds.), *Theories in second language acquisition* (2nd ed., pp. 34–53). Routledge.

Wickens, C. (1992). *Engineering psychology and human performance* (2nd ed.). HarperCollins.

Willingham, D. B., & Goedert-Eschmann, K. (1999). The relation between implicit and explicit learning: Evidence for parallel development. *Psychological Science, 10,* 531–534.

INDEX

A not B error 51
ability, stability of 164
abstract thought 373
academic buoyancy 140, 208
academic self-efficacy (ASE) 102
acceptance within a class group 319
acceptance and commitment therapy (ACT) 180
acculturation 151
accumulative stress 151
acquiescent responding (AR) 381–2
acquisition 406
acquisition-learning hypothesis 406
acting 180
action research 249
action tendencies 179
action zone in the classroom 291
acts as products of determinants 341
acts of kindness 327, 328
adaptations, characteristic 126
adaptive control of thought (ACT) theory 409, 410–11
adaptive control of thought-rational (ACT-R) theory 8, 9
adaptive reaching 56
affect 177
affective empathy 327
affective engagement 141, 142
affective filter hypothesis 39
affective regulation 179
age factor 77–8, 82
agency 250–4, 276; affordances in 252; personal 127; research on 253, 254
agentic engagement questionnaire (AEQ) 142
agreeableness 114, 118
Albert, Ágnes 339
alienated group members 287
alignment to environment 357
Allport, G.W. 341
altruism 325, 328

ambiguity, tolerance of 115, 118
ambiverts 113
American Psychological Association 313
amygdala 182–3
anger 318, 327
anthropologists 354
anti-depressants 51
anti-ought-to self 152, 154
anxiety 38, 51, 67, 183–4, 339; language 117, 183–4, 314, 316, 341–2, 383; proneness 341; situation-specific 341, 342; social 314; as a trait 115
approach versus avoidance motivation 128
aptitude 77, 339; dynamic conceptualization of 344; "malleability" 344; profiles 400
aptitude models 393, 395–7
aptitude-treatment interactions (ATI) 400, 401
Aristotle 192
Arnold, Jane 36
arousal of emotion 181
article usage 56
artificial intelligence 352, 353
Asher, James 44
Asian culture 263
associationism 352
associative memory 393
asylum seekers 308
at-risk populations 200
attention 316, 407–8, 410
attitude and motivation test battery (AMTB) 127, 150, 152
attitudes 149, 150, 302
attractor states 49, 50, 52, 55
attribution 106, 164; intra- and inter-personal comparisons 168; research 166–9, 175–6; theory 106, 161, 162–3
attribution-mindset relation 164
authorial voice 57
authoritarian teachers 209
autocratic leadership 287

Index

automatization 8, 9, 11, 408–9, 410
autonomous learning behavior 223–4
autonomy 39, 142, 245–50, 276; definitions 247, 248; learner 247, 248, 249; teacher 249
axioms 365
Ayers-Glassey, Samantha 61

backchannelling 142, 144
Bacon, Francis 351, 367
Bandura, Albert: 100–2, 105, 106, 107, 354, 357
Bayesian hypothesis testing 386
behavior 141, 219, 223–4, 287, 314, 409; automatic 236, 409; challenging 277, 280; helpless 166; intergroup 326; prosocial 325, 326; silent 276, 314, 315–16, 319; of teachers 277
behavior formula 287
behavior therapy 181
behavioral engagement 142, 144
behavioral psychology 352
behaviorist theories 22
beliefs 151, 152; and agency 253; about oneself 164; of teachers 151
beliefs about language learning inventory (BALLI) 151
belonging: to groups 286, 288–9; at school 288–9, 290, 292; sense of 143, 288
belongingness hypothesis 288–9
bias: agreement 381–2; implicit 150–1; in research 133, 384, 381
biased errors 364
big five traits of personality 113, 114, 340; "new big five" 126
bilingualism 76
bilinguals 75, 76, 181, 210
biomarkers 194
"black box" theory (linguistic) 364
"black box thinking" (motivation) 125, 126
blocked practice 14, 15, 17
bodily state 183
brain 78, 352, 364, 408; activity 365, 412; components 9, 38, 114, 182–3, 365; motor area 370–1
"broaden-and-build" theory 181
Bronfenbrenner's ecological systems theory 196
buoyancy 140, 208

cameras, point-of-view (POV) 145
"can-do" 100, 105
capital (power) 92, 93, 94
Carroll's aptitude model 393
case studies as evidence 379
causal attribution 106, 165
causal dimensions 162, 165; scale II 167
causal search 162
causal thinking and emotions 163
challenging behaviors 277, 280
change, capacity for 218
character strengths 64
characteristic adaptations 126
check and connect 144

children, kindergarten 281
Chinese culture 262
choice 127, 143, 246, 248, 267
Chomsky, Noam 352, 355, 364
circular seating 291
clarification requests 412
classes online 96, 144, 263
classmates providing information 385
classroom dynamics 281
classroom environment 263, 280
classroom management 144, 145
classroom observation 265
cliques 316, 319
cogito ergo sum 363, 367
cognition, teacher 151
cognitive abilities 395, 396
cognitive ability for novelty as applied to foreign language test (CANAL-FT) 394
cognitive ability for novelty in language acquisition-foreign (CANAL-F) theory 394
cognitive approaches 314, 352–3, 355–6
cognitive change strategies 317
cognitive control 75
cognitive ecosystem 58
cognitive elements 353
cognitive empathy 327
cognitive engagement 141, 142
cognitive impairment 314
cognitive linguistics 368
cognitive perspective 350
cognitive processes, unconscious 219, 302
cognitive reappraisal 317
cognitive-interactionist approach 410
cohort studies 379
"cold calling" 278
collaborative for academic, social and emotional learning (CASEL) 186
collective agency 107
collective efficacy 107, 288, 290
collectivist-oriented trait 286
color-naming 30
color-word stimuli 75
coma patients 365
common European framework of reference for languages (CEFR) 39, 105
communicating, joy of 268
communication apprehension 342
communication, nonverbal 369, 372; facial expressions 369, 371; gestures 27, 30, 368–9, 371, 374
communication and positive evaluation 261
communicative competence 264, 267
communicative language teaching (CLT) 43, 391
communities of practice (CoPs) 292–3
communities, resilient 213
Community Language Learning (CLL) 43
comorbidity 51
compassion 182, 327–8, 330
competence 143, 246, 264, 267, 276

420

Index

complex dynamic systems theory (CDST) 48–57, 78–9, 266, 357, 400
complexity-accuracy-fluency (CAF) 17
computational perspective of the mind 364
computer aided learning 224, 248, 263–4, 364
computer-assisted language learning (CALL) 248
computing 352, 353
concept-based language instruction (CBLI) 28–9, 31
conceptual metaphor 367–8, 372
conceptual thinking 24
conceptualization for speech production 75, 373
confidence and lack of 55, 103
conflict and solutions 286
confounders (variables) 79, 380
confrontation 327
congruent goals 234
connotation 364
conscientiousness 113–14, 117
consciousness 354, 363, 364, 365, 366, 370; below 302; hard problem of 366, 371; phenomenal 363, 364, 365, 366, 367, 374
consistency 280
contemplative practices 329
content and language integrated learning (CLIL) 197, 199, 263, 267
content-based instruction settings (CBI) 197
continuous visual memory task 11
contributors viii–xiii
controllability of outcome 162, 163
conversation flow 265
cool intelligence 179
cooperative learning 209
co-orientational ICC model 306–7
coping 179, 200
corrective feedback (CF) 406, 410, 413
corrective reformulation 410, 412
correlation 54, 384
co-speech gestures 27, 30, 369
counseling learning 43
courage 180
Cramer, Dr A. O. J. 51, 52
creativity 339, 341, 344–5
Crick, Francis 364
critical cultural awareness 307
critical cultural theory 301
critical participatory looping (CPL) 291
critical period hypothesis (CPH) 81
cross-linguistic interference 75–6
Csíkszentmihályi, Mihaly 192
Csizér, Kata 339
Cuisenaire rods 44
cultural awareness 307
cultural beliefs 184
cultural difference 303–4
cultural empathy 114, 119
cultural iceberg 302
cultural identity 301, 303
cultural influence 263
cultural mediators 184

cultural misunderstandings 318
cultural predispositions 301
cultural-historical psychology (CHP) 22
culture 302, 303, 304, 305
culture, Asian 263
culture Chinese 262
culture clash 374
culture and language 303, 305–6
culture, large and small concept 304
culture and nation 301
culture teaching, purpose of 305 *see also* intercultural
current self 232, 239
cybernetics 353

Daniels, Lia M. 161
Darvin, Ron 89
decision to communicate 264
decision-making 277, 364
declarative knowledge 8, 408, 411
declarative memory 7, 8, 9, 11, 22
declarative/procedural model of learning (Ullman) 8–9
deduction 411
deep acting 180
democratic leadership 287, 294
demonstrable risk 206
demotivation 131, 210
denotation 364
depression 51, 57, 64
deprivation, children raised in 205–6
Descartes, René 351, 363, 367
desire 93
development 24, 50–1
Dewaele, Jean-Marc 112
Dewey, John 40
diagnostic and statistical manual of mental disorders (DSM-5) 52
differences, accepting 328
difficult learners 280
digital contexts for learning 263–4
digital storytelling 95
digital tools 144, 224
Dilthey, Wilhelm 353
directed motivational currents (DMCs) 68, 131–2, 236
disadvantaged groups 308, 327
disappointment 317
disappointment-related words 371
discipline 278
discrimination 150, 331
displaced people 308
disposition 340
dispositional traits 126
disruptive classes and seating 288
divergent thinking 344–5
DNA, discovery of 364
Dörnyei, Z. 8, 222, 237
dorsal language stream 370
dorsolateral prefrontal cortex 114

drama, use of 211, 213
dual-memory system 9
dyads 261, 264
dynamic assessment (DA) 25–6, 28
dynamic systems theory (CDST) 48–9, 52–7, 78–9, 266, 357, 400
dynamic testing 25
dynamic usage-based (DUB) theory 79
dynamogenic factors 289

ecological approach 356
ecological psychology 353
ecological systems theory (Bronfenbrenner) 196
ecosystems 58, 213
education, holistic 329
education, teachers' 332
educational data mining 145
educational psychology 194–5
EEG 365
efficacy, collective 107, 288, 290
"effort" 140
elaboration in thinking 344
electrophysiological (ERP) measures 413
eliminativism 364
embarrassment 314, 317
embodiment 355, 362, 366, 368, 372–3
emergentist theories 355
emotion families 179, 180
emotional danger zone 314
emotional experience 179, 288, 317
emotional intelligence (EI) 107, 114–15, 118, 179–80, 184, 279, 327
emotional intensity 181, 318
emotional labor 178, 180, 184, 318
emotional management 316
emotional pain 288
emotional regulation 179, 184–5, 316, 317
emotional stability 113, 114, 117, 120
emptional trait 179
emotional well-being, teachers 197
emotions 163, 178–81, 181, 183, 186
emotions, appropriate 181
emotions, basic 180, 369
emotions expression 180
emotions, negative/fire-fighting 66–7, 141, 163, 181, 183, 185, 219
emotions, positive 39–40, 66–7, 141, 163, 181, 183, 210
emotions beyond self 182
emotions, teachers' 39, 317, 318, 319
EMPATHICS 66, 69, 108, 196, 198, 208
empathy 40, 180, 326, 327–8, 330; cognitive 327; cultural 114, 119
empirical human sciences 353
enculturation 302, 355
engagement 137, 138, 140, 141, 142, 144–5
engagement antecedents 137, 142–3
engagement, behavioral 140, 142
engagement, cognitive 141, 142

engagement models 138–9; in-the-moment 137, 140
engagement versus disaffection with learning measure (EVDL) 142
engine model of well-being 193–4
English, attitudes towards 153
English medium instruction (EMI) 197
English-as-a-Foreign-Language (EFL) 17, 191
enjoyment 67, 118, 181, 266
Enlightenment 363
entitativity ("groupiness") 288
entity theorists 163
environment, role on learning 25
epiphenomenalism 364, 373, 374
episodic future thinking 234
episodic memory 408
EPPI-Center 380
errors, biased 364
essentialization 301
ethnic protection 151
ethnocultural empathy 328
ethnomethodology 354
eudemonic well-being dimensions 193
Eurocentrism 307
everyday language 267
everyday and scientific concepts (Vygotsky) 26
evidence: hierarchies 379, 382, 386; quality 378–9, 380, 382; shortcomings 379; weights 380
excitement 264
executive working memory (EWM) 398
existential courage 180
exosystems 276
expectancy-value models 128
expectations by teachers 280
expected/likely self 232
experience 63, 101, 180, 278
experience sampling method (ESM) 345
experiential learning 329–30
experimental studies 379
expert opinion 379
explicit attitudes 149, 150
explicit instruction 411, 412
explicit knowledge 408, 409, 410, 412
explicit learning 76, 407, 408
explicitness and implicitness as a continuum 411
exploratory factor analyses (EFAs) 151
exploratory talk 141
extraversion 55, 113, 116, 117, 261
extraverts 113, 340
extreme responding (ER) 381, 382
extrinsic motivation 128
eye contact 291
eye tracking 145, 411
Eysenck, Hans 113, 116, 117

face 314, 318
face-to-face and online comparison 263
face-to-face seating 291
face-to-face use of language 368

facial expressions 369, 371
failure: experience of 163; fear of 166
fairness 280
Falout, Joseph 285
fantasies, positive 232–4
fear: of ambiguity 151; of failure 166; of negative evaluation 342
feared self 232
feedback 106–7, 226, 280, 412; corrective 406, 410, 413
feeling good 193
feeling rules 184, 318
feelings 38, 179
Feryok, Anne 350
Festman, Julia 74
Fidel chart 44
fight-or-flight decisions 181
fitness, wearable devices 145
Five Graces Group 357
fixed mindset 152
flexibility 114, 119, 344
flourishing 181
flow 68, 142, 182, 341, 345
fluency: in speaking skills 17; in divergent thinking 344
fMRI scans 365
focus on form 410
followers 287
Foncubierta, José Manuel 36
Fordyce's Happiness measure 193
foregrounding 368
foreign language classroom anxiety (FLCA) 117, 314, 316; link with neuroticism 117; scale (FLCAS) 342, 383
forethought 101
forgetting 408
formula for behaviour 295
fossilized (stationary) learning 54
free riding 286, 289
French grammar 10
Fukada, Yoshifumi 285
Fukuda, Tetsuya 285
functioning well 193
fundamental differences hypothesis 395
future selves 68, 291, 292

Gadotti 36
Galen 340
Galileo 363, 367
Gal'perin, Piotr 26
Ganassin, Sara 300
Gardner, Howard 41, 68
gender, group belonging 286
generalizability 383
generative grammar 354
geosemiotics 368, 372
geriatric psychology 313–14
gestalt 353
Gestalt psychology 22, 352, 353, 354

gestures 30, 368–9, 371, 374; accompanying speech 27, 30, 369
Gkonou, Christina 275
global neuronal workspace hypothesis 364
global orientation 151
globalization 151
goal self-concordance 233–7; lack of 237; and vision 234
goals 234; self-defining 238, 239; self-enhancing 238–9; self-relevant 239
goal-selection 234, 238
goal-setting 236, 267
God 363
grade-level expectations 25
grades 384
grading of recommendations easement, development and evaluation (GRADE) 379
grammar, French 10
grammar, generative 355
grammar learning 9, 11, 13, 29
grammar teaching 414
grammatical sensitivity 393
grammatical structure 366
gratitude 182, 327, 329
grit 385
group analysis, levels of 295
group behavior 326
group cohesion 286, 287, 290
group culture 288
group dynamics 43, 277, 285–8, 289, 293, 319
group members, advantaged and disadvantaged 287, 308, 326, 327
"groupiness" 288
grouping participants 81–2
grower relationships 50, 54
growth mindset 152, 164–5, 166, 168, 169, 170
guilt 317, 327

hand reaching behavior 56
happiness 180
happiness measure (Fordyce) 193
hard problem of consciousness 366, 371
hardiness 208–9
hazukashii (embarrassment) 314
hedonic well-being 193, 195
helpless learning behaviors 166
Henry, Alastair 231
Hepford, Elizabeth 48
"here-and-now" self 232
heritage languages (HL) 210
heuristic model of WTC 261
hierarchical structures 276
hierarchy of needs (Maslow) 37, 288
high-level language aptitude battery (hi-LAB model) 397
highly automatized knowledge 409
Hippocrates 340
Hiver, Phil 205
holistic education 329

Index

"hot" intelligence 179
human development 24, 50–1
humanism 36–9
humanistic approaches 42, 357
humanistic language teaching (HLT) 39, 358
humanistic psychology 355, 357
humor, using 278, 280
Husserl, Edmund 363
hybrid schedule (grammar)14, 15
hypothesis testing (Bayesian) 386

ideal classmates 294
ideal classmates priming (ICP) 291–2
ideal self 68, 152, 232, 235, 239, 291–2
"ideasthesia" 371
identical twins development 52
identities 89–90, 91; holding on to 152; multiple 92–5; relevance 233; of teachers 94; texts 95
identity theorists 94
ideologies 92, 93
illocutionary force 316
images 42, 231–2
imagination, limits to 366
imagined community 91
immersion students 263, 265
immigrants, difficulties for 373
implicit association test (IAT) 150
implicit attitudes 150
implicit bias 150–1
implicit instruction 411, 412
implicit knowledge 408, 409–10, 312
implicit learning 76, 407, 408
implicit theories 165
impression management 316, 318
inclusivity 40–1
incremental theorists 163
individual differences 11, 49, 77, 82, 339, 341–2, 381
induction 411
inductive language learning ability 393
inequality 316, 331, 391
inert knowledge problem 406
infant development 50, 56
influences, social 221
information from classmates 385
informational language versus commands 246
information-processing approach (Esterman & Rothlein) 407
inhibitory control (IC) Model 75
initiation-response-feedback (IRF) 319
innate learning aptitude 166
inner peace 330
inner sense 370
inner speech 30, 31, 370, 371
input enhancement 412
input-interaction-output (IIO) model 355, 357
Institute of Education, University College London 380
integrated information theory (IIT) 365, 374
integrationist perspective 368

integrative life narratives 126
"integrativeness" 117, 152
intellect 38, 114
intelligence, emotional (EI) 114–15, 118, 179–80, 184, 279, 327; model 179–80
intelligences 41, 179, 279
intentionality 101
interaction hypothesis 410
interactionist approaches 314
interactions with fellow learners 316
intercultural attitudes 307
intercultural communication 304
intercultural competence (IC) 306–7
intercultural encounters 308
intercultural language teaching 305 *see also* culture
interdisciplinary collaboration 104, 105
interest 126
interference effect, vocabulary learning 15
intergroup behavior 326
interlanguage 80, 82
interleaved practice (grammar) 14, 15, 17
internalization 23–4, 30, 370
international posture (IP) 262, 307
internet 92
internet of things (IoT) devices 145
interpersonal perception 318
interpreting skills 307
interpretivist approaches 300–1
inter-session interval (ISI) 13
inter-session interval-retention interval (ISI-RI) ratio, optimal 13
intervention programs 144
intraclass correlation coefficient (ICC) models 306–7
intrinsic motivation 128
introspection 351
introversion 55, 261
introverts 113, 116
intuition 117–18, 409
investment 91–3, 94–5, 132
Irie, Kay 100
ISI-RI ratio, optimal 13
isolation 288
iterative processes 49, 50–1

James, William 62, 231, 232
journal keeping 293
judging, absence of 328
judicial framework in research 382
justice building and teaching 330

Kalaja, Paula 245
kanji learning 224–65
Kant, Immanuel 246, 351–20, 353, 363
kindness, acts of 327, 328
King, Jim 313
knowledge 8, 11
knowledge, automatized 411
knowledge, declarative and procedural 9, 10
knowledge, explicit 9, 408, 409, 410, 412

knowledge HOW 8, 408, 411
knowledge, implicit 9
knowledge retention 406
knowledge (savoir) 307
knowledge THAT 8, 408, 411
Koch, Christof 363, 365
Krashen's Input Hypothesis 355

L1 acquisition and learning 152, 355
L1 erosion 373, 374
L1-L2 link 393–4
L1-LX hybrid 27, 30, 31
L2 and acculturation 302–3
L2 aptitude, components 394
L2 learning 8, 9, 13
L2 motivational self system (L2MSS) 129, 152, 156, 234–5
L2 socialization (SLS) 356
L2 teachers 308
L2 willingness to communicate 261, 262–6
laissez-faire leadership 287
languaculture 305–7, 367, 368
language acquisition 76, 119
language analytic ability 396
language anxiety 117, 183–4, 314, 316, 341–2, 383
language and culture 305–6
language enjoyment 183
language exchange partnerships 106
language induction ability 393
language learning ability 393
language learning aptitude 166, 343–4, 400, 401
language learning, attitudes towards 154
language learning, computer aided 224, 248, 263–4, 363
language learning device 398
language learning motivation 342–3
language learning, space, place, and autonomy in 249
language learning strategies (LLSs) 222
language learning, technology-enhanced 224
language loss 210
language in the mind 369
language of peace approach (LPA) 330
language processor/parser 398
language production 75
language resilience 211
language of science 367
language shift, cross-generational 210
language teaching, communicative (CLT) 43, 391
language teaching, humanistic (HLT) 39, 358
language-related episodes 141
languages other than English (LOTEs) 153–4
large culture concept 304
latent variable theory 51
leadership 286–7, 294
learner autonomy 247, 248
learner behavior 384
learner beliefs 262–3
learner bonding and lack of 289, 290
learner capabilities, assessment 25

learner confidence levels, fluctuating 55
learner diversity 40–1
learner engagement 137, 138
learner grit 385
learner leadership 319
learner, older 152
learner reticence 280, 318, 319
learner research 236
learner self-assessment 385
learner silence 315–16, 319
learner well-being 197–8, 199
learner-centered teaching practices 294
learner/teacher relationships 275, 276–7, 278, 280, 317, 318
learning 101, 209, 406
learning and acquisition 407
learning analytics 147
learning aptitude 168
learning development 53–4, 55
learning, elements of 36
learning, experiential 329–30
learning and extraversion 117
learning, implicit 76, 407, 408
learning management systems (LMS) 145
"learning in the wild" 373
legitimate peripheral participation 293
Lewin, Kurt 354
Lewin's field theory 287, 295
lexico-phonological rules 14
life narratives 126
Likert-scale 105, 113, 114, 150
linguaculture 305–6, 367, 368
linguistic coding differences hypotheses (LCDH) 393–4
linguistic competence 303
linguistic interdependence hypothesis (Cummins) 393–4
linguistic relativity 373
linguistic threshold hypothesis 394
linguistical mediation 371
LLAMA test battery (Meara) 395
locus of causality 162
Long's interaction hypothesis 355
long-term memory 7, 8, 9, 11, 12, 13, 396
looping cycle 291
Lou, Nigel Mantou 161
Lozanov, Georgi 43
LX development and inner speech 31

MacIntyre, Peter D. 61
macrosystems 276
major depressive disorder (MDD) 51
Mandarin speakers 373
market research 149
Maslow, Abraham 41, 62, 182; hierarchy of needs 37, 288
Massimini, Marcello 365
mastery experience 101, 104, 106
matrix of evidence approach 380

McCafferty, Steven G. 362
mediating variables 412
mediation in agency 252
mediation, linguistic 371
mediator 28
memory 7–8, 9, 11, 22, 393
memory for contingent speech 395–6
memory, declarative 7, 8, 9, 11, 22
memory, episodic 408
memory, executive working (EWM) 398
memory, long-term 7, 8, 9, 11, 12, 13, 396
memory, phonological working (PWM) 397–8
memory, short-term 408
memory systems, long-term 7–8, 9, 396
memory, working 7, 8, 77, 395–6, 397, 398–9, 407
mental contrasting 233
mental disorders and diagnoses 51–2
mental imagery 231–32, 233, 235
mental processes 7
mental time travel 232, 234
mentoring programs 144
mesosystems 276
metaaffective strategies 222
metacognition 220
metacognitive control breakdown 223
metacognitive strategies 222
metacognitive strategies questionnaire (MSQ) 142
metaknowledge 223
metaphor, conceptual 367–8, 372
metaphysical psychology 351
metastrategies 222–3
microsystems 276
migrants' acquisition of official language 91
Milgram's obedience experiment 340
mind: computational perspective of 364; properties of 366; subsystems 183
mind-body connections in different languages 372
mindset 143, 163, 165, 168
mindset, fixed 152, 164–6, 168, 169
mindset, growth 152, 164–6, 168, 169, 170
mindset theory 161, 163–4
mindset-attribution relation 164
min/max graphs 52, 53
mirror neurons 369
missing at random (MAR) 384
mistakes, responses to 316
model, engagement 138, 140
model for interpersonal teacher behavior 277
model, SCT triadic causal 100–1
model of self-regulation (Rose) 223
model of well-being 193–4
modern language aptitude test (MLAT) 11, 391, 392–3, 394, 396, 400
momentum 237, 238
monitor theory (Krashen) 406
monitoring by teachers 144
monolingual approach 75
mood 179
morphemes 8

Morris, Sam 313
Moskowitz, Gertrude 40, 41
mother-infant interactions 313
motivated strategies for learning questionnaire (MSLQ) 102, 142
motivation 101, 125, 126, 127, 342–3
motivation, approach versus avoidance 128
motivation, fluctuation of 343
motivation, group framing of 290
motivation, intrinsic and extrinsic 128
motivation partnerships 107
motivation, self-system 68
motivation, state 343
motivation, teachers' 132
motivation, time and context variables 343
motivation, tripartite model 128
motivational conglomerates 126, 130
motivational factors questionnaire (MFQ) 155
motivational psychologists 125
motives, conscious and unconscious 132
movement, use of 42
moving averages 52, 53
moving correlations 53
Muir, Christine 124
multicultural acquisition 151
multicultural personality questionnaire (MPQ) 114, 119, 120
multilingualism and anxiety 119
multilinguals 119–20, 210
multiple identities 95
multiple intelligence theory 41
Murphey, Tim 285
music, use of 42, 43
Myers-Briggs Type Indicator (MBTI) 116, 118

Nakamura, Sachiko 137
names, using 278
narrative-bonding 290, 291
national comorbidity survey replication (NCS-R) 51
"native speaker" models of learning 307, 309
natural kinds theory 180
natural sciences, experimental 353
naturalistic language acquisition 76
nature-versus-nurture 23
near-peer role models (NPRMs) 106, 290–1
need to relate 279
needs, hierarchy of 37, 288
negative energy 287
negative/fire-fighting emotions 66–7, 141, 163, 181, 183, 210, 219; healthy/unhealthy 185
Neisser, Ulric 353
nested systems 266, 267, 279
neural system 352
neurobiological learning model 8
neurobiological structures 9, 38, 114, 182, 365
neurocorrelates 363, 371; of consciousness 364, 365
neuromotor development 56
neurons, mirror 369
neuropsychological tests 76

neuroscience 352, 363
neuroticism 113, 117; and FLCA link 117
"new big five" regarding personality 126
newsletters 290
Night Train to Lisbon (novel) 115
Noels, Kimberly A. 161
noise, effect on work 288
non-concordant goals 234
nonconscious processes 234, 302
non-response errors 384
nonverbal behaviors 291, 314, 319
nonverbal communication 369, 372; facial expressions 369, 371; gestures 27, 30, 368–9, 371, 374
Norton, Bonny 89
noticing hypothesis (Schmidt) 410

object relative clauses (OR) 14, 15
observational information 385
observational studies 379
observers' rating with self-reports 384–5
Olivero, M. Matilde 325
online practices 96, 144, 263
ontological stance 301
ontology 366
openness-to-experience 114, 117–18, 119
oppression 331
optimal distinctiveness theory 286
oral exams and extraversion 116
oral picture descriptive task 17
"ordinary magic" 207
originality in thinking 344
orthographic decoding skill 393
"othering" 301
ought-to self 68, 93, 152, 235
out-groups 326
output hypothesis 410
output-inducing 412
overlaps 142
overlearning 12–13
Oxford, Rebecca L. 178, 197–8, 222, 223, 328

panpsychism 366
parameters in dynamic systems 49, 52
parental support 104
participation-identification model (Finn) 138
past selves 292
Pawlak, Miroslaw 406
peacebuilding activities 330
peak experiences 182
peer reactions, hypersensitivity to 314
peer scaffolding 28
perezhivanie 25, 29, 31, 370
performance 23, 220; anxiety 342; avoidance 171
peripheral participation 293
PERMA 42, 63, 69, 181, 194–6, 197–8
permanence of knowledge 407
persistence 166, 238
personal action 327
personal agency 127

personal determinants for self-efficacy 101
personal experiences, sharing 278
personality 11
personality, big five traits of 113, 114, 340; "new big five" 126
personality dispositions/traits 340, 341
personality and language acquisition 119
personality psychology 340
personality study 385
personality types 116, 340
personification 372
"person-in-context" 129, 304
perturbations 49, 55, 365
Pfenninger, Simone E. 74
phase shift/transition 49, 50, 53
phenomenal consciousness 363, 364, 365, 366, 367, 374
phenomenal experience 374
phenomenological distinctions 365
phenomenology 352, 353, 363
Phi 365
phonetic coding ability 393, 396
phonological/executive hypothesis (P/E model) 397, 398
phonological working memory (PWM) 397–8
phonology/orthography skills 394
physiological and affective states 101, 104, 106, 107
Piaget, Jean 51
pilot surveys 384, 385
pineal gland 363
place, in language learning 249
Plonsky, Luke 378
plurals 56
political action 327
polynomial trendlines 52, 53
PolyVagal theory 182
population (surveys) 383
portfolio assessment 225
position 89–90, 91, 93, 94, 95
positive and negative affect scale (PANAS) 193
positive education (PE) 194–5
positive emotions 39–40, 66–7, 141, 163, 181, 183, 210
positive language education (PLE) 192
positive psychology 37, 61–3; and SLA 65–6
positive psychology interventions (PPIs) 195, 196
positive slant 233
positivist approaches 300, 301
possible selves 129, 232, 237, 238–9, 292
power dynamics 91, 95, 287, 316
power of law learning curve 9, 10
practice 11, 16
pragmatics 287
Prague School of linguistics 354
predictions of automatization of knowledge 11
pre-experience 232, 234
preposition "in" 368
present community of imagination (PCOIz) 292

Index

presentation-practice-production (PPP) procedure 413–14
pride-related words 371
primary language erosion 373, 374
probability and non-probability sampling 383
procedural knowledge 8, 408, 411
procedural memory 8, 9, 11, 22
proceduralization 8, 9, 411
processing of information 407
progmax-regmin graphs 53, 54
prognostication 400–1
project-based learning 107
prompts 412
pronunciation learning 14
prosocial behavior 325, 326
protective systems, human 207
proximity 291
psycholinguistics 74–8
psychological disorders 288
psychological momentum 237
psychological needs 142–3, 245, 276
psychological predicate 369–70
psychological well-being (PWB) 193, 198; and biomarkers 194
psychologists, motivational 125
psychology behavioral 352
psychology, ecological 353
psychology, Gestalt 22, 352, 353, 354
psychology, history of 351–2
psychology, humanistic 355, 357
psychology of language learning (PLL) 378
psychology of language learning and teaching (PLLT) 198, 245
psychology, metaphysical 351
psychology, scientific 351
psychology, social approaches in 353–4
psychoticism 113
public self-image 314
pushed output 410

qualia 365, 366, 369, 370, 371, 372; structure 372
qualitative modelling 400
questionnaire of English self-efficacy (QESE) 104, 105
questionnaires 113, 381, 382–3, 386

random selection and sampling 383
random variability 80
randomized control trials (RCTs) 379
Rasch modeling 292, 295
rational emotive behavior therapy (REBT) 181, 185
reaching behavior (infants) 56
Read Talbot, Kyle 191
recasts 410, 412
reciprocal idealizing 292
reconceptualization 373
recovery aspect 206
reductionism 352, 367
re-experience 232, 364

refugees 200, 307
regression in learning, temporary 53, 54, 55, 56
Reinders, Hayo 137
relatedness 143, 246, 276
relating skills 307
relationships, forming 276
relationships, long-term caring 288
relationships, positive or hostile 276
relationships between learners and faculty 289
relationships, teacher/learner 275, 276–7, 278, 280, 317, 318
relative clauses 14, 15
repetition 209
research 206, 207, 208, 210, 213, 379
research on action 249
research on agency 253, 254
research on autonomy 250
Research Centre for Group Dynamics 285
research of heritage language 210
research, individual versus collective 212
research on language 211
research in learning contexts 209–11
research on resilience 205, 209
research, teachers' 211
research on willingness to communicate 262–6
respect 306
response errors 384
response modulation 179; strategies 317
responsibility 38, 264; for own learning 143
retention interval (RI) 13
retention, long-term 12, 13
reticent learners 318, 319
retrieval 12, 13
retrodictive qualitative modeling 400
risk 118, 206, 207, 213
Rivers, Wilga 40
Rogers, Carl 36, 37, 41, 395
Rose's model of self-regulation 223
row-and-column seating 288, 291
Ruohotie-Lyhty, Maria 245

samples (surveys) 383–4
Sánchez Solarte, Ana Clara 205
sarcasm 277
satisfaction with life scale (SWLS) 193
Saussure, Ferdinand de 354
savoirs (factors) 306–7
scaffolding 28, 285
scales of psychological well-being (SPWB) 193
scaling in surveys 105
Schartner, Alina 300
schema for the complete orienting basis for action (SCOBA) 26
school, belonging to 288–9, 290, 292
science, language of 367
scientific psychology 351
seating arrangements 288, 291, 319
second language development (SLD) 48, 49, 55; teacher knowledge about L1 56; modelling 55–6

second language socialization (SLS) 356
second language tolerance of ambiguity (SLTA) 118
security 264
segregationist perspective 368
selection of samples 383
self-access learning centers (SALCs) 292, 293
self-actualization 37, 38, 62
self-anchoring striving scale 193
self-assessment 101, 385
self-concept 101–2
self-concordance vision 234, 237
self-construal 180, 314
self-control factor 114–15
self-determination theory (SDT) 39, 128, 246
self-efficacy 100–1, 102, 103–5, 106–7; academic (ASE) 102; teacher (TSE) 100, 103, 104
self-esteem 101, 288, 391
self-focused image 315–16
selfhood, social psychology of 90
self-identity 90
self-image 314
self-organization in a system 49, 50–1
self-reactiveness 101
self-reflection 101, 220
self-regulated learning (SRL) 100, 220, 221–5
self-regulation 103, 218–23
self-regulation, effects of gender 224
self-regulation failure 219, 221
self-regulation, key features 220, 222, 223
self-regulation models 220–1, 222, 223; phases 220
self-reports 141–2, 381, 382, 384–5
self-schema 239
self-system model of motivational development (SSMMD) 142
"self-talk" 30, 31, 369, 370, 371
self-transcendent emotions 186
Seligman, Martin 63, 181, 192
Seligman and Csíkszentmihályi 37
selves, current 232, 239
selves, future 68, 291, 292
selves, ideal 68, 152, 232, 235, 239, 291–2
selves, ought-to 68, 93, 154, 235
selves, possible 129, 232, 237, 238–9, 291
selves, types of 152, 154, 232, 292
semantic contexts 370
semantic memory 408
semantic-differential scale 149–50
semantics 15, 16, 364, 368
semiotics 368
sense of autonomy 39
service-industry workers 180
service-learning encounter 373
"sheep" (group members) 287
short-term memory 408
shy learners 280
significant others, interactions with 279
silence from others 276, 314, 315–16, 319; teachers' wait time 319
silent inner vocalizations 30, 31, 369, 370, 371

Silent Way, The 44
simulation theory 369
situation-specific anxiety 341, 342
Skehan's staged model 396–7
skill acquisition and learning 8–11, 410, 411
skills of discovery and interaction 307
skills of interpreting and relating 307
small culture formation 304
sociability 115
social anxiety 314
social approaches 353–4, 356–7
social cognition 149
social cognitive theory (SCT) 100–1, 354
social discomfiture 314
social ecosystem 58
social emotional and academic learning (SEAL) 186
social emotional learning (SEL) 186
social engagement 141, 142, 145
social facilitation 289
social identity 288
social influences 220
social initiative 114, 117, 119
social intelligence 279
social interaction 313, 314–17
social interpretence 368
social justice 325, 327
social loafing 289
social media 92
social motivation 326
social network analysis processes 145
social perspective 350–1
social persuasion 101, 104, 106–7
social psychology 339, 340
social relations 38
social scientists 302
social transformation 307
social variables 356
social/cognitive split 350, 354–5, 356; efforts to overcome 357
socially desirable responding (SDR) 381, 382
sociocognitive approach 357
sociocultural interaction rules 318
sociocultural theory, Vygotsky (SCT) 22–30, 31, 356
socio-economic divide 225, 277
socio-educational model (Gardner) 68, 127
socio-emotional development (SED) 195
sociofugal spaces 288, 291
sociopetal spaces 288
somatic marker 183
somatosensory input, loss of 371
space, place, and autonomy in language learning 249
spaced learning (vocabulary) 15
spaces, visually attractive 287–8
Spanish 154–5
Sparks and Ganschow 394
spatiotemporal conceptualization 373
speaking skills development 17
speech 369; avoidance 314; inner 30, 31, 369, 370, 371; preparation for 75, 373

Spinoza, Baruch (Benedict) 363, 367
stable dispositions (traits) 113, 339, 340
stable/unstable cause 162
Stanford prison experiment 340
star followers 287
state motivation 343
states 340
state-trait anxiety inventory (STAI) 115, 341
statistical correlations 54
statistical learning 407
status inequalities 316
stereotyping 301
stimulus appraisal system 183
stimulus-response (S-R) reactions 22, 23
storytelling 95, 211, 213, 373
strategic self-regulation (S²R) model 222, 223
strategy training 235
stress 151, 342; of teachers 67–8, 277, 278
stressors 196–7, 200, 209
Stroop task 75
structural equation modeling (SEM) 262, 263, 264, 295
structural violence 331
structure of intellect model 344
student engagement 137, 138; databases 144
student engagement instruments (SEI) 142, 144
student-centered teaching practices 294
study-abroad experience 101
subjective relative clauses (SRC) 14, 15
subjective well-being (SWB) 193, 195; teachers' 196, 200
subjectivity in communities 91
subordinating clauses 54
Sudina, Ekaterina 378
"suggestology" 43
suggestopedia 43
sulking, stylized 316
supportive services 207
surface acting 180, 184
survey-based research 382, 384
surveys 149–50, 384, 385
surveys, accuracy of 381, 382, 384
surveys, design 383
surveys as evidence 379
surveys about learners' behaviour 381
surveys, non-response to 384
surveys, pilot 384, 385
surveys, purpose of 382, 383
surveys, self-reports 141–2, 381
Suzuki, Yuichi 7
Swain's comprehensible output hypothesis 355
"switchers" and "non-switchers" 76
sympathy 182, 327
synesthesia 371, 373
syntax 364, 368
systematic and deliberate practice 15, 16
systemic functional linguistics 368
systemic reviews 379

systemic theoretical instruction (STI) model 26, 28, 29

tandem-learning 106
target language (TL) 291, 410, 413
task analysis 220
task aptitudes 400
task-based language teaching (TBLT) 17, 142
task-level engagement 137, 140
teacher autonomy 249
teacher behavior 277, 278
teacher beliefs 151
teacher cognition 151
teacher qualities 37
teacher resilience 211
teacher self-efficacy (TSE) 100, 103, 104
teacher silence (wait time) 319
teacher stress 67–8, 277, 278
teacher types 66, 209
teacher well-being 67–8, 196–7, 200, 277
teacher/learner relationships 275, 276–7, 278, 279, 280, 317–18
teachers' education 281, 332
teachers' emotional rewards 197, 279
teachers' emotions 39, 317, 318, 319
teachers' professional development 281
teachers providing information 385
teachers and significant others 279
teaching English to speakers of other languages (TESOL) 186
teaching of foreign languages and justice building 330
teaching practices, learner-centered 294
teasing 317
technology-enhanced language learning 224
Teimouri, Yasser 378
temperature, effect on work 288
"temporary disharmony" 278
tense-aspect-mood distinction 14
test anxiety 342
testing 11
thalamocortical region 365
theory of attribution (Weiner) 162–3
theory of momentum (Adler) 237
theory of self-determination (SDT) 233
thinking, elaboration in 344
"thinking for speaking" 75, 373
Thompson, Amy S. 149
thought, abstract 373
Three Blessings/Good Things 64
time organization 373
Tomasello 350
Tononi, Gulilo 365
total physical response (TPR) 42, 44, 372
trait emotional intelligence (TEI) 118
traits 113, 114–15, 126, 339, 340; Big Five of personality 113, 114, 340; dispositional 126
trait/state (person/situation) 339
trajectory graphs 52, 53
transcranial magnetic stimulation 365

Index

transduction 364
transfer appropriate processing 411
transformative approaches 329
Turkish learner of English 53

Ursulu 394
Ushioda, Ema 304

vagus nerve 182, 185
valence of emotion 180, 181, 232
values in action (VIA) classification of strengths 63, 64
van Compernolle, Remi A. 22
variability 80
variable interaction 50, 52, 54
variables in learning development 53–4
variables, mediating 412
verbal mediation 369
verbal working memory 77
verbalization 26–7, 29
verb-framed versus satellite-framed languages 27
verbs 8, 49
vicarious experience 101, 104, 106
victim blaming 240
videos 290, 373
violence, structural 331
virtues 64
vision 231–33, 234–6, 237
visionary images 231–2
visionary training 238
visualization 52–3, 235–6, 267
visuospatial working memory 77
vocabulary learning 12, 15, 54
voice, paralinguistic elements 314
volunteerism 326
von Helmholtz, Hermann 352

Vygotskian sociocultural theory (SCT) 22–30, 31, 356
Vygotsky, Lev S. 314, 354, 369, 370

Wang, Isobel Kai-Hui 218
"watchful "other" 314
wearable devices 145
Weiner's theory of attribution 162–3
well-being 62, 63, 114, 193–5, 199
well-being, fluctuations 200
well-being, learner 197–8, 199
well-being, psychological (PWB) 193, 198
well-being, subjective (SWB) 193, 195, 196, 200
well-being, teacher 67–8, 196–7, 200, 277
Wen, Zhisheng (Edward) 391
western educated industrialized rich democratic (WEIRD) samples 81
who, whom, which distinctions 14
wh-questions 9–10
willingness to communicate (WTC) 54–5, 118, 260, 265–8; decision to 264; heuristic model 261
willingness to engage (WTE) 142
working in groups 285, 289
working memory 7, 8, 77, 395–6, 397, 398–9, 407
Wulff, Christian 351
Wundt, Wilhelm 352

Yashima, Tomoko 260
yes-people 287
Young, Tony Johnstone 300

Zhang, Xijia 161
Zimmerman's self-regulated learning model 220, 221, 223
Zone of Proximal Development (ZPD) 24–6, 28
Zoom 145